RADICAL CHART

347	345	343						
313	312	311						
278	275	265	264	261	261	259	252	251
239	238	235	224	**4**	319	348	241	223
223	221	217	202	196	191	190	187	187
186	182	182	179	175	174	173	172	171
168	168	166	165	163	160	148	145	142
136	132	130	128	121	116	101	**3**	99
99	95	93	92	91	91	87	86	85
85	79	72	68	66	65	64	63	60
56	54	51	32	29	26	24	22	**2**
	20	19	18	17	15	14	1	**1**

KODANSHA'S
ELEMENTARY
KANJI
DICTIONARY

KODANSHA'S ELEMENTARY KANJI DICTIONARY

KODANSHA INTERNATIONAL
Tokyo • New York • London

Note: Previously published as *Kodansha's Pocket Kanji Guide*, this dictionary is an abridgment of *Kodansha's Compact Kanji Guide*.

Distributed in the United States by Kodansha America, Inc., 575 Lexington Avenue, New York, N.Y. 10022, and in the United Kingdom and continental Europe by Kodansha Europe Ltd., 95 Aldwych, London WC2B 4JF.

Published by Kodansha International Ltd., 17-14, Otowa 1-chome, Bunkyo-ku, Tokyo 112-8652 and Kodansha America, Inc.

First Edition, 2001
01 02 03 04 05 06 07 08 09 10   10 9 8 7 6 5 4 3 2 1

www.thejapanpage.com

CONTENTS

CONTENTS

PUBLISHER'S NOTE

Kodansha's Elementary Kanji Dictionary is an up-to-date dictionary of Shin-kyōiku Kanji, the 1,006 characters that form the core of elementary school education in Japan. It aims to be as comprehensive as possible within self-imposed limits, but at the same time, and most importantly, to be portable and handy. Moreover, maximum priority has been given to ease of access: first, by listing the characters according to their most familiar, traditional radicals; second, by providing three types of indices to facilitate the often time-consuming task of locating the desired character. Definitions of individual characters and kanji compounds are given in clear, straightforward English. Distinctions are made between noun and verb forms of character compounds for utmost precision.

In the realm of kanji compounds, particular attention has been paid to combinations that appear frequently in contemporary newspapers, magazines, and other forms of mass media, but which are sometimes neglected in Japanese-English dictionaries. Thus, the dictionary does not confine itself to the standard selection of compounds. It chooses, rather, to include any kanji combination that is likely to be a problem for the student of modern Japanese.

This convenient and handy format has been achieved by focusing on a judicious selection of general and specialized kanji compounds, to the exclusion of rarer and more archaic words and meanings. The result is a compact and portable dictionary designed to serve the needs of the increasing number of people throughout the world who are learning to read and write Japanese.

In the compilation of the dictionary, numerous domestic Japanese and Japanese-English character dictionaries were consulted, the most important of which are listed below. Meanings given for characters and compounds follow modern domestic and Japanese-English practice.

Nelson, Andrew Nathaniel. *The Modern Reader's Japanese-English Character Dictionary*. Second revised edition. Tokyo: Charles E. Tuttle Company, 1974.

Nishio Minoru et al. *Iwanami Kokugo Jiten*. Tokyo: Iwanami Shoten, 1986.

Onoue Kanehide et al. *Ōbunsha Shōgaku Kanji Saishin Jiten*. Tokyo: Obunsha, 1990.

Ōmura Hama et al. *Sanseidō Shōgaku Kanwa Jiten*. Tokyo: Sanseido, 1989.

Masuda, Koh, et al. *Kenkyusha's New Japanese-English Dictionary*. Fourth edition. Tokyo: Kenkyusha, 1974.

Spann, M., and W. Hadamitzky. *Japanese Character Dictionary: With Compound Lookup via any Kanji*. Tokyo: Nichigai Associates, 1989.

Suzuki Shūji et al. *Kadokawa Saishin Kanwa Jiten*. Tokyo: Kadokawa Shoten, 1990.

Umesao Tadao et al. *Nihongo Daijiten*. Tokyo: Kodansha, 1989.

Yamaguchi Akiho et al. *Iwanami Kango Jiten*. Tokyo: Iwanami Shoten, 1987.

Global Management Group. *Shin Bijinesu Eigo Daijiten*. Tokyo: PMC, 1990.

INTRODUCTION TO THE JAPANESE WRITING SYSTEM

Stefan Kaiser

1. A Mixed Writing System

Japanese is written with a combination of kanji (Chinese characters) and two sets of phonetic syllabaries or *kana*, known as *hiragana* and *katakana*. Apart from a few exceptions, such as children's books (written in *hiragana*), Japanese Braille (*hiragana* based), and telegrams (traditionally written in *katakana*), these components are rarely used independently in running text.

Kanji, *hiragana*, and *katakana* are therefore not three separate writing systems but rather three different but complementary scripts used in conjunction within the Japanese writing system. They can be broadly defined as follows: (1) Kanji. Used for elements that carry meaning (or content), such as proper and common nouns, and the stem part of verbs and adjectives. (2) *Katakana* (the angular *kana* script). Used in a similar way to that of italics in English: namely, for foreign words and names (other than those that have been rendered into kanji), certain scientific and technical terms (such as names of species), and for emphasis of a particular word or phrase in a sentence. (3) *Hiragana* (the cursive *kana* script). Used for functional elements expressing grammatical relations (case particles, conjunctions, etc.) and inflectional endings.

In sum, kanji and *katakana* can be grouped together as expressing content units (often compared to building blocks), whereas *hiragana* is used to hold units (blocks) together within sentences like mortar.

この自動車はデザインがたいへん優れている。
"The design of this car is quite outstanding."

Here, the noun *jidōsha* "car" and the stem of the verb *sugureru* "be outstanding" are written in kanji; the foreign word *dezain* "design" is written in *katakana*; and grammatical elements such as the determiner *kono* "this," the adverb of degree *taihen* "quite," the topic and subject particles *wa* and *ga*, and the inflectional ending *-te iru* are written in *hiragana*. (For an explanation of *hiragana* usage for the penultimate syllable *re* in vowel-stem verbs, see section 4, below.)

2. The Function of Kanji in Running Japanese Text

As Japanese does not mark word boundaries in text, the use of visually distinct kanji (and *katakana*) within the basic *hiragana* script itself functions as an indicator of a word boundary. As kanji are used for content words, a typical unit of meaning begins with a kanji and ends with *hiragana* (particles or inflectional endings etc.).

3. Readings

As the term "Chinese characters" implies, kanji were originally imported from China, along with Buddhism (in its Chinese form) and Chinese culture, accompanied by a large number of Chinese loanwords pertaining to these areas. A kanji therefore entered Japan accompanied by its Chinese pronunciation, in a form adapted to the Japanese sound system; this is called its ON (音) reading. Later, Japanese readings developed for many kanji by using them to express a Japanese word of equivalent or related meaning. This is called the KUN (訓) reading. Thus, the Chinese word for "child" acquired the KUN reading こ ("child" in native Japanese) in addition to its ON reading シ. Sometimes several Japanese words became attached to one kanji, as in the following example which has a total of two ON and eight KUN readings:

上
ジョウ・ショウ
うえ・うわ・かみ・あ（げる）・あ（がる）・の（ぼる）・の（ぼせ
る）・の（ぼす）

There are some kanji that have more than one ON reading. This is because readings entered Japan from China in three major waves, at different times and from different areas in China, or in other cases, such as 楽, because the kanji had more than one meaning attached to it in the original Chinese. 楽 has two ON readings: pronounced ガク, it means "music"; pronounced ラク, "easy, happy."

Kanji with multiple readings, however, are infrequent: of the 1,945 Jōyō Kanji, about two-thirds have either only a single ON reading or one ON and one KUN reading.

4. The Use of *Okurigana*

Most verbs and adjectives have their (unchanging) stems written in kanji, and their (changing) inflectional endings written in *hiragana*.

VERBS
consonant-stem: 読む・読んだ・読めば
vowel-stem: 起きる・起きた・起きれば
　　　　　食べる・食べた・食べれば

ADJECTIVES
-i: 早い・早かった・早ければ
-shii: 新しい・新しかった・新しければ

This use of *hiragana* is referred to as *okurigana*, which literally means "*kana* suffix." There are a number of conventions to be observed when using *okurigana*, whose main function, as alluded to above, is to show the inflectional ending of a verb or adjective. The following points should also be noted: *okurigana* does not always show the inflectional ending clearly (*yom-u*, for example, would be a better analysis of a consonant-stem verb than *yo-mu*). Likewise, vowel-stem verbs and -*shii* adjectives follow a stylistic convention whereby the penultimate syllable, though not being strictly a part of the inflectional ending, is written as *okurigana*. Further examples of adjectives whose penultimate syllables conventionally appear in the *kana* script are 大きい and 小さい.

5. Readings: Single Elements and Compounds (熟語 *Jukugo*)

• ON or KUN?

Kanji are used to write either Chinese loanwords (漢語 *kango*) or native Japanese words (和語 *wago*). There is a marked difference between their usage in that, while *kango* are usually found as compounds comprising two or more single elements, *wago* most commonly consist of a single kanji.

When used in *kango*, therefore, kanji typically represent what we may call "the building blocks of word formation," whereas *wago* free-words are commonly expressed by one kanji (although it is not uncommon to find *wago* compounds in written Japanese). To illustrate this point with an example given earlier, the kanji for "child" can only be used alone in its *wago* form, as in the following sentence:

この子は大きい子だ。
"This child is a big child."

Used in *kango*, however, it can only be used in compounds.

子孫 シソン "descendant"
子宮 シキュウ "uterus"
子音 シオン "vowel"
母子 ボシ "mother and child"
分子 ブンシ "element; molecule"

This use of kanji proved invaluable during the introduction of Western technology in the nineteenth century, when in both China and Japan a great many new terms had to be coined in order to convey new ideas and technology. Take, for instance, the element 圧 ア ツ "pressing down; pressure."

圧縮 アッシュク "compression"
圧搾 アッサク "constriction"
圧力 アツリョク "pressure"
気圧 キアツ "atmospheric pressure"
血圧 ケツアツ "blood pressure"
高圧 コウアツ "high pressure"
水圧 スイアツ "water/hydraulic pressure"

電圧 デンアツ "voltage"

Thus, given the fact that a compound can be either a *kango* or *wago* combination, the learner of Japanese often has trouble deciding the correct reading of a kanji in running text (is it ON or is it KUN?). Unfortunately, there is no foolproof way to determine the right reading, but some statistical tendencies do help in forming a number of ground rules.

Ground Rule 1

Groups of kanji do not generally mix in their readings; i.e., they are read as either ON or KUN.

ON: 教育学概論 キョウイクガクガイロン　制度化 セイドカ
KUN: 安値 やすね　閏年 うるうどし

Ground Rule 2

A kanji that is part of a compound is almost always read in its ON reading.

音楽 オンガク　政治改革 セイジカイカク

Ground Rule 3

If a compound contains *okurigana*, it normally has a KUN reading.

乗り換える のりかえる　引き渡す ひきわたす

Ground Rule 4

A kanji that stands alone is normally read in its KUN reading.

この子は大きい子だ。

Although there are exceptions to these rules, they can nevertheless serve as useful guidelines to the beginner while he or she learns to determine how a kanji is read from experience.

• *Ateji*

One area of kanji usage whose unpredictable nature makes it particularly difficult for the learner is *ateji*. *Ateji* are kanji that are used to represent Japanese sounds regardless of their meaning or, conversely, meanings regardless of their sounds.

乙女 オトめ "maiden," where the first part of the Japanese word is similar in sound to the kanji's ON reading (オツ).

意気地なし イくジなし "spineless," where the first and third syllables represent ON readings, and the second, an approximation of the kanji's KUN reading.

Sometimes kanji with auspicious meanings are chosen for *ateji*; this is particularly common in the case of personal names.

美千代 Michiyo ("beauty" + "one thousand" + "generations")

Ateji include cases where a compound made from two kanji elements is equated with a Japanese word of equal or similar meaning.

悪戯 いたずら "mischief"
悪阻 つわり "morning sickness"

6. How Many Kanji Does One Need?

The Japan Industrial Standard (JIS) kanji codes of 1978 (rev. 1983) list well over 6,000 kanji, a number that may be regarded as the upper level of kanji usage in Japan. In newspapers and magazines, the total number used has been counted at approximately 3,300 or so. In contrast, the Shin-kyōiku Kanji number only 1,006. How useful is this number for reading Japanese?

Because the more frequent kanji are encountered over and over again, one can in fact achieve a great deal with a limited number of kanji; thus, the most frequent 500 cover about eighty percent of newspaper kanji; that figure increases to ninety-four percent if you know the top 1,000 kanji.

7. Kanji Composition

The majority (about two-thirds) of Jōyō Kanji are "phonetic compounds"; these are made up from a "radical" indicating the field of meaning to which the kanji belongs, and a "phonetic," which gives an indication of the ON reading. These two elements are arranged in a variety of combinations (the shaded section is the radical; examples are at right).

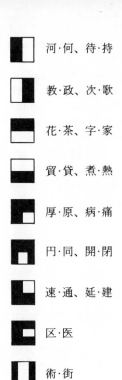

河・何、待・持

教・政、次・歌

花・茶、字・家

貿・貸、煮・熱

厚・原、病・痛

円・同、開・閉

速・通、延・建

区・医

術・街

回・因

The reminder can be divided into simple kanji and non-phonetic compounds. Simple kanji are typically stylized drawings of objects.

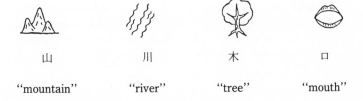

山	川	木	口
"mountain"	"river"	"tree"	"mouth"

There is a correlation between the frequency of use of a kanji and its complexity in terms of number of strokes. Simply put, the kanji with the fewest strokes are the most frequently used. The implications of this fact are that a significant proportion of simple kanji (which give no phonetic clues and need to be memorized on the basis of their shape) are composed of a limited number of strokes and do not, for that reason, put an undue strain on the learner's memory. Furthermore, they are encountered so often that they are easily retained.

Non-phonetic compounds consist of two or four simple kanji put together to indicate a new idea.

roof + pig = house 家
tree + tree = woods 林
tree + tree + tree = forest 森

8. Phonetic Compounds and Kanji Learning Strategy

The proportion of phonetic compounds in which the phonetic indicator gives a perfect indication of the kanji's ON reading is almost fifty-eight percent (a), while a partly reliable indication is achieved in nearly thirty-three percent (b); just under ten percent of cases provide no useful indication (c).

a) 寺 ジ 持 ジ
b) 古 コ　苦 ク
c) 十 ジュウ　針 シン

It is, therefore, quite possible to make an "educated guess" about the ON reading of an unknown kanji (and the field of meaning to which it belongs).

Apart from its use in guesswork, the phonetic indicator can also be used a a tool in the memorization process that is inevitably associated with kanji learning. An efficient way of committing new kanji to memory is to relate the phonetic indicator to known elements with the same or similar ON readings, keeping in separate drawers identical or similar elements with different ON.

9. Kanji Made in Japan: *Kokuji*

A number of kanji have been made up by the Japanese on the Chinese model. The composition of these kanji is mostly of the non-phonetic compound variety, such as 畑 はたけ (burning + field = dry field), and 峠 とうげ (mountain + high/low = mountain pass), and therefore tend not to have an ON reading. However, some have both ON and KUN, like 働 ドウ　はたらく・く, and some even have ON readings only, such as 塀 ヘイ and 錠 ジョウ. Although not part of the Jōyō Kanji list, there are many more such characters, of which a good number are names of indigenous fish and vegetation.

10. Kanji and Writing Styles

Finally, a word should be said about the stylistic dimension of kanji in general and Jōyō Kanji in particular. The use of kanji in a text can be regarded as a broad indicator of technical content, as they typically express Sino-Japanese vocabulary. This explains why kanji are used liberally in scientific articles etc. but only sparingly in poetry.

Insofar as the Jōyō Kanji are concerned, the media and even many academic periodicals tend, by and large, to abide by the official list. Literature, on the other hand, is quite a different story, making good use of *ateji* and other kanji not officially recognized. Some authors even go out of their way to dot their texts with rare and abstruse kanji, employing their multifunctional nature (variant readings etc.) as stylistic devices.

USER'S MANUAL

This section offers you a few tips on how to use *Kodansha's Elementary Kanji Dictionary*—how to get the information you need as efficiently as possible. It is organized into the following sections: (1) keywords, (2) the organization of the book, (3) how to look up the characters, (4) how to look up the compounds, (5) sample entries with explanatory notes, and (6) abbreviations.

1. Keywords

This section sets out to explain the meaning of the following keywords and how they are used throughout this dictionary: kanji, radical, stroke number, stroke order, ON reading, KUN reading, *jukugo*, and *gojūon-jun*.

Kanji　漢字
"Kanji" (literally "Han letters") is the term used by the Japanese for the ideographs borrowed from China. They are ideographs in the sense that each character symbolizes a single idea and, by extension, represents the sound associated with that idea. Characters are used alongside the native phonetic syllabaries, *hiragana* and *katakana*, to express meaning as opposed to indicating the grammatical form of a word or phrase.

Radical　部首
A "radical" (*bushu*) is that part of a character that indicates the field of meaning to which the kanji belongs. It may appear at the left- or right-hand side of a kanji, at the top or bottom, or it may be an enclosure. Alternatively, as in the case of simple kanji, the character itself may be a radical. Chinese characters have been classified according to their radicals for nearly three centuries, and like most domestic character dictionaries for Japanese consumption, *Kodansha's Elementary Kanji Dictionary* orders kanji by radical. It is

therefore quite important for the student of written Japanese to be able to identify a radical both promptly and correctly.

Some radicals have variants. A variant is an abbreviated form of a radical, usually with a lower stroke count. A complete list of the radicals and their variants, arranged strictly by stroke count, has been collected together in the Radical Chart printed inside the back cover of the book. In contrast to the Radical Chart, both the Radical Index and the running column of radicals in the margin of the body of the book list variants according to the number of strokes of their parent radical, not the abbreviated number of strokes of the variant itself. For example, the variant 扌, which has three strokes, is listed under its parent radical 手, which has four.

Stroke Number 画数

"Stroke number" (*kakusū*) is the term that refers to the total number of strokes that make up a single character. The kanji listed in *Kodansha's Elementary Kanji Dictionary* contain between 1 and 20 strokes. Over two-thirds of these have a stroke number of between 9 and 12 strokes. As kanji are often listed according to their stroke number, we have appended an index that classifies the Shin-kyōiku Kanji by the total number of strokes. In addition, within each radical section all characters have been put in stroke-number order.

Stroke Order 書き順

The strokes of a Chinese character are written in a set sequence, known as "stroke order" (*kakijun*). It is essential to learn the correct stroke order if you wish to write kanji. The stroke order for all 1,006 Shin-Kyōiku Kanji is shown at the head of each entry.

ON Reading 音読み

Nearly all kanji entered Japan accompanied by a Chinese pronunciation in a form adapted to the Japanese sound system; this is called an ON reading (*on-yomi*). All ON readings are shown in *katakana*.

KUN Reading 訓読み

Kanji acquired further readings used to express native Japanese words of equivalent or related meaning, often called KUN readings (*kun-yomi*). In order to distinguish between ON and KUN readings, all KUN readings are given here in *hiragana*.

Jukugo 熟語

Two or more kanji can be combined in the form of a compound to make new words. These compounds are known as *jukugo*. Here the term *jukugo* refers to those compounds where all the kanji are read with their ON reading.

Gojūon-jun 五十音順

Gojūon-jun refers to the standard order of the two Japanese phonetic syllabaries. Literally it means the "order of the fifty sounds" and is reproduced below for both *hiragana* and *katakana*. Japanese words appearing in *Kodansha's Elementary Kanji Dictionary* are generally listed according to the *gojūon-jun* standard.

Hiragana

あ	か	さ	た	な	は	ま	や	ら	わ	ん
い	き	し	ち	に	ひ	み		り		
う	く	す	つ	ぬ	ふ	む	ゆ	る		
え	け	せ	て	ね	へ	め		れ		
お	こ	そ	と	の	ほ	も	よ	ろ	を	

Katakana

ア	カ	サ	タ	ナ	ハ	マ	ヤ	ラ	ワ	ン
イ	キ	シ	チ	ニ	ヒ	ミ		リ		
ウ	ク	ス	ツ	ヌ	フ	ム	ユ	ル		
エ	ケ	セ	テ	ネ	ヘ	メ		レ		
オ	コ	ソ	ト	ノ	ホ	モ	ヨ	ロ	ヲ	

Note: The tables are read from top to bottom, left to right: i.e., *a, i, u, e, o, ka, ki, ku*, etc.

2. About the Organization of the Book

This section deals with the structure and organization of *Kodansha's Elementary Kanji Dictionary*.

Shin-kyōiku Kanji

In 1992 the Japanese Ministry of Education issued a list of 1,006 "Education Characters" (Shin-kyōiku Kanji) which form the core of kanji education in all elementary schools in Japan. Accordingly each of the 1,006 Shin-kyōiku Kanji is explained in a separate entry in this dictionary.

Arrangement of Characters

As mentioned above, it is most convenient to arrange kanji according to their radicals, and in fact most character dictionaries, both for native Japanese speakers and foreign learners as well, are structured in this way. All entry characters in *Kodansha's Elementary Kanji Dictionary* are listed by their traditionally attributed radical. Thus the 1,006 Shin-kyōiku Kanji are divided into 202 radical sections. The radical sections themselves are arranged by stroke number, the first radical being of a single stroke and the final radical containing fourteen strokes. Within each radical section, the kanji are also arranged by their stroke number, a character of a lower stroke number coming before one of a higher stroke number.

Compounds

It is possible in most cases to combine two or more characters together and make a compound. *Kodansha's Elementary Kanji Dictionary* lists a generous selection of commonly used compounds for each entry character where compounds exist. However, such compounds are listed only when the entry character is the first kanji in the compounds. Within each entry there are two categories of compounds.

a) *Jukugo* Group, where the entry character is read in its ON reading
b) KUN Group, where the entry character is read in its KUN reading

Compounds within each category are arranged in *gojūon-jun* order.

3. How to Look Up the Characters

There are three ways to look up characters in *Kodansha's Elementary Kanji Dictionary* by radical, by ON/KUN reading, and by stroke number.

Radical

Perhaps the quickest way to find a kanji is by using the Radical Chart printed inside the back cover. The Radical Chart is a table showing the radicals and their variants in stroke-number order and indicating the page on which each radical section begins. Looking up a character in this way depends on your skill at being able to identify a radical correctly (see "Kanji Composition," p. xiv). The procedure for looking up a character in this way is as follows: (a) determine the radical; (b) count the number of strokes contained in the radical; (c) locate the radical in the Radical Chart; (d) go to the page number as indicated in the chart; (e) and, last of all, find the character within its radical section.

There will be occasions when you will waste a lot of time looking for a character in the wrong radical section. This sometimes happens because the character in question has two or more possible radicals. In such cases, use of the Radical Index is recommended. This is a very useful index. Not only does it show all the characters that belong to a particular radical section, but it also lists those characters whose radicals are easily mistaken. Take the character 頭 "head," for instance. It contains two possible radicals: the radical 豆 "bean" and the radical 頁 "page." Unless you know that the correct radical for 頭 is 豆, then you will not be able to find the character by using just the Radical Chart. However, 頭 is listed under both radicals in the Radical Index. Consequently, unless you are absolutely sure of a kanji's correct radical, you should first check in the Radical Index.

ON/KUN Reading

If you know either the ON or KUN reading of a Chinese character, then it may be quicker to go to the ON/KUN Index. Here the regular ON/KUN readings, as established by the Japanese Ministry of Education, are listed in *gojūon-jun* order, together with the kanji number. As elsewhere in the book, ON readings are shown in *katakana* and KUN readings in *hiragana*.

Stroke Number

When you have problems determining the correct radical and don't know the ON or KUN reading of a kanji, you should refer to the Stroke Index. Here the characters are classified according to their stroke number. You simply count the number of strokes contained in the character, and then look it up in the corresponding list in the Stroke Index.

The various ways of looking up characters are summarized in the diagram printed inside the front cover.

4. How to Look Up the Compounds

Once you have learned how to look up characters, finding a compound is a relatively easy task. The first thing to remember is that all compounds in *Kodansha's Elementary Kanji Dictionary* are listed under the character that is the initial kanji in the compound. For example, the compound 洗脳 "brainwashing" is listed under the character 洗, not the character 脳. The second thing to have in mind is that, where applicable, there are two separate compound groups:

a) *Jukugo* Group (clue: first kanji is read with its ON reading)
b) KUN Group (clue: first kanji is read with its KUN reading)

Take, for example, the compound 断言 ダンゲン "assertion; affirmation; declaration." This compound will be found under the entry for the character 断. When you go to this entry you will find that there are two compound groups—the *jukugo* and KUN groups. In this case, however, the first kanji is used with its ON reading and will therefore be located in the *jukugo* group, marked by the symbol 熟 .

Again, take the compound 旅人 たびびと "traveler; wayfarer; pilgrim," which is listed under the entry for 旅. Here, the first kanji is read in KUN and so it can be found in the KUN group, marked with the symbol 訓 .

5. Sample Entries with Explanatory Notes

This section deals with the typography used throughout *Kodansha's Elementary Kanji Dictionary*.

Radical Section Header

① This digit represents the radical or variant's stroke number.
② Radical or variant.
③ Traditional Japanese name of radical or variant.
④ Given English name of radical or variant.

Character Entry

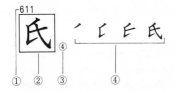

① Kanji number. This is the number that is used to identify the character in each of the indices that have been appended at the back of the book.
② Kanji box. An enlarged example of the entry character in a box.
③ Stroke number. The total number of strokes contained in the entry character.
④ Stroke order The order of strokes when writing the entry character.

ON Reading

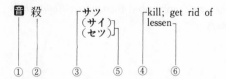

① ON reading symbol—the character for ON 音 in a black box.
② Entry character illustrated in standard type.
③ Regular ON reading.
④ Meaning attached to the regular ON reading.
⑤ Irregular ON reading.
⑥ Meaning attached to the irregular ON reading.

Compounds (*Jukugo*)

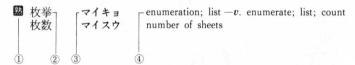

Compounds are listed as shown above in *gojūon-jun* order. The compound can be made into a verb by adding the verb *suru* "to do" when a verb form (indicated by the abbreviations *v* or *vt*) is included in the definition.

① *Jukugo* symbol—the character for *juku* 熟 in a black box.
② Compound.
③ Regular reading of compound.
④ Definition/explanation of the meaning and usage of the compound.

KUN Reading and KUN Compounds

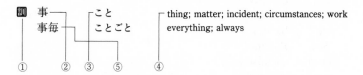

① KUN reading symbol—the character for KUN 訓 in a black box.
② Entry character.
③ Regular KUN reading.
④ Meaning attached to this KUN reading.
⑤ Regular KUN compound.

6. Abbreviations

adj.	adjective
bas.	baseball
bio.	biology
Bud.	Buddhist
chem.	chemistry
clas.	classical
col.	colloquial
derog.	derogatory
fig.	figurative(ly)
hist.	historical
hon	honorific
hum.	humble
math.	mathematics
med.	medicine
n.	noun
phy.	physics
v.	verb
vi.	intransitive verb
vt.	transitive verb

THE SHIN-KYŌIKU KANJI

一 ｜ 、 ノ 乙 ｣

音 一	イチ	one; equal; the first; whole
	イツ	one; entirely
熟 一因	イチイン	one cause among many; a single factor
一員	イチイン	a member of a group; one member
一円	イチエン	the whole area; all over; one yen
一応	イチオウ	tentatively; provisionally; anyhow; once; in outline; for the time being
一月	イチガツ	January
一丸	イチガン	one lump
一群	イチグン	one group
一芸	イチゲイ	one art; one of the arts
一合目	イチゴウめ	arbitrary tenth of the height of a mountain; beginning of a mountain climb
一言	イチゴン	(one) word/phrase; utterance
一次	イチジ	the first *math.* linear
一時	イチジ	for a time; (at) one time; once; one o'clock
一日	イチジツ	one/some day; first day of the month
一日千秋	イチジツ センシュウ	feel as if a day were so many years; waiting impatiently
一助	イチジョ	aid; some help
一条	イチジョウ	one line; one of a series of articles in a document; an event
一場	イチジョウ	one scene/place
一族	イチゾク	one's whole family; one's kinsmen
一存	イチゾン	one's own will/opinion
一代	イチダイ	one life/dynasty; one/first generation
一大事	イチダイジ	serious matter/affair
一団	イチダン	body; group; crowd of people
一段落	イチダンラク	pause; one pause for the present —*vi.* pause; suspend
一同	イチドウ	all present; all persons concerned; everybody
一読	イチドク	a reading —*v.* read over; read through once
一日	イチニチ	some day; all day; one day
一任	イチニン	delegation; trust —*v.* leave a matter to a person; entrust
一人前	イチニンまえ	grown-up; adult; one adult portion (of food)

1

一｜
、ノ
乙しＬ
亅

一年	イチネン	one year
一念	イチネン	zeal; enthusiasm; concentration
一部	イチブ	one part/section/book
一部始終	イチブシジュウ	the whole story from beginning to end; all the details
一望	イチボウ	one view —v. look out; take in the view
一望千里	イチボウセンリ	a fine view of a boundless plain; a clear view in the distance
一味	イチミ	the same group/party; a single flavor
一名	イチメイ	one person; another name; alias
一命	イチメイ	(one) life
一面	イチメン	one side
一文	イチモン	old Japanese coin; one tenth of a sen; tiny sum of money
一門	イチモン	whole family; one clan
一問一答	イチモンイットウ	question and answer —vi. give an immediate answer to each question
一夜	イチヤ	one night; some night; single night
一様	イチヨウ	even; equality
一覧	イチラン	a look; a glance —v. look over; take a look; glance through
一理	イチリ	some truth; a truth
一利一害	イチリイチガイ	advantages and disadvantages
一律	イチリツ	equality; monotony; uniformity
一流	イチリュウ	first or highest in a group; unique; first class
一両日	イチリョウジツ	a day or two
一輪	イチリン	one flower/wheel; the next full moon
一例	イチレイ	an example
一連	イチレン	series; ream
一路	イチロ	road; straight
一割	イチワリ	ten percent
一家	イッカ	family; master; an authority
一画	イッカク	a stroke in writing; building lot
一級	イッキュウ	first/top class; first rate
一挙一動	イッキョイチドウ	one's every action
一挙両得	イッキョリョウトク	kill two birds with one stone
一計	イッケイ	plan; idea
一見	イッケン	(one) glance —v. have a look; glance; take a quick look
一件	イッケン	affair; matter; item
一考	イッコウ	consideration —v. consider
一行	イッコウ	one event; party; group
一刻	イッコク	moment; instant

2

一切	イッサイ	all; entire; whole
一策	イッサク	plan; idea
一昨日	イッサクジツ	the day before yesterday
一式	イッシキ	complete set
一首	イッシュ	one poem
一種	イッシュ	one kind/type
一周	イッシュウ	a round; one lap —*v.* go round
一笑	イッショウ	laugh —*v.* laugh at
一生	イッショウ	one's (whole) life
一身	イッシン	oneself; one's whole body
一身上	イッシンジョウ	personal; private
一新	イッシン	renewal —*v.* renew; change completely
一進一退	イッシンイッタイ	advance and retreat; ebb and flow
一心不乱	イッシンフラン	heart and soul; concentration
一世	イッセ	one existence (past, present, or future)
一世	イッセイ	a life; era; the first monarch in line of succession; first generation of immigrants
一席	イッセキ	meeting; sitting; first place
一石二鳥	イッセキニチョウ	kill two birds with one stone
一節	イッセツ	one paragraph/phrase
一説	イッセツ	another opinion/view; one opinion; one way of looking at things
一線	イッセン	a line; the front line
一層	イッソウ	even more; all the more
一体	イッタイ	one body; a style; a form; (who/what) on earth?
一帯	イッタイ	tract of land; whole area
一朝一夕	イッチョウ イッセキ	brief space of time
一長一短	イッチョウ イッタン	merits and demerits
一直線	イッチョクセン	straight line
一対	イッツイ	pair
一手	イッテ	move in go or *shōgi;* monopoly
一定	イッテイ	fixed; definite; certain —*v.* fix; set; settle; define
一転	イッテン	change; complete change —*vi.* make a complete change
一等	イットウ	first place/prize/class
一時	イットキ	short time
一派	イッパ	school of thought
一筆	イッピツ	one uninterrupted stroke of a pen; brief note
一服	イップク	dose of medicine; puff of a cigarette; rest —*v.* have/take a rest

一片	イッペン	piece; fragment of a thin object
一辺	イッペン	one side
一変	イッペン	(complete) change —*v.* change (completely)
一歩	イッポ	step; footstep
一方	イッポウ	one side/part; on one hand
一方的	イッポウテキ	one-sided; unilateral
一本気	イッポンギ	single-minded
一本調子	イッポンチョウシ	a monotone; monotony

訓 一つ	ひとつ	one
一	ひと	(prefix) one; single
一雨	ひとあめ	shower; rainfall
一息	ひといき	breath; rest; breather
一重	ひとえ	single; onefold
一際	ひときわ	in general; one time (long ago)
一昔	ひとむかし	decade
一休み	ひとやすみ	brief rest; breather; break —*vi.* take a rest; take a breather

---

2

七 ② 一 七

音 七	シチ	seven
熟 七月	シチガツ	July
七五三	シチゴサン	(celebration of) a child's third, fifth, and seventh years
七五調	シチゴチョウ	the seven-and-five-syllable meter in Japanese poetry
七福神	シチフクジン	Seven Gods of Good Fortune
七面鳥	シチメンチョウ	turkey
訓 七	なな	seven
七つ	ななつ	seven
七日	なのか	seventh day (of the month); 7th

3

丁 ② 一 丁

音 丁	チョウ	leaf; page; block; even number
	テイ	youth; servant; the fourth of the ten calendar signs; polite
熟 丁度	チョウド	exactly; just; right; quite

丁場	チョウば	the distance between stages
丁半	チョウハン	odd and even numbers
丁字	テイジ	T
丁字形	テイジケイ	T-shaped
丁字路	テイジロ	T junction
丁重	テイチョウ	polite; courteous; civil; respectful; reverent

一 丨 丶 丿 乙 亅

4

下 ③ 一 丁 下

音	下	カ	under; lower part; descend; below; lower; go down; fall
		ゲ	below; lower part; be inferior; lower
熟	下位	カイ	lower rank; subordinate position
	下院	カイン	Lower House
	下記	カキ	the following; undermentioned; below
	下級	カキュウ	lower class/grade
	下降	カコウ	descent; fall; drop —*vi.* descend; fall; drop; decline
	下層	カソウ	lower classes
	下等	カトウ	low grade; meanness; inferiority
	下半身	カハンシン	lower half of the body
	下部	カブ	lower part
	下流	カリュウ	lower part of a river; downstream
	下界	ゲカイ	the earth; here below
	下戸	ゲコ	teetotaler; nondrinker
	下校	ゲコウ	leaving school for the day; coming home from school —*vi.* leave school for the day; come home from school
	下山	ゲザン	descent of a mountain —*vi.* climb down a mountain
	下車	ゲシャ	alighting —*vi.* alight from a train, car, bus
	下宿	ゲシュク	lodgings; boarding house —*vi.* lodge; board; take up lodgings
	下水	ゲスイ	sewage; sewer; drainage
	下船	ゲセン	disembarkation; going ashore —*vi.* leave a ship; go ashore
	下足	ゲソク	footwear
	下段	ゲダン	lowest step; lower berth
	下馬評	ゲバヒョウ	common talk; gossip; rumor
	下品	ゲヒン	coarse; rude; vulgar
	下落	ゲラク	fall; decline; drop; deterioration —*v.* fall; decline; drop; deteriorate

1 訓

下	した	low; inferior to; below; under; young
下絵	したえ	rough sketch; undersketch; design
下書き	したがき	rough draft
下着	したぎ	underwear; undergarments
下心	したごころ	ulterior motive
下地	したヂ	groundwork; preparations; first coat (of paint/lacquer); aptitude
下調べ	したしらべ	preliminary inquiry; preparations
下積み	したづみ	goods at the bottom of a pile; lowest social classes; the lowest
下手	したて (したで)	inferiority; downwards
下火	したび	fire that has burnt out; decline
下町	したまち	*shitamachi* (traditional working-class neighborhood)
下見	したみ	preliminary examination; clapboard; narrow board thicker at one edge than the other used for sliding
下役	したヤク	petty official; underling
下りる	おりる	*vi.* come down; get off/down/out
下ろす	おろす	*vt.* take down; grate; put down
下す	くだす	*vt.* let down; subdue; give; issue; pass; have loose bowels
下る	くだる	*vi.* descend; go down; pass
下り	くだり	descent; going down; away from the center of town
下さる	くださる	*vt.* **hon.** give; receive; oblige; favor with
下がる	さがる	*vi.* come down; leave; hang down; fall
下げる	さげる	*vt.* take down; lower; hang
下	しも	low; lower part; the governed; lower classes; lower half of the body
下座	しもザ	lower seat
下々	しもじも	the masses; lower classes
下手	しもて	downwards; right side of a stage; actor's right
下	もと	under; base

第一画
一、ノ乙し亅

5
三 ３
一 二 三

音	三	サン	three
熟	三角	サンカク	triangle
	三角関係	サンカクカンケイ	eternal triangle; love triangle
	三角形	サンカクケイ	triangle
	三角州	サンカクス	delta
	三月	サンガツ	March

6

三権	サンケン	three branches of government
三原色	サンゲンショク	three primary colors
三次元	サンジゲン	three-dimensional (3-D)
三方	サンポウ	three directions/sides; small wooden stand
三面記事	サンメンキジ	city news; police news

訓

三つ	みっつ	three
三	み	three
三日	みっか	third day (of the month); 3rd
三日月	みかづき	new/crescent moon
三つ	みつ	three

6

上 ③ ｜ ｜ 上

音 上 　ジョウ　　　　upper part; good; first; rise; get on
　　　　（ショウ）

熟

上位	ジョウイ	superior/higher rank
上映	ジョウエイ	movie screening/showing —*v*. screen; show/put on a movie
上演	ジョウエン	performance; presentation —*v*. perform; present
上官	ジョウカン	senior officer; superior
上記	ジョウキ	the above; the above-mentioned
上気	ジョウキ	blushing; rush of blood to the cheeks —*vi*. have a rush of blood to the head; blush; go red in the cheeks
上級	ジョウキュウ	upper grade; upper; higher; senior
上京	ジョウキョウ	going to Tokyo —*vi*. come up to Tokyo
上下	ジョウゲ	vertical; up and down; top and bottom; fluctuation; social standing —*v*. go up and down; rise and fall; fluctuate
上下関係	ジョウゲカンケイ	social standing
上下動	ジョウゲドウ	up-and-down movement; vertical earthquake
上限	ジョウゲン	upper limit; maximum
上戸	ジョウゴ	heavy drinker
上告	ジョウコク	final appeal —*vi*. make a final appeal
上司	ジョウシ	one's superior/boss
上質	ジョウシツ	fine/choice quality
上述	ジョウジュツ	the above; the above-mentioned
上々	ジョウジョウ	excellent; the very best
上申	ジョウシン	report —*v*. report to one's superiors
上申書	ジョウシンショ	written report
上水	ジョウスイ	water supply; tap/city water

一
丨
丶
丿
乙
亅

上水道	ジョウスイドウ	water works
上席	ジョウセキ	seniority; upper rank
上奏	ジョウソウ	report —*v.* report to the emperor
上層	ジョウソウ	upper class/layer/stratum/air
上体	ジョウタイ	upper part of the body
上代	ジョウダイ	in old/ancient times
上達	ジョウタツ	advancement; progress; improvement —*vi.* make progress; advance; improve; become proficient
上段	ジョウダン	upper section/deck/berth
上程	ジョウテイ	lay before/introduce/present to the Diet
上出来	ジョウでき	good work; well-made; well-done
上等	ジョウトウ	fine/top quality; excellent
上人	ショウニン	saint; holy priest
上半身	ジョウハンシン	upper half of the body
上品	ジョウヒン	elegant; refined; in good taste
上部	ジョウブ	upper part; top
上物	ジョウもの	choice/high quality goods
上陸	ジョウリク	landing; disembarkation —*vi.* land; make a landing; go on shore
上流	ジョウリュウ	upper reaches of a river; upstream; upper classes
訓 上がり	あがり	rise; income; returns; proceeds
上がる	あがる	*vi.* rise; go up; come in; enter; be promoted; (rain) stops **hon.** eat
上げる	あげる	*v.* raise; lift; invite; send; give; be promoted; vomit
上	うえ	top; upper part; above; over; on; upon; older; senior; better
上	うわ	(prefix) upper; up-
上書き	うわがき	address
上着	うわぎ	coat; jacket
上手	うわて	upper part/course
上の空	うわのそら	absentmindedly
上辺	うわべ	surface; outward; seeming
上回る	うわまわる	*vi.* exceed; be better; surpass
上向き	うわむき	upward; looking up
上目使い	うわめづかい	upturned eyes/glance
上役	うわヤク	one's superior
上	かみ	up a river; upstream
上方	かみがた	Kyoto and vicinity; the Kyoto-Osaka area
上座	かみザ	front seat; seat of honor; top of the class
上手	かみて	upper part/course; right hand side of the stage
上せる	のぼせる	*vt.* put in; put on record *vi.* feel dizzy

| 上り | のぼり | ascent; going up; toward the center of town |
| 上る | のぼる | *vi.* climb; go up; reach; amount to |

7 万 ③ 一 フ 万

音	万	バン	countless; myriad; all
		マン	ten thousand; myriad
熟	万感	バンカン	flood of emotions; various emotions
	万古	バンコ	perpetuity; eternity
	万国	バンコク	all nations
	万策	バンサク	every means; all possible ways
	万事	バンジ	everything; all
	万障	バンショウ	all obstacles; various problems/business
	万象	バンショウ	the universe; all things; everything
	万全	バンゼン	perfect; sure
	万難	バンナン	innumerable difficulties; all obstacles
	万人	バンニン	all people; everybody
	万能	バンノウ	almighty; omnipotent; all-around; all-purpose
	万物	バンブツ	all things; all creation
	万民	バンミン	all the people; nation
	万有	バンユウ	all things; all creation; universal
	万有引力	バンユウ インリョク	universal gravitation
	万一	マンイチ	by any chance; should happen to
	万年	マンネン	eternity; perpetuity; ten thousand years
	万年筆	マンネンヒツ	fountain-pen
	万引き	マンびき	shoplifting; shoplifter
	万病	マンビョウ	all kinds of diseases; all diseases
	万力	マンリキ	vise

8 不 ④ 一 フ ァ 不

音	不	フ	not
		ブ	
熟	不安	フアン	uneasy; uncertain; insecure; suspenseful; fearful; nervous
	不安定	フアンテイ	instability; lack of stability
	不案内	フアンナイ	ignorance; unfamiliarity

不意	フイ	suddenly; unexpectedly
不運	フウン	misfortune
不可	フカ	bad; wrong; improper; impossible
不可解	フカカイ	mysterious; beyond comprehension; inscrutable
不可欠	フカケツ	indispensable; essential; vital
不可思議	フカシギ	strange; mysterious
不可分	フカブン	inseparable; indivisible; undetachable
不快	フカイ	unpleasant; rotten; disagreeable; offensive; sickness
不快指数	フカイシスウ	discomfort index
不覚	フカク	negligent; improvident; unprepared; unexpected
不規則	フキソク	irregular; unsystematic
不気味	ブキミ	weird; eerie; ominous; uncanny
不急	フキュウ	nonurgent; not pressing
不興	フキョウ	displeasure; ill humor; disgrace
不義理	フギリ	ingratitude; dishonesty; injustice
不器量	ブキリョウ	plain; ugly; homely
不具	フグ	*derog.* deformed; malformed; crippled
不景気	フケイキ	depression (esp. economic)
不経済	フケイザイ	uneconomical; wasteful; extravagant; expensive
不潔	フケツ	dirty; smutty; unclean; impure
不言実行	フゲンジッコウ	work before talk; action before words
不孝	フコウ	undutiful; disobedient; impious; thankless; ungrateful
不幸	フコウ	unhappy; unfortunate; unlucky; death of a close relative
不合格	フゴウカク	failure; disqualification
不合理	フゴウリ	irrational; illogical; unreasonable; preposterous
不心得	フこころえ	indiscreet; imprudent; unwise
不在	フザイ	absence; being away
不在投票	フザイトウヒョウ	absentee voting
不作	フサク	poor crop; bad harvest
不作法	ブサホウ	bad manners/form; rudeness
不治	フジ	incurable; malignant (disease)
不時	フジ	emergency; unexpectedness; sudden
不思議	フシギ	mysterious; wonderful; marvelous; strange; uncanny
不自然	フシゼン	unnatural; artificial
不時着	フジチャク	forced/emergency landing
不実	フジツ	unfaithful; insincere; cold-hearted; untruth; falsehood
不始末	フシマツ	mismanagement; misconduct; malpractice; improvidence
不死身	フジみ	immortal; invincible; indomitable

不自由	フジユウ	inconvenient; uncomfortable —*vi.* be troubled by
不純	フジュン	impure; foul; mixed
不承不承	フショウブショウ	unwillingly; reluctantly; grudgingly
不信	フシン	distrust; mistrust; disbelief; insincerity; fidelity
不信任	フシンニン	lack of confidence
不正	フセイ	injustice; unfairness; wrong; illegality
不世出	フセイシュツ	rare
不成績	フセイセキ	poor results; bad record; underachievement
不全	フゼン	imperfect; incomplete
不戦勝	フセンショウ	unearned win; win by default
不相応	フソウオウ	unsuitable; unfit; inappropriate; unbecoming
不足	フソク	lack; insufficiency; shortage; need; want; discontent; dissatisfaction —*vi.* lack; be short of; be discontented
不測	フソク	unforeseen; unexpected
不断	フダン	ceaseless; incessant; continual; usually; habitually
不調	フチョウ	bad condition; rupture; failure; fiasco
不通	フツウ	interruption; suspension (of traffic); unreliable; hard to understand; unclear
不都合	フツゴウ	inconvenient; inexpedient
不定	フテイ	indefinite; uncertain; unsettled; unfixed
不定期	フテイキ	irregular (time period)
不体裁	フテイサイ	unseemly; unsightly; indecent; improper
不敵	フテキ	brave; daring; intrepid; fearless
不出来	フデき	poor work; failure; bungle
不適合	フテキゴウ	incongruent
不手際	フてぎわ	clumsy; awkward; inept
不当	フトウ	injustice; wrongfulness; impropriety; unreasonableness
不同	フドウ	unequal; uneven; irregular; dissimilar
不動	フドウ	immovability; immobility; firmness; stability
不統一	フトウイツ	disorganized; disunited; divided; chaotic
不徳	フトク	vice; immorality; delinquency
不慣れ	フなれ	inexperience
不人情	フニンジョウ	unkind; unfeeling; inhuman; cold-hearted
不燃	フネン	incombustible; fireproof
不能	フノウ	inability; impotence
不敗	フハイ	invincible; undefeated; unbeatable
不発	フハツ	misfire; backfire
不備	フビ	deficiency; imperfection; inadequacy; lack; defect
不評	フヒョウ	unpopular; disreputable

1	不平等	フビョウドウ	unequal; unfair
	不服	フフク	dissatisfaction; discontentment; disagreement; objection; protest
	不平	フヘイ	complaint; grievance; discontent; displeasure
	不変	フヘン	unchangeable; invariable; constant
	不便	フベン	inconvenient
	不法	フホウ	unlawful; illegal; unjust
	不本意	フホンイ	reluctant; unwilling
	不満	フマン	discontent; dissatisfaction faction; displeasure
	不向き	ふむき	unsuitable; unfit; ill-fitting
	不明	フメイ	unknown; obscure; unclear; vague; ambiguous
	不毛	フモウ	unproductive; sterile; infertile; barren (land, projects, etc.)
	不問	フモン	ignore; disregard
	不夜城	フヤジョウ	nightless quarter; city that never sleeps
	不要	フヨウ	unnecessary; useless; needless
	不用	フヨウ	useless; unnecessary
	不用意	フヨウイ	unprepared; not organized
	不用心	ブヨウジン	careless; imprudent; insecure; unsafe
	不養生	フヨウジョウ	neglect of one's health
	不利	フリ	disadvantage
	不良	フリョウ	badness; inferiority; deliquency
	不漁	フリョウ	poor catch (of fish)
	不老不死	フロウフシ	eternal youth; immortality
	不和	フワ	discord; trouble; differences; disharmony

一 丨 、 丿 乙 乚 亅

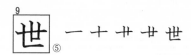

世⑤ 9   一 十 卅 卋 世

音	世	セ	world; life
		セイ	
熟	世紀	セイキ	century
	世界	セカイ	world; earth; circle; sphere
	世界的	セカイテキ	worldwide; international
	世間	セケン	the world; people; the public; circle of acquaintances
	世間体	セケンテイ	decency; appearances
	世間話	セケンばなし	chat; small talk
	世情	セジョウ	worldly matters; the ways of the world
	世相	セソウ	social conditions/aspects
	世帯	セタイ	household
	世代	セダイ	generation

世論	セロン（よロン）	public opinion; consensus of opinion
世話	セワ	aid; help; assistance; service; care; trouble; everyday life —v. help; assist; serve; care
お世辞	おセジ	compliment
訓 世	よ	society; times; life
世の中	よのなか	in the world/society; at large

10

両 ⑥　一　厂　丙　丙　両　両

音 両	リョウ	both; two; _ryō_ (old Japanese coin); (counter for cars, carriages, rolling stock)
熟 両院	リョウイン	both houses (of parliament/congress); upper and lower houses
両極	リョウキョク	the two poles; both extremities
両軍	リョウグン	two armies
両日	リョウジツ	both/two days
両者	リョウシャ	both people
両親	リョウシン	parents
両性	リョウセイ	both sexes; male and female
両生類	リョウセイルイ	amphibia (animal)
両断	リョウダン	divided into two —v. cut in two
両刀	リョウトウ	two swords
両得	リョウトク	double profit
両人	リョウニン	two/both people
両方	リョウホウ	both
両面	リョウメン	both faces/sides
両用	リョウヨウ	serving a double purpose
両様	リョウヨウ	two/both ways
両立	リョウリツ	coexistence; compatibility —vi. coexist; be compatible
両輪	リョウリン	two wheels

1	｜ ぼう rod; stick; line

一｜
、ノ
乙し
亅

11
中④ 丶 冂 口 中

音	中	チュウ	center; middle; medium; mediocrity; average
熟	中央	チュウオウ	center; middle; heart
	中学生	チュウガクセイ	junior high school student
	中学校	チュウガッコウ	junior high/middle school
	中型	チュウがた	medium-size
	中間	チュウカン	middle; midway
	中期	チュウキ	middle period
	中級	チュウキュウ	medium grade
	中近東	チュウキントウ	The Near and Middle East
	中位	チュウくらい	medium size; middling; moderate; passable
	中古	チュウコ	the middle ages; second hand; old
	中古車	チュウコシャ	used/second hand car
	中国	チュウゴク	China
	中座	チュウザ	leaving in the middle of a meeting —*vi.* leave before the meeting is over
	中産階級	チュウサンカイキュウ	the middle class
	中止	チュウシ	discontinuance; interruption; suspension; stoppage —*v.* discontinue; interrupt; suspend; stop
	中傷	チュウショウ	slander; libel; malicious gossip —*v.* slander; libel
	中心	チュウシン	center; middle; heart; balance
	中世	チュウセイ	Middle Ages
	中性	チュウセイ	neuter
	中性子	チュウセイシ	*phy.* neutron
	中絶	チュウゼツ	abortion; interruption; suspension; intermission; stoppage —*v.* interrupt; suspend; stop; abort
	中退	チュウタイ	dropping out of school
	中段	チュウダン	middle of the stairs; middle berth
	中断	チュウダン	interruption; discontinuance; suspension —*v.* interrupt; discontinue; suspend
	中東	チュウトウ	Middle East
	中道	チュウドウ	halfway; middle of the road
	中毒	チュウドク	poisoning; toxication; intoxication —*v.* be poisoned
	中二階	チュウニカイ	mezzanine floor

	中肉中背	チュウニク チュウぜい	medium height and build; middle-sized person
	中日	チュウニチ	equinox; China and Japan
	中年	チュウネン	middle age; middle-aged person
	中腹	チュウフク	heart of the mountain
	中米	チュウベイ	Central America
	中立	チュウリツ	neutrality; neutral; independent —***vi***. be neutral/independent
	中立国	チュウリツコク	neutral power/country
	中流	チュウリュウ	midstream; middle class
	中和	チュウワ	neutralization; counteraction —***v***. neutralize; counteract
	お中元	おチュウゲン	*ochūgen* (midyear gift)
訓	中	なか	interior; middle; inside; contents; among; mean
	中入り	なかいり	recess; intermission; interval
	中身	なかみ	interior; contents; substance
	中休み	なかやすみ	rest; recess; break
	中指	なかゆび	middle finger

1 丶 てん dot; point

12

丸 ③ ノ 九 丸

音	丸	ガン	ball; round
熟	丸薬	ガンヤク	pill
訓	丸	まる	ball; circle; whole; castle tower
	丸い	まるい	round; globular; spherical
	丸暗記	まるアンキ	memorize everything just as it is
	丸損	まるゾン	complete loss
	丸太	まるタ	log
	丸出し	まるだし	exposed; uncovered
	丸々	まるまる	completely; entirely; wholly
	丸見え	まるみえ	fully exposed to view; in plain sight
	丸める	まるめる	***vt***. round; shave; make round; make a circle

13

主 ⑤　　丶　一　二　主　主

一
丶
ノ
乙
乚
亅

音	主	シュ	master; lord; the Lord; first concern; chief; main; principle
		（ス）	master

熟	主位	シュイ	position of leadership; central position
	主因	シュイン	primary/main cause; main factor
	主演	シュエン	star of a movie or a play
	主客	シュカク（シュキャク）	host and guest; primary and subordinate
	主観	シュカン	subjectivity
	主観的	シュカンテキ	subjective
	主管	シュカン	supervision; superintendence —*v.* supervise; have charge of
	主眼	シュガン	main point; principal objective
	主義	シュギ	principle; doctrine; belief
	主君	シュクン	one's lord/master
	主計	シュケイ	accountant; accounting
	主権	シュケン	sovereignty
	主権在民	シュケンザイミン	sovereignty rests with the people
	主権者	シュケンシャ	sovereign; supreme ruler
	主語	シュゴ	*gram.* subject
	主査	シュサ	chief examiner/investigator
	主事	シュジ	director; superintendent
	主治医	シュジイ	family doctor; attending physician
	主従	シュジュウ	master and servant; employer and employee
	主将	シュショウ	captain; supreme commander; commander-in-chief
	主唱	シュショウ	advocacy —*v.* advocate
	主食	シュショク	staple/principal food
	主人	シュジン	one's husband; head of the family; owner; proprietor
	主人公	シュジンコウ	hero; heroine; protagonist
	主席	シュセキ	the Chairman (as used in China—Chairman Mao, etc.)
	主体	シュタイ	main constituent; subject
	主題	シュダイ	theme; subject
	主張	シュチョウ	assertion; insistence; emphasis; advocacy —*v.* assert; insist; emphasize; advocate; lay stress on
	主導	シュドウ	leadership
	主任	シュニン	chief; head; manager

16

主犯	シュハン	principal offender; ring leader
主筆	シュヒツ	editor-in-chief; chief editor
主婦	シュフ	housewife
主部	シュブ	main part; subject
主役	シュヤク	leading part; starring role; star
主要	シュヨウ	principal; chief; main
主流	シュリュウ	main current/stream
主力	シュリョク	main force
訓 主	おも	chief; principal; leading
主	ぬし	master; owner

---

1 ノ の at the top; *no* (katakana)

14

久 ③ ノ ク 久

音 久	キュウ （ク）	long; long-standing
熟 久遠	クオン	eternity
訓 久しい	ひさしい	long; long-continued; long time

15

乗 ⑨ 一 ニ 二 千 千 垂 垂 乗 乗

音 乗	ジョウ	get on; ride; multiply
熟 乗じる	ジョウじる	*v.* take advantage of (weakness, darkness, etc.); multiply
乗員	ジョウイン	crew; crew member
乗客	ジョウキャク	passenger
乗降	ジョウコウ	getting on and off —*vi.* get on and off
乗算	ジョウサン	*math.* multiplication
乗車	ジョウシャ	taking a train/taxi —*vi.* take a train/taxi
乗車賃	ジョウシャチン	fare; busfare; trainfare
乗除	ジョウジョ	multiplication and division —*v.* multiply and divide
乗数	ジョウスウ	*math.* multiplier
乗船	ジョウセン	boarding ship; embarkation —*vi.* get on; board; embark

	乗馬	ジョウバ	riding; horseback riding —*vi.* ride/mount a horse
	乗法	ジョウホウ	*math.* multiplication
	乗務員	ジョウムイン	train crew; crew member
訓	乗る	のる	*vi.* get/step onto; take; board; mount; ride
	乗せる	のせる	*vt.* help a person get on; give a person a lift; take someone in
	乗り合い	のりあい	riding together; fellow passenger; partnership
	乗り入れる	のりいれる	*v.* ride; drive into
	乗り気	のりキ	interest; enthusiasm
	乗り切る	のりきる	*vi.* ride out; weather; survive
	乗組員	のりくみイン	crew
	乗り捨てる	のりすてる	*v.* get out of a vehicle
	乗り手	のりて	rider; passenger
	乗り場	のりば	stop; place to get on
	乗り物	のりもの	vehicle; vessel; aircraft; ride (at an amusement park)

---

1 乙 おつ second

16
九 ② ノ 九

音	九	キュウ	nine
		ク	nine
熟	九官鳥	キュウカンチョウ	myna bird; hill myna
	九死	キュウシ	narrowly escape death
	九月	クガツ	September
	九九	クク	*math.* multiplication table
訓	九つ	ここのつ	nine
	九日	ここのか	ninth day (of the month); 9th

17

乱 ⑦ 　ノ　ニ　千　舌　舌　舌　乱

音	乱	ラン	disorder; riot; rebellion
熟	乱交	ランコウ	orgy
	乱雑	ランザツ	disorder; confusion
	乱視	ランシ	astigmatism
	乱射	ランシャ	random shooting —*vi*. fire/shoot at random
	乱心	ランシン	derangement; insanity —*vi*. become mentally deranged/insane
	乱世	ランセ	tumultuous times
	乱戦	ランセン	confused/free-for-all fight
	乱造	ランゾウ	overproduction; careless manufacture —*v*. overproduce
	乱丁	ランチョウ	mixed-up collation
	乱読	ランドク	indiscriminate reading —*v*. read indiscriminately
	乱入	ランニュウ	intrusion; trespassing (in large numbers) —*vi*. intrude/trespass (in large numbers)
	乱売	ランバイ	dumping/selling at a loss —*v*. dump/sell at a loss
	乱筆	ランピツ	hasty writing; scrawl
	乱暴	ランボウ	violence; rough; reckless —*vi*. be violent/rough/reckless
	乱脈	ランミャク	confusion; chaos
	乱用	ランヨウ	abuse; misuse; misappropriation —*v*. abuse; misuse; missappropriate
	乱立	ランリツ	profusion —*vi*. profuse; flood
訓	乱れる	みだれる	*vi*. be in disorder; be confused/disorganized
	乱す	みだす	*vt*. put in disorder

18

乳 ⑧ 　ノ　く　く　か　ザ　孚　孚　乳

音	乳	ニュウ	milk
熟	乳液	ニュウエキ	milky liquid
	乳化	ニュウカ	emulsification —*vt*. emulsify
	乳牛	ニュウギュウ	cow in milk; dairy cow
	乳酸	ニュウサン	lactic acid

一
|
、
ノ
乙
し
•し
•」

乳歯	ニュウシ	milk tooth
乳児	ニュウジ	baby; infant; suckling
乳製品	ニュウセイヒン	dairy product
乳頭	ニュウトウ	nipple; teat
乳糖	ニュウトウ	milk sugar; lactose
乳白色	ニュウハクショク	milky white
乳幼児	ニュウヨウジ	infants

訓
乳	ちち	mother's milk; breast
乳	ち	milk
乳首	ちくび	nipple; teat
乳飲み子	ちのみご	unweaned baby; suckling child

---

1 亅 はねぼう feathered stick; hook; barb

19
事⑧　一　丶　𠄌　𠃌　亐　耳　事　事

音 事 ジ matter; work
　　　（ズ）

熟
事業	ジギョウ	work; undertaking; business; enterprise
事件	ジケン	event; happening; incident; matter; affair
事故	ジコ	accident; mishap; hitch; incident
事後	ジゴ	after the event/fact
事実	ジジツ	fact; the truth; actually; really; as a matter of fact
事実無根	ジジツムコン	groundless; false; unfounded
事象	ジショウ	matter; aspect; phase
事情	ジジョウ	reasons; circumstances; the situation; the case; conditions
事前	ジゼン	beforehand; in advance
事前調査	ジゼンチョウサ	feasibility study
事態	ジタイ	situation; state of affairs
事大主義	ジダイシュギ	submission to power; toadyism
事典	ジテン	encyclopedia
事物	ジブツ	things
事変	ジヘン	incident; disturbance
事務	ジム	office/clerical work; business
事務員	ジムイン	clerk
事務所	ジムショ	office

事務的	ジムテキ	clerical; businesslike	**1**
事由	ジユウ	reason; cause	
事例	ジレイ	precedent; case; example	
訓 事	こと	thing; matter; incident; circumstances; work	
事毎	ことごと	everything; always	

一
｜
丶
ノ
乙
し
亅 •

2 二 に two

20

二 一 二 ②

音	二	ニ	two; twice; again; next; (prefix) bi-
熟	二回	ニカイ	twice; two times; again
	二階	ニカイ	second floor; upstairs
	二月	ニガツ	February
	二級	ニキュウ	second-class
	二元	ニゲン	duality
	二号	ニゴウ	number two; concubine; mistress
	二言	ニゴン	duplicity; double-dealing; say something twice
	二次	ニジ	second (time)
	二次試験	ニジシケン	secondary examination
	二次的	ニジテキ	secondary
	二重	ニジュウ	duplicated; double
	二重人格	ニジュウジンカク	dual personality
	二乗	ニジョウ	*math*. square of a number —*v*. square (a number)
	二世	ニセイ	second generation; second generation of Japanese immigrants
	二足	ニソク	two legs/feet/pairs
	二束三文	ニソクサンモン	dirt-cheap
	二度	ニド	twice; two times
	二等	ニトウ	second-class/rate
	二等分	ニトウブン	bisection —*v*. bisect
	二の次	ニのつぎ	secondary importance
	二倍	ニバイ	double; twice; two-fold; as much again
	二番	ニバン	second; number two; runner-up
	二百十日	ニヒャクとうか	210th day; first day of spring
	二部	ニブ	two parts/copies
	二分	ニブン	division into two parts; bisection —*v*. divide into two parts; halve; bisect
	二枚	ニマイ	two leaves/sheets
	二枚舌	ニマイじた	double-tongued; duplicity; equivocation
	二毛作	ニモウサク	two crops a year; double cropping
	二流	ニリュウ	second-rate
	二輪	ニリン	two wheels/flowers
	二輪車	ニリンシャ	two-wheeled vehicle; bicycle

訓	二つ	ふたつ	two
	二	ふた	(prefix) two; bi-; double
	二重	ふたえ	fold; two-layered; double
	二心	ふたごころ	duplicity; double-dealing; treachery
	二葉	ふたば	seed leaf; bud; sprout

21 五 ④ 一 丁 五 五

音	五	ゴ	five
熟	五月	ゴガツ	May
	五感	ゴカン	the five senses
	五色	ゴシキ	the five colors (blue, red, yellow, white, and black)
	五十音図	ゴジュウオンズ	*gram*. systematic table of the fifty sounds of the Japanese language
	五体満足	ゴタイマンゾク	person who is without any physical defect
	五分	ゴブ	five percent; half
	五分五分	ゴブゴブ	fifty-fifty
	五輪大会	ゴリンタイカイ	Olympic games
訓	五つ	いつつ	five
	五	いつ	five

22 来 ⑦ 一 ㄷ 口 亚 平 来 来

音	来	ライ	come; next; since
熟	来意	ライイ	purpose of one's visit
	来客	ライキャク	visitor; caller
	来月	ライゲツ	next month
	来校	ライコウ	coming to school —*vi*. come to school
	来航	ライコウ	arrival of ships/by ships —*vi*. arrive by ship
	来週	ライシュウ	next week
	来春	ライシュン	next spring
	来場	ライジョウ	attendance —*vi*. attend; be in attendance
	来信	ライシン	received letter
	来世	ライセ	afterlife; next world
	来朝	ライチョウ	*clas*. visit/arrival in Japan —*v*. visit/arrive in Japan
	来店	ライテン	visit to a store/shop —*vi*. visit a store/shop

来日	ライニチ	coming to Japan —*vi.* come to Japan
来年	ライネン	next year
来訪	ライホウ	visit; call —*vi.* come visiting/calling

訓	来る	くる	come
	来る	きたる	*vi.* come; be forth coming
	来す	きたす	*vt.* cause/bring about (unpleasant circumstances)

---

2 亠 なべぶた kettle lid

23

亡 ③   ` 亠 亡

| 音 | 亡 | ボウ (モウ) | dead |

熟	亡君	ボウクン	one's deceased lord
	亡兄	ボウケイ	one's late elder brother
	亡国	ボウコク	ruined country; destruction/ruination (of a country)
	亡妻	ボウサイ	one's late wife
	亡失	ボウシツ	loss —*v.* lose; be lost
	亡夫	ボウフ	one's late husband
	亡父	ボウフ	one's late father
	亡母	ボウボ	one's late mother
	亡命	ボウメイ	escaping one's native country for political reasons; defecting —*vi.* flee one's country; defect
	亡命者	ボウメイシャ	exile; émigré; refugee; defector
	亡者	モウジャ	ghost; the dead
訓	亡びる	ほろびる	*vi.* perish; come to ruin
	亡ぼす	ほろぼす	*vt.* destroy; bring to ruin
	亡い	ない	the late/deceased
	亡き	なき	the late/deceased
	亡くなる	なくなる	*vi.* die; pass away

24

交 ⑥   ` 亠 产 六 亥 交

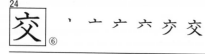

| 音 | 交 | コウ | intercourse; exchange; cross; mix |

熟	交易	コウエキ	trade; commerce; barter —*v.* trade; exchange; barter
	交差	コウサ	crossing; point of intersection —*v.* cross; intersect
	交差点	コウサテン	crossing; intersection; junction
	交際	コウサイ	intercourse; association; society; company; fellowship —*vi.* associate/fraternize with; keep company with
	交渉	コウショウ	negotiation; bargaining; relationship —*vi.* negotiate; bargain; discuss; have a relationship
	交戦	コウセン	war; hostilities; combat; action —*vi.* fight; engage in hostilities/combat
	交替	コウタイ	relief; change; shift —*vi.* take turns; alternate; rotate; relieve
	交通	コウツウ	traffic; communication; transportation; navigation
	交通機関	コウツウキカン	transit system
	交通費	コウツウヒ	traveling expenses; fare
	交配	コウハイ	crossbreeding; hybridization; crossfertilization —*v.* hybridize; cross; crossbreed; interbreed
	交番	コウバン	police box
	交付	コウフ	delivery; grant; transfer; service —*v.* deliver; grant; transfer; service
	交友	コウユウ	friend; acquaintance
	交遊	コウユウ	companionship; friendship —*vi.* associate with; keep company with
	交流	コウリュウ	alternating current (AC); interchange
訓	交わす	かわす	*vt.* exchange; cross; intersect
	交う	かう	(suffix) cross; intersect
	交ざる	まざる	*vi.* mix; mingle; blend
	交える	まじえる	*vt.* mix; cross; exchange
	交じる	まじる	*vi.* be mixed/mingled/blended; mix; mingle; join
	交わる	まじわる	*vi.* associate with; keep company with; cross; intersect; join
	交ぜる	まぜる	*vt.* blend; mix; include

25

京 ⑧ ′ 亠 亠 产 古 宁 京 京

音	京	キョウ	capital; metropolis; Kyoto; Tokyo; ten quadrillion
		ケイ	
熟	京風	キョウフウ	Kyoto-style (food)

訓 京　　みやこ　　capital; metropolis

---

2 人　ひと　man

26

人② ノ 人

音 人　　ジン　　　　man
　　　　ニン　　　　man; character

熟 人員　　ジンイン　　number of persons; staff; personnel
　人家　　ジンカ　　　house; dwelling
　人格　　ジンカク　　personality; character
　人格化　ジンカクカ　personification —*v.* personify
　人絹　　ジンケン　　rayon; artificial silk
　人権　　ジンケン　　human rights
　人権宣言 ジンケンセンゲン Declaration of Human Rights
　人件費　ジンケンヒ　personnel expenses
　人後　　ジンゴ　　　next person
　人工　　ジンコウ　　artificial; man-made
　人工衛星 ジンコウエイセイ artificial satellite
　人工栄養 ジンコウエイヨウ bottle feeding
　人工呼吸 ジンコウコキュウ artificial respiration; mouth-to-mouth
　　　　　　　　　　　resuscitation —*vi.* give mouth-to-mouth
　　　　　　　　　　　resuscitation
　人工受精 ジンコウジュセイ artificial insemination —*vi.* be artificially
　　　　　　　　　　　inseminated
　人工知能 ジンコウチノウ artificial intelligence
　人工的　ジンコウテキ artificial; man-made
　人口　　ジンコウ　　population
　人口密度 ジンコウミツド population density
　人災　　ジンサイ　　disaster caused by human error
　人材　　ジンザイ　　talent; ability
　人士　　ジンシ　　　man of good breeding; gentleman
　人事　　ジンジ　　　personnel affairs
　人事不省 ジンジフセイ unconscious; fainting; coma
　人種　　ジンシュ　　race; ethnic group
　人種差別 ジンシュサベツ racial discrimination —*vi.* discriminate on
　　　　　　　　　　　the basis of race
　人心　　ジンシン　　the people's mind; public feeling
　人生　　ジンセイ　　life

人生観	ジンセイカン	view of life; outlook on life
人選	ジンセン	selection of a suitable person —*vi*. select a suitable person
人造	ジンゾウ	artificial; manmade; imitation; synthetic
人造人間	ジンゾウニンゲン	robot
人造皮革	ジンゾウヒカク	artificial leather
人体	ジンタイ	human body
人知	ジンチ	human intelligence/knowledge/understanding
人的	ジンテキ	human
人道	ジンドウ	humanity
人道主義	ジンドウシュギ	humanitarianism
人道的	ジンドウテキ	humane
人頭税	ジントウゼイ	poll tax
人徳	ジントク	natural virtue
人品	ジンピン	character; personality; appearance
人物	ジンブツ	character; person; figure
人物画	ジンブツガ	portrait
人物画家	ジンブツガカ	portrait painter
人文	ジンブン ジンモン	humanity; civilization; culture
人文科学	ジンブンカガク	the humanities
人望	ジンボウ	popularity
人民	ジンミン	the people/citizens
人名	ジンメイ	person's name
人命	ジンメイ	human life; people's lives
人力車	ジンリキシャ	rickshaw
人力	ジンリョク	human power/strength
人類	ジンルイ	human race; mankind; humanity
人類学	ジンルイガク	anthropology
人気	ニンキ	popularity
人気歌手	ニンキカシュ	pop singer/idol
人気作家	ニンキサッカ	popular writer
人魚	ニンギョ	mermaid
人形	ニンギョウ	doll; puppet
人間	ニンゲン	man; human being; mankind
人間衛星	ニンゲンエイセイ	manned satellite
人間関係	ニンゲンカンケイ	human relations
人間国宝	ニンゲンコクホウ	living national treasure
人間性	ニンゲンセイ	humanity
人間味	ニンゲンミ	warm-hearted
人情	ニンジョウ	humaneness; human feelings
人参	ニンジン	carrot

二人へイ儿入八冂冖冫几凵刀刂力勹匕匚十卩卩厂厶又ク マ

人数	ニンズウ	number of persons
人相	ニンソウ	looks; physiognomy
人足	ニンソク	*derog*. laborer; navvy
人夫	ニンプ	*derog*. laborer; navvy

訓

人	ひと	man; person; people
人気	ひとけ	sign/presense of people
人事	ひとごと	other people's affairs
人殺し	ひとごろし	murder —*v*. murder
人里	ひとざと	village; human dwellings
人質	ひとジチ	hostage
人手	ひとで	help; hand
人出	ひとで	crowds; crowded
人並み	ひとなみ	ordinary; commonplace; average
人波	ひとなみ	surging crowd
人々	ひとびと	people; each person
人前	ひとまえ	in public; in the presence of others
人任せ	ひとまかせ	leaving (work) to someone else
人見知り	ひとみしり	bashful/shy (in front of strangers)
人目	ひとめ	notice; attention

27

以 ⑤ ㇏ ㇏ ㇏ 以 以

音	以	イ	by; since; with
熟	以遠	イエン	beyond; farther
	以下	イカ	less than; below; not more than
	以外	イガイ	except; outside of; excluding; besides
	以後	イゴ	after this; from now on; hereafter; henceforth; since
	以降	イコウ	from that time; from now on
	以上	イジョウ	not less than; or more; and over; more than
	以心伝心	イシンデンシン	communion of mind with mind; telepathy; empathy
	以前	イゼン	formerly; before
	以内	イナイ	within; less than; not more than
	以来	イライ	since then; from that time on; ever since
訓	以て	もって	by means of
	以ての外	もってのほか	outrageous; preposterous; scandalous

2 **亠** やね roof

28

今 ノ 人 今 今 ④

音	今	キン	present
		コン	now; this time
熟	今回	コンカイ	lately; this time
	今月	コンゲツ	this month
	今後	コンゴ	after this; henceforth; hereafter
	今昔	コンジャク	past and present
	今週	コンシュウ	this week
	今度	コンド	this/next time
	今日	コンニチ	today
	今晩	コンバン	this evening
訓	今	いま	now

29

令 ノ 人 今 今 令 ⑤

音	令	レイ	rule; order; command (honorific prefix)
熟	令室	レイシツ	*hon*. your wife
	令状	レイジョウ	warrant; writ
	令息	レイソク	*hon*. your son
	令夫人	レイフジン	*hon*. Mrs.; Lady; Madam; your wife

30

会 ノ 人 人 合 会 会 ⑥

音	会	エ	meet; memorial service
		カイ	meet; meeting; society
熟	会得	エトク	comprehension; understanding —*v*. comprehend; understand
	会員	カイイン	member; membership
	会館	カイカン	hall; assembly hall
	会議	カイギ	conference; meeting —*vi*. have a conference/meeting

	会合	カイゴウ	meeting; gathering; assembly —*vi.* meet; gather; assemble
	会社	カイシャ	company; corporation
	会食	カイショク	dining together —*vi.* dine together
	会則	カイソク	rules of an association
	会談	カイダン	talk; conference; conversation —*vi.* talk together; have a conference
	会報	カイホウ	bulletin; report
	会話	カイワ	conversation; talk —*vi.* converse; talk
訓	会う	あう	*vi.* meet

31

全⑥　ノ　入　ヘ　今　午　全　全

音	全	ゼン	all; complete
熟	全域	ゼンイキ	the whole area
	全員	ゼンイン	all the members; the whole staff/crew
	全快	ゼンカイ	full recovery —*vi.* recover fully
	全額	ゼンガク	sum total
	全権	ゼンケン	full authority
	全校	ゼンコウ	whole school; all the schools
	全国	ゼンコク	the whole country; nationwide; national
	全集	ゼンシュウ	complete/collected works
	全書	ゼンショ	complete book; compendium
	全焼	ゼンショウ	total destruction by fire —*vi.* be totally destroyed by fire
	全勝	ゼンショウ	complete victory —*vi.* win a complete victory
	全身	ゼンシン	the whole body
	全盛	ゼンセイ	prime; height of prosperity
	全盛期	ゼンセイキ	one's prime period
	全然	ゼンゼン	utterly; entirely; not at all
	全速力	ゼンソクリョク	full speed; top speed
	全体	ゼンタイ	the whole; in all
	全治	ゼンチ	complete cure —*vi.* fully recover; heal completely
	全長	ゼンチョウ	overall length
	全土	ゼンド	the whole country
	全能	ゼンノウ	omnipotent; all powerful
	全敗	ゼンパイ	complete defeat —*vi.* be defeated completely
	全部	ゼンブ	all; whole; entirely
	全文	ゼンブン	full text; whole sentence
	全面的	ゼンメンテキ	full; general

全訳	ゼンヤク	complete/unabridged translation —*v.* make a complete and unabridged translation
全容	ゼンヨウ	full story/picture
全力	ゼンリョク	all one's power; one's every effort; full capacity
訓 全うする	まっとうする	*vt.* accomplish; fulfil
全く	まったく	entirely; completely; truly; indeed

32

 余 ⑦ ノ 人 人 会 全 弁 余

音 余	ヨ	remainder; the rest; other; more than; myself; I
熟 余技	ヨギ	hobby; avocation
余儀なく	ヨギなく	unavoidable; obliged to
余興	ヨキョウ	entertainment; side show
余計	ヨケイ	unnecessary; more than enough; extra; uncalled for
余罪	ヨザイ	other crimes
余人	ヨジン	other people; others
余生	ヨセイ	the rest of one's life
余勢	ヨセイ	surplus energy
余談	ヨダン	digression
余地	ヨチ	room; place; margin; scope
余熱	ヨネツ	lingering summer heat
余念	ヨネン	thinking of other matters
余波	ヨハ	after/secondary effects; consequences
余白	ヨハク	blank; space; margin
余病	ヨビョウ	complications; secondary disease
余分	ヨブン	extra; excess
余程	ヨほど	very; much; to a great degree
余命	ヨメイ	the rest of one's life
余力	ヨリョク	remaining strength; surplus energy
訓 余る	あまる	*vi.* remain; be more than enough; exceed
余り	あまり	remainder; surplus; more than; very; as a result of
余す	あます	*vt.* leave; save

| ノ | 入 | 入 | 全 | 全 | 全 | 舎 | 舎 | | |

⑧

音	舎	シャ	inn; building
熟	舎兄	シャケイ	*hum.* my elder brother
	舎弟	シャテイ	*hum.* my younger brother
	舎利	シャリ	*Bud.* one's remains/ashes; rice (in sushi bar)

34

倉 ⑩

| ノ | 入 | 入 | 今 | 今 | 今 | 仝 | 倉 | 倉 | 倉 |

音	倉	ソウ	warehouse; storehouse
熟	倉庫	ソウコ	warehouse
訓	倉	くら	warehouse; storehouse
	倉主	くらぬし	warehouse owner

2 イ にんべん man to the left

| ノ | イ | イ | 化 | | |

④

音	化	カ	transform; change
		ケ	die; civilize; change
熟	化学	カガク	chemistry
	化学肥料	カガクヒリョウ	chemical fertilizer
	化学兵器	カガクヘイキ	chemical weapons
	化合	カゴウ	*chem.* chemical combination; compound —*vi.* combine to make a compound out of two or more elements
	化成	カセイ	transformation —*vi.* transform
	化石	カセキ	fossil
	化身	ケシン	incarnation/manifestation of a god or buddha; reincarnation
訓	化ける	ばける	*vi.* transform; disguise oneself
	化かす	ばかす	*vt.* bewitch; enchant; deceive
	化けの皮	ばけのかわ	disguise
	化け物	ばけもの	apparition; goblin; monster

36 仁 ④ ノ イ 仁 仁

音	仁	ジン （ニ）	compassion
熟	仁愛	ジンアイ	benevolence
	仁義	ジンギ	humanity and justice; duty; respect
	仁術	ジンジュツ	benevolent act; caring profession; art of healing
	仁徳	ジントク	benevolence
	仁王	ニオウ	the two Deva kings

37 仏 ④ ノ イ 仏 仏

音	仏	フツ	France; French
		ブツ	Buddha; Buddhism
熟	仏閣	ブッカク	Buddhist temple
	仏教	ブッキョウ	Buddhism
	仏具	ブツグ	Buddhist altar articles
	仏寺	ブツジ	Buddhist temple
	仏事	ブツジ	Buddhist memorial service
	仏式	ブッシキ	Buddhist rite
	仏舎利	ブッシャリ	Buddha's ashes
	仏心	ブッシン	Buddha's heart/character
	仏前	ブツゼン	before/in front of Buddha/the tablet of the deceased; Buddhist altar offerings
	仏像	ブツゾウ	Buddhist image
	仏頂面	ブッチョウづら	sour face; pout; scowl
	仏典	ブッテン	Buddhist scripture/literature
	仏道	ブツドウ	Buddhism
	仏法	ブッポウ	Buddhism
	仏間	ブツマ	Buddhist altar room
	仏門	ブツモン	Buddhism; Buddhist priesthood
訓	仏	ほとけ	Buddha; Buddhist image; the dead
	仏心	ほとけごころ	merciful; kindhearted (like Buddha)
	仏様	ほとけさま	Buddha; dead person

二 亠 人 � ⺅ • 儿 入 八 冂 冖 冫 几 凵 刀 刂 力 勹 匕 匚 十 卜 卩 厂 厶 又 夕 宀

38

仕 ⑤ ノ イ 仆 什 仕

音	仕	シ ジ	serve; work; to do
熟	仕上げる	シあげる	*vt.* finish; complete
	仕打ち	シうち	treatment; behavior; action; conduct
	仕送り	シおくり	allowance; remittance —*v.* send/remit money; make an allowance
	仕返し	シかえし	revenge; retaliation —*vi.* avenge oneself; retaliate
	仕官	シカン	government service —*vi.* enter government service
	仕切り	シきり	dividing line; boundary; partition
	仕草	シぐさ	behavior; acting; gestures
	仕事	シごと	occupation; work; job; business
	仕立て	シたて	tailoring
	仕立てる	シたてる	*vt.* sew; tailor; prepare; train
訓	仕える	つかえる	*vi.* serve; work under; be clogged/blocked

39

他 ⑤ ノ イ 仆 休 他

音	他	タ	other; another; outside; different
熟	他意	タイ	another intention; ulterior motive; secret purpose
	他界	タカイ	death; demise; the other world; another world —*vi.* die; pass away
	他国	タコク	strange land; foreign country; another province
	他言	タゴン	disclosure —*v.* divulge; reveal; let out; disclose
	他殺	タサツ	murder; homicide; manslaughter
	他人	タニン	another person; others; unrelated person; outsider; third party; stranger
	他方	タホウ	the other hand/side; another side/place
	他面	タメン	the other/another side
	他力本願	タリキホンガン	salvation through faith in the Amida Buddha
訓	他	ほか	other; another

34

代 ⑤ ノ イ 仁 代 代

音	代	タイ	
		ダイ	substitution; proxy; reign; era
熟	代案	ダイアン	alternative plan
	代議員	ダイギイン	representative; delegate
	代議士	ダイギシ	congressman; dietman; member of Parliament
	代数	ダイスウ	*math*. algebra
	代打	ダイダ	*bas*. pinch hitter —*vi*. pinch hit
	代々	ダイダイ	from generation to generation
	代読	ダイドク	reading by proxy —*v*. read by proxy; read on behalf of someone else
	代筆	ダイヒツ	writing by proxy —*v*. write on behalf of someone else
	代表	ダイヒョウ	representative; delegation; deputation —*v*. represent; be representative of; stand/act for
	代表的	ダイヒョウテキ	representative; typical
	代弁	ダイベン	speaking by proxy; agency; commission; payment by proxy —*v*. speak/pay by proxy
	代名詞	ダイメイシ	*gram*. pronoun
	代役	ダイヤク	substitution; substitute; understudy
	代用	ダイヨウ	substitution —*v*. substitute
	代理	ダイリ	representation; agency; proxy —*v*. act for; represent; deputy
訓	代える	かえる	*vt*. change; alter; convert; renew; reform
	代わる	かわる	*vi*. take the place of; replace; be substituted
	代わり	かわり	substitute; deputy; alternative; compensation
	代	よ	the world; society; age; era; rule; reign

付 ⑤ ノ イ 仁 付 付

音	付	フ	attach
熟	付する	フする	*vt*. add; attach; wear; apply; use; refer to
	付加	フカ	addition; annexation; supplement; appendix —*v*. add; annex; supplement; append
	付記	フキ	written addition; additional/supplementary (written) remark —*v*. add in writing; append
	付近	フキン	neighborhood; vicinity; environs

付属	フゾク	belonging to; adjunctive; incidental; subsidiary; branch school —*vi.* be attached/belong to
付着	フチャク	adherence; sticking; adhesion; cohesion —*vi.* adhere to; stick; attach
付録	フロク	supplement in a book/magazine; appendix
訓 付く	つく	*vi.* stick; adhere; touch; reach; come; set; be dyed/colored; be decided
付き合う	つきあう	*vi.* accompany; socialize; go out together
付ける	つける	*vt.* add; attach; append; fix; put on; wear; apply; use; add; join; attend to; name; light a fire; load

42 仮 ⑥ ノ イ 仁 仟 仮 仮

音 仮	カ	temporary; provisional; forgive
	（ケ）	false; feigned
熟 仮死	カシ	*med.* suspended animation; asphyxia; temporary suspension of the vital functions
仮借	カシャク	pardoning; leniency; forgiveness; borrowing —*v.* pardon; be lenient; borrow; forgive
仮性	カセイ	(prefix) false; psuedo-
仮設	カセツ	temporary construction —*v.* put up a temporary construction; construct temporarily
仮説	カセツ	hypothesis
仮装	カソウ	disguise; fancy clothes —*vi.* disguise oneself; wear fancy clothes
仮定	カテイ	supposition; assumption; presumption —*v.* suppose; assume; presume
仮名	カな	*kana* (Japanese syllabary)
仮名	カメイ	pseudonym; assumed name; alias
仮面	カメン	mask
仮病	ケビョウ	feigned illness
訓 仮	かり	temporary

43 休 ⑥ ノ イ 仁 什 休 休

音 休	キュウ	resting; taking a break; giving up; quitting
熟 休会	キュウカイ	adjournment; recess —*vi.* adjourn
休学	キュウガク	temporary absence from school —*vi.* be absent from school for a time
休火山	キュウカザン	dormant volcano

36

	休刊	キュウカン	suspension/discontinuation of publication —*vi.* suspend publication
	休校	キュウコウ	closing down of school —*vi.* close; be closed
	休講	キュウコウ	cancelling a lecture —*vi.* cancel a lecture
	休止	キュウシ	pause; standstill; suspension; stoppage —*v.* cease; pause; suspend; stop
	休日	キュウジツ	holiday; day off
	休戦	キュウセン	armistice; truce; ceasefire —*vi.* conclude an armistice; cease firing
	休息	キュウソク	rest; repose; relaxation; respite —*vi.* rest; take a rest; relax
	休養	キュウヨウ	rest; relaxation; recuperation —*vi.* rest; take a rest; recuperate
訓	休み	やすみ	rest; respite; break; repose; holiday
	休む	やすむ	*vi.* rest from; stop; suspend; be absent

44
件⑥　ノ　イ　イ　仁　仵　件

音	件	ケン	matter; case (counter for cases)
熟	件数	ケンスウ	number of cases

45
仲⑥　ノ　イ　仆　仲　仲　仲

音	仲	チュウ	relations; relationships; terms
熟	仲裁	チュウサイ	arbitration; mediation; intervention; intercession —*v.* arbitrate; mediate; intervene; interceed
訓	仲	なか	relations; relationship; terms
	仲居	なかい	parlormaid; waitress
	仲買	なかがい	broking; brokerage
	仲買人	なかがいニン	broker; middleman; agent
	仲立ち	なかだち	mediation; matchmaking —*v.* mediate; matchmake
	仲直り	なかなおり	reconciliation; peacemaking; restoration of friendship —*vi.* reconcile; make up; make the peace
	仲間	なかま	company; party; set; circle; friends
	仲良し	なかよし	intimacy; familiar terms; intimate friend

伝 ⑥ ／ イ 仁 仁 伝 伝

音	伝	デン	convey; transmit; communicate; legend; tradition; life; biography
熟	伝記	デンキ	biography; life
	伝言	デンゴン	message —*v.* leave word; give/send a message
	伝言板	デンゴンバン	message board
	伝授	デンジュ	initiation; instruction —*v.* initiate; instruct
	伝承	デンショウ	oral tradition; transmission; handing down —*v.* hand down; transmit by word of mouth
	伝心	デンシン	mutual understanding of mutual thoughts
	伝説	デンセツ	legend; tradition
	伝染	デンセン	contagion; infection; communication of disease —*vi.* be contagious/infectious/infective
	伝染病	デンセンビョウ	contagious disease
	伝送	デンソウ	transmission —*v.* transmit
	伝達	デンタツ	transmission; conveyance; communication; propagation —*v.* transmit; convey; communicate; deliver; notify
	伝統	デントウ	tradition; conversion
	伝統的	デントウテキ	traditional; conventional
	伝道	デンドウ	missionary work; evangelism —*vi.* evangelize; engage in missionary work
	伝導	デンドウ	conduction; transmission —*v.* conduct; transmit
	伝票	デンピョウ	chit; slip; ticket
	伝聞	デンブン	rumor; hearsay; report —*v.* hear from others; be informed; learn by hearsay
	伝来	デンライ	introduction; transmission —*vi.* be transmitted/ handed down/introduced
	伝令	デンレイ	message
訓	伝える	つたえる	*vt.* convey; report; deliver; communicate; transmit; teach
	伝わる	つたわる	*vi.* be handed down/transmitted/conveyed/ introduced
	伝う	つたう	*vi.* go along
	伝え	つたえ	legend
	伝わり	つたわり	propagation
	伝	つて	intermediary; introducer; medium

任 ⑥ ノ イ イ仁仁仟任

音	任	ニン	trust, duty
熟	任じる	ニンじる	appoint; nominate; assume; profess; pose
	任意	ニンイ	option; pleasure; discretion
	任官	ニンカン	appointment; installation; commission —*vi*. be appointed/installed/commissioned
	任期	ニンキ	term/period of office
	任地	ニンチ	place of one's appointment; one's post
	任務	ニンム	duty; office; task; function; mission
	任命	ニンメイ	appointment; nomination; designation; commission —*v*. appoint; nominate; designate; commission
	任用	ニンヨウ	employment; appointment —*v*. employ; appoint
訓	任せる	まかせる	*vt*. entrust; delegate; commission
	任す	まかす	*vt*. entrust; delegate; commission

位 ⑦ ノ イ 仁 仁 什 位 位

音	位	イ	rank; position; grade
熟	位相	イソウ	*math*. topology *phy*. phase
	位置	イチ	position; situation; location —*vi*. be positioned/situated/located
訓	位	くらい	grade; rank; dignity; the throne; about; approximately
	位する	くらいする	*vi*. rank; be ranked/located/placed

何 ⑦ ノ イ 仁 仁 佢 佢 何

音	何	カ	what
訓	何	なに	what; anything else
		（なん）	what
	何事	なにごと	what; everything; whatever
	何者	なにもの	who; what
	何十	なんジュウ	(how) many; tens of
	何度	なんド	how many degrees; how many times; how often

何人	なんニン	how many (people)
何分	なにぶん	please, at any rate; somewhat
何故	なにゆえ	why

50 作⑦ ノ イ イ 仁 竹 作 作

音 作	サ	working
	サク	make; work; harvest
熟 作業	サギョウ	work; operations —*vi.* work; operate
作業員	サギョウイン	worker
作業時間	サギョウジカン	working hours
作意	サクイ	intentional; deliberate
作詞	サクシ	lyrical writing —*v.* write lyrics
作詩	サクシ	poetry composition —*vi.* write poetry/verse
作者	サクシャ	author; writer; poet
作図	サクズ	drawing figures; construction of diagrams —*v.* draw a diagram; construct a shape
作製	サクセイ	manufacture; production —*v.* manufacture; production
作成	サクセイ	preparation; drawing up —*v.* make; prepare; draw up
作戦	サクセン	tactics; operations; action; strategy
作品	サクヒン	work (of art, literature, etc.)
作風	サクフウ	literary style; style
作文	サクブン	composition; essay
作物	サクモツ	crops; farm produce
作家	サッカ	novelist; writer; author
作曲	サッキョク	musical composition —*v.* compose/write music
作曲家	サッキョクカ	composer
作法	サホウ	manners; etiquette
作用	サヨウ	action; effect —*vi.* act on
訓 作る	つくる	*vt.* make; manufacture; grow; till; form; establish; cook
作り	つくり	composition; workmanship
作り出す	つくりだす	*vt.* make; manufacture

51 似⑦ ノ イ 化 化 似 似 似

| 音 似 | ジ | resemble |

訓	似合う	にあう	*vi*. go well with; look good with
	似顔絵	にがおえ	portrait
	似る	にる	*vi*. resemble; look like

52

住⑦ ノ イ イ 仁 什 住 住

音	住	ジュウ	live
熟	住居	ジュウキョ	residence; house; home
	住所	ジュウショ	address
	住職	ジュウショク	chief priest (of a Buddhist temple)
	住宅	ジュウタク	house; residence
	住人	ジュウニン	inhabitant; resident
	住民	ジュウミン	inhabitant; resident
訓	住む	すむ	*vi*. live; dwell; be resident
	住まい	すまい	house; residence; home
	住まう	すまう	*vi*. live; dwell; be resident

53

体⑦ ノ イ イ 仕 休 休 体

音	体	タイ	body; style; form; substance; center
		テイ	appearance
熟	体位	タイイ	physique; posture; body position
	体育	タイイク	physical education/training
	体温	タイオン	temperature; body temperature/heat
	体温計	タイオンケイ	thermometer
	体格	タイカク	physique; constitution; frame
	体形	タイケイ	form; figure
	体系	タイケイ	system; organization; scheme
	体験	タイケン	experience; personal experience —*v*. have an experience; experience; undergo
	体質	タイシツ	one's physical constitution
	体重	タイジュウ	(body) weight
	体制	タイセイ	structure; system; organization; order; the Establishment
	体勢	タイセイ	posture; stance
	体積	タイセキ	volume; capacity
	体操	タイソウ	gymnastics; physical exercises; calisthenics —*vi*. practice gymnastics/calisthenics

二十人へイ几入八冂冖冫几凵刀刂力勹匕匚十卩巳厂厶又々マ

	体得	タイトク	realization; experience; comprehension; mastering —*v.* realize; learn; comprehend; master
	体内	タイナイ	inside the body
	体面	タイメン	honor; dignity; prestige; reputation; appearances
	体力	タイリョク	physical strength; stamina
	体裁	テイサイ	appearance; decency; form; style
訓	体	からだ	body

54 低 ⑦　ノ イ 亻 仁 作 低 低

音	低	テイ	low
熟	低圧	テイアツ	low pressure/tension/voltage
	低位	テイイ	low position/rank/degree
	低音	テイオン	low voice; bass; low pitched sound
	低温	テイオン	low temperature
	低下	テイカ	lowering; fall; decline; drop; dip; depreciation; deterioration —*v.* fall; drop; dip; decline; lower; depreciate; deteriorate
	低額	テイガク	small amount
	低気圧	テイキアツ	low atmospheric pressure
	低級	テイキュウ	low grade/class
	低空	テイクウ	low altitude
	低血圧	テイケツアツ	*med.* low blood pressure
	低減	テイゲン	fall; depreciation; reduction; decrease
	低質	テイシツ	low quality
	低速	テイソク	low speed
	低地	テイチ	low-lying land; lowlands; flats
	低調	テイチョウ	dull; weak; inactive; bearish
	低能	テイノウ	weak intellect; low intelligence; feeble mindedness
	低木	テイボク	shrub
	低迷	テイメイ	overhanging; threatening; floundering —*v.* overhang; threaten; flounder
	低落	テイラク	fall; depreciation; slump —*v.* fall; depreciate; decline; go down
	低率	テイリツ	low rate/ratio
訓	低い	ひくい	low; short; humble; mean
	低まる	ひくまる	*vi.* sink; become lower
	低める	ひくめる	*vt.* lower; make low; bring down

55

価 ⑧ ノ　イ　イ　价　佰　佰　価　価

音	価	カ	price; value
熟	価値	カチ	value; worth
訓	価	あたい	price; value —*vi*. price; put a price on; value; praise

56

供 ⑧ ノ　イ　イ　件　件　供　供　供

音	供	キョウ（ク）	offer; submit; serve (a meal); supply
熟	供する	キョウする	*vt*. offer; submit; serve (a meal); supply
	供給	キョウキュウ	supply; service —*v*. supply; provide; furnish; serve
	供述	キョウジュツ	testimony; statement; deposition; confession —*v*. testify; state; confess (to a fact)
	供物	クモツ	offering (to ancestors)
	供養	クヨウ	memorial service —*v*. hold a memorial service
訓	供える	そなえる	*vt*. offer (to a god); make an offering
	供	とも	attendant; servant retinue

57

使 ⑧ ノ　イ　イ　仁　佇　佢　伊　使

音	使	シ	use; messenger
熟	使者	シシャ	messenger; envoy
	使節	シセツ	envoy; delegate; delegation; mission (to a foreign country)
	使徒	シト	apostle; disciple
	使命	シメイ	mission
	使用	シヨウ	use —*v*. use; make use of; employ
	使用人	シヨウニン	person who works under his/her master; employee; servant
訓	使う	つかう	*vt*. use; handle; employ
	使い	つかい	errand; messenger
	使い方	つかいかた	usage; how to use
	使い捨て	つかいすて	disposable

二
十
人
へ
イ
儿
入
八
冂
一
冫
几
凵
刀
刂
力
勹
匕
匚
十
卜
卩
厂
厶
又
ク
マ

| 使い手 | つかいて | user; consumer |
| 使い道 | つかいみち | way of using |

58

例⑧ ノ イ 彳 仔 仔 例 例 例

音	例	レイ	example; precedent; practice
熟	例会	レイカイ	regular meeting
	例外	レイガイ	exception
	例証	レイショウ	example; illustration —v. show by example; illustrate
	例題	レイダイ	exercise; example
	例年	レイネン	every year; normal/average year
	例文	レイブン	example sentence (in a dictionary, etc.)
訓	例えば	たとえば	for example
	例話	たとえばなし	verbal example
	例える	たとえる	vt. show by example; illustrate

59

係⑨ ノ イ 仁 仁 係 係 係 係 係

音	係	ケイ	connection; involve; concern; affect
熟	係争	ケイソウ	dispute; conflict; conflagration; litigation —vi. dispute; be in conflict
訓	係	かかり	the person in charge/responsible
	係る	かかる	vi. affect; engender; modify
	係わり	かかわり	involvement; connection
	係わる	かかわる	vi. have to do with; be involved with

60

信⑨ ノ イ 仁 信 信 信 信 信 信

音	信	シン	fidelity; trust; letter
熟	信じる	シンじる	vt. believe; trust; have faith in
	信義	シンギ	faith; loyalty; honor
	信教	シンキョウ	religious belief; religion
	信号	シンゴウ	signal; traffic lights
	信実	シンジツ	sincerity
	信者	シンジャ	believer in a religion

信書	シンショ	correspondence; letter
信条	シンジョウ	belief; creed; principle
信心	シンジン	faith; belief; piety —*v.* believe; worship
信徒	シント	adherent; believer
信任	シンニン	confidence; trust —*v.* place confidence in; trust
信念	シンネン	belief; faith; conviction
信服	シンプク	self-conviction —*vi.* convince oneself; be convinced
信望	シンボウ	confidence; popularity
信用	シンヨウ	confidence; trust; faith; reliance; reputation —*v.* believe; trust; have faith in; have confidence in; be reliable/reputable

61

便⑨ ノ イ 仁 仨 佰 佰 佰 便 便

音 便	ビン	mail; transport; flight; opportunity
	ベン	convenience; facilities; excrement; feces
熟 便乗	ビンジョウ	getting in a car or on a boat (with someone); taking advantage of —*vi.* get in a car (with someone); take advantage of
便意	ベンイ	urge to go to the toilet; call of nature
便益	ベンエキ	convenience; benefit; advantage
便器	ベンキ	toilet; urinal
便所	ベンジョ	toilet; lavatory
便通	ベンツウ	bowel movement
便秘	ベンピ	constipation
便法	ベンポウ	convenient/easy way
便覧	ベンラン（ビンラン）	handbook; manual
便利	ベンリ	convenient; handy
便利屋	ベンリヤ	handyman
訓 便り	たより	news; tidings

62

保⑨ ノ イ 仁 佢 但 保 保 保

音 保	ホ	keep; preserve; maintain
熟 保安	ホアン	maintenance of public peace and security
保育	ホイク	childcare; —*v.* bring up/raise a child
保育園	ホイクエン	nursery (school)

二
亻
人
へ
イ
儿
入
八
冂
冖
冫
几
凵
刀
刂
力
勹
匕
匚
十
卜
卩
厂
厶
又
勹
マ

● イ

保育所	ホイクジョ	nursery (school)
保温	ホオン	keeping warm; heat maintenance —*vi.* keep warm
保管	ホカン	custody; deposit; storage —*v.* keep in custody; store
保険	ホケン	insurance; assurance
保健	ホケン	health preservation; hygiene
保健所	ホケンジョ	health center
保護	ホゴ	protection; shelter —*v.* protect; shelter
保護国	ホゴコク	protectorate
保護者	ホゴシャ	guardian; protector
保護色	ホゴショク	protective coloration
保持	ホジ	maintenance; preservation —*v.* maintain; preserve; keep (a memory, etc.)
保持者	ホジシャ	(record) holder
保守	ホシュ	conservation —*v.* conserve; preserve; maintain
保守的	ホシュテキ	conservative
保守党	ホシュトウ	conservative party
保証	ホショウ	guarantee —*v.* guarantee; promise
保障	ホショウ	guarantee; security —*v.* guarantee; assure
保身	ホシン	self-protection
保全	ホゼン	preservation —*v.* preserve; conserve
保存	ホゾン	preservation —*v.* preserve; conserve
保母	ホボ	kindergarten teacher
保有	ホユウ	possession; ownership —*v.* possess; own; hold; maintain
保有者	ホユウシャ	owner; holder
保養	ホヨウ	recreation; recuperation; health preservation —*vi.* recreate; recuperate
保養所	ホヨウジョ	sanatorium; rest home
保養地	ホヨウチ	health resort
保留	ホリュウ	reservation; putting on hold —*v.* reserve; defer

訓 保つ　たもつ　*vt.* keep; preserve; maintain

63

個 ⑩　ノ イ 亻 仃 何 個 個 個 個 個

音	個	コ	piece (counter for small objects)
熟	個々	ココ	separately; individually
	個人	コジン	individual
	個人差	コジンサ	difference among individuals

個人主義	コジンシュギ	individualism
個人的	コジンテキ	individually; personally; privately
個数	コスウ	number of items
個性	コセイ	personality; individuality; originality
個展	コテン	personal exhibition; one-man show
個別	コベツ	individually; separately; one by one

64 候 ⑩ ノ 亻 亻 仁 伫 伫 伫 侯 候 候

音	候	コウ	attend; season
熟	候補	コウホ	candidacy
	候補者	コウホシャ	candidate; applicant
訓	候	そうろう	*vi. clas.* be; exist

65 借 ⑩ ノ 亻 亻 仁 什 併 併 借 借 借

音	借	シャク	borrow
訓	借りる	かりる	*vt.* borrow; have a loan; get into debt
	借り	かり	debt; loan
	借り主	かりぬし	borrower

66 修 ⑩ ノ 亻 亻 仃 俨 俨 俢 修 修 修

音	修	シュウ	learn; repair
		（シュ）	
熟	修業	シュウギョウ	studying; learning —*v.* study; learn
	修士	シュウシ	master's degree
	修築	シュウチク	building repairs —*v.* make repairs to a building
	修道院	シュウドウイン	monastery; abbey; religious house
	修道士	シュウドウシ	monk; friar
	修得	シュウトク	acquisition of skills —*v.* acquire; learn; master
	修理	シュウリ	repair; mending —*v.* repair; mend; fix
	修練	シュウレン	training; practice —*v.* train; practice; rehearse
	修行	シュギョウ	training; religious training —*v.* practice asceticism

2

訓	修まる	おさまる	*vi.* conduct oneself well
	修める	おさめる	*vt.* study; master; behave oneself

---

67 値 ⑩
ノ　イ　伫　伫　仵　佔　佔　佔　値　値

音	値	チ	value; price; cost
訓	値する	あたいする	*vi.* be worth; be worthy; deserve; merit
	値	あたい	price; cost; value; worth; merit
	値	ね	price; cost; figure; value
	値打ち	ねうち	price; value
	値段	ねダン	price; cost

---

68 俳 ⑩
ノ　イ　彳　仴　付　俏　侢　俳　俳　俳

音	俳	ハイ	performer; haiku poetry
熟	俳句	ハイク	haiku poem
	俳号	ハイゴウ	haiku poet's pen name
	俳人	ハイジン	haiku poet
	俳優	ハイユウ	actor; actress

---

69 倍 ⑩
ノ　イ　イ′　仒　仒　佔　佔　倍　倍　倍

音	倍	バイ	times
熟	倍加	バイカ	doubling; great/marked increase —*v.* double; increase twofold; add much to
	倍額	バイガク	double the price
	倍数	バイスウ	*math.* multiple
	倍増	バイゾウ	redoubling; double —*v.* redouble; double
	倍率	バイリツ	magnification

---

70 俵 ⑩
ノ　イ　伫　仹　伨　佯　俈　俵　俵　俵

音	俵	ヒョウ	straw bag (counter for sacks)
訓	俵	たわら	straw bag

48

71

健 ⑪ ノ イ 亻 亻ㄱ 亻ㅋ 亻ㅋ 亻彐 伊 律 律 健 健

音	健	ケン	health
熟	健康	ケンコウ	health
	健康的	ケンコウテキ	healthy
	健康保健	ケンコウホケン	health insurance
	健在	ケンザイ	in good health; alive and well
	健全	ケンゼン	healthy; normal; sound; wholesome
訓	健やか	すこやか	healthy; fit; well

72

側 ⑪ ノ イ 亻 们 伫 伊 但 俱 俱 側 側

音	側	ソク	side
熟	側線	ソクセン	siding; sidetrack; side lines
	側面	ソクメン	side; flank
	側近	ソッキン	close associate
訓	側	かわ	side

73

停 ⑪ ノ イ 亻 广 仁 仃 位 停 停 停 停

音	停	テイ	stop
熟	停学	テイガク	suspension from school
	停止	テイシ	suspension; stoppage; stay; prohibition; temporary ban; standstill; stop; halt; deadlock; stalemate; interruption; cessation —*v.* suspend; stop; prohibit; cease; come to an end
	停車	テイシャ	stop; stoppage —*vi.* stop; come to a halt
	停戦	テイセン	truce; ceasefire; armistice —*v.* cease fire; stop fighting
	停電	テイデン	power failure/cut —*v.* have a power cut
	停留	テイリュウ	stoppage; stop —*v.* stop; halt
	停留所	テイリュウジョ	stop; stand; station; depot
訓	停まる	とまる	*vi.* stop; cease; be stopped/suspended
	停める	とめる	*vt.* stop; suspend

74

備 ⑫ ノ イ イ イ イ 伴 伴 伴 借 借 備 備 備

音	備	ビ	provide; furnish; preparation
熟	備考	ビコウ	note; remarks
	備品	ビヒン	fixture; equipment; kit
	備忘録	ビボウロク	memorandum; notebook
訓	備える	そなえる	*vt.* provide; possess; equip
	備え	そなえ	provision; preparations; preparedness; equipment
	備え付ける	そなえつける	*vt.* provide; furnish; equip; fit; outfit
	備わる	そなわる	*vi.* be furnished/provided/equipped

75

傷 ⑬ ノ イ イ イ 仁 仵 作 佢 俥 俥 傷 傷 傷

音	傷	ショウ	wound; injure; damage
熟	傷害	ショウガイ	injury
	傷害保険	ショウガイホケン	accident insurance
	傷心	ショウシン	broken heart; heartbreak; grief; sorrow
	傷病	ショウビョウ	injuries and illness
訓	傷む	いたむ	*v.* be damaged/hurt/bruised/spoilt
	傷める	いためる	*vt.* damage; hurt; spoil
	傷	きず	injury; wound; cut; flaw; defect
	傷口	きずぐち	wound; sore
	傷付く	きずつく	*vi.* be hurt/injured/damaged
	傷付ける	きずつける	*vt.* wound; injure; bruise; scratch; crack
	傷物	きずもの	defective article

76

働 ⑬ ノ イ イ イ 仁 仵 侮 侮 侮 偅 働 働

音	働	ドウ	work
訓	働く	はたらく	*vi.* work
	働き	はたらき	work; labor; achievements; function; effect; workings
	働き口	はたらきぐち	job; position
	働き者	はたらきもの	hard worker

77 像 ⑭　イ イ イ´ イ˝ 伃 俏 像 像 傍 像 像 像

音 像　ゾウ　image

78 億 ⑮　イ イ˝ イ´ イ˝ イ˝ 俨 侉 倍 倍 億 億

音 億　オク　one-hundred million; 100,000,000

熟 億万長者　オクマン　billionaire; multimillionaire
　　　　　　　チョウジャ

79 優 ⑰　イ イ´ イ´ 俨 佰 佰 偅 偃 憂 憂 傻 優

音 優　ユウ　superior; gentle; actor

熟 優位　ユウイ　high position
　　優勝　ユウショウ　championship; victory —*v.* win
　　優勢　ユウセイ　predominance; superiority
　　優先　ユウセン　preference; superiority —*vi.* be prior to;
　　　　　　　　　　have preference to
　　優先的　ユウセンテキ　preferential
　　優待　ユウタイ　generous/preferential treatment
　　　　　　　　　—*v.* treat generously; receive hospitality
　　優等　ユウトウ　excellent; superior
　　優美　ユウビ　graceful; elegant
　　優良　ユウリョウ　excellent; superior

訓 優れる　すぐれる　*vi.* excel; surpass
　　優しい　やさしい　graceful; gentle; kind

---

2 儿　ひとあし　legs

80 元 ④　一 二 テ 元

音 元　ガン

二
ー
人
ヘ
イ
儿
・ 入
八
冂
冖
冫
几
凵
刀
刂
力
勹
匕
匚
十
卜
卩
厂
厶
又
ク
マ

		ゲン	the origin; background; cause
熟	元日	ガンジツ	New Year's Day
	元祖	ガンソ	originator; founder; ancestor; forerunner
	元年	ガンネン	first year of an imperial era
	元来	ガンライ	originally; essentially; by nature
	元気	ゲンキ	healthy; happy; jolly; cheerful
	元首	ゲンシュ	head of state
	元素	ゲンソ	*chem.* element
	元服	ゲンプク	coming of age day for boys —*v.* celebrate one's coming of age
	元老	ゲンロウ	elder statesman
訓	元	もと	origin; originally; background; cause; former; ex-
	元帳	もとチョウ	ledger
	元通り	もとどおり	former; as it used to be
	元々	もともと	originally; from the outset; by nature

81

兄 ⑤ ㇒ 口 口 尸 兄

音	兄	ケイ	elder brother; elder brother of one's spouse
		（キョウ）	elder brother
熟	兄弟	キョウダイ	brother(s); brothers and sisters
	兄弟姉妹	ケイテイシマイ	brothers and sisters
訓	兄	あに	one's elder brother
	兄弟子	あにでし	senior fellow disciple/pupil

82

光 ⑥ ㇒ ㇔ ⺌ 半 尤 光

音	光	コウ	light; shine; brilliance; time
熟	光栄	コウエイ	honor; glory; privilege
	光化学	コウカガク	photochemistry
	光学	コウガク	optics; optical science
	光景	コウケイ	scene; sight; spectacle; scenery; view
	光源	コウゲン	*phy.* light source
	光合成	コウゴウセイ	photosynthesis
	光線	コウセン	light; ray/beam of light
	光度	コウド	*phy.* luminous intensity; light intensity; brightness; luminosity

	光年	コウネン	light-year
	光波	コウハ	*phy*. light waves
	光明	コウミョウ	hope; light; bright future
訓	光	ひかり	light; ray; beam; lumisary; influence; power
	光る	ひかる	*vi*. shine; be bright/brilliant; illuminate; glitter

83

先 ⑥　ノ　 ⸜ ⸜ 生 牛 先

音	先	セン	future; priority; precedence
熟	先覚者	センカクシャ	pioneer (in a particular field)
	先客	センキャク	previous visitor/customer
	先月	センゲツ	last month
	先見	センケン	foresight
	先刻	センコク	while ago; already
	先史時代	センシジダイ	prehistoric times
	先日	センジツ	the other day
	先週	センシュウ	last week
	先人	センジン	ancestor; predecessor
	先進国	センシンコク	advanced/developed nation
	先生	センセイ	teacher; master; doctor
	先祖	センゾ	ancestor
	先代	センダイ	predecessor; previous age/generation
	先達	センダツ	pioneer (in a field); leader; guide
	先着	センチャク	first arrival
	先手	センテ	first move; initiative
	先天的	センテンテキ	inborn; congenital; hereditary
	先頭	セントウ	head; lead
	先導	センドウ	guidance; leadership —*v*. guide; lead
	先入観	センニュウカン	prejudice; preconception; preoccupation
	先年	センネン	former years; a few years ago
	先発	センパツ	starting in advance —*vi*. start in advance; go ahead
	先方	センポウ	the other part; the other member/partner
	先約	センヤク	previous engagement
	先例	センレイ	precedent
訓	先	さき	tip; point; end; lead; the future; recent
	先立つ	さきだつ	*vi*. coming forward; precede; die before (someone)
	先細り	さきぼそり	gradual decline —*vi*. decline gradually
	先回り	さきまわり	*vi*. beat (a person) to it

二亠人ᛌイ几
•几入八冂冫冫几凵刀刂力勹匕匚十卩巴厂厶又夂マ

84

兆 ⑥   ノ ノ ノ タ 北 北 兆

音	兆	チョウ	sign; indication; sympton; omen; trillion; 1,000,000,000
熟	兆候	チョウコウ	sign; indication; omen; symptom
訓	兆し	きざし	signs; symptoms; indication; sprouting; germination
	兆す	きざす	*vi*. show signs of; indicate; show symptons; sprout; germinate

85

児 ⑦   ノ ハ バ 旧 旧 尹 児

音	児	ジ	infant; child
		(ニ)	infant
熟	児童	ジドウ	child; elementary school pupil
	児童憲章	ジドウケンショウ	The Children's Charter
	児童文学	ジドウブンガク	children's literature

2 入 いる enter

86

入 ②   ノ 入

音	入	ニュウ	enter
熟	入院	ニュウイン	hospitalization; admittance into a hospital —*vi*. be hospitalized; go into hospital
	入営	ニュウエイ	enrollment/enlistment (in the army) —*vi*. enlist/enroll/volunteer (for the army)
	入会	ニュウカイ	admission/entrance/enrollment (into a club) —*vi*. register/join a club; become a club member)
	入閣	ニュウカク	entry into the Cabinet —*vi*. enter the Cabinet
	入学	ニュウガク	entrance into a school; matriculation —*vi*. enter/be admitted into a school; matriculate
	入居	ニュウキョ	occupancy —*vi*. move (into a flat, house, etc.)
	入居者	ニュウキョシャ	tenant

入金	ニュウキン	receipt of money —*vi.* receive money; make a part payment
入港	ニュウコウ	arrival in port —*vi.* enter/make port
入国	ニュウコク	entry into a country; immigration —*vi.* gain entry into a country
入社	ニュウシャ	joining a company —*vi.* join a company; become a member of a company
入手	ニュウシュ	receipt; aquisition; procurement —*v.* procure; obtain; come by
入所	ニュウショ	entrance; admission (to a training school, laboratory, prison, etc.) —*vi.* enter; be admitted; be put into prison
入賞	ニュウショウ	winning a prize —*vi.* win a prize
入場	ニュウジョウ	entrance; admission; admittance; —*vi.* enter; get in; be admitted
入植	ニュウショク	immigration; settlement —*vi.* immigrate; settle
入信	ニュウシン	religious conversion —*vi.* be converted; come to believe
入選	ニュウセン	winning —*vi.* be accepted/selected
入隊	ニュウタイ	joining the army; enlistment; enrollment —*vi.* join; enlist
入団	ニュウダン	joining an organization; enlistment —*vi.* join an organization; enlist
入湯	ニュウトウ	taking a hot bath —*vi.* take/have a bath
入念	ニュウネン	careful
入梅	ニュウバイ	beginning of the rainy season
入費	ニュウヒ	expenditure; expenses
入部	ニュウブ	admission into a club —*vi.* enter/be admitted into a club
入門	ニュウモン	becoming a disciple; learner's book —*vi.* become a pupil
入門書	ニュウモンショ	guide; primer; manual; introduction
入用	ニュウヨウ	need; want; demand; necessity
入浴	ニュウヨク	bath; bathing —*vi.* take a bath; bathe
入力	ニュウリョク	input —*v.* input
入れる	いれる	*vt.* put in; insert; employ; make tea
入れ歯	いれば	false tooth/teeth
入れ物	いれもの	receptable; container
入る	いる	*v.* go/come in; set; sink; begin; attain; crack
入口	いりぐち	entrance
入る	はいる	*vi.* enter; come in; break in; join; begin

訓

2 八 はち eight

87 八 ②　ノ 八

音	八	ハチ	eight
熟	八月	ハチガツ	August
	八十八夜	ハチジュウハチヤ	eighty-eighth day from the beginning of spring
	八頭身	ハットウシン	well-proportioned figure
	八方	ハッポウ	every side; all around
	八方美人	ハッポウビジン	everybody's friend
訓	八	や	eight
	八重	やえ	eightfold
	八重歯	やえば	double/extra tooth
	八つ	やつ	eight
	八つ	やっつ	eight

88 公 ④　ノ 八 公 公

音	公	コウ (ク)	the public; duke
熟	公家	クゲ	court noble
	公安	コウアン	public peace
	公園	コウエン	park
	公演	コウエン	public performance —*vi.* perform in public
	公海	コウカイ	open sea; international waters
	公開	コウカイ	open to the public —*v.* be open to the public
	公害	コウガイ	pollution
	公休日	コウキュウび	legal/public holiday
	公共	コウキョウ	the public
	公告	コウコク	public notice —*v.* give notice to the public
	公算	コウサン	probability
	公私	コウシ	public and private matters
	公使	コウシ	vice-ambassador
	公式	コウシキ	***math.*** formula
	公衆	コウシュウ	the public

	公衆衛生	コウシュウ エイセイ	public health
	公職	コウショク	public office
	公正	コウセイ	justice
	公選	コウセン	election by popular vote —*v.* elect by popular vote
	公然	コウゼン	open; public; not secret
	公道	コウドウ	public road
	公認	コウニン	official recognition; authorized —*v.* recognize officially
	公判	コウハン	public/open trial
	公費	コウヒ	public expenses
	公表	コウヒョウ	public announcement —*v.* announce publicly
	公布	コウフ	promulgation; proclamation —*v.* promulgate; proclaim
	公平	コウヘイ	fairness
	公報	コウホウ	official gazette —*v.* keep an official gazette
	公民	コウミン	citizen
	公民館	コウミンカン	community center
	公務	コウム	public duties
	公務員	コウムイン	civil servant
	公明正大	コウメイセイダイ	fairness; fair and square; just and right
	公用	コウヨウ	official business
	公立	コウリツ	public foundation/institution
訓	公	おおやけ	the public

89

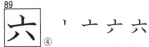

六 ④   ノ 亠 六 六

音	六	ロク (リク)	six
熟	六合	リクゴウ	universe; cosmos
	六書	リクショ	the six styles of Chinese characters
	六月	ロクガツ	June
	六三制	ロクサンセイ	6-3 educational system (six years of elementary school and three years of junior high school)
	六角形	ロッカクケイ	*math.* hexagon
	六法全書	ロッポウゼンショ	Compendium of Laws; the statute books
訓	六つ	むっつ	six
	六	む	six
	六つ	むつ	six

二十人へイ几入八冂冖几凵刀刂力勹匕匚十卜卩巴厂厶又ク マ

90

共 ⑥ 　一 十 艹 芉 共 共

音	共	キョウ	together; common; joint; (prefix) co-
熟	共栄	キョウエイ	mutual prosperity —*vi*. prosper
	共演	キョウエン	costar —*vi*. costar
	共学	キョウガク	coeducation
	共感	キョウカン	sympathy —*vi*. feel sympathy
	共済組合	キョウサイくみあい	benefit society
	共産主義	キョウサンシュギ	Communism
	共存	キョウゾン	coexistence —*vi*. coexist
	共通	キョウツウ	common —*vi*. commune; be common
	共通語	キョウツウゴ	common language
	共同	キョウドウ	cooperation; union —*vi*. cooperate; collaborate
	共犯	キョウハン	complicity
	共鳴	キョウメイ	resonance; agreement; sympathy —*vi*. agree; sympathize
	共有	キョウユウ	common ownership —*v*. own communally
	共用	キョウヨウ	common use —*v*. use communally
	共和国	キョウワコク	republic
訓	共	とも	together; common; joint; co-

91

 ⑦ 　ˊ ̆ ̆ ̆ 丘 乒 兵

音	兵	ヘイ	soldier; weapon; warfare
		ヒョウ	
熟	兵員	ヘイイン	military strength; numerical strength of an army
	兵営	ヘイエイ	barracks
	兵役	ヘイエキ	military service
	兵器	ヘイキ	arms; weapon
	兵士	ヘイシ	soldier
	兵舎	ヘイシャ	barracks
	兵隊	ヘイタイ	troops; soldier
	兵法	ヘイホウ（ヒョウホウ）	military tactics; strategy
	兵力	ヘイリョク	military force; troop strength

92 具 ⑧ ⟮ ⊓ ⊟ 月 目 且 具 具

音	具	グ	equipment; tool; utensil; detail
熟	具合	グアイ	condition; circumstances
	具体案	グタイアン	definite/concrete plan
	具体化	グタイカ	embodiment; materialization —*v.* embody; manifest
	具体的	グタイテキ	concrete; definite; tangible

93 典 ⑧ ⟮ ⊓ 巾 曲 曲 曲 典 典

音	典	テン	book; model; ceremony; celebration; code
熟	典型	テンケイ	model; type; pattern
	典型的	テンケイテキ	typical; representative; model; ideal
	典礼	テンレイ	ceremony

94 興 ⑯ ′ 亻 乇 臼 臼 臼 臼 舁 臼 舁 舁 舁 興 興

音	興	キョウ	interest
		コウ	spring up
熟	興じる	キョウじる	*vi.* amuse oneself; have fun; make merry
	興味	キョウミ	interest
	興行	コウギョウ	public entertainment; entertainment industry; performance —*v.* give a performance; produce; show; exhibit
	興奮	コウフン	excitement; stimulation —*vi.* be excited/aroused/stimulated
	興亡	コウボウ	rise and fall; ups and downs; existence; destiny
訓	興す	おこす	*vt.* revive; resuscitate
	興る	おこる	*vi.* rise; flourish; be prosperous

2 冂　どうがまえ　upside–down box

95 円 ④ 丨 冂 冂 円

音	円	エン	round; circle; yen (unit of currency)
熟	円形	エンケイ	circular; round
	円周	エンシュウ	circumference
	円周率	エンシュウリツ	**math**. pi; π
	円熟	エンジュク	maturity; mellowness —**vi**. be matured/well-rounded
	円柱	エンチュウ	column; pillar
	円満	エンマン	harmony; peaceful; perfect; well-roundedness
訓	円い	まるい	round; circular; spherical; globular

96 内 ④ 丨 冂 内 内

音	内	ナイ （ダイ）	inside
熟	内裏	ダイリ	imperial palace
	内意	ナイイ	secret intention; private opinion
	内科	ナイカ	internal medicine
	内海	ナイカイ	inland sea
	内外	ナイガイ	inside and outside; interior and exterior; some; about
	内角	ナイカク	**math**. interior angle
	内閣	ナイカク	Cabinet; administration
	内規	ナイキ	bylaw; customary rules
	内勤	ナイキン	office duty; indoor service; desk work —**vi**. work in an office
	内外科	ナイゲカ	internal medicine and surgery
	内向	ナイコウ	introversion
	内向的	ナイコウテキ	introverted; unsociable
	内妻	ナイサイ	common-law wife
	内在	ナイザイ	immanence; indwelling; inherence —**vi**. be immanent; indwell; inhere
	内在的	ナイザイテキ	immanent; indwelling; inherent; intrinsic
	内耳	ナイジ	**med**. internal ear; labyrinth

内実	ナイジツ	facts; truth
内出血	ナイシュッケツ	*med.* internal bleeding; internal hemorrhage —*vi. med.* bleed internally
内助	ナイジョ	wife's help; internal assistance —*v.* help one's husband; get inside help
内情	ナイジョウ	internal conditions; inside affairs
内職	ナイショク	side job —*vi.* do another job on the side; moonlight
内心	ナイシン	one's heart/real intention; inner center
内申	ナイシン	unofficial report —*v.* make an unofficial report
内申書	ナイシンショ	report on a pupil; secret school report
内政	ナイセイ	internal/domestic affairs
内省	ナイセイ	reflection; introspection; inward-looking; self-examination —*v.* introspect; reflect on oneself
内省的	ナイセイテキ	introspective; reflective; indrawn
内戦	ナイセン	civil war
内線	ナイセン	interior wiring; (telephone) extension
内蔵	ナイゾウ	built-in; containing —*v.* contain; have built-in
内臓	ナイゾウ	internal organs
内談	ナイダン	private talk; personal conversation —*vi.* have a private talk/word
内地	ナイチ	inland; the interior; back country
内通	ナイツウ	secret communication/understanding; treachery; betrayal —*vi.* collude; conspire; betray
内定	ナイテイ	informal/tentative decision —*v.* decide tentatively; make an informal decision
内的	ナイテキ	inner; internal; intrinsic
内々	ナイナイ	private; secret; confidential
内燃機関	ナイネンキカン	internal-combustion engine
内部	ナイブ	interior; inner part; inside
内服	ナイフク	*med.* internal use (of medicine) —*v.* take (medicine) internally
内服薬	ナイフクヤク	internal medicine; medicine for internal use
内分	ナイブン	*math.* interior division —*v. math.* divide internally
内聞	ナイブン	secret; secrecy; privacy
内包	ナイホウ	connotation; comprehension —*v.* connote; contain; involve
内密	ナイミツ	secret; private; confidential; backdoor; under-the-table
内務	ナイム	home/domestic affairs
内面	ナイメン	inside; interior
内約	ナイヤク	private contract; tacit agreement —*v.* make a private agreement; have a tacit understanding

	内容	ナイヨウ	contents; substance; details; depth
	内乱	ナイラン	civil war; insurrection; rebellion
	内覧	ナイラン	preview; preliminary inspection —*v.* preview; give a preliminary inspection
	内陸	ナイリク	inland
訓	内	うち	inside; interior; house; within
	内気	うちキ	reserved; shy; timid
	内金	うちキン	money paid on account; deposit; down payment
	内幕	うちマク	inside; inner workings
	内輪	うちわ	inside; family circle; moderate; conservative
	内訳	うちわけ	items; details; breakdown; classification

97

冊 ⑤ 丿 冂 冂 冊 冊

音	冊	サク	
		サツ	book; volume (counter for books)
熟	冊子	サッシ	book; booklet; pamphlet

98

再 ⑥ 一 厂 冂 丙 再 再

音	再	サイ	again; repeat; second; (prefix) re-
		（サ）	
熟	再演	サイエン	repeat/second performance —*v.* perform again; give a second performance
	再会	サイカイ	reunion; meeting again —*vi.* meet again
	再開	サイカイ	reopening; resumption —*v.* reopen; resume
	再刊	サイカン	republication; reissue —*v.* republish; reissue
	再起	サイキ	comeback; recovery —*vi.* make a comeback; recover; resume
	再挙	サイキョ	second attempt; comeback
	再建	サイケン	reconstruction; rebuilding —*v.* reconstruct; rebuild
	再現	サイゲン	reappearance; reproduction; reincarnation —*v.* reappear; reproduce; reincarnate
	再検討	サイケントウ	reexamination; reconsideration; review; reppraisal —*v.* reexamine; reconsider; review; reppraise
	再考	サイコウ	reconsideration; second thought; reflection —*v.* reconsider; reflect; think over again

再々	**サイサイ**	often; repeatedly; over and over
再三再四	サイサンサイシ	repeatedly; time and time again
再出発	サイシュッパツ	restart; fresh start
再生	サイセイ	regeneration; restoration; recycle —*v.* come to life again; recycle; regenerate; playback a recording
再生産	サイセイサン	reproduction —*v.* reproduce
再製	サイセイ	recycling —*v.* remanufacture; remake; recycle
再選	サイセン	reelection —*v.* reelect
再度	サイド	second time; twice; again
再読	サイドク	second reading —*v.* reread; read a book again
再入国	サイニュウコク	reentry (into a country) —*vi.* reenter (a country)
再入国許可	サイニュウコク キョカ	reentry permit
再任	サイニン	reappointment; reinstatement —*vi.* reappoint; reinstate
再認識	サイニンシキ	recognizing anew —*v.* recognize anew; realize
再燃	サイネン	recurrence; revival —*vi.* recur; revive; be revived
再発	サイハツ	recurrence; relapse —*vi.* recur; come back
再発見	サイハッケン	rediscovery
再版	サイハン	reprint; second impression —*v.* reprint; print a second edition
再犯	サイハン	second offense —*v.* recidivate
再放送	サイホウソウ	repeat of a program; rebroadcast; rerun —*v.* repeat; show a rerun
再来	サイライ	second coming —*vi.* come again
訓 再び	ふたたび	again; once more

---

2 冖 わかんむり wa crown; *wa* (katakana)

99

写 ⑤   ' ''' 冖 写 写

音 写	シャ	copy; film; photograph
熟 写実	シャジツ	realism
写実的	シャジツテキ	realistic
写植	シャショク	photocomposition; phototypesetting
写真	シャシン	photograph; photo
写真家	シャシンカ	photographer; cameraman

| 写生 | シャセイ | sketch; sketching |
| 写本 | シャホン | written copy; manuscript |

訓
| 写す | うつす | *vt.* copy; reproduce; take a photo |
| 写る | うつる | *vi.* be taken (a photo); come out; appear; be projected on a screen |

---

2 冫 にすい ice

100

冷 ⑦ 　 丶 冫 冫 冷 冷 冷 冷

音 冷 　レイ 　cold

熟
冷害	レイガイ	cold-weather damage
冷気	レイキ	cold; chill; cold weather
冷血	レイケツ	coldhearted; cold-blooded
冷血動物	レイケツドウブツ	cold-blooded animal
冷笑	レイショウ	sneer; scornful laugh —*v.* sneer; laugh scornfully
冷水	レイスイ	cold/ice water
冷静	レイセイ	calm; cool
冷戦	レイセン	cold war
冷蔵	レイゾウ	cold storage; refrigeration —*v.* keep in cold storage; refrigerate
冷蔵庫	レイゾウコ	refrigerator

訓
冷たい	つめたい	cold
冷える	ひえる	*vi.* get cold
冷	ひや	cold water/saké/rice
冷やかす	ひやかす	*vt.* tease; banter
冷やす	ひやす	*vt.* cool; refrigerate
冷ます	さます	*vt.* let cool
冷める	さめる	*vi.* get cold; cool down

二十人へイ儿入八冂宀冫儿凵刀刂力勹匕匚十卜卩厂ム又夂マ

101
風 ⑨　丿 几 几 凡 同 同 同 風 風 風

音 風	フウ	wind; air; look; appearance; fashion; style; type	
	（フ）		
熟 風圧	フウアツ	wind pressure	
風雨	フウウ	wind and rain; rainstorm	
風雲	フウウン	winds and clouds; times of change	
風雲児	フウウンジ	adventurer; soldier of fortune	
風化	フウカ	weathering —*vi.* weather	
風害	フウガイ	storm damage; gale damage	
風格	フウカク	personality; character; style	
風変わり	フウがわり	eccentric; peculiar	
風紀	フウキ	public morals	
風景	フウケイ	scenery; landscape; view	
風月	フウゲツ	wind and moon; the beauty of nature	
風光	フウコウ	scenery; natural beauty	
風車	フウシャ	windmill	
風習	フウシュウ	customs; manners; ways	
風水害	フウスイガイ	storm and flood damage	
風雪	フウセツ	blizzard; snow storm	
風説	フウセツ	rumor	
風船	フウセン	balloon	
風速	フウソク	wind velocity	
風速計	フウソクケイ	anemometer	
風潮	フウチョウ	tide; trend of the times; social climate	
風体	フウテイ	appearance; looks; attitude	
風土	フウド	climate; topography; natural features	
風土病	フウドビョウ	endemic disease	
風波	フウハ	wind and waves; storm; rough seas; fight; disagreement	
風評	フウヒョウ	rumor	
風物	フウブツ	scenery; nature; natural objects; seasonal scenery	
風物詩	フウブツシ	nature poem; poem about a season	
風聞	フウブン	rumor; report	
風味	フウミ	taste; flavor	

二 ｣ 人 ヘ イ 几 入 八 冂 ｀冫 几 凵 刀 刂 力 勹 匕 匸 匚 十 卩 卪 厂 厶 ク マ

風流	フウリュウ	elegant; refined
風力	フウリョク	wind force
風情	フゼイ	taste; appearance; air

訓 風 （かざ） (prefix) wind

風足	かざあし	wind velocity
風上	かざかみ	windward
風下	かざしも	leeward
風見	かざみ	weathercock; weather vane
風向き	かざむき	wind direction *fig.* situation; condition; (bad) temper
風	かぜ	wind
風当たり	かぜあたり	force of the wind; criticism; opposition

---

2 凵 うけばこ open box

102
⑤ 丨 屮 屮 出 出

| **音** 出 | シュツ | go/put out; exit |
| | （スイ） | |

熟

出演	シュツエン	stage/TV appearance —*vi.* appear on the stage/TV
出火	シュッカ	outbreak of fire; fire —*vi.* break out in flames; catch fire
出荷	シュッカ	shipment; shipping —*v.* ship; forward
出願	シュツガン	application —*v.* apply
出金	シュッキン	contribution; expenses; investment —*vi.* pay; contribute; invest
出家	シュッケ	Buddhist priest —*vi.* become a priest; renounce the world
出血	シュッケツ	bleeding —*vi.* bleed
出欠	シュッケツ	attendance
出現	シュツゲン	appearance; emergence —*vi.* appear; emerge; come into existence
出航	シュッコウ	departure —*vi.* sail; leave; fly; take off
出港	シュッコウ	departure from a port —*vi.* leave from a port
出国	シュッコク	leaving a country —*vi.* leave/get out of a country
出札	シュッサツ	ticket issue —*vi.* issue a ticket
出産	シュッサン	childbirth —*v.* give birth to
出所	シュッショ	source; release from prison —*vi.* be released from prison

出生	シュッセイ （シュッショウ）	birth —*vi*. give birth
出生地	シュッセイチ	birthplace
出生率	シュッセイリツ	birth rate
出場	シュツジョウ	participation —*vi*. participate; take part
出色	シュッショク	eminent; outstanding; remarkable; excellent
出身	シュッシン	one's hometown
出世	シュッセ	success in life; promotion —*vi*. rise; be promoted
出席	シュッセキ	presence; attendance —*vi*. be present; attend
出題	シュツダイ	question setting —*vt*. set test questions
出張	シュッチョウ	business trip —*vi*. take a business trip
出典	シュッテン	source (of a quote, etc.)
出頭	シュットウ	appearance; presentation —*vi*. appear; present oneself
出動	シュツドウ	dispatch —*vi*. dispatch; call in; alert
出馬	シュツバ	in person —*vi*. run for; go in person
出発	シュッパツ	start; departure —*vi*. depart; leave
出版	シュッパン	publication; publishing —*v*. publish
出品	シュッピン	exhibition; exhibit —*v*. exhibit; enter; be on display
出兵	シュッペイ	troop dispatchment —*vt*. dispatch troops
出漁	シュツリョウ	fishing (on a boat) —*vi*. go out fishing (on a boat)
出力	シュツリョク	output

訓

出す	だす	*vt*. let out; show; hold out
出る	でる	*vi*. go out; start; leave; rise; appear; protrude
出会う	であう	*vi*. meet; run into; encounter
出足	であし	start; initial charge (in sumo)
出来事	できごと	happening; affair; incident; event
出来物	できもの	swelling; tumor
出来る	できる	*vi*. be finished/ready/made from; come into being; can; be possible

103

 一 ⺁ ⺊ 而 両 面 画 画
⑧

音 画	ガ	picture; painting
	カク	stroke in calligraphy; division; plan
熟 画家	ガカ	painter; artist
画一的	カクイツテキ	uniform; uniformized
画策	カクサク	plan; scheme —*v*. plan; scheme

二 亠 人 ヘ イ 几 入 八 冂 冖 冫 几 凵 刀 刂 力 勹 ヒ 匚 十 卜 卩 厂 ム 又 夂 マ

画数	カクスウ	number of strokes (in a Chinese character)
画然	カクゼン	distinct; clear cut
画材	ガザイ	painting materials
画商	ガショウ	picture/art dealer
画像	ガゾウ	portrait
画題	ガダイ	title/subject of a painting
画期的	カッキテキ	epoch-making
画風	ガフウ	style of painting
画面	ガメン	picture; (television) screen
画用紙	ガヨウシ	drawing paper
訓 画	え	picture; painting

---

2 刀   かたな   knife; sword

104

刀 ②   フ 刀

音	刀	トウ	sword
熟	刀工	トウコウ	swordmaker; swordsmith
	刀身	トウシン	sword blade
	刀自	トジ	Madame; lady; matron; mistress
訓	刀	かたな	sword; blade; knife

105

切 ④   一 七 切 切

音	切	セツ	cut
		（サイ）	all
熟	切開	セッカイ	incision *med.* section; operation —*v.* make an incision; carry out a surgical operation
	切実	セツジツ	pressing; acute; keen; urgent; earnest
	切除	セツジョ	cutting off; removal *med.* excision —*v.* cut off; remove *med.* excise
	切々	セツセツ	ardent; earnest; sincere
	切断	セツダン	cutting; section; amputation —*v.* cut; sever; amputate
	切ない	セツない	melancholic
	切に	セツに	desperately; very much

| 切腹 | セップク | hara-kiri; suicide by disembowelment —*vi.* commit hara-kiri; disembowel oneself |
| 切望 | セツボウ | earnest desire; yearning —*v.* desire earnestly; yearn for |

訓

切る	きる	*v.* cut; give up; finish
切れる	きれる	*vi.* break; cut well; be sharp
切り上げる	きりあげる	*vt.* stop doing something
切手	きって	postage stamp

106

分 ④　ノ 八 分 分

音 分

	ブ	rate; percentage; one percent; thickness; *bu* (unit of length, approx. 3.03 cm)
	フン	minute (of time or arc); *fun* (unit of weight, approx. 375 mg)
	ブン	dividing; portion

熟

分化	ブンカ	specialization; differentiation —*vi.* specialize; differentiate
分解	ブンカイ	resolution; decomposition; dissection —*v.* be resolved; decompose; dissect; fall apart; take apart
分割	ブンカツ	division; partition —*v.* divide; partition
分業	ブンギョウ	division of labor —*v.* divide an operation into separate tasks
分極化	ブンキョクカ	polarization —*vi.* polarize
分家	ブンケ	branch family —*vi.* move out and set up a branch family
分権	ブンケン	decentralization of power/authority
分光	ブンコウ	*phy.* spectrum —*v.* separate a ray of light into a spectrum
分校	ブンコウ	branch school
分際	ブンザイ	one's status/position
分冊	ブンサツ	division of a book into separate volumes; volume —*v.* divide into separate volumes
分散	ブンサン	dispersion —*vi.* disperse; be dispersed; break up
分詞	ブンシ	*gram.* participle
分子	ブンシ	*chem.* molecule *math.* numerator *n.* elements; function
分室	ブンシツ	branch office; partitioned room
分宿	ブンシュク	separate hotels, etc. —*vi.* stay at separate hotels, etc.
分乗	ブンジョウ	separate cars/buses —*vi.* ride in separate cars /buses
分身	ブンシン	child; branch(of a family/organization)

二
亠
人
ヘ
イ
几
入
八
冂
冖
冫
几
凵
• 刀
刂
力
勹
匕
匸
十
卜
卩
厂
厶
又
ク
マ

分水	ブンスイ	diversion/shedding of water; diverted water —*vi.* divert/shed water
分水界	ブンスイカイ	watershed; (continental) divide
分数	ブンスウ	*math.* fraction
分節	ブンセツ	decomposition; division; articulation —*v.* break something down into its constituent parts; divide a sentence into clauses; articulate (each syllable)
分隊	ブンタイ	squad; division; detachment
分担	ブンタン	division; share; assignment —*v.* divide; share; assign; allot
分団	ブンダン	branch; chapter; group
分銅	ブンドウ	balance weight
分度器	ブンドキ	protractor
分納	ブンノウ	installment —*v.* pay in installments
分派	ブンパ	branch; faction; sect; denomination; separation; division —*vi.* branch out into factions/sects; separate; divide
分売	ブンバイ	separate sales —*v.* sell separately; break up and sell
分配	ブンパイ	distribution; division; share —*v.* distribute; divide; share
分筆	ブンピツ	subdivision (of a lot) —*vi.* subdivide land
分布	ブンプ	distribution —*v.* distribute
分別	フンベツ	discretion; good sense —*v.* be discrete
分別	ブンベツ	classification —*v.* classify; sort; separate
分母	ブンボ	*math.* denominator
分野	ブンヤ	field; sphere; realm
分立	ブンリツ	separation; independence —*v.* separate; make independent; act separately/independently
分流	ブンリュウ	tributary; branch
分留	ブンリュウ	fractional distillation —*v.* carry out fractional distillation
分量	ブンリョウ	quantity; amount; dose
分類	ブンルイ	classification —*v.* classify; sort; break down
訓 分ける	わける	*vi.* divide into; separate; classify; share
分け合う	わけあう	*vt.* share
分け前	わけまえ	one's share; cut
分け目	わけめ	part; parting
分かる	わかる	*vi.* understand; see; appreciate; know; find out; recognize
分らず屋	わからずや	obstinate person; blockhead; bovine
分かれる	わかれる	*vi.* branch off; separate; be divided; disperse; break up
分かれ道	わかれみち	branch/forked road
分かれ目	わかれめ	turning point; dividing line

107
| 初 ⑦ | ` ラ イ ネ ネ 初 初 |

音	初	ショ	beginning
熟	初夏	ショカ	early summer; beginning of summer
	初回	ショカイ	the first time; the beginning
	初刊	ショカン	first publication
	初期	ショキ	early days; first stages
	初級	ショキュウ	beginner's class
	初産	ショサン（ういザン）	first birth
	初志	ショシ	original intention/purpose
	初秋	ショシュウ	early fall/autumn
	初春	ショシュン	early spring; beginning of spring
	初心	ショシン	original intention; immaturity; inexperience
	初心者	ショシンシャ	beginner; novice
	初代	ショダイ	first generation; the first
	初対面	ショタイメン	first meeting
	初潮	ショチョウ	*med*. one's first menstruation
	初冬	ショトウ	early winter; beginning of winter
	初等	ショトウ	elementary
	初七日	ショなのか	seventh day from a person's death
	初日	ショニチ	first day; the start
	初版	ショハン	first edition
	初犯	ショハン	first offense
	初歩	ショホ	the first step; rudiments; elements
	初夜	ショヤ	wedding night
	初老	ショロウ	middle-aged; elderly
訓	初め	はじめ	beginning; outset
	初めて	はじめて	for the first time
	初	はつ	first
	初荷	はつに	first cargo of the New Year
	初耳	はつみみ	news heard for the first time
	初物	はつもの	first product of the season
	初雪	はつゆき	first snowfall of the year
	初夢	はつゆめ	one's dream on the second day of the New Year
	初める	そめる	*vt*. start; begin

二十人へイ儿入八冂冖冫几凵刀刂力勹匕匚十卜卩巳厂厶又ク マ

108

券 ⑧

` ` ` 丷 丷 彐 ゠ 夹 券 券

音	券	ケン	ticket

---

2 刂　りっとう　standing sword

109

刊 ⑤

一 二 千 刊 刊

音	刊	カン	publish
熟	刊行	カンコウ	publication —*vt*. publish; issue; bring out
訓	刊む	きざむ	*vt*. engrave; chisel; carve

110

列 ⑥

一 ア 歹 歹 列 列

音	列	レツ	line; row; queue
熟	列する	レッする	*v*. line up; queue
	列記	レッキ	written list; enumeration —*v*. list; enumerate
	列挙	レッキョ	list; enumeration —*v*. list; enumerate
	列強	レッキョウ	treaty/world powers
	列国	レッコク	nations; the powers
	列車	レッシャ	train
	列席	レッセキ	attendance; presence —*vi*. attend; be present
	列伝	レツデン	biographies
	列島	レットウ	chain of islands; archipelago
訓	列なる	つらなる	*vi*. lie in a row
	列ねる	つらねる	*vt*. put/lie in a row

111

判 ⑦

` ` ` 丷 丷 ゠ 半 半 判

音	判	ハン	judge; decide; seal; stamp; format
		バン	

熟	判決	ハンケツ	judgment; judicial decision —v. judge; pass judgment
	判事	ハンジ	judge; justice
	判然	ハンゼン	clear; evident
	判断	ハンダン	judgment; decision; conclusion; divination —v. judge; make judgment; decide; conclude
	判定	ハンテイ	judgment; decision; adjudication —v. judge; decide; adjudicate
	判読	ハンドク	interpretation; reading; decipherment (of unclear writing) —v. interpret; read; decipher (unclear writing)
	判別	ハンベツ	discrimination; distinction —v. distinguish; discriminate
	判明	ハンメイ	clear; confirmed —vi. become clear; be ascertained/confirmed
	判例	ハンレイ	precedent; leading case

112

別 ⑦ 　 丶 口 口 号 号 別 別

音	別	ベツ	different; separate; another; special; parting; farewell
熟	別格	ベッカク	special; exceptional
	別館	ベッカン	annex; separate building
	別記	ベッキ	stated elsewhere —v. be stated elsewhere
	別居	ベッキョ	(legal) separation (of a married couple); living apart —vi. live separately; be separated
	別口	ベツくち	different kind/item
	別個	ベッコ	separate; different
	別冊	ベッサツ	separate volume; supplement
	別紙	ベッシ	attached sheet; enclosure
	別辞	ベツジ	parting words; farewell speech
	別室	ベッシツ	separate/special room
	別種	ベッシュ	another/different kind
	別状	ベツジョウ	something unusual/different
	別人	ベツジン	another/different person
	別世界	ベッセカイ	another world
	別席	ベッセキ	different/special seat; different/special room
	別送	ベッソウ	by separate mail; under separate cover —v. send by separate mail
	別宅	ベッタク	second home/residence
	別段	ベツダン	special; particular
	別天地	ベッテンチ	another world

二
十
人
へ
イ
儿
入
八
冂
冖
冫
几
凵
刀
●刂
力
勹
匕
匸
十
卜
卩
厂
厶
又
ク
マ

別納	ベツノウ	payment made at different time or in a different way —*v.* pay at a different time; pay in a different way
別便	ベツビン	by separate mail
別封	ベップウ	by separate cover —*v.* send by separate cover
別々	ベツベツ	separate; individual
別法	ベッポウ	different way/method
別棟	ベツむね	separate/different building; annex
別名	ベツメイ	another name (used in biology when referring to the different names used for the same animal or plant)
別物	ベツもの	something else; exception; special case
訓 別ける	わける	*vt.* divide; separate; distinguish
別れ道	わかれみち	forked road; crossroads
別れ目	わかれめ	turning point; junction
別れる	わかれる	*vi.* part company with; leave; separate; get divorced; diverge
別つ	わかつ	*vt.* divide; separate; distinguish

113

利⑦　　一　二　千　禾　禾　利　利

音 利	リ	profit; advantage; interest
熟 利する	リする	*v.* profit; benefit; do (a person) good
利害	リガイ	advantages and disadvantages; interests
利器	リキ	sharp-edged/useful tool; convenience
利権	リケン	rights; interests; concession
利己	リコ	egoism; self-interest
利己主義	リコシュギ	egoism; selfishness
利口	リコウ	smart; clever; bright
利点	リテン	advantage; point in favor
利得	リトク	profit; benefit; gain
利発	リハツ	cleverness; intelligence
利用	リヨウ	utilization; application —*v.* utilize; apply; make use of
訓 利く	きく	*vi.* take effect; work
利かす	きかす	*vt.* make effective; use; exercise

114

刻 ⑧ 　 ` 　 亠 　 ナ 　 歺 　 亥 　 亥 　 亥 　 刻′ 　 刻

音	刻	コク	carve
熟	刻一刻	コクイッコク	gradually; moment by moment
	刻印	コクイン	carved seal —*v*. impress a seal
	刻限	コクゲン	fixed/appointed time
	刻々	コクコク	every moment; moment by moment; gradually
	刻苦	コック	hard work; arduous labor —*vi*. work hard; be arduous
訓	刻む	きざむ	*vt*. carve; engrave; sculpt

115

刷 ⑧ 　 ⊓ 　 コ 　 ㇷ゚ 　 尸 　 月 　 吊 　 刷′ 　 刷

音	刷	サツ	print; reform
熟	刷新	サッシン	reform —*v*. reform
訓	刷る	する	*vt*. print

116

制 ⑧ 　 ′ 　 ⻗ 　 ㇸ 　 仁 　 台 　 告 　 制′ 　 制

音	制	セイ	regulation; control
熟	制する	セイする	*vt*. control; command; dominate
	制圧	セイアツ	control —*v*. gain control; suppress
	制海権	セイカイケン	maritime control
	制球	セイキュウ	*bas*. ball control —*vi*. have ball control
	制空権	セイクウケン	air superiority
	制限	セイゲン	limit; restriction; limitation —*v*. limit; restrict; control
	制裁	セイサイ	punishment; sanction; penalty —*v*. punish; sanction; penalize
	制裁金	セイサイキン	penalty; fine
	制作	セイサク	work; production —*v*. produce; make
	制作者	セイサクシャ	producer
	制止	セイシ	check; control; restrain —*v*. control; restrain; hold back; check
	制定	セイテイ	enactment; establishment —*v*. enact; establish; create

制度	セイド	system; institution; organization
制度化	セイドカ	systematization; organization —*v.* systematize; organize
制動	セイドウ	brake; braking —*v.* brake
制動機	セイドウキ	brake
制服	セイフク	uniform
制約	セイヤク	restriction; limitation; condition —*v.* restrict; limit
制令	セイレイ	regulations

117

前 ⑨ 、 ツ 丷 丷 亠 产 前 前 前 前 前

音	前	ゼン	before; fornt
熟	前衛	ゼンエイ	vanguard; advance guard; avant-guarde
	前回	ゼンカイ	last time
	前科者	ゼンカもの	person's criminal record
	前記	ゼンキ	above-mentioned
	前期	ゼンキ	first term; preceeding period
	前言	ゼンゲン	one's previous remarks
	前後	ゼンゴ	about; approximately; order; sequence; front and back —*vi.* reverse order
	前座	ゼンザ	minor performer; opening performance
	前菜	ゼンサイ	hors d'oeuvres
	前史	ゼンシ	prehistory
	前日	ゼンジツ	previous day; day before
	前者	ゼンシャ	the former
	前述	ゼンジュツ	the above-mentioned —*vi.* mention above
	前身	ゼンシン	one's form in a previous existence; previous form; former position
	前進	ゼンシン	advance; drive; progress —*vi.* advance; drive forward; progress
	前世	ゼンセ	previous existence
	前線	ゼンセン	front lines; the front; front (meteorology)
	前奏	ゼンソウ	prelude (in music)
	前奏曲	ゼンソウキョク	prelude; overture
	前代	ゼンダイ	previous generation; former ages
	前代未聞	ゼンダイミモン	news heard for the first time
	前兆	ゼンチョウ	omen; portent; sign
	前提	ゼンテイ	premise; prerequiste
	前任	ゼンニン	former official; previous job
	前年	ゼンネン	preceeding year; last year

前半	ゼンハン	first half
前文	ゼンブン	preamble; the above statement
前面	ゼンメン	front
前夜	ゼンヤ	last night; previous night
前夜祭	ゼンヤサイ	celebration held on the eve of an anniversary or event
前略	ゼンリャク	first part omitted (salutation in letter)
前例	ゼンレイ	precedent
前歴	ゼンレキ	one's past record
訓 前	まえ	before; front
前売り	まえうり	advance sale —*vi*. sell in advance
前置き	まえおき	introductory remark; preliminary —*vi*. make introductory remarks

---

118

則 ⑨ ⎹ ⎠ 目 月 目 目 貝 則 則

| 音 則 | ソク | rule |

119

副 ⑪ 一 厂 后 后 戸 쿄 쿄 畐 畐 副 副

音 副	フク	accompany; vice-; deputy; assistant
熟 副官	フクカン	adjutant; aide
副業	フクギョウ	side job
副作用	フクサヨウ	*med*. ill/side effect
副産物	フクサンブツ	byproduct
副詞	フクシ	*gram*. adverb
副次的	フクジテキ	secondary
副収入	フクシュウニュウ	additional/side income
副賞	フクショウ	extra/supplementary prize
副将	フクショウ	second-in-command; vice-captain
副食	フクショク	side dish (to be eaten with rice)
副題	フクダイ	subtitle; subheading
副読本	フクドクホン	supplementary reader
副本	フクホン	duplicate; copy (of a written work)

120

割 ⑫ 　`　宀　宀　宀　宀　宀　宔　宔　害　害　害　割

音	割	カツ	divide; cut
熟	割愛	カツアイ	omission —*v.* omit; part with
	割腹	カップク	*hara-kiri* (self-disembowelment) —*vi.* disembowel oneself
	割礼	カツレイ	circumcision
訓	割る	わる	*vt.* break; divide; split; water; allot
	割	わり	rate; one tenth; ten percent; division
	割り当てる	わりあてる	*vt.* assign; allot; distribute
	割り切る	わりきる	*vt.* divide; leave no doubt; give a clear-cut solution (for a problem)
	割れる	われる	*vi.* break; be divisible; crack; be torn
	割く	さく	*vt.* tear; sever; estrange; spare

121

創 ⑫ 　ノ　ハ　ケ　今　今　今　毎　倉　倉　倉　倉　創

音	創	ソウ	create; originate; make; wound; injury
熟	創案	ソウアン	original idea —*v.* come up with an original idea
	創意	ソウイ	originality; inventiveness
	創刊	ソウカン	first edition —*v.* start/launch a magazine
	創業	ソウギョウ	inauguration; establishment —*v.* found; establish
	創建	ソウケン	foundation; establishment —*v.* found; establish
	創作	ソウサク	creation; work —*v.* create; write a novel/story
	創始	ソウシ	origination; creation —*v.* originate; create; found
	創世	ソウセイ	creation of the world
	創世記	ソウセイキ	Genesis
	創設	ソウセツ	foundation; establishment —*v.* found; establish
	創造	ソウゾウ	creation —*v.* create
	創立	ソウリツ	foundation; establishment

122

劇 ⑮ 　`　宀　宀　广　虍　虍　庐　虍　虏　虏　豦　劇

| 音 | 劇 | ゲキ | play; drama; the theater; acute; sharp |

熟	劇化	ゲキカ	dramatization —*vi.* dramatize
	劇画	ゲキガ	comics with a realistic narrative
	劇作家	ゲキサッカ	dramatist
	劇場	ゲキジョウ	theater; play house
	劇団	ゲキダン	troupe; theatrical company
	劇中劇	ゲキチュウゲキ	play within a play
	劇的	ゲキテキ	dramatic; dramatically
	劇毒	ゲキドク	deadly poison
	劇薬	ゲキヤク	powerful drug

---

2 力　ちから　strength; power

123

| 力 ② | フ カ |

音	力	リキ	strength; force; power
		リョク	strength; force; power
熟	力演	リキエン	superb performance —*vi.* give a superb performance
	力学	リキガク	dynamics; mechanics
	力作	リキサク	great work; masterpiece
	力士	リキシ	sumo wrestler
	力説	リキセツ	emphasis; stress —*v.* emphasize; stress
	力走	リキソウ	sprinting; fast running —*vi.* run as fast as one can; sprint
	力点	リキテン	fulcrum; emphasis
	力む	リキむ	*vi.* exert one's strength; strain; bear down
	力量	リキリョウ	ability; capacity; physical strength
訓	力	ちから	force; power; strength
	力仕事	ちからシごと	physical labor
	力試し	ちからだめし	trial of one's strength; test of one's ability
	力づける	ちからづける	*vt.* encourage; cheer up
	力持ち	ちからもち	man of great (physical) strength

124

| 加 ⑤ | フ カ カ 加 加 |

| 音 | 加 | カ | add; increase; join; participate; Canada; California |

79

二
亠
人
亻
儿
入
八
冂
冖
冫
几
凵
刀
刂
● 力
勹
匕
匸
十
卩
巴
厶
又
ク
マ

熟	加害	カガイ	assault; violence
	加害者	カガイシャ	assailant
	加減	カゲン	addition and subtraction; degree; extent; adjustment —*v.* allow for; make allowances for; adjust; moderate
	加護	カゴ	divine protection —*v.* receive divine protection
	加算	カサン	*math.* addition —*v.* add; include
	加重	カジュウ	weighted (average) —*vt.* add weight/intensity
	加勢	カセイ	help; aid; support; assistance —*vi.* help; aid; support; assist
	加速	カソク	acceleration —*v.* accelerate
	加速度	カソクド	acceleration rate
	加担	カタン	support; help; assistance; participation —*v.* support; help; assist; participate
	加入	カニュウ	joining; admission; entry; affiliation —*vi.* join; enter; affiliate
	加入者	カニュウシャ	member; subscriber
	加熱	カネツ	heating —*v.* heat up
	加筆	カヒツ	correction; revision (of an essay, a painting, etc.) —*v.* correct; revise
	加法	カホウ	*math.* addition
	加味	カミ	flavoring; seasoning —*v.* flavor; season
	加盟	カメイ	affiliation; participation —*vi.* join; affiliate; participate
訓	加える	くわえる	*vt.* add; increase; include
	加わる	くわわる	*vi.* join; participate; take part

125

功 ⑤

一 丁 工 功 功

音	功	コウ（ク）	exploit; achievement; merit
熟	功徳	クドク	act of charity; blessings
	功罪	コウザイ	merits and demerits; pros and cons
	功績	コウセキ	meritorious deed; services; merits; achievement
	功名	コウミョウ	great exploit; distinguished services
	功名心	コウミョウシン	ambition; aspiration; love of fame
	功利的	コウリテキ	utilitarian; matter of fact
	功労	コウロウ	merits; service; exploit
	功労者	コウロウシャ	person of distinguished service

助 ⑦ 　 亅 冂 冃 目 且 助刁 助

音	助	ジョ	help
熟	助演	ジョエン	supporting performance/role —*v.* play a supporting role
	助教授	ジョキョウジュ	assistant professor
	助言	ジョゲン	advice; counsel —*vi.* advise; counsel
	助詞	ジョシ	*gram.* particle
	助手	ジョシュ	helper; assistant
	助成	ジョセイ	aid; help with research or an enterprise —*v.* help; aid; assist
	助勢	ジョセイ	aid; support —*vi.* back; help
	助走	ジョソウ	run-up; approach run —*vi.* run up; make an approach run
	助長	ジョチョウ	promotion; encouragement —*v.* promote; encourage
	助動詞	ジョドウシ	*gram.* auxiliary verb
	助命	ジョメイ	sparing a person's life —*v.* spare a person's life
	助役	ジョヤク	assistant stationmaster; deputy mayor
	助力	ジョリョク	aid; help assistance; cooperation; support
訓	助	すけ	help; aid; assistance
	助太刀	すけだち	help; assistance; support
	助っ人	すけっと	helper; assistant
	助平	すけベイ	lechery; lewdness
	助かる	たすかる	*vi.* be helped/saved/rescued
	助ける	たすける	*vt.* help; assist; rescue; save

努 ⑦ 　 く 夕 女 奵 奴 努刁 努

音	努	ド	effort; endeavor
熟	努力	ドリョク	effort; endeavor; exertion; labor; strain; industry —*vi.* endeavor; do one's best; strive; make efforts
訓	努める	つとめる	*vt.* endeavor; make efforts; strive; apply oneself; try hard

二ユ人ヘイ儿入八冂宀冫几凵刀刂力勹匕匚十卜卩厂厶又ケ マ

128 労 ⑦

丶 ゛ ツ ⺍ 学 学 労

音	労	ロウ	work; labor; toil
熟	労役	ロウエキ	labor; work; toil
	労苦	ロウク	labor; pains; toil
	労作	ロウサク	laborious work; toil; labor
	労賃	ロウチン	labor cost
	労働	ロウドウ	labor; work; toil —*vi.* labor; work; toil
	労働者	ロウドウシャ	laborer; worker
	労働力	ロウドウリョク	labor; manpower; workforce
	労務者	ロウムシャ	worker; laborer
	労力	ロウリョク	labor; effort; trouble
訓	労る	いたわる	*vt.* sympathize with; be kind to; treat well; *vi.* get sick/ill

129 効 ⑧

丶 一 ナ 六 交 交 効 効

音	効	コウ	effect; efficacy; efficiency
熟	効果	コウカ	effect; effectiveness; efficiency
	効果的	コウカテキ	effective; effectual; successful
	効能	コウノウ	efficacy; effect; virtue; benefit; effectiveness
	効用	コウヨウ	effect; use; usefulness; utility; benefit
	効率	コウリツ	utility factor; efficiency
	効力	コウリョク	effect; efficacy; value; validity; force
訓	効き目	ききめ	effect; virtue; efficacy
	効く	きく	*vi.* be effective; work; act

130 勇 ⑨

マ マ マ マ 乛 丂 角 甬 勇 勇

音	勇	ユウ	courage; bravery; heroism
熟	勇気	ユウキ	courage; bravery; valor; nerve; audacity
	勇士	ユウシ	brave man; hero
	勇姿	ユウシ	brave/gallant figure
	勇者	ユウシャ	brave man; hero; man of valor
	勇将	ユウショウ	brave general; great soldier

	勇退	ユウタイ	voluntary retirement —*v*. retire voluntarily; bow out
	勇断	ユウダン	resolute decision
訓	勇ましい	いさましい	courageous; valiant
	勇む	いさむ	*vi*. cheer up; be in high spirits

131

勉 ⑩ 　ノ　ク　ケ　夕　台　台　户　免　免　勉

音	勉	ベン	diligence
熟	勉学	ベンガク	diligent study —*v*. study hard
	勉強	ベンキョウ	studying; diligence *col*. selling cheap —*v*. study; be diligent *col*. sell cheaply

132

動 ⑪ 　一　二　一　一　一　一　一　一　一　一　一

音	動	ドウ	movement; motion
熟	動じる	ドウじる	*vi*. be upset/perturbed/confused
	動員	ドウイン	mobilization —*v*. mobilize; set in motion
	動機	ドウキ	motive; inducement; incentive
	動議	ドウギ	motion (of a meeting)
	動向	ドウコウ	trend; tendency; movement
	動作	ドウサ	movement; motion; action
	動詞	ドウシ	*gram*. verb
	動静	ドウセイ	movements; state of things; conditions
	動的	ドウテキ	dynamic; kinetic
	動転	ドウテン	fright —*vi*. be frightened
	動物	ドウブツ	animal; beast
	動物園	ドウブツエン	zoo; zoological gardens
	動脈	ドウミャク	artery
	動乱	ドウラン	disturbance; upheaval; agitation; commotion; riot
	動力	ドウリョク	power; dynamic force; moment
訓	動かす	うごかす	*vt*. move; stir; put in motion; inspire; touch; impress
	動く	うごく	*vi*. move; stir; budge; shake; work; operate; be moved/touched

133

務 ⑪　⁻ ⁻ ⁻ 了 矛 矛 矛 矛 敄 務 務

音	務	ム	serve; work
訓	務め	つとめ	work; responsibility
	務める	つとめる	*vt.* work; serve

134

勤 ⑫　一 十 卄 ザ 芇 苩 茟 革 堇 堇 勤 勤

音	勤	キン	work; hold a post; exert oneself; endeavor; be diligent; try hard
		ゴン	
熟	勤勉	キンベン	diligence; industry; hard work
	勤労	キンロウ	labor; work; service; industry
訓	勤まる	つとまる	*vi.* be fit for; be equal to
	勤める	つとめる	*vt.* serve; work; hold a position; be diligent
	勤め先	つとめさき	one's place of work; the office

135

勝 ⑫　丿 刀 月 月 月 月 胖 胖 胖 胖 勝 勝

音	勝	ショウ	win; excel
熟	勝因	ショウイン	the cause of victory
	勝運	ショウウン	one's winning luck
	勝機	ショウキ	winning opportunity/chance
	勝算	ショウサン	chance of success; prospects; odds; chances
	勝者	ショウシャ	winner; victor
	勝敗	ショウハイ	victory or defeat; win or lose; the outcome
	勝負	ショウブ	match; game; contest —*vi.* play; have a game; have a match
	勝利	ショウリ	victory; triumph
訓	勝つ	かつ	*vi.* win; beat; defeat
	勝ち気	かちき	unyielding spirit
	勝ち目	かちめ	chances of winning
	勝る	まさる	*vi.* excel; be superior to

136

勢 ⑬ 　一　十　土　夫　去　杢　幸　幸丸　執　執　勢　勢

音	勢	セイ	power; force; energy; vigor
熟	勢力	セイリョク	influence; force
訓	勢い	いきおい	force; energy; vigor

2　勹　つつみがまえ　wrapping

137

包 ⑤ 　ノ　ク　勹　匂　包

音	包	ホウ	wrap; cover; envelop; conceal
熟	包囲	ホウイ	siege; surrounding (the enemy) —*v.* besiege; surround (the enemy)
	包装	ホウソウ	packing; packaging; wrapping —*v.* pack; package; wrap
	包蔵	ホウゾウ	concealment —*vt.* contain; imply; hold
	包帯	ホウタイ	bandage; dressing
	包丁	ホウチョウ	kitchen knife; cooking knife
	包皮	ホウヒ	outer skin; foreskin
	包容	ホウヨウ	tolerance; implication; comprehension —*v.* tolerate; comprehend imply
	包容力	ホウヨウリョク	capacity; tolerance; broad–mindedness
訓	包み紙	つつみがみ	wrapping paper
	包む	つつむ	*vt.* wrap; cover; envelop; conceal

2　匕　ひ　spoon; *hi* (katakana)

138

北 ⑤ 　一　十　丰　扎　北

音	北	ホク	north
熟	北上	ホクジョウ	going north —*vi.* go north
	北天	ホクテン	northern sky

2

二 ー 人 ヘ イ 儿 入 八 冂 冖 冫 几 凵 刀 刂 力 勹 • 匕 匸 • 十 卜 卩 厂 厶 又 ク マ

北部	ホクブ	north; northern part
北米	ホクベイ	North America
北辺	ホクヘン	northern regions/extremes
北洋	ホクヨウ	northern sea
北海道	ホッカイドウ	Hokkaido
北極	ホッキョク	North Pole
北極星	ホッキョクセイ	North Star; Polaris
北氷洋	ホッピョウヨウ	Arctic Ocean
北方	ホッポウ	north; northward; northern

訓

北	きた	north
北回帰線	きたカイキセン	Tropic of Cancer
北風	きたかぜ	north wind
北大西洋	きたタイセイヨウ	North Atlantic
北半球	きたハンキュウ	Northern Hemisphere
北向き	きたむき	facing north

2 匚　はこがまえ　box on side

139

④ 一 フ ヌ 区

音	区	ク	divide; punctuate; partition; borough; ward; diverse
熟	区域	クイキ	the limits; boundary; domain
	区画	クカク	division; demarcation —*v.* divide; demarcate
	区間	クカン	section between two points; territory
	区分	クブン	division; demarcation —*v.* divide; demarcate
	区別	クベツ	distinguishing; discrimination —*v.* distinguish; discriminate
	区民	クミン	ward/borough citizens
	区役所	クヤクショ	ward office
	区立	クリツ	funded/run and organized by the ward/borough

140

医　⑦ 一 ア 丆 匸 矢 医

| 音 | 医 | イ | heal; cure; doctor; medicine |
| 熟 | 医院 | イイン | physician's office; doctor's surgery |

医学	イガク	medical science; medicine
医師	イシ	doctor; physician
医務	イム	medical affairs
医薬品	イヤクヒン	medicine; drugs

---

2 十 じゅう ten; cross

141

十　② 　一 十

音	十	ジュウ	ten
熟	十一月	ジュウイチガツ	November
	十月	ジュウガツ	October
	十五夜	ジュウゴヤ	full-moon night
	十字	ジュウジ	cross
	十字軍	ジュウジグン	Crusaders
	十字路	ジュウジロ	crossroads
	十二月	ジュウニガツ	December
	十二支	ジュウニシ	twelve signs of the Chinese/Japanese zodiac
	十二分	ジュウニブン	more than enough
	十人十色	ジュウニンといろ	everyone to his own taste; to each his own
	十人並	ジュウニンなみ	average; ordinary
	十年一日	ジュウネンイチジツ	without any change over a long period
	十八番	ジュウハチバン	what one is best at
	十分	ジュウブン	enough; plenty
	十中八九	ジュッチュウハック	almost
訓	十	と	ten
	十	とお	ten
	十日	とおか	tenth day (of the month); 10th

142

千　③ 　一 二 千

音	千	セン	thousand
熟	千金	センキン	lot of money
	千差万別	センサバンベツ	infinite variety; various kinds

二 十 人 へ イ ル 入 八 冂 冖 冫 几 凵 刀 刂 力 勹 匕 匚 十 卜 卩 厂 厶 又 夂 マ

二
十
人
へ
イ
几
入
八
冂
冖
冫
几
凵
刀
刂
力
勹
匕
匚
●
十
卜
卩
厂
厶
又
夂
マ

	千秋楽	センシュウラク	the last day of a play, sumo, etc.
	千里眼	センリガン	clairvoyance
訓	千	ち	one thousand

143

午 ④ 　ノ 　　ニ 午

音	午	ゴ	noon
熟	午後	ゴゴ	afternoon; p.m.
	午前	ゴゼン	morning; a.m.

144

半 ⑤ 　丶 　丷 丷 半

音	半	ハン	half
熟	半永久的	ハンエイキュウテキ	semipermanent
	半円	ハンエン	semicircle; half-circle
	半音	ハンオン	semitone; halftone
	半開	ハンカイ	half open; partly open; semi-civilized
	半額	ハンガク	half the sum; half price
	半期	ハンキ	half year; half term
	半旗	ハンキ	flag at half-mast
	半休	ハンキュウ	half-holiday
	半球	ハンキュウ	hemisphere
	半径	ハンケイ	*math*. radius
	半月	ハンゲツ	half moon; half-month
	半減	ハンゲン	reduction by half —*v*. reduce by half; halve; take off half
	半紙	ハンシ	common Japanese paper
	半死半生	ハンシハンショウ	more dead than alive; all but dead; half dead
	半周	ハンシュウ	semicircle —*vi*. go half way around a circuit, etc.
	半熟	ハンジュク	half-boiled; half-done; half-ripe
	半身	ハンシン	half the body
	半信半疑	ハンシハンギ	incredulous; half in doubt; dubious
	半数	ハンスウ	half the number (of objects)
	半生	ハンセイ	half one's life; half a lifetime
	半世紀	ハンセイキ	half a century
	半田	ハンだ	solder; pewter

半月	ハンつき	half a month; half-month
半島	ハントウ	peninsula
半時	ハンとき	about an hour; short time; short while; half an hour
半年	ハンとし	half a year; half year
半日	ハンニチ	half a day; half day
半値	ハンね	half price
半白	ハンパク	salt and pepper hair
半々	ハンハン	half and half; fifty-fifty
半分	ハンブン	half
半面	ハンメン	one side; half; profile
訓 半ば	なかば	half; semi-; middle; center; in part; partially

145

協 ⑧ 一 十 忄 忄ワ 忄カ 恊 協 協 協

音	協	キョウ	cooperation; group; organization
熟	協会	キョウカイ	association; league; society
	協議	キョウギ	conference; council; consultation —*v*. confer; consult; deliberate
	協賛	キョウサン	support; cooperation —*v*. support; cooperate
	協商	キョウショウ	entente —*vi*. reach agreement
	協奏曲	キョウソウキョク	concerto
	協調	キョウチョウ	cooperation; harmony; conciliation —*v*. cooperate; act in union/harmony/concert
	協定	キョウテイ	agreement; convention; pact —*v*. agree upon; arrange; make an agreement
	協同	キョウドウ	cooperation; collaboration; union —*v*. cooperate with; collaborate; work together
	協約	キョウヤク	agreement; convention; pact
	協力	キョウリョク	cooperation; collaboration; working together —*vi*. cooperate; work together; collaborate
	協和	キョウワ	harmony —*vi*. be in harmony

146

卒 ⑧ 丶 宀 广 宀 卉 卆 卒 卒

音	卒	ソツ	soldier; private; sudden; come to an end; die; graduate
熟	卒業	ソツギョウ	graduation —*v*. graduate
	卒中	ソッチュウ	*med*. apoplexy; cerebral stroke

89

147 南 ⑨

一 十 广 内 内 肉 南 南 南

音	南	ナン	south
熟	南下	ナンカ	going south —*vi.* go down south
	南極	ナンキョク	South Pole
	南船北馬	ナンセンホクバ	constant traveling; being on the move
	南中	ナンチュウ	southing; culmination —*vi.* go south; cross the meridian; culminate
	南氷洋	ナンピョウヨウ	Antarctic Ocean
	南米	ナンベイ	South America
	南洋	ナンヨウ	South Seas
訓	南	みなみ	south
	南回帰線	みなみカイキセン	Tropic of Capricorn
	南十字星	みなみジュウジセイ	Southern Cross
	南半球	みなみハンキュウ	Southern Hemisphere

148 博 ⑫

一 十 广 扩 沪 博 博 博 博 博

音	博	ハク	broad; doctor; professor
		（バク）	gambling
熟	博する	ハクする	*vt.* gain/win (reputation); win/enjoy (credit/confidence)
	博愛	ハクアイ	philantropy; charity; benevelonce; humanity
	博学	ハクガク	erudition; extensive learning; wide knowledge
	博士	ハクシ（ハカセ）	doctor; professor
	博士号	ハクシゴウ（ハカセゴウ）	doctorate
	博識	ハクシキ	wide knowledge; erudition
	博徒	バクト	professional gambler
	博物	ハクブツ	extensive knowledge; natural sciences (term used in prewar Japanese schools)
	博物館	ハクブツカン	museum
	博覧	ハクラン	wide reading; extensive knowledge —*vi.* be widely read; have extensive knowledge
	博覧会	ハクランカイ	fair; exhibition; exposition

2 卩 わりふ／ふしづくり joint; seal

149

印 ⑥ 　 ´ ㇒ ㇇ ㇕ 印 印

音	印	イン	stamp; printing; seal
	印刷	インサツ	printing —*v.* print
	印紙	インシ	revenue stamp
	印字	インジ	printing —*v.* print
	印象	インショウ	impression
	印象的	インショウテキ	impressive; memorable
	印税	インゼイ	royalty (on a book)
訓	印	しるし	sign; proof; signal
	印す	しるす	*vt.* mark; inscribe

150

卵 ⑦ 　 ´ ㇄ ㇟ 身 卯 卵 卵

音	卵	ラン	egg
熟	卵黄	ランオウ	yolk
	卵管	ランカン	*med.* fallopian tube
	卵子	ランシ	*med.* ovum; egg cell
	卵生	ランセイ	*med.* oviparity
	卵巣	ランソウ	*med.* ovary
	卵白	ランパク	white of an egg; albumin
訓	卵	たまご	spawn; egg

2 㔾 わりふ／ふしづくり crooked seal

151

危 ⑥ 　 ㇒ ㇀ 㕻 产 危 危

音	危	キ	dangerous; hurt
熟	危害	キガイ	harm; injury
	危機	キキ	crisis; emergency

2

二十人へイ儿入八冂冖冫几凵刀刂力勹匕匚十卜卩厂
● 厶又マ

	危険	キケン	danger; hazard; risk
訓	危ない	あぶない	dangerous; doubtful; risky
	危うい	あやうい	dangerous; critical; hazardous; risky
	危ぶむ	あやぶむ	*vi.* fear; be apprehensive/afraid

2 厂 　がんだれ　cliff

152 厚 ⑨　一 厂 厂 厂 厓 厍 厚 厚 厚

音	厚	コウ	thick; kind; tender
熟	厚意	コウイ	favor; kind intentions; kindness
	厚顔	コウガン	impudence; shamelessness
	厚情	コウジョウ	kindness
訓	厚い	あつい	thick; heavy; bulky; kind; cordial; tender; warm; deep
	厚着	あつぎ	thick/warm clothes —*vi.* be thick/warmly dressed
	厚手	あつで	thick; bulky

153 原 ⑩　一 厂 厂 厂 厛 原 原 原 原 原

音	原	ゲン	plain; field; source; origin; crude
熟	原案	ゲンアン	original bill/plan
	原因	ゲンイン	cause; factor
	原画	ゲンガ	original picture
	原形	ゲンケイ	original form
	原型	ゲンケイ	model; prototype; archetype
	原語	ゲンゴ	original language; the original
	原告	ゲンコク	prosecutor; plaintiff; complainant
	原材料	ゲンザイリョウ	raw materials
	原作	ゲンサク	original story; the original; the book
	原産	ゲンサン	country of origin; native
	原始	ゲンシ	genesis; primitive; primeval
	原始時代	ゲンシジダイ	primitive age
	原始人	ゲンシジン	primitive man
	原始的	ゲンシテキ	primitive; primeval

92

原子	ゲンシ	atom
原子力	ゲンシリョク	atomic energy; nuclear power
原子力発電所	ゲンシリョクハツデンショ	nuclear power plant
原紙	ゲンシ	stencil paper; stencil
原住民	ゲンジュウミン	natives; aborigines
原書	ゲンショ	original book; the original; in the original
原色	ゲンショク	primary color
原図	ゲンズ	original drawing/plan/map
原寸	ゲンスン	actual size; life-size; full-size
原生動物	ゲンセイドウブツ	*bio.* protozoa
原生林	ゲンセイリン	primeval forest
原則	ゲンソク	general/fundamental rule; principle
原典	ゲンテン	original text
原点	ゲンテン	starting point; origin
原動力	ゲンドウリョク	motivating power; driving force
原文	ゲンブン	original text; the original
原木	ゲンボク	raw lumber
原野	ゲンヤ	wilderness; field; plain
原油	ゲンユ	crude oil; petroleum
原理	ゲンリ	principle
原料	ゲンリョウ	raw materials
訓 原	はら	plain; field

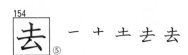

2 ム　む　*mu* (katakana)

154
去 ⑤　一 十 土 去 去

音 去	キョ	depart; go away; leave; the past; remove; clear away
	コ	
熟 去就	キョシュウ	one's course of action
去勢	キョセイ	emasculation —*vt.* emasculate
去年	キョネン	last year
去来	キョライ	coming and going; recurrence —*vi.* recur
訓 去る	さる	*vi.* take off; remove; eliminate; take away; get rid of; divorce; leave; depart from; pass; elapse; be over

2

ㄴ ㄙ ㄙ 予 弁

音	弁	ベン	speech; dialect; valve; petal; distinguish between; braid; bind
熟	弁じる	ベンじる	*vi.* speak; talk; debate; discriminate; pledge; vow; solve; finish; arrange
	弁解	ベンカイ	explanation; justification; defense; excuse; apology —*v.* explain; justify; excuse; apologize
	弁護	ベンゴ	defense; pleading for —*v.* defend; plead for
	弁護士	ベンゴシ	lawyer; attorney
	弁護団	ベンゴダン	the defense counsel (composed of several attorneys-at-law)
	弁護人	ベンゴニン	counsel; defender; lawyer
	弁才	ベンサイ	oratorical talents; eloquence
	弁済	ベンサイ	compensation; settlement; return of a borrowed item —*vi.* compensate; settle; return
	弁士	ベンシ	speaker; orator; silent movie narrator
	弁証法	ベンショウホウ	logical argumentation; dialectic
	弁舌	ベンゼツ	speech; eloquence
	弁天	ベンテン	Sarasvati (Indian goddess of music, eloquence, wisdom, and wealth)
	弁当	ベントウ	(box) lunch; packed lunch
	弁別	ベンベツ	discrimination; distinction —*v.* discriminate; distinguish
	弁務官	ベンムカン	commissioner (in colony/commonwealth country)
	弁明	ベンメイ	explanation; justification —*vi.* explain; justify
	弁理	ベンリ	management; dealing
	弁理士	ベンリシ	patent attorney (lawyer, agent)
	弁論	ベンロン	argument; debate —*vi.* argue; debate

ㄴ ㄙ ㄙ 予 矢 糸 参 参

音	参	サン	visit; go; worship; join; assemble
熟	参じる	サンじる	*vi.* go; visit
	参加	サンカ	participation —*vi.* participate in; take part; enter
	参賀	サンガ	congratulatory visit to the imperial palace —*vi.* visit the imperial palace to express congratulations
	参会	サンカイ	attendance at a meeting —*vi.* attend a meeting

参画	サンカク	participation in planning
参観	サンカン	visit; observation —*v*. visit; observe
参議院	サンギイン	House of Councilors; Upper House
参考	サンコウ	reference; consultation
参考書	サンコウショ	reference book
参考人	サンコウニン	witness
参集	サンシュウ	gathering; collecting —*vi*. gather; collect
参照	サンショウ	reference; consultation; comparison —*v*. refer; consult; compare
参上	サンジョウ	*hum*. visit —*vi*. *hum*. visit; go to see
参政権	サンセイケン	suffrage; right to vote; franchise
参戦	サンセン	participation in a war —*vi*. enter a war
参道	サンドウ	approach/path leading to a shrine
参拝	サンパイ	worship at a shrine or temple —*vi*. go and worship at a shrine or temple
参列者	サンレツシャ	attendant; one of those present
訓 参る	まいる	*hum. vi*. come; go; visit; worship

2 又　また　again

157

収 ④　丨　丩　収　収

音 収	シュウ	receive payment; harvest; store; keep
熟 収拾	シュウシュウ	control; reinstating order —*v*. put under control; settle
収集	シュウシュウ	collection; collecting —*v*. collect; gather; amass
収縮	シュウシュク	shrinkage; contraction —*v*. shrink; contract
収束	シュウソク	conclusion; convergence —*v*. gather and bundle; conclude; converge
収納	シュウノウ	receipt of payment/goods —*v*. receive payment/goods
収納家具	シュウノウカグ	cabinet
収納庫	シュウノウコ	shed; closet
収容	シュウヨウ	accommodation of people/things in a place —*v*. accommodate; send
収容所	シュウヨウジョ	concentration camp
収録	シュウロク	record; recording —*v*. record music/pictures (on magnetic tape, etc.)
訓 収まる	おさまる	*vi*. hold; contain; settle down
収める	おさめる	*vt*. put away/back; include; obtain; pay a bill

反 ④ 一 厂 厉 反

二人人 ヘ イ 几 入 八 冂 冖 冫 几 凵 刀 刂 力 勹 匕 匚 十 卜 卩 厂 厶 又 ⺍ マ

音	反	ハン	return; disobey
		（タン）	dry goods; drapery
		（ホン）	
熟	反する	ハンする	*vi*. be opposed/contrary to; go against
	反物	タンもの	dry goods; drapery
	反意語	ハンイゴ	*gram*. antonym
	反映	ハンエイ	reflection; influence —*v*. reflect; be reflected; influence
	反感	ハンカン	ill feeling; antipathy; adverse sentiment
	反旗	ハンキ	standard of revolt; banner of rebellion
	反逆	ハンギャク	treason; treachery; insurrection; rebellion; mutiny —*vi*. turn traitor; rebel; revolt
	反共	ハンキョウ	anti-communist
	反語	ハンゴ	rhetorical question; irony
	反作用	ハンサヨウ	*phy*. reaction; counterreaction
	反射	ハンシャ	reflection; reflex —*v*. reflect
	反証	ハンショウ	counterevidence; proof to the contrary; disproof —*v*. disprove; prove to the contrary
	反省	ハンセイ	reflection; self-examination; introspection; reconsideration —*v*. examine oneself; reflect; introspect; reconsider
	反戦	ハンセン	antiwar
	反則	ハンソク	foul; irregularity; violation of rules
	反対	ハンタイ	opposition; resistance; contrast; reverse; inverse —*vi*. oppose; resist; contrast
	反転	ハンテン	turning over; reversal —*v*. turn around; be reversed
	反動	ハンドウ	reaction; counteraction
	反応	ハンノウ	reaction; response; effect —*vi*. react/respond to; act upon
	反発	ハンパツ	repulsion; opposition; resistance; rebellion —*v*. repel; repulse; oppose; resist; rebel
	反比例	ハンピレイ	inverse proportion —*vi*. be inversely proportionate
	反復	ハンプク	repetition —*v*. repeat; do over again
	反面	ハンメン	other side; reverse
	反目	ハンモク	antagonism; variance; hostility; enmity; feud —*vi*. be at odds; feud with
	反乱	ハンラン	rebellion; revolt; insurrection —*vi*. rebel; revolt; rise up
	反論	ハンロン	refutation; counterargument —*v*. refute

| 訓 | 反らす | そらす | *vt*. bend; warp; curve |
| | 反る | そる | *vi*. warp; be warped/curved |

159

友 ④　一 ナ 方 友

音	友	ユウ	friend
熟	友愛	ユウアイ	friendship; brotherly love
	友軍	ユウグン	friendly troops; allied army
	友好	ユウコウ	friendship; amity
	友情	ユウジョウ	friendship; fellowship
	友人	ユウジン	friend
訓	友	とも	friend
	友達	ともだち	friend

160

取 ⑧　一 丆 下 F 耳 耳 耵 取

音	取	シュ	take
熟	取材	シュザイ	data collection; gathering material —*vi*. collect data; gather material
	取材記者	シュザイキシャ	reporter
	取捨	シュシャ	choice; selection
	取得	シュトク	acquisition —*v*. acquire
訓	取る	とる	*vt*. take; remove; gather; get
	取り上げる	とりあげる	*vt*. pick up; take up; adopt; take away; deliver a baby
	取り入る	とりいる	*vi*. ingratiate oneself; curry favor; flatter
	取り入れる	とりいれる	*vt*. take in; harvest; introduce; accept; adopt
	取り組む	とりくむ	*vi*. wrestle; tackle
	取り消す	とりけす	*vt*. cancel; withdraw; retract
	取り下げる	とりさげる	*vt*. withdraw
	取り次ぎ	とりつぎ	intermediation; agency
	取り付ける	とりつける	*vt*. install; fit; be equipped
	取り外す	とりはずす	*vt*. take down; remove; detach; dismantle

受 ⑧

161

丿 乛 乛 爫 爫 严 受 受

左欄（縦書き）:
二 亠 人 ∧ イ 儿 入 八 冂 冖 冫 几 凵 刀 刂 力 勹 匕 匸 匚 十 卜 卩 厂 厶 又 夕 マ

	受	ジュ	accept
音			
熟	受益	ジュエキ	in receipt of benefits —*vi.* receive benefits
	受給	ジュキュウ	in receipt of salary/pension —*vt.* receive a salary/pension
	受験	ジュケン	examination —*v.* sit an examination
	受講	ジュコウ	lecture attendance —*v.* attend a lecture
	受賞	ジュショウ	receiving a prize; prize winning —*v.* receive a prize; win a prize; be awarded a prize
	受賞作品	ジュショウサクヒン	prize-winning novel or work
	受信	ジュシン	reception of telecommunications —*v.* receive
	受信人	ジュシンニン	addressee
	受精	ジュセイ	*bio.* fertilization; pollination —*vi.* be fertilized/pollinated
	受像	ジュゾウ	on T.V. —*v.* receive a picture/image
	受注	ジュチュウ	acceptance of an order —*v.* accept/receive an order
	受動的	ジュドウテキ	passive
	受難	ジュナン	sufferings; ordeals; Passion of Christ
	受粉	ジュフン	pollination —*vi.* pollinate
	受理	ジュリ	acceptance of forms, papers, etc. —*v.* accept; receive
	受話器	ジュワキ	telephone receiver
訓	受かる	うかる	*vi.* pass an examination
	受け入れる	うけいれる	*vt.* receive; accept
	受け売り	うけうり	retailing; borrowing; parrot learning
	受け皿	うけざら	saucer
	受付	うけつけ	information; reception
	受け付ける	うけつける	*vt.* accept; receive
	受け取る	うけとる	receive
	受身	うけみ	defensive fall; break-fall; negative; passive; *gram.* passive voice
	受け持つ	うけもつ	*vt.* take charge of; be in charge of
	受ける	うける	*vt.* be given; receive; get; obtain; suffer; accept

2 ク く *ku* (katakana)

162

争 ⑥ ノ ク ク 气 争 争

音	争	ソウ	conflict; dispute; argue
熟	争議	ソウギ	dispute; strife; conflict
	争乱	ソウラン	rioting; disturbance
訓	争う	あらそう	*vt.* compete; dispute; argue

2 マ ま *ma* (katakana)

163

予 ④ フ マ ヌ 予

音	予	ヨ	previously; beforehand myself; I
熟	予価	ヨカ	intended price; overcharge
	予覚	ヨカク	premonition; hunch —*v.* have a hunch
	予感	ヨカン	premonition; hunch —*v.* have a premonition/ hunch
	予期	ヨキ	anticipation; expectation —*v.* anticipate; expect
	予見	ヨケン	forecast; foreknowledge —*v.* foresee; foreknow
	予言	ヨゲン	prediction —*v.* predict
	予行	ヨコウ	rehearsal —*v.* rehearse
	予告	ヨコク	advance notice; preview —*v.* notify beforehand
	予習	ヨシュウ	lesson preparation —*v.* prepare lessons
	予選	ヨセン	preliminary selection/screening; championship
	予想	ヨソウ	expectation; anticipation; conjecture —*v.* expect; anticipate; conjecture; imagine; guess
	予測	ヨソク	forecast; estimate; prediction —*v.* forecast; estimate; predict
	予断	ヨダン	prediction; guess —*v.* predict; guess
	予知	ヨチ	foreknowledge —*v.* foresee; foretell; predict
	予定	ヨテイ	plan; prearrangement; expectation —*v.* make a plan; prearrange
	予備	ヨビ	in reserve; spare; preliminary; preparatory
	予備校	ヨビコウ	preparatory school
	予備知識	ヨビチシキ	preliminary/background knowledge

2

二 亠 人 ヘ イ 几 入 八 冂 冖 冫 几 凵 刀 刂 力 勹 匕 匚 十 卩 卩 厂 厶 又 ⼡ マ
●

予報	ヨホウ	forecast; prediction —*v.* forecast; predict
予防	ヨボウ	prevention; protection —*v.* prevent; protect
予防接種	ヨボウセッシュ	**med**. inoculation
予約	ヨヤク	reservations; booking; advance order; subscription; appointment —*v.* make a reservation; book previously

3 口　くち／くちへん　mouth

164

口　　丶　冂　口
③

音	口	ク	
		コウ	mouth; speak; entrance
熟	口調	クチョウ	tone of voice
	口伝	クデン	oral instruction; by word of mouth —*v.* instruct/tell orally
	口外	コウガイ	uttering; telling —*v.* utter; tell; let out
	口径	コウケイ	diameter; aperture; caliber
	口語	コウゴ	*gram.* spoken colloquial language
	口語体	コウゴタイ	*gram.* colloquial style
	口座	コウザ	bank account
	口実	コウジツ	excuse
	口上	コウジョウ	statement; prologue
	口頭	コウトウ	orally
	口頭試問	コウトウシモン	oral test
	口答	コウトウ	oral answer/reply —*v.* answer orally
	口論	コウロン	quarrel —*v.* quarrel; row
訓	口	くち	mouth; entrance
	口当たり	くちあたり	taste
	口絵	くちえ	frontispiece
	口金	くちがね	bottle cap; top (of a jar, etc.); metal clasp (on a handbag)
	口車	くちぐるま	coaxing; flattering; honeyed words
	口答え	くちごたえ	back talk; retort —*vi.* talk back
	口先	くちさき	glib talk
	口出し	くちだし	poking one's nose —*vi.* meddle/chip in
	口止め	くちどめ	muzzle; hush money —*vi.* muzzle
	口走る	くちばしる	*vt.* let/blurt out
	口火	くちび	fuse (on a stick of dynamite, etc.)
	口下手	くちべた	poor in expressing oneself; poor talker
	口約束	くちやくそく	verbal promise; one's word

口口土士夕夕大女子宀寸小⺌⺍尤尸山川工己巾干幺广廴廾弓彡彳艹辶阝⺶忄扌犭氵

165 右 ⑤　ノ ナ オ 右 右

音 右	ウ	
	ユウ	right; right hand
熟 右往左往	ウオウサオウ	in all directions —*vi*. go right and left; go this way and that way
右折	ウセツ	right turn —*vi*. make a right turn
右党	ウトウ	right-wing party
右派	ウハ	the right; rightists
右方	ウホウ	the right; the right side
訓 右	みぎ	right; right-hand
右利き	みぎきき	right-handed
右巻き	みぎまき	clockwise
右回り	みぎまわり	clockwise

166 古 ⑤　一 十 十 古 古

音 古	コ	old; ancient; antique; classic
熟 古語	コゴ	archaic word
古今	ココン	ancient and modern times; all ages
古参	コサン	seniority; old-timer
古式	コシキ	ancient rite; traditional ritual
古人	コジン	the ancients; men of old
古代	コダイ	ancient times; antiquity
古典	コテン	classics; classical literature
古都	コト	ancient capital/city
古風	コフウ	antique; old-fashioned; archaic; classic
古文	コブン	ancient writings; classics
古米	コマイ	old rice; rice stored from a previous year's harvest
古来	コライ	from ancient times; time-honored
古老	コロウ	old man; elderly person
訓 古い	ふるい	old
古傷	ふるきず	old wound; (a person's) misdeeds/scandals
古す	ふるす	(suffix) used; worn out
古巣	ふるす	old nest
古めかしい	ふるめかしい	old; old-fashioned

167

台 ⑤ 　ㄥ ㄥ ㄥ 台 台

音	台	タイ	
		ダイ	stately mansion; stand; basis; (counter for vehicles, machines, etc.)
熟	台紙	ダイシ	pasteboard
	台地	ダイチ	plateau
	台帳	ダイチョウ	ledger; register; script
	台所	ダイどころ	kitchen
	台無し	ダイなし	ruined; spoiled; coming to nothing
	台風	タイフウ	typhoon
	台本	ダイホン	script; scenario; screenplay

168

各 ⑥ 　丿 ク 夂 冬 各 各

音	各	カク	each; every
熟	各位	カクイ	every one; all the members concerned
	各自	カクジ	each person; everyone
	各人各様	カクジンカクヨウ	in all their respective ways
訓	各(各々)	おのおの	each; every one

169

后 ⑥ 　一 厂 ㇒ 斤 后 后

| 音 | 后 | コウ | empress; emperor's wife |

170

合 ⑥ 　丿 𠆢 ム 合 合 合

音	合	ガッ	
		ゴウ	combine; join; union; fit; match
		（カッ）	
熟	合作	ガッサク	joint work/production; collaboration —*v.* collaborate; produce jointly
	合衆国	ガッシュウコク	United States

口 口 土 士 夂 夕 大 女 子 宀 寸 小 ㇑ 丷 尢 尸 山 川 工 己 巾 干 幺 广 廴 弋 弓 彡 彳 艹 辶 阝 丷 忄 扌 犭 氵

口口土士夂夕大女子宀寸小ㅆ�尢尸山川工己巾干幺广廴弋弓彡彳艹辶阝卩丬扌犭氵

合宿	ガッシュク	communal lodgings —*vi*. lodge together; be billeted together
合唱	ガッショウ	chorus; ensemble —*v*. sing together/in chorus
合奏	ガッソウ	concert; ensemble —*v*. play in concert
合点	ガッテン（ガテン）	understanding; comprehension —*vi*. understand; comprehend; grasp the meaning
合羽	カッパ	raincoat; mackintosh
合意	ゴウイ	mutual consent/agreement; concurrence —*vi*. come to mutual agreement; concur
合一	ゴウイツ	unity; union; oneness —*v*. unite; be united; act as one
合格	ゴウカク	success in an examination; passing an examination —*vi*. pass an examination
合議	ゴウギ	conference; consultation; counsel —*v*. confer; consult; hold a conference
合金	ゴウキン	alloy; compound metal
合計	ゴウケイ	total; aggregate —*v*. add up; total
合成	ゴウセイ	composition; synthesis —*v*. compose; compound; synthesize
合同	ゴウドウ	union; combination; amalgamation; merger; fusion —*v*. combine; unite; amalgamate; incorporate; merge
合板	ゴウバン	plywood; veneer board
合理化	ゴウリカ	rationalization —*v*. rationalize
合理的	ゴウリテキ	rational; logical; reasonable
合流	ゴウリュウ	confluence; conflux; linking; union —*vi*. join; link; unite

訓 合う	あう	*vi*. fit; suit; agree; be agreeable; be right; be correct
合図	あいズ	signal; sign; alarm
合わす	あわす	*vt*. expose/subject to
合わせる	あわせる	*vt*. expose/subject to

171

名 ⑥　ノ ク タ タ 名 名

音 名	ミョウ	
	メイ	name; fame; reputation
熟 名字	ミョウジ	surname
名代	ミョウダイ	proxy; deputy; representative
名案	メイアン	good idea
名医	メイイ	famous doctor; skilled physician
名園	メイエン	famous garden
名家	メイカ	distinguished family; celebrity

名歌	メイカ	famous/excellent poem or song
名画	メイガ	famous picture; masterpiece
名義	メイギ	official name; moral duty
名曲	メイキョク	famous music
名句	メイク	famous haiku; well-put phrase
名月	メイゲツ	harvest moon
名言	メイゲン	wise saying; apt remark
名工	メイコウ	master craftsman
名作	メイサク	literary masterpiece
名産	メイサン	noted product/speciality of a particular area
名山	メイザン	famous mountain
名士	メイシ	prominent figure; celebrity
名詞	メイシ	*gram*. noun
名実	メイジツ	in name and fact
名手	メイシュ	expert
名酒	メイシュ	famous/renowned saké
名所	メイショ	place of interest
名将	メイショウ	famous general/military commander
名称	メイショウ	name
名勝	メイショウ	scenic spot
名人	メイジン	master; expert; virtuoso
名声	メイセイ	fame; reputation
名著	メイチョ	famous work; great book
名店街	メイテンガイ	street of famous shops
名刀	メイトウ	fine sword; famed blade
名馬	メイバ	fine horse
名物	メイブツ	noted product of a particular area; standout
名文	メイブン	excellent composition; fine prose
名分	メイブン	moral duty; justice
名目	メイモク	name; pretext; nominal; ostensible
名門	メイモン	famous family; prestigious school
名訳	メイヤク	excellent/famous translation
名優	メイユウ	famous actor; star
訓 名	な	name; fame; reputation
名残	なごり	traces; remains; vestiges
名指す	なざす	*vt*. name; call by a name
名代	なだい	fame
名高い	なだかい	famous; renowned
名付ける	なづける	*vt*. name; call; entitle
名無し	ななし	nameless; anonymous; unknown
名主	なぬし	*hist*. village headman (Edo period)

| 名札 | なふだ | name plate/tag |
| 名前 | なまえ | name |

172 君 ⑦

ㄱ ㄱ ㅋ 尹 尹 君 君

音	君	クン	you; lord; splendid person; (suffix) attached to the names of young men
熟	君子	クンシ	gentleman; man of virture
	君主	クンシュ	monarch
	君主国	クンシュコク	monarchy
	君臨	クンリン	reigning —*vi.* reign
訓	君	きみ	you (used among friends, by teachers to students, by seniors to juniors, etc.)

173 告 ⑦

丿 ㇄ 屮 生 生 告 告

音	告	コク	tell; announce; inform
熟	告示	コクジ	notification; notice; bulletin —*v.* notify; proclaim; announce
	告知	コクチ	notice; announcement —*v.* notify; announce
	告白	コクハク	confession; avowal; admission —*v.* confess; admit; declare
	告発	コクハツ	prosecution; indictment; accusation —*v.* prosecute; indict; accuse; charge
	告別	コクベツ	leave-taking; parting —*vi.* take leave of; bid farewell
訓	告げる	つげる	*vt.* notice; inform; proclaim
	告げ口	つげぐち	telling tales —*vi.* tell tales; rat on
	お告げ	おつげ	announcement

174 否 ⑦

一 ㇇ 不 不 不 否 否

音	否	ヒ	no; negative; refuse; decline
熟	否決	ヒケツ	rejection; voting against —*v.* reject; vote against
	否定	ヒテイ	denial; negation —*v.* deny; negate
	否定的	ヒテイテキ	negative; contradictory

否認	ヒニン	denial; repudiation —v. deny; repudiate

訓 否　いな　no

否や　いなや　as soon as; no sooner than; yes or no; objection; if; whether

否　いや　no; nay; yes; well

否々　いやいや　grudgingly; by no means

否応なし　いやオウなし　whether one likes it or not

175

喜 ⑫　一 十 土 丰 吉 吉 声 喜 壴 責 喜 喜

音 喜　キ　gladness; joy; happiness

熟 喜歌劇　キカゲキ　comic opera; musical comedy

喜劇　キゲキ　comedy

喜色　キショク　countenance; mood; humor; feelings; happy expression

訓 喜び　よろこび　joy; happiness

喜ぶ　よろこぶ　*vi.* rejoice; be glad/happy

176

善 ⑫　丶 丷 丷 䒑 兰 羊 羊 美 美 善 善 善

音 善　ゼン　good

熟 善悪　ゼンアク　good and evil

善意　ゼンイ　good faith; well-intentioned; good will

善行　ゼンコウ　good conduct/deed

善後策　ゼンゴサク　remedial measures

善処　ゼンショ　appropriate action —*vi.* take appropriate action

善戦　ゼンセン　good fight —*vi.* put up a good fight

善男善女　ゼンナンゼンニョ　devout men and women

善導　ゼンドウ　edification —*vt.* edify

善人　ゼンニン　good man/people

善良　ゼンリョウ　good; good-natured; virtuous

訓 善い　よい　right; fine; good

177

吸 ⑥　丶 口 口 叨 吸 吸

音 吸　キュウ　inhale; suck; smoke

口口土士夂夕大女子宀寸小⺌⺍尤尸山川工己巾干幺广廴弋弓彡彳艹辶阝⺍忄扌犭氵

熟	吸引	キュウイン	absorption; suction —v. absorb; suck
	吸気	キュウキ	air supply; ventilation
	吸収	キュウシュウ	absorption; imbibition —v. absorb; imbibe
	吸着	キュウチャク	absorption —vi. absorb
	吸入	キュウニュウ	inhalation —v. breathe in; inhale
	吸盤	キュウバン	sucker; cupule
訓	吸う	すう	vt. breathe in; inhale; imbibe; smoke
	吸い上げる	すいあげる	vt. suck/pump up
	吸い出す	すいだす	vt. suck out; aspirate
	吸い付く	すいつく	vi. stick/cling to; adhere
	吸い物	すいもの	suimono (Japanese clear soup)

178
呼 ⑧ ノ 丨 口 口′ 叩′ 叩′ 呰 呼

音	呼	コ	call; expire; exhale; breathe out
熟	呼応	コオウ	shouting; agreement; correlation —v. shout to each other; agree; go together; correlate; act in concert
	呼気	コキ	expiration; exhalation
	呼吸	コキュウ	breathing; respiration —v. breathe
	呼吸器	コキュウキ	med. respiratory organs
訓	呼ぶ	よぶ	vt. call; ring for; invite; name
	呼び子	よびこ	whistle
	呼び声	よびごえ	call; cries
	呼び捨て	よびすて	calling a person by name without any honorific title
	呼び出す	よびだす	vt. ask to come; call up; summon
	呼び水	よびみず	priming water (for a pump)

179
味 ⑧ ノ 口 口 口一 口二 吽 昧 味

音	味	ミ	taste; flavor
熟	味覚	ミカク	taste; sense of taste
	味方	ミかた	friend; ally; supporter
	味読	ミドク	read with appreciation
訓	味	あじ	taste; flavor
	味気ない	あじケない	dull; wearisome; dreary; wretched
	味付け	あじつけ	seasoning; salting —v. season; salt

味わう　　あじわう　　*vt*. taste; experience; relish; appreciate

180

唱⑪　丶　口　口　口　叩　叩　吚　吗　唱　唱　唱

音	唱	ショウ	recite; sing; advocate
熟	唱歌	ショウカ	singing; songs
	唱和	ショウワ	chorus —*vi*. sing in chorus/unison
訓	唱える	となえる	*vt*. recite; chant; advocate; urge; preach

181

可⑤　一　丁　㕚　可　可

音	可	カ	possible; can; permit; good
熟	可動	カドウ	movable; mobile
	可燃性	カネンセイ	inflammability; combustibility
	可燃物	カネンブツ	inflammable/combustible substance
	可能	カノウ	possible
	可能性	カノウセイ	possibility
	可否	カヒ	right or wrong; pro and con; for and against
	可愛い	カワイい	cute; pretty; dear; darling; charming

182

句⑤　丿　勹　匇　句　句

音	句	ク	phrase; part of a sentence; haiku poem
熟	句会	クカイ	haiku gathering; meeting for the purpose of reading haiku
	句集	クシュウ	haiku anthology
	句点	クテン	period; full stop
	句読点	クトウテン	punctuation marks

183

号⑤　丷　口　口　昙　号

音	号	ゴウ	shout; cry; name; sign; title; order; command
熟	号外	ゴウガイ	extra/special edition (of a newspaper, magazine, periodical, etc.)

	号泣	ゴウキュウ	wailing; lamentation; moaning; weeping —*vi*. wail; lament; moan; weep bitterly
	号数	ゴウスウ	number (of editions)
	号令	ゴウレイ	order; command —*vi*. order; command; give an order

184

史 ⑤ 　ノ 口 口 史 史

音	史	シ	history
熟	史家	シカ	historian
	史学	シガク	history; historical studies
	史実	シジツ	historical fact
	史書	シショ	historical writing
	史上	シジョウ	in history; historical
	史料	シリョウ	historical records
	史論	シロン	historical thesis

185

司 ⑤ 　フ ヲ ヨ 司 司

音	司	シ	official; officer; control; manage
熟	司会	シカイ	presiding; taking the chair —*v*. preside; take the chair
	司会者	シカイシャ	master of ceremonies (MC); chairman
	司祭	シサイ	Roman Catholic priest
	司書	シショ	librarian
	司法	シホウ	the judiciary
	司法官	シホウカン	judicial officer; judges and prosecutors
	司法行政	シホウギョウセイ	judicial administration; the judiciary
	司法権	シホウケン	right to justice
	司令	シレイ	command; commander —*v*. command
	司令部	シレイブ	military headquarters

186

向 ⑥ 　ノ イ 内 向 向 向

| 音 | 向 | コウ | face; front; opposite; the other side |
| 熟 | 向学心 | コウガクシン | love of learning; desire to learn |

| 向上 | コウジョウ | improvement; elevation; rise —*vi.* rise; be elevated; become higher; improve; advance |

訓 向かう　むかう　*vi.* face; front; look at; be opposite; meet; confront; approach

向き	むき	direction; quarter; exposure; aspect
向く	むく	*vi.* turn; look to; face; point; tend; suit
向ける	むける	*vt.* turn; face; direct; point; aim; send; address; refer
向こう	むこう	the other side; beyond; one's destination; the other party

187

同 ⑥　｜ 冂 冂 同 同 同

音 同　ドウ　same; similar

熟

同意	ドウイ	same meaning/opinion; agreement; consent —*vi.* agree with; consent to; approve
同意語	ドウイゴ	*gram.* synonym
同一	ドウイツ	identity; sameness; oneness; equality; indiscrimination
同一視	ドウイツシ	*vt.* regard A in the same light as B; look at things indiscriminately
同音語	ドウオンゴ	*gram.* homophone
同化	ドウカ	adaptation; assimilation —*v.* adapt; assimilate
同格	ドウカク	same rank; equal footing; equality
同感	ドウカン	same sentiment; sympathy; empathy; agreement; concurrence
同期	ドウキ	same period/class; synchronism
同義	ドウギ	synonymy; same meaning
同義語	ドウギゴ	*gram.* synonym
同居	ドウキョ	living together —*vi.* live together
同郷	ドウキョウ	same province/village
同業	ドウギョウ	same trade/business
同権	ドウケン	equal rights
同行	ドウコウ	going/traveling together —*vi.* go/travel together
同好	ドウコウ	same tastes; liking the same thing
同士	ドウシ	fellow; companion
同志	ドウシ	same mind; congenial spirit; like-minded person
同乗	ドウジョウ	riding together; sharing a carriage —*vi.* ride together; share a carriage
同乗者	ドウジョウシャ	fellow passenger
同情	ドウジョウ	sympathy; compassion; fellow feeling —*vi.* sympathize; be sympathetic; have compassion

口 口 土 士 夂 夕 大 女 子 宀 寸 小 ⺌ ⺍ 尢 尸 山 川 工 己 巾 干 幺 广 廴 弋 弓 彐 彡 彳 艹 辶 阝 阝 ⺾ 扌 犭 氵

同人	ドウジン	same person; coterie; clique; fraternity; club
同性	ドウセイ	same sex
同性愛	ドウセイアイ	homosexuality
同席	ドウセキ	sitting with/together —*vi*. sit with
同然	ドウゼン	same
同窓	ドウソウ	alumnus
同調	ドウチョウ	alignment; conformity —*vi*. align oneself; conform; follow suit; fall into line
同等	ドウトウ	equality; parity
同盟	ドウメイ	alliance; league; union; confederation —*v*. ally with; form an alliance/union
同様	ドウヨウ	same; similar; identical
同類	ドウルイ	same kind/class
訓 同じ	おなじ	same

188

周 ⑧　　丿 冂 冂 冂 門 用 用 周 周

音 周	シュウ	round; surround; Zhou/Chou dynasty
熟 周囲	シュウイ	circumference; girth; periphery; surroundings; the environment
周回	シュウカイ	lap; going around —*v*. go around
周期	シュウキ	period; cycle
周航	シュウコウ	sailing around; circumnavigation —*vi*. sail around; circumnavigate
周知	シュウチ	well-known; widely-known
周到	シュウトウ	careful; scrupulous; meticulous
周年	シュウネン	(suffix) whole year; anniversary
周波	シュウハ	cycle; frequency
周波数	シュウハスウ	frequency
周辺	シュウヘン	outskirts; around; environs
周遊	シュウユウ	tour; excursion
訓 周り	まわり	surroundings; neighborhood; environment; those around one

189

命 ⑧　　丿 人 亼 合 合 命 命 命

音 命	ミョウ	
	メイ	life; destiny; fate order; command
熟 命じる	メイじる	order; command

命運	メイウン	fate
命数	メイスウ	one's natural life span; destiny
命題	メイダイ	proposition
命中	メイチュウ	hit —*vi*. hit (the target)
命日	メイニチ	anniversary of a death
命脈	メイミャク	life
命名	メイメイ	naming; christening; calling —*vi*. name; christen; call
命令	メイレイ	order; command —*v*. order; command

訓 命　いのち　life

命知らず	いのちしらず	recklessness; daredevil
命取り	いのちとり	fatal
命拾い	いのちびろい	narrow escape from death

190

和⑧　一　ニ　千　禾　禾　和　和

音 和	ワ (オ)	peace; harmony; Japan

熟 和英	ワエイ	Japanese and English languages; Japan and England
和音	ワオン	chord (in music)
和歌	ワカ	*tanka* (31-syllable poem)
和解	ワカイ	amicable settlement; compromise; reconciliation —*vi*. be reconciled; settle one's differences
和気	ワキ	harmony; peacefulness; calm (sea, wind, etc.)
和議	ワギ	peace talks; settlement (to avoid declaring bankruptcy)
和合	ワゴウ	harmony; concord; concord of husband and wife —*vi*. be in harmony/concord
和裁	ワサイ	Japanese dress-making; sewing kimono
和紙	ワシ	*washi* (Japanese paper)
和室	ワシツ	Japanese-style room
和食	ワショク	Japanese cuisine
和声	ワセイ	harmony (in music)
和製	ワセイ	made in Japan
和装	ワソウ	Japanese dress
和風	ワフウ	Japanese style
和服	ワフク	kimono; Japanese clothes
和文	ワブン	something written in Japanese; Japanese writing (especially *kana*)
和平	ワヘイ	peace

口 口 土 士 夂 夕 大 女 子 宀 寸 小 ⺌ 尢 尸 山 川 工 己 巾 干 幺 广 廴 弋 弓 彐 彡 彳 艹 辶 阝 丬 忄 扌 氵 犭

和訳	ワヤク	translation into Japanese —v. translate into Japanese
和洋	ワヨウ	Japanese and Western
和様	ワヨウ	Japanese style
訓 和む	なごむ	v. become calm; calm down vt. calm down; moderate
和やか	なごやか	peaceful; calm
和らぐ	やわらぐ	vi. soften; become soft/gentle/peaceful vt. soften; moderate
和らげる	やわらげる	vt. soften; lessen; relieve; pacify; moderate; modify

191

品 ⑨ 、 ロ ロ ロ ロ ロ 品 品 品

音 品	ヒン	article; refinement
熟 品	ヒン	elegance; grace; refinement; dignity; article; piece; item; course
品位	ヒンイ	dignity; nobility; grade; carat
品格	ヒンカク	dignity; nobility
品行	ヒンコウ	conduct; behavior; actions
品行方正	ヒンコウホウセイ	well-mannered; exemplary conduct
品詞	ヒンシ	gram. part of speech
品質	ヒンシツ	quality
品種	ヒンシュ	kind; variety; type; grade; breed
品性	ヒンセイ	character
品評会	ヒンピョウカイ	competitive show/exhibition; fair
品目	ヒンモク	item; list of articles
訓 品	しな	article; goods; wares; quality; personality
品書き	しながき	catalog; menu
品切れ	しなぎれ	out of stock; sold out
品物	しなもの	article; thing; goods; wares; stuff; stock

192

員 ⑩ 、 ロ ロ ア ア 月 月 目 目 員

| **音** 員 | イン | member; staff |
| **熟** 員数 | インズウ | the number of persons or things |

---

193 商 ⑪ 　`丶 亠 产 产 产 产 产 商 商 商`

- 音 商　ショウ　trade; merchant; business; commerce
- 熟 商科　ショウカ　commercial department; department of business and commerce
- 　商船　ショウセン　merchant ship/marine
- 　商店　ショウテン　store; shop
- 　商店街　ショウテンガイ　shopping center/mall
- 　商人　ショウニン　merchant; tradesman; dealer
- 訓 商う　あきなう　*vt.* sell; deal; trade

194 問 ⑪ 　`丨 冂 冂 冃 冃 冐 門 門 問 問 問`

- 音 問　モン　question; problem
- 熟 問罪　モンザイ　accusation; indictment —*vi.* accuse; indict
- 　問責　モンセキ　censure; reprimand —*v.* censure; reprimand
- 　問題　モンダイ　question; problem; issue
- 　問答　モンドウ　questions and answers —*v.* question and answer
- 訓 問う　とう　*vt.* inquire; ask; care about; accuse
- 　問い　とい　question; inquiry
- 　問い合わせる　といあわせる　*vt.* inquire; ask about

195 器 ⑮ 　`丶 口 口 叩 叩 罒 罗 哭 哭 器 器 器`

- 音 器　キ　receptacle; vessel; organ
- 熟 器械　キカイ　instrument; appliance
- 　器械体操　キカイタイソウ　gymnastics
- 　器楽　キガク　instrumental music
- 　器官　キカン　*med.* body organ
- 　器具　キグ　implement; appliance; apparatus
- 　器材　キザイ　materials; tools and materials
- 　器物　キブツ　utensil; vessel; container
- 　器用　キヨウ　skillfulness; dexterity
- 　器量　キリョウ　countenance; talent; ability

口 口 土 士 夂 夕 大 女 子 宀 寸 小 ⺌ ⺍ 尢 尸 山 川 工 己 巾 干 幺 广 廴 弋 弓 彑 彳 艹 辶 阝 䒑 忄 扌 犭 氵

3	訓 器	うつわ	vessel; container; utensil; capacity

___

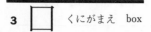

3 □ くにがまえ box

左side vertical kanji list:
● 口
● 囗
土 士 夂 夕 大 女 子 宀 寸 小 ⺌ ⺍ 尢 尸 山 川 工 己 巾 干 幺 广 廴 弋 弓 彐 彡 彳 艹 辶 阝 丷 忄 扌 氵 犭

___

196

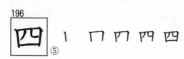

四 ⑤　一 冂 円 四 四

音	四	シ	four
熟	四角	シカク	square
	四角四面	シカクシメン	stiff; serious; stuffy; prim
	四月	シガツ	April
	四季	シキ	the four seasons
	四苦八苦	シクハック	struggling —*vi*. struggle; sweat blood
	四散	シサン	dispersion; scatter —*vi*. disperse; scatter
	四捨五入	シシャゴニュウ	***math***. rounding off —*v*. round off
	四方	シホウ	in all directions
	四六時中	シロクジチュウ	day and night; twenty-four hours a day ***fig***. always; often
訓	四	よん	four
	四	よ	four
	四	よつ	four
	四日	よっか	fourth day (of the month); 4th
	四	よっつ	four

197

因 ⑥　一 冂 冂 因 因 因

音	因	イン	cause
熟	因果	インガ	cause and effect; retribution; karma; fate
	因果応報	インガオウホウ	reward in accordance with deed; law of cause and effect
訓	因る	よる	*vi*. be caused by; be due to

198

回 ⑥　一 冂 冂 冋 回 回

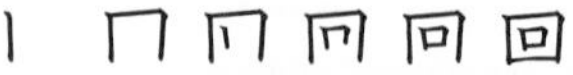

音	回	カイ	pass; turn; go round; circumference

116

	（エ）		turn round; service
熟	回帰線	カイキセン	the tropics
	回教	カイキョウ	Islam
	回収	カイシュウ	withdrawal; collection; recovery —v. withdraw from circulation; recover; collect
	回数	カイスウ	frequency; common occurence
	回数券	カイスウケン	coupon (commutation) ticket
	回送	カイソウ	forwarding; transportation —v. forward; send on; transport
	回想	カイソウ	retrospection; reminiscence; recollection —v. retrospect; recollect
	回虫	カイチュウ	*med.* roundworm; intestinal worm
	回転	カイテン	rotation —vi. revolve; rotate; turn around
	回答	カイトウ	reply; answer; response —vi. reply; answer; respond
	回復	カイフク	restoration; recovery —v. restore; recover
	回復期	カイフクキ	convalescence
	回覧	カイラン	circulation —v. circulate; send around
	回路	カイロ	electric circuit
訓	回る	まわる	*vi.* go around; pass; spread
	回す	まわす	*vt.* turn; pass; revolve
	回り	まわり	circumference; surroundings; by way of
	回り道	まわりみち	making a detour

199

団 ⑥ 丨 冂 冂 用 困 団

	団	ダン（トン）	body; group; corps; organization; association
音	団	ダン（トン）	body; group; corps; organization; association
熟	団員	ダンイン	group member
	団結	ダンケツ	unity; union; solidarity; combination —vi. unite; be united; stand together; combine
	団子	ダンゴ	dumpling
	団体	ダンタイ	party; company; group; body; organization; association
	団地	ダンチ	housing development; public housing complex
	団長	ダンチョウ	leader; head of a group

3

口口土士夕夕大女子宀寸小⺌⺍尢尸山川工己巾干幺广廴弋弓彡彳艹辶阝阝牛扌犭氵

200

囲 ⑦ 〡 冂 冃 冃 冄 囬 囲

音	囲	イ	surround; enclose
訓	囲む	かこむ	**vt.** enclose; surround; encircle
	囲う	かこう	**vt.** enclose; fence
	囲い	かこい	enclosure; fence
	囲み	かこみ	surrounding the enemy; enclosure

201

困 ⑦ 〡 冂 冃 冄 困 困 困

音	困	コン	suffer; distress
熟	困苦	コンク	hardships; adversity; trials; suffering
	困難	コンナン	difficulty; hurdle; trouble; distress
訓	困る	こまる	**vi.** suffer; be in trouble; have a problem

202

図 ⑦ 〡 冂 冂 冋 冈 図 図

音	図	ズ	drawing; picture; plan; figure
		ト	plan
熟	図案	ズアン	design; device; sketch; plan
	図画	ズガ	drawing; sketching
	図解	ズカイ	illustration; explanatory diagram —**v.** illustrate; explain with diagrams
	図形	ズケイ	figure; device; diagram
	図示	ズシ	illustration; graphic representation —**v.** illustrate; represent graphically
	図式	ズシキ	diagram; graph; chart; figure
	図版	ズハン	figure; illustration; plate
	図板	ズバン	drafting/drawing board
	図表	ズヒョウ	diagram; chart; graph
	図法	ズホウ	drawing; draftmanship
	図面	ズメン	drawing; sketch; map
	図書	トショ	books
	図書館	トショカン	library
訓	図る	はかる	**vt.** plan; devise; contrive; design; plot

203

固 ⑧ 丨 冂 冂 冃 冃 冄 固 固

音	固	コ	hard; solid; obstinate
熟	固形	コケイ	solid body; solid
	固持	コジ	persistence —v. be persistent; hold to; stand by; stick to
	固辞	コジ	categorical refusal —v. categorically refuse; refuse flatly
	固守	コシュ	adherence; persistence; insistence —v. adhere to; persist in; insist on
	固体	コタイ	solid; solid matter
	固定	コテイ	fixed; settled —v. fix; settle
	固有	コユウ	peculiar; characteristic; indigenous; particular
	固有名詞	コユウメイシ	*gram.* proper noun
訓	固い	かたい	hard; tough; tight; firm; strict; obstinate; rigid
	固まる	かたまる	*vi.* harden; become stiff; congeal; coagulate; thicken
	固める	かためる	*vt.* make hard; strengthen; fortify; solidify

204

国 ⑧ 丨 冂 冂 冃 用 国 国 国

音	国	コク	state; country; nation; province
熟	国営	コクエイ	state/government management
	国外	コクガイ	outside the country
	国学	コクガク	study of classical Japanese literature, history, and thought (late Edo period)
	国技	コクギ	national sport
	国語	コクゴ	one's mother tongue; the Japanese language
	国際	コクサイ	international
	国際化	コクサイカ	internationalization —v. internationalize
	国際的	コクサイテキ	international; universal; cosmopolitan
	国際連合	コクサイレンゴウ	United Nations
	国策	コクサク	national policy
	国産	コクサン	domestic production
	国史	コクシ	national history
	国字	コクジ	Japanese script; *kanji* invented in Japan
	国事	コクジ	affairs of state; national affairs
	国情	コクジョウ	conditions of a country; state of affairs
	国政	コクセイ	national administration; government

口口土士夂夕大女子宀寸小⺌⺍尢尸山川工已巾干幺广廴弋弓彡彳⺾辶阝亠忄扌犭氵

国勢	コクセイ	state of a country
国勢調査	コクセイチョウサ	census
国体	コクタイ	polity; national structure
国土	コクド	country; territory; realm; domain
国道	コクドウ	national road/highway
国内	コクナイ	internal; domestic
国費	コクヒ	national expenditure
国文学	コクブンガク	Japanese literature
国宝	コクホウ	national treasure
国防	コクボウ	national defense
国民	コクミン	nation; people; nationality
国民性	コクミンセイ	national character
国務	コクム	affairs of state; state affairs
国立	コクリツ	national
国力	コクリョク	national power/resourses
国家	コッカ	state; nation; country
国家主義	コッカシュギ	nationalism
国家的	コッカテキ	national; state
国歌	コッカ	national anthem
国花	コッカ	national flower
国会	コッカイ	Diet; national assembly; congress; parliament
国旗	コッキ	national flag
国境	コッキョウ	border; frontier
国交	コッコウ	diplomatic relations

訓 国　くに　state; nation; country; province

205

園 ⑬　｜ 冂 冋 冂 同 同 周 周 周 園 園 園

音	園	エン	garden; park
熟	園芸	エンゲイ	gardening; horticulture; floriculture
	園児	エンジ	kindergarten pupils
	園長	エンチョウ	head zookeeper; head of a kindergarten
	園遊会	エンユウカイ	garden party
訓	園	その	garden

3 土 つち／つちへん earth

206

土 ③ 一 十 土

音	土	ト	
		ド	soil; earth; dirt
熟	土方	ドかた	construction worker; navvy
	土管	ドカン	earthen pipe
	土器	ドキ	earthenware; crockery
	土下座	ドゲザ	prostrating oneself; paying obeisance —*vi.* prostrate oneself; apologize; show respect; pay obeisance
	土建	ドケン	civil engineering and construction
	土工	ドコウ	construction worker; navvy
	土左衛門	ドザエモン	drowned person
	土質	ドシツ	soil quality
	土砂	ドシャ	earth and sand
	土砂降り	ドシャぶり	pouring/heavy rain
	土人	ドジン	native; aboriginal
	土製	ドセイ	earthen; made of clay
	土星	ドセイ	the planet Saturn
	土蔵	ドゾウ	warehouse; storehouse
	土足	ドソク	with one's shoes on
	土台	ドダイ	foundation; groundwork; base; basis; cornerstone
	土地	トチ	earth; land
	土着	ドチャク	native; aboriginal; indigenous
	土手	ドて	embankment; dike
	土俵	ドヒョウ	sandbag; ring for sumo wrestling
	土木	ドボク	engineering/public works
	土間	ドマ	unfloored part of the house; earthen floored room; pit in a theater
	土民	ドミン	natives; aborigines
	土用	ドヨウ	dog days; midsummer; hottest period of summer
	土曜日	ドヨウび	Saturday
訓	土	つち	Mother Earth; earth; soil; ground; clay

口
口
土
士
夂
夕
大
女
子
宀
寸
小
⺌
⺌
尢
尸
山
川
工
已
巾
干
幺
广
廴
弋
弓
彡
彳
⻌
阝
⺾
忄
扌
犭
氵

207

圧 ⑤　一 厂 厂 圧 圧

音	圧	アツ	pressure; press down
熟	圧する	アッする	*vt*. press; press down; oppress
	圧死	アッシ	death from crushing —*v*. be crushed to death; be suffocated
	圧縮	アッシュク	compression; constriction; condensation —*v*. compress; constrict; make compact; condense
	圧勝	アッショウ	landslide win; sweeping victory —*vi*. defeat decisively; win a landslide victory
	圧力	アツリョク	pressure; stress

208

在 ⑥　一 ナ ナ 右 存 在

音	在	ザイ	be
熟	在外	ザイガイ	being abroad/overseas
	在学	ザイガク	enrolled —*vi*. be in school; be a student at; be enrolled at
	在勤	ザイキン	while working —*vi*. be working; be at work
	在庫	ザイコ	stock; inventory
	在住	ザイジュウ	living; in residence —*vi*. live; be in residence at
	在住者	ザイジュウシャ	resident
	在職	ザイショク	in the office; at work —*vi*. be in office
	在宅	ザイタク	at home —*vi*. be at home
	在来	ザイライ	usual; common; conventionally
	在留	ザイリュウ	in residence —*vi*. reside; live
訓	在る	ある	*vi*. be; exist; live; be situated; be located

209

垂 ⑧　一 二 二 千 壬 垂 垂 垂

音	垂	スイ	droop; hang down
熟	垂訓	スイクン	teaching; instruction
	垂線	スイセン	perpendicular (line)
	垂直	スイチョク	perpendicular; vertical; plumb; sheer; at right angles

訓	垂らす	たらす	*vt*. hang down; suspend; slouch
	垂れる	たれる	*v*. hang down; droop; drop; drip
	垂氷	たるひ	icicle
	垂水	たるみ	waterfall

210 報 ⑫

一 十 土 圡 耂 耂 幸 幸 幸 幸ⁿ 虾 郣 報

音	報	ホウ	news; report; reward
熟	報じる	ホウじる	*v*. repay; requite; report; inform
	報恩	ホウオン	showing gratitude; repaying a kindness
	報国	ホウコク	service to one's country
	報告	ホウコク	report —*v*. report; make a report
	報告書	ホウコクショ	(written) report/statement
	報知	ホウチ	information; news; intelligence —*v*. inform; make known; announce
	報道	ホウドウ	reporting; news coverage —*v*. report; inform; make known
	報徳	ホウトク	showing gratitude; repaying a kindness
	報復	ホウフク	revenge; vengence —*vi*. take revenge; revenge oneself
訓	報いる	むくいる	*vt*. reward; repay; retaliate; avenge oneself

211 型 ⑨

一 ニ チ 开 开 刑 刑 型 型

音	型	ケイ	pattern; model; shape; form
訓	型	かた	model; pattern; mold; shape; form
	型紙	かたがみ	paper pattern
	型通り	かたどおり	in due/correct form; formal; formulaic (speech)
	型破り	かたやぶり	unconventional; unusual; break with tradition
	型	がた	(suffix) -type; -model

212 基 ⑪

一 十 艹 艹 艹 甘 苴 其 其 基 基

音	基	キ	foundation; radical
熟	基金	キキン	fund; endowment
	基準	キジュン	standard; criterion

口口土士夂夕大女子宀寸小⺌
⺌尢尸山川工己巾干幺广廴弋弓彡彳
⻌阝⺌忄扌犭氵

基数	キスウ	*math*. cardinal numbers
基地	キチ	(military) base
基調	キチョウ	keynote; underlying tone/theme
基点	キテン	*math*. cardinal/reference point
基本	キホン	basis; foundation
基本的	キホンテキ	basically; fundamentally

訓
基	もと	basis; base
基	もとい	basis; foundation
基づく	もとづく	*vi*. be based on; originate; be due to

213

堂 ⑪　　丶　丶　⺌　⺌　⺌　㳕　常　常　営　営　堂

音
| 堂 | ドウ | palace; temple |

熟
| 堂宇 | ドウウ | temple eaves; temple |
| 堂々 | ドウドウ | stately; imposing; dignified |

214

墓 ⑬　　一　艹　艹　芍　昔　昔　莒　莫　莫　莫　墓　墓

音
| 墓 | ボ | tomb; grave |

熟
墓穴	ボケツ	grave
墓参	ボサン	visiting a grave —*vi*. visit a grave
墓所	ボショ	graveyard; cemetery
墓前	ボゼン	before the grave; in front of a grave
墓地	ボチ	graveyard; cemetery
墓標	ボヒョウ	grave post

訓
墓	はか	tomb; grave
墓石	はかいし	gravestone; headstone
墓場	はかば	graveyard; cemetery
墓守	はかもり	gravekeeper
お墓参り	おはかまいり	visiting a grave —*vi*. visit a grave

215

地 ⑥　　一　十　土　圠　圠　地

音
| 地 | ジ | earth; ground; soil; land; spot; place; district; region |
| | チ | |

124

熟	地上げ	ジあげ	forcing a landowner to sell his land against his will (through violence)
	地金	ジがね	metal; ore; one's true character/colors
	地声	ジごえ	one's natural voice
	地所	ジショ	land; ground; piece of land
	地蔵	ジゾウ	Jizō (Buddhist guardian deity of children)
	地主	ジぬし	landlord; landowner
	地味	ジミ	plain; simple; quiet; sober; conservative
	地道	ジみち	the honest way; beaten track
	地面	ジメン	ground; earth's surface
	地元	ジもと	local
	地元民	ジもとミン	local people; people of the district
	地位	チイ	position; status; standing; place
	地域	チイキ	area; region; zone
	地下	チカ	underground
	地階	チカイ	basement; cellar
	地下資源	チカシゲン	underground resources
	地下水	チカスイ	ground water
	地下鉄	チカテツ	subway; the underground
	地下道	チカドウ	underpass
	地球	チキュウ	earth; globe
	地区	チク	area; district; region; zone
	地形	チケイ	topography
	地質	チシツ	geology; geological features
	地上	チジョウ	on the ground; on earth
	地図	チズ	map; atlas; chart; plan
	地勢	チセイ	topography; geographical features; physical aspect
	地層	チソウ	layer; stratum
	地帯	チタイ	zone; area; region; belt
	地点	チテン	spot; point; place; position
	地熱	チネツ	terrestrial heat
	地表	チヒョウ	earth's surface
	地平線	チヘイセン	horizon; skyline
	地方	チホウ	district; region; area; locality
	地方化	チホウカ	localization —*v.* localize
	地方裁判所	チホウサイバンショ	district court
	地方自治	チホウジチ	local autonomy; self-government; home rule
	地方色	チホウショク	local color
	地方新聞	チホウシンブン	local newspaper
	地方税	チホウゼイ	local taxes
	地方分権	チホウブンケン	decentralization of power

口
口
土 •
士
夂
夕
大
女
子
宀
寸
小
⺍
⺌
尤
尸
山
川
工
己
巾
干
幺
广
廴
弋
弓
彡
彳
⺾
辶
阝
阝
⺌
忄
扌
犭
氵

口口土士夂夕大女子宀寸小⺌⺍尢尸山川工己巾干幺广廴弋弓彡彳艹辶阝疒忄扌犭氵

216

均 ⑦   一 十 土 ナ 圴 圴 均

音	均	キン	equal; identical; the same
熟	均一	キンイツ	uniformity; equality
	均衡	キンコウ	equilibrium; balance
	均質	キンシツ	homogeneity
	均整	キンセイ	symmetry
	均斉	キンセイ	symmetry
	均等	キントウ	equality; uniformity; evenness —*v.* be equal/uniform/even
	均分	キンブン	equal division —*v.* divide equally

217

坂 ⑦   一 十 土 圹 圻 坂 坂

音	坂	ハン	slope
訓	坂	さか	slope
	坂道	さかみち	sloping road; slope

218

城 ⑨   一 十 土 圠 圹 圻 城 城 城

音	城	ジョウ	castle
	城下町	ジョウカまち	castle town
	城主	ジョウシュ	feudal lord; lord of a castle
訓	城	しろ	castle; fort

219

域 ⑪   一 十 土 圵 圹 圹 垣 垣 域 域 域

音	域	イキ	district; region; boundary; scope
熟	域外	イキガイ	outside the region/scope
	域内	イキナイ	within the region/scope

220

場 ⑫   一 十 土 圵 圯 圯 坦 坦 坦 場 場 場

音	場	ジョウ	place; scene
熟	場外	ジョウガイ	outside of the grounds/premises

	場内	ジョウナイ	in the hall/grounds
訓	場	ば	place; spot; room; space; scene; field
	場合	ばあい	situation; circumstances; conditions; case; occasion
	場数	ばかず	experience
	場所	ばショ	place; spot; site; location; room; space
	場末	ばすえ	the suburbs/outskirts; off the beaten track
	場面	ばメン	scene; sight

221

塩 ⑬ 一 十 土 圤 圹 圹 垆 垆 垆 坫 塩 塩

音	塩	エン	salt
熟	塩化	エンカ	*chem*. chloridation; saltification —*vi. chem*. chloridate; saltify
	塩酸	エンサン	*chem*. hydrochloric acid
	塩水	エンスイ (しおみず)	salt water; brine
	塩素	エンソ	*chem*. chlorine
	塩田	エンデン	salt field/farm
	塩分	エンブン	saltiness; amount of salt; salt content
訓	塩	しお	salt

222

境 ⑭ 土 圵 圹 圹 圹 垆 垆 培 培 垆 境 境

音	境	キョウ (ケイ)	barrier; border; place; fortune; chance; fate; circumstances
熟	境界	キョウカイ	boundary; border; frontier
	境地	キョウチ	state; stage
	境内	ケイダイ	precincts; grounds; compound
訓	境	さかい	border; boundary; frontier

223

増 ⑭ 土 圵 圵 圹 圹 增 增 增 增 増 増 増

音	増	ゾウ	increase
熟	増員	ゾウイン	personnel increase —*v*. increase the staff
	増加	ゾウカ	increase; addition; rise; growth —*v*. increase; add; rise; grow
	増額	ゾウガク	increase —*v*. increase; raise

3

口口土士夕夕大女子宀寸小ソソ尢尸山川工己巾干幺广廴弋弓彡彳艹辶阝丷忄扌犭氵

127

増刊	ゾウカン	special edition; extra number —*v.* publish a special edition
増強	ゾウキョウ	reinforcement —*v.* reinforce; augment; beef up
増結	ゾウケツ	additional cars/carriages —*v.* add cars/carriages (to a train)
増減	ゾウゲン	increase and decrease —*v.* increase or decrease; vary (in quantity)
増刷	ゾウサツ	reprinting; additional printing —*v.* reprint; print additional copies
増進	ゾウシン	improvement; increase —*v.* improve; increase; further
増水	ゾウスイ	rising/swelling (of a river); flooding —*v.* swell; rise; flood
増設	ゾウセツ	extension —*v.* build on; extend; establish; install more
増大	ゾウダイ	increase; enlargement —*v.* increase; enlarge
増築	ゾウチク	extension —*v.* build on; extend; enlarge
増長	ゾウチョウ	*v.* grow presumptuous/impudent
増発	ゾウハツ	extra train; extra issue (of bonds) —*v.* put on an extra train; issue extra (bonds)
増兵	ゾウヘイ	reinforcements —*v.* reinforce
増補	ゾウホ	enlargement; supplement —*v.* enlarge; supplement
訓 増える	ふえる	*vi.* increase; rise; raise
増やす	ふやす	*vi.* increase; rise; raise
増す	ます	*vi.* increase; rise; raise

---

3 士 さむらい samurai; gentleman

224

士 ③ 一 十 士

音 士	シ	samurai; warrior; man; gentleman
熟 士官	シカン	military officer
士気	シキ	morale
士族	シゾク	samurai family; descendant of a samurai
士農工商	シノウコウショウ	*hist.* the military, agricultural, industrial, and mercantile classes of feudal Japan (Edo period)

225

声 ⑦ 　一　十　士　±　声　声　声　声

音	声	セイ	voice; reputation
		（ショウ）	
熟	声域	セイイキ	voice range; register
	声楽	セイガク	vocal music; singing
	声楽家	セイガクカ	vocalist
	声帯	セイタイ	vocal chords
	声望	セイボウ	popularity; fame; reputation
	声明	セイメイ	declaration; proclamation —v. declare; proclaim
	声明書	セイメイショ	statement; public/official statement
	声優	セイユウ	actor/actress specializing in dubbing films
	声量	セイリョウ	volume
訓	声	こえ	voice
	声	こわ	(prefix) voice; vocal
	声高	こわだか	loud voice
	声音	こわね	tone of voice

226

売 ⑦ 　一　十　士　±　声　声　売

音	売	バイ	sell
熟	売春	バイシュン	prostitution; harloty; streetwalking —vi. prostitute; walk the streets; sell oneself for money
	売春婦	バイシュンフ	prostitute; street girl
	売店	バイテン	stand; stall; booth
	売買	バイバイ	buying and selling; trade; dealing; transaction —v. buy and sell; trade/deal in; market; handle
	売名	バイメイ	self-advertisement
	売約	バイヤク	sales contract
訓	売る	うる	vt. sell; deal offer; deceive
	売り	うり	sale; selling;
	売り切れ	うりきれ	being sold out; exhausted supplies; sold out
	売り出す	うりだす	vt. offer for sale; become popular
	売り主	うりぬし	seller; vendor
	売り場	うりば	counter; shop; store
	売れる	うれる	vi. sell; be in demand; be well know/popular
	売れ口	うれくち	market; outlet; one's place of employment

口口土士夂夕大女子宀寸小⺌⺍尤尸山川工己巾干幺广廴弋弓彡彳艹⻌阝⺌忄扌犭氵

3

口 口 土 士 夂 夕 大 女 子 宀 寸 小 ⺌ ⺍ 尢 尸 山 川 工 已 巾 干 幺 广 廴 弋 弓 彡 彳 辶 阝 艹 忄 扌 氵

売れっ子　うれっこ　　popular singer/actor
売れ行き　うれゆき　　market; sale; demand

---

3 夂　ふゆがしら／なつあし　winter

227

処 ⑤　ノ ク 夂 処 処

音	処	ショ	place; deal with
熟	処する	ショする	*vi*. face; conduct; deal with; manage
	処子	ショシ	virgin; innocent child
	処女	ショジョ	virgin
	処女作	ショジョサク	maiden work
	処世訓	ショセイクン	the secret of getting along in the world
	処断	ショダン	ruling; judgment
	処置	ショチ	treatment; disposal; measures —*v*. dispose; deal with; take measures; treat
	処分	ショブン	disposal; punishment; measure —*v*. dispose of; deal with; punish
	処方	ショホウ	*med*. prescription —*v*. prescribe
	処理	ショリ	management —*v*. deal with; handle

228

冬 ⑤　ノ ク 夂 冬 冬

音	冬	トウ	winter
熟	冬季	トウキ	winter
	冬期	トウキ	wintertime
	冬至	トウジ	winter solstice
訓	冬	ふゆ	winter
	冬ごもり	ふゆごもり	winter confinement; wintering —*vi*. stay indoors for the winter
	冬物	ふゆもの	winter clothing/wear
	冬休み	ふゆやすみ	winter vacation

229

麦 ⑦　一 十 キ 圭 丰 麦 麦

音	麦	バク	barley; wheat

熟	麦芽	バクガ	malt; germ wheat; barley
訓	麦	むぎ	wheat; barley; oats; rye

230

変 ⑨　`　亠　ナ　方　亦　亦　亦　変　変

音	変	ヘン	change; strange; mishap; accident; flat (in music)
熟	変じる	ヘンじる	*v.* change; alter; renew
	変圧器	ヘンアツキ	transformer (voltage)
	変移	ヘンイ	change; alteration —*v.* change; alter
	変異	ヘンイ	change; fluctuation; variation; mishap —*vi.* change; fluctuation; be different
	変化	ヘンカ	change; transformation —*vi.* change; transform
	変革	ヘンカク	reformation; change; revolution —*v.* reform; change; be revolutionized
	変化	ヘンゲ	goblin; apparition; god that has taken on human form
	変形	ヘンケイ	transformation; modification; deformation —*v.* transform; modify; deform
	変死	ヘンシ	unnatural death (by accident, murder, suicide, etc.) —*vi.* die an unnatural death
	変事	ヘンジ	mishap; accident; incident
	変質	ヘンシツ	deterioration; degeneration —*vi.* be degenerate
	変質者	ヘンシツシャ	pervert; deviant
	変種	ヘンシュ	variety; strain
	変色	ヘンショク	discoloration; change of color —*v.* change the color; discolor
	変身	ヘンシン	metamorphosis; transformation —*vi.* metamorphose; transform
	変心	ヘンシン	change of mind/heart; fickleness —*vi.* change one's mind; be fickle
	変人	ヘンジン	odd person; eccentric
	変数	ヘンスウ	*math.* variable
	変成	ヘンセイ	metamorphosis; change of shape/form —*v.* change shape/form
	変節	ヘンセツ	change of seasons; apostasy
	変装	ヘンソウ	disguise —*vi.* be disguised
	変造	ヘンゾウ	alteration; defacement; forgery
	変速	ヘンソク	changing speed/gears
	変則	ヘンソク	irregular; abnormal
	変態	ヘンタイ	metamorphosis; abnormal; perverted
	変調	ヘンチョウ	change of tone/key; irregular; abnormal
	変転	ヘンテン	great changes; vicissitudes —*vi.* change

口口土士夂夕大女子宀寸小丷尢尸山川工己巾干幺广廴弋弓彡彳艹辶阝⺌忄扌犭氵

unpredictably

	変動	ヘンドウ	change; fluctuation —*vi.* change; fluctuate
	変名	ヘンメイ (ヘンミョウ)	assumed name; name change —*vi.* change one's name; assume an alias
	変容	ヘンヨウ	changed appearance —*v.* change appearance
	変乱	ヘンラン	upheaval; disturbance
訓	変える	かえる	*vt.* change; alter; move
	変わる	かわる	*vi.* change; be different/strange
	変わり種	かわりだね	exceptional case; different from the rest
	変わり 果てる	かわりはてる	*vi.* change completely
	変わり目	かわりめ	change; turning point; transition
	変わり者	かわりもの	odd person; eccentric

231

夏 ⑩   一 一 ァ 丆 丙 丙 百 百 戸 亨 夏 夏

音	夏	カ	summer
		(ゲ)	summer
熟	夏季	カキ	summer season
	夏期	カキ	summer period
	夏至	ゲシ	summer solstice
訓	夏	なつ	summer
	夏場	なつば	summertime; summer resort
	夏休み	なつやすみ	summer holiday/vacation

3   夕   た／ゆうべ   *ta* (katakana); evening

232

夕 ③   ノ ク 夕

音	夕	セキ	evening
訓	夕	ゆう	evening
	夕方	ゆうがた	evening
	夕刊	ゆうカン	evening paper/edition
	夕暮れ	ゆうぐれ	evening
	夕食	ゆうショク	dinner; evening meal
	夕立	ゆうだち	sudden shower in the evening or late afternoon

夕飯	ゆうハン	dinner; evening meal
夕日	ゆうひ	setting sun
夕焼け	ゆうやけ	sunset

233 外 ⑤ 　ノ ク タ 列 外

音	外	ガイ	appearance; outside; unfasten
		ゲ	outside
熟	外圧	ガイアツ	external/foreign pressure
	外界	ガイカイ	external world; outside; physical world
	外海	ガイカイ（そとうみ）	open sea
	外角	ガイカク	*bas.* outcorner; external angle
	外観	ガイカン	external appearance
	外気	ガイキ	open air
	外勤	ガイキン	outside duty; canvassing
	外見	ガイケン	outward appearance; faces
	外交	ガイコウ	diplomacy
	外交官	ガイコウカン	diplomat
	外耳	ガイジ	*med.* external ear; concha
	外出	ガイシュツ	going out; outing; airing —*vi.* go out
	外傷	ガイショウ	external wound
	外食	ガイショク	eating/dining out —*vi.* dine/eat out
	外人	ガイジン	foreigner
	外地	ガイチ	foreign area; overseas land
	外電	ガイデン	foreign telegram; dispatch from overseas
	外部	ガイブ	outside; outer; external
	外米	ガイマイ	imported/foreign rice
	外面	ガイメン	outward appearance; the outside; exterior
	外遊	ガイユウ	foreign travel —*vi.* take a trip abroad
	外洋	ガイヨウ	ocean
	外用薬	ガイヨウヤク	external remedy; medicine for external use
	外来	ガイライ	from abroad; outpatients
	外来語	ガイライゴ	*gram.* adopted word; loanword
	外科	ゲカ	surgery; department of surgery in a hospital
	外道	ゲドウ	non-Buddhist beliefs; demon(-mask)
訓	外	そと	outside
	外す	はずす	*vt.* remove; miss; avoid
	外れる	はずれる	*vi.* be off; be contrary to; miss
	外	ほか	other; another

234 多 ⑥ 丶 ク タ タ 多 多

音	多	タ	many; much; multiple
熟	多額	タガク	large sum/amount
	多角的	タカクテキ	many sided; versatile; diversified; multilateral
	多角形	タカッケイ	polygon
	多感	タカン	sensibility; susceptibility; sentimentality
	多義	タギ	polysemy; diverse meanings
	多芸	タゲイ	versatility; well versed in the arts
	多元	タゲン	pluralism
	多才	タサイ	versatility; versatile talents
	多事	タジ	eventfulness; pressure of business
	多種	タシュ	various kinds
	多種多様	タシュタヨウ	variety; diversity
	多少	タショウ	more or less; approximately; some; a few
	多情	タジョウ	wanton; fickle; inconstant; licentious
	多数	タスウ	large number; multitude; majority; predominance
	多数決	タスウケツ	majority rule
	多勢	タゼイ	great numbers; numerical superiority
	多大	タダイ	great quantity; large amount
	多読	タドク	wide/extensive reading —v. be widely read; read extensively
	多難	タナン	full of difficulties
	多人数	タニンズウ	great number of people
	多年	タネン	many years; number of years
	多分	タブン	plenty; much; many; a great deal; probably; perhaps; maybe
	多方面	タホウメン	many quarters/directions
	多面	タメン	many faces/sides
	多量	タリョウ	large quantities; abundance; a great deal
訓	多い	おおい	many; much; a lot of

235 夜 ⑧ 丶 亠 广 疒 疗 疖 夜 夜

音	夜	ヤ	night
熟	夜会	ヤカイ	evening party; ball
	夜学	ヤガク	night school; evening classes

夜間	ヤカン	night; night time
夜気	ヤキ	night air; stillness of the night
夜曲	ヤキョク	nocturne
夜勤	ヤキン	night duty/shift —*vi*. do night duty; work at night
夜具	ヤグ	bedding
夜景	ヤケイ	night view
夜警	ヤケイ	night watch
夜行	ヤコウ	night train/travel
夜光虫	ヤコウチュウ	night-glowing insect
夜半	ヤハン	midnight; dead of night
夜分	ヤブン	night; evening
夜来	ヤライ	since last night; overnight

訓

夜	よ	night
夜明かし	よあかし	staying up all night —*vi*. stay up overnight
夜明け	よあけ	dawn; daybreak
夜通し	よどおし	overnight
夜中	よなか	midnight; dead of night
夜目	よめ	watching in the dark
夜	よる	night

236

夢 ⑬　一　艹　艹　芦　芦　芦　茜　苗　莇　莇　夢　夢

音

夢	ム	dream

熟

夢想	ムソウ	dream; vision; fantasy —*v*. dream; fantasize; have a vision
夢中	ムチュウ	rapture; absorption; intentness; frantic
夢遊病	ムユウビョウ	sleepwalking

訓

夢	ゆめ	dream
夢心地	ゆめごこち	trance; ecstasy
夢路	ゆめじ	dream; dreaming

口
口
土
士
夂
夕 ●
大
女
子
宀
寸
小
⺍
⺌
尢
尸
山
川
工
己
巾
干
幺
广
廴
弋
弓
彡
彳
艹
辶
阝
⺍
忄
扌
犭
氵

135

口口土士夂夕大女子宀寸小ツ尢尸山川工己巾干幺广廴弋弓彡彳艹辶阝爿忄扌犭氵

3 大 だい big

237
大 ③ 一 ナ 大

音	大	タイ	large; many; importance; whole
		ダイ	big; excellent; dimension; prosperity
熟	大安	タイアン（ダイアン）	lucky/auspicious day (on the Japanese calendar)
	大意	タイイ	gist; purport; substance; ration; holocaust
	大家	タイカ	mansion; illustrious family; master; authority
	大火	タイカ	great fire; conflagration
	大会	タイカイ	mass meeting; tournament; convention
	大学	ダイガク	university; college
	大学院	ダイガクイン	graduate school
	大学生	ダイガクセイ	university/college student
	大観	タイカン	general/philosophical/comprehensive view —*v.* take a general view; make a general survey; have a broad outlook
	大寒	ダイカン	the coldest season (the latter part of January); very cold weather
	大気	タイキ	atmosphere; air
	大器	タイキ	great talent; large vessel
	大規模	ダイキボ	large-scale; mass
	大挙	タイキョ	in great force —*vi.* come in great force
	大局	タイキョク	the whole situation; main issue
	大工	ダイク	carpenter
	大軍	タイグン	large army
	大群	タイグン	large crowd
	大国	タイコク	large/great country
	大差	タイサ	great difference; striking contrast
	大罪	ダイザイ	great crime; felony; mortal sin
	大作	タイサク	major work; masterpiece
	大志	タイシ	ambition; aspiration
	大使	タイシ	ambassador
	大使館	タイシカン	embassy
	大師	ダイシ	great teacher of Buddhism; Kobo Daishi
	大事	ダイジ	important; grave; serious; valuable
	大衆	タイシュウ	masses; crowd of people
	大将	タイショウ	general; admiral

大勝	タイショウ	great/landslide victory —*vi*. win by a landslide	**3**
大小	ダイショウ	large and small size	
大乗	ダイジョウ	Great Vehicle; Mahayana Buddhism	
大静脈	ダイジョウミャク	*med*. main vein	
大食	タイショク	gluttony; heavy eating —*vi*. eat heavily; eat like a horse	
大臣	ダイジン	minister of state	
大成	タイセイ	completion; accomplishment —*v*. complete; accomplish; attain; mature	
大勢	タイセイ	general trend/tendency/situation	
大切	タイセツ	important; valuable	
大体	ダイタイ	outline; summary; generally; essentially	
大々的	ダイダイテキ	on a large scale; great; grand; gigantic; immense	
大多数	ダイタスウ	majority	
大地	ダイチ	earth; ground	
大敵	タイテキ	powerful enemy	
大同小異	ダイドウショウイ	general similarity	
大動脈	ダイドウミャク	**med**. main artery	
大統領	ダイトウリョウ	president (of a republic)	
大任	タイニン	important charge/position	
大破	タイハ	ruin; dilapidation; havoc —*v*. be crippled/wrecked/in ruins	
大敗	タイハイ	terrible defeat —*vi*. sustain a terrible defeat	
大半	タイハン	greater part; majority; bulk	
大病	タイビョウ	serious/major illness	
大分	ダイブ	very; much	
大仏	ダイブツ	great Buddha (statue)	
大部分	ダイブブン	the majority (of); mostly; for the most part	
大別	タイベツ	broad classification —*v*. make a general classification; divide into main classes	
大変	タイヘン	very; greatly; awfully	
大便	ダイベン	feces; stool	
大枚	タイマイ	large sum of money	
大名	ダイミョウ	*daimyo* (feudal lords of the Edo period)	
大役	タイヤク	important task; heavy duty	
大洋	タイヨウ	ocean	
大陸	タイリク	continent	
大量	タイリョウ	large quantity; magnanimity; generosity; liberality	
大量生産	タイリョウ セイサン	mass production —*v*. mass produce	
大漁	タイリョウ	large catch of fish	
大輪	タイリン	large flower/wheel	

口 口 土 士 夂 夕 **大** 女 子 宀 寸 小 ⺌ � 尢 尸 山 川 工 己 干 幺 广 廴 弋 弓 彡 彳 艹 辶 阝 阝 ⺍ 忄 扌 氵

	大老	タイロウ	*hist.* Shogun's chief minister (Edo period)
訓	大	おお	big; large; great
	大きい	おおきい	big; large; great; grand
	大きさ	おおきさ	size; dimensions; magnitude
	大型	おおがた	large size
	大筋	おおすじ	outline
	大手	おおて	front gate of a castle; major company
	大道具	おおドウグ	stage setting
	大判	おおバン	large sheet of paper; *ōban* (coinage used during the Edo period)
	大水	おおみず	flood; overflow
	大物	おおもの	big figure; important person
	大家	おおや	landlord; landlady
	大いに	おおいに	very; much; far; greatly

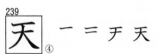

238
太 ④ 一 ナ 大 太

	太	タ	big; fat; thick
音		タイ	big; fat; thick; deep; beginning
熟	太古	タイコ	remote ages; ancient times; prehistoric days
	太鼓	タイコ	drum
	太子	タイシ	crown prince; prince
	太平洋	タイヘイヨウ	Pacific Ocean
	太陽	タイヨウ	sun
	太陽熱	タイヨウネツ	solar heat; heat of the sun's rays
	太刀	タチ	long sword
訓	太い	ふとい	big; large; fat; thick
	太さ	ふとさ	thickness
	太る	ふとる	*vi.* grow fat; put on weight

239
天 ④ 一 二 テ 天

	天	テン	sky; air; the heavens; heaven; nature; fate; destiny
音			
熟	天王星	テンオウセイ	the planet Jupiter
	天下	テンカ	whole country; land; realm
	天下一品	テンカイッピン	beyond comparison; unrivalled
	天気	テンキ	the weather/elements; atmospheric conditions

138

天気予報	テンキヨホウ	weather forecast
天球	テンキュウ	celestial sphere
天狗	テング	*tengu* (long-nosed goblin)
天空	テンクウ	the sky/air/firmament
天候	テンコウ	weather; elements
天国	テンゴク	heaven
天才	テンサイ	genius
天災	テンサイ	natural disaster/calamity; act of God
天子	テンシ	son of heaven; emperor
天使	テンシ	angel
天守閣	テンシュカク	castle tower; donjon; keep
天上	テンジョウ	the heavens
天職	テンショク	mission; vocation
天神	テンジン	heavenly gods
天性	テンセイ	nature; by nature; naturally
天体	テンタイ	heavenly body
天地	テンチ	heaven and earth; top and bottom
天頂	テンチョウ	zenith
天女	テンニョ	celestial nymph
天人	テンニン	angel; heavenly being
天然	テンネン	nature; spontaneity
天然記念物	テンネンキネンブツ	natural monument
天然資源	テンネンシゲン	natural resources
天然色	テンネンショク	natural color
天皇	テンノウ	emperor (Japanese only)
天火	テンび	oven
天引き	テンびき	deduction; deduction in advance —*v.* deduct; knock off
天分	テンブン	one's nature; natural gifts
天変地異	テンペンチイ	natural disasters
天幕	テンマク	tent; pavilion; marquee; awning
天窓	テンまど	skylight
天命	テンメイ	will of the gods; fate; destiny; life
天文	テンモン	astronomy; astrology
天文学	テンモンガク	astronomy
天文台	テンモンダイ	astronomical observatory
天理教	テンリキョウ	Tenriism (new religion)
訓 天	あま	the heavens; heaven
天下り	あまくだり	descent from heaven *fig.* appointment of a former official to an important post in a private company (through influence from above)

139

口
口
土
士
夂
夕
•大
女
子
宀
寸
小
ツ
ソ
尢
尸
山
川
工
己
巾
干
幺
广
廴
弋
弓
彡
彳
艹
辶
阝
阝
忄
扌
犭
氵

天照大神	あまてらす おおみかみ	Sun Goddess (in Japanese mythology)
天の河	あまのがわ	Milky Way
天	あめ	heaven; the sky; the heavens

240

夫 ④ 一 二 夫 夫

音 夫	フ （フウ）	husband
熟 夫婦	フウフ	man and wife; husband and wife; married couple
夫妻	フサイ	husband and wife
夫人	フジン	woman; lady; female
訓 夫	おっと	husband; man

241

央 ⑤ ノ 冂 冂 央 央

音 央	オウ	center; middle

242

失 ⑤ ノ ー 二 牛 失

音 失	シツ	lose; error; failure
熟 失する	シッする	vt. miss; forget
失意	シツイ	disappointment
失火	シッカ	accidental fire —vi. catch on fire accidentally
失格	シッカク	disqualification; elimination —vi. disqualify; eliminate
失禁	シッキン	incontinence —vi. be incontinent
失敬	シッケイ	rudeness; theft —vi. steal; take; help oneself to
失言	シツゲン	slip of the tongue —vi. make a slip of the tongue
失効	シッコウ	invalidation —vi. lapse; lose validity; expire; run out
失策	シッサク	error; mistake —vi. err; blunder
失笑	シッショウ	spontaneous laughter —vi. burst out laughing
失職	シッショク	unemployment —vi. lose one's job; become unemployed

失神	シッシン	faint —*vi.* faint; lose consciousness
失政	シッセイ	misgovernment; misrule
失速	シッソク	stall —*vi.* stall
失態	シッタイ	blunder
失敗	シッパイ	failure; mistake; blunder —*vi.* fail; blunder; be unsuccessful
失望	シツボウ	disappointment; despair —*vi.* be disappointed
失明	シツメイ	loss of sight; blindness —*vi.* lose one's eyesight; become blind
失礼	シツレイ	impoliteness; rudeness; bad manners —*vi.* be impolite/rude; have bad manners
訓 失う	うしなう	*vt.* lose; miss

243

一 二 三 声 夫 表 麦 奏 奏 ⑨

音 奏	ソウ	play; present; report; take effect
熟 奏する	ソウする	*vt.* play a musical instrument; report to the emperor
奏楽	ソウガク	instrumental music
奏功	ソウコウ	achieving one's aim —*vi.* succeed in achieving the aim
奏効	ソウコウ	effectiveness —*vi.* be effective
奏上	ソウジョウ	reporting to the emperor —*v.* report to the emperor
訓 奏でる	かなでる	*vt.* play (a musical instrument)

244

大 大 木 衣 卒 奔 奮 奮 奮 奮 奮 奮 ⑯

音 奮	フン	be enlivened/invigorated
熟 奮起	フンキ	inspiration —*vi.* rouse oneself; be inspired
奮戦	フンセン	hard fighting —*vi.* fight hard/furiously
奮然	フンゼン	vigorously; courageously; resolutely
奮発	フンパツ	exertion; strenuous efforts; extravagance with money —*vi.* exert oneself; splurge
訓 奮う	ふるう	screw up courage; be inspired; wield; flourish
奮って	ふるって	voluntarily; willingly; heartily

口
口
土
士
夂
夕
大 ●
女
子
宀
寸
小
ツ
ツ
尢
尸
山
川
工
己
巾
干
幺
广
廴
弋
弓
彡
彳
艹
辶
阝
阝
忄
扌
氵

141

3 女 おんな／おんなへん woman

245

女 ③ く 女 女

音	女	ジョ	woman; girl; female
		ニョ	woman; girl
		（ニョウ）	
熟	女医	ジョイ	woman doctor
	女王	ジョオウ	queen
	女系	ジョケイ	female line; maternal relatives
	女子	ジョシ	girl; woman
	女子学生	ジョシガクセイ	female student
	女史	ジョシ	Mrs.; Ms.; Miss
	女児	ジョジ	girl
	女色	ジョショク	amorous involvement with women
	女性	ジョセイ	woman; female
	女性的	ジョセイテキ	feminine; womanish; effeminate
	女装	ジョソウ	women's clothing —*vi.* dress up like a woman; put on women's clothing
	女中	ジョチュウ	maid
	女難	ジョナン	woman trouble
	女優	ジョユウ	actress
	女流	ジョリュウ	women; female
	女流作家	ジョリュウサッカ	woman writer
	女人	ニョニン	woman
訓	女	おんな	woman; female
	女盛り	おんなざかり	peak of womanhood
	女手	おんなで	woman's handwriting
	女	め	woman
	女神	めがみ	goddess

246

委 ⑧ 一 二 千 千 禾 禾 委 委

音	委	イ	leave to; entrust; minute; detailed
熟	委細	イサイ	details; particulars; circumstances
	委縮	イシュク	shrivelling; atrophy —*vi.* shrivel up; waste away

	委任	イニン	proxy; trust; charge; commission; delegation —*v.* entrust; commission; charge; delegate
訓	委せる	まかせる	*vt.* entrust; leave to; delegate
	委ねる	ゆだねる	*vt.* commit; entrust; delegate

247

妻 ⑧　一 ⼾ ⼾ ⼾ ⼾ 妻 妻 妻

音	妻	サイ	wife
熟	妻子	サイシ	one's wife and children
	妻女	サイジョ	one's wife and daughter(s); women
	妻帯	サイタイ	married; connubial; matrimonial —*vi.* get married; marry
	妻帯者	サイタイシャ	married man
訓	妻	つま	wife

248

姿 ⑨　丶 冫 ⼎ 广 カ 次 次 姿 姿

音	姿	シ	figure
熟	姿勢	シセイ	posture; attitude; profile
	姿態	シタイ	figure; pose
訓	姿	すがた	figure; image; appearance; looks
	姿見	すがたみ	full-length mirror

249

好 ⑥　く 乄 女 女 奷 好

音	好	コウ	good; favorable; prefer; like; love
熟	好意	コウイ	goodwill; good wishes; regard; kindness; favor; friendliness
	好感	コウカン	favorable/good impression; good feeling/will
	好機	コウキ	good opportunity/time
	好色	コウショク	sensuality; amorousness; lust; eroticism
	好人物	コウジンブツ	good-natured person; good fellow; nice chap
	好調	コウチョウ	good condition; favorable; satisfactory; promising
	好都合	コウツゴウ	favorable; convenient; fortunate; prosperous

143

口口土士夂夕大女子宀寸小⺌⺍尤尸山川工己巾干幺广廴弓彡彳艹辶阝䒑忄扌犭氵

好適	コウテキ	suitable; ideal; good best
好敵手	コウテキシュ	good match; worthy opponent
好転	コウテン	favorable turn; change for the better; improvement —*vi.* take a favorable turn; change for the better; improve
好評	コウヒョウ	favorable criticism/comment; public favor
好物	コウブツ	favorite; delight; favorite food

訓

好む	このむ	*vt.* like; fancy; be fond of; love; care for; prefer
好ましい	このましい	desirable; welcome; nice; good
好み	このみ	taste; liking; choice; preference
好き	すき	like; favorite; preference
好く	すく	*vt.* like; love; be fond of; care for

250

姉 ⑧ く 夕 女 女' 女 女 妒 妒 姉

音 姉	シ	elder sister; lady
熟 姉妹	シマイ	sisters
姉妹都市	シマイトシ	sister city; twin town
訓 姉	あね	one's elder sister

251

始 ⑧ く 夕 女 女 女 女 始 始

音 始	シ	beginning; start; origin
熟 始球式	シキュウシキ	*bas.* opening ceremony of a baseball game in which an honorary guest throws the first ball
始業	シギョウ	beginning of work or class —*vi.* start work or class
始業式	シギョウシキ	opening ceremony for school or work
始終	シジュウ	whole story; from beginning to end; always; constantly; frequently; the beginning and the end
始祖	シソ	founder; ancestor
始動	シドウ	starting an engine —*v.* start up an engine
始発	シハツ	station of origin; first train of the day
始発駅	シハツエキ	station of origin; first station on a line
始末	シマツ	ordering; taking care of —*v.* put in order; take care of; come to pass
始末書	シマツショ	written explanation/apology (for an accident, etc.)

144

訓	始まり	はじまり	opening; beginning; start
	始まる	はじまる	*vi*. begin; start; date from
	始める	はじめる	*vt*. begin; start; commence
	始め	はじめ	beginning; founding; origin

252

妹 ⑧　く　夕　女　女　女ᅳ　奸　奸　妹

| 音 | 妹 | マイ | younger sister |
| 訓 | 妹 | いもうと | younger sister |

253

婦 ⑪　く　夕　女　女ᄀ　女ᄏ　女ᄏ　姈　娼　娼　婦

音	婦	フ	woman; wife
熟	婦警	フケイ	policewoman
	婦女	フジョ	woman
	婦人	フジン	woman; lady
	婦人用	フジンヨウ	for ladies; women's
	婦長	フチョウ	head nurse

3 　子　こ／こへん　child

254

子 ③　ᅳ　了　子

音	子	シ	child; son; man; Confucius
熟	子宮	シキュウ	*med*. womb; uterus
	子細	シサイ	details; particulars; reasons; circumstances; meaning
	子息	シソク	son
	子孫	シソン	posterity; descendant
	子弟	シテイ	boys; children; younger people
	子葉	シヨウ	*bio*. cotyledon
訓	子	こ	child
	子供	こども	child; children
	子分	こブン	follower; henchman

口口土士夂夕大女子宀寸小⺌⺍尢尸山川工己巾干幺广廴弋弓彡彳艹辶阝阝丷忄扌犭氵

145

子持ち	こもち	parent
子守	こもり	baby-sitting
子役	こヤク	child actor

255

字 ⑥ 　 ＼ ＂ 宀 ウ 宁 字

音 字	ジ	letter; character
熟 字音	ジオン	the Japanized pronunciation of a Chinese character
字義	ジギ	meaning of a Chinese character
字句	ジク	words; phrases; wording; expression; letters and phrases
字書	ジショ	dictionary
字体	ジタイ	form of a character; typeface
字典	ジテン	dictionary
字引	じびき	dictionary
字幕	ジマク	movie subtitle
訓 字	あざ	section of a village

256

存 ⑥ 　 一 ナ 才 存 存 存

音 存	ソン	be; exist
	ゾン	be; exist
熟 存外	ゾンガイ	unexpectedly; beyond expectations; contrary to expectations
存在	ソンザイ	existence —*v.* exist
存続	ソンゾク	continued existence; duration —*v.* continue (to exist); endure; last
存念	ゾンネン	idea; thought; concept
存分	ゾンブン	to one's heart's content; as much as one wants; without reserve
存命	ゾンメイ	living —*v.* be alive
存立	ソンリツ	existence; substistence —*v.* exist; subsist

257

孝 ⑦ 　 一 十 土 耂 考 考 孝

| 音 孝 | コウ | filial piety; obedience to one's parents |

熟 孝行	コウコウ	filial piety; obedience to one's parents —*vi.* be dutiful to one's parents; be a good son/daughter

258

学 ⑧　　丶　　丷　　⺍　　⺍　　ヅ　学　学　学

音 学	ガク	study; science
熟 学位	ガクイ	academic degree
学園	ガクエン	school; educational institution
学業	ガクギョウ	studies; schoolwork
学芸	ガクゲイ	art and science
学士	ガクシ	bachelor's degree
学資	ガクシ	educational fund
学識	ガクシキ	scholarship; learning
学者	ガクシャ	scholar; learned person
学習	ガクシュウ	study; learning —*v.* study; learn
学術	ガクジュツ	science; learning
学生	ガクセイ	student
学制	ガクセイ	educational system
学説	ガクセツ	theory; doctrine
学長	ガクチョウ	chancellor/president of a university
学徒	ガクト	students and pupils
学童	ガクドウ	schoolchild; pupil
学年	ガクネン	school year; grade
学費	ガクヒ	school expenses; tuition fees
学名	ガクメイ	scientific name
学問	ガクモン	learning and research —*vi.* pursue learning
学友	ガクユウ	schoolmate
学用品	ガクヨウヒン	school supplies
学力	ガクリョク	academic ability
学歴	ガクレキ	school career; educational background
学割	ガクわり	student discounts
学科	ガッカ	school subject; branch of learning
学会	ガッカイ	learned society; academia; meeting of scholars
学界	ガッカイ	academic world; academia
学期	ガッキ	school term
学区	ガック	school precincts
訓 学ぶ	まなぶ	*vt.* learn; study

口口土士夂夕大女子宀寸小⺌⺍尢尸山川工己巾干幺广廴弋弓彑彡彳艹阝⺌扌犭氵

259

季 ⑧ 一 ニ 千 千 禾 禾 季 季

音	季	キ	season
熟	季刊	キカン	quarterly publication
	季節	キセツ	season
	季節風	キセツフウ	monsoon

260

孫 ⑩ ﻨ 了 子 孑 孖 孫 孫 孫 孫 孫

音	孫	ソン	descendants
訓	孫	まご	grandchild
	孫子	まごこ	children and grandchildren; descendants

---

3 宀 うかんむり *u* (katakana)

261

安 ⑥ ﺀ ﺀ 宀 安 安 安

音	安	アン	safe; stable; easy; peaceful; inexpensive
熟	安易	アンイ	easy; simple; straightforward; easygoing; carefree
	安価	アンカ	cheapness; low price
	安産	アンザン	easy birth/delivery —*v.* have an easy birth; give birth easily
	安住	アンジュウ	peaceful living —*vi.* live in peace
	安心	アンシン	peace of mind; relief; safety —*vi.* feel at rest/relieved/assured
	安静	アンセイ	free from activity or labor; rest; quiet; repose
	安全	アンゼン	free from harm or risk; safety; security
	安全第一	アンゼンダイイチ	safety first
	安全地帯	アンゼンチタイ	safety zone
	安息	アンソク	repose; rest —*vi.* rest; take a break
	安置	アンチ	installation —*v.* install; enshrine
	安着	アンチャク	comfort; safe arrival —*vi.* arrive safely
	安直	アンチョク	inexpensive

安定	アンテイ	stability; stabilization; steadiness —*vi.* be stable/steady/balanced/settled
安定性	アンテイセイ	stability
安否	アンピ	safety; welfare
安楽死	アンラクシ	painless death; mercy killing; euthanasia
訓 安い	やすい	cheap; easy; calm
安上がり	やすあがり	doing something cheaply
安らか	やすらか	peaceful; tranquil; calm
安らぎ	やすらぎ	peace of mind; serenity; calmness
安んじる	やすんじる	*v.* be reassured; have peace of mind; be contented

---

262

宇 ⑥   ⟍ ⟍ 宀 宀 宇 宇

音 宇	ウ	expanse; universe; cosmos; space; eaves; roof
熟 宇宙	ウチュウ	the universe; outer space
宇宙船	ウチュウセン	spaceship; spacecraft
宇宙飛行士	ウチュウヒコウシ	astronaut; spaceman

263

守 ⑥   ⟍ ⟍ 宀 宀 守 守

音 守	シュ	defend
	（ス）	protect
熟 守衛	シュエイ	guard; doorman; doorkeeper
守護	シュゴ	protection —*v.* protect; guard
守護神	シュゴシン	guardian diety
守勢	シュセイ	defensive
守備	シュビ	defense —*v.* defend; guard
訓 守る	まもる	*vt.* defend; protect; keep one's word; abide by
守り	まもり	defense; protection; safeguard
守	もり	nursemaid

264

宅 ⑥   ⟍ ⟍ 宀 宀 宅 宅

| 音 宅 | タク | home; house; residence; our home; my husband |
| 熟 宅地 | タクチ | building lot; land for housing; residential land |

3

口口土士夕大女子宀寸小⺌⺍尤尸山川工己巾干幺广廴弋弓彡彳艹辶阝⺌忄扌犭氵

完 ⑦ 　 ′ ′′ 宀 宀 宁 宁 完

音	完	カン	complete; perfect
熟	完結	カンケツ	completion; conclusion; termination —v. complete; conclude; finish; end
	完済	カンサイ	full payment of debts —vt. pay off one's all debts
	完勝	カンショウ	complete victory —vi. defeat decisively; win a landslide victory
	完成	カンセイ	completion; accomplishment; perfection —v. complete; conclude; finish; accomplish
	完全	カンゼン	perfection; completeness
	完投	カントウ	**bas**. pitching a whole game —**vi**. pitch a whole game
	完納	カンノウ	full payment —v. pay in full
	完敗	カンパイ	complete defeat —vi. suffer a complete defeat
	完備	カンビ	perfection; completion —v. be perfect/complete

266

官 ⑧ 　 ′ ′′ 宀 宀 宁 宁 官 官

音	官	カン	official; government; senses
熟	官軍	カングン	government forces; Imperial Army
	官公庁	カンコウチョウ	government and municipal offices
	官舎	カンシャ	official residence
	官職	カンショク	government/official post
	官製	カンセイ	government manufacture
	官庁	カンチョウ	government office
	官能	カンノウ	senses; sensual
	官能的	カンノウテキ	sensual
	官報	カンポウ	official gazette

267

実 ⑧ 　 ′ ′′ 宀 宀 宁 宁 実 実

音	実	ジツ	substance; sincerity; truth; reality; actual
熟	実印	ジツイン	registered seal
	実益	ジツエキ	practical use; usefulness; actual profit
	実演	ジツエン	stage show; demonstration

150

実家	ジッカ	one's parents' home
実害	ジツガイ	actual harm
実学	ジツガク	practical science; studies of use in everyday life
実感	ジッカン	actual feeling; atmosphere —v. realize
実技	ジツギ	actual technique; practical skills; technical skill
実兄	ジッケイ	one's real brother
実権	ジッケン	real power; actual control
実験	ジッケン	experimentation; experiment; test —v. experiment
実験室	ジッケンシツ	laboratory
実験的	ジッケンテキ	experimental
実現	ジツゲン	realization; materialization —v. be realized; materialize
実行	ジッコウ	practice; action; execution —v. carry out; put into practice; execute
実行可能	ジッコウカノウ	practical; feasible
実際	ジッサイ	in practice; fact; truth; reality; actuality; really; indeed
実在	ジツザイ	real/actual existence —vi. exist
実在論	ジツザイロン	realism
実子	ジッシ	one's real/own child
実質	ジッシツ	substance; essence
実写	ジッシャ	photograph or movie of actual scenery or people —v. photograph or film actual scenery or people
実社会	ジッシャカイ	the real world
実習	ジッシュウ	practical training —v. practice; have training
実証	ジッショウ	proof —v. prove; demonstrate
実情	ジツジョウ	actual conditions
実数	ジッスウ	*math*. real/actual number
実績	ジッセキ	actual results; achievements
実戦	ジッセン	actual fighting/service; combat
実測	ジッソク	actual survey/measurement —v. measure; survey
実存	ジツゾン	existence —vi. exist
実存主義	ジツゾンシュギ	existentialism
実体	ジッタイ	substance; solid
実態	ジッタイ	actual condition
実地	ジッチ	in actual practice; the scene (of a crime)
実直	ジッチョク	honest; steady; conscientious
実費	ジッピ	actual expenses
実否	ジッピ	true or not
実父	ジップ	one's real/own father
実物	ジツブツ	the real thing; the genuine article; real life
実物大	ジツブツダイ	actual/life/full size

口 口 土 士 夂 夕 大 女 子 宀 寸 小 ⺌ ⺌ 尢 尸 山 川 工 己 巾 幺 广 廴 弋 弓 彡 彳 艹 辶 阝 阝 忄 扌 氵 犭

口
口
土
士
夂
夕
大
女
子
宀
寸
小
⺌
⺍
尢
尸
山
川
工
己
巾
干
幺
广
廴
弋
弓
彡
彳
艹
辶
阝
艹
忄
扌
犭
氵

実母	ジツボ	one's real/own mother
実名	ジツメイ	one's real name
実用	ジツヨウ	practical use
実用化	ジツヨウカ	practicality —*v.* put a thing to practical use
実用主義	ジツヨウシュギ	pragmatism
実用的	ジツヨウテキ	practical
実用品	ジツヨウヒン	daily necessities; domestic articles
実利	ジツリ	utility; actual benefit
実利的	ジツリテキ	utilitarian
実力	ジツリョク	real ability; force; arms
実力行使	ジツリョクコウシ	use of force
実力者	ジツリョクシャ	influential person; powerful figure
実例	ジツレイ	instance; example
実録	ジツロク	true record
実話	ジツワ	true story; story taken from real life

訓 実	み	seed; berry; fruit; nut; ingredients; content; substance
実る	みのる	*vi.* bear fruit; bear fruitful results
実り	みのり	ripening; fruitful; productive

268

宗 ⑧　　'　丷　宀　宀　宁　宁　宗　宗

| 音 宗 | シュウ | sect; religion; denomination |
| | ソウ | founder; head; leader |

熟 宗教	シュウキョウ	religion
宗教家	シュウキョウカ	man of religion
宗祖	シュウソ	founder of a sect
宗徒	シュウト	believer; adherent
宗派	シュウハ	sect; denomination
宗家	ソウケ	head family; originator

269

宙 ⑧　　'　丷　宀　宀　宁　宙　宙　宙

| 音 宙 | チュウ | sky; air; space |
| 熟 宙返り | チュウがえり | somersault; looping the loop —*vi.* turn a somersault; turn loops |

定 ⑧ ⎞⎞　丶　ノ　宀　宀　宀　宇　定　定

音	定	テイ	fixed; constant; regular
		ジョウ	
熟	定規	ジョウギ	ruler; scale
	定圧	テイアツ	constant pressure
	定員	テイイン	capacity; seating/passenger capacity; regular staff
	定期	テイキ	fixed period
	定期券	テイキケン	pass; season ticket
	定期船	テイキセン	liner
	定義	テイギ	definition —*v.* define
	定休日	テイキュウび	regular holiday
	定形	テイケイ	fixed form; regular shape
	定型	テイケイ	type; definite form
	定型的	テイケイテキ	typical; stereotyped
	定見	テイケン	definite view; firm conviction
	定限	テイゲン	fixed limit; limits; limitation; restriction —*v.* limit; restrict; confine
	定刻	テイコク	appointed hour; scheduled time
	定時	テイジ	regular/fixed time
	定住	テイジュウ	settlement; domicile —*v.* settle down; reside
	定住者	テイジュウシャ	permanent resident; settler
	定食	テイショク	set meal
	定数	テイスウ	fixed number; constant; invariable; fate
	定説	テイセツ	established theory
	定足数	テイソクスウ	quorum
	定置	テイチ	fixing in a set position —*vt.* fix; set; station
	定着	テイチャク	fixing; fastening; fixation; anchoring —*v.* fix; fasten; anchor; take root
	定点	テイテン	fixed point
	定年	テイネン	age limit; retirement age
	定評	テイヒョウ	established reputation; fixed opinion
	定本	テイホン	standard/authentic text
	定理	テイリ	theorem
	定率	テイリツ	fixed rate
	定量	テイリョウ	fixed quantity; measurement; dose —*v.* measure
	定例	テイレイ	established usage; precedent
訓	定まる	さだまる	*vi.* be decided/determined/fixed/settled
	定める	さだめる	*vt.* decide; determine; appoint; set; lay down

口
口
土
士
夂
夕
大
女
子
宀 ●
寸
小
ツ
尢
尸
山
川
工
己
巾
干
幺
广
廴
弋
弓
彡
彳
艹
辶
阝
亠
忄
扌
氵

3　定か　さだか　certain; fixed

口口土士夕夕大女子宀寸小ᵛ···尤尸山川工己巾干幺广廴弋弓彡彳艹辶阝衤扌氵

271

宝 ⑧　　　ヽ 丷 宀 宀 宀 宀 宝 宝

音	宝	ホウ	treasure
熟	宝玉	ホウギョク	jewel; gem; precious stone
	宝庫	ホウコ	treasure house
	宝石	ホウセキ	jewel; gem; precious stone
	宝典	ホウテン	valued/useful book; book of Buddhist sutras
	宝刀	ホウトウ	treasured sword
	宝物	ホウモツ	treasure
訓	宝	たから	treasure
	宝島	たからじま	treasure island
	宝物	たからもの	treasure

272

宣 ⑨　　　ヽ 丷 宀 宀 宀 宀 宣 宣 宣

音	宣	セン	declare; edict; announce
熟	宣教師	センキョウシ	missionary
	宣言	センゲン	declaration; statement —*v.* declare; state
	宣誓	センセイ	oath; vow; pledge —*v.* make an oath; vow; pledge
	宣戦	センセン	declaration of war —*vi.* declare war
	宣伝	センデン	propaganda; advertising; publicity —*v.* propagate; advertise; publicize

273

客 ⑨　　　ヽ 丷 宀 宀 宀 宎 客 客 客

音	客	キャク (カク)	guest; visitor; visiting; traveler; customer; client; the past
熟	客死	カクシ (キャクシ)	dying away from home; dying in a foreign country —*vi.* die away from home; die overseas
	客員教授	キャクイン キョウジュ	visiting/guest professor
	客受け	キャクうけ	customer appeal
	客室	キャクシツ	guest room
	客車	キャクシャ	passenger vehicle; coach; carriage

客商売	キャクショウバイ	service industry
客筋	キャクすじ	quality of clientele
客席	キャクセキ	audience seat
客船	キャクセン	passenger vessel/liner
客引き	キャクひき	barker —*vi.* pull in/attract customers
客間	キャクま	drawing room; parlor; guest room
客観	キャッカン	object (in philosophy)
客観的	キャッカンテキ	objective

274

室 ⑨ ` ` ㆑ ㆑ ㆑ ㆑ ㆑ ㆑ 室

音	室	シツ	room; wife; concubine
熟	室温	シツオン	room temperature
	室外	シツガイ	outside the room
	室内	シツナイ	inside the room
	室内楽	シツナイガク	chamber music
訓	室	むろ	cellar; hot house; drying room
	室町	むろまち	*hist.* Muromachi period/culture (1338-1573)

275

家 ⑩ ` ` ㆑ ㆑ ㆑ ㆑ ㆑ 家 家 家

音	家	カ	house; family
		ケ	house; family
熟	家屋	カオク	house
	家業	カギョウ	one's trade or business
	家具	カグ	furniture
	家系	カケイ	family line; lineage
	家計	カケイ	household economy; housekeeping expenses
	家財	カザイ	household goods
	家事	カジ	housework
	家臣	カシン	*hist.* retainer/vassal (Edo period)
	家政	カセイ	housekeeping
	家政婦	カセイフ	housekeeper
	家族	カゾク	family
	家庭	カテイ	home; household; family
	家伝	カデン	handed down from father to son; hereditary
	家内	カナイ	family; one's wife

口
口
土
士
夂
夕
大
女
子
宀
寸
小
⺌
⺍
尢
尸
山
川
工
己
巾
干
幺
广
廴
弋
弓
彡
彳
⺍
⻌
⻏
⺌
忄
扌
犭
氵

口口土士夂夕大女子宀寸小ⵯⵯ尢尸山川工己巾干幺广廴弋弓彡彳艹辶阝兺忄扌犭氵

家風	カフウ	family custom
家宝	カホウ	heirloom
家名	カメイ	family name
家老	カロウ	*hist.* chief/principal retainer (Edo period)
家来	ケライ	subordinates loyal to a lord; vassal; retinue

訓 家　いえ　house; home; ancestry
家主　いえぬし（やぬし）　landlady; landlord; houseowner
家元　いえもと　*hist.* the head of a school (of a traditional art)
家　や　house
家賃　やチン　rent for a house, apartment, etc.

276

害 ⑩　　' 宀 宀 宀 中 宔 宔 害 害 害

音 害　ガイ　harm; damage
熟 害する　ガイする　*vt.* injure; harm; hurt; impair
害悪　ガイアク　evil; vice
害虫　ガイチュウ　harmful/noxious insect
害毒　ガイドク　evil influence; evil; harm

277

宮 ⑩　　' 宀 宀 宀 宫 宮 宮 宮 宮 宮

音 宮　キュウ　palace; imperial dwelling; shrine
グウ
（ク）
熟 宮城　キュウジョウ　imperial palace
宮内庁　クナイチョウ　Imperial Household Agency
訓 宮　みや　(Shinto) shrine; imperial prince

278

容 ⑩　　' 宀 宀 宀 宀 宀 容 容 容 容

音 容　ヨウ　form; appearance; content
熟 容易　ヨウイ　easy; simple
容器　ヨウキ　vessel; container
容疑　ヨウギ　suspicion (of a crime)

容疑者	ヨウギシャ	suspect
容姿	ヨウシ	face and figure; looks; appearances
容色	ヨウショク	features; looks; personal appearance
容積	ヨウセキ	capacity; volume
容体	ヨウダイ	condition (of an illness)
容認	ヨウニン	admission; approval; acceptance —*v.* admit; approve; accept
容量	ヨウリョウ	capacity; volume

279
寄 ⑪ 　`　丶　宀　宀　宀　宇　宇　宙　害　害　寄

音	寄	キ	call at; depend on; approach; contribute; donation
熟	寄港	キコウ	port call —*vi.* call at port
	寄宿舎	キシュクシャ	dormitory
	寄食	キショク	dependence —*vi.* sponge off one friends or relatives
	寄進	キシン	donation; contribution —*vt.* make a donation
	寄生	キセイ	parasitism —*vi.* be parasitic; be a parasite
	寄付	キフ	contribution; donation —*v.* contribute; donate
	寄与	キヨ	contribution; services —*v.* contribute; render services
	寄留	キリュウ	sojourn; temporary residence —*vi.* sojourn; reside temporarily
訓	寄る	よる	*vi.* draw near; drop in; come together; stop at a place
	寄せる	よせる	*v.* allow (a person); put (a thing) aside; send (a letter); be dependent on (a person); contribute an article (to a magazine)
	寄り合い	よりあい	meeting; assembly; gathering
	寄り道	よりみち	dropping in on the way —*vi.* drop in on the way

280
宿 ⑪ 　`　丶　宀　宀　宀　宁　宿　宿　宿　宿

音	宿	シュク	inn; stay
熟	宿願	シュクガン	long-cherished desire; dream
	宿舎	シュクシャ	dormitory; housing; lodgings; accomodations
	宿題	シュクダイ	homework; assignment
	宿直	シュクチョク	night duty

口口土士夂夕大女子宀寸小⺌⺍尢尸山川工己巾干幺广廴廾弋弓彐彡彳辶阝艹卄扌氵犭

	宿敵	シュクテキ	old foe; archenemy
	宿命	シュクメイ	fate; destiny
	宿命論	シュクメイロン	fatalism
訓	宿	やど	inn; hotel; lodgings; shelter
	宿る	やどる	*vi*. dwell; live; stay; lodge; harbor
	宿す	やどす	*vt*. be pregnant; harbor; give lodgings to
	宿帳	やどチョウ	hotel register
	宿賃	やどチン	hotel bill
	宿無し	やどなし	homeless person; vagabond; tramp
	宿屋	やどや	inn; hotel

281

密 ⑪ `ヽ 丷 宀 宀 宀 灾 灾 灾 宓 密 密`

	密	ミツ	close; dense; crowded; minute; fine; secret
熟	密画	ミツガ	detailed drawing
	密会	ミッカイ	clandestine meeting —*vi*. meet secretly; have a secret rendezvous
	密議	ミツギ	secret conference/consultation
	密航	ミッコウ	stow away; secret passage on a ship —*vi*. stowaway
	密行	ミッコウ	prowling —*v*. prowl about; go secretly
	密告	ミッコク	secret information —*v*. provide secret information
	密告者	ミッコクシャ	informer; betrayer
	密事	ミツジ	secret
	密室	ミッシツ	secret/locked room
	密集	ミッシュウ	crowd —*vi*. mass together
	密書	ミッショ	secret written message
	密生	ミッセイ	thick/luxurious growth —*vi*. grow thick/luxuriantly
	密接	ミッセツ	close; intimate —*vi*. be close/intimate
	密造	ミツゾウ	illegal manufacture —*v*. manufacture illegally
	密談	ミツダン	secret talk —*vi*. take part in secret conversations
	密着	ミッチャク	sticking; adherence —*vi*. stick/adhere to
	密通	ミッツウ	adultery; secret relationship —*vi*. commit adultery; have an affair
	密度	ミツド	density
	密入国	ミツニュウコク	illegal immigration —*vi*. enter a country illegally
	密売	ミツバイ	illicit sale; smuggling; bootlegging —*v*. smuggle; bootleg

密閉	ミッペイ	shut tight —*v.* seal airtight
密約	ミツヤク	secret agreement —*vi.* make a secret agreement
密輸	ミツユ	smuggling; contraband —*v.* smuggle
密漁	ミツリョウ	fish poaching —*v.* poach fish
密林	ミツリン	jungle; dense forest

282

寒 ⑫   ` ` 宀 宀 宀 宙 宙 宝 実 実 寒 寒 寒

音	寒	カン	cold; poor
熟	寒気	カンキ	cold weather
	寒暑	カンショ	heat and cold; temperature
	寒村	カンソン	remote/lonely village
	寒帯	カンタイ	frigid zone; arctic regions
	寒暖	カンダン	hot and cold; temperature
	寒暖計	カンダンケイ	thermometer
	寒中	カンチュウ	midwinter; depth of winter
	寒波	カンパ	cold wave
	寒流	カンリュウ	cold current
	寒冷	カンレイ	coldness; chill
訓	寒い	さむい	cold; chilly
	寒気	さむケ	chill; cold fit; rigor
	寒さ	さむさ	coldness; the cold

283

富 ⑫   ` ` 宀 宀 宀 宁 官 官 宫 宫 富 富 富

音	富	フ	wealth; rich; affluent; ample
		（フウ）	
熟	富貴	フウキ	wealth and rank
	富強	フキョウ	rich and powerful（country）
	富鉱	フコウ	rich ore/deposit
	富国	フコク	rich country
	富農	フノウ	wealthy farmer
	富有	フユウ	wealthy; affluent; rich
	富力	フリョク	wealth; resources
訓	富	とみ	wealth; resources; assets
	富む	とむ	*vi.* be rich; abound in

口口土士夂夕大女子宀 ● 寸小⺌ ⺌ 尢尸山川工己巾干幺广廴弋弓彡彳艹辶阝⺖忄扌犭氵

284

察 ⑭ 　宀 宀 宀 宁 宛 宛 宛 宛 窓 窓 察 察

音	察	サツ	investigate; guess
熟	察する	サッする	***vt.*** investigate; guess
	察知	サッチ	perception; sense —*v.* perceive; sense; gather; infer

---

3 寸　すん　inch

285

寸 ③ 　一 十 寸

音	寸	スン	*sun* (unit of length, approx. 3.03 cm); small; tiny
熟	寸劇	スンゲキ	short play; sketch; skit
	寸志	スンシ	small present (small amount of money)
	寸前	スンゼン	just/right/immediately before
	寸断	スンダン	***vt.*** tear/cut to pieces
	寸評	スンピョウ	short review; brief comment
	寸分	スンブン	bit; little
	寸法	スンポウ	measure; measurements; dimensions; plan

286

寺 ⑥ 　一 十 土 士 寺 寺

音	寺	ジ	temple
熟	寺院	ジイン	temple
	寺社	ジシャ	shrines and temples
訓	寺	てら	Buddhist temple

287

対 ⑦ 　丶 ユ ナ 文 文 対 対

| 音 | 対 | タイ ツイ | set; couple; response; oppose; face |

熟	対する	タイする	*vi*. be against; oppose; face
	対応	タイオウ	correspondence; equivalence; counterpart —*vi*. correspond to; be equivalent to; tackle; deal with; cope
	対角線	タイカクセン	diagonal (line)
	対決	タイケツ	confrontation; face-to-face meeting —*vi*. confront; have a showdown; stand face-to-face
	対向	タイコウ	opposite
	対策	タイサク	countermeasure; counterplan; countermove
	対処	タイショ	coping; dealing; tackling —*vi*. cope/deal with; tackle
	対象	タイショウ	object; subject; target
	対照	タイショウ	contrast; comparison —*v*. contrast; compare
	対戦	タイセン	competition —*vi*. compete; oppose
	対談	タイダン	talk; conversation; dialog; interview —*vi*. talk/converse with; have an interview with
	対等	タイトウ	equality; equal footing; equal terms; parity
	対比	タイヒ	contrast; comparison; opposition; analogy —*v*. contrast; compare; oppose; analogize
	対面	タイメン	interview; meeting —*vi*. interview; meet; see; have an interview
	対立	タイリツ	opposition; confrontation; contrast —*vi*. be opposed/confronted with
	対話	タイワ	dialog; conversation —*vi*. have a dialog/conversation with
	対句	ツイク	antithesis; parallelism
	対語	ツイゴ	*gram*. antonym

288

専⑨ 一 厂 冂 冃 冃 甫 車 専 専

音	専	セン	solely; exclusive
熟	専横	センオウ	despotism; tyranny
	専科	センカ	special course (of study)
	専業	センギョウ	profession; main occupation
	専従	センジュウ	exclusive obedience; full-time employment
	専心	センシン	devotion; concentration; undivided attention —*vi*. be devoted; concentrate; give one's undivided attention
	専制	センセイ	absolutism; autocracy
	専制政治	センセイセイジ	absolute/despotic government
	専任	センニン	full-time
	専念	センネン	close/undivided attention —*vi*. give one's close/undivided attention

口口土士夂夕大女子宀寸小⺌⺌尢尸山川工已巾干幺广廴弋弓彡彳艹辶阝扌艹犭

専売	センバイ	monopoly —*v*. monopolize
専務	センム	managing director
専門	センモン	specialty
専門家	センモンカ	person specialized in certain fields
専門店	センモンテン	specialty store
専有	センユウ	exclusive possession; monopoly —*v*. possess exclusively; monopolize
専用	センヨウ	exclusive use; private/personal use —*v*. have exclusive use of
訓 専ら	もっぱら	exclusively

289

射 ⑩ 丶 亻 仃 仃 自 身 身 身 射 射

音	射	シャ	archery; fire
熟	射角	シャカク	angle of fire
	射幸	シャコウ	speculation
	射幸心	シャコウシン	speculative spirit
	射幸的	シャコウテキ	speculative
	射殺	シャサツ	death by shooting —*v*. shoot to death
	射手	シャシュ	marksman; archer
	射出	シャシュツ	ejection; radiation; discharge —*v*. fire; eject; spout; radiate
	射精	シャセイ	ejaculation; seminal emission —*vi*. ejaculate
	射程	シャテイ	shooting/firing range
	射的	シャテキ	target practice
	射利心	シャリシン	mercenary spirit
訓	射る	いる	*vt*. shoot; fire

290

将 ⑩ 丨 丬 丬 丬 扩 扩 护 护 将 将

音	将	ショウ	commander; general
熟	将軍	ショウグン	shogun; military dictator; general
	将来	ショウライ	the future

	尊	ソン	esteem; value; respect
熟	尊敬	ソンケイ	respect; esteem; honor —v. respect; hold in esteem; honor
	尊厳	ソンゲン	dignity
	尊大	ソンダイ	haughty; arrogant; self-important
	尊重	ソンチョウ	respect; esteem —v. respect; hold in esteem
	尊王	ソンノウ	reverence for the emperor; advocacy of imperial rule
	尊父	ソンプ	*hon.* your father
訓	尊い	たっとい	exalted; valuable; precious; noble
	尊ぶ	たっとぶ	*vt.* respect; esteem; value
	尊い	とうとい	noble; precious; exalted; valulable
	尊ぶ	とうとぶ	*vt.* respect; value; esteem

	導	ドウ	guide; transmit; conduct
熟	導火線	ドウカセン	fuse; cause; agency; impetus; incentive
	導線	ドウセン	leading wire
	導体	ドウタイ	conductor (of electricity, heat, etc.)
	導入	ドウニュウ	introduction; induction; invitation —v. introduce; induce; invite
訓	導き	みちびき	guidance; showing the way; instruction
	導く	みちびく	*vt.* guide; lead; conduct; show; introduce; instruct

3 小 しょう small

	小	ショウ	small; little; younger; (prefix) sub-
熟	小異	ショウイ	minor differences

3

口口土士夕夕大女子宀寸
●小ソ丷尢尸山川工己巾干幺广廴弋弓彡彳艹辶阝丬忄扌氵

小学生	ショウガクセイ	elementary school pupil
小学校	ショウガッコウ	elementary/primary school
小休止	ショウキュウシ	break; breather —v. take a break/breather
小計	ショウケイ	subtotal
小康	ショウコウ	lull; letup; remission
小国	ショウコク	little country; minor power
小差	ショウサ	narrow margin
小冊子	ショウサッシ	pamphlet; booklet
小市民	ショウシミン	petty bourgeois
小食	ショウショク	light eating
小心	ショウシン	timidity; cowardice
小心者	ショウシンもの	coward; timid person
小数	ショウスウ	*math*. decimal
小数点	ショウスウテン	*math*. decimal point
小生	ショウセイ	*hum*. I; me
小節	ショウセツ	bar of music; measure
小説	ショウセツ	novel; fiction
小説家	ショウセツカ	novelist
小児	ショウニ	small child; infant
小児科	ショウニカ	*med*. pediatrics
小便	ショウベン	urine; piss; pee —vi. pass urine; piss; pee
訓 小さい	ちいさい	small; little; tiny; young
小	お	(prefix) small; little; sub-
小	こ	(prefix) small; little; sub-
小型	こがた	small size; small; compact
小型化	こがたカ	miniature; small; compact —v. miniaturize; compact
小言	こごと	scolding; rebuke; preaching; lecture; grumbling
小細工	こザイク	cheap/petty tricks
小雨	こさめ	light/fine rain; drizzle
小銭	こぜに	small change
小包	こづつみ	parcel; package
小手先	こてさき	cheap/petty tricks
小話	こばなし	short tale; anecdote
小人	こびと	dwarf; pygmy
小間使い	こまづかい	maid
小間物屋	こまものや	notions dealer; haberdasher
小麦	こむぎ	wheat
小麦粉	こむぎこ	flour
小屋	こや	hut; shed; shack; cabin

164

294

少 ④   ⌿ ⼃ 小 少

音	少	ショウ	few; young
熟	少額	ショウガク	small sum/amount of money
	少女	ショウジョ	girl
	少々	ショウショウ	just a little; few
	少食	ショウショク	light eating; small appetite
	少数	ショウスウ	small number
	少年	ショウネン	boy; juvenile
	少量	ショウリョウ	small quantity; morsel
訓	少ない	すくない	few; not many; little
	少し	すこし	little; not much

3   ⼃⼂ さかさしょう small on top

295

当 ⑥   ⼃ ⼆ ⼩ 当 当 当

音	当	トウ	right; justice; fairness; this; the present; the current; right now
熟	当局	トウキョク	authorities; the powers that be
	当座	トウザ	the time being; the present
	当時	トウジ	at the present time; then; in those days
	当事者	トウジシャ	party concerned; interested party
	当日	トウジツ	that/the day; the appointed day
	当初	トウショ	at first; at the beginning
	当世	トウセイ	present day; the day/age/era
	当選	トウセン	winning; return to office; election —*vi.* be elected/returned to office; win an election
	当然	トウゼン	naturally; justly; properly; as a matter of course
	当地	トウチ	this place/area here
	当直	トウチョク	being on duty/watch —*vi.* be on duty; keep watch
	当人	トウニン	the said person; the person in question; the man himself
	当年	トウネン	this year; that year; those days

口口土士夂夕大女子宀寸小尢尸山川工己巾干幺广廴弋弓彡彳艹阝爿忄扌犭氵

当番	トウバン	being on duty/watch/guard
当否	トウヒ	right or wrong; justice; propriety; fitness; suitability
当分	トウブン	for the time being
当方	トウホウ	our part; I; we
当面	トウメン	present; urgent; pressing; immediate —*vi*. face; confront
当落	トウラク	result of an election

訓 当たる　あたる　hit; strike; touch; be touched; be equal; match; *col.* have food poisoning

当たり	あたり	hit; success; strike
当たり前	あたりまえ	proper; right; just; fair; common; normal; usual
当てる	あてる	apply; lay; hold; hit; strike; guess; succeed; expose

---

296

党 ⑩　丶　ソ　ツ　ᨈ　ᨈ　ᨈ　尚　尚　党　党

音 党　トウ　company; (political) party

熟
党員	トウイン	party member
党規	トウキ	(political) party regulations
党紀	トウキ	(political) party discipline
党議	トウギ	party policy; platform; party decision
党首	トウシュ	party leader
党派	トウハ	party/action/school of thought
党風	トウフウ	(political) party character
党利	トウリ	party interests
党略	トウリャク	party platform/policy

3　ᨈ　つ　*tsu* (katakana)

297

単 ⑨　丶　ᨈ　ᨈ　ᨈ　ᨈ　ᨈ　当　当　単

音 単　タン　single; simple

熟
単位	タンイ	unit
単元	タンゲン	unit
単語	タンゴ	word

単行本	タンコウボン	separate volume; one volume (not a series, etc.); hardcover book
単純	タンジュン	simplicity
単身	タンシン	alone; by oneself; unaccompanied
単数	タンスウ	singular number
単線	タンセン	single track
単調	タンチョウ	monotony; dullness; humdrum
単刀直入	タントウ チョクニュウ	straightforward; direct; frank; to the point
単独	タンドク	singleness; independence; separateness
単文	タンブン	simple sentence

298

巢 ⑪ 　丶　ヾ　ヾ　ヾ　ヾ　ヾ　当　当　単　単　巢

音	巢	ソウ	nest; web; hive
訓	巢	す	nest; shelter; web; hive
	巢くう	すくう	*vi*. build a nest
	巢立つ	すだつ	*vi*. leave the nest; graduate; start out in life

299

営 ⑫ 　丶　ヾ　ヾ　ヾ　ヾ　労　労　労　労　営　営

音	営	エイ	run; manage; administer
訓	営み	いとなみ	business; trade
	営む	いとなむ	*vt*. run a business; engage in commercial activities

300

厳 ⑰ 　ヾ　ヾ　产　产　产　产　产　岸　岸　岸　厳　厳

音	厳	ゲン（ゴン）	strict; severe; stern; solemn
熟	厳格	ゲンカク	strict; severe; stern; rigid
	厳禁	ゲンキン	strict prohibition —*v*. be strictly prohibited
	厳守	ゲンシュ	strict observance —*v*. keep strictly to; adhere rigidly; obey
	厳重	ゲンジュウ	stern; severe; strict; tight; close
	厳正	ゲンセイ	strict; rigid; fair; impartial
	厳選	ゲンセン	careful selection —*v*. select carefully; hand pick

口 口 土 士 夂 夕 大 女 子 宀 寸 小 ⺌ ⺌ 尢 尸 山 川 工 己 巾 干 幺 广 廴 弋 弓 彡 彳 艹 辶 阝 丷 扌 氵 犭

口口土士夂夕大女子宀寸小ㅚㅗ
●●●尢尸山川工己巾干幺广廴廾弓彡彳
辶阝艹 忄扌氵

厳然	ゲンゼン	grim; grave; solemn
厳冬	ゲントウ	severe/hard winter
厳父	ゲンプ	strict father; (another person's) father
厳密	ゲンミツ	strict; close; clear cut;
厳命	ゲンメイ	strict command —*v.* give a strict command
訓 厳か	おごそか	solemn; stately
厳しい	きびしい	severe; strict; stern

---

3 尢 だいのまげあし crooked leg

301

就⑫ 、 亠 亠 产 古 亨 京 京 京 京 尌 就 就

音 就	シュウ (ジュ)	get a job; install; study with; set out
熟 就役	シュウエキ	going into commission —*vi.* go into commission; undergo punishment
就学	シュウガク	entering/starting school —*vi.* enter/start school
就学率	シュウガクリツ	percentage of pupils attending school
就航	シュウコウ	commission/service (of ships/aircraft)
就任	シュウニン	inauguration/installation in a new position —*vi.* take up a position
就任式	シュウニンシキ	inauguration; inaugural ceremony
訓 就く	つく	*vi.* get a job; become; study under
就ける	つける	*vt.* seat; appoint a person; install

---

3 尸 しかばね corpse; flag

302

 ④ ㄱ ㄱ 尸 尺

音 尺	シャク	*shaku* (unit of measurement, approx. 30.3 cm)
熟 尺度	シャクド	measure; standard; criterion
尺八	シャクハチ	*shakuhachi* (bamboo flute)

303

局 ⑦

一 コ ヲ 尸 局 局 局

音	局	キョク	part; bureau; chamber
熟	局所	キョクショ	local; part of the body (normally sexual organs)
	局地	キョクチ	locality
	局部	キョクブ	limited part; section
	局面	キョクメン	position; situation; phase

304

居 ⑧

一 コ ヲ 尸 尸 尸 屏 居 居

音	居	キョ	be; live; sit
熟	居住	キョジュウ	residence; abode; dwelling —*vi.* reside; dwell
	居所	キョショ	one's abode; one's place of residence
	居留地	キョリュウチ	settlement; concession
訓	居心地	いごこち	comfortable; at ease; cosy; smug
	居酒屋	いざかや	tavern; bar
	居間	いま	living room
	居る	いる	*vi.* be; exist; live; sit
	居留守	いルス	pretend to be out

305

届 ⑧

一 コ ヲ 尸 尸 尸 届 届 届

音	届	（カイ）	send; report
訓	届く	とどく	*vi.* reach; attain
	届ける	とどける	*vt.* report; notify; send; forward
	届け	とどけ	report; notice; forwarding; delivery
	届け出で	とどけいで	notification; entry
	届け先	とどけさき	destination; receiver's address; consignee
	届け出る	とどけでる	*vt.* submit/give notice

306

屋 ⑨

一 コ ヲ 尸 尸 尸 屏 屏 屋 屋

音	屋	オク	house; roof

口口土士夂夕大女子宀寸小⺌⺍尢尸山川工己巾干幺广廴弋弓彡彳艹辶阝⺍忄扌犭氵

熟	屋外	オクガイ	the outdoors/open air
	屋上	オクジョウ	rooftop; roof
	屋内	オクナイ	indoors
訓	屋	や	house; roof; store name; seller
	屋号	やゴウ	store name
	屋台	やタイ	pushcart/mobile stall
	屋根	やね	roof

307

展 ⑩ 一 コ コ 尸 尸 尸 尸 屈 屈 展 展

音	展	テン	display; spread
熟	展開	テンカイ	unfolding; development; evolution; discovery; deployment —v. unfold; develop; evolve; deploy
	展示	テンジ	display; exhibition —v. exhibit; display; have on view
	展望	テンボウ	view; prospect; outlook; review —v. have a view of; look over; survey; review; pass
	展望鏡	テンボウキョウ	telescope
	展望台	テンボウダイ	observatory; observation post
	展覧	テンラン	exhibition; show —v. exhibit; display; show
	展覧会	テンランカイ	exhibition; exhibit; show

308

属 ⑫ 一 コ 尸 尸 尸 尸 尸 尼 属 属 属 属

音	属	ショク	
		ゾク	belong to; be attached to; genus
熟	属目	ショクモク	attention; observation
	属性	ゾクセイ	attribute
	属地	ゾクチ	territory; possession
	属領	ゾクリョウ	territory; possession; dependency
	属国	ゾッコク	dependency; vassal state

309

層 ⑭ 尸 尸 尸 尸 尽 屈 屈 屈 層 層 層 層

音	層	ソウ	layer; class; stratum

3 山　やま　mountain

310

山③　｜　山　山

音	山	サン	mountain
熟	山河	サンガ	mountains and rivers
	山間	サンカン	in the mountains
	山菜	サンサイ	edible wild plants
	山水画	サンスイガ	landscape (painting)
	山積	サンセキ	pile; accumulation —*vi.* pile up; accumulate
	山村	サンソン	mountain village
	山頂	サンチョウ	mountaintop; summit; peak
	山腹	サンプク	hillside; mountainside
	山脈	サンミャク	mountain range
	山門	サンモン	temple gate; main gate of a Buddhist temple
	山野	サンヤ	hills and fields; countryside
	山林	サンリン	forest in the mountains; mountains and forest
訓	山	やま	mountain; hill; mine; heap; pile; climax; peak; crisis (of an illness)
	山男	やまおとこ	woodsman; mountain laborer
	山小屋	やまごや	mountain hut/lodge
	山里	やまざと	mountain hamlet/village
	山師	やまし	prospecter; miner; speculator; imposter; swindler
	山積み	やまづみ	heap; huge amount
	山の手	やまのて	uptown; residential
	山登り	やまのぼり	mountain-climbing —*vi.* climb mountains

311

岩⑧　｜　山　山　屵　屵　岩　岩　岩

音	岩	ガン	rock
熟	岩塩	ガンエン	rock salt
	岩石	ガンセキ	rock; crag; stones and rocks
	岩頭	ガントウ	top of a rock; rock head

口口土士夂夕大女子宀寸小⺌⺍尢尸山川工己巾干幺广廴弋弓彡彳艹辶阝忄扌犭氵

3

	訓	岩	いわ	rock; crag; reef
		岩清水	いわしみず	spring water
		岩場	いわば	rock face; cliff
		岩屋	いわや	cave; cavedwelling

312

岸 ⑧　ᐟ　丷　屵　屵　屵　岸　岸　岸

音	岸	ガン	shore
訓	岸	きし	seashore; cliff

313

島 ⑩　ᐟ　亻　宀　户　户　皀　鸟　鸟　島　島

音	島	トウ	island
熟	島民	トウミン	islanders; natives of an island
訓	島	しま	island
	島国	しまぐに	island nation
	島国根性	しまぐにコンジョウ	insular spirit; insularism
	島田	しまだ	(traditional Japanese coiffure for unmarried women)
	島流し	しまながし	exile; banishment

3 川　かわ　river

314

川 ③　丿　川　川

音	川	セン	river
訓	川	かわ	river
	川上	かわかみ	upper stream
	川下	かわしも	lower stream
	川面	かわも	surface of a river

315

州　　　`ヽ ﾉ ｲ 小 州 州`
⑥

音	州	シュウ	province; state; continent
訓	州	す	sand bank

---

3 工　え　*e* (katakana)

316

工　　　`一 丁 工`
③

音	工	コウ （ク）	artisan; work; craft; construction
熟	工夫	クフウ	device; idea
	工面	クメン	contrivance; management —*v.* contrive; manage
	工員	コウイン	factory worker
	工学	コウガク	engineering
	工業	コウギョウ	industry; manufacturing
	工具	コウグ	tool; implement
	工芸	コウゲイ	industrial arts
	工作	コウサク	handicraft; handiwork; construction —*v.* make; construct
	工事	コウジ	construction work
	工場	コウジョウ （コウば）	factory
	工賃	コウチン	pay; wages
	工程	コウテイ	process

317

左　　　`一 ナ 左 左 左`
⑤

音	左	サ	left
熟	左官	サカン	plasterer
	左記	サキ	the following; the above
	左折	サセツ	left turn —*vi.* make a left turn; turn to the left
	左折禁止	サセツキンシ	No Left Turn (road marking)

口口土士夊夕大女子宀寸小⺌⺍尤尸山川工己巾干幺广廴廾弓彡彳艹辶阝⺍忄扌犭氵

左派 サハ left-wing party; the left
左右 サユウ right and left; both ways; opposite directions —*v.* control; influence

訓 左 ひだり left
左手 ひだりて left hand
左前 ひだりまえ wrong way; adversity; downward course

318

差 ⑩ 、 丷 ュ ㄚ 差 羊 羊 羊 差 差 差

音 差 サ point; indicate; difference; distinguish
熟 差異 サイ difference
差額 サガク balance; margin; difference
差別 サベツ discrimination; prejudice —*v.* discriminate (against)
差別用語 サベツヨウゴ discriminatory language; derogatory term
訓 差す さす *v.* pour; fill; add; apply; offer; point at -*vi.* shine
差し上げる さしあげる *vi.* give; present; offer
差し入れる さしいれる *vt.* insert; put into
差し金 さしがね instigation; suggestion
差出人 さしだしニン sender
差し支える さしつかえる *vi.* interfere
差止め さしどめ prohibition; ban; suspension
差し引く さしひく *vt.* deduct
差向い さしむかい face to face

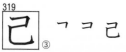

3 己 おのれ self; snake

319

己 ③ ㄱ コ 己

音 己 キ myself
コ self
訓 己 おのれ oneself *col.* you bastard (term of abuse)

320

巻⑨ 丶 丷 凵 屵 屵 券 巻 巻

音	巻	カン	volume; scroll
熟	巻頭	カントウ	beginning of a book
	巻末	カンマツ	end of a book
訓	巻き	まき	roll; volume; tome; book
	巻き貝	まきがい	snail; conch
	巻紙	まきがみ	wrapping paper
	巻き舌	まきじた	trilling (one's r's)
	巻き尺	まきジャク	tape measure
	巻物	まきもの	scroll
	巻く	まく	*v*. roll; coil

3 巾 はば／はばへん width; cloth

321

市⑤ 丶 亠 广 方 市

音	市	シ	market; city; municipality; urban; municipal
熟	市営	シエイ	municipal management
	市街	シガイ	the streets; the city
	市外	シガイ	outskirts of a town; out of town
	市議会	シギカイ	city assembly/council
	市制	シセイ	municipal organization
	市政	シセイ	municipal government/administration
	市長	シチョウ	mayor
	市民	シミン	citizen
	市民権	シミンケン	citizenship
	市役所	シヤクショ	city hall; municipal office
	市立	シリツ (いちリツ)	municipal
訓	市	いち	market; fair
	市場	いちば	market
	市松模様	いちまつモヨウ	checked pattern

175

口口土士攵夕大女子宀寸小⺌⺍尢尸山川工己巾干幺广廴弋弓彡彳⻌阝阝艹忄扌氵

322 布 ⑤ ノ ナ ナ 右 布

音	布	フ	cloth; spread
熟	布教	フキョウ	propagation of religion; missionary work —*v.* propagate religion
	布告	フコク	declaration; proclamation; notification —*v.* declare; proclaim; announce; decree
	布石	フセキ	initial stage in a go match; arrangements; preparations
	布団	フトン	futon; quilt; mattress
訓	布	ぬの	cloth; material
	布地	ぬのジ	cloth; material

323 希 ⑦ ノ メ ㄨ 产 产 希 希

音	希	キ	rare; wish
熟	希少	キショウ	scarce; rare
	希少価値	キショウカチ	scarcity value
	希代	キダイ	rarity; uniqueness
	希望	キボウ	hope; wish; desire; ambition —*v.* hope; wish; desire; aspire to

324 帰 ⑩ ⼁ ⼃ ⼃⼃ ⼃⼃⼃ ⼃⼅ ⼃⼅ ⼃⼅⼅ ⼃⼅⼅ 帰 帰

音	帰	キ	return
熟	帰化	キカ	naturalization —*vi.* become naturalized
	帰京	キキョウ	returning to Tokyo —*vi.* return to Tokyo
	帰郷	キキョウ	going home; returning to one's home town —*vi.* return to one's home town
	帰結	キケツ	conclusion; end; result; consequence —*vi.* be concluded; end
	帰国	キコク	return to one's country —*vi.* return/come back to one's country; go/come home
	帰省	キセイ	coming home; homecoming —*vi.* go/come/return home; visit one's native place
	帰着	キチャク	return; coming back; conclusion —*vi.* return; come back; conclude; bring to a conclusion
	帰路	キロ	homeward journey

| 訓 | 帰す | かえす | *vt*. dismiss; release |
| | 帰る | かえる | *vi*. return; go home; leave |

325

師 ⑩　＇ イ ⺹ ⺹ ⺀ 自 自 師 師 師

音	師	シ	army; teacher; missionary
熟	師事	シジ	studying under a person —*vi*. study under a person; become a person's student
	師団	シダン	division of soldiers
	師弟	シテイ	master and pupil; teacher and student

326

席 ⑩　＇ 宀 广 广 广 庐 庐 庐 席 席

音	席	セキ	seat; place
熟	席次	セキジ	ranking; precedence; seating order
	席上	セキジョウ	at the meeting; on the occasion
	席巻	セッケン	sweeping; conquest

327

帯 ⑩　一 十 卄 卅 世 世 带 帯 帯 帯

音	帯	タイ	belt; band; wear; zone
熟	帯出	タイシュツ	borrowing —*v*. carry out; take out; borrow
訓	帯	おび	*obi* (sash used to tie around a kimono); belt; sash; girdle
	帯状	おびジョウ	long, narrow strip
	帯びる	おびる	*vt*. wear; put on; bear; carry; be entrusted/vested with

---

328

常 ⑪　＇ ⺌ ⺍ ⺌ 尚 尚 常 常 常 常 常

音	常	ジョウ	ordinary; common; normal
熟	常温	ジョウオン	normal/room/average/uniform temperature
	常客	ジョウキャク	regular customers; a regular
	常勤	ジョウキン	full-time/regular employment —*vi*. be in

口
口
土
士
夕
大
女
子
宀
寸
小
⺌
⺌
尢
尸
山
川
工
己
巾
干
幺
广
廴
弋
弓
彡
彳
辶
阝
丷
忄
扌
氵

full-time/regular employment

常時	ジョウジ	always; habitually
常識	ジョウシキ	common sense/decency/practice; reasonable; sensible
常習	ジョウシュウ	bad habit —*v.* be in the habit of
常習者	ジョウシュウシャ	addict
常習犯	ジョウシュウハン	habitual offender; confirmed criminal
常食	ジョウショク	diet; staple food —*v.* eat everyday; live on a diet of
常人	ジョウジン	ordinary man
常数	ジョウスウ	*math.* constant
常設	ジョウセツ	permanent; standing —*v.* establish permanently
常態	ジョウタイ	normal condition
常道	ジョウドウ	regular/usual way; proper behavior/conduct
常任	ジョウニン	permanent; regular; standing
常備	ジョウビ	standing; reserve —*v.* have always ready; be provided with
常用	ジョウヨウ	common/everyday use —*v.* use commonly/regularly; have everyday use of
常用漢字	ジョウヨウカンジ	*jōyō kanji* (the 1,945 Chinese characters in common use)
常緑樹	ジョウリョクジュ	evergreen tree
常連	ジョウレン	regular customer; frequenters

常	つね	common; everyday; ordinary; normal; always; constantly
常々	つねづね	always; at all times
常	とこ	(prefix) everlasting; permanent
常夏	とこなつ	everlasting/permanent summer

329

帳 ⑪ 丨 口 巾 帄 帄 帄 帄 帳 帳 帳

帳	チョウ	curtain; book; register; album
帳場	チョウば	counter; counting house; office; front desk
帳面	チョウメン	notebook; register; account book

330

幕 ⑬ 一 艹 艹 芢 芦 苩 苩 莫 莫 莫 幕 幕

| 幕 | バク | Japanese feudal government |
| | マク | curtain; act |

熟	幕府	バクフ	shogunate; military government
	幕末	バクマツ	*hist*. last years of the Tokugawa shogunate
	幕間	マクあい	intermission
	幕開き	マクあき	start of a play
	幕内	マクうち	senior-grade sumo wrestler
	幕切れ	マクぎれ	end
	幕下	マクした	junior-grade sumo wrestler
	幕の内	マクのうち	behind the curtain

3 干 かん dry; one ten

331
干 ③ 一 二 干

音	干	カン	dry; concern; perpetrate; ebb
熟	干害	カンガイ	drought disaster/damage
	干潮	カンチョウ	ebb/low tide
	干満	カンマン	ebb and flow; tide
訓	干物	ひもの	dried fish
	干る	ひる	*vi*. dry; parch; recede; fall; ebb
	干す	ほす	*vt*. dry; drain; drink up

332
平 ⑤ 一 一 こ 乃 平

音	平	ヘイ	flat; level; even; calm; ordinary; common; peaceful
		ビョウ	
熟	平等	ビョウドウ	equality; impartiality
	平安	ヘイアン	peace; safety and security *hist*. Heian period/court (794-1185)
	平易	ヘイイ	easy; simple; straightforward
	平温	ヘイオン	usual temperature
	平気	ヘイキ	calm; unconcerned; nonchalant
	平均	ヘイキン	average; mean
	平原	ヘイゲン	plain; prairie
	平行	ヘイコウ	parallel —*vi*. be parallel
	平行線	ヘイコウセン	parallel line

平日	ヘイジツ	weekdays; every day apart from Sundays and National Holidays
平常	ヘイジョウ	usual; common; everyday
平身低頭	ヘイシンテイトウ	bowing; prostration —*vi.* bow to the ground; prostrate oneself
平静	ヘイセイ	tranquillity; calmness; peacefulness
平生	ヘイゼイ	usual; everyday; ordinary
平然	ヘイゼン	calmness; nonchalance
平素	ヘイソ	usual; commonplace; ordinary
平地	ヘイチ	level/flat land; even surface
平熱	ヘイねつ	normal body temperature
平年	ヘイネン	normal year; not a leap year
平服	ヘイフク	plain/everyday clothes
平方	ヘイホウ	*math.* square of a number; square (meter, etc.) —*v.* square a number
平方根	ヘイホウコン	*math.* square root
平民	ヘイミン	common people
平野	ヘイヤ	plain; open field
平和	ヘイワ	peace

訓

平ら	たいら	flat; level
平	ひら	common; ordinary; average
平謝り	ひらあやまり	humble apology
平泳ぎ	ひらおよぎ	breast stroke
平仮名	ひらがな	*hiragana* (the cursive syllabary)
平たい	ひらたい	flat; level
平屋	ひらや	one-story house

333

⑥ 　 ノ　ケ　ヒ　乍　乍　年

音

| 年 | ネン | year; age |

熟

年賀	ネンガ	New Year's greetings
年賀状	ネンガジョウ	New Year's greeting card
年月日	ネンガッぴ	date; year, month, and date
年刊	ネンカン	yearly publication; annual
年間	ネンカン	period of a year
年季	ネンキ	apprenticeship; experience; training
年期	ネンキ	period of years; length of time (in years)
年月	ネンゲツ	a long period of time
年限	ネンゲン	period of years; length of time (in years)
年功	ネンコウ	long experience/service

年号	ネンゴウ	name of an era
年始	ネンシ	beginning of the year
年次	ネンジ	annual; yearly
年収	ネンシュウ	yearly income; annual salary
年中	ネンジュウ	whole year; always; perpetually
年中行事	ネンチュウ ギョウジ	annual functions; regular events
年少	ネンショウ	youth
年代	ネンダイ	era; age; epoch; period
年長	ネンチョウ	seniority
年度	ネンド	year; term; fiscal/financial year
年頭	ネントウ	beginning of the year
年内	ネンナイ	within the year; before the year is out
年表	ネンピョウ	chronological table
年別	ネンベツ	annual variation; classification by year
年報	ネンポウ	annual report
年末	ネンマツ	year-end; end of the year
訓 年	とし	year; age; years
年上	としうえ	older
年子	としご	children born in consecutive years
年下	としした	younger

334

幸 ⑧　　一　十　土　圡　㞢　㐀　幸　幸　幸

音 幸	コウ	happiness; good luck; felicity
熟 幸運	コウウン	good fortune/luck; happiness
幸福	コウフク	happiness; felicity; well-being; bliss
訓 幸い	さいわい	happiness; felicity; bliss; good luck/fortune
幸	さち	happiness; fortune; luck
幸せ	しあわせ	happiness; felicity; bliss

335

幹 ⑬　　一　十　十　古　古　吉　直　卓　車　斡　幹　幹　幹

音 幹	カン	tree trunk; body; ability
熟 幹事	カンジ	manager; secretary; person in charge of a party
幹線	カンセン	trunk/main line
訓 幹	みき	tree trunk; important part

3 幺 いとがしら short thread

336 幼 ⑤ ⟨ ⟨ 幺 幻 幼

音	幼	ヨウ	infant; small child
熟	幼魚	ヨウギョ	young fish
	幼児	ヨウジ	infant; toddler; baby
	幼時	ヨウジ	childhood; infancy
	幼少	ヨウショウ	childhood; infancy
	幼虫	ヨウチュウ	larva
	幼年	ヨウネン	childhood; infancy; child
	幼名	ヨウメイ	one's infant name
訓	幼い	おさない	young; infantile; childish
	幼な顔	おさながお	how one looked as a baby
	幼子	おさなご	little child; baby
	幼心	おさなごころ	child's mind/heart

3 广 まだれ dotted cliff

337 広 ⑤ ⟨ 亠 广 広 広

音	広	コウ	wide; broad; spacious; spread
熟	広義	コウギ	broad sense
	広言	コウゲン	big talk; brag; boast; boasting —*vi*. talk big; brag; boast
	広原	コウゲン	vast plain; open country
	広告	コウコク	advertisement; notice; announcement —*v*. advertise; announce; give publicity to
	広大	コウダイ	vast; extensive; immense; huge
	広報	コウホウ	public information; publicity; public relations
訓	広い	ひろい	wide; broad; spacious; large
	広場	ひろば	open space; square; plaza
	広々	ひろびろ	wide; open; vast
	広間	ひろま	hall; saloon
	広がる	ひろがる	*vi*. spread out; expand; extend; stretch

広げる	ひろげる	*vt.* extend; expand; enlarge; widen; unfold; open; lay out
広さ	ひろさ	area; extent; dimensions
広まる	ひろまる	*vi.* spread; be diffused/propagated
広める	ひろめる	*vt.* extend; widen; broaden; spread; diffuse; propagate

---

338

庁 ⑤ 　 ， 一 广 户 庁

| 音 | 庁 | チョウ | agency; office; board |
| 熟 | 庁舎 | チョウシャ | government building |

339

序 ⑦ 　 ， 一 广 庐 庐 庑 序

音	序	ジョ	introduction
熟	序曲	ジョキョク	overture
	序文	ジョブン	preface; foreword; introduction
	序幕	ジョマク	opening/first act
	序列	ジョレツ	order; rank; ranking
	序論	ジョロン	introduction

340

底 ⑧ 　 ， 一 广 广 广 庐 底 底

音	底	テイ	bottom; base; kind; sort
熟	底止	テイシ	cessation —*v.* cease; stop; end
	底辺	テイヘン	*math.* base (of a triangle) *fig.* bottom/lower levels (of society)
	底本	テイホン	original text; source book
	底流	テイリュウ	undercurrent; underflow
訓	底	そこ	base; bottom; lower part
	底力	そこぢから	latent energy; hidden power

341

店 ⑧ 　 ， 一 广 广 庐 庐 店 店

| 音 | 店 | テン | shop |

183

口口土士夂夕大女子宀寸小⺌⺍尢尸山川工己巾干幺广廴弋弓彡彳艹辶阝⺮扌犭氵

熟	店員	テンイン	clerk; shop assistant; salesman; saleswoman
	店主	テンシュ	shopkeeper; storekeeper; store owner
	店頭	テントウ	shop front; counter; shop; store
	店屋物	テンやもの	dishes from a caterer; dishes prepared at a store
訓	店	みせ	stall; shop; office; place of business
	店先	みせさき	storefront
	店番	みせバン	tending a store; store tender; salesman
	店開き	みせびらき	opening of business —v. open business

342

府 ⑧

丶 亠 广 广 庁 疒 府 府

音	府	フ	capital; prefecture (used only for Osaka and Kyoto)
熟	府議会	フギカイ	prefectural assembly
	府庁	フチョウ	prefectural office
	府立	フリツ	prefectural

343

度 ⑨

丶 亠 广 广 庐 庐 庐 度 度

音	度	ド (タク) (ト)	degree; frequency; extent; measure; time
熟	度合い	ドあい	degree; extent; rate
	度外視	ドガイシ	neglect; disregard —v. neglect; disregard; overlook; ignore
	度胸	ドキョウ	courage; pluck; mettle; guts; nerve
	度数	ドスウ	number of times; frequency; incidence; degree
	度量	ドリョウ	generosity; liberality; magnamity; length and volume
訓	度	たび	time; occasion; every time
	度重なる	たびかさなる	vi. be repeated/repetitive
	度々	たびたび	often; repeatedly; over and over

344

庫 ⑩

丶 亠 广 广 庐 庐 店 肩 盲 庫

| 音 | 庫 | コ (ク) | warehouse; store |

345

座 ⑩ 　 丶 一 广 广 庐 庐 庐 床 座 座

音	座	ザ	sitting; gathering; theater
熟	座金	ザがね	metal washer
	座興	ザキョウ	joke; entertainment; fun
	座高	ザコウ	one's height when sitting
	座席	ザセキ	seat
	座像	ザゾウ	seated statue; seated figure
	座談	ザダン	conversation; discussion —*vi.* converse; discuss
	座長	ザチョウ	chairman; chairperson
	座標	ザヒョウ	coordinates
	座右	ザユウ	at one's side; within arm's reach
訓	座る	すわる	*vi.* sit down; be seated

346

庭 ⑩ 　 丶 一 广 广 庐 庭 庭 庭 庭 庭

音	庭	テイ	garden
熟	庭園	テイエン	garden; park
	庭球	テイキュウ	tennis
	庭前	テイゼン	garden
訓	庭	にわ	garden
	庭石	にわいし	garden stone
	庭先	にわさき	in the garden
	庭師	にわシ	landscape gardener; garden designer

347

康 ⑪ 　 丶 一 广 广 庐 庐 庐 庐 庐 康 康

| 音 | 康 | コウ | peaceful; healthy |

3

3 えんにょう stretching

口
口
土
士
夂
夕
大
女
子
宀
寸
小
⺍
⺌
尢
尸
山
川
工
己
巾
干
幺
广
廴
廾
弓
彡
彳
⺍
辶
阝
阝
忄
扌
氵
氵

348

延 ⑧   一 ｨ ｨ ｨｰ 正 ｨ正 延 延

音	延	エン	extend; lengthen; postpone
熟	延引	エンイン	delay; postponement; procrastination —*vi.* be delayed/postponed/put off
	延期	エンキ	delay; postponement; procrastination —*v.* delay; postpone; procrastinate; put off
	延焼	エンショウ	spread of a fire —*vi.* spread; catch fire
	延着	エンチャク	delayed/late arrival —*vi.* arrive late; be delayed
	延長	エンチョウ	extension; continuation —*v.* lengthen in time, scope, or range; extend; continue; prolong
訓	延ばす	のばす	*vt.* lengthen; stretch; extend; postpone; put off
	延びる	のびる	*vi.* lengthen; stretch; extend; be put off; be delayed
	延び	のび	postponement; putting off; stretching; growth; extension
	延び延び	のびのび	long delay
	延べる	のべる	*vt.* spread; extend; postpone; put off
	延べ	のべ	total; aggregate

349

建 ⑨   ｱ ｺ ｺ ｺ ⺕ ⺕ 聿 ｨ聿 建 建

音	建	ケン （コン）	build
熟	建国	ケンコク	foundation of a state
	建設	ケンセツ	construction; building; establishment —*v.* construct; build; establish
	建造	ケンゾウ	building; construction —*v.* build; construct
	建造物	ケンゾウブツ	structure
	建築	ケンチク	building; construction; architecture —*v.* build; construct
	建築家	ケンチクカ	architecture
	建立	コンリュウ	erection/construction (of a shrine or a temple) —*v.* erect/construct (a shrine or temple)
訓	建つ	たつ	*vi.* be built/set up/erected
	建てる	たてる	*vt.* build; construct; erect
	建具	たてグ	door; sliding door; window frames; fittings

建具屋	たてグや	joiner
建て前	たてまえ	*tatemae* (principle); roof-raising ceremony
建物	たてもの	building

---

3 弋 しきたすき／しきがまえ ceremony

350

式 ⑥ 　一 二 〒 王 式 式

音	式	シキ	ceremony; formula; system; equation; expression
熟	式辞	シキジ	address (at a ceremony)
	式日	シキジツ	day of a ceremony
	式場	シキジョウ	ceremonial hall
	式台	シキダイ	step in a Japanese entryway
	式典	シキテン	ceremony
	式服	シキフク	formal/ceremonial dress

---

3 弓 ゆみ／ゆみへん bow

351

弓 ③ 　⊃ コ 弓

音	弓	キュウ	bow; bow-shaped
熟	弓術	キュウジュツ	archery; bowmanship
	弓状	キュウジョウ	bow-shaped; arched
	弓道	キュウドウ	*kyūdō* (Japanese archery)
訓	弓	ゆみ	bow
	弓矢	ゆみや	bow and arrow

352

引 ④ 　⊃ コ 弓 引

| 音 | 引 | イン | pull; attract; guide; lead |
| 熟 | 引火 | インカ | ignition; combustion —*vi*. ignite; set fire to; combust |

口口土士夕夕大女子宀寸小丷丷尢尸山川工己巾干幺广廴弋弓彡彳艹辶阝艹忄扌犭氵

引責	インセキ	assumption of responsibility —*vi.* assume responsibility
引率	インソツ	leadership; command —*v.* lead; head; command
引退	インタイ	retirement —*vi.* retire; withdraw from public life
引用	インヨウ	quotation; citation —*v.* quote; cite
引力	インリョク	gravitation
引例	インレイ	quotation; citation
訓 引く	ひく	*vt.* pull; draw; reduce; retire; drag; lay on; refer to
引き受ける	ひきうける	*vt.* accept an offer; assume; take over; guarantee
引き算	ひきザン	*math.* subtraction
引き出し	ひきだし	drawer
引き立てる	ひきたてる	*vt.* make (someone/something) stand out
引き取る	ひきとる	*vt.* take over
引き分ける	ひきわける	*v.* draw; tie
引け目	ひけめ	inferiority complex
引っ張る	ひっぱる	*vt.* pull

353

⑦ 　丶　丷　ᶜ　ᶜ　ᶜ　弟　弟

音 弟	テイ	younger brother
	（ダイ）	
	（デ）	
熟 弟妹	テイマイ	younger brothers and sisters
弟子	デシ	disciple
訓 弟	おとうと	younger brother

354

⑩ 　フ　コ　弓　弓　弓　弓ˊ　弓ˊ　弱　弱　弱

音 弱	ジャク	weak
熟 弱酸	ジャクサン	weak acid
弱視	ジャクシ	weak sight; amblyopia
弱小	ジャクショウ	small and weak; young
弱卒	ジャクソツ	weak soldier/subordinate
弱体	ジャクタイ	weak body/system
弱敵	ジャクテキ	unworthy enemy

弱点	ジャクテン	weakness; weak point; shortcoming; defect
弱電機	ジャクデンキ	light electric appliance
弱肉強食	ジャクニクキョウショク	survival of the fittest; law of the jungle
弱年	ジャクネン	youth
弱化	ジャッカ	weakening —v. weaken

訓

弱い	よわい	weak; frail; feeble; poor; bad
弱気	よわキ	timid; fainthearted
弱腰	よわごし	weak attitude
弱音	よわね	complaint
弱火	よわび	slow flame; low heat
弱虫	よわむし	coward; weakling
弱々しい	よわよわしい	feeble; faint; frail; delicate; fragile
弱さ	よわさ	weakness; feebleness; frailty
弱まる	よわまる	vi. get weak; abate; drop; calm down
弱み	よわみ	weak position; vulnerability; weak point
弱める	よわめる	vt. weaken; impair; decrease; turn down; lower; dilute
弱る	よわる	vi. grow weak; weaken; be at a loss what to do; be in a fix
弱り果てる	よわりはてる	vi. be weak with exhaustion; be annoyed; be fed up

355

強 ⑪ フ コ 弓 弘 弘 弘 弘 弥 強 強 強

音 強

| 強 | キョウ | strong; strengthen; force |
| | ゴウ | strong |

熟

強化	キョウカ	strengthening; intensification; reinforcement —v. strengthen; solidify; build up; intensify
強健	キョウケン	robust health; strong constitution
強権	キョウケン	authority; state power
強固	キョウコ	firmness; stability; solidity; security; strength
強行	キョウコウ	enforcement; force —v. enforce; force
強勢	キョウセイ	emphasis; stress
強制	キョウセイ	compulsion; coercion; duress —v. compel; force; coerce
強大	キョウダイ	mighty; powerful; strong
強調	キョウチョウ	emphasis —v. emphasize
強度	キョウド	intensity; strength
強要	キョウヨウ	persistent demand; extortion —v. exact; compel; force; coerce
強力	キョウリョク	power; might
強引	ゴウイン	force

口口土士夂夕大女子宀寸小平灬尢尸山川工己巾干幺广廴弋弓彡彳艹辶阝阝丷忄扌犭氵

189

口 口 土 士 夕 大 女 子 宀 寸 小 ⺌ ⺍ 尤 尸 山 川 工 己 巾 干 幺 广 廴 弋 弓 彡 彳 艹 辶 阝 扌 忄 扌 氵 犭

	強情	ゴウジョウ	obstinacy; stubbornness
	強欲	ゴウヨク	avarice; greed; greediness
訓	強い	つよい	strong
	強まる	つよまる	*vi.* become strong; be intensified; increase; be emphasized
	強める	つよめる	*vt.* strengthen; intensify; increase; emphasize
	強いる	しいる	*vt.* force; compel; press

356

張 ⑪ ⌐ ⌐ 弓 引 引 引 引 引 張 張 張

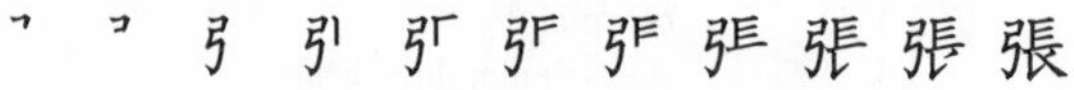

	張	チョウ	stretch
熟	張本人	チョウホンニン	ringleader
	張力	チョウリョク	tension; tensile force
訓	張る	はる	*v.* stretch; spread; extend; strain; tighten
	張り合う	はりあう	*vi.* rival; emulate; compete
	張り切る	はりきる	*vi.* be in high spirits
	張り子	はりこ	papier-mâché

---

3 彡 さんづくり short hair

357

形 ⑦ 一 �ニ テ 开 形 形 形

	形	ケイ	shape; form; appearance
		ギョウ	form; figure; model
熟	形相	ギョウソウ	looks; figure; face
	形式	ケイシキ	formation
	形式的	ケイシキテキ	formally; perfunctory
	形状	ケイジョウ	shape; state
	形勢	ケイセイ	situation; state of affairs
	形成	ケイセイ	formation —*v.* form; build/make up
	形成外科	ケイセイゲカ	plastic/cosmetic surgery
	形態	ケイタイ	form; shape
	形容	ケイヨウ	description; qualification; modification —*v.* describe; modify; qualify
	形容詞	ケイヨウシ	*gram.* adjective

形容動詞　ケイヨウドウシ　*gram.* adjectival verb (verb used to qualify/modify a noun)

訓	形	かた	shape; form; model; pattern
	形	かたち	shape; form
	形見	かたみ	keepsake; memento

3　彳　ぎょうにんべん　going man

358

役⑦　ノ　ク　イ　イ　伇　役　役

音	役	エキ	war; battle; service
	役	ヤク	post; role; duty; charge
熟	役者	ヤクシャ	actor
	役所	ヤクショ	government office
	役立つ	ヤクだつ	*vi.* be useful; serve a purpose
	役立てる	ヤクだてる	*vt.* put to use; make use of
	役人	ヤクニン	officer
	役場	ヤクば	town office
	役割	ヤクわり	part; role

359

往⑧　ノ　ク　イ　イ　彳　行　往　往

音	往	オウ	go; former; past
熟	往々	オウオウ	sometimes; occasionally; now and then
	往時	オウジ	the past; things past
	往生	オウジョウ	death; submission —*vi.* die; pass away; submit
	往信	オウシン	outgoing letter; letter sent
	往年	オウネン	former years; formerly; the past
	往復	オウフク	round/return trip —*v.* go and come back; make a round trip
	往来	オウライ	coming and going; street traffic —*vi.* come and go
	往路	オウロ	outward trip/journey
訓	往く	ゆく	*vi.* go

口
口
土
士
夂
夕
大
女
子
宀
寸
小
䒑
⺍
尢
尸
山
川
工
己
巾
干
幺
广
廴
弋
弓
彡
彳
⺾
辶
阝
⺍
忄
扌
犭
氵

口
口
土
士
夕
大
女
子
宀
寸
小
⺌
尢
尸
山
川
工
己
巾
干
幺
广
廴
弋
弓
彡
彳
艹
辶
阝
阝
丷
忄
扌
犭
氵

360

径 ⑧ 　 丶 ク 彳 彳 彷 径 径 径

| 音 | 径 | ケイ | lane; small road; path; diameter |
| 熟 | 径路 | ケイロ | course; route; process |

361

後 ⑨ 　 丶 ク 彳 彳 彳 彿 移 移 後

音	後	ゴ （コウ）	after; post; later
熟	後学	コウガク	future scholars; future reference
	後記	コウキ	postscript
	後期	コウキ	latter period
	後見人	コウケンニン	guardian
	後者	コウシャ	latter
	後進	コウシン	reversing —v. reverse; back up; go backwards
	後進国	コウシンコク	developing country
	後世	コウセイ	future generations; ages to come
	後続	コウゾク	following; succeeding; next
	後退	コウタイ	retreat; recession; retrogression; step back —vi. retreat; retrogress; go backwards; step back
	後天的	コウテンテキ	acquired; postnatal
	後任	コウニン	successor
	後年	コウネン	future years; in years to come; later; afterwards
	後半	コウハン	latter/second half
	後半生	コウハンセイ	the latter half of life
	後部	コウブ	back end; rear
	後家	ゴケ	widow
	後光	ゴコウ	halo
	後妻	ゴサイ	second wife
	後日	ゴジツ	later date; later on; in the future
	後手	ゴて	one step behind; too late; second player (in go or shōgi)
訓	後	あと	later; after; next; the rest
	後始末	あとシマツ	settlement
	後ずさり	あとずさり	stepping back —vi. step back
	後回し	あとまわし	postponement; putting off

後ろ	うしろ	back; behind
後ろめたい	うしろめたい	feel uneasy/guilty; have a bad conscience
後ろ指	うしろゆび	suspicion
後れる	おくれる	*vi.* be late; be backward
後	のち	later; afterwards; in the future

362

待 ⑨ ⸍ ⸗ 彳 彳 彳 彳 徏 待 待

音	待	タイ	wait; treat
熟	待機	タイキ	waiting for a chance —*vi.* watch and wait; wait and see
	待望	タイボウ	eager waiting —*v.* wait eagerly
訓	待つ	まつ	*vt.* wait
	待合室	まちあいシツ	waiting room

363

律 ⑨ ⸍ ⸗ 彳 彳 彳 彳 律 律 律

音	律	リツ (リチ)	law; regulation; rhythm
熟	律する	リッする	*vt.* judge; measure
	律動	リツドウ	rhythm —*vi.* have rhythm; be rhythmic
	律法	リッポウ	law; rule
	律令	リツリョウ	code of laws; laws and orders

364

従 ⑩ ⸍ ⸗ 彳 彳 彳 彳 徉 徉 従

音	従	ジュウ (ジュ) (ショウ)	obey; follow; engage in / junior grade
熟	従業員	ジュウギョウイン	employee
	従軍	ジュウグン	going to the front with the army —*vi.* go to the front with the army
	従事	ジュウジ	engagement; involvement —*vi.* engage in; be involved in
	従順	ジュウジュン	obedience; submission

口 口 土 士 夂 夕 大 女 子 宀 寸 小 ⺌ ⺌ 尢 尸 山 川 工 己 巾 干 幺 广 廴 弋 弓 彐 彡 彳 • 艹 辶 阝 亠 忄 扌 氵 犭

口口土士夕夕大女子宀寸小丷
尢尸山川工己巾干幺广廴弋弓彡彳
⺾辶阝⺍扌犭

| 従属 | ジュウゾク | subordination —*vi.* be subordinate to |
| 従来 | ジュウライ | hitherto; as in the past; as usual |

訓 | 従う | したがう | *vi.* follow; accompany; obey; conform; comply |
| 従える | したがえる | *vt.* be attended/followed by |
| 従って | したがって | accordingly; consequently; therefore; in obedience to; as; in proportion to |

365

徒 ⑩ ／ ク 彳 彳 彳 衸 徏 徏 徒 徒

音 | 徒 | ト | on foot; empty; vain; companions; disciple; punishment |

熟 | 徒競争 | トキョウソウ | footrace; race on foot |
徒弟	トテイ	apprentice; disciple
徒党	トトウ	faction; conspirators; league
徒歩	トホ	walking; going on foot
徒労	トロウ	futile effort; vain attempt; fruitless labor

366

得 ⑪ ／ ク 彳 彳 彳 彳 彳 得 得 得 得

音 | 得 | トク | obtain; acquire; ability |

熟 | 得する | トクする | *vi.* obtain; acquire; get |
得意	トクイ	pride; triumph; forte; strong point; customer; patron
得策	トクサク	good policy; best plan
得失	トクシツ	relative merits; advantages and disadvantages; profit and loss
得心	トクシン	conviction; consent; compliance —*vi.* consent to; comply with; be convinced of
得点	トクテン	score; marks obtained —*vi.* score; gain marks
得票	トクヒョウ	polling score —*vi.* poll; gain/win votes
得票数	トクヒョウスウ	number of votes polled

訓 | 得る | うる | *vt.* obtain; acquire; get; can; be able to |
| 得る | える | *vt.* get; have; obtain; acquire; can; be able to |
| 得手 | えて | strong point; forte |

367

復 ⑫ ／ ク 彳 彳 彳 衧 衧 衧 衧 伊 復 復

音 | 復 | フク | return; repeat; be restored |

熟	復する	フクする	*v.* return; be restored; reply; take revenge
	復位	フクイ	restoration; reinstatement —*vi.* be restored/reinstated
	復員	フクイン	demobilization —*v.* be demobilized and sent home
	復元	フクゲン	restoration (to the original state) —*v.* restore; reconstruct
	復習	フクシュウ	review; revision —*v.* review; revise
	復唱	フクショウ	repeat —*v.* repeat an order aloud
	復職	フクショク	reinstatement; reappointment —*vi.* be reinstated/reappointed in one's job
	復命	フクメイ	report —*v.* report (to one's superior)
	復路	フクロ	return trip
	復活	フッカツ	rebirth; revival —*v.* be reborn/brought back to life
	復活祭	フッカツサイ	Easter
	復刊	フッカン	republication; reissue —*v.* republish; reissue
	復帰	フッキ	return; reinstatement —*vi.* return; reinstate; come back
	復旧	フッキュウ	restoration; recovery —*v.* restore; be restored
	復古	フッコ	restoration (of the old regime/situation) —*v.* restore; be restored
	復古調	フッコチョウ	reactionary mood
	復興	フッコウ	reconstruction; revival —*v.* reconstruct; revive
	復刻	フッコク	republication; reissue —*v.* republish; reissue

368

德 ⑭ 彳 彳 彳 彳 彳 彳 德 德 德 德 德 德

音	德	トク	virtue; goodness; grace; character
熟	德育	トクイク	moral education/training
	德政	トクセイ	benevolent administration
	德性	トクセイ	morality
	德操	トクソウ	strong moral sense/character
	德望	トクボウ	moral influence
	德目	トクモク	individual article of ethics
	德用	トクヨウ	economical
	德利	トクリ	flask; liquor bottle; turtleneck
	德化	トッカ	*v.* influence by good moral example
	德行	トッコウ	virtuous conduct; virtue; goodness

3 艹　くさかんむり　grass crown

口口土士夂夕大女子宀寸小⺌⺍尢尸山川工己巾干幺广廴弋弓彡彳⺾辶阝阝忄扌犭氵

369 花 ⑦
一 ヤ サ ヤ ヤ 花 花

音	花	カ	flower; gaudy
熟	花鳥風月	カチョウフウゲツ	beauties of nature; elegant pursuits
	花粉	カフン	pollen
	花弁	カベン	petal
訓	花	はな	flower; cherry blossoms; gratuity; flower arrangement
	花形	はながた	floral pattern; celebrity; popular star
	花束	はなたば	bouquet; bunch of flowers
	花火	はなび	fireworks
	花見	はなみ	cherry-blossom viewing

370 芸 ⑦
一 ヤ サ 艹 芏 芸 芸

音	芸	ゲイ	learning; art; entertainment
熟	芸者	ゲイシャ	geisha
	芸術	ゲイジュツ	art; the arts
	芸当	ゲイトウ	feat; trick; stunt; performance
	芸道	ゲイドウ	art; accomplishments
	芸人	ゲイニン	artist; entertainer; public performer
	芸能	ゲイノウ	public entertainment; performing arts
	芸名	ゲイメイ	stage name

371 英 ⑧
一 ヤ サ 艹 苎 苎 英 英

音	英	エイ	brilliant; eminent; England; English
熟	英気	エイキ	virility; energy; vigor
	英語	エイゴ	the English language
	英国	エイコク	England; Britain
	英才	エイサイ	genius; talent
	英断	エイダン	decisive judgment

英知	エイチ	wisdom; intelligence
英文	エイブン	English writing
英文学	エイブンガク	English literature
英米	エイベイ	England and America; English and American
英訳	エイヤク	English translation —*v.* translate into English

372

芽 ⑧　一　十　艹　艹　芒　芦　芽　芽

音	芽	ガ	bud
訓	芽	め	bud; good luck
	芽生え	めばえ	sprout; bud
	芽生える	めばえる	*vi.* spring up; sprout

373

苦 ⑧　一　十　艹　艹　芒　芋　苦　苦

音	苦	ク	bitter; pain; hard work
熟	苦学	クガク	self-support through university —*vi.* pay one's way/work through university
	苦境	クキョウ	distressed circumstances; dire straits
	苦行	クギョウ	penance; aseticism —*vi.* do penance; practice aseticism
	苦言	クゲン	outspoken advice; bitter counsel
	苦笑	クショウ	wry smile; strained laugh —*vi.* smile wryly
	苦情	クジョウ	complaint; grievance; objection
	苦心	クシン	pains; effort; labor; trouble; hard work —*vi.* make painstaking efforts
	苦戦	クセン	hard fight; desperate battle —*vi.* fight hard; battle desperately
	苦痛	クツウ	pain; anguish
	苦難	クナン	distress; suffering; affliction
	苦肉の策	クニクのサク	last resort; desperate/clumsy measure taken under the pressure of necessity
	苦楽	クラク	joys and sorrows
	苦労	クロウ	trouble; hardship; suffering —*vi.* be troubled; suffer hardship
訓	苦しい	くるしい	painful; hard; difficult; embarrassing
	苦しむ	くるしむ	*vi.* suffer from; groan; agonize; be troubled with; worry oneself; be at a loss
	苦しめる	くるしめる	*vt.* torment; torture; distress; trouble; inflict pain

口
口
土
士
夂
夕
大
女
子
宀
寸
小
ⵝ
ⵞ
尤
尸
山
川
工
己
巾
干
幺
广
廴
弋
弓
彡
彳
艹
辶
阝
阝
艹
忄
扌
犭
氵

苦い	にがい	bitter; hard; trying
苦手	にがて	weak point; be bad (at)
苦り切る	にがりきる	*vi*. pull a sour face

374

若 ⑧ 一 ㅗ 艹 艹 艻 芏 若 若

音	若	ジャク （ニャク）	young
熟	若年	ジャクネン	youth
	若干	ジャッカン	some; a few
訓	若い	わかい	young; immature; green
	若草	わかくさ	green/young grass
	若気	わかゲ	youthful impatience
	若様	わかさま	prince
	若衆	わかシュウ	young person
	若造	わかゾウ	stripling
	若作り	わかづくり	making oneself up to look young; mutton dressed up as lamb
	若手	わかて	young person
	若向き	わかむき	suitable for younger people
	若者	わかもの	young man/people; youth
	若し	もし	if; in case of; suppose
	若しくは	もしくは	or; either

375

草 ⑨ 一 ㅗ 艹 艹 芍 苎 苩 草 草

音	草	ソウ	grass; small plants; original; draft; cursive handwriting
熟	草案	ソウアン	(rough) draft; rough copy
	草原	ソウゲン	grassy plain; grass land
	草書	ソウショ	cursive form of a Chinese character
	草食	ソウショク	herbivorous
	草々	ソウソウ	In haste (closing words of a letter)
	草創	ソウソウ	inauguration; inception; beginning of construction of a temple or shrine
	草木	ソウモク	plants and trees; vegetation
訓	草	くさ	grass; small plants
	草分け	くさわけ	early settler; pioneer

376

一 十 サ 艾 芝 苎 芩 苓 茶 茶 ⑨

音	茶	チャ	tea plant; tea; light brown
		サ	tea
熟	茶会	サカイ / チャカイ	gathering for tea ceremony
	茶道	サドウ	tea ceremony
	茶飯事	サハンジ	everyday affair
	茶話会	サワカイ	tea party
	茶色	チャいろ	brown
	茶器	チャキ	tea ceremony paraphernalia
	茶室	チャシツ	tea arbor; tea ceremony room
	茶所	チャどころ	tea-growing district; tea-producing center
	茶の間	チャのま	living/sitting room
	茶番	チャバン	tea maker; farce
	茶目	チャめ	playful

377

一 十 サ 艹 艹 芏 芐 芐 荷 荷 荷 ⑩

音	荷	カ	load; burden; cargo
熟	荷担	カタン	help; assistance; support; aid —*vi.* help; assist; support; aid
訓	荷	に	load; burden
	荷札	にふだ	luggage tag
	荷物	にモツ	load; burden; luggage; baggage

378

一 十 サ 艹 艹 荳 荳 荳 荳 荳 菜 ⑪

音	菜	サイ	vegetables; greens
熟	菜園	サイエン	vegetable/kitchen garden
	菜根	サイコン	vegetable roots; simple meal
	菜食	サイショク	vegetable diet; vegetarian meal —*vi.* live on vegetables; follow a vegetarian diet
	菜食主義者	サイショク シュギシャ	vegetarian
訓	菜	な	vegetables; greens

3

| 菜種 | なたね | rapeseed |
| 菜の花 | なのはな | rape blossoms |

379

著 ⑪　一 ナ ナ 世 世 萝 茅 茅 著 著 著

音	著	チョ	work; written by; author; remarkable
熟	著作	チョサク	literary work; writing; authorship —*v.* write (a novel, etc.)
	著作権	チョサクケン	copyright; literary property
	著作者	チョサクシャ	author; writer
	著者	チョシャ	author; writer
	著述	チョジュツ	writing books; book; literary work —*v.* write a book
	著書	チョショ	literary work; book
	著名	チョメイ	prominence; eminence; distinction; celebrity
	著明	チョメイ	renowned; famous
訓	著す	あらわす	*vt.* write; publish
	著しい	いちじるしい	remarkable; distinguished; striking

380

葉 ⑫　一 ナ ナ 世 世 芏 苹 茟 葉 莘 葉 葉 葉

音	葉	ヨウ	leaf; (counter for flat, thin objects)
熟	葉脈	ヨウミャク	vein (of a leaf)
	葉緑素	ヨウリョクソ	chlorophyl
訓	葉	は	leaf
	葉書	はがき	postcard
	葉末	はずえ	leaf tip
	葉月	はづき	eighth lunar month
	葉巻	はまき	cigar

381

落 ⑫　一 ナ ナ 世 サ 芢 芝 茨 莎 茨 落 落

音	落	ラク	fall; fail; be defeated
熟	落書き	ラクがき	graffiti —*v.* scribble; scrawl; doodle
	落語	ラクゴ	*rakugo* (comic story telling)

口 口 土 士 夂 夕 大 女 子 宀 寸 小 ⺌ ⺍ 尢 尸 山 川 工 已 巾 干 幺 广 廴 弋 弓 彡 彳 艹 辶 阝 ⺍ 忄 扌 氵

200

落差	ラクサ	water head/level; difference in height
落日	ラクジツ	setting sun
落城	ラクジョウ	fall of a castle —*vi.* fall; surender
落成	ラクセイ	completion of construction —*vi.* be completed/finished/ready for occupancy
落成式	ラクセイシキ	building-completion ceremony
落選	ラクセン	defeat in an election; failure to get elected —*vi.* be defeated/unsuccessful in an election
落第	ラクダイ	failure in an examination —*vi.* fail to pass an examination
落着	ラクチャク	settlement —*vi.* come to a settlement; be settled
落丁	ラクチョウ	missing pages (in a book)
落馬	ラクバ	fall from one's horse —*vi.* fall/be thrown off one's horse
落命	ラクメイ	death —*vi.* die; pass away; be killed
落葉	ラクヨウ	fallen leaves —*vi.* shed/cast leaves
落葉樹	ラクヨウジュ	deciduous tree
落陽	ラクヨウ	setting sun
落下	ラッカ	fall; descend; drop —*vi.* fall; descend; drop
落花生	ラッカセイ	peanuts
訓 落ちる	おちる	*vi.* fall; fail
落ち着く	おちつく	calm/settle down
落ち目	おちめ	decline of fortune; adversity
落とす	おとす	*vt.* drop; let fall; lose
落とし穴	おとしあな	pitfall; pit; trap; tricky
落とし子	おとしご	illegitimate child
落とし物	おとしもの	lost article; article accidentally dropped

382

一 艹 艹 艿 芽 苂 苹 莢 蒸 蒸 蒸 蒸 ⑬

音 蒸	ジョウ	vapor
熟 蒸気	ジョウキ	steam; vapor
蒸気機関	ジョウキキカン	steam engine
蒸発	ジョウハツ	evaporation; vaporization —*vi.* evaporate; vaporize
蒸留	ジョウリュウ	distillation —*v.* distill
蒸留酒	ジョウリュウシュ	distilled/hard liquor
訓 蒸す	むす	*v.* steam; be sultry; be hot and humid
蒸し暑い	むしあつい	muggy; sultry; hot and humid
蒸し焼き	むしやき	baking; roasting

| 蒸らす | むらす | **vt**. steam |
| 蒸れる | むれる | **vi**. be steamed/stuffy; get sticky |

383

蔵 ⑮　　サ ナ 广 疒 芹 芹 芹 芦 萨 茊 蔵 蔵 蔵

音	蔵	ゾウ	warehouse; storehouse; repository
熟	蔵書	ゾウショ	private library; book collection
訓	蔵	くら	warehouse

384

薬 ⑯　　 サ サ サ ヤ 甘 甘 昔 消 淋 漱 蒅 薬 薬

音	薬	ヤク	medicine; chemical
熟	薬学	ヤクガク	pharmacology
	薬草	ヤクソウ	medicinal herbs
	薬品	ヤクヒン	drugs; chemicals
	薬方	ヤクホウ	prescription
	薬味	ヤクミ	spices; seasoning
	薬用	ヤクヨウ	medicinal
	薬局	ヤッキョク	pharmacy; chemist's shop
	薬効	ヤッコウ	effect of medicine
訓	薬	くすり	medicine; drugs; chemicals
	薬屋	くすりや	drugstore; chemist's shop
	薬指	くすりゆび	ring/fourth finger

3 辶　しんにょう　road

385

辺 ⑤　　フ 刀 刀 辺 辺

音	辺	ヘン	edge; boundary; border; vicinity; neighborhood; surrounding area
熟	辺境	ヘンキョウ	remote frontier; border country
	辺地	ヘンチ	remote place; out-of-the-way location
	辺土	ヘンド	place long way away from the city; remote region

訓	辺り	あたり	neighborhood; surrounding area; vicinity
	辺	べ	neighborhood; surrounding area; vicinity

386

近 ⑦　　ノ　ノ　┌　斤　斤　近　近

音	近	キン	near; approach; recent; close
熟	近刊	キンカン	recent publication/issue
	近眼	キンガン	nearsightedness; myopia
	近々	キンキン	shortly; before long
	近郊	キンコウ	suburbs; outskirts
	近視	キンシ	nearsightedness; myopia
	近日	キンジツ	soon; shortly; in a few days
	近所	キンジョ	neighborhood; vicinity
	近親	キンシン	close relation
	近世	キンセイ	modern/recent times
	近接	キンセツ	approach; contiguity —*vi.* approach; be contiguous
	近代	キンダイ	the modern age
	近代化	キンダイカ	modernization
	近代的	キンダイテキ	modern
	近年	キンネン	recent years
	近辺	キンペン	neighborhood; vicinity
訓	近い	ちかい	close; nearby
	近々	ちかぢか	before long
	近づく	ちかづく	*vi.* come/go near; approach
	近道	ちかみち	short cut

387

返 ⑦　　一　厂　反　反　返　返　返

音	返	ヘン	return
熟	返事	ヘンジ	answer; reply; response —*vi.* answer; reply; respond
	返書	ヘンショ	letter of reply
	返上	ヘンジョウ	returning; sending back —*v.* return; send back; give back
	返信	ヘンシン	letter of reply
	返送	ヘンソウ	sending back; returning —*v.* send back; return
	返電	ヘンデン	telegram in reply

口
口
土
士
夂
夕
大
女
子
宀
寸
小
㣺
⺍
尢
尸
山
川
工
己
巾
干
幺
广
廴
弋
弓
彐
彡
彳
艹
⻌
阝
阝
⺍
扌
氵
犭

返答	ヘントウ	answer; reply; response —*vi.* answer; reply; respond
返本	ヘンポン	returning unsold books to the publisher; returns —*v.* return unsold books to the publisher
返礼	ヘンレイ	return present; giving a present in return for a previously received gift —*vi.* make a gift in return for a previous gift/favor

訓

返す	かえす	*vt.* return; give/send/bring back
返す返す	かえすがえす	repeat; do over and over again
返り討ち	かえりうち	die while trying to kill an enemy
返る	かえる	*vi.* return; be given/sent back; come back

388

述 ⑧ 一 十 オ 才 木 朮 㐱 述 述

音	述	ジュツ	state; mention; say
熟	述懐	ジュッカイ	recollection; expression (of one's thoughts); relation —*v.* express one's thoughts; relate; reminisce
	述語	ジュツゴ	*gram.* predicate
訓	述べる	のべる	*vt.* state; describe; mention

389

逆 ⑨ 丶 丷 䒑 芏 屰 㳀 逆 逆

音	逆	ギャク	opposite; reverse
熟	逆効果	ギャクコウカ (ギャッコウカ)	adverse reaction; boomerang effect
	逆光	ギャクコウ	against the light
	逆算	ギャクサン	inverse operation —*v.* operate inversely
	逆上	ギャクジョウ	dizziness; vertigo; frenzy; madness —*vi.* be dizzy; suffer from vertigo; go mad
	逆説	ギャクセツ	paradox
	逆手	ギャクテ	dirty trick; backhander; using an opponent's strength against him
	逆転	ギャクテン	reversal; turnabout —*v.* reverse positions; turn about
	逆風	ギャクフウ	headwind; adverse wind
	逆用	ギャクヨウ	reverse use —*v.* use in an opposite way
	逆流	ギャクリュウ	countercurrent; counterflow —*vi.* flow against the current
	逆境	ギャッキョウ	adversity; adverse circumstances
	逆行	ギャッコウ	retrogression; retrogradation —*vi.* retrogress

訓	逆	さか	inverse; upside down
	逆さま	さかさま	inverse; inverted; upside down; topsy-turvy
	逆夢	さかゆめ	dreaming the opposite of reality
	逆らう	さからう	**vi.** oppose; go against; act contrary to

390

送 ⑨ 　 丶　ソ　ソ　ゝ　关　关　关　送　送

音	送	ソウ	send
熟	送球	ソウキュウ	passing/throwing a ball —**vi.** pass/throw a ball
	送金	ソウキン	remittance —**vi.** send a remittance/money
	送検	ソウケン	being sent to the procurator's office —**v.** send to the procurator's office
	送信	ソウシン	(radio/wireless) transmission —**v.** transmit
	送電	ソウデン	power transmission —**v.** transmit power
	送付	ソウフ	sending; forwarding —**v.** send; forward; remit
	送別	ソウベツ	farewell; send off —**v.** see someone off; say farewell
	送料	ソウリョウ	postage; shipping charges
	送話器	ソウワキ	transmitter (of sound)
訓	送る	おくる	**vt.** send
	送り仮名	おくりがな	inflectional *kana* ending

391

退 ⑨ 　 フ　ヨ　ヨ　艮　艮　艮　艮　退　退

音	退	タイ	retreat; recede; withdraw; expel; drive away; refuse
熟	退位	タイイ	abdication —**vi.** abdicate
	退院	タイイン	leaving hospital; discharge from hospital —**vi.** be discharged from hospital
	退化	タイカ	degeneration; degradation; regression —**vi.** degenerate; degrade; retrograde
	退学	タイガク	leaving school/college; expulsion —**vi.** leave school; withdraw from college; be expelled
	退去	タイキョ	leaving; quitting; withdrawl; evacuation —**v.** leave; quit; withdraw; evacuate
	退校	タイコウ	dismissal/expulsion from school —**vi.** give up school; be expelled
	退散	タイサン	dispersion; melting —**vi.** disperse; break up; melt
	退治	タイジ	subdual; subjugation; elimination; crusade —**v.** subdue; subjugate; suppress; eliminate

口口土士夂夕大女子宀寸小⺌尢尸山川工己巾干幺广廴弋弓彡彳艹⻌阝广忄扌犭

退社	タイシャ	retirement from a company; leaving the office —*vi*. retire; leave the office
退出	タイシュツ	leaving; withdrawal —*vi*. leave; withdraw
退場	タイジョウ	exit; leaving; walk out —*vi*. leave; go away; make one's exit; walk out
退席	タイセキ	leaving one's seat; retirement; withdrawal —*vi*. leave one's seat; retire; withdraw
退任	タイニン	retirement —*v*. retire

訓 退く しりぞく *vi*. retreat; recede; withdraw; retire
退ける しりぞける *vt*. drive; send away; repel; expel; retire; refuse

392

追 ⑨ 　 ′ ⺁ ⼾ ⼾ 𠂤 𠂤 ⺫ 㠯 追 追

音 追 ツイ run/hunt after

熟 追加 ツイカ addition; addendum; appendix; supplement —*v*. add; append; supplement
追求 ツイキュウ pursuit; chase; search —*v*. pursue; chase; follow
追究 ツイキュウ close inquiry; thorough investigation —*v*. inquire into; investigate closely; cross-examine
追従 ツイジュウ following; servility —*vi*. follow; be servile; kowtow
追従 ツイショウ flattery; adulation; sycophancy —*vi*. flatter; adulate
追想 ツイソウ remembrance; recollection; retrospection; reminiscence —*v*. remember; recollect; retrospect; reminisce
追認 ツイニン ratification; confirmation —*v*. ratify; confirm
追放 ツイホウ banishment; eviction; exile; deportation; purge —*v*. banish; exile; evict; deport; purge

訓 追う おう *vt*. drive away; pursue; chase; follow
追い返す おいかえす *vt*. repel; repulse; beat off; drive back
追い出す おいだす *vt*. expel; turn out; throw out; discharge; dismiss

393

迷 ⑨ 　 ′ ⼆ ⼆ 半 米 米 ⺶ 迷 迷

音 迷 メイ get lost; go astray; be perplexed

熟 迷宮 メイキュウ labyrinth; maze
迷信 メイシン superstition
迷想 メイソウ illusion; fallacy

迷路	メイロ	labyrinth; maze
訓 迷う	まよう	*vi.* hesitate; lose one's way
迷い	まよい	perplexity; doubt; delusion
迷わせる	まよわせる	*vt.* perplex; lead astray; charm; seduce

394

造 ⑩   ノ 亠 丿 生 牛 告 告 告 造 造

音 造	ゾウ	build; make; produce
熟 造営	ゾウエイ	erection; building; construction —*v.* erect; build; construct
造花	ゾウカ	artificial flowers
造形	ゾウケイ	molding; modeling —*v.* mold; model
造作	ゾウサ	trouble; difficulty
造作	ゾウサク	fixtures; facial features
造成	ゾウセイ	construction —*v.* construct; build
造船	ゾウセン	shipbuilding —*v.* build/construct a ship
造林	ゾウリン	forestation
訓 造る	つくる	*vt.* make; build; produce

395

速 ⑩   一 厂 戸 日 市 束 束 束 速 速

音 速	ソク	fast
熟 速成	ソクセイ	intensive training; short course —*v.* train quickly; give intense training
速達	ソクタツ	express/special delivery
速度	ソクド	speed; velocity
速報	ソクホウ	bulletin; news flash —*v.* report promptly; announce quickly
速力	ソクリョク	speed; velocity
速記	ソッキ	shorthand —*v.* write/take down in shorthand
速効	ソッコウ	quick effect
訓 速い	はやい	fast
速める	はやめる	*vt.* quicken; accelerate
速やか	すみやか	prompt; speedy

通 ⑩ 　 ⌐ マ ア 冎 冎 甬 甬 涌 涌 通

口口土士夊夕大女子宀寸小⺌⺍尢尸山川工己巾干幺广夂弋弓彡彳⺾●⻌阝⺣忄扌犭氵

音	通	ツウ（ツ）	pass; go to and from; inform; know thoroughly
熟	通じる	ツウじる	*vi.* pass; run; be open to traffic; transmit; be understood
	通じて	ツウじて	through; throughout; all over; in total; together with
	通院	ツウイン	regular hospital visits —*vi.* go to hospital regulary
	通運	ツウウン	transportation; forwarding; express
	通過	ツウカ	passage; passing; pass; transit; carriage —*vi.* pass; pass/go through
	通学	ツウガク	attending school —*vi.* attend school
	通気	ツウキ	ventillation; draft; airing; aeration
	通勤	ツウキン	commuting; going to work —*vi.* commute; go to work
	通行	ツウコウ	traffic; passing; passage; transit —*vi.* pass; go past/through
	通告	ツウコク	notification; notice; announcement; warning —*v.* notify; give notice; announce; warn
	通算	ツウサン	sum total; aggregate; summing-up —*v.* total; include; aggregate; sum up
	通常	ツウジョウ	usually; normally; generally
	通信	ツウシン	correspondence; communication; intelligence; dispatch; news —*vi.* correspond; communicate
	通説	ツウセツ	common opinion; popular view
	通達	ツウタツ	notification; communication; circular notice —*v.* notify; communicate
	通知	ツウチ	notice; notification; communication; information; advice —*v.* notify; communicate; inform; advise
	通帳	ツウチョウ	bankbook; passbook
	通読	ツウドク	reading (a book) from cover to cover —*v.* read from cover to cover
	通報	ツウホウ	report; dispatch; advice; bulletin; information —*vi.* report; notify; advise
	通訳	ツウヤク	interpretation; interpreter —*v.* interpret; act as an interpreter
	通用	ツウヨウ	common/popular use; circulation; currency —*vi.* be in common use; circulate; run current
	通例	ツウレイ	usually; commonly; generally; as a rule
	通路	ツウロ	path; passageway
	通話	ツウワ	telephone call/conversation

通夜	ツヤ	wake; vigil
訓 通う	かよう	*vi.* go to and from; frequent; attend (school, lessons, etc.)
通る	とおる	*vi.* go along; pass by
通す	とおす	*vt.* pass through; pierce; admit; let a person pass
通り	とおり	road; street; passage; understanding; way; manner
通り過ぎる	とおりすぎる	*vi.* go past/by

397

連 ⑩　一　厂　万　盲　盲　亘　車　車　連　連

音 連	レン	company; relation
熟 連記	レンキ	list —*v.* list up; make a list
連休	レンキュウ	consecutive holidays
連係	レンケイ	connection; liaison; contact
連結	レンケツ	connection; coupling; consolidated —*v.* connect; couple; consolidate
連呼	レンコ	repeated calls/shouts —*v.* call/shout repeatedly
連行	レンコウ	escorting/accompanying (a criminal, etc.) —*v.* escort/accompany (a criminal etc.)
連合	レンゴウ	union; league; federation —*v.* be in alliance/league with
連座	レンザ	involvement; accompanying —*vi.* be involved in; accompany
連作	レンサク	repeated cultivation of the same crop; linked short stories/*tanka* —*v.* plant (a field) with same crop every year
連山	レンザン	mountain range
連日	レンジツ	day after day; every day
連勝	レンショウ	consecutive victories; winning streak —*vi.* keep on winning; be on a winning streak
連戦	レンセン	series of battles; battle after battle
連想	レンソウ	association of ideas —*v.* associate (A with B); be reminded of
連続	レンゾク	continuation; consecutive; in a row —*v.* continue; be consecutive
連打	レンダ	repeated blows —*v.* hit back; offer repeated blows/strikes
連帯	レンタイ	solidarity
連中	レンチュウ	particular group of people; they; crowd
連動	レンドウ	gears; linkage; drive —*vi.* link; drive
連破	レンパ	successive wins; winning streak

口
口
土
士
攵
夕
大
女
子
宀
寸
小
丷
尢
尸
山
川
工
己
巾
干
幺
广
廴
弓
彡
彳
艹
辶
阝
阝
忄
扌
氵
犭

209

口口土士夊夕大女子宀寸小⺌⺍尢尸山川工己巾干幺广廴廾弓彡彳艹辶阝阝⺌艹扌犭氵

—*v.* win successively; keep on winning; have a winning streak

連敗	レンパイ	successive defeats; losing streak —*vi.* keep on losing; suffer a losing streak
連発	レンパツ	rapid machine-gun fire —*v.* fire shots rapidly one after another
連名	レンメイ	joint signature
連盟	レンメイ	league; federation; union
連綿	レンメン	unbroken; consecutive
連夜	レンヤ	night after night; nightly
連立	レンリツ	alliance; coalition —*v.* make an alliance/coalition

訓

連なる	つらなる	*vi.* stand in a row
連ねる	つらねる	*vt.* put in a row
連れる	つれる	*v.* take along; accompany
連れ	つれ	companion
連れ子	つれこ	child by a previous marriage

398

週 ⑪   丿 几 冂 月 門 用 用 周 周 冎 週 週

音 週　シュウ　week

熟

週間	シュウカン	week
週刊	シュウカン	weekly publication
週刊誌	シュウカンシ	weekly magazine
週休	シュウキュウ	weekly holiday
週給	シュウキュウ	weekly pay/salary
週日	シュウジツ	weekdays (mon-sat)
週番	シュウバン	week-long duty
週末	シュウマツ	weekend

399

進 ⑪   丿 亻 彳 彳 仸 仹 隹 隹 進 進

音 進　シン　advance

熟

進化	シンカ	evolution —*vi.* evolve; develop
進学	シンガク	educational progress; development —*vi.* go on to the next stage of one's education
進学志望者	シンガク シボウシャ	applicants to high school or college

進学率	シンガクリツ	ratio of students who go on to higher education
進級	シンキュウ	promotion —*vi.* be promoted
進軍	シングン	advance; march; marching —*vi.* advance; march on
進言	シンゲン	advice; counsel; proposal —*v.* advise; counsel; make a proposal
進行	シンコウ	advance; progress —*vi.* move forward; advance; make progress
進航	シンコウ	progress of a boat or ship
進取	シンシュ	enterprising; enterprise
進出	シンシュツ	advance —*vi.* advance; make inroads into; go into
進退	シンタイ	advance or retreat; movement; behavior
進展	シンテン	development; progress —*vi.* develop; progress
進度	シンド	progress; degree of progress
進入	シンニュウ	entry; approach —*vi.* march; make their way; enter; approach
進歩	シンポ	progress; advance; improvement —*vi.* make progress; advance; improve
進歩的	シンポテキ	progressive; advanced
進物	シンモツ	gift
進路	シンロ	course; route; way
訓 進む	すすむ	*vi.* advance; progress; travel; go forward *vt.* lead; move; go ahead
進める	すすめる	*vt.* lead; move; advance; proceed; go ahead; be promoted

400

運 ⑫   ' 一 冖 冖 冖 月 月 亘 軍 軍 運 運

音 運	ウン	carry; ship; transport; fate; luck; destiny
熟 運営	ウンエイ	management; operation; administration —*v.* manage; operate; administer
運河	ウンガ	canal
運休	ウンキュウ	suspension (of a scheduled train, flight, etc.) —*v.* suspend (a train, flight) etc.
運行	ウンコウ	revolution; movement; motion —*vi.* revolve; orbit; move around
運航	ウンコウ	shipping; airline service —*vi.* operate; run; ply
運勢	ウンセイ	one's stars; fortune; luck
運送	ウンソウ	transportation; conveyance; shipping; transporting; traffic —*v.* transport; convey; carry; forward; ship
運賃	ウンチン	freight; shipping charge; tarrif; passenger fare; (goods) rate

口 口 土 士 夂 夕 大 女 子 宀 寸 小 ⺌ ⺌ 尢 尸 山 川 工 己 巾 干 幺 广 廴 弋 弓 彑 彳 艹 辶 阝 阝 ⺌ 忄 扌 犭 氵

211

3

口 囗 土 士 夂 夕 大 女 子 宀 寸 小 ⺌ ⺍ 尢 尸 山 川 工 己 巾 干 幺 广 廴 弋 弓 彡 彳 艹 ●辶 阝 阝 ⺾ 忄 扌 犭 氵

	運転	ウンテン	driving; operation —*v*. drive; operate
	運転手	ウンテンシュ	driver
	運動	ウンドウ	motion; exercise; canvassing; campaign —*vi*. move; exercise; canvass; campaign
	運命	ウンメイ	destiny; fate; luck; fortune; the inevitable
	運輸	ウンユ	transport; traffic
訓	運ぶ	はこぶ	*vt*. carry; ship; progress

401

過 ⑫

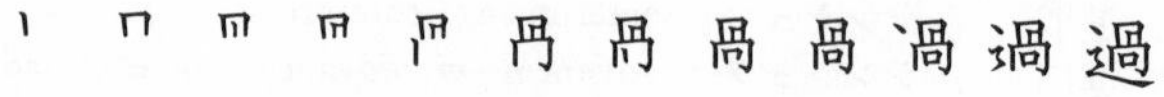

音	過	カ	pass; spend; error; excessive
熟	過激	カゲキ	extreme/radical (thought or action)
	過去	カコ	the past; one's past life ***gram***. past tense
	過言	カゴン	saying too much; exaggeration
	過失	カシツ	unintentional mistake; error; negligence
	過日	カジツ	the other day; some days ago
	過重	カジュウ	too great a load; overload
	過小	カショウ	too small
	過少	カショウ	too few/little
	過信	カシン	overconfidence —*v*. have too much confidence
	過多	カタ	excess; surplus; too much/many
	過大	カダイ	too big; excessive
	過程	カテイ	process; course
	過度	カド	beyond a reasonable limit; excess
	過熱	カネツ	overheating —*v*. overheat
	過半数	カハンスウ	majority
	過不足	カフソク	excess or deficiency
	過分	カブン	generous; excessive; unworthy
	過密	カミツ	overcrowded; overpopulated
	過労	カロウ	overwork; overexertion
訓	過ぎる	すぎる	*vi*. pass; exceed
	過ごす	すごす	*vt*. pass/spend (time); live; stay
	過ち	あやまち	mistake; fault; error
	過つ	あやまつ	*vt*. err; make a mistake

402

達 ⑫

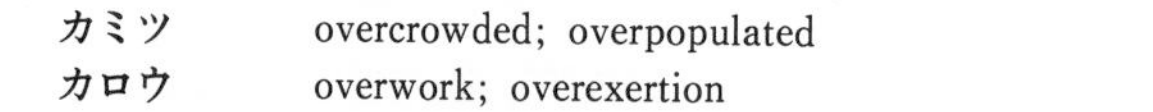

音	達	タツ	lead; deliver; announcement

熟	達する	タッする	v. reach; attain; achieve
	達観	タッカン	farsighted-view; philosophic view —v. take a farsighted view
	達者	タッシャ	healthy; well; strong; expert; proficient; clever
	達人	タツジン	expert; master
	達成	タッセイ	attainment; achievement; accomplishment —v. achieve; attain; accomplish
	達筆	タッピツ	good handwriting/writing style

403

道 ⑫

、 ゛ ヽ ゛ 产 首 首 首 首 首 道 道

音	道	ドウ (トウ)	road; reason; method; district; way
熟	道義	ドウギ	morality; morals; moral principles
	道具	ドウグ	instrument; appliance; tool; furniture
	道具箱	ドウグばこ	tool box
	道化	ドウケ	buffoonery; tomfoolery
	道化師	ドウケシ	clown
	道場	ドウジョウ	drill hall for martial arts
	道中	ドウチュウ	on a journey; travel on a tour
	道程	ドウテイ	distance; journey
	道徳	ドウトク	morality
	道破	ドウハ	declaration; strong statement —v. declare; state strongly
	道標	ドウヒョウ (みちしるべ)	guidepost; signpost
	道楽	ドウラク	hobby; pastime; dissipation; debauchery
	道楽者	ドウラクもの	playboy
	道理	ドウリ	reason; right; justice; truth
	道路	ドウロ	road; way; street
	道路標識	ドウロヒョウシキ	road sign
訓	道	みち	road; way; street; journey; distance; duty; morality
	道案内	みちアンナイ	guidance; guide
	道草を食う	みちくさをくう	vi. loiter/tarry on the way —fig. lose/waste time
	道順	みちじゅん	route; itinerary

口 口 土 士 夂 夕 大 女 子 宀 寸 小 ⺌ ⺌ 尢 尸 山 川 工 己 巾 干 幺 广 廴 弓 彐 彳 ⺾ ⻌ ⻏ ⺍ 忄 扌 氵

口口土士夕夕大女子宀寸小⺌⺍尢尸山川工已巾干幺广廴弋弓彡彳⺌⻌⻏⻏⺾忄扌氵

404

遊 ⑫

丶 ユ ⺈ ㄏ ㄈ 疒 疒 挤 斿 斿 游 遊

音	遊	ユウ (ユ)	play; tour; enjoy; oneself; be idle
熟	遊泳	ユウエイ	swimming
	遊園地	ユウエンチ	amusement park; recreation area; playground
	遊学	ユウガク	studying away from home —v. study away from home
	遊休	ユウキュウ	idle; unused
	遊星	ユウセイ	planet
	遊説	ユウゼイ	canvassing; campaign —vi. canvass; campaign
	遊牧民	ユウボクミン	nomads
	遊覧	ユウラン	sightseeing; excursion —vi. go sightseeing; go on an excursion
	遊山	ユサン	picnic/outing/excursion to the mountains
訓	遊ぶ	あそぶ	vi. play; enjoy oneself; be idle
	遊び	あそび	play; game; sport; amusement; recreation
	遊ばせる	あそばせる	amuse; let play; leave something as it is

405

遠 ⑬

一 十 土 ⼟ 吉 吉 吉 吉 専 亨 袁 遠 遠

音	遠	エン (オン)	distant; far; profound; perspective / far; eternity
熟	遠因	エンイン	remote cause; underlying factor; indirect cause
	遠泳	エンエイ	long-distance swim
	遠海	エンカイ	the open sea; the deep
	遠近	エンキン	far and near; distance
	遠景	エンケイ	distant view
	遠視	エンシ	farsightedness; hyperopia
	遠日点	エンジツテン	aphelion
	遠心力	エンシンリョク	centrifugal force
	遠足	エンソク	excursion; day-trip; school trip
	遠大	エンダイ	having wide range or effect; far-reaching
	遠望	エンボウ	distant view; perspective —v. view from a distance
	遠方	エンポウ	faraway
	遠洋	エンヨウ	the open sea; the deep
	遠来	エンライ	coming from afar

遠路	エンロ	long way; roundabout way
訓 遠浅	とおあさ	shallow for a considerable distance; shoal
遠い	とおい	far; remote; distant
遠回し	とおまわし	indirect; roundabout; vague
遠回り	とおまわり	detour

406 適 ⑭

丶 亠 产 产 产 商 商 商 商 滴 適

音 適	テキ	suit
熟 適する	テキする	*vi.* fit; suit; agree; be adapted/qualified
適応	テキオウ	adaptation; accommodation; conformity —*v.* be adaptable; be suitable/fitted to
適応性	テキオウセイ	adaptability; flexibility
適格	テキカク	competency
適合	テキゴウ	conformity; agreement; compatibility —*v.* conform; suit; fit; be compatible
適材適所	テキザイテキショ	right man in the right place
適時	テキジ	timely; opportune
適正	テキセイ	proper; appropriate; right; just
適正化	テキセイカ	rationalization
適性	テキセイ	aptitude
適性検査	テキセイケンサ	aptitude test —*v.* give an aptitude test
適切	テキセツ	pertinent; fit; suitable; adequate; proper; relevent
適中	テキチュウ	hit
適度	テキド	moderation; proper degree; temperance; measure
適当	テキトウ	suitable; fit; proper; adequate
適任	テキニン	fitness; suitability; competence
適否	テキヒ	propriety; suitability; fitness; aptitude
適法	テキホウ	legality; lawfulness
適役	テキヤク	fit post/role
適用	テキヨウ	application —*v.* apply
適量	テキリョウ	proper quantity/dose; dosage
適例	テキレイ	good example

407 遺 ⑮

丶 口 口 虫 虫 串 書 書 書 貴 遺 遺

音 遺	イ (ユイ)	leave; abandon

口口土士夂夕大女子宀寸小䒑⺌尢尸山川工己巾干幺广廴弋弓彡彳⺾●辶阝⻏⺌扌攵氵

熟	遺業	イギョウ	work left unfinished by the deceased; unfinished work
	遺訓	イクン	maxims left by the dead
	遺骨	イコツ	(one's) ashes; skeletal remains
	遺作	イサク	posthumous work
	遺産	イサン	inheritance; legacy; estate; bequest
	遺志	イシ	one's dying wish; unfulfilled wish of a dying person
	遺児	イジ	child of the deceased; orphaned child
	遺失	イシツ	loss —*v.* lose; leave behind
	遺失物	イシツブツ	lost article/property
	遺書	イショ	note left behind by a dead person; suicide note
	遺族	イゾク	bereaved family; family of the deceased; survivors
	遺体	イタイ	dead body; corpse; remains
	遺伝	イデン	heredity; hereditary transmission; genetic inheritance —*vi.* be inherited; be transmitted; be handed down
	遺伝子	イデンシ	gene
	遺品	イヒン	article left by the departed
	遺物	イブツ	relic; remains; antiquity; memento
	遺言	ユイゴン	(one's) will; will and testament; one's spoken will and testament —*v.* leave/make a will

408

⑮ ㇀ ㇆ 甲 巴巴 巴巴 巴巴 巽巽 巽巽 巽巽 巽選 選

音	選	セン	choose; select
熟	選外	センガイ	left out; not chosen
	選挙	センキョ	election —*v.* elect
	選挙権	センキョケン	right to vote; suffrage
	選考	センコウ	selection; screening —*v.* select; screen
	選者	センジャ	selector; judge
	選手	センシュ	sports player; athlete
	選手権	センシュケン	championship title
	選集	センシュウ	selection; anthology
	選出	センシュツ	election; select —*v.* elect; select; pick out
	選定	センテイ	selection; choice —*v.* select; choose
	選別	センベツ	selection; grading; sorting —*v.* select; grade; sort
	選良	センリョウ	the elite; member of a parliament
訓	選ぶ	えらぶ	*vt.* choose; select

3 阝 こざとへん left village

409

防 ⑦

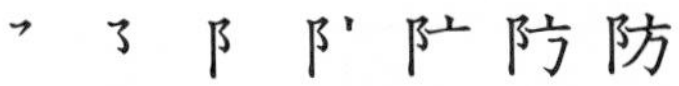

音	防	ボウ	defend; protect; prevent; (prefix) anti-; -proof; -resistant
熟	防衛	ボウエイ	defense —*v*. defend
	防音	ボウオン	soundproof —*vi*. be soundproof
	防火	ボウカ	fire prevention; fire fighting; fireproof
	防寒	ボウカン	protection against the cold
	防寒服	ボウカンフク	winter/arctic clothing
	防具	ボウグ	armor; protective gear
	防空	ボウクウ	air defense
	防護	ボウゴ	protection; custody —*v*. protect (against injury)
	防災	ボウサイ	prevention of disaster
	防止	ボウシ	prevention —*v*. prevent
	防縮	ボウシュク	shrinkage prevention —*vi*. prevent shrinkage
	防水	ボウスイ	waterproof; watertight —*v*. make waterproof/watertight
	防雪	ボウセツ	snow protection
	防雪林	ボウセツリン	snowbreak (forest)
	防戦	ボウセン	defensive battle/fight —*vi*. fight a defensive battle
	防虫	ボウチュウ	insect repellent
	防毒	ボウドク	gasproof
	防犯	ボウハン	crime prevention
	防備	ボウビ	defensive preparations —*v*. make preparations to defend/protect (against an enemy attack)
	防風	ボウフウ	wind protection/shelter
	防風林	ボウフウリン	windbreak (forest)
訓	防ぐ	ふせぐ	***vt***. defend; prevent; protect (from)

410

限 ⑨

音	限	ゲン	limit; boundary; restriction
熟	限界	ゲンカイ	limit; boundary; margin
	限外	ゲンガイ	beyond the limit; excessive

口口土士夂夕大女子宀寸小⺌⺍尢尸山川工己巾干幺广廴弋弓彡彳艹⻌阝阝⺆⺍扌犭氵

	限局	ゲンキョク	strict limitation; limit strictly
	限定	ゲンテイ	limitation; restriction —v. limit; restrict
	限度	ゲンド	limit
訓	限る	かぎる	vt. restrict; limit
	限り	かぎり	limits; restriction

411 院 ⑩

＇ ㇆ ㇘ ㇘' ㇘' ㇘⺁ ㇘宀 ㇘宀 ㇘宀 院

音	院	イン	public place or building (such as hospital or Diet)
熟	院議	インギ	parliamentary/Diet decision
	院長	インチョウ	the director (of a hospital)

412 降 ⑩

＇ ㇆ ㇘ ㇘' ㇘⺁ ㇘⺁ 降 降 降 降

音	降	コウ	fall; descend; alight; drop; surrender
熟	降雨	コウウ	rainfall; precipitation
	降下	コウカ	descent; falling; dropping; fall; landing —vi. descend; fall; drop; land
	降参	コウサン	surrender; submission; capitulation —vi. surrender; submit; capitulate
	降車	コウシャ	alighting; getting off —vi. alight; get off/down
	降水量	コウスイリョウ	amount of precipitation/rainfall
	降雪	コウセツ	snowfall; snow
	降誕	コウタン	nativity; birth; advent; incarnation —vi. be born; be incarnated; see the light
訓	降りる	おりる	vi. come/get down; descend; alight; leave; quit
	降ろす	おろす	vt. take down; lower; bring down; drop; have an abortion; grate
	降る	ふる	vi. fall; come down; descend; rain; snow

413 除 ⑩

＇ ㇆ ㇘ ㇘' ㇘⺁ 除 除 除 除 除

音	除	ジョ (ジ)	remove; divide
熟	除外	ジョガイ	exception; exclusion —v. exclude; leave out
	除去	ジョキョ	removal; riddance —v. remove; get rid of

除雪	ジョセツ	snow removal —*vi.* clear away the snow
除草	ジョソウ	weeding —*vi.* weed
除幕式	ジョマクシキ	unveiling ceremony
除名	ジョメイ	expulsion —*v.* expel from (association, political party, etc.)
除夜	ジョヤ	New Year's Eve
訓 除く	のぞく	*vt.* remove; exclude; expel; leave/take out

414 陛 ⑩
`⁊ ⻖ ⻖ ⻖⁻ ⻖ヒ ⻖ヒ⁻ ⻖比 陛 陛 陛`

| 音 陛 | ヘイ | stairway in the imperial palace; (honorific word used to describe a monarch) |
| 熟 陛下 | ヘイカ | His/Her/Your Majesty |

415 険 ⑪
`⁊ ⻖ ⻖ ⻖⁻ ⻖⁀ 险 险 険 険 険`

音 険	ケン	steep
熟 険悪	ケンアク	threatening; hostile; cross
訓 険しい	けわしい	steep; stern; sharp

416 陸 ⑪
`⁊ ⻖ ⻖ ⻖⁻ ⻖⁺ 陆 陆 陸 陸 陸`

音 陸	リク	land
熟 陸運	リクウン	land transport
陸軍	リクグン	army
陸上競技	リクジョウキョウギ	field and track events
陸続	リクゾク	in succession; continuously
陸地	リクチ	land
陸路	リクロ	overland route
陸橋	リッキョウ	overpass; viaduct

417 階 ⑫
`⁊ ⻖ ⻖ ⻖⁻ ⻖ヒ ⻖ヒ⁻ ⻖比 ⻖比 階 階 階`

| 音 階 | カイ | stairs; floor; staircase; rank |

219

熟	階下	カイカ	downstairs
	階級	カイキュウ	class
	階上	カイジョウ	upstairs
	階層	カイソウ	class; layer; stratum
	階段	カイダン	stairs

418

隊 ⑫ ' ⻖ 阝 阝 阝 阝 阼 阼 陊 隊 隊 隊

音	隊	タイ	crew; party
熟	隊員	タイイン	crew member
	隊商	タイショウ	caravan
	隊長	タイチョウ	captain; leader; commanding officer
	隊列	タイレツ	file; rank

419

陽 ⑫ ' ⻖ 阝 阝 阝 阝 阳 阳 陽 陽 陽

音	陽	ヨウ	the sun; positive; yang
熟	陽気	ヨウキ	weather; cheerful; gay; happy
	陽極	ヨウキョク	positive pole; anode
	陽光	ヨウコウ	sunlight; sunshine
	陽子	ヨウシ	proton
	陽春	ヨウシュン	warm spring; New Year (of the lunar calendar)
	陽性	ヨウセイ	cheerful; positive
	陽転	ヨウテン	positive reaction (to a medical test) —*vi*. react positively (to a medical test)
	陽暦	ヨウレキ	solar calendar

420

際 ⑭ 阝 阝 阝 阝 阝 阝 隊 隊 際 際 際 際

音	際	サイ	case; associate; mix; limit; occasion
熟	際限	サイゲン	limits; bounds
訓	際	きわ	brink; verge
	際立つ	きわだつ	*vi*. stand out; be conspicuous
	際どい	きわどい	risky; close; narrow; indecent
	際物	きわもの	seasonal goods

421
障 ⑭
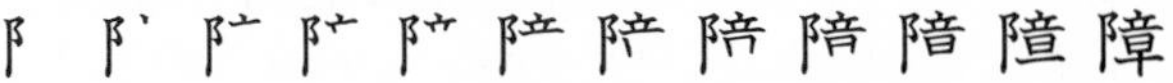

音	障	ショウ	obstacle; hurdle
熟	障害	ショウガイ	obstacle; hindrance; difficulty; handicap; disorder; impediment
	障害者	ショウガイシャ	handicapped person
	障害物	ショウガイブツ	obstacle; hurdle
	障子	ショウジ	*shōji* (paper sliding door)
訓	障る	さわる	***vi.*** interfere; obstruct; be bad for
	障り	さわり	obstacle; obstruction

3 阝 おおざと right village

422
郡 ⑩
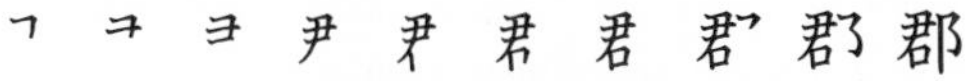

音	郡	グン	territorial division; (suffix) *-gun* (county; district)
熟	郡部	グンブ	rural section; suburban districts; districts classified as *gun*

423
郷 ⑪

音	郷	キョウ ゴウ	town; hometown; country; province
熟	郷土	キョウド	one's hometown/town of birth
	郷土色	キョウドショク	local color
	郷里	キョウリ	one's hometown

424
都 ⑪

音	都	ト	city; Tokyo
		ツ	all

口口土士夂夕大女子宀寸小⺌⺍尢尸山川工己巾干幺广廴弋弓彡彳艹辶阝丬牜犭氵

熟	都合	ツゴウ	arrangements; circumstances
	都度	ツド	every time; each occasion; whenever
	都営	トエイ	metropolitan Tokyo-run (subway)
	都下	トカ	metropolis; capital; Tokyo
	都会	トカイ	city; town
	都市	トシ	city; town; urban area
	都心	トシン	city center
	都内	トナイ	within Tokyo
	都立	トリツ	metropolitan; municipal
訓	都	みやこ	capital; metropolis; seat of government
	都落ち	みやこおち	rustification —*vi.* flee the capital city

425

部⑪　丶 ユ 宀 ヸ 立 产 咅 音 音 剖 部

音	部	ブ	section; department; club; category; (counter for copies of books, etc.)
熟	部員	ブイン	staff; member of a club
	部下	ブカ	subordinate (worker)
	部首	ブシュ	radicals of Chinese characters
	部署	ブショ	one's post/duty/station
	部数	ブスウ	number of copies; circulation
	部族	ブゾク	tribe
	部隊	ブタイ	(military) unit; corps; detachment
	部長	ブチョウ	department head; head of a club
	部分	ブブン	part
	部落	ブラク	village; community
	部類	ブルイ	classification; category

426

郵⑪　一 二 三 垂 垂 垂 垂 垂 郵 郵 郵

音	郵	ユウ	mail; post
熟	郵政	ユウセイ	postal system
	郵税	ユウゼイ	postage; rate of postage
	郵送	ユウソウ	mailing —*v.* mail; post
	郵便	ユウビン	mail; post
	郵便局	ユウビンキョク	post office
	郵便箱	ユウビンばこ	mailbox

3 丷 そいち lining up (artificial radical)

427

並 ⑧ 丶 丷 丷 丷 丷 丷 並 並

音	並	ヘイ	side-by-side; together; ordinary
熟	並行	ヘイコウ	parallel; side-by-side; together —*vi*. line up in a row; occur simultaneously
	並存	ヘイゾン (ヘイソン)	coexistence —*vi*. coexist
	並立	ヘイリツ	standing side-by-side —*vi*. stand side-by-side
	並列	ヘイレツ	parallel (circuit); arranged in a row —*v*. arrange in a row
訓	並	なみ	ordinary; average; regular
	並木	なみき	row of trees on either side of a street
	並外れる	なみはずれる	*vi*. be out of the ordinary
	並ぶ	ならぶ	*vi*. be in a row; rank with; queue up
	並べる	ならべる	*vt*. arrange/place in a row; display; lay out; compare
	並びに	ならびに	both; and; as well as

3 小 see ⇨p.233

3 扌 see ⇨p.241

3 犭 see ⇨p.348

3 氵 see ⇨p.319

4 心 こころ heart 忄 (p.233)

428

心 ④ `、 心 心 心`

音	心	シン	mind; core; heart; soul
熟	心音	シンオン	*med.* heart beat
	心外	シンガイ	regrettable; unexpected; unthinkable
	心眼	シンガン	mind's eye; insight
	心機一転	シンキイッテン	changing one's mind; turning over a new leaf —*v.* change one's mind; turn over a new leaf
	心境	シンキョウ	state of mind; feelings
	心中	シンジュウ	double/lovers' suicide —*vi.* commit suicide together
	心証	シンショウ	firm belief; conviction; impression
	心象	シンショウ	image; mental picture
	心情	シンジョウ	feelings; emotions
	心身	シンシン	body and mind; mentally and physically
	心臓	シンゾウ	*med.* heart
	心臓外科	シンゾウゲカ	open heart surgery
	心中	シンチュウ	at heart; inwardly; feelings
	心痛	シンツウ	worry; concern —*v.* be worried/concerned
	心的	シンテキ	mental; psychological
	心電図	シンデンズ	*med.* electrocardiogram (ECG)
	心配	シンパイ	anxiety; worry; care —*v.* be worried/troubled; worry; care
	心理	シンリ	mentally; mental state; psychology
	心理学	シンリガク	psychology
	心理的	シンリテキ	psychological; mental
	心労	シンロウ	cares; anxieties; worries
訓	心	こころ	mind; heart; feeling; consideration; attention
	心当たり	こころあたり	in mind; could think of
	心有る	こころある	thoughtful; considerate; sensible; sensitive
	心意気	こころイキ	spirit; determination
	心得	こころえ	knowledge; understanding; rules; regulations; directions; instructions
	心得る	こころえる	*vt.* know; understand; regard; think; be aware of
	心配り	こころくばり	consideration; thoughtfulness
	心苦しい	こころぐるしい	feeling sorry/bad about

心して	こころして	determinedly; carefully
心強い	こころづよい	reassuring; encouraging
心残り	こころのこり	regret
心細い	こころぼそい	lonely; helpless; hopeless; discouraging

429 必 ⑤　　丶 ソ 必 必 必

音	必	ヒツ	certain; sure; necessary
熟	必見	ヒッケン	required reading/viewing
	必殺	ヒッサツ	inevitable killing; deadly
	必死	ヒッシ	certain death; desperate; frantic; with all one's might
	必至	ヒッシ	inevitable; desperate; frantic
	必修科目	ヒッシュウカモク	required/obligatory/compulsory subject
	必勝	ヒッショウ	sure victory; desperate to win
	必定	ヒツジョウ	inevitable; unavoidable
	必然	ヒツゼン	inevitability; necessity; certainty
	必然性	ヒツゼンセイ	necessity; inevitability
	必然的	ヒツゼンテキ	inevitable; of necessity; as a matter of course
	必着	ヒッチャク	required arrival time
	必中	ヒッチュウ	always hits the target —*vi*. never fails to hit the target
	必読	ヒツドク	required reading
	必要	ヒツヨウ	necessary; essential
	必要悪	ヒツヨウアク	necessary evil
	必要条件	ヒツヨウ ジョウケン	necessary condition
訓	必ず	かならず	surely; certainly; without fail; certainly

430 応 ⑦　　丶 一 广 广 応 応 応

音	応	オウ	respond; meet; consent
熟	応じる	オウじる	*vi*. respond to; act in accordance with; consent; be suitable
	応急	オウキュウ	emergency
	応接	オウセツ	reception —*vi*. receive/see a guest
	応接間	オウセツま	waiting room; reception
	応戦	オウセン	returning fire; fight back —*vi*. return fire; fight back

心 ⺗ 戈 戸 手 扌 支 攵 文 斗 斤 方 日 曰 月 肉 月 木 欠 止 歹 殳 母 毌 比 毛 氏 气 水 氷 氵 火 灬 父 片 牛 犬 犭 王 礻 耂

心 忄 戈 戸 手 扌 支 攵 文 斗 斤 方 日 曰 月 肉 月 木 欠 止 歹 殳 母 毋 比 毛 氏 气 水 氺 氵 火 灬 父 片 牛 犬 犭 王 衤 耂

応対	オウタイ	reception —*vi*. see one's guests; grant an interview
応答	オウトウ	reply; response; answer —*vi*. reply; respond; answer
応分	オウブン	fitting; suitable; appropriate; reasonable
応用	オウヨウ	application; adaptation; improvement —*v*. apply; adapt; put into practice
訓 応える	こたえる	*vi*. respond to; have effect on

431

志 ⑦ 　一 十 士 士 志 志 志

音 志	シ	will; intention; desire; wish
熟 志願	シガン	wish; desire; ambition —*v*. apply; volunteer; wish; want
志願者	シガンシャ	applicant; candidate
志願兵	シガンヘイ	volunteer soldier
志向	シコウ	intention —*v*. intend
志望	シボウ	wish; desire; ambition —*v*. wish for; desire; aspire
志望者	シボウシャ	applicant; candidate
訓 志	こころざし	will; resolution; aim; purpose; intention; wish; gift; kindness; consideration
志す	こころざす	*vi*. intend; aim; aspire; make up one's mind

432

忘 ⑦ 　、 ㇜ 亡 亡 忘 忘 忘

音 忘	ボウ	forget
熟 忘恩	ボウオン	ingratitude
忘我	ボウガ	self-oblivion; trance; ecstasy
忘年会	ボウネンカイ	year-end party
訓 忘れる	わすれる	*v*. forget
忘れ形見	わすれがたみ	memento; keepsake; posthumous child
忘れ物	わすれもの	lost property; item left behind accidentally

433

忠 ⑧ 　、 ㇆ 口 口 中 忠 忠 忠

| 音 忠 | チュウ | loyalty; devotion; fidelity; faithfulness |

熟	忠義	チュウギ	loyalty; fidelity; devotion
	忠孝	チュウコウ	loyalty and filial piety
	忠告	チュウコク	advice; warning; caution; admoniton —*v.* advise; warn; caution; admonish
	忠実	チュウジツ	honesty; faithfulness; devotion; fidelity; faith
	忠臣	チュウシン	loyal retainer
	忠誠	チュウセイ	allegiance; loyalty; fidelity; devotion; integrity
	忠節	チュウセツ	loyalty; allegiance; fidelity; devotion

434

念 ⑧   ノ 入 今 今 念 念 念

音	念	ネン	think
熟	念じる	ネンじる	*vt.* wish; pray
	念願	ネンガン	wish; desire; prayer —*v.* wish; desire; pray
	念頭	ネントウ	mind
	念仏	ネンブツ	Buddhist prayer
	念力	ネンリキ	willpower; will; faith

435

急 ⑨   ノ ク 勹 刍 刍 急 急 急 急

音	急	キュウ	make haste; hasten; acute
熟	急激	キュウゲキ	sudden; abrupt; precipitous
	急行	キュウコウ	express (train/bus) —*vi.* hasten; go posthaste
	急降下	キュウコウカ	nose dive —*vi.* nose-dive
	急告	キュウコク	urgent notice
	急死	キュウシ	sudden death —*vi.* die suddenly
	急所	キュウショ	vital part of the body
	急進	キュウシン	rapid progress —*vi.* make rapid progress
	急性	キュウセイ	acute (sickness)
	急送	キュウソウ	dispatching hurriedly —*v.* send a thing in haste
	急増	キュウゾウ	sudden increase; jump —*vi.* increase rapidly/suddenly
	急速	キュウソク	rapid; swift; prompt
	急停止	キュウテイシ	sudden stop —*vi.* stop suddenly
	急転	キュウテン	sudden change —*vi.* change suddenly; take a sudden turn
	急場	キュウば	emergency; crisis
	急病	キュウビョウ	sudden attack of illness

急変	キュウヘン	sudden change/transition —*vi.* change suddenly
急報	キュウホウ	urgent message/report —*v.* send an urgent message; report promptly
急務	キュウム	urgent business; pressing need
急用	キュウヨウ	urgent business; business demanding immediate attention
急流	キュウリュウ	rapidly flowing stream
訓 急ぐ	いそぐ	*vi.* hasten; hurry up; go quickly

436
思 ⑨　ー 口 皿 卅 田 甲 思 思 思

音 思	シ	think; thought; idea
熟 思案	シアン	thought; consideration; reflection; worry —*v.* think; consider; reflect; worry
思考	シコウ	thought; thinking —*v.* think
思春期	シシュンキ	puberty; adolescence
思想	シソウ	thought; idea; thoughts
思想家	シソウカ	thinker
訓 思う	おもう	*vt.* think; consider; suspect; wonder; guess; suppose; imagine; fancy; be in love; wish; desire; recall; remember
思う存分	おもうゾンブン	as much as one likes
思い	おもい	thought; feeling; wish; desire; love
思い切って	おもいきって	bravely
思い出す	おもいだす	*vt.* recall; remember
思い出	おもいで	memory; recollections

437
恩 ⑩　ー 口 月 円 因 因 恩 恩 恩 恩

音 恩	オン	kindness; favor; grace
熟 恩返し	オンがえし	repayment of a favor
恩義	オンギ	favor; obligation; moral obligation
恩給	オンキュウ	pension
恩恵	オンケイ	favor; benefit
恩師	オンシ	one's former teacher
恩賜	オンシ	imperial gift
恩赦	オンシャ	amnesty; general pardon
恩情	オンジョウ	compassion
恩知らず	オンしらず	ingratitude; ingrate

恩人	オンジン	benefactor; patron
恩寵	オンチョウ	grace; favor
恩典	オンテン	grace; act of grace

438

息 ⑩ ′ 亻 竹 白 自 自 自 息 息 息

音	息	ソク	breath; son
熟	息災	ソクサイ	healthy; safety; safe and sound
	息女	ソクジョ	daughter
訓	息	いき	breath

439

悪 ⑪ 一 一 一 一 亜 亜 亜 亜 悪 悪 悪

音	悪	アク	wrong; incorrect; bad; evil; immoral; ugly; poor quality; inferior; hate
		オ	hate
熟	悪意	アクイ	evil intention; wrongful intent
	悪運	アクウン	the devil's luck
	悪行	アクギョウ	evildoing; wicked act
	悪事	アクジ	evil deed; wrongdoing; wrong; crime
	悪質	アクシツ	full of faults; vicious; corrupt; of poor quality; faulty; defective
	悪習	アクシュウ	bad habit; abuse; vice
	悪性	アクセイ	evil nature; malignancy; malevolence
	悪態	アクタイ	foul language; curse; slander; abuse
	悪党	アクトウ	bad person; villain; scoundrel; rogue
	悪徳	アクトク	vice; corruption; immorality
	悪人	アクニン	wicked person; wrongdoer
	悪筆	アクヒツ	poor handwriting
	悪評	アクヒョウ	ill repute; bad reputation; notoriety
	悪風	アクフウ	bad custom; vice
	悪文	アクブン	poor writing; writing that is difficult to understand
	悪夢	アクム	nightmare; bad dream
	悪名	アクメイ	bad reputation; infamy; notoriety
	悪用	アクヨウ	abuse; misuse —*v.* abuse; misuse; put to a bad use
	悪化	アッカ	worsening; deterioration —*vi.* get worse; become impaired; deteriorate

心 小 戈 戸 手 扌 支 攵 文 斗 斤 方 日 曰 月 肉 月 木 欠 止 歹 殳 母 毋 比 毛 氏 气 水 氷 氵 火 灬 父 片 牛 犬 犭 王 礻 耂

229

	悪寒	オカン	chill; cold
訓	悪い	わるい	wrong; bad; inferior; ugly
	悪気	わるギ	malice; spite; ill will; harm
	悪口	わるくち	abuse; slander; foul language
	悪者	わるもの	bad person; rogue; villain

440

悲 ⑫　ノ フ ヲ ヨ 킈 非 非 非 非 悲 悲 悲

	悲	ヒ	sad
熟	悲運	ヒウン	misfortune; bad/ill luck
	悲歌	ヒカ	elegy; sad tune; plaintive melody
	悲観	ヒカン	pessimism; disappointment —*v.* be pessimistic/disappointed
	悲願	ヒガン	Buddhist prayer for mankind; earnest wish
	悲喜	ヒキ	joy and sorrow
	悲境	ヒキョウ	adversities; unhappy situation; plight
	悲劇	ヒゲキ	tragedy; tragic play
	悲痛	ヒツウ	bitter; grief; sorrow
	悲報	ヒホウ	sad news
	悲鳴	ヒメイ	scream; shrier
	悲話	ヒワ	sad story
訓	悲しい	かなしい	sorrowful; sad
	悲しむ	かなしむ	*vt.* grieve; mourn; sorrow

441

愛 ⑬　ノ ィ ィ ぃ 쯩 产 产 忍 恶 愛 愛 愛

	愛	アイ	love; affection; attraction; attachment
熟	愛する	アイする	*vt.* love; be attracted to; cherish; hold dear
	愛護	アイゴ	protection; preservation; conservation —*v.* protect; preserve; conserve
	愛好	アイコウ	love; liking —*v.* love; like; be a lover of; be fond of
	愛国心	アイコクシン	patriotism; nationalism
	愛妻	アイサイ	one's beloved/darling wife
	愛妻家	アイサイカ	devoted husband; husband who loves and cares for his wife
	愛児	アイジ	beloved/favorite child
	愛情	アイジョウ	feeling of love; affection; attachment; devotion

愛人	アイジン	lover; sexual partner
愛想	アイソ（ウ）	amiablity; sociability; friendliness; congeniality
愛着	アイチャク	attachment; affection; love —*v.* become attached to; hold dear
愛読	アイドク	enjoyable/regular reading —*v.* enjoy reading; read regularly
愛用	アイヨウ	habitual/regular use —*v.* use habitually

442

 ⑬ ` ー ｆ ﾎ 立 产 产 音 音 音 音 意 意

音	意	イ	mind; feeling; thought; idea; intention; opinion; reason; meaning
熟	意外	イガイ	unexpected; unforeseen; surprising
	意気	イキ	spirits; disposition; temperament; humor
	意気投合	イキトウゴウ	mutual understanding; sympathy; affinity —*vi.* get on well with; have an affinity for; be like minded
	意気地なし	イクジなし	coward; lack of courage or resolution
	意義	イギ	meaning; sense; significance
	意見	イケン	opinion; view; idea; suggestion —*v.* give advice; admonish; reprove
	意向	イコウ	intention; inclination; disposition
	意志	イシ	will; volition
	意思	イシ	intention; intent; purpose
	意地	イジ	temper; obstinacy; pride; nature; dispositon
	意地悪	イジわる	ill-natured; malevolent; spiteful
	意識	イシキ	consciousness; awareness; senses —*v.* be conscious; feel; be aware
	意中	イチュウ	one's mind/thoughts/feelings
	意図	イト	intent; intention; aim; idea —*v.* intend; design; aim
	意表	イヒョウ	unexpectedness; surprise
	意味	イミ	meaning; sense; significance; implication —*v.* mean; signify; imply
	意訳	イヤク	free translation —*v.* translate freely
	意欲	イヨク	will; desire; volition

443

 ⑬ ） 厂 厂 厂 后 后 咸 咸 咸 感 感 感

| 音 | 感 | カン | feel; feeling; inspiration; sensation; sentiment; emotion |

心
忄
戈
戸
手
扌
支
攵
文
斗
斤
方
日
曰
月
肉
月
木
欠
止
歹
殳
母
毋
比
毛
氏
气
水
氺
氵
火
灬
父
片
牛
犬
犭
王
礻
爿

熟	感じる	カンじる	v. be conscious of; suffer; be impressed; feel
	感化	カンカ	inspiration; influence —v. inspire; influence
	感覚	カンカク	sense; sensibility; feeling
	感激	カンゲキ	deep emotion; impression; enthusiasm —vi. be deeply moved/impressed
	感光	カンコウ	exposure to light
	感謝	カンシャ	thanks; appreciation; gratitude —v. thank; be thankful/grateful for
	感受性	カンジュセイ	sensibility; receptivity
	感傷	カンショウ	sentimentality
	感情	カンジョウ	feeling; sentiment; emotion
	感染	カンセン	infection —v. be infected
	感想	カンソウ	impressions; thoughts
	感知	カンチ	perception; awareness —v. perceive; become aware of
	感づく	カンづく	vi. suspect; sense; get wind of
	感電	カンデン	electric shock —vi. receive an electric shock
	感度	カンド	sensitivity; sensibility
	感動	カンドウ	impression; emotion; inspiration —vi. be impressed/moved/inspired
	感服	カンプク	admiration —vi. be impressed by

444

 想 ⑬   一 十 才 木 朼 相 相 相 相 相 想 想

音	想	ソウ (ソ)	idea; thought
熟	想起	ソウキ	recollection; remembrance
	想像	ソウゾウ	imagination —v. imagine
	想定	ソウテイ	supposition; hypothesis —v. suppose; make a hypothesis
	想念	ソウネン	idea; conception

445

 態 ⑭   ⺌ 厶 台 台 育 育 能 能 能 態 態

音	態	タイ	figure; posture; attitude
熟	態勢	タイセイ	attitude; condition
	態度	タイド	attitude; behavior

446

憲 ⑯ 　 丶 宀 宀 宀 宀 宀 害 害 害 害 憲 憲

音	憲	ケン	constitution
熟	憲章	ケンショウ	charter
	憲法	ケンポウ	constitution
訓	憲	のり	law; rule; regulation

---

3 忄 りっしんべん　heart to the left

447

快 ⑦ 　 丶 丷 忄 忄 忄 快 快

音	快	カイ	comfort; pleasure
熟	快活	カイカツ	cheerfulness; liveliness
	快感	カイカン	pleasant sensation; pleasure
	快挙	カイキョ	brilliant achievement; heroic deed
	快勝	カイショウ	easy victory —*vi.* win an easy victory
	快晴	カイセイ	fine weather
	快走	カイソウ	fast running —*vi.* run fast
	快速	カイソク	high/great speed
	快調	カイチョウ	excellent condition; harmony
	快適	カイテキ	comfortable; delightful; agreeable
	快方	カイホウ	convalescence; recovery from illness
	快報	カイホウ	good/welcome news
	快楽	カイラク	pleasure; enjoyment
訓	快い	こころよい	pleasant; comfortable

448

性 ⑧ 　 丶 丷 忄 忄 忄 忄 性 性

音	性	セイ	nature; sex; gender
		ショウ	nature
熟	性根	ショウネ	nature; character
	性分	ショウブン	nature; disposition
	性愛	セイアイ	sexual love

心
忄
戈
戸
手
扌
支
攵
文
斗
斤
方
日
曰
肉
月
木
欠
止
歹
殳
母
毋
比
毛
氏
气
水
氺
氵
火
灬
父
片
牛
犬
犭
王
礻
耂

4

心 忄 戈 戸 手 扌 支 攵 文 斗 斤 方 日 曰 月 肉 月 木 欠 止 歹 殳 母 毋 比 毛 氏 气 水 氺 氵 火 灬 父 片 牛 犬 犭 王 礻 夊

性格	セイカク	character; personality
性器	セイキ	sexual organs; genitals
性急	セイキュウ	hasty; impatient
性教育	セイキョウイク	sex education
性交	セイコウ	intercourse; sex; coitus —*vi.* have sex; make love
性向	セイコウ	disposition; nature
性行	セイコウ	character and conduct
性質	セイシツ	nature; disposition; property
性的	セイテキ	sexual
性能	セイノウ	performance; efficiency
性病	セイビョウ	venereal disease
性病科	セイビョウカ	department for the treatment of venereal diseases
性別	セイベツ	distinction of sex; gender
性本能	セイホンノウ	sex drive/impulse
性欲	セイヨク	sexual desire; lust

449

 情 ⑪   丶 丶 忄 忄 忄 忄 忄 忄 情 情 情

音 情	ジョウ	feeling; sentiment; emotions; heart; affection; love
	(セイ)	
熟 情愛	ジョウアイ	affection; love; compassion
情感	ジョウカン	emotion
情景	ジョウケイ	scene
情交	ジョウコウ	sexual intercourse
情死	ジョウシ	lover's suicide —*vi.* carry out a suicide pact
情事	ジョウジ	love affair
情実	ジョウジツ	private considerations; favoritism
情状	ジョウジョウ	circumstances; allowances
情勢	ジョウセイ	situation; state of affairs; conditions
情操	ジョウソウ	sentiments
情熱	ジョウネツ	passion; ardor; enthusiasm
情熱的	ジョウネツテキ	passionate; ardent; enthusiastic
情念	ジョウネン	sentiments; feelings
情夫	ジョウフ	male lover
情婦	ジョウフ	female lover
情報	ジョウホウ	information; news; data; report
情報機関	ジョウホウキカン	secret service
情報処理	ジョウホウショリ	data processing

| 情欲 | ジョウヨク | sexual desire; lust |
| 情理 | ジョウリ | reason and sentiment |

訓 情け　なさけ　sympathy; pity; compassion; charity; love
情けない　なさけない　deplorable; shameful; heartless; miserable; disgraceful

450 慣 ⑭

忄 忄 忄 忄 忄 忄 慣 慣 慣 慣 慣

音 慣　カン　custom; get used to

熟
慣行	カンコウ	customary practice; traditional way
慣習	カンシュウ	rules and conventions
慣性	カンセイ	inertia
慣用	カンヨウ	usage; common use
慣例	カンレイ	custom; usage; convention

訓
| 慣れる | なれる | *vi.* get used to; grow accustomed to |
| 慣らす | ならす | *vt.* tame; domesticate; accustom; familiarize |

4 戈 ほこがまえ tasseled spear

451 成 ⑥

ノ 厂 厂 成 成 成

音 成　セイ　be completed; achieve; accomplish
　　（ジョウ）

熟
成就	ジョウジュ	accomplishment; attainment —*v.* accomplish; attain
成仏	ジョウブツ	death; Buddhahood —*vi.* enter Nirvana; die; pass away
成育	セイイク	growth; development —*v.* grow; develop; raise
成因	セイイン	origin; cause
成果	セイカ	result; fruits; achievement
成句	セイク	set phrase; idiomatic expression; common saying; proverb
成形	セイケイ	molding —*v.* mold
成型	セイケイ	casting —*v.* cast
成功	セイコウ	success; achievement —*vi.* succeed; be successful; pass; achieve
成熟	セイジュク	maturity; ripeness —*vi.* ripen; mature

心忄戈戸手扌支攵文斗斤方日曰月肉月木欠止歹殳母毋比毛氏气水氺氵火灬父片牛犬犭王礻牙

成熟期	セイジュクキ	adolescence; puberty; period of maturity
成人	セイジン	adult; grown-up —*vi.* grow-up; attain adulthood
成人教育	セイジンキョウイク	adult education
成人式	セイジンシキ	*seijinshiki* (coming-of-age ceremony)
成績	セイセキ	result; record; grade; mark; performance; showings
成虫	セイチュウ	imago
成長	セイチョウ	growth; development —*vi.* grow; grow up; develop
成長率	セイチョウリツ	growth rate
成年	セイネン	adult age; majority
成敗	セイハイ	success and failure
成敗	セイバイ	judgment; punishment —*v.* judge; punish
成否	セイヒ	success or failure; result
成分	セイブン	ingredient; component; constituent
成立	セイリツ	formation —*vi.* come into existence/being; be organized/concluded

訓

成す	なす	*vt.* accomplish; achieve; take shape; form
成る	なる	*vi.* become; be completed; consist; be made up; be promoted
成り上がり者	なりあがりもの	upstart
成金	なりキン	upstart; newly rich
成り立ち	なりたち	history; the origin; structure; formation
成り行き	なりゆき	course of events; developments

452

 我 ⑦ ノ 一 千 千 扎 我 我

音 我	ガ	self; selfish; ego; obstinacy
熟 我意	ガイ	self-will; obstinacy
我田引水	ガデンインスイ	drawing water for one's own field *fig.* promoting one's own interests
我流	ガリュウ	self-taught method; one's own way (of doing something)
訓 我	わ	I
我	われ	I; one's side
我等	われら	we; our; us
我々	われわれ	we; our; us

戦 ⑬ 　〃　〃　ヾ　ヾ　ヾ　ヾ　単　単　戦　戦　戦

音	戦	セン	war; battle
熟	戦域	センイキ	war zone; theater of war
	戦火	センカ	(the flames of) war
	戦記物	センキもの	account of a war
	戦局	センキョク	war situation
	戦後	センゴ	after the war; post war (in particular, World War Ⅱ)
	戦国	センゴク	country torn apart by civil war
	戦国時代	センゴクジダイ	*hist.* era of civil wars (1467-1568)
	戦災	センサイ	war devastation
	戦士	センシ	warrior; soldier
	戦死	センシ	death in battle; killed in action —*vi.* be killed/die in action
	戦時	センジ	wartime; war period
	戦車	センシャ	tank
	戦術	センジュツ	tactics
	戦勝	センショウ	victory —*vi.* be victorious in battle
	戦傷	センショウ	war wound —*vi.* be wounded in battle
	戦場	センジョウ	battlefield; front
	戦績	センセキ	war record
	戦線	センセン	battle line; front
	戦前	センゼン	before the war; prewar (in particular, World War Ⅱ)
	戦争	センソウ	war —*vi.* fight; go to war
	戦隊	センタイ	corps; squadron
	戦地	センチ	battlefield; front
	戦中	センチュウ	during the war
	戦犯	センパン	war crime/criminal
	戦費	センピ	costs of war
	戦友	センユウ	con/comrade-in-arms rade-in-arms
	戦乱	センラン	upheavals of war
	戦利品	センリヒン	war spoils; booty
	戦略	センリャク	strategy
	戦力	センリョク	war fighting capacity
	戦歴	センレキ	war experience; combat record
	戦列	センレツ	ranks; battle line
訓	戦う	たたかう	*vt.* fight; wage war
	戦	いくさ	war

心 忄 戈 戸 手 扌 支 攵 文 斗 斤 方 日 曰 月 肉 月 木 欠 止 歹 殳 母 毋 比 毛 氏 气 水 氷 氵 火 灬 父 片 牛 犬 犭 王 礻 耂

4

4 戸 と door

454

| 戸 ④ | 一 ⇒ ⇒ 戸 |

454

戸 ④　　一　ⴞ　ⴗ　戸

音	戸	コ	door; house; (counter for houses and buildings)
熟	戸外	コガイ	outdoors; out of doors; open air
	戸別	コベツ	from door to door; each house
訓	戸	と	door

455

所 ⑧　　一　ⴞ　ⴗ　戸　ⴶ　所　所　所

音	所	ショ	place
熟	所管	ショカン	jurisdiction
	所感	ショカン	impressions; thoughts; feelings
	所見	ショケン	one's view/opinion
	所在	ショザイ	site; one's whereabouts; location
	所産	ショサン	product; fruit of one's efforts
	所持	ショジ	possession —*v*. possess; have; store/put away one's possessions
	所信	ショシン	one's beliefs/opinions/views
	所蔵	ショゾウ	possession —*v*. possess; own; store/put away one's possessions
	所属	ショゾク	one's position —*vi*. belong to; be with; be attached to
	所存	ショゾン	thoughts; intentions
	所帯	ショタイ	property; household
	所長	ショチョウ	the head
	所定	ショテイ	fixed; appointed
	所望	ショモウ	desire; wish; request —*v*. wish; desire; ask for; request
	所有	ショユウ	ownership; possession —*vt*. own; possess
	所有権	ショユウケン	ownership; title
	所用	ショヨウ	business
訓	所	ところ	place; spot; locality

心忄戈戸手扌支攵文斗斤方日曰月肉月木欠止歹殳母毋比毛氏气水氺氵火灬父片牛犬犭王礻耂

238

4 手 て hand 扌 (p.241)

456

手 ④ 一 二 三 手

音	手	シュ	hand

熟	手記	シュキ	note; memorandum; private papers
	手芸	シュゲイ	handicrafts
	手工業	シュコウギョウ	handicraft/manual industry
	手術	シュジュツ	*med.* operation; surgery —*v.* operate; perform an operation
	手段	シュダン	means; step; measure
	手動	シュドウ	manual operation
	手法	シュホウ	technique; technical skill
	手練	シュレン	skill; dexterity

訓	手	て	hand; handle; trouble; means
	手足	てあし	hands and feet; arms and legs; limbs
	手当たり次第	てあたりシダイ	at random
	手当	てあて	medical treatment/care; salary; allowance; cover; provision —*v.* treat (a burn, etc.)
	手書き	てがき	handwriting —*v.* write; draft
	手数	てかず（てスウ）	trouble
	手紙	てがみ	letter; note
	手軽	てがる	light; simple
	手際	てぎわ	skill
	手口	てぐち	method; way; trick; *modus operandi*
	手首	てくび	wrist
	手心（を加える）	てごころ（をくわえる）	consideration; allowance —*v.* consider; allow for
	手応え	てごたえ	effect; resistance; response
	手強い	てごわい	strong; tough; formidable
	手細工	てザイク	handiwork; handicraft
	手先	てさき	fingertips
	手探り	てさぐり	groping
	手提げ	てさげ	handbag; bag
	手下	てした	underling; henchmen
	手品	てじな	magic; conjuring trick; sleight of hand
	手品師	てじなシ	magician; conjurer
	手順	てジュン	order; plan; arrangements; process; procedure

心忄戈戸手扌支攵文斗斤方日曰月肉月木欠止歹殳母毋比毛氏气水氺氵火灬父片牛犬犭王礻㐬

手製	てセイ	handmade; homemade
手相	てソウ	palmistry
手出し	てだし	interference —*vi.* meddle; interfere; make advances; dabble
手立て	てだて	means; process; order
手近	てぢか	close at hand; within reach
手帳	てチョウ	notebook; pocket diary
手作り	てづくり	homemade; handmade
手伝う	てつだう	*vt.* help; assist; aid
手続き	てつづき	procedure; formalities
手並み	てなみ	skill; dexterity
手習い	てならい	practice; learning
手慣れる	てなれる	*vi.* get used (to); get skillful (in)
手荷物	てにモツ	baggage
手配	てハイ	arrangements; preparations; search —*v.* arrange; prepare
手放す	てばなす	*vt.* dispose; do away with; part; sell
手引き	てびき	guidance; guide; introduction; manual
手解き	てほどき	initiation
手本	てホン	copy; model; copy book
手前	てまえ	before; near; in front
手間取る	てまどる	*vi.* take time; be delayed; be kept long
手回し	てまわし	preparation; arrangements
手短か	てみじか	brief; short
手持ち	てもち	on a hand; in stock; holdings
手元	てもと	at hand
手料理	てリョウリ	home cooking

457

 ⑧   一 了 了 尹 手 承 承 承

音	承	ショウ	consent; agree; accept
熟	承知	ショウチ	consent; agreement; assent —*v.* know; understand; be aware; consent; agree; permit; allow
	承認	ショウニン	approval; consent; assent —*v.* approve; consent; acknowledge
	承服	ショウフク	submission —*v.* yield to; accept; consent
訓	承る	うけたまわる	*vt.* hear; understand; comply; consent

458

、 ゛ ゛゛ ⺍ ⺌ 兴 兴 兴 挙 挙 ⑩

音	挙	キョ	raise; lift; enumerate; list; happen; occur; move; shake
熟	挙行	キョコウ	performance; celebration —*v.* perform (a ceremony); hold (a reception); celebrate (a marriage)
	挙式	キョシキ	(bridal) ceremony; celebration —*vi.* hold a ceremony; celebrate
	挙手	キョシュ	raising one's hand; show of hands —*vi.* raise one's hand; give a show of hands
	挙動	キョドウ	behavior; conduct; demeanor
	挙兵	キョヘイ	raising an army; taking up arms —*vi.* raise an army; take up arms
訓	挙がる	あがる	*vi.* raise; be lifted/elevated
	挙げる	あげる	*vt.* raise; lift; elevate

3　扌　てへん　hand at left

459

才 ③ 一 十 才

音	才	サイ	wit; talent; ability
熟	才覚	サイカク	wit; resources; contrivance; device
	才気	サイキ	quick-witted; gifted; brilliant
	才女	サイジョ	talented woman
	才能	サイノウ	talent; ability; gift

460

打 ⑤ 一 十 扌 扩 打

音	打	ダ	beat; bat; strike; hit; shoot
熟	打開	ダカイ	breakthrough; development; solution —*v.* breakthrough; effect a development
	打楽器	ダガッキ	percussion instrument
	打球	ダキュウ	***bas.*** batting
	打算的	ダサンテキ	calculating; selfish; self-centered; mercenary

241

心忄戈戸手扌支攵文斗斤方日曰肉月木欠止歹殳母毋比毛氏气水氺氵火灬父片牛犬犭王礻耂

心忄戈戸手扌
支攵文斗斤方
日曰月肉月木
欠止歹父母毋
比毛氏气水氺
氵火灬父片牛
犬犭王礻耂

打者	ダシャ	*bas*. batter
打順	ダジュン	*bas*. batting order
打席	ダセキ	*bas*. at bat
打線	ダセン	*bas*. the batting line-up
打破	ダハ	breaking; destruction; defeat; conquest; overthrow —*v*. break down; overthrow; conquer; destroy; defeat
打率	ダリツ	*bas*. batting average

訓 打つ　うつ　*vt*. hit; strike; shoot; make noodles; send a telegram; gamble

打ち勝つ　うちかつ　*vi*. overcome; get over; conquer

打ち切る　うちきる　*vt*. stop doing something; call off

461
技 ⑦　一　扌　扌　扩　扩　技　技

音 技　ギ　skill; art; craft

熟 技師　ギシ　engineer; technician

技術　ギジュツ　technique; technology; technical skill

技能　ギノウ　technical skill; ability

技法　ギホウ　technique

技量　ギリョウ　skill; ability; talent; capability

訓 技　わざ　art; trick; skill

462
折 ⑦　一　扌　扌　扩　扩　折　折

音 折　セツ　break; divide; be folded

熟 折角　セッカク　kindly; with much effort; go to the trouble of

折半　セッパン　halving —*v*. halve; divide into two

訓 折る　おる　*v*. fold; break; bend

折れる　おれる　*vi*. break; be folded; bend; turn; yield

折　おり　occasion; opportunity

折り合う　おりあう　*vi*. agree; come to terms

折り返す　おりかえす　*v*. make a turn; turn back

463

投 ⑦ 一 十 扌 扌 扩 抄 投

音	投	トウ	throw; fling; cast
熟	投下	トウカ	dropping; throwing down —*v.* drop; throw down
	投球	トウキュウ	*bas.* pitching —*v. bas.* throw; pitch
	投降	トウコウ	surrender —*vi.* surrender; lay down one's arms
	投合	トウゴウ	agreement; coincidence —*vi.* agree/coincide with
	投資	トウシ	investment —*vi.* invest; make investments
	投宿	トウシュク	registering/staying at a hotel —*vi.* register/stay at a hotel
	投書	トウショ	contribution; reader's letter; letter to the editor —*vi.* write a letter to the editor; contribute to (a magazine, newspaper, etc.)
	投身	トウシン	suicide by drowning —*vi.* commit suicide by drowning
	投石	トウセキ	stone throwing —*vi.* throw stones
	投入	トウニュウ	investment; capital injection; commitment —*v.* invest in; commit to
	投票	トウヒョウ	vote; suffrage; poll; ballot; voting; election —*vi.* ballot; cast a vote; elect; vote
	投薬	トウヤク	prescription —*v.* prescribe medicine; medicate
訓	投げる	なげる	*vt.* throw; fling; cast; abandon; give up

464

批 ⑦ 一 十 扌 扌 扑 扑 批

音	批	ヒ	criticize
熟	批判	ヒハン	criticism; comment; critique —*v.* criticize; comment
	批評	ヒヒョウ	criticism; critique; critical essay —*v.* criticize; comment
	批評家	ヒヒョウカ	critic; reviewer
	批評眼	ヒヒョウガン	critical eye
	批難	ヒナン	negative criticism; blame —*vt.* denounce; blame

465

拡 ⑧ 一 十 扌 扌 扩 扩 拡 拡

音	拡	カク	expand; spread

心
忄
戈
戸
手
扌
支
攵
文
斗
斤
方
日
曰
月
肉
月
木
欠
止
歹
殳
母
毋
比
毛
氏
气
水
氷
氵
火
灬
父
片
牛
犬
犭
王
礻
耂

心 忄 戈 戸 手 扌 支 攵 文 斗 斤 方 日 曰 月 肉 月 木 欠 止 歹 殳 母 毋 比 毛 氏 气 水 氺 氵 火 灬 父 片 牛 犬 犭 王 礻 耂

熟	拡散	カクサン	proliferation; diffusion —*v*. spread; proliferate
	拡声器	カクセイキ	loudspeaker
	拡大	カクダイ	enlargement; magnification —*v*. magnify; expand
	拡張	カクチョウ	extension; expansion; enlargement —*v*. extend; expand; enlarge; increase
訓	拡げる	ひろげる	*vt*. spread; widen; expand

466 招 ⑧ 　一 ナ 扌 扒 护 护 招 招

音	招	ショウ	invite
熟	招集	ショウシュウ	call/invitation to a group of people —*v*. call/invite a group of people
	招待	ショウタイ	invitation —*v*. invite; get an invitation
	招待状	ショウタイジョウ	(letter of) invitation
訓	招く	まねく	*vt*. call; beckon; invite

467 担 ⑧ 　一 ナ 扌 扣 扣 扫 担 担

音	担	タン	shoulder; carry; bear
熟	担当	タントウ	charge; duty; person in charge —*v*. take charge; assume responsibility
	担任	タンニン	charge; duty; homeroom teacher —*v*. take charge; be in charge; be in charge of a homeroom class; be a class teacher
訓	担ぐ	かつぐ	*vt*. carry on one's shoulder; shoulder; bear
	担う	になう	*vt*. carry on one's shoulder; bear; shoulder responsibility

468 拝 ⑧ 　一 ナ 扌 扩 扩 拝 拝 拝

音	拝	ハイ	worship; pray; bow; look; witness; (prefix to make an expression humble)
熟	拝する	ハイする	*vt*. worship —***hon***. receive; see
	拝観	ハイカン	***hum***. inspection; visit to a temple, etc. —*v*. ***hum***. see; inspect; look at; view
	拝顔	ハイガン	***hum***. seeing/meeting (someone) —*v*. ***hum***. see/meet (someone)

拝見	ハイケン	*hum.* looking; inspection —*v.* *hum.* have the honor of seeing; see; inspect
拝察	ハイサツ	*hum.* guess
拝借	ハイシャク	*hum.* borrowing; loan —*v.* *hum.* have a loan; borrow
拝受	ハイジュ	*hum.* acceptance —*v.* *hum.* receive; accept
拝読	ハイドク	*hum.* reading —*v.* *hum.* read; note
拝復	ハイフク	*hum.* in reply to your letter
拝礼	ハイレイ	worship —*v.* worship
訓 拝む	おがむ	*vt.* *hum.* look; view; witness; worship; pray; bow; implore

指⑨ 一 十 才 扌 扩 护 指 指 指

音 指	シ	finger; point; indicate
熟 指圧	シアツ	*shiatsu* (form of massage) —*v.* give *shiatsu*
指揮	シキ	command; direction —*v.* command; direct; lead; conduct an orchestra
指揮者	シキシャ	conductor
指示	シジ	instructions; indications; directions —*v.* indicate; instruct; direct
指針	シシン	guide; indicator; pointer; compass needle
指数	シスウ	*math.* index; exponent
指定	シテイ	appointment; specification; designation —*v.* appoint; specify; designate; reserve
指定席	シテイセキ	reserved seat
指導	シドウ	guidance; leadership; coaching —*v.* lead; guide; coach
指導者	シドウシャ	leader; guide
指導力	シドウリョク	leadership
指南	シナン	instruction; teaching —*v.* teach; instruct; coach
指標	シヒョウ	index
指名	シメイ	nomination; designation —*v.* nominate; designate
指令	シレイ	order —*v.* order; instruct; give instructions
訓 指す	さす	*vt.* point to; indicate
指図	さしズ	direction; directions
指	ゆび	finger; toe
指折り	ゆびおり	leading; prominent
指先	ゆびさき	fingertip
指差す	ゆびさす	*vt.* point

心 忄 戈 戸 手 扌 支 攵 文 斗 斤 方 日 曰 月 肉 月 木 欠 止 歹 殳 母 毋 比 毛 氏 气 水 氺 氵 火 灬 父 片 牛 犬 犭 王 礻 耂

心忄戈戸手扌支攵文斗斤方日曰月肉月木欠止歹殳母毋比毛氏气水氺冫火灬父片牛犬犭王礻耂

---

470 持 ⑨
一 十 寸 扌 扩 扩 拦 拝 持 持

音	持	ジ	have; hold
熟	持する	ジする	have; hold
	持久	ジキュウ	endurance; perserverance; tenacity —*vi.* endure; perservere
	持久戦	ジキュウセン	protracted war
	持久力	ジキュウリョク	tenacity; stamina; staying power
	持参	ジサン	bringing; taking —*v.* bring; take
	持参金	ジサンキン	dowry
	持説	ジセツ	one's cherished opinion
	持続	ジゾク	continuing; lasting —*v.* continue; last
	持続性	ジゾクセイ	durability
	持続的	ジゾクテキ	continuous; lasting
	持病	ジビョウ	chronic disease
	持論	ジロン	pet theory
訓	持つ	もつ	*v.* have; hold; take; carry; own; possess
	持ち	もち	durability; wear
	持ち上げる	もちあげる	*vt.* lift; raise; flatter
	持ち味	もちあじ	characteristic; peculiar flavor
	持ち合わせる	もちあわせる	*vt.* carry with oneself
	持ち家	もちいえ	one's own house
	持ち主	もちぬし	owner; proprietor
	持ち場	もちば	one's place/position/territory

---

471 拾 ⑨
一 十 寸 扩 扒 拎 拎 拾 拾

音	拾	シュウ	pick up
熟	拾得	シュウトク	picking up from the ground; finding something that has been dropped —*v.* find/pick up something that has been dropped
	拾得物	シュウトクブツ	thing found (on the road); found article; find; windfall
訓	拾う	ひろう	*vt.* pick up; gather; find
	拾い読み	ひろいよみ	scanning —*vt.* scan; read here and there

採 ⑪ 一 十 扌 扌 扌 扩 扩 扩 护 抒 抒 採

音	採	サイ	choose; take
熟	採決	サイケツ	vote; parlimentary decision —*v.* vote; take a vote
	採血	サイケツ	***med.*** blood sample/collection —*vi.* collect blood; take a blood sample
	採光	サイコウ	lighting
	採鉱	サイコウ	mining —*vi.* work a mine; mine
	採取	サイシュ	collecting; extracting; collection; extract —*v.* gather; pick; collect; extract
	採集	サイシュウ	collecting; gathering; hunting —*v.* collect; hunt; gather
	採炭	サイタン	coal mining —*vi.* mine coal
	採点	サイテン	marking papers; grading assignments —*v.* give marks; grade exams or papers
	採否	サイヒ	adoption or rejection; employment and rejection; result; decision
	採用	サイヨウ	adoption; employment; usage —*v.* adopt; employ; use; choose
訓	採る	とる	*vt.* adopt; employ; select; choose; prefer

捨 ⑪ 一 十 扌 扌 扩 扩 抖 拴 拴 捨 捨

音	捨	シャ	throw away
訓	捨てる	すてる	*vt.* throw away; dump; abandon; desert
	捨て金	すてがね	wasted money
	捨て子	すてご	abandoned child; foundling
	捨て値	すてね	dirt-cheap; giveaway price
	捨て身	すてみ	wholeheartedly

授 ⑪ 一 十 扌 扌 扩 扩 扩 扩 护 拧 授

音	授	ジュ	grant; give; teach
熟	授業	ジュギョウ	lesson; lecture —*vi.* teach/give a lecture
	授産所	ジュサンジョ	work center; labor exchange; place for the unemployed to find work
	授受	ジュジュ	transmission —*vt.* transfer

授賞	ジュショウ	prize-giving —*vi*. give/award a prize
授精	ジュセイ	fertilization; insemination; pollination
授乳	ジュニュウ	nursing (a baby); breast-feeding —*vi*. nurse (a baby); breastfeed
訓 授かる	さずかる	*vi*. be given/granted/taught
授ける	さずける	*vt*. give; grant; teach; instruct

475

推 ⑪

一 扌 扌 扌 扩 扩 扩 拊 拊 推 推

音 推	スイ	propel; recommend
熟 推移	スイイ	transition; change; progress —*vi*. change; undergo a change; shift; progress
推挙	スイキョ	proposal; recommendation —*v*. propose; recommend
推計	スイケイ	estimation —*v*. estimate
推考	スイコウ	speculation —*v*. speculate
推察	スイサツ	conjecture; guess; inference; surmise —*v*. guess; conjecture; infer; surmise
推参	スイサン	unvited visit —*vi*. barge in, crash a party
推進	スイシン	propulsion; drive —*v*. propel; drive forward; promote; further
推進力	スイシンリョク	thrust; impulse; driving force
推測	スイソク	conjecture; surmise; supposition —*v*. conjecture; surmise; suppose
推定	スイテイ	presumption; assumption; inference —*v*. presume; assume; infer
推理	スイリ	reasoning; deduction; detection —*v*. reason; deduct; detect
推理小説	スイリショウセツ	detective story; mystery; thriller
推量	スイリョウ	guess; conjecture —*v*. guess; conjecture
推力	スイリョク	*phy*. thrust; driving force
推論	スイロン	reasoning; inference; induction; deduction —*v*. reason; infer; induce; deduce
訓 推す	おす	*vt*. infer; deduce; conclude; recommend; propose; nominate
推し量る (推し測る)	おしはかる	*vt*. guess; conjecture

接 ⑪　一 扌 扌 扌' 扩 扩 护 护 接 接 接

音	接	セツ	contact; join; near; touch
熟	接する	セッする	*v.* make contact; touch
	接角	セッカク	*math.* adjacent angles
	接近	セッキン	approaching; drawing near —*v.* approach; draw near
	接合	セツゴウ	joining; union —*v.* join; put together; unite
	接骨医	セッコツイ	bone setter; bonesetting —*v.* set bones
	接写	セッシャ	close-up photo —*v.* take close-up pictures
	接種	セッシュ	inoculation; vaccination —*v.* inoculate; vaccinate
	接収	セッシュウ	requisition; take over —*v.* requisite; take over
	接戦	セッセン	close combat/contest
	接線	セッセン	*math.* tangent
	接続	セツゾク	connection; joining —*v.* connect; join
	接続詞	セツゾクシ	*gram.* conjunction
	接待	セッタイ	reception; welcome; serving; offering —*v.* give a reception; welcome; serve; offer
	接着	セッチャク	adhesion —*v.* be adhesive; adhere to; stick
	接点	セッテン	point of tangency; contact
	接頭語	セットウゴ	*gram.* prefix
訓	接ぐ	つぐ	*vt.* join; piece
	接ぎめ	つぎめ	joint; seam

探 ⑪　一 扌 扌 扌 扩 扩 护 捽 探 探 探

音	探	タン	search; inquire; investigate; explore
熟	探究	タンキュウ	research; investigation; inquiry; study —*v.* investigate; inquire into; explore; research into
	探求	タンキュウ	quest; search; pursuit —*v.* search for; pursue
	探検	タンケン	exploration; expedition; —*v.* explore; make an exploration; go on an expedition
	探知	タンチ	detection —*v.* detect; spy; trace
	探訪	タンボウ	inquiry —*v.* make inquiries into; inquire into
訓	探す	さがす	*vt.* search/look for; trace; locate
	探る	さぐる	*vt.* search; look for; explore; spy
	探り	さぐり	spy; probe

心 忄 戈 戸 手 扌 •
支 攵 文 斗 斤 方 日 曰 月 肉 月 木 欠 止 歹 殳 母 毋 比 毛 氏 气 水 氺 氵 火 灬 父 片 牛 犬 犭 王 礻 耂

心
忄
戈
戸
手
扌
支
攵
文
斗
斤
方
日
曰
月
肉
月
木
欠
止
歹
殳
母
毋
比
毛
氏
气
水
氺
氵
火
灬
父
片
牛
犬
犭
王
礻
耂

478

揮 ⑫

一 亅 扌 扌 扩 扩 护 护 捔 揎 揎 揮

音	揮	キ	wield; command
熟	揮発	キハツ	volatilization —*vi*. volatize
	揮発油	キハツユ	gasoline; benzine

479

提 ⑫

一 亅 扌 扌 扩 护 护 押 押 捍 捍 提

音	提	テイ	present
熟	提案	テイアン	proposal; offer; suggestion; overture —*v*. propose; suggest; make a proposal
	提起	テイキ	institution; lodging —*v*. institute; lodge
	提議	テイギ	proposal; proposition; suggestion —*v*. propose; make a proposition; suggest; recommend
	提供	テイキョウ	offer; proffer; tender —*v*. offer; make an offer; produce evidence
	提示	テイジ	presentation —*v*. exhibit; present
	提出	テイシュツ	presentation; introduction; exhibition; production —*v*. present; introduce; submit
	提唱	テイショウ	advocacy; proposal —*v*. advocate; put forward; advance; lecture
	提要	テイヨウ	summary; compendium
訓	提げる	さげる	*vt*. carry in one's hand

480

損 ⑬

亅 扌 扌 扩 护 护 捐 捐 捐 捐 損 損

音	損	ソン	loss; damage; disadvantage
熟	損害	ソンガイ	damage; loss; injury —*v*. damage; loss; injure
	損失	ソンシツ	loss —*v*. lose
	損傷	ソンショウ	damage; injury —*v*. damage; injure
	損得	ソントク	loss and gain; advantages and disadvantages
	損料	ソンリョウ	rental fee
訓	損なう	そこなう	*vt*. harm; spoil; hurt
	損ねる	そこねる	*vt*. injure; hurt; harm

481

操 ⑯　一 扌 扌 扌 扩 扩 护 护 操 撡 撡 撡 操

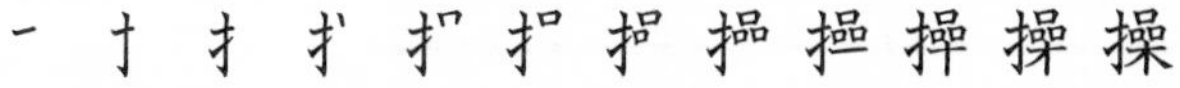

🔊 操	ソウ	manipulate; operate
🔥 操業	ソウギョウ	operation; work
操業短縮	ソウギョウタンシュク	curtailment of operations
操行	ソウコウ	conduct; department
操作	ソウサ	operation; handing; control —*v.* operate; handle; control
操車	ソウシャ	operation (of trains)
操縦	ソウジュウ	handling; manipulation; control —*v.* handle; manipulate; control; operate
操練	ソウレン	military exercises; drill
📖 操る	あやつる	*vt.* manipulate; operate
操	みさお	chastity; virginity; constancy; fidelity; honor

4　支 じゅうまた／しにょう／えだにょう　branch

482

支 ④　一 十 � 支

🔊 支	シ	branch; separate; pay; support; prop up
🔥 支給	シキュウ	supply —*v.* provide; issue; supply
支局	シキョク	branch office
支持	シジ	support; backing —*v.* support; back; stand by
支社	シシャ	branch office (of a company)
支障	シショウ	hindrance; trouble
支度	シタク	preparations; arrangements —*v.* prepare; arrange
支柱	シチュウ	support; prop; mainstay
支店	シテン	branch store/office
支点	シテン	fulcrum
支配	シハイ	rule; control; direction; management —*v.* rule; control; direct; manage
支配人	シハイニン	manager (of hotels, restaurants, etc.)
支部	シブ	branch/local office; chapter (of an organization)
支流	シリュウ	branch (of a river or family); tributary; faction; splinter group

心忄戈戸手扌支攵文斗斤方日曰月肉月木欠止歹殳母毋比毛氏气水氷氵火灬父片牛犬犭王礻耂

訓 支える　ささえる　**vt**. support; prop up; hold

---

4 攵　のぶん　_no_ (katakana); literature

483
改 ⑦　㇒　㇇　己　己　己　改　改

音	改	カイ	improve; change; reform
熟	改悪	カイアク	change for the worse; deterioration —*v*. get worse; deteriorate
	改革	カイカク	reform; reformation —*v*. reform; reorganize
	改行	カイギョウ	new line/paragraph —*vi*. start a new line/paragraph
	改元	カイゲン	change of an imperial era —*v*. change an imperial era
	改作	カイサク	adaptation; recomposition —*v*. adapt; recompose; remodel
	改札	カイサツ	ticket inspection —*v*. inspect tickets
	改札口	カイサツぐち	ticket gate; wicket
	改宗	カイシュウ	conversion; proselytism —*vi*. be converted; change one's religion
	改修	カイシュウ	repair; improvement —*v*. repair; fix; improve
	改心	カイシン	reform; mending one's ways —*vi*. reform; mend one's ways
	改新	カイシン	renovation; reformation —*v*. renovate; reform
	改正	カイセイ	revision; amendment —*v*. revise; amend
	改選	カイセン	reelection —*v*. reelect
	改善	カイゼン	improvement —*v*. improve; make better
	改装	カイソウ	remodeling; refurbishing; modification —*v*. remodel; refurbish; modify
	改造	カイゾウ	reconstruction; reorganization —*v*. reconstruct; reorganize
	改築	カイチク	rebuilding; reconstruction —*v*. rebuild; reconstruct
	改訂	カイテイ	revision of (manuscript, etc.) —*v*. revise
	改名	カイメイ	name change —*vi*. change one's name
	改良	カイリョウ	improvement; reformation —*v*. improve; reform
訓	改まる	あらたまる	*vi*. be renewed
	改める	あらためる	*vt*. renew; improve; change

⑧

丶 ユ ゥ 方 方 方 放 放

音	放	ホウ	let go; release; fire (a gun); emit
熟	放歌	ホウカ	loud singing —*vi.* sing loudly
	放火	ホウカ	arson —*vi.* deliberately set on fire
	放火犯	ホウカハン	arson; arsonist
	放課後	ホウカゴ	after school
	放言	ホウゲン	unreserved talk; speaking without thinking —*v.* talk without reservations; speak without thinking
	放校	ホウコウ	expulsion from school —*v.* expel from school
	放散	ホウサン	radiation; diffusion; evaporation —*vi.* radiate; diffuse; evaporate
	放射	ホウシャ	radiation; emission; discharge —*v.* radiate; emit; discharge
	放射線	ホウシャセン	radiation
	放射線科	ホウシャセンカ	*med.* radiology
	放射能	ホウシャノウ	radioactivity; radiation
	放出	ホウシュツ	emittance; release; discharge —*v.* emit; release; discharge
	放心	ホウシン	absent-mindedness; uncertain psychological state —*vi.* be absent-minded; have one's mind on other things; relax; feel reassured
	放水	ホウスイ	drainage; pour water on a fire with a hose —*vi.* drain; be drained; put a fire out with a hose
	放送	ホウソウ	broadcasting; broadcast —*v.* broadcast
	放送局	ホウソウキョク	broadcasting station
	放題	ホウダイ	(verb suffix) all you can (eat, drink, sing, etc.)
	放談	ホウダン	unreserved talk —*vi.* talk without any reservations
	放置	ホウチ	leaving something as it is —*v.* leave as is; leave to chance; let alone
	放電	ホウデン	electric discharge —*vi.* discharge electricity
	放任	ホウニン	nonintervention; indifference —*v.* do not intervene; be indifferent
	放熱	ホウネツ	radiant heat —*vi.* radiate heat
	放熱器	ホウネツキ	radiator
	放念	ホウネン	relaxed mind —*vi.* feel at ease; relax; have no worries
	放物線	ホウブツセン	*math.* parabola
	放牧	ホウボク	grazing —*v.* let graze; put out to pasture
	放牧地	ホウボクチ	grazing land; pasture

心 忄 戈 戸 手 扌 支 攵 文 斗 斤 方 日 曰 月 肉 月 木 欠 止 歹 殳 母 毋 比 毛 氏 气 水 氷 氵 火 灬 父 片 牛 犬 犭 王 礻 耂

心忄戈戸手扌支攵文斗斤方日曰月肉月木欠止歹殳母毋比毛氏气水氷氵火灬父片牛犬犭王礻耂

放流	ホウリュウ	stocking (rivers with fish); draining (a river)
放る	ホウる	*vt.* throw; leave as is
放ったらかす	ホッたらかす	*vt.* neglect; lay aside; leave undone

訓 放す　はなす　*vt.* set free; release; let go

放つ　はなつ　*vt.* set free; release; fire (a gun); emit; set fire to; chase away

放れる　はなれる　get free; be released/fired (arrow/bullet, etc.)

485

故 ⑨　一 十 寸 古 古 古 甴 故 故

音 故　コ　intentional; deliberate; willful; knowingly; (prefix) late; deceased

熟 故意　コイ　intentional; deliberate; wilful; knowingly

故郷　コキョウ　one's hometown

故国　ココク　one's homeland/native country

故事　コジ　historical fact; tradition; folklore

故実　コジツ　ancient practices/customs

故障　コショウ　hindrance; obstacle; trouble; breakdown; failure; damage —*v.* break down; fail; be out of order

故人　コジン　the deceased/departed

訓 故　ゆえ　reason; cause; meaning

486

政 ⑨　一 丁 下 正 正 正 政 政 政

音 政　セイ　govern
　　　（ショウ）　government

熟 政界　セイカイ　political world/circles; politics

政局　セイキョク　political situation

政経　セイケイ　politics and economics

政見　セイケン　political views

政権　セイケン　political power; government; administration

政策　セイサク　policy

政治　セイジ　government; politics

政治家　セイジカ　statesman; politician; strategist

政情　セイジョウ　political situation

政争　セイソウ　political conflict

政敵　セイテキ　political enemy/opponent

政党	セイトウ	political party
政府	セイフ	government; administration
政変	セイヘン	political change; change in government; cabinet reshuffle
政務	セイム	State affairs; affairs of State
政略	セイリャク	political tactics/maneuvers
政令	セイレイ	government ordinance
訓 政	まつりごと	administration; government; politics

487

救 ⑪　一　十　十　才　求　求　求　求　救　救　救

音 救	キュウ	assistance; help; aid
熟 救急	キュウキュウ	first aid
救護	キュウゴ	relief; aid —*v.* relieve; help; aid
救済	キュウサイ	relief; help; aid; redemption —*v.* relieve; help; aid; redeem
救出	キュウシュツ	rescue; saving; relief —*v.* rescue; save; relieve
救助	キュウジョ	rescue; relief —*v.* rescue; relieve
救世主	キュウセイシュ	savior; Jesus Christ
救命	キュウメイ	lifesaving
訓 救う	すくう	*vt.* rescue

488

教 ⑪　一　十　土　耂　耂　考　孝　孝　孝　教　教

音 教	キョウ	teach; instruction
熟 教育	キョウイク	education —*v.* educate
教員	キョウイン	teacher; member of the teaching staff
教化	キョウカ	culture; enlightenment; edification —*v.* culture; enlighten; edificate
教科	キョウカ	subject; course of study; curriculum
教科書	キョウカショ	textbook; school book
教会	キョウカイ	Christian church
教官	キョウカン	teacher; instructor; faculty; teaching staff
教義	キョウギ	doctrine; dogma; tenet; creed
教訓	キョウクン	teachings; lesson; injunction
教材	キョウザイ	teaching materials
教師	キョウシ	schoolteacher; schoolmaster; schoolmistress
教示	キョウジ	instruction; teaching —*v.* instruct; teach

心忄戈戸手扌支攵文斗斤方日曰月肉月木欠止歹殳母毋比毛氏气水氺氵火灬父片牛犬犭王礻歩

教室	キョウシツ	classroom
教授	キョウジュ	teachings; instruction; professor —*v.* teach; instruct
教習所	キョウシュウジョ	training school/institute
教書	キョウショ	message
教職	キョウショク	teaching profession
教祖	キョウソ	founder of a religion
教徒	キョウト	believer in a religion; convert
教養	キョウヨウ	culture; education
教理	キョウリ	principles; teachings; doctrine (of a religion)

訓
教える	おしえる	*vt.* teach; instruct; inform
教え子	おしえご	one's pupil
教わる	おそわる	*vt.* be taught/informed

489

敗 ⑪

丿 冂 冂 冃 目 貝 貝 貯 貯 敗 敗

音	敗	ハイ	be defeated

熟
敗因	ハイイン	cause of defeat
敗軍	ハイグン	defeated army
敗者	ハイシャ	defeated person; the vanquished; loser
敗色	ハイショク	signs of defeat
敗戦	ハイセン	defeat; lost battle/war —*vi.* be defeated; lose the war
敗走	ハイソウ	flight; rout; debacle —*vi.* take to flight; be routed; flee
敗退	ハイタイ	defeat; setback —*vi.* retreat; be defeated
敗北	ハイボク	defeat; loss; setback —*vi.* be defeated/beaten; suffer a setback

訓
敗れる	やぶれる	*vi.* be beaten/defeated; lose

490

敬 ⑫

一 十 丗 芐 芀 芀 苟 苟 苟 苟 敬 敬

音	敬	ケイ	respect

熟
敬愛	ケイアイ	love and respect —*v.* love and respect
敬意	ケイイ	respect; reverence; tribute
敬遠	ケイエン	at a distance —*v.* keep at a distance
敬具	ケイグ	Truly yours; Yours respectfully/faithfully (closing phrase of a letter)
敬語	ケイゴ	*gram.* honorific expression; term of respect

敬服	ケイフク	admiration; regard —*vi.* admire; have great regard for
敬礼	ケイレイ	salute; bow —*vi.* salute; bow; greet
敬老	ケイロウ	respect for the aged —*vi.* respect the aged
訓 敬う	うやまう	*vt.* respect; hold in high esteem; look up to

491

散 ⑫ 一 十 卄 丗 产 苫 昔 昔 背 背 散 散

音 散	サン	scatter; spread; messy; powder
熟 散会	サンカイ	adjournment —*vi.* adjourn; break up
散開	サンカイ	deployment —*vi.* spread out; deploy
散在	サンザイ	scattered; spread about —*vi.* be scattered; be spread about
散財	サンザイ	squandering; waste of money —*vi.* squander; waste money
散策	サンサク	walk —*vi.* take a walk
散々	サンザン	severely; utterly; thoroughly
散水	サンスイ	watering —*vi.* water; spray/sprinkle water
散水機	サンスイキ	water sprinkler
散発	サンパツ	scattering; occasional happenings —*v.* scatter; occur sporadically; happen occasionally
散布	サンプ	scattering; sprinkling; spraying —*v.* scatter; sprinkle; spray
散文	サンブン	prose
散歩	サンポ	walk; stroll —*vi.* take a walk; have a stroll; stroll
散乱	サンラン	scattered; littered —*vi.* be scattered about; diffuse; be littered
訓 散る	ちる	*vi.* fall; scatter; disperse; spread
散らす	ちらす	*vt.* scatter; shower; distract
散らかす	ちらかす	*vt.* scatter about; leave in disorder
散らかる	ちらかる	*vi.* be scattered; be all over the place; be in a mess

492

数 ⑬ 丶 丷 ⺷ 半 米 米 娄 娄 娄 数 数 数

音 数	スウ	number; count
	（ス）	number; count
熟 数回	スウカイ	several times
数学	スウガク	mathematics

心忄戈戸手扌支攵文斗斤方日曰月肉月木欠止歹殳母毋比毛氏气水氺氵火灬父片牛犬犭王礻耂

	数日	スウジツ	several days
	数値	スウチ	numerical value; result
	数量	スウリョウ	quantity; volume
訓	数	かず	number; figure
	数々	かずかず	numerous; many; varied
	数える	かぞえる	*vt*. count

493

敕⑮ ` ㇒ 宀 疒 肖 肖 商 商 商 啇 敵 敵

音	敵	テキ	enemy; foe; opponent; adversary; rival; competitor
熟	敵する	テキする	*vi*. turn/fight against; antagonize
	敵意	テキイ	enmity; hostility; animosity
	敵視	テキシ	enmity; hostility —*v*. be hostile; regard somone as an enemy
	敵情	テキジョウ	enemy movements
	敵対	テキタイ	hostility; contention; antagonism —*v*. be hostile to; turn against
	敵地	テキチ	enemy country
訓	敵	かたき	enemy; foe; opponent
	敵討ち	かたきうち	revenge; vendetta

494

整⑯ 一 ㇀ 戸 肀 束 敕 敕 敕 整 整 整 整

音	整	セイ	arrange
熟	整形	セイケイ	*med*. orthopedics; orthopedic surgery; plastic/cosmetic surgery —*v*. have plastic surgery
	整形外科	セイケイゲカ	*med*. orthopedic surgery
	整形手術	セイケイシュジュツ	*med*. plastic/cosmetic surgery —*v*. undergo cosmetic surgery
	整合	セイゴウ	adjustment; coordination —*v*. adjust; coordinate
	整骨	セイコツ	*med*. bonesetting; osteopathy
	整数	セイスウ	*math*. integral number
	整然	セイゼン	orderly; regular; systematic
	整地	セイチ	ground leveling; soil preparation —*vi*. prepare the land for construction of a house
	整備	セイビ	full equipment —*v*. be fully equipped; maintain; equip
	整理	セイリ	arrangement; adjustment; reorganization —*v*. arrange; adjust; reorganize

| 整列 | セイレツ | array; line up —*vi.* array; stand in a line; line up |

| **訓** 整う | ととのう | *vi.* be put in order/arranged/prepared |
| 整える | ととのえる | *vt.* put in order; arrange; prepare |

---

4 文 ぶん literature

495

文 ④ 　 ' 　 亠 　 ナ 　 文

音 文	ブン	writing; composition; sentence; text; style; literature
	モン	character; word; design; *mon* (former unit of currency); *mon* (unit of measurement, approx. 2.4cm)
熟 文案	ブンアン	draft; rough copy
文意	ブンイ	meaning of (a passage/sentence)
文化	ブンカ	culture
文化遺産	ブンカイサン	cultural heritage
文化交流	ブンカコウリュウ	cultural exchange
文化祭	ブンカサイ	cultural/school festival
文化財	ブンカザイ	cultural assets/properties
文化人	ブンカジン	cultivated person; man of culture
文化人類学	ブンカジンルイガク	cultural anthoropology
文化水準	ブンカスイジュン	cultural level; level/standard of culture
文化生活	ブンカセイカツ	civilized life
文化的	ブンカテキ	cultural
文科	ブンカ	liberal arts
文学	ブンガク	literature
文官	ブンカン	civil servant; public official; civil service
文教	ブンキョウ	education
文具	ブング	stationery
文型	ブンケイ	*gram.* sentence pattern
文芸	ブンゲイ	literature and the arts; liberal arts; literature
文芸映画	ブンゲイエイガ	film based on a literary classic
文芸家	ブンゲイカ	literary man; man of letters
文芸学	ブンゲイガク	study of literature
文芸批評	ブンゲイヒヒョウ	literary criticism
文庫	ブンコ	library; collection of books; pocket-sized book

心 忄 戈 戸 手 扌 支 攵 文 斗 斤 方 日 曰 月 肉 月 木 欠 止 歹 殳 母 毋 比 毛 氏 气 水 氺 氵 火 灬 父 片 牛 犬 犭 王 礻 爿

文庫本	ブンコボン	pocket-sized book
文語	ブンゴ	written/literary/classic language
文語体	ブンゴタイ	literary style (classical, etc.)
文才	ブンサイ	literary talent; talent for writing
文士	ブンシ	writer; man of letters
文集	ブンシュウ	anthology; collection of works
文書	ブンショ	document; record; archives
文章	ブンショウ	sentence; writing; composition
文人	ブンジン	literary man; man of letters
文節	ブンセツ	*gram*. minimum division in a Japanese sentence
文選	ブンセン	typesetting —*v*. typeset
文体	ブンタイ	(writing) style
文題	ブンダイ	theme; subject (of an essay)
文通	ブンツウ	correspondence —*vi*. write/exchange letters
文頭	ブントウ	beginning of a sentence; opening passage
文筆	ブンピツ	literary pursuits/career; writing
文武	ブンブ	civil and military affairs; the pen and the sword
文武両道	ブンブリョウドウ	literary and military arts
文法	ブンポウ	grammar
文末	ブンマツ	end of a sentence; closing sentence
文脈	ブンミャク	context
文明	ブンメイ	civilization
文明国	ブンメイコク	civilized country/nation
文明社会	ブンメイシャカイ	civilized society
文面	ブンメン	contents of a letter
文楽	ブンラク	Bunraku (puppet show/performance)
分理	ブンリ	literature and science
文例	ブンレイ	model sentence; example sentence
文字	モジ	letter; writing; character
文句	モンク	words; expression; phrase; complaint; objection
文無し	モンなし	broke; penniless
訓 文	ふみ	letter; note

4　斗　とます　dots and cross

496

料 ⑩

`、` `ヽ` `ソ` `半` `米` `米` `米` `米` `料` `料`

音	料	リョウ	material; charge; fee
熟	料金	リョウキン	charge; fee; fare
	料簡	リョウケン	idea; forgive
	料理	リョウリ	cooking; cuisine; dish; food —*v.* cook
	料理屋	リョウリや	restaurant

4　斤　おのづくり　ax

497

断 ⑪

`、` `ヽ` `ソ` `半` `米` `米` `迷` `断` `断` `断` `断`

音	断	ダン	decision; judgment; resolution; sever; refuse
熟	断じる	ダンじる	*vt.* decide; judge; resolve
	断言	ダンゲン	assertion; affirmation; declaration —*vi.* assert; affirm; declare
	断固	ダンコ	firm; decisive; resolute
	断交	ダンコウ	break in relations; rupture —*vi.* break off relations
	断行	ダンコウ	decisive action; resolute enforcement —*v.* carry out; execute; effect; enforce
	断食	ダンジキ	fast; fasting —*vi.* fast
	断じて	ダンじて	definitely
	断水	ダンスイ	suspension of water supply —*vi.* cut off the water supply
	断絶	ダンゼツ	extinction; discontinuation; severance; rupture —*v.* become extinct; cease to exist; sever; cut off
	断然	ダンゼン	positively; resolutely; absolutely; without hesitation
	断層	ダンソウ	geological fault; throw; dislocation; shift; jump
	断続	ダンゾク	intermittence —*vi.* be intermittent
	断腸	ダンチョウ	heartbreak; broken heart
	断定	ダンテイ	conclusion; decision —*v.* conclude; decide; come to a conclusion

心
忄
戈
戸
手
扌
支
攵
文
斗
斤
方
●
日
曰
月
肉
月
木
欠
止
歹
殳
母
毋
比
毛
氏
气
水
氺
氵
火
灬
父
片
牛
犬
犭
王
礻
耂

断念	ダンネン	abandonment; relinquishment; despair —*v.* give up; abandon; forgo; relinquish
断片	ダンペン	piece; fragment; shred; scrap
断片的	ダンペンテキ	fragmentary; scrappy; piecemeal
断面	ダンメン	section; phase; profile
訓 断る	ことわる	*vt.* decline; ask to be excused; apologize; dismiss; prohibit
断つ	たつ	*vt.* sever; cut; chop/break off; abstain; exterminate

498

新 ⑬   ㇒ ㇒ ㇒ 立 立 辛 辛 亲 亲 新 新 新

音 新	シン	new; novel; (prefix) neo-
熟 新案	シンアン	new device/design/idea
新入り	シンいり	newcomer
新開地	シンカイチ	newly developed land
新型	シンガタ	new/latest style; new model
新館	シンカン	new building/wing
新刊	シンカン	new publication/book
新規	シンキ	new; anew
新機軸	シンキジク	innovation; new departure/direction
新旧	シンキュウ	old and new
新居	シンキョ	new house/home
新教	シンキョウ	Protestantism
新劇	シンゲキ	*shingeki* (Western plays put on by Japanese players)
新月	シンゲツ	new moon
新語	シンゴ	new word; newly coined word
新興	シンコウ	newly risen; rising; burgeoning
新興国	シンコウコク	rising nation
新興宗教	シンコウシュウキョウ	new religion
新興都市	シンコウトシ	new town
新作	シンサク	new work/composition
新参	シンザン	newcomer; new hand
新式	シンシキ	new type/style/method
新春	シンシュン	New Year
新進	シンシン	new face; up-and-coming
新人	シンジン	new member/figure/face
新人作家	シンジンサッカ	budding writer
新制	シンセイ	new system

新星	シンセイ	nova	
新生	シンセイ	new birth; rebirth	
新生児	シンセイジ	newborn infant	
新設	シンセツ	newly established; new —*v*. found; establish; set up; organize	
新説	シンセツ	new theory/view	
新装	シンソウ	redecoration; refurbishment —*v*. redecorate; refurbish	
新卒	シンソツ	new graduate	
新大陸	シンタイリク	the New World	
新築	シンチク	new house; newly built	
新茶	シンチャ	first tea of the season	
新着	シンチャク	new arrivals; newly imported	
新調	シンチョウ	newly made; brand-new —*v*. make new (clothes, etc.)	
新天地	シンテンチ	new world; new field of activity	
新任	シンニン	newly appointed —*v*. appoint a new person	
新年	シンネン	new year	
新派	シンパ	new school	
新品	シンピン	new article; brand-new; new	
新婦	シンプ	bride	
新風	シンプウ	new life; fresh current	
新聞	シンブン	newspaper; the press	
新聞記者	シンブンキシャ	newspaper reporter	
新聞社	シンブンシャ	newspaper company	
新聞発表	シンブンハッピョウ	press release —*v*. send out a press release	
新米	シンマイ	new rice; first rice of the season *fig*. newcomer; beginner	
新味	シンミ	novelty; fresh; novel; original	
新芽	シンメ	sprout; shoot; bud	
新緑	シンリョク	fresh verdure; new green leaves	
新しい	あたらしい	new; novel; fresh; modern	
新た	あらた	new; renewed	
新手	あらて	new member/player; innovation	
新	にい	(prefix) new-	
新妻	にいづま	newly married woman	

4

心 忄 戈 戸 手 扌 支 攵 文 斗 斤 方 日 曰 月 肉 月 木 欠 止 歹 殳 母 毋 比 毛 氏 气 水 氺 氵 火 灬 父 片 牛 犬 犭 王 礻 耂

心
忄
戈
戸
手
扌
支
攵
文
斗
斤
• 方
日
曰
月
肉
月
木
欠
止
歹
殳
母
毋
比
毛
氏
气
水
氺
氵
火
灬
父
片
牛
犬
犭
王
礻
爿

4 方　ほう／ほうへん　direction; side

499 方 ④ 　 ᐟ 亠 方 方

音	方	ホウ	direction; side; square
熟	方位	ホウイ	direction; bearing (based on the four points of the compass)
	方円	ホウエン	round and/or square
	方角	ホウガク	direction; bearing
	方眼紙	ホウガンシ	graph paper
	方形	ホウケイ	square; regular quadrilateral
	方言	ホウゲン	dialect
	方向	ホウコウ	direction; destination —*fig.* one's aim
	方策	ホウサク	plan
	方式	ホウシキ	formula; method; system
	方針	ホウシン	compass needle; course; policy
	方図	ホウズ	end; limit
	方寸	ホウスン	1 square *sun* (unit of area, approx. 3㎠); very small area; heart; mind; intention
	方程式	ホウテイシキ	*math.* equation
	方便	ホウベン	expedient; means; instrument
	方法	ホウホウ	method; way; means
	方法論	ホウホウロン	methodology
	方々	ホウボウ	all directions; all over the place; everywhere
	方面	ホウメン	general direction; district; standpoint
訓	方	かた	*hon.* person; direction; way; means; (mother's/father's) side of a family
	〜方	〜がた	*hon.* plural suffix to denote people

500 旅 ⑩ 　 ᐟ 亠 方 方 方 方 方 旅 旅 旅

音	旅	リョ	travel; trip journey
熟	旅客	リョカク／リョキャク	traveler
	旅館	リョカン	hotel; inn
	旅券	リョケン	passport
	旅行	リョコウ	journey; trip; travel —*vi.* make a trip; journey; travel

旅行案内	リョコウアンナイ	travel/tour guide
旅行記	リョコウキ	travel journal
旅情	リョジョウ	one's mood while traveling
旅装	リョソウ	traveling clothes
旅団	リョダン	(military) brigade
旅程	リョテイ	itinerary; distance to be covered
旅費	リョヒ	traveling expenses

訓
旅	たび	travel; trip; journey
旅芸人	たびゲイニン	itinerant performer
旅心	たびごころ	one's mood while traveling
旅先	たびさき	destination
旅路	たびジ	journey
旅立つ	たびだつ	*vi*. start on a journey
旅人	たびびと	traveler; wayfarer; pilgrim

501

族 ⑪   ` �亠 ⺇ 方 扩 扩 扩 疒 族 族 族

音
族	ゾク	family; tribe

502

旗 ⑭   �亠 ⺇ 方 扩 扩 疒 斿 斿 旃 旃 旗 旗

音
旗	キ	flag
熟
旗手	キシュ	standard bearer; ensign
訓
旗	はた	flag
旗印	はたじるし	flag mark
旗日	はたび	national holiday

---

4 日 ひ／ひへん sun

503

日 ④   丨 冂 日 日

音
日	ニチ	sun; day; Japan
	ジツ	sun; day

心
忄
戈
戸
手
扌
支
攵
文
斗
斤
方
日
曰
月
肉
月
木
欠
止
歹
殳
母
毋
比
毛
氏
气
水
氷
氵
火
灬
父
片
牛
犬
犭
王
礻
耂

4

心
忄
戈
戸
手
扌
支
攵
文
斗
斤
方
● 日
日
曰
月
肉
月
木
欠
止
歹
殳
母
毋
比
毛
氏
气
水
氺
氵
火
灬
父
片
牛
犬
犭
王
礻
耂

熟	日印	ニチイン	Indo-Japanese
	日英	ニチエイ	Anglo-Japanese
	日時	ニチジ	date and time
	日常	ニチジョウ	usually; daily; everyday
	日常生活	ニチジョウセイカツ	everyday/daily life
	日米	ニチベイ	Japanese-American
	日夜	ニチヤ	day and night; constantly; around the clock
	日曜日	ニチヨウび	Sunday
	日用品	ニチヨウヒン	daily necessities
	日課	ニッカ	daily work/schedule
	日刊	ニッカン	daily publication
	日記	ニッキ	diary; journal
	日給	ニッキュウ	daily wages
	日系	ニッケイ	Japanese (-related)
	日光	ニッコウ	sunlight
	日光浴	ニッコウヨク	sunbathing —*vi.* sunbathe
	日誌	ニッシ	diary; journal
	日射病	ニッシャビョウ	sunstroke
	日照	ニッショウ	sunshine
	日章旗	ニッショウキ	national flag of Japan; the Rising Sun
	日食	ニッショク	solar eclipse
	日進月歩	ニッシンゲッポ	ever-progressing; constantly advancing
	日赤 （日本 赤十字社）	ニッセキ （ニホン セキジュウジシャ）	Red Cross (Society)
	日中	ニッチュウ	in the daytime; China and Japan; Sino-Japanese
	日直	ニッチョク	day duty
	日程	ニッテイ	day's program/schedule; agenda for the day
	日当	ニットウ	daily wages/allowance
	日本画	ニホンガ	Japanese painting
	日本語	ニホンゴ	the Japanese language
	日本	ニホン （ニッポン）	Japan
訓	日	か	day
	日	ひ	sun; sunshine; day; date
	日帰り	ひがえり	day trip; excursion
	日付	ひづけ	date; dating
	日の出	ひので	sunrise
	日焼け	ひやけ	sunburn; suntan —*vi.* tan
	日和	ひより	weather; fine weather; perfect day

旧 ⑤ 丨 丨丨 丨丨丨 丨日 丨日

音	旧	キュウ	old; previous; former; classic; old calendar
熟	旧家	キュウカ	old family
	旧教	キュウキョウ	Roman Catholicism; Roman Catholic Church
	旧交	キュウコウ	old/former relationship
	旧式	キュウシキ	old type; old-fashioned; classic
	旧制度	キュウセイド	old/former system; ancient regime
	旧石器時代	キュウセッキジダイ	Stone Age; Paleolithic Period
	旧知	キュウチ	old friend/acquaintance
	旧道	キュウドウ	old road
	旧年	キュウネン	the old year; last year
	旧約聖書	キュウヤクセイショ	Old Testament
	旧友	キュウユウ	old friend

早 ⑥ 丨 冂 日 日 旦 早

音	早	ソウ （サッ）	swift; early; fast
熟	早期	ソウキ	early stage/phase
	早急	ソウキュウ	urgently; without delay
	早計	ソウケイ	premature; hasty; rash (plan or idea)
	早産	ソウザン	premature birth
	早熟	ソウジュク	precocious; maturing early
	早春	ソウシュン	early spring
	早々	ソウソウ	quickly; early; immediately
	早退	ソウタイ	leaving early —*vi.* leave earlier than usual
	早朝	ソウチョウ	early morning
	早天	ソウテン	sky at dawn
	早晩	ソウバン	sooner or later
訓	早い	はやい	quick; early; fast
	早合点	はやガテン （はやガッテン）	jumping to a conclusion —*vi.* jump to a conclusion
	早口	はやくち	speaking fast
	早まる	はやまる	*vi.* be hasty/in a hurry
	早道	はやみち	shortcut

心忄戈戸手扌支攵文斗斤方日 ● 曰月肉月木欠止歹殳母毋比毛氏气水氷冫火灬父片牛犬犭王礻疒

心
↑
戈
戸
手
扌
支
攵
文
斗
斤
方
●日
日
曰
月
肉
月
木
欠
止
歹
殳
母
毋
比
毛
氏
气
水
氷
氵
火
灬
父
片
牛
犬
犭
王
礻
⺾

早見表	はやみヒョウ	chart; table
早耳	はやみみ	quick-eared; in the know
早目	はやめ	a little early
早める	はやめる	*vt*. hasten; accelerate

506 易 ⑧

一 口 日 日 尸 号 号 易 易

音	易	イ	easy; simple
		エキ	trade; divination
熟	易々	イイ	easy; easily
	易者	エキシャ	fortuneteller
訓	易しい	やさしい	easy; simple; soft

507 昔 ⑧

一 十 艹 芒 芒 昔 昔 昔

音	昔	セキ	old times
		（シャク）	
熟	昔日	セキジツ	old times; formerly; in the past
訓	昔	むかし	long ago; formerly; in the past
	昔話	むかしばなし	fairy/folk tale

508 春 ⑨

一 二 三 夫 夫 未 春 春 春

音	春	シュン	spring
熟	春夏秋冬	シュンカ シュウトウ	the four seasons; all year around
	春季	シュンキ	springtime; spring
	春期	シュンキ	spring
	春秋	シュンジュウ	spring and fall; year; years; age
	春風	シュンプウ	spring breeze
	春分	シュンブン	vernal/spring equinox
訓	春	はる	spring; springtime of life; prime; puberty
	春先	はるさき	early spring
	春雨	はるさめ	spring rain; sticks of bean jelly
	春巻き	はるまき	spring roll

509

星⑨　　丶　冂　冂　日　尸　戸　昌　星　星

音	星	セイ （ショウ）	star
熟	星雲	セイウン	nebula
	星座	セイザ	constellation
	星団	セイダン	star cluster
訓	星	ほし	star; spot; mark; asterisk; aim
	星空	ほしぞら	starry sky

510

昼⑨　　乛　コ　尸　尺　尺　尽　昼　昼　昼

音	昼	チュウ	daytime; noon; lunch
熟	昼食	チュウショク	lunch; luncheon
	昼夜	チュウヤ	day and night
訓	昼	ひる	daytime; noon
	昼下がり	ひるさがり	early afternoon
	昼過ぎ	ひるすぎ	early afternoon
	昼間	ひるま	day; daytime
	昼飯	ひるめし	lunch
	昼休み	ひるやすみ	lunchbreak

511

景⑫　　丶　冂　冂　日　旦　早　景　昌　景　景　景

音	景	ケイ	scenery; appearance; looks
熟	景観	ケイカン	scenery
	景勝	ケイショウ	picturesque scenery; scenic beauty
	景品	ケイヒン	gift; premium

心 忄 戈 戸 手 扌 支 攵 文 斗 斤 方 日 曰 月 肉 月 木 欠 止 歹 殳 母 毋 比 毛 氏 气 水 氷 氵 火 灬 父 片 牛 犬 犭 王 礻 耂

512

暑 ⑫

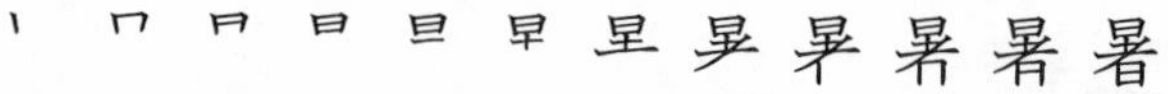

音	暑	ショ	hot; summer
熟	暑中	ショチュウ	hot season; height of summer
訓	暑い	あつい	hot; warm

513

暮 ⑭

音	暮	ボ	get dark; come to an end
熟	暮雨	ボウ	evening rain
	暮景	ボケイ	evening scenery
	暮秋	ボシュウ	late fall/autumn
	暮春	ボシュン	late spring
	暮色	ボショク	evening twilight
	暮夜	ボヤ	evening; night
訓	暮れ	くれ	nightfall; year-end; end of a season
	暮れる	くれる	***vi.*** get dark; become night; come to the end of (a day, year)
	暮らす	くらす	***vi.*** live; dwell
	暮らし	くらし	(daily) living
	暮らし向き	くらしむき	(financial) circumstances; livelihood

514

暴 ⑮

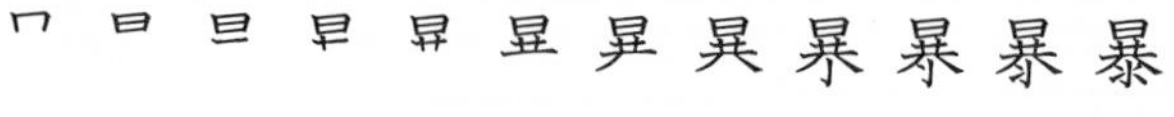

音	暴	ボウ	violence; sudden
		(バク)	expose; reveal
熟	暴飲	ボウイン	heavy excessive drinking —***vi.*** drink to excess
	暴漢	ボウカン	ruffian; goon; thug
	暴挙	ボウキョ	violence; recklessness; riot
	暴君	ボウクン	tyrant; despot
	暴言	ボウゲン	violent/abusive language
	暴行	ボウコウ	violence; rape; assault —***vi.*** use violence/force; rape; assault
	暴食	ボウショク	gluttony; gorging oneself —***vi.*** be gluttonous; gorge oneself; eat too much
	暴政	ボウセイ	tyranny; oppressive rule

暴走	ボウソウ	wild; (running) out of control; joyride —*vi.* run wild/out of control; take a car for a joyride
暴走族	ボウソウゾク	motorbike gang; bikers
暴徒	ボウト	mob; rioters
暴動	ボウドウ	riot; disturbance; uprising
暴発	ボウハツ	sudden/spontaneous occurrence; accidental firing of a gun —*vi.* occur suddenly/spontaneously; go off accidentally (pistols, guns, etc.)
暴風	ボウフウ	wind storm; high winds
暴風雨	ボウフウウ	rainstorm
暴利	ボウリ	profiteering; excessive profits; illegal profit
暴力	ボウリョク	violence; force
暴力団	ボウリョクダン	gangster organization
暴論	ボウロン	irrational/wild argument

訓
| 暴く | あばく | *vt.* disclose; expose; bring to light; dig up |
| 暴れる | あばれる | *vi.* act violently; rage; rampage |

515

明 ⑧

丨 冂 月 日 日 明 明 明

音
明	ミョウ	light; next; following
	メイ	light
	（ミン）	Ming dynasty

熟
明春	ミョウシュン	next spring
明星	ミョウジョウ	the morning star; the planet Venus
明神	ミョウジン	gracious god
明朝	ミョウチョウ	tomorrow morning
明日	ミョウニチ	tomorrow; next/following day
明年	ミョウネン	next year
明晩	ミョウバン	tomorrow evening
明暗	メイアン	light and dark; shading; happiness and sadness
明快	メイカイ	clear; lucid
明解	メイカイ	clear
明確	メイカク	clear; distinct; well-defined
明記	メイキ	clearly written/stated —*v.* stipulate; specify (in writing)
明君	メイクン	wise ruler
明言	メイゲン	declaration; assertion —*v.* declare; assert
明細	メイサイ	details; particulars
明示	メイジ	clear statement/indication —*v.* state/indicate clearly

心 忄 戈 戸 手 扌 支 攵 文 斗 斤 方 日 ● 曰 月 肉 月 木 欠 止 歹 殳 母 毋 比 毛 氏 气 水 氺 氵 火 灬 父 片 牛 犬 犭 王 礻 耂

左 心 忄 戈 戸 手 扌 支 攵 文 斗 斤 方 ● 日 日 月 肉 月 木 欠 止 歹 殳 母 毋 比 毛 氏 气 水 氺 氵 火 灬 父 片 牛 犬 犭 王 礻 玊

明治	メイジ	*hist.* Meiji (period/emperor 1868-1912)
明度	メイド	brightness; luminosity
明答	メイトウ	definite answer
明白	メイハク	clear; unmistakable
明朗	メイロウ	cheerful; clear; open

訓

明かす	あかす	*vt.* pass; spend the night; confide; divulge
明らむ	あからむ	*vi.* become light
明かり	あかり	light; clearness
明るい	あかるい	bright; cheerful; knowledgeable
明るむ	あかるむ	*vi.* become light
明らか	あきらか	clear; definite
明く	あく	*vi.* be open; be visible
明くる	あくる	next; following
明ける	あける	*vi.* dawn; (a new year) begin; expire (a term of office) *vt.* open (up)

516

映 ⑨　丨 冂 冂 日 日 旷 旷 映 映

| 音 | 映 | エイ | project; reflect |

熟	映画	エイガ	motion picture; movie; film
	映画館	エイガカン	movie theater; cinema
	映画俳優	エイガハイユウ	movie actor
	映写	エイシャ	projection —*v.* project an image onto a screen
	映像	エイゾウ	reflection; image; video

訓	映す	うつす	*vt.* reflect
	映る	うつる	*vi.* reflect; match; harmonize
	映える	はえる	*vi.* shine; gleam

517

昨 ⑨　丨 冂 日 日 旷 旷 昨 昨

| 音 | 昨 | サク | yesterday |

熟	昨日	サクジツ	yesterday
	昨年	サクネン	last year
	昨晩	サクバン	last night
	昨夜	サクヤ	last night
	昨今	サッコン	these days; lately; recently

518

昭 ⑨ ｜ 冂 月 日 日⁷ 昭 昭 昭 昭

| 音 | 昭 | ショウ | clear |
| 熟 | 昭和 | ショウワ | Showa (period/emperor 1925-1988) |

519

時 ⑩ ｜ 冂 月 日 日⁻ 旷 旷 昨 時 時

音	時	ジ	time; hour; opportunity
熟	時間	ジカン	time; hour
	時期	ジキ	time; timing; season
	時機	ジキ	opportunity; chance
	時給	ジキュウ	payment by the hour
	時局	ジキョク	situation; current state of affairs
	時限	ジゲン	closing time; time limit; deadline
	時効	ジコウ	prescription (in the legal sense); statute of limitations
	時候	ジコウ	seasonal weather
	時刻	ジコク	time; the hour; appointed time
	時差	ジサ	time difference
	時事	ジジ	current events
	時々刻々	ジジコクコク	every moment; hour to hour; moment to moment
	時制	ジセイ	*gram*. tense
	時勢	ジセイ	trend of the times; the times
	時世	ジセイ	the times; the day; the age
	時節	ジセツ	the season; the times; the occasion; the moment; good opportunity
	時速	ジソク	speed per hour
	時代	ジダイ	the times; era; age; antiquity
	時点	ジテン	point in time; instant
	時分	ジブン	time; season; opportunity
	時報	ジホウ	time signal; current news
訓	時	とき	time; hour; case; opportunity; then; the times; the season
	時折	ときおり	sometimes; occasionally
	時々	ときどき	sometimes
	時めく	ときめく	*vi*. prosper; flourish
	時計	とケイ	watch; clock

4

心 忄 戈 戸 手 扌 支 攵 文 斗 斤 方 日 ● 曰 月 肉 月 木 欠 止 歹 殳 母 毋 比 毛 氏 气 水 氺 氵 火 灬 父 片 牛 犬 犭 王 衤 耂

520 晴 ⑫

丨 冂 月 日 日⁻ 日⁺ 日ᵗ 日ᵗ 晴 晴 晴 晴

音	晴	セイ	clear
熟	晴雨	セイウ	rain or shine; weather
	晴耕雨読	セイコウウドク	plowing on fine days and reading on wet days; free life-style
	晴天	セイテン	fine weather; blue sky
訓	晴れる	はれる	*vi.* clear; be dispelled
	晴れ	はれ	sunny/fine weather; clear skies
	晴れ着	はれぎ	one's best clothes; one's Sunday best
	晴れやか	はれやか	radiant; beaming; cheerful
	晴らす	はらす	*vt.* clear oneself; avenge oneself; dispel; remove (doubts, etc.)

521 晩 ⑫

丨 冂 月 日 日ʼ 日ʼʼ 日ʼʼ 晩 晩 晩 晩 晩

音	晩	バン	evening; late
熟	晩夏	バンカ	late summer; latter part of summer
	晩学	バンガク	learning late in life; late education
	晩秋	バンシュウ	late autumn; latter part of autumn
	晩春	バンシュン	late spring; latter part of spring
	晩冬	バントウ	late winter; latter part of winter
	晩年	バンネン	one's closing years; last part of one's life

522 暗 ⑬

丨 冂 日 日ʼ 日⁻ 日⁻ 日⁻ 暗 暗 暗 暗 暗

音	暗	アン	dark; dull; secret; hidden; learn by heart; foolish
熟	暗雲	アンウン	dark clouds
	暗記	アンキ	memorizing; learning by heart —*v.* memorize; learn by heart
	暗号	アンゴウ	code; cipher; cryptograph; passssword
	暗黒	アンコク	darkness; blackness
	暗殺	アンサツ	assassination —*v.* assassinate
	暗算	アンザン	*math.* mental arithmetic —*v.* do sums in one's head

	暗示	アンジ	hint; suggestion; reminder —v. hint; suggest; remind
	暗唱	アンショウ	recital; recitation —v. recite
	暗然	アンゼン	tearful; doleful; gloomy
	暗幕	アンマク	blackout curtain
	暗夜	アンヤ	dark night
訓	暗い	くらい	dark; black

523

暖⑬　丨　Π　日　日ˊ　日ˇ　日ˇ　日ˇˇ　日ˡˡ　日ˡˡ　暖　暖　暖

音	暖	ダン	warmth; heat
熟	暖気	ダンキ	warmth; warm weather
	暖色	ダンショク	warm colors
	暖帯	ダンタイ	subtropical zone
	暖地	ダンチ	warm region
	暖冬	ダントウ	mild winter
	暖流	ダンリュウ	warm sea current
訓	暖か	あたたか	warmly; kindly
	暖かい	あたたかい	warm; mild; kind; friendly
	暖まる	あたたまる	vi. warm oneself; get warm
	暖める	あたためる	vt. warm; heat; heat up

524

曜⑱　Π　日　日ˀ　日ˀ　日ˀ　日ˀˀ　日ˀˀ　曜　曜　曜　曜　曜

| 音 | 曜 | ヨウ | day of the week |
| 熟 | 曜日 | ヨウび | day of the week |

4　曰　いわく／ひらび　flat sun

525

曲⑥　丨　冂　冂　冉　曲　曲

音	曲	キョク	bend; wrong; detail; unusual; song; play
熟	曲芸	キョクゲイ	acrobatics; trick; stunt
	曲折	キョクセツ	winding; meandering; bending —vi. wind;

275

心
忄
戈
戸
手
扌
支
攵
文
斗
斤
方
日　•
曰　•
月
肉
月
木
欠
止
歹
殳
母
毋
比
毛
氏
气
水
氺
氵
火
灬
父
片
牛
犬
犭
王
礻
耂

心忄戈戸手扌支攵文斗斤方日曰月肉月木欠止歹殳母毋比毛氏气水氺火灬父片牛犬犭王礻

meander; bend

曲線	キョクセン	curved line; curve	
曲目	キョクモク	musical program; one's repertoire; musical number	
曲解	キョッカイ	perversion; distortion —*v.* pervert; distort	
訓 曲がる	まがる	*vi.* bend; twist; turn; wind	
曲げる	まげる	*vt.* bend; twist; turn; wind	

526

書 ⑩   ⁻ ⁻¹ ⁻¹¹ ⁻¹¹¹ ⁻¹¹¹¹ 聿 書 書 書 書

音 書	ショ	write; letter; book	
熟 書画	ショガ	paintings and calligraphic works	
書簡	ショカン	letter; correspondence; note	
書記	ショキ	clerk; secretary	
書記長	ショキチョウ	secretary-general (of the UN, Japanese Communist Party, etc.)	
書庫	ショコ	library	
書式	ショシキ	set way of writing or filling out (forms, etc.)	
書写	ショシャ	transcription	
書状	ショジョウ	letter	
書生	ショセイ	student; houseboy	
書体	ショタイ	style of handwriting/type	
書店	ショテン	bookstore; bookshop; publisher	
書道	ショドウ	calligraphy	
書評	ショヒョウ	book review	
書風	ショフウ	style of calligraphy	
書名	ショメイ	title of a book	
書面	ショメン	letter; writing; document	
書物	ショモツ	book	
書類	ショルイ	documents; papers	
訓 書く	かく	*vt.* write; spell; compose	
書き入れる	かきいれる	*vt.* enter; fill out (a form)	
書き置き	かきおき	note left behind; memo; message	
書き初め	かきぞめ	first calligraphy of the New Year (Japanese custom)	
書留	かきとめ	registered mail	

4

音	最	サイ	utmost; the most
熟	最愛	サイアイ	one's dearest/closest
	最悪	サイアク	worst
	最下位	サイカイ	lowest rank; last place; bottom
	最強	サイキョウ	strongest
	最近	サイキン	lately; recently
	最敬礼	サイケイレイ	most respectful bow —*vi.* bow most respectfully
	最古	サイコ	oldest
	最後	サイゴ	last; end; final; in conclusion
	最期	サイゴ	one's death/last moment
	最高	サイコウ	highest; best; maximum
	最高裁判所	サイコウ サイバンショ	Supreme Court
	最高潮	サイコウチョウ	climax; peak; the height
	最終	サイシュウ	last; final
	最終駅	サイシュウエキ	terminal station; last station
	最初	サイショ	first; beginning; start; initial
	最小	サイショウ	smallest; minimum
	最少	サイショウ	least; smallest; lowest
	最上	サイジョウ	best; finest; highest
	最新	サイシン	latest; newest; most up to date
	最盛期	サイセイキ	golden age; heyday
	最前	サイゼン	foremost; forefront
	最善	サイゼン	best; ideal
	最多	サイタ	most
	最大	サイダイ	maximum; largest; biggest
	最短	サイタン	shortest
	最中	サイチュウ	in the middle; while
	最長	サイチョウ	longest
	最低	サイテイ	lowest; minimum
	最適	サイテキ	best; most suitable; perfect; optimum
	最年少	サイネンショウ	youngest
	最年長	サイネンチョウ	oldest
	最良	サイリョウ	best; ideal
訓	最も	もっとも	most

最 ⑫ 丶 冂 冂 日 旦 昌 昌 昌 昻 昻 最 最

心 忄 戈 戸 手 扌 支 攵 文 斗 斤 方 日 曰 月 肉 月 木 欠 止 歹 殳 母 毋 比 毛 氏 气 水 氺 氵 火 灬 父 片 牛 犬 犭 王 礻 耂

心忄戈戸手扌支攵文斗斤方日曰月肉月木欠止歹殳母毋比毛氏气水氺氵火灬父片牛犬犭王礻爿

4 月 つき／つきへん　moon　　月 (にくづき) ⇨p.281

528

月 ④ 　ノ 几 月 月

音	月	ゲツ	month; moon
		ガツ	month; moon
熟	月刊	ゲッカン	monthly issue
	月光	ゲッコウ	moonlight; moonshine
	月謝	ゲッシャ	monthly tuition/fee
	月食	ゲッショク	lunar eclipse
	月曜日	ゲツヨウび	Monday
	月例	ゲツレイ	monthly
訓	月	つき	moon; month
	月並み	つきなみ	conventional; commonplace; hackneyed
	月日	つきひ	time; days; years

529

有 ⑥ 　ノ ナ オ 冇 有 有

音	有	ユウ	possession
		ウ	existence; being
熟	有する	ユウする	*vt.* have; possess; own
	有象無象	ウゾウムゾウ	rabble; riff-raff
	有頂天	ウチョウテン	exaltation; rapture; ecstacy
	有無	ウム	existence; presence; yes or no
	有意義	ユウイギ	significant
	有益	ユウエキ	beneficial; profitable; instructive; edifying
	有害	ユウガイ	harmful; noxious; destructive
	有機	ユウキ	organic
	有給	ユウキュウ	salaried
	有形	ユウケイ	concrete; material; visible
	有限	ユウゲン	limited; finite
	有権者	ユウケンシャ	qualified person; electorate
	有効	ユウコウ	validity; efficiency; effectiveness
	有罪	ユウザイ	guilt; criminality
	有志	ユウシ	volunteer; interest; sympathy
	有史以来	ユウシイライ	since the dawn of history

有識者	ユウシキシャ	intellectual person
有終	ユウシュウ	perfection; fine conclusion
有色人種	ユウショク ジンシュ	colored race
有数	ユウスウ	leading; prominent; distinguished
有線	ユウセン	cable; wire
有段者	ユウダンシャ	grade holder (of Japanese go, shōgi or martial arts)
有毒	ユウドク	poisonous; toxic
有能	ユウノウ	able; capable; efficient
有望	ユウボウ	promising; good prospects
有名	ユウメイ	famous; well-known; notorious; proverbial
有名無実	ユウメイムジツ	nominal; titular
有用	ユウヨウ	useful; available; serviceable
有利	ユウリ	profitable; advantageous
有料	ユウリョウ	charge; toll
有力	ユウリョク	influential; powerful
訓 有る	ある	*vi.* be; have; exist; occur; be located; consist of
有り様	ありさま	situation; circumstances; sight; the naked truth

530

服⑧ ） 刀 月 月 𦨎 𦨏 服 服

音 服	フク	clothes; dress; dose; obey; serve; admit to
熟 服する	フクする	*v.* obey; submit; serve; drink; wear; put on
服役	フクエキ	penal servitude; military service —*vi.* serve a prison sentence; do military service
服罪	フクザイ	pleading guilty; acceptance of punishment —*vi.* plead guilty; admit one's crime and accept punishment
服地	フクジ	cloth; fabric; material
服従	フクジュウ	obedience; submission —*vi.* obey; submit to
服装	フクソウ	dress; attire
服毒	フクドク	taking poison —*vi.* take poison
服務	フクム	service; duties —*vi.* serve; be on duty
服薬	フクヤク	taking medicine —*vi.* take medicine
服用	フクヨウ	taking (medicine) —*vi.* take (medicine)

心 忄 戈 戸 手 扌 支 攵 文 斗 斤 方 日 曰 月 肉 月 木 欠 止 歹 殳 母 毋 比 毛 氏 气 水 氷 氵 火 灬 父 片 牛 犬 犭 王 礻 耂

心忄戈戸手扌支攵文斗斤方日曰月肉月木欠歹殳母毋比毛氏气水氺氵火灬父片牛犬犭王礻耂

531

丶　ㄅ　ㅋ　ㅋ　自　良　良）　朗　朗　朗

⑩

音	朗	ロウ	clear; bright; cheerful
熟	朗読	ロウドク	recitation —*v.* read aloud
	朗報	ロウホウ	good news; glad tidings
	朗々	ロウロウ	clear; sonorous
訓	朗らか	ほがらか	clear; bright; cheerful

532

丶　亠　亡　亡）　切　朝　朝　望　望　望　望

⑪

音	望	ボウ	hope; desire; look into the distance; full moon
		モウ	
熟	望遠鏡	ボウエンキョウ	telescope
	望外	ボウガイ	unexpected; not even dreamed of
	望郷	ボウキョウ	nostalgia; homesickness
	望見	ボウケン	watching from afar —*v.* watch from afar
訓	望む	のぞむ	*vt.* desire; hope for; look into the distance; look up; long for
	望み通り	のぞみどおり	as desired

533

期

一　十　卄　艹　甘　其　其　其　期）　期　期　期

⑫

音	期	キ	time; period
		（ゴ）	time; period
熟	期間	キカン	period; time
	期限	キゲン	time limit; term; deadline
	期日	キジツ	fixed date
	期待	キタイ	expectation —*v.* expect; hope
	期末	キマツ	end of a term

534

一　十　十　士　古　甴　直　卓　朝　朝　朝　朝

⑫

| 音 | 朝 | チョウ | morning; court; dynasty; reign; regime; period; |

era

熟	朝会	チョウカイ	morning assembly
	朝刊	チョウカン	morning edition/newspaper
	朝食	チョウショク	breakfast
	朝夕	チョウセキ	morning and evening; day and night; always; usually
	朝礼	チョウレイ	morning assembly/gathering; morning meetings (at school or a company)
訓	朝	あさ	morning
	朝晩	あさバン	morning and evening
	朝日	あさひ	morning sun

---

6 にく meat　　月 (p.281)

535

肉 〡 冂 内 内 肉 肉 ⑥

音	肉	ニク	flesh; muscles; meat
熟	肉眼	ニクガン	naked eye
	肉食	ニクショク	meat diet; meat-eating; flesh-eating —*vi.* eat meat; live on a meat diet
	肉親	ニクシン	blood relation; flesh and blood
	肉声	ニクセイ	natural/human voice
	肉体	ニクタイ	body; flesh
	肉団子	ニクダンご	meat dumpling/ball
	肉筆	ニクヒツ	autograph; one's own handwriting
	肉太	ニクぶと	full-faced; bold-faced; thick type
	肉片	ニクヘン	piece of meat
	肉欲	ニクヨク	lust; animal passions; carnal desire; sexual appetite

---

4 にくづき meat; body　　月 (つきへん) ⇨P.278

536

育 ⼀ 亠 ㄊ ㄊ 产 育 育 育 ⑧

| 音 | 育 | イク | bring up; grow up; breed; train |

４

心忄戈戸手扌支攵文斗方日曰月肉月木欠止歹殳母毋比毛氏气水氺氵火灬父片牛犬犭王礻耂

	育英	イクエイ	cultivation of young talent; education and scholarship
熟	育児	イクジ	child/baby care; infant rearing
	育成	イクセイ	rearing; upbringing —v. bring up; rear; raise; foster
訓	育つ	そだつ	vi. grow up; be brought up; be bred
	育てる	そだてる	vt. bring up; rear; raise; nurture
	育む	はぐくむ	vt. bring up; nurse; foster; cultivate

537

胃 ⑨ 丶 丨 冂 冂 甲 田 甲 胃 胃 胃

音	胃	イ	stomach
熟	胃液	イエキ	med. gastric juice
	胃散	イサン	stomach powder
	胃腸	イチョウ	med. stomach and intestines; gastrointestinal tract; digestive organs
	胃腸科	イチョウカ	gastrointestinal medicine; hospital department for diseases of the gastrointestinal tract

538

背 ⑨ 一 丬 キ 土 北 北 背 背 背

音	背	ハイ	back; height; rebel
熟	背泳	ハイエイ	backstroke
	背教	ハイキョウ	renegation; apostasy
	背景	ハイケイ	background; scenery; setting
	背後	ハイゴ	back; rear
	背信	ハイシン	betrayal; infidelity —v. betray a person's confidence
	背徳	ハイトク	immorality; corruption
	背任	ハイニン	breach of trust; malpractice
	背反	ハイハン	rebellion; revolt —vi. rebel; revolt
	背面	ハイメン	rear; back
	背理	ハイリ	irrationality; absurdity; preposterous
訓	背	せ	back; stature; height; ridge
	背	せい	stature; height
	背負う	せおう	vt. carry (a burden) on one's back; shoulder (a burden)
	背泳ぎ	せおよぎ	backstroke
	背筋	せすじ	line of the backbone; seam of the back

背広	せびろ	gentleman's suit
背骨	せぼね	backbone; spine; spinal column
背く	そむく	*v.* go against; be contrary; disobey; violate; rebel; revolt
背ける	そむける	*vt.* turn one's face away; look away

539

能 ⑩　ㄥ　ㄙ　ㄟ　台　台　台　台　能　能　能

音	能	ノウ	talent; faculty; ability; Noh drama
熟	能楽	ノウガク	Noh drama
	能動	ノウドウ	activity
	能動的	ノウドウテキ	active
	能筆	ノウヒツ	good writing/writer
	能弁	ノウベン	eloquence; oratory
	能面	ノウメン	Noh mask
	能率	ノウリツ	efficiency
	能力	ノウリョク	ability; capacity; capability

540

肥 ⑧　丿　刀　月　月　月ㄱ　月ㄲ　月ㄲ　肥

音	肥	ヒ	grow fat/fertile
熟	肥育	ヒイク	fattening —*v.* fatten
	肥大	ヒダイ	fleshiness; corpulence ***med.*** hypertrophy —*vi.* get fat; become corpulent/fleshy; swell
	肥満	ヒマン	fatness; corpulence; obesity —*vi.* grow corpulent/stout; become fat
	肥料	ヒリョウ	fertilizer; manure
訓	肥	こえ	manure; night soil
	肥える	こえる	*vi.* grow fat/fertile; gain experience
	肥やし	こやし	manure; fertilizer
	肥やす	こやす	*vt.* fertilize; fatten (livestock); enrich
	肥る	ふとる	*vi.* get fat

541

肺 ⑨　丿　刀　月　月　月'　月ㄫ　月ㄫ　肺　肺

| 音 | 肺 | ハイ | lung |

心 忄 戈 戸 手 扌 支 攵 文 斗 斤 方 日 曰 月 肉 月 木 欠 止 歹 殳 母 毋 比 毛 氏 气 水 氺 氵 火 灬 父 片 牛 犬 犭 王 礻 耂

•

心忄戈戸手扌支攵文斗斤方日曰月肉月木欠止歹殳母毋比毛氏气水氺氵火灬父片牛犬犭王礻耂

熟	肺活量	ハイカツリョウ	*med.* breathing/lung capacity
	肺臓	ハイゾウ	*med.* lungs
	肺病	ハイビョウ	*med.* lung disease

542

胸 ⑩) 刀 月 月 肝 肑 肑 胸 胸 胸

音	胸	キョウ	chest; bosom; heart
熟	胸囲	キョウイ	chest measurement; girth of the chest
	胸像	キョウゾウ	bust
	胸中	キョウチュウ	feelings; thoughts; intent
訓	胸	むね	chest; bosom; heart
	胸	むな	(prefix) chest; bosom; heart; feelings
	胸算用	むなザンヨウ	mental arithmetic; expectation; anticipation
	胸元	むなもと	pit of the stomach; bosom; breast

543

脈 ⑩) 刀 月 月 肝 肵 肵 胪 脈 脈

音	脈	ミャク	blood vessel; pulse; vein
熟	脈打つ	ミャクうつ	*vi.* pulsate; beat
	脈管	ミャクカン	*med.* blood vessel; duct
	脈動	ミャクドウ	*med.* pulsation —*vi.* pulsate; beat
	脈々	ミャクミャク	continuous; unbroken

544

脳 ⑪) 刀 月 月 月 肝 肝 肸 胳 脳 脳

音	脳	ノウ	brain
熟	脳外科	ノウゲカ	*med.* brain surgery
	脳出血	ノウシュッケツ	*med.* cerebral hemorrhage
	脳天	ノウテン	pate; crown
	脳貧血	ノウヒンケツ	*med.* cerebral anemia
	脳裏	ノウリ	one's mind/memory

545 腸 ⑬

) 刀 月 月' 肝 肥 胛 胛 胛 腭 腸 腸

| 音 | 腸 | チョウ | intestines; entrails; gut |
| 訓 | 腸 | はらわた | bowels; intestines; entrails; gut |

546 腹 ⑬

) 刀 月 月' 肝 肝 腑 腑 胪 胪 腹 腹

音	腹	フク	belly; stomach; heart; mind
熟	腹案	フクアン	(secret) plan; forethought
	腹式呼吸	フクシキコキュウ	abdominal breathing
	腹心	フクシン	confidant; trusted associate
	腹痛	フクツウ	*med*. stomachache; abdominal pain
	腹部	フクブ	*med*. abdomen; belly
	腹話術	フクワジュツ	ventriloquism
	腹筋	フッキン	*med*. abdominal muscles
訓	腹	はら	belly; stomach; heart; mind
	腹切	はらきり	suicide by disembowlment; hara-kiri
	腹立つ	はらだつ	*vi*. get angry
	腹八分	はらハチブ	moderate eating
	腹巻	はらまき	stomach wrapper

547 臓 ⑲

刀 月 肝 肝 胪 胪 胪 腑 膧 臓 臓 臓

音	臓	ゾウ	entrails; internal organs
熟	臓器	ゾウキ	*med*. internal organs; viscera
	臓器移植	ゾウキイショク	*med*. organ transplant
	臓物	ゾウモツ	entrails; giblets

心 忄 戈 戸 手 扌 支 攵 文 斗 斤 方 日 曰 月 肉 月 木 欠 止 歹 殳 母 毋 比 毛 氏 气 水 氺 氵 火 灬 父 片 牛 犬 犭 王 礻 耂

心忄戈戸手扌支攵文斗斤方日曰月肉月●木欠止歹殳母毋比毛氏气水氺冫火灬父片牛犬犭王礻耂

4 木 き／きへん tree

548
木④ 一 十 オ 木

音	木	ボク	tree; wood
		モク	tree; wood
熟	木刀	ボクトウ	wooden sword
	木魚	モクギョ	wooden temple drum
	木材	モクザイ	wood; lumber
	木質	モクシツ	ligneous
	木製	モクセイ	wooden; made of wood
	木星	モクセイ	the planet Jupiter
	木造	モクゾウ	wooden; made of wood
	木像	モクゾウ	wooden image
	木炭	モクタン	charcoal
	木彫	モクチョウ	wood carving
	木馬	モクバ	wooden/rocking/carousel/vaulting horse
	木版	モクハン	woodblock printing/print
	木片	モクヘン	block/chip/splinter of wood
	木目	モクめ	wood grain
	木曜日	モクヨウび	Thursday
	木工	モッコウ	carpenter; woodworker; carpentry; woodworking
	木綿	モメン	cotton (cloth)
訓	木	き	tree; wood
	木戸	きど	gate; wicket; entrance; castle gate
	木	こ	(prefix) wood; tree
	木立	こだち	grove; thicket

549
本⑤ 一 十 オ 木 本

音	本	ホン	book; this; main; origin; (counter for long objects)
熟	本意	ホンイ	one's real intention
	本院	ホンイン	main institution; this institution
	本営	ホンエイ	(military) headquarters
	本格的	ホンカクテキ	full-scale; genuine; in earnest

本官	ホンカン	one's permanent/principal function; I (used by officials); the present official
本気	ホンキ	serious; in earnest
本義	ホンギ	true meaning; basic principle
本決まり	ホンぎまり	final decision
本給	ホンキュウ	basic/regular salary
本業	ホンギョウ	one's main occupation
本家	ホンケ	main family; originator
本校	ホンコウ	this school
本国	ホンゴク	one's own country
本山	ホンザン	head temple; this temple
本紙	ホンシ	this newspaper
本誌	ホンシ	this magazine
本式	ホンシキ	regular; orthodox
本質	ホンシツ	essence
本日	ホンジツ	today
本社	ホンシャ	head office; main shrine; this shrine
本州	ホンシュウ	Honshu
本性	ホンショウ	true nature/character
本職	ホンショク	one's regular occupation; expert
本心	ホンシン	one's right mind/senses; real intention/motive; conscience
本筋	ホンすじ	plot (of a story)
本線	ホンセン	main (railway) line
本尊	ホンゾン	**Bud**. main image (of worship); idol
本体	ホンタイ	true form
本隊	ホンタイ	main body (of troops)
本題	ホンダイ	main (this) issue/subject/problem
本宅	ホンタク	principal residence
本調子	ホンチョウシ	proper key (of an instrument); regular form
本店	ホンテン	head office; main store; this store
本土	ホンド	mainland
本当	ホントウ	true; real
本島	ホントウ	main island; this island
本堂	ホンドウ	main temple building
本人	ホンニン	the person himself; the said person; the principal figure
本音	ホンね	real intention; underlying motive
本年	ホンネン	this year
本能	ホンノウ	instinct
本場	ホンば	the best place for (a product); the place where something is produced (food, etc.)
本箱	ホンばこ	bookcase

心
⼘
戈
戸
手
扌
支
攵
文
斗
斤
方
日
曰
月
肉
月
木 ●
欠
止
歹
殳
母
毋
比
毛
氏
气
水
氺
氵
火
灬
父
片
牛
犬
犭
王
礻
⺹

心忄戈戸手扌支攵文斗斤方日曰月肉月木欠止歹殳母毋比毛氏气水氺氵火灬父片牛犬犭王礻老

本番	ホンバン	actual performance (not a rehearsal)
本文	ホンブン	main text; body of a letter
本分	ホンブン	duty (as a student, soldier, etc.)
本丸	ホンまる	castle proper; donjon; keep
本名	ホンミョウ	one's real name
本務	ホンム	duty (as a student, soldier, etc.)
本命	ホンメイ	probable winner; favorite (to win)
本望	ホンモウ	satisfaction; long cherished desire
本物	ホンもの	real thing; genuine article
本屋	ホンや	bookstore; bookshop
本来	ホンライ	in essence; naturally; originally; primarily
本流	ホンリュウ	mainstream
本領	ホンリョウ	characteristic; nature; true ability
本論	ホンロン	main subject/discussion; this subject
訓 本	もと	the origin; former

550

末⑤ 一 二 亖 才 末

音 末	マツ バツ	end; powder
熟 末期	マッキ	last/closing years; last stage
末期	マツゴ	one's last dying moments
末座	マツザ	lowest-ranking seats
末日	マツジツ	last day
末子	マッシ（バッシ）	youngest child
末世	マッセ	future ages —**Bud**. last days of the world
末席	マッセキ	lowest-ranking seats
末代	マツダイ	all ages to come; eternity; the next world; future ages
末筆	マッピツ	closing written remarks
末葉	マツヨウ	close; end of an era
末流	マツリュウ	descendants; lower reaches of a river
末路	マツロ	last days; end; end of one's life; old age
訓 末	すえ	end; future; descendant; youngest child; trivialities
末っ子	すえっこ	youngest child

未⑤ 一 二 キ 牛 未

音	未	ミ	not yet; (prefix) un-
熟	未開	ミカイ	uncivilized; barbarous; undeveloped
	未開発	ミカイハツ	undeveloped
	未解決	ミカイケツ	unsolved; unsettled
	未刊	ミカン	unpublished
	未完	ミカン	incomplete; unfinished
	未完成	ミカンセイ	incomplete; unfinished
	未決	ミケツ	undecided; pending; unsettled
	未見	ミケン	unacquainted; unknown
	未済	ミサイ	unpaid; unsettled; outstanding
	未熟	ミジュク	unripe; inexperienced; premature; immature
	未成年	ミセイネン	underage; minority; minor
	未然	ミゼン	before it happens; beforehand
	未知	ミチ	unknown; strange
	未知数	ミチスウ	unknown quantity
	未着	ミチャク	not yet arrived
	未定	ミテイ	undecided; pending
	未納	ミノウ	nonpayment; default; arrears
	未亡人	ミボウジン	widow
	未満	ミマン	less than; below
	未明	ミメイ	early dawn before sunrise
	未聞	ミモン	unheard of; unknown
	未来	ミライ	future *gram.* future tense
	未練	ミレン	regret; lingering affection

条⑦ ノ ク タ タ 冬 条 条

音	条	ジョウ	branch; reason
熟	条件	ジョウケン	condition; prerequisite; terms; requirement
	条文	ジョウブン	provision; the text; notes
	条約国	ジョウヤクコク	treaty power/nation
	条理	ジョウリ	reason
	条例	ジョウレイ	ordinance; rules; regulation

右側余白（部首索引）: 心 忄 戈 戸 手 扌 支 攵 文 斗 斤 方 日 曰 月 肉 月 木 ● 欠 止 歹 殳 母 毋 比 毛 氏 气 水 氷 氵 火 灬 父 片 牛 犬 犭 王 礻 耂

4

心忄戈戸手扌支攵文斗斤方日日月肉月木欠止歹殳母毋比毛氏气水氷氵火灬父片牛犬犭王礻耂

553

束 ⑦

一 厂 厂 丏 束 束 束

音	束	ソク	bundle; sheaf; ream
訓	束	たば	bundle; bunch; sheaf
	束ねる	たばねる	*vt.* bundle; govern; manage; control
	束	つか	handbreadth; span; brief time; thickness
	束ねる	つかねる	*vt.* tie in bundles; fold (one's arms)

554

果 ⑧

丨 冂 日 日 旦 甲 果 果

音	果	カ	fruit; effect; complete
熟	果実	カジツ	fruit
	果樹	カジュ	fruit tree
	果然	カゼン	as expected; sure enough
	果報	カホウ	good fortune; luck; reward
訓	果たして	はたして	as expected; sure enough
	果たす	はたす	*vt.* carry out; accomplish; finish; complete; effect
	果て	はて	limits; end; outcome
	果てる	はてる	*vi.* terminate; end; die

555

東 ⑧

一 厂 厂 丏 丏 market 車 東 東

音	東	トウ	east
熟	東海道	トウカイドウ	Tokaido (route between Kyoto and Tokyo)
	東京	トウキョウ	Tokyo
	東宮	トウグウ	crown prince
	東経	トウケイ	east longitude
	東国	トウゴク	eastern country; Kanto provinces
	東洋	トウヨウ	Orient
訓	東	ひがし	east

栄 ⑨ 　 丶 　ゝ　 ⸊ 　⸊⸊　 ⸌⸍　 ⸌⸍⸍　 栄　 栄　 栄

音	栄	エイ	prosper; thrive; glory
熟	栄光	エイコウ	glory; honor
	栄転	エイテン	promotion; transference —*vi.* be promoted; be transferred to another post
	栄養	エイヨウ	nutrition
	栄養価	エイヨウカ	nutritive value
訓	栄える	さかえる	*vi.* prosper; be prosperous; flourish
	栄え	はえ	glory
	栄える	はえる	*vi.* shine; be brilliant

査 ⑨ 　 一　 十　 オ　 木　 木　 杏　 杏　 杳　 査

音	査	サ	investigation; inquiry
熟	査察	ササツ	inspection —*v.* inspect
	査察官	ササツカン	inspector
	査証	サショウ	visa —*v.* grant a visa
	査定	サテイ	assessment —*v.* assess; make an assessment
	査問	サモン	inquiry —*v.* inquire

染 ⑨ 　 丶　 ⸊　 ⸍　 汀　 汍　 汃　 染　 染

音	染	セン	dye; color
熟	染色	センショク	dyeing; staining —*v.* dye; stain
	染料	センリョウ	dyestuff
訓	染み	しみ	stain; blot; smudge
	染みる	しみる	*vi.* be influenced/infected; hurt
	染まる	そまる	*vi.* be dyed/imbued with
	染める	そめる	*vt.* dye; color

4

心忄戈戸手扌支攵文斗斤方日曰月肉月
●木欠止歹殳母毋比毛氏气水氺氵火灬父片牛犬犭王礻耂

559 案 ⑩ ` ´ ´ ˊ ゙ 宀 安 安 安 窣 窣 案

音	案	アン	desk; investigate; idea; plan; proposal; draft
熟	案じる	アンじる	*vt.* worry over; be anxious; be concerned; devise; consider
	案	アン	plan; draft; idea
	案外	アンガイ	contrary to expectations; unexpectedly; unforeseen
	案内	アンナイ	guidance; conduct; lead; information —*v.* guide; conduct; lead; notify; inform
	案内状	アンナイジョウ	letter of invitation; advice note

560 森 ⑫ 一 十 才 木 木 木 杰 森 森 森 森 森

音	森	シン	forest
熟	森林	シンリン	forest
訓	森	もり	wood; forest

561 楽 ⑬ ` ´ ˊ ̊ 白 白 泊 泊 泊 泊 楽 楽 楽

音	楽	ガク	music
		ラク	pleasure; ease; comfort; relief
熟	楽隊	ガクタイ	band; orchestra
	楽団	ガクダン	band; orchestra
	楽典	ガクテン	rules of musical composition
	楽屋	ガクや	dressing room; backstage; behind the scenes; secret
	楽器	ガッキ	musical instrument
	楽園	ラクエン	paradise
	楽勝	ラクショウ	easy victory —*vi.* win an easy victory
	楽天	ラクテン	optimism
	楽天家	ラクテンカ	optimist
	楽天的	ラクテンテキ	optimistic; cheerful
	楽々	ラクラク	comfortably; with great ease
	楽観	ラッカン	optimism —*v.* be optimistic; look on the bright side

楽観的	ラッカンテキ	optimistic; hopeful
訓 楽しい	たのしい	fun; enjoyable; pleasant
楽しむ	たのしむ	*vt*. enjoy
楽しみ	たのしみ	pleasure; enjoyment; delight; happiness

562

業⑬　　丶　丷　丷　丱　业　业　业　芈　芈　芈　業

音 業	ギョウ	work; duty; enterprise; achievement; karma
	ゴウ	
訓 業	わざ	work; deed; act

563

札⑤　　一　十　才　木　札

音 札	サツ	card; ticket; bill; bank note
訓 札	ふだ	card; ticket
札所	ふだショ	***Bud***. temple from which amulets may be obtained
札付き	ふだつき	price label/ticket; (person with) bad reputation

564

机⑥　　一　十　才　木　朾　机

音 机	キ	desk
熟 机下	キカ	in front of you; your desk
机上	キジョウ	on the desk; on top of a desk
机上の空論	キジョウの クウロン	unrealistic/impractical idea
訓 机	つくえ	desk; table

565

材⑦　　一　十　才　木　朾　村　材

音 材	ザイ	material; talent
熟 材木	ザイモク	lumber; wood; timber
材料	ザイリョウ	materials; raw materials; data; factor; ingredients

心忄戈戸手扌支攵文斗斤方日曰月肉月木欠止歹殳母毋比毛氏气水氺氵火灬父片牛犬犭王礻耂

566 村 ⑦

一　十　才　木　木　村　村

音	村	ムラ	village
熟	村議会	ソンギカイ	village assembly
	村長	ソンチョウ	village mayor
	村民	ソンミン	villagers
	村落	ソンラク	village; hamlet
	村立	ソンリツ	established by the village
訓	村	むら	village
	村雨	むらさめ	passing shower
	村八分	むらハチブ	social ostracism
	村人	むらびと	villager

567 枝 ⑧

一　十　才　木　木　杧　杫　枝

音	枝	シ	branch
熟	枝葉	ショウ（えだは）	branches and leaves *fig.* minor details
	枝葉末節	ショウマッセツ	trivia; minor details
訓	枝	えだ	branch
	枝豆	えだまめ	green soybeans

568 松 ⑧

一　十　才　木　朳　朳　松　松

音	松	ショウ	pine
熟	松竹梅	ショウチクバイ	pine, bamboo, and plum
訓	松	まつ	pine tree

569 板 ⑧

一　十　才　木　朾　朸　板　板

音	板	バン	board
		ハン	
熟	板金	バンキン	sheet metal

294

板書	バンショ	writing on a blackboard —*v.* write on the blackboard
訓 板	いた	board; plank; plate; the stage
板紙	いたがみ	paper covering a board on which food is served; cardboard
板前	いたまえ	cook/chef (who prepares Japanese food)
板目	いため	wood grain of a plank

570

枚⑧ 一 十 オ オ 木 杉 朽 枚 枚

音 枚	マイ	sheet; (counter for flat, thin objects)
熟 枚挙	マイキョ	enumeration; list —*v.* enumerate; list; count
枚数	マイスウ	number of sheets

571

林⑧ 一 十 オ オ 木 村 材 林

音 林	リン	forest; wood
熟 林間学校	リンカンガッコウ	camp; outdoor school
林業	リンギョウ	forestry
林産物	リンサンブツ	forest products
林地	リンチ	forest region
林道	リンドウ	forest road/trail
林野	リンヤ	forests and fields; woodlands
林立	リンリツ	standing close together —*vi.* stand close together
訓 林	はやし	wood; forest

572

柱⑨ 一 十 オ オ 札 杧 杧 柱 柱

音 柱	チュウ	pillar; cylinder
熟 柱石	チュウセキ	mainstay; pillar; prop; support
訓 柱	はしら	pillar; support

4

心 忄 戈 戸 手 扌 支 攵 文 斗 斤 方 日 曰 月 肉 月 木 欠 止 歹 殳 母 毋 比 毛 氏 气 水 氺 氵 火 灬 父 片 牛 犬 犭 王 礻 耂

4

心忄戈戸手扌支攵文斗斤方日曰月肉月木欠止歹殳母毋比毛氏气水氺氵火灬父片牛犬犭王礻爿

573

桜 ⑩　一 十 才 才 木 栌 栌 松 桜 桜

音	桜	オウ	cherry tree; cherry
熟	桜花	オウカ	cherry blossoms
訓	桜	さくら	cherry tree
	桜色	さくらいろ	pink; cerise
	桜肉	さくらニク	horsemeat

574

格 ⑩　一 十 才 木 木 杉 杉 格 格 格

音	格	カク	character; syntactic case; rank
		（コウ）	
熟	格言	カクゲン	maxim; proverb; adage; saying
	格式	カクシキ	formality; social status
	格段	カクダン	special; marked difference
	格調	カクチョウ	style and tone of poetry
	格納庫	カクノウコ	aircraft hangar
	格好	カッコウ	shape; form; appearance; dress; style
	格子	コウシ	lattice; latticework

575

株 ⑩　一 十 才 木 木 杵 杵 件 株 株

| 音 | 株 | （シュ） | stump; root; share; stocks |
| 訓 | 株 | かぶ | stump; root; share; stocks |

576

校 ⑩　一 十 才 木 杉 栌 栌 栌 栌 校

音	校	コウ	school; correct; compare
熟	校医	コウイ	school doctor
	校旗	コウキ	school banner/flag
	校訓	コウクン	school precepts/motto
	校舎	コウシャ	school house/building
	校正	コウセイ	proofreading —*v.* proofread; correct

校則	コウソク	school regulations/rules
校長	コウチョウ	principal; headmaster
校庭	コウテイ	school grounds; schoolyard; campus
校風	コウフウ	school spirit/tradition
校友	コウユウ	schoolmate

577

根 ⑩ 一 十 オ オ 札 柏 柏 柏 根 根 根

音	根	コン	root; foundation; basis
熟	根幹	コンカン	basis; root; nucleus
	根気	コンキ	patience; perseverance; endurance; stamina
	根源	コンゲン	origin; root; source
	根治	コンジ（コンチ）	radical/permanent cure —v. cure permanently/radically
	根性	コンジョウ	nature; disposition; spirit; mind; willpower
	根絶	コンゼツ	extermination; eradication —v. exterminate; eradicate
	根底	コンテイ	root; bottom; foundation
	根本	コンポン	root; source; origin; foundation; basis
	根本的	コンポンテキ	fundamental; cardinal; basic
	根負け	コンまけ	losing stamina/patience —vi. have one's patience exhausted
訓	根	ね	root; origin; nature
	根深い	ねぶかい	deep-rooted; ingrained; incurable
	根元	ねもと	root; base

578

梅 ⑩ 一 十 オ オ 材 杧 栌 梅 梅 梅

音	梅	バイ	plum tree
熟	梅雨	バイウ	rain in the wet/rainy season
	梅園	バイエン	plum tree garden
	梅毒	バイドク	*med.* syphillis
	梅林	バイリン	plum orchard/grove
訓	梅	うめ	plum; plum tree
	梅酒	うめシュ	plum wine
	梅干し	うめぼし	pickled plum

579

械 ⑪ 　一 十 オ 才 木 杧 枛 枛 械 械 械

| 音 | 械 | カイ | device; apparatus |
| 訓 | 械 | かせ | shackles; handcuffs |

580

極 ⑫ 　一 十 オ 才 木 朾 朾 柯 柯 極 極 極

音	極	キョク	go to extremes; the end; the poles; magnetic/electrical poles
		ゴク	
熟	極言	キョクゲン	so far as to say —v. go so far as to say; go to the length of saying
	極限	キョクゲン	utmost limits; bounds
	極地	キョクチ	polar region; wilderness
	極度	キョクド	highest degree; utmost
	極東	キョクトウ	far east
	極力	キョクリョク	to the utmost; to the best of one's ability
	極論	キョクロン	carrying logic to extremes —v. carry logic to extremes
	極悪	ゴクアク	atrocity; brutality; villainy
	極意	ゴクイ	the secret; the mystery; the essence
	極上	ゴクジョウ	first rate; premier quality
	極道	ゴクドウ	wicked; dissipated
	極秘	ゴクヒ	top secret
	極楽	ゴクラク	paradise; heaven
訓	極まる	きわまる	vi. end; terminate; be at an end; reach an extreme
	極める	きわめる	vt. go to the end; go to the extremes
	極み	きわみ	height; apex; end; limit

581

検 ⑫ 　一 十 オ 才 木 朾 朾 枠 枠 検 検

音	検	ケン	investigate; examine; test; inspect
熟	検眼	ケンガン	eye test —vi. examine a person's eyes
	検挙	ケンキョ	arresting —v. arrest
	検挙者	ケンキョシャ	person in custody/under arrest

検査	ケンサ	test; inspection; examination; audit —v. inspect; examine; check; test; audit
検察	ケンサツ	investigation; examination; prosecution
検察側	ケンサツがわ	the prosecution
検察庁	ケンサツチョウ	Public Prosecutor's Office
検算	ケンザン	verification of accounts —v. check/verify the accounts
検事	ケンジ	public prosecutor; the prosecution
検出	ケンシュツ	detection —v. detect; find
検証	ケンショウ	verification; inspection —v. verify; inspect
検針	ケンシン	meter inspection —v. read a meter
検定	ケンテイ	official approval —v. give official approval; sanction; authorize
検討	ケントウ	examination; investigation; consideration —v. examine; investigate; consider; discuss
検分	ケンブン	survey; inspection; examination —v. inspect; examine
検便	ケンベン	stool test —vi. examine a stool sample
検問	ケンモン	check; inspection —v. check; inspect; examine

582

植 ⑫ 一 十 才 才 才 杧 柿 柿 柿 植 植 植

音	植	ショク	plant; cultivate; set type
熟	植字	ショクジ	typesetting —vi. set type
	植樹	ショクジュ	tree planting —vi. plant a tree
	植物	ショクブツ	plant; vegetation
	植物園	ショクブツエン	botanical garden
	植物学	ショクブツガク	botany
	植民	ショクミン	colonization; settler; colonial —vi. colonize
	植民地	ショクミンチ	colony
	植林	ショクリン	afforestation —vi. plant trees
訓	植える	うえる	vt. plant; grow
	植わる	うわる	vi. be planted
	植木	うえき	garden plant

583

棒 ⑫ 一 十 才 才 才 杧 杧 栚 栈 棒 棒 棒

| 音 | 棒 | ボウ | stick; pole |
| 熟 | 棒暗記 | ボウアンキ | indiscriminate memorization; memorization |

299

心 忄 戈 戸 手 扌 支 攵 文 斗 斤 方 日 曰 月 肉 月 ● 木 欠 止 歹 殳 母 毋 比 毛 氏 気 水 氺 氵 火 灬 父 片 牛 犬 犭 王 礻 艹

without understanding —*v.* memorize indiscriminately; memorize without understanding

棒組	ボウぐみ	typesetting
棒術	ボウジュツ	(martial art using long staffs)
棒状	ボウジョウ	cylindrical; stick
棒立ち	ボウだち	frozen in an upright position with shock
棒読み	ボウよみ	monotone reading

584

構 ⑭ 十 扌 扌 扗 扸 扸 搆 搆 構 構 構 構

音	構	コウ	structure; attitude; concern
熟	構外	コウガイ	outside the premises
	構図	コウズ	composition; plot
	構成	コウセイ	composition; organization; construction —*v.* make; compose; organize; construct
	構想	コウソウ	plan; plot; conception; idea —*v.* plan; plot; conceive an idea
	構造	コウゾウ	structure; construction; framework; organization
	構築	コウチク	construction; structure —*v.* build; construct; erect
	構内	コウナイ	premises; precincts; grounds
訓	構う	かまう	*vi.* mind; care about; be concerned; meddle; interfere; entertain
	構える	かまえる	*vt.* keep; set up; build; pose; feign; pretend
	構え	かまえ	structure; construction; posture; position; attitude

585

模 ⑭ 十 扌 扌 扗 扸 扸 槒 槒 模 模 模 模

音	模	ボ	model; copy; imitation
		モ	model; copy; imitation
熟	模する	モする	*vt.* model; copy; imitate
	模型	モケイ	model; mold
	模写	モシャ	copy; replica —*v.* copy; make a replica
	模造	モゾウ	imitation —*v.* imitate; copy
	模様	モヨウ	pattern; design; appearance; situation

586

様 ⑭ 十 オ オ オ' オ゙ オ゙ オ゙ 栟 样 样 样 様 様

音	様	ヨウ	way; manner; similar; like; condition
熟	様式	ヨウシキ	mode; form; style
	様子	ヨウス	situation; appearance; aspect
	様相	ヨウソウ	phase; aspect; condition
	様態	ヨウタイ	situation; condition
訓	様	さま	appearance
	様々	さまざま	various; varied

587

横 ⑮ 十 オ オ オ゙ オ゙ 栏 栏 楛 横 横 横 横

音	横	オウ	side; direction; dishonesty
熟	横行	オウコウ	swaggering; walking sideways —*vi.* overrun; swagger; walk sideways
	横隊	オウタイ	rank; line
	横断	オウダン	crossing; intersection —*v.* cross; intersect
	横断歩道	オウダンホドウ	pedestrian/zebra crossing
	横着	オウチャク	cunning; wayward; dishonest —*vi.* be cunning/wayward/dishonest
	横転	オウテン	turning sideways; rolling —*vi.* turn sideways; roll
	横暴	オウボウ	oppression; tyranny; violence
	横領	オウリョウ	usurpation; embezzlement; misappropriation —*v.* usurp; embezzle; misappropriate
訓	横	よこ	width; side; wicked; dishonest
	横顔	よこがお	face in profile; profile
	横書き	よこがき	horizontal writing
	横切る	よこぎる	*vi.* go across; cross
	横たえる	よこたえる	*vt.* lay
	横たわる	よこたわる	*vi.* lie
	横町	よこチョウ	alleyway; alley
	横取り	よこどり	snatching; stealing —*v.* take away
	横腹	よこばら	side; flank
	横笛	よこぶえ	flute
	横道	よこみち	byroad; sidetrack
	横文字	よこモジ	Western language/alphabet

心 忄 戈 戸 手 扌 支 攵 文 斗 斤 方 日 曰 月 肉 月 木 欠 止 歹 殳 母 毋 比 毛 氏 气 水 氷 氵 火 灬 父 片 牛 犬 犭 王 礻 耂

心
忄
戈
戸
手
扌
支
攵
文
斗
斤
方
日
曰
月
肉
月
● 木
欠
止
歹
殳
母
毋
比
毛
氏
气
水
氺
氵
火
灬
父
片
牛
犬
犭
王
礻
耂

588

権 ⑮　十 才 オ オ 杧 杧 杧 杧 栌 栌 梻 権 権

音	権	ケン	authority
		ゴン	secondary
熟	権限	ケンゲン	authority; power
	権利	ケンリ	right; rights; claim
	権力	ケンリョク	power; authority
	権化	ゴンゲ	incarnation; embodiment; personification

589

標 ⑮　十 才 杧 杧 杧 柟 柟 栖 標 標 標 標

音	標	ヒョウ	mark; sign
熟	標記	ヒョウキ	mark; heading —*vt*. mark
	標語	ヒョウゴ	slogan; motto
	標高	ヒョウコウ	above sea level
	標識	ヒョウシキ	mark; sign; beacon
	標準	ヒョウジュン	standard; criterion; level; average; normal
	標準語	ヒョウジュンゴ	standard language
	標準時	ヒョウジュンジ	standard time
	標的	ヒョウテキ	target
	標本	ヒョウホン	sample; specimen

590

機 ⑯　十 才 オ 栌 栌 栌 樴 樴 樴 樴 機 機 機

音	機	キ	mechanism; loom; machine; chance
熟	機運	キウン	fortune; opportunity; chance
	機会	キカイ	opportunity; chance
	機械	キカイ	machine; machinery
	機械化	キカイカ	mechanization —*v*. mechanize; introduce machinery
	機械的	キカイテキ	mechanical
	機関	キカン	engine; organ; agency; institution
	機器	キキ	machinery; tools; apparatus
	機構	キコウ	mechanism; system; organization; structure
	機首	キシュ	nose of a plane

機種	キシュ	type of airplane
機上	キジョウ	aboard an aircraft; in flight
機知	キチ	wit
機長	キチョウ	captain; chief pilot
機転	キテン	wit; tact
機能	キノウ	function; faculty —*v.* function; work; operate
機密	キミツ	secret; secrecy
訓 機	はた	loom

591

橋 ⑯　十 オ オ ギ ギ ギ 杼 杼 杼 栝 橋 橋 橋

音 橋	キョウ	bridge
訓 橋	はし	bridge

592

樹 ⑯　十 オ オ ギ ギ 柱 桂 桂 桂 梪 梪 樹 樹

音 樹	ジュ	tree; establish
熟 樹下	ジュカ	beneath the trees
樹海	ジュカイ	sea of trees; broad expanse of dense woodland
樹氷	ジュヒョウ	rime on trees; coat of ice of tree branches
樹木	ジュモク	trees
樹立	ジュリツ	establishment; founding —*v.* establish; found
樹林	ジュリン	forest; lignosae (woody plants)

4　欠　かける／あくび　yawning

593

欠 ④　ノ ケ ケ 欠

音 欠	ケツ	lack
熟 欠員	ケツイン	vacancy
欠勤	ケッキン	absence —*vi.* be absent from work
欠航	ケッコウ	flight/ship cancellation —*vi.* cancel a sailing/a flight
欠場	ケツジョウ	failure to make an appearance

4

心 忄 戈 戸 手 扌 支 攵 文 斗 斤 方 日 曰 月 肉 月 木 欠 止 歹 殳 母 毋 比 毛 氏 气 水 氷 氵 火 灬 父 片 牛 犬 犭 王 礻 耂

•
•

303

左側縦書き: 心 忄 戈 戸 手 扌 支 攵 文 斗 方 日 曰 月 肉 月 木 **・欠** 止 歹 殳 母 毋 比 毛 氏 气 水 氺 氵 火 灬 父 片 牛 犬 犭 王 礻 耂

欠席	ケッセキ	absence —*vi.* be absent
欠損	ケッソン	loss; deficit —*vi.* lose
欠点	ケッテン	defect; fault; shortcoming; drawback
欠番	ケツバン	missing number
欠落	ケツラク	lack —*v.* lack
訓 欠く	かく	*vt.* break; chip; lack; be wanting in; fail to carry out
欠ける	かける	*vi.* break/chip off; wane; lack; miss; be short
欠け	かけ	fragment; broken piece
欠かす	かかす	lack; be deficient

594

次 ⑥   丶 冫 冫 ゲ 次 次

音 次	ジ	next; order
	シ	order
熟 次回	ジカイ	next time
次官	ジカン	vice-minister; undersecretary
次期	ジキ	next period/term/session
次元	ジゲン	dimension; sphere
次席	ジセキ	second position/place; deputy of a bureau/department
次第	シダイ	order; process; reason; circumstances
次第に	シダイに	gradually
次点	ジテン	second-best mark
次男	ジナン	second son
訓 次	つぎ	next; following; adjoining
次ぐ	つぐ	*vi.* rank next to; follow
次々	つぎつぎ	one after another; in rapid succession

595

欲 ⑪   ノ ハ グ 父 父 谷 谷 谷 谷 欲 欲

音 欲	ヨク	desire
熟 欲情	ヨクジョウ	passions; desires
欲得	ヨクトク	selfishness; self-interest
欲念	ヨクネン	desires; wishes; passions
欲張り	ヨクばり	greed; covetousness

欲望	ヨクボウ	desire; craving
欲目	ヨクめ	favorable view; partiality; favoritism
欲求	ヨッキュウ	desires; wants —*v.* desire; want
欲求不満	ヨッキュウフマン	frustration
訓 欲しい	ほしい	want
欲する	ほっする	*vt.* want

596 歌 ⑭

一 哥 哥 哥 哥 哥 哥 哥 歌 歌 歌

音 歌	カ	song; sing; poem
熟 歌曲	カキョク	song
歌劇	カゲキ	opera
歌詞	カシ	lyrics
歌手	カシュ	singer
歌集	カシュウ	collection of *tanka* poems; collection of odes
歌人	カジン	*tanka* poet
歌道	カドウ	the art of *waka* poetry; poetry
歌風	カフウ	poetical style
訓 歌	うた	*tanka* poem; song
歌う	うたう	*vt.* sing
歌声	うたごえ	singing voice

---

4 止 とめる stop

597 止 ④

丨 卜 止 止

音 止	シ	stop
熟 止血	シケツ	*med.* hemostasis —*v.* stop the bleeding
訓 止まる	とまる	*vi.* stop; come to an end
止める	とめる	*vt.* stop; put an end to; check

598

正⑤　一 丁 下 止 正

心 忄 戈 戸 手 扌 支 攵 文 斗 斤 方 日 曰 月 肉 月 木 欠 止 歹 殳 母 毋 比 毛 氏 气 水 氺 氵 火 灬 父 片 牛 犬 犭 王 礻 耂

音	正	ショウ	right; just
		セイ	just; correct; formal
熟	正気	ショウキ	sanity; soberness; consciousness
	正午	ショウゴ	noon; noontime; midday
	正直	ショウジキ	honest; upright; square
	正体	ショウタイ	true character/form; consciousness
	正札	ショウフダ	price mark/tag
	正味	ショウミ	net; clear; the actual amount
	正面	ショウメン	front; facade
	正課	セイカ	regular subject/curriculum; compulsory subject
	正解	セイカイ	right answer; correct interpretation —*v.* interpret correctly; give a right answer
	正確	セイカク	accuracy; precision; exactness; correctness
	正規	セイキ	regularity; formality; rule
	正義	セイギ	justice; right; righteousness; correct meaning
	正誤	セイゴ	correction
	正座	セイザ	*seiza* (formal kneeling position) —*vi.* sit upright; sit square; sit in the correct manner; kneel in the Japanese manner
	正視	セイシ	looking straight at —*v.* look in the face; face up to
	正式	セイシキ	formal; proper; regular; official
	正常	セイジョウ	normal; regular
	正数	セイスウ	*math.* positive number
	正々堂々	セイセイドウドウ	fair and square; open and above board
	正装	セイソウ	full/formal dress —*vi.* dress up; be in full uniform
	正当	セイトウ	just; justifiable; warrantable; right; rightful
	正当防衛	セイトウボウエイ	legal defense; legitimate self-defense
	正統	セイトウ	legitimacy; orthodoxy; direct line; lineal descent
	正道	セイドウ	right track; path of righteousness
	正反対	セイハンタイ	exact opposite/reverse
	正否	セイヒ	right or wrong
	正比例	セイヒレイ	direct proportion —*vi.* be in direct proportion
	正方形	セイホウケイ	square; four-square; quadrate
	正論	セイロン	just argument
訓	正しい	ただしい	right; just; correct; formal
	正す	ただす	*vt.* correct; rectify; put right; redress
	正	まさ	right; exact; true

| 正に | まさに | just; exactly; precisely; surely; certainly |
| 正夢 | まさゆめ | dream that comes true; prophetic dream |

599

武 ⑧ 一 二 ナ テ チ 正 武 武

| 音 | 武 | ブ | military |
| | | ム | |

熟	武器	ブキ	arms; weapon
	武家	ブケ	samurai
	武芸	ブゲイ	martial arts
	武骨	ブコツ	boorish; uncouth; rude
	武士	ブシ	samurai; warrior
	武士道	ブシドウ	samurai code of chivalry
	武術	ブジュツ	martial arts
	武将	ブショウ	military commander
	武装	ブソウ	arming for war —*vi*. arm oneself; militarize
	武道	ブドウ	martial arts
	武門	ブモン	military family; samurai family
	武勇	ブユウ	valor; bravery
	武力	ブリョク	military force
	武者	ムシャ	warrior; samurai

600

歩 ⑧ 丨 ト 止 止 牛 牛 歩 歩

音	歩	ホ	walk; step; pace
		ブ	rate; one percent; *bu* (unit of area, approx. 3.3㎡)
		（フ）	pawn (in shogi)

熟	歩行	ホコウ	walking; ambulatory —*vi*. walk
	歩行者	ホコウシャ	pedestrian
	歩測	ホソク	measurement by paces —*v*. measure off a distance by pacing
	歩調	ホチョウ	pace; step
	歩道	ホドウ	sidewalk; footpath; pavement
	歩道橋	ホドウキョウ	pedestrian overpass
	歩兵	ホヘイ	infantry; foot soldier

| 訓 | 歩く | あるく | *vi*. walk |
| | 歩む | あゆむ | *vi*. walk; progress step-by-step; tread |

| 歩み | あゆみ | step; pace; walking; progress |
| 歩み寄る | あゆみよる | *vi.* walk towards; converge on; compromise |

601

歴 ⑭　一 厂 厂 厂 厅 厤 厤 厤 厤 厤 歴 歴 歴

音	歴	レキ	continuation; passage of time; successive; clear
熟	歴史	レキシ	history
	歴然	レキゼン	clear; unmistakable
	歴代	レキダイ	successive generations
	歴任	レキニン	successively holding various posts —*v.* hold various post in succession
	歴訪	レキホウ	round of calls/visits —*v.* make a round of calls/visits

4

歹　いちたへん／かばねへん　death

602

死 ⑥　一 厂 ア 歹 歹 死

音	死	シ	die; death; inactivity
熟	死因	シイン	cause of death
	死角	シカク	blind spot; dark corner
	死火山	シカザン	extinct/dead volcano
	死活問題	シカツモンダイ	matter of life and death
	死期	シキ	hour/time of death
	死去	シキョ	death —*vi.* die
	死後	シゴ	after one's death; posthumously
	死語	シゴ	dead language
	死罪	シザイ	capital punishment/crime
	死産	シザン	*med.* stillbirth —*vi.* give birth to a stillborn baby
	死者	シシャ	dead person; the dead; the deceased
	死守	シシュ	defense to the death/last —*v.* defend to the death/last
	死傷	シショウ	casualities
	死相	シソウ	look like a dead person; shadow of death; face of a dead person
	死蔵	シゾウ	shutting/locking up; storing away —*v.* shut/lock up; store away

死体	シタイ	dead body; corpse; cadaver
死地	シチ	jaws of death; death trap; place to die
死人	シニン	dead person
死病	シビョウ	fatal disease
死別	シベツ	bereavement —*vi.* be bereaved; lose someone close
死亡	シボウ	death —*vi.* die
死亡率	シボウリツ	death rate
死力	シリョク	desperate efforts

訓
死ぬ	しぬ	*vi.* die; pass away; be lifeless; be unusable
死なす	しなす	*vt.* let die; kill
死に顔	しにがお	face of a dead person
死に絶える	しにたえる	*vi.* die out; become extinct
死に目	しにめ	the moment a person dies

603

残 ⑩ 一 ァ ゙ ゙ ゙ ゙ ゙ ゙ 歹 歹= 歹= 残 残 残

音
残	ザン	remain; survive; cruel; brutal

熟
残額	ザンガク	account balance
残業	ザンギョウ	overtime work —*vi.* work overtime
残暑	ザンショ	lingering summer heat
残照	ザンショウ	twilight; traces; vestiges
残雪	ザンセツ	remaining/unmelted snow
残像	ザンゾウ	afterimage; lingering impression
残存	ザンゾン	survival —*vi.* survive; remain; be extant
残念	ザンネン	regrettable; disappointing; vexing; pity
残飯	ザンパン	leftover rice; leftover food; leftovers
残部	ザンブ	remainder; the rest
残余	ザンヨ	the rest; residue
残留	ザンリュウ	remaining; stay behind —*vi.* remain; stay behind

訓
残る	のこる	*vi.* be left; remain; stay; remain; survive
残す	のこす	*vt.* leave; save
残り	のこり	remainder; the rest
残り物	のこりもの	leftovers

心 忄 戈 戸 手 扌 支 攵 文 斗 斤 方 日 曰 月 肉 月 木 欠 止 歹 殳 母 毋 比 毛 氏 气 水 氺 氵 火 灬 父 片 牛 犬 犭 王 礻 爻

心忄戈戸手扌支攵文斗斤方日曰月肉月木欠止歹殳母毋比毛氏气水氺氵火灬父片牛犬犭王礻耂

4 殳 るまた　windy again

604

段 ⑨　　＇　亻　彳　牟　牟　牟　段　段　段

音	段	ダン	steps; stairs; column; grade; degree; extent
熟	段階	ダンカイ	steps; grade; rank
	段々	ダンダン	gradually; increasingly; growingly; more and more
	段々畑	ダンダンばたけ	terraced farm/fields; field in terraces
	段取り	ダンどり	program; plan; arrangements
	段落	ダンラク	end of a paragraph; conclusion; ending

605

殺 ⑩　　ノ　メ　ㄨ　乎　米　杀　杀　杀　杀　殺

音	殺	サツ	kill; get rid of
		（サイ）	lessen
		（セツ）	
熟	殺意	サツイ	murderous intent; urge to kill
	殺気	サッキ	thirst for blood; stormy atmosphere
	殺傷	サッショウ	killing and wounding; blood shedding —*v*. kill and wound; shed blood
	殺人	サツジン	murder; manslaughter; homicide
	殺人罪	サツジンザイ	murder; homicide
	殺人的	サツジンテキ	deadly
	殺人犯人	サツジンハンニン	murderer
	殺風景	サップウケイ	desolate; bleak; dreary; drab; prosaic; matter-of-fact; unimaginative
	殺生	セッショウ	slaughter; cruelty —*v*. kill; take life
訓	殺す	ころす	*vt*. kill; murder; surpress; restrain
	殺し文句	ころしモンク	clincher; killing expression

4 母 ははのかん／なかれ　mother　　　母 はは　mother

606

母 ⑤　　し　乙　口　므　母　母

音	母	ボ	mother
熟	母音	ボイン	vowel
	母系	ボケイ	maternal line (of a family)
	母系制度	ボケイセイド	matriarchal system
	母校	ボコウ	*alma mater*
	母国	ボコク	mother/native country
	母国語	ボコクゴ	mother/native tongue
	母子	ボシ	mother
	母性	ボセイ	motherhood; maternity
	母船	ボセン	mother ship
	母体	ボタイ	mother's body; parent organization
	母堂	ボドウ	*hon.* mother
	母乳	ボニュウ	mother's milk
訓	母	はは	one's mother
	母上	ははうえ	*hon.* mother
	母親	ははおや	mother
	母君	ははぎみ	*hon.* mother
	母屋(母家)	おもや	main building/house

607

毎 ⑥　　ノ　ㅗ　と　勾　毎　毎

音	毎	マイ	every; each
熟	毎回	マイカイ	every time
	毎号	マイゴウ	every issue
	毎時	マイジ	per hour; every hour
	毎週	マイシュウ	every week; weekly
	毎食	マイショク	each meal; at mealtime
	毎月	マイつき	every month; monthly
	毎度	マイド	each time; frequently; always
	毎日	マイニチ	every day; daily
	毎年	マイネン (マイとし)	every year; annually

311

心 ↑ 戈 戸 手 扌 支 攵 文 斗 斤 方 日 曰 月 肉 月 木 欠 止 歹 殳 母 毌 比 毛 氏 气 水 氷 氵 火 灬 父 片 牛 犬 犭 王 礻 耂

左余白（縦書き部首一覧）: 心 忄 戈 戸 手 扌 支 攵 文 斗 斤 方 日 曰 月 肉 月 木 欠 止 歹 殳 母 毋 ・ ・ 比 毛 氏 气 水 氺 氵 火 灬 父 片 牛 犬 犭 王 礻 艹

608

毒 ⑧　一　十　卉　主　毒　毒　毒　毒

音	毒	ドク	poison; toxicant; virus; germ; harm
熟	毒する	ドクする	*vt.* poison; corrupt; contaminate
	毒気	ドクケ	poisonous character; virulence; malice; spite
	毒殺	ドクサツ	death by poisoning —*v.* poison; kill by poison
	毒舌	ドクゼツ	spiteful/malicious tongue
	毒素	ドクソ	toxin; poisonous matter
	毒々しい	ドクドクしい	poisonous-looking
	毒物	ドクブツ	poisonous substance; poison; toxicant
	毒味(毒見)	ドクミ(ドクみ)	tasting for poison
	毒虫	ドクむし	poisonous insect
	毒矢	ドクヤ	poison arrow/dart
	毒薬	ドクヤク	poisonous drug; poison

4　比　くらべる／ならびひ　comparing

609

比 ④　一　匕　比　比

音	比	ヒ	compare; ratio; the Philippines
熟	比する	ヒする	*vt.* compare
	比重	ヒジュウ	*phy.* specific gravity
	比熱	ヒネツ	*phy.* specific heat
	比率	ヒリツ	percentage; rate; ratio
	比類	ヒルイ	parallel; equal
	比例	ヒレイ	proportion; ratio —*vi.* be proportioned/proportionate
訓	比べる	くらべる	*vt.* compare

4 毛 け hair; fur

610

毛 ④ 一 二 三 毛

音	毛	モウ	hair; tiny amount; 1/10,000 yen
熟	毛細血管	モウサイケッカン	capillary
	毛頭	モウトウ	person with uncropped hair; acolyte; young samurai
	毛頭ない	モウトウない	by no means; not at all
	毛布	モウフ	blanket
訓	毛	け	hair; fur; wool
	毛糸	けいと	woolen yarn; worsted
	毛色	けいろ	color of hair; nature; type; kind
	毛織物	けおりもの	woolen goods
	毛皮	けがわ	fur; skin; pelt
	毛並み	けなみ	lie of the hair *fig.* social standing/status of a family; birth; stock
	毛虫	けむし	caterpillar

4 氏 うじ clan

611

氏 ④ ′ Ĺ Ĕ 氏

音	氏	シ	clan; family; Mr.
熟	氏族	シゾク	family; clan
	氏族制度	シゾクセイド	family system
	氏名	シメイ	one's full name
訓	氏	うじ	family name; birth; lineage
	氏神	うじがみ	tutelary deity; patron god
	氏子	うじこ	local residents under the protection of the same guardian deity

心忄戈戸手扌支攴文斗斤方日曰月肉月木欠止歹殳母毋比毛氏气水氺氵火灬父片牛犬犭王礻爿

612

民 ⑤ 一 ㄱ ㄹ 尸 民

音	民	ミン	the people
熟	民家	ミンカ	private house
	民間	ミンカン	private (not public)
	民芸	ミンゲイ	folk art/craft
	民権	ミンケン	civil rights
	民事	ミンジ	civil affairs; civil
	民主	ミンシュ	democratic
	民主主義	ミンシュシュギ	democracy
	民主的	ミンシュテキ	democratic
	民衆	ミンシュウ	the people; populace; the masses
	民宿	ミンシュク	lodging house
	民情	ミンジョウ	public sentiment
	民心	ミンシン	popular sentiment; the people's feelings
	民生委員	ミンセイイイン	district welfare officer
	民族	ミンゾク	race; a people
	民度	ミンド	level of popular sophistication
	民兵	ミンペイ	militia
	民法	ミンポウ	the civil law/code
	民有	ミンユウ	privately owned
	民力	ミンリョク	national strength
	民話	ミンワ	folk tale; folklore
訓	民	たみ	the people
	民草	たみぐさ	the people; the populace

4 气 きがまえ steam

613

気 ⑥ ′ ⌒ ⌐ 气 気 気

音	気	キ	air; weather; feeling
		ケ	sign; appearance
熟	気圧	キアツ	atmospheric pressure
	気圧配置	キアツハイチ	distribution of atmospheric pressure
	気運	キウン	tendency

314

気後れ	キおくれ	diffidence; self-distrust; timidity —*vi.* be timid/diffident
気温	キオン	temperature
気化	キカ	evaporation; vaporization —*vi.* evaporate; vaporize
気構え	キがまえ	expectation; preparedness
気軽	キがる	lighthearted; cheerful
気管	キカン	*med.* trachea; windpipe
気管支	キカンシ	*med.* bronchial tubes
気球	キキュウ	balloon
気苦労	キグロウ	worries; care; anxiety
気候	キコウ	climate
気質	キシツ	temperament; disposition
気性	キショウ	temper; nature; disposition
気象	キショウ	atmospheric phenomena; meteorology
気色	キショク	countenance; feeling
気勢	キセイ	spirit; ardor
気絶	キゼツ	fainting —*vi.* faint; pass out; black out
気体	キタイ	gas; vapor
気付	キつけ	encouragement; resurrection
気の毒	キのドク	pitiable; regrettable; feeling sorry for
気乗り	キのり	interest; inclination —*vi.* be interested in; feel inclined
気晴らし	キばらし	diversion; recreation
気品	キヒン	nobility; dignity; grace
気風	キフウ	character; disposition; temper
気分	キブン	feeling; mood; atmosphere
気前	キまえ	generosity; liberality
気味	キミ	feeling; sensation; touch of; tinge
気短か	キみじか	short-tempered; rash; impatient
気持ち	キもち	feeling; sensation; mood
気休め	キやすめ	relieving one's conscience
気楽	キラク	feeling at ease; carefree; easygoing
気流	キリュウ	air current/steam
気力	キリョク	spirit; guts; vitality
気色	ケシキ	appearance; countenance
気配	ケハイ	sign; indication

心
忄
戈
戸
手
扌
支
攵
文
斗
斤
方
日
曰
月
肉
月
木
欠
止
歹
殳
母
毋
比
毛
氏
气 ●
水
氺
氵
火
灬
父
片
牛
犬
犭
王
礻
耂

4 水 みず water   氷 (p.318) 氵 (p.319)

614
水 ④   ┃ ゔ 才 水

音	水	スイ	water; river; Wednesday
熟	水圧	スイアツ	water/hydraulic pressure
	水位	スイイ	water level
	水域	スイイキ	water area
	水運	スイウン	water transport; transportation by water
	水泳	スイエイ	swimming; bathing —*vi.* swim; bathe; have a swim
	水温	スイオン	water temperature
	水化	スイカ	hydration —*v.* hydrate
	水化物	スイカブツ	hydrate
	水害	スイガイ	flood disaster/damage
	水銀	スイギン	*chem.* mercury; quicksilver
	水源	スイゲン	riverhead; fountain head; source of water supply; reservoir
	水郷	スイゴウ	riverside/lakeside district
	水産	スイサン	fishing
	水死	スイシ	drowning
	水質	スイシツ	water quality
	水車	スイシャ	water mill/wheel
	水準	スイジュン	level; standard; water level
	水準器	スイジュンキ	level
	水蒸気	スイジョウキ	steam; water vapor
	水深	スイシン	depth of water
	水星	スイセイ	the planet Mercury
	水勢	スイセイ	force of water; current
	水生動物	スイセイドウブツ	aquatic animal
	水洗	スイセン	flushing; washing; rinsing
	水素	スイソ	*chem.* hydrogen
	水族館	スイゾクカン	aquarium
	水中	スイチュウ	in the water; underwater
	水田	スイデン	rice paddy
	水道	スイドウ	water works/supply/way
	水難	スイナン	drowning; disaster at sea; shipwreck
	水分	スイブン	water; moisture; humidity; juice; sap
	水兵	スイヘイ	seaman; sailor

心忄戈戸手扌支攵文斗斤方日曰月肉月木欠止歹殳母毋比毛氏气 ●水氷氵火灬父片牛犬犭王礻尹

316

水平	スイヘイ	horizontally
水平線	スイヘイセン	horizon; horizontal line
水防	スイボウ	flood control/prevention
水面	スイメン	water surface
水門	スイモン	floodgate; sluice gate
水薬	スイヤク	liquid medicine
水曜日	スイヨウび	Wednesday
水浴	スイヨク	bathing —*vi.* bathe
水利	スイリ	water facility/supply; irrigation; navigability
水量	スイリョウ	water volume; quantity of water
水量計	スイリョウケイ	water gauge
水力	スイリョク	water/hydraulic power
水力学	スイリョクガク	hydraulics; hydrodynamics
水路	スイロ	waterway; water course/conduit
訓 水	みず	water; flood; inundation
水足	みずあし	speed of flowing water
水鏡	みずかがみ	reflective surface of water
水着	みずぎ	swimsuit; bathing costume
水先案内	みずさきアンナイ	pilot; pilotage; piloting
水商売	みずショウバイ	night-time entertainment business such as bars, clubs

615

 ⑤ 　`　丁　疒　永　永

音 永	エイ	long; eternal; forever
熟 永遠	エイエン	eternity; perpetuity; infinity; permanence; immortality
永久	エイキュウ	permanence; eternity; perpetuity
永久歯	エイキュウシ	permanent/second teeth
永住	エイジュウ	domiciliation; permanent residence —*vi.* settle down; take up permanent residence
永世中立	エイセイチュウリツ	permanent neutrality
永続	エイゾク	permanence; perpetuity; perpetuation —*vi.* last long; endure; remain; perpetuate
永年	エイネン	many years; eternity; a long time
訓 永い	ながい	long; lengthy

心
忄
戈
戸
手
扌
支
攵
文
斗
斤
方
日
曰
月
肉
月
木
欠
止
歹
殳
母
毋
比
毛
氏
气
水
氺
氵
火
灬
父
片
牛
犬
犭
王
礻
耂

心忄戈戸手扌支攵文斗斤方日曰月肉月木欠止歹殳母毋比毛氏气●水氺氵火灬父片牛犬犭王礻爿

616

氷 ⑤ 丨 丬 𠬝 氺 氷

音	氷	ヒョウ （ヒ）	ice
熟	氷河	ヒョウガ	glacier
	氷河時代	ヒョウガジダイ	ice age
	氷海	ヒョウカイ	frozen sea
	氷解	ヒョウカイ	cleared away; dispelled —*vi.* be cleared (of suspision, etc.); be dispelled
	氷結	ヒョウケツ	frozen over; icebound —*vi.* freeze
	氷原	ヒョウゲン	ice field
	氷山	ヒョウザン	iceberg
	氷室	ヒョウシツ	icehouse; ice room
	氷人	ヒョウジン	go-between; matchmaker
	氷雪	ヒョウセツ	ice and snow
	氷柱	ヒョウチュウ	icicle; ice pillar placed in a room in summer
	氷点	ヒョウテン	*chem.* freezing point
訓	氷	こおり	ice

617

泉 ⑨ 丿 丶 ⼧ 白 白 𡭴 泉 泉 泉

音	泉	セン	spring
熟	泉下	センカ	underworld
	泉水	センスイ	ornamental pond; pond of spring water
訓	泉	いずみ	spring

5 したみず water at bottom

618

求 ⑦ 一 寸 寸 寸 𣥂 求 求

音	求	キュウ	request; search; want; desire; demand
熟	求愛	キュウアイ	amorous advances —*vi.* court; woo
	求心力	キュウシンリョク	centripetal force

訓 求める　　もとめる　　*vt*. want; wish for; desire; request; demand; pursue

---

3　氵　さんずい　water at left

619
池 ⑥　　` 丶 氵 氵 汁 沖 池

音	池	チ	pond; lake
訓	池	いけ	pond; lake

620
汽 ⑦　　` 丶 氵 氵 氵 沪 沪 汽

音	汽	キ	steam; vapor
熟	汽圧	キアツ	steam pressure
	汽車	キシャ	(steam) train
	汽船	キセン	steam ship
	汽笛	キテキ	steam whistle

621
決 ⑦　　` 丶 氵 氵 沪 沪 決 決

音	決	ケツ	fix; settle; decide, collapse
熟	決する	ケッする	fix; settle; decide
	決起	ケッキ	going into action —*vi*. rise and go into action
	決行	ケッコウ	execution —*v*. carry out; go ahead
	決裁	ケッサイ	sanction; approval —*v*. sanction; approve
	決死	ケッシ	desperate; ready to die
	決勝	ケッショウ	finals (of a competition)
	決心	ケッシン	determination; resolution —*vi*. determine; be determined; make up one's mind; resolve
	決戦	ケッセン	decisive battle
	決然	ケツゼン	determinedly; decisively; resolutely
	決断	ケツダン	decision; determination —*vi*. decide; make a decision
	決着	ケッチャク	conclusion; the end; settlement —*vi*. conclude; end; settle

心 忄 戈 戸 手 扌 支 攵 文 斗 斤 方 日 曰 月 肉 月 木 欠 止 歹 殳 母 毋 毌 比 毛 氏 气 水 氺 氵 火 灬 父 片 牛 犬 犭 王 礻 耂

● ●

心
忄
戈
戸
手
扌
支
攵
文
斗
斤
方
日
曰
月
肉
月
木
欠
止
歹
殳
母
毋
比
毛
氏
气
水
氺
氵
火
灬
父
片
牛
犬
犭
王
礻
歩

決定	ケッテイ	decision; conclusion; determination —*v.* decide; determine; set; fix
訓 決まる	きまる	*vi.* be decided/settled
決める	きめる	*vt.* decide; fix; settle; determine

622

泳 ⑧ 丶 冫 氵 氵 汀 汈 泳 泳

音 泳	エイ	swimming
熟 泳者	エイシャ	swimmer
訓 泳ぎ	およぎ	swimming; swim
泳ぐ	およぐ	*vi.* swim

623

沿 ⑧ 丶 冫 氵 氵 氿 氿 沿 沿

音 沿	エン	lie along; go along; run parallel
熟 沿海	エンカイ	coast
沿革	エンカク	history; chronicle; development; changes
沿岸	エンガン	coast; shore
沿線	エンセン	along a railroad
沿道	エンドウ	roadside; route; course
訓 沿う	そう	*vi.* go/lie along; run parallel

624

河 ⑧ 丶 冫 氵 氵 氵 沪 沪 河

音 河	カ	river; Yellow River
熟 河岸	カガン	riverbank
河口	カコウ	mouth of a river; river mouth
河川	カセン	rivers
訓 河	かわ	river
河原	かわら	dry riverbed; river beach

625

泣 ⑧ 　 丶　丶　氵　氵　汀　汁　泣　泣

音	泣	キュウ	crying; weeping
訓	泣く	なく	*vi*. cry; weep
	泣き声	なきごえ	tearful voice; whine
	泣き言	なきごと	complaint; grievance; whimper
	泣き上戸	なきジョウゴ	sentimental drinker; crying drunk
	泣き虫	なきむし	crybaby

626

治 ⑧ 　 丶　丶　氵　汁　汋　治　治

音	治	チ ジ	govern; rule; cure; heal; remedy; recover
熟	治安	チアン	public peace and order
	治外法権	チガイホウケン	extraterritoriality; extraterritorial rights
	治水	チスイ	flood control; river improvement —*vi*. carry out flood control work
訓	治まる	おさまる	*vi*. be at peace; be tranquil; calm down
	治める	おさめる	*vt*. rule; govern; administer; manage; put down; suppress
	治す	なおす	*vt*. mend; repair; put in order; reform; correct; cure; heal; remedy
	治る	なおる	*vi*. get well/better; recover; be cured

627

注 ⑧ 　 丶　丶　氵　氵　汴　汴　注

音	注	チュウ	annotation; notes; comments; flow into; pour
熟	注意	チュウイ	attention; observation; note; notice; care; caution —*vi*. pay attention; give heed; observe; take note; be cautious
	注意人物	チュウイジンブツ	dangerous person; suspicious character
	注意力	チュウイリョク	attentiveness
	注記	チュウキ	note; entry —*v*. note; make entries; write down
	注視	チュウシ	gaze; close observation; scrutiny —*v*. watch carefully; contemplate; scrutinize
	注射	チュウシャ	injection; shot; inoculation —*v*. inject; syringe; inoculate

心 忄 戈 戸 手 扌 支 攵 文 斗 斤 方 日 曰 月 肉 月 木 欠 止 歹 殳 母 毋 比 毛 氏 气 水 氺 氵 火 灬 父 片 牛 犬 犭 王 礻 耂

●

321

注射器	チュウシャキ	injector; syringe
注水	チュウスイ	watering; pouring water —*vi.* pour water; water
注入	チュウニュウ	injection; infusion; infiltration —*v.* pour into; inject; impregnate; infuse; implant
注目	チュウモク	attention; observation; notice; remark —*v.* pay attention; observe; remark; notice
注文	チュウモン	order; commission; request; demand; wish; desire —*v.* order; request; demand; desire; wish
注油	チュウユ	oiling; lubrication —*v.* oil; lubricate
訓 注ぐ	そそぐ	*v.* pour into; irrigate; flow into; drain

628

波 ⑧ `、 ㇀ 氵 ㇒ 沪 沪 波 波`

音 波	ハ	wave
熟 波状	ハジョウ	wave; undulation
波長	ハチョウ	wavelength
波動	ハドウ	undulation; fluctuation —*vi.* undulate; fluctuate; wave
波乱	ハラン	trouble; disturbance; commotion; storm
訓 波	なみ	wave; sea; billow; surge
波風	なみかぜ	wind and waves; trouble; discord; quarrel
波立つ	なみだつ	*vi.* be choppy; run high; billow

629

法 ⑧ `、 ㇀ 氵 氵 汁 汢 法 法`

音 法	ホウ	law; method; religion
	（ホ）	
	（ハ）	
熟 法度	ハット	ban; law; prohibition
法衣	ホウイ	***Bud.*** vestments; priestly robes
法医学	ホウイガク	forensic medicine
法王	ホウオウ	Pope
法皇	ホウオウ	ex-emperor who has become a monk
法貨	ホウカ	legal tender
法外	ホウガイ	unreasonable; preposterous
法学	ホウガク	law; jurisprudence
法官	ホウカン	judicial officer; judge
法規	ホウキ	laws and regulations

法権	ホウケン	legal right
法号	ホウゴウ	(priest's or posthumous) Buddhist name
法師	ホウシ	*Bud*. priest
法事	ホウジ	*Bud*. memorial service
法式	ホウシキ	regulation; rite; rule
法制	ホウセイ	legislation; laws
法則	ホウソク	law; rule
法治国	ホウチコク	constitutional state
法定	ホウテイ	legal; prescribed by law
法典	ホウテン	law code
法名	ホウミョウ	(priest's or posthumous) Buddhist name
法要	ホウヨウ	*Bud*. memorial service
法力	ホウリキ	merits/powers of Buddhism
法律	ホウリツ	law
法律上	ホウリツジョウ	legally
法令	ホウレイ	laws and (cabinet or ministerial) orders

630

油⑧　　丶 丶 氵 沪 沪 油 油 油

音	油	ユ	oil
熟	油断	ユダン	carelessness; inattentiveness
	油田	ユデン	oil field
訓	油	あぶら	oil
	油絵	あぶらエ	oil painting
	油ぎる	あぶらぎる	*vi*. be oily/fatty; glisten with oil
	油っこい	あぶらっこい	oily; fatty

631

海⑨　　丶 丶 氵 氵 汇 泸 海 海 海

音	海	カイ	sea
熟	海王星	カイオウセイ	the planet Neptune
	海外	カイガイ	abroad; overseas; foreign countries
	海岸	カイガン	seaside
	海軍	カイグン	the navy
	海国	カイコク	maritime country/power
	海産物	カイサンブツ	marine products
	海図	カイズ	nautical chart

心 忄 戈 戸 手 扌 支 攵 文 斗 斤 方 日 曰 月 肉 月 木 欠 止 歹 殳 母 毋 比 毛 氏 气 水 氷 氵 火 灬 父 片 牛 犭 王 衤 耂

心 忄 戈 戸 手 扌 支 攵 文 斗 斤 方 日 曰 月 肉 月 木 欠 止 歹 殳 母 毋 比 毛 氏 气 水 氺 氵 火 灬 父 片 牛 犬 犭 王 礻 耂

海水	カイスイ	sea water
海水浴	カイスイヨク	swimming at the beach
海風	カイフウ	sea wind/breeze
海綿	カイメン	sponge
海洋	カイヨウ	ocean
海里	カイリ	nautical mile; knot
海流	カイリュウ	ocean current
海路	カイロ	sea route
訓 海	うみ	sea; lake; well of an inkstone

632

活 ⑨ 　 丶 氵 氵 汒 汗 汗 活 活

音 活	カツ	vivid; live; life
熟 活火山	カッカザン	active/live volcano
活気	カッキ	vigor; liveliness; activity
活字	カツジ	printing type
活字体	カツジタイ	typeface
活動	カツドウ	activity; action —*vi*. be active; lead an active life; play an active part
活発	カッパツ	lively; brisk; active
活版	カッパン	typography; letterpress
活用	カツヨウ	practical use; application —*v*. apply; utilize; put to practical use
活力	カツリョク	vitality; vigor
活路	カツロ	means of escape; way out
訓 活き	いき	freshness
活きる	いきる	*vi*. live; be alive
活ける	いける	*vt*. arrange flowers

633

洗 ⑨ 　 丶 氵 氵 氵 汁 泙 泙 洗

音 洗	セン	wash
熟 洗眼	センガン	eyewashing
洗顔	センガン	washing one's face —*vi*. wash one's face
洗車	センシャ	car wash —*vi*. wash the car
洗脳	センノウ	brainwashing —*v*. brainwash
洗面	センメン	washing one's face —*vi*. wash one's face
洗面台	センメンダイ	wash basin

洗礼	センレイ	baptism
洗練	センレン	refinement; polishing —*v*. refine; polish
訓 洗う	あらう	***vt***. wash; probe

634 浅 ⑨
`丶 冫 氵 沙 浅 浅 浅 浅`

音 浅	セン	shallow
熟 浅学	センガク	shallow learning; superficial knowledge
訓 浅い	あさい	shallow
浅ましい	あさましい	shameful; mean

635 派 ⑨
`丶 冫 氵 沪 沪 泥 派 派`

音 派	ハ	group; school; sect; denomination
熟 派出	ハシュツ	dispatch —*v*. send out; dispatch; detach
派出所	ハシュツジョ	branch office; police office/box
派生	ハセイ	derivation —*vi*. derive; be derived from; originate
派手	ハで	showy; gaudy; flashy; vain
派兵	ハヘイ	dispatch of troops —*vi*. dispatch troops

636 洋 ⑨
`丶 冫 氵 ジ 沣 泮 洋 洋`

音 洋	ヨウ	ocean; foreign; western
熟 洋画	ヨウガ	Western picture/movie
洋学	ヨウガク	Western learning
洋楽	ヨウガク	Western music
洋館	ヨウカン	Western-style building
洋行	ヨウコウ	travels to the US or Europe —*vi*. go to the US or Europe
洋裁	ヨウサイ	Western-style dressmaking
洋式	ヨウシキ	Western-style
洋室	ヨウシツ	Western-style room; non-*tatami* room
洋酒	ヨウシュ	Western liquors
洋書	ヨウショ	foreign/Western book
洋上	ヨウジョウ	on the sea; seagoing

心 忄 戈 戸 手 扌 支 攵 文 斗 斤 方 日 曰 月 肉 月 木 欠 止 歹 殳 母 毋 比 毛 氏 气 水 氷 氵 火 灬 父 片 牛 犬 犭 王 礻 尹

心忄戈戸手扌支攵文斗斤方日曰月肉月木欠止歹殳母毋比毛氏气水氺氵火灬父片牛犬犭王礻耂

洋食	ヨウショク	Western food
洋装	ヨウソウ	Western dress —*v.* wear Western dress
洋品店	ヨウヒンテン	haberdashery; hosier
洋風	ヨウフウ	Western-style
洋服	ヨウフク	(Western-type) clothes
洋間	ヨウま	Western-style room
洋々たる	ようようたる	wide; broad; vast

637

消 ⑩ 　丶 丶 氵 氵 氵 氵 汁 消 消 消

音	消	ショウ	vanish; extinguish; consume
熟	消火	ショウカ	fire extinguisher —*vi.* extinguish a fire
	消化	ショウカ	digestion; consumption; absorption —*v.* digest; consume; absorb
	消極的	ショウキョクテキ	negative; passive; half-hearted
	消失	ショウシツ	disappearance; vanishing —*vi.* disappear; vanish
	消息	ショウソク	news; information
	消灯	ショウトウ	lights off —*vi.* put out/turn off the lights
	消毒	ショウドク	disinfection; sterilization; fumigation —*v.* disinfect; sterilize; fumigate
	消費	ショウヒ	consumption; expenditure —*v.* consume; use up
	消防	ショウボウ	fire fighting —*v.* fight a fire
訓	消える	きえる	*vi.* go out; die; disappear; go/fade away
	消す	けす	*vt.* put out; extinguish; switch/turn off; erase; liquidate
	消印	けしイン	postmark
	消しゴム	けしゴム	pencil eraser
	消し止める	けしとめる	*vt.* put out; extinguish

638

浴 ⑩ 　丶 丶 氵 氵 氵 氵 汁 浴 浴 浴

音	浴	ヨク	bathe; bath
熟	浴室	ヨクシツ	bathroom
	浴場	ヨクジョウ	bathroom; bath house
訓	浴びる	あびる	*vt.* pour over oneself; bathe in
	浴びせる	あびせる	*vt.* pour on; shower upon

`丶 冫 氵 浐 浐 浐 浐 済 流`

音	流	リュウ（ル）	flow; wander; style; school; rank; class

熟	流域	リュウイキ	river basin/valley
	流会	リュウカイ	adjournment —*vi*. be adjourned/called off
	流感	リュウカン	influenza; flu
	流血	リュウケツ	bloodshed
	流言	リュウゲン	false rumor
	流行	リュウコウ	fashionable; popular; prevalent —*vi*. be in fashion; be popular/prevalent/epidemic
	流行病	リュウコウビョウ	epidemic
	流産	リュウザン	miscarriage —*v*. suffer a miscarriage
	流失	リュウシツ	washed away —*vi*. be washed away
	流出	リュウシュツ	outflow —*vi*. outflow; flow out
	流星	リュウセイ	shooting star; meteor
	流説	リュウセツ	rumor; idle talk
	流線型	リュウセンケイ	streamline
	流体	リュウタイ	*phy*. fluid
	流通	リュウツウ	circulation; distribution —*vi*. circulate; distribute
	流動	リュウドウ	flowing; liquid (assets); current —*vi*. flow; be liquid/current
	流動体	リュウドウタイ	fluid
	流入	リュウニュウ	influx —*vi*. flow in
	流派	リュウハ	school (of thought/art)
	流氷	リュウヒョウ	drift ice; ice floe
	流木	リュウボク	driftwood
	流民	リュウミン	refugees
	流用	リュウヨウ	multipurpose —*v*. use for other purposes
	流量	リュウリョウ	*phy*. volume of floating fluid
	流罪	ルザイ	banishment; exile
	流転	ルテン	constant change; wandering; vagrancy; reincarnation —*vi*. change constantly; wander
	流布	ルフ	circulation; dissemination —*vi*. circulate; spread; disseminate

訓	流す	ながす	*vt*. let flow
	流し	ながし	sink
	流れる	ながれる	*vi*. flow
	流れ	ながれ	stream

心 忄 戈 戸 手 扌 支 攵 文 斗 斤 方 日 曰 月 肉 月 木 欠 止 歹 殳 母 毋 比 毛 氏 气 水 氺 氵 火 灬 父 片 牛 犬 犭 王 礻 耂

640 液 ⑪

` ミ ミ ジ 汽 汽 汴 汴 泧 液 液 液

音	液	エキ	liquid; fluid; juice; sap
熟	液化	エキカ	liquefaction —*v.* be liquefied
	液状	エキジョウ	liquid form
	液体	エキタイ	liquid substance; fluid
	液肥	エキヒ	liquid fertilizer

641 混 ⑪

` ミ ミ ジ 沪 沪 沪 渭 混 混 混

音	混	コン	mix
熟	混血児	コンケツジ	half-breed; child of mixed blood
	混合	コンゴウ	mixture —*v.* mix; mingle; blend; compound
	混雑	コンザツ	congestion; confusion; disorder —*vi.* be congested/confused; be in disorder
	混戦	コンセン	confused/free fight —*vi.* fight in confusion
	混線	コンセン	cross; contact; entanglement —*vi.* be crossed; be mixed up; be entangled
	混同	コンドウ	mixing; confusion; merger —*v.* confuse; confound; mix-up
	混入	コンニュウ	mixing; mixture; blending —*v.* mix; mingle; blend
	混用	コンヨウ	composite —*v.* mingle; use together
	混乱	コンラン	confusion; disorder; chaos —*vi.* be confused/chaotic; be mixed up
訓	混ざる	まざる	*vi.* be mixed/blended
	混じる	まじる	*vi.* mix; mingle; blend
	混ぜる	まぜる	*vt.* blend; mix

642 済 ⑪

` ミ ミ ジ 沪 沪 泲 済 済 済 済

音	済	サイ	relieve; help; end; finish; repay
熟	済度	サイド	**Bud.** salvation; redemption —*v.* **Bud.** save; redeem
訓	済ます	すます	*vt.* finish; repay; payback; make do; manage; settle; solve
	済む	すむ	*vi.* be over; finish; be paid; settle; complete

643

深⑪　`ミミ汀汀汀汀沪涇深深

音	深	シン	deep
熟	深遠	シンエン	profound; deep
	深海	シンカイ	deep sea
	深紅	シンク	deep red
	深呼吸	シンコキュウ	deep breathing —*vi.* breathe deeply
	深刻	シンコク	serious; grave; critical
	深山	シンザン	deep mountains
	深謝	シンシャ	hearty thanks; sincere apology —*v.* express one's gratitude; make a sincere apology
	深窓	シンソウ	tender care; happy family circumstances
	深層	シンソウ	the depths
	深長	シンチョウ	profound; deep
	深度	シンド	depth
	深部	シンブ	depth
	深夜	シンヤ	midnight; dead of night
	深緑	シンリョク	dark green
訓	深い	ふかい	deep; profound; late; serious
	深まる	ふかまる	*vi.* become deep; deepen
	深める	ふかめる	*vt.* make deep; deepen
	深入り	ふかいり	deeply involved —*vi.* be deeply involved

644

清⑪　`ミミ汀汁汗浐清清清清

音	清	セイ	pure; clear; clean
		（ショウ）	
熟	清教徒	セイキョウト	Puritan
	清潔	セイケツ	clean; untainted
	清算	セイサン	liquidation; settlement; clearance —*v.* settle; clear; liquidate
	清酒	セイシュ	refined saké
	清純	セイジュン	purity; innocence
	清書	セイショ	fair/clean copy —*v.* write a clean copy
	清々	セイセイ	relief —*vi.* feel relieved
	清貧	セイヒン	honest poverty

心忄戈戸手扌支攵文斗斤方日曰月肉月木欠止歹殳母毋比毛氏气水氺氵火灬父片牛犬犭王礻耂

心
忄
戈
戸
手
扌
支
攵
文
斗
斤
方
日
日
月
肉
月
木
欠
止
歹
殳
母
毋
比
毛
氏
气
水
氺
氵
火
灬
父
片
牛
犬
犭
王
礻

| 清流 | セイリュウ | limpid/clear stream |

訓
清い	きよい	clean; clear; pure
清まる	きよまる	*vi*. become clean; be purified
清める	きよめる	*vt*. cleanse; make clean; purify; purge

645

温 ⑫ 丶 冫 氵 氵 沪 沪 沪 沪 洹 渭 温 温

音
| 温 | オン | warmth; temperature; gentle |

熟
温顔	オンガン	warm expression
温厚	オンコウ	gentle; courteous
温室	オンシツ	hothouse; greenhouse
温室効果	オンシツコウカ	greenhouse effect
温順	オンジュン	obedient; gentle; submissive; docile
温情	オンジョウ	warm; cordial; kind
温泉	オンセン	hot spring; spa
温存	オンゾン	preservation; maintenance —*v*. preserve; retain; keep
温帯	オンタイ	temperate zone
温暖	オンダン	mild; warm; temperate
温度	オンド	temperature
温良	オンリョウ	gentle; amiable
温和	オンワ	pleasantly mild; gentle hearted

訓
温かい	あたたかい	warm; mild; genial; kind
温か	あたたか	warm; mild
温まる	あたたまる	*vi*. get warm
温める	あたためる	*vt*. warm; heat; keep

646

減 ⑫ 丶 冫 氵 氵 沪 沪 沪 減 減 減 減 減

音
| 減 | ゲン | decrease; reduce |

熟
減額	ゲンガク	reduction; cut —*v*. reduce; cut
減収	ゲンシュウ	decrease in income; drop in revenue
減少	ゲンショウ	decrease; diminution —*v*. fall off; go down; drop; diminish; be decreased/reduced
減食	ゲンショク	diet —*vi*. eat less; cut down; diet
減水	ゲンスイ	fall in water level —*v*. drop; fall; reduce
減速	ゲンソク	speed reduction; deceleration —*v*. reduce speed; decelerate; slow down

減退	ゲンタイ	decline —*vi.* decline; fall off; weaken; fail
減点	ゲンテン	demerit marks; deducted points
減量	ゲンリョウ	weight loss; losing weight —*v.* lose weight
訓 減る	へる	*vi.* decrease; diminish; run short; dwindle; drop; lose
減らす	へらす	*vt.* reduce; decrease; cut down; take away

647

湖 ⑫ ` ` 氵 氵 汁 汁 沽 沽 油 湖 湖 湖

音 湖	コ	lake
熟 湖水	コスイ	lake
訓 湖	みずうみ	lake

648

港 ⑫ ` ` 氵 氵 汁 汁 洪 洪 洪 港 港

音 港	コウ	port; harbor
熟 港口	コウコウ	harbor entrance
訓 港	みなと	port; harbor

649

測 ⑫ ` ` 氵 汁 汋 汋 泪 泪 淠 測 測

音 測	ソク	measure
熟 測算	ソクサン	measuring and calculating
測地	ソクチ	land surveying; geodetic
測定	ソクテイ	measurement —*v.* measure
測度	ソクド	measurement; gauging
測量	ソクリョウ	survey; measurement —*v.* survey; measure
測候所	ソッコウジョ	weather station
訓 測る	はかる	*vt.* measure; estimate

4

心 忄 戈 戸 手 扌 支 攵 文 斗 斤 方 日 曰 月 肉 月 木 欠 止 歹 殳 母 毋 比 毛 氏 气 水 氺 氵 ● 火 灬 父 片 牛 犬 犭 王 礻 耂

331

4

湯 ⑫ 　 丶 丶 氵 氵 沪 沪 沪 浔 浔 湯 湯 湯

音	湯	トウ	hot water
熟	湯治	トウジ	hot-spring cure; taking the baths —*v.* take the baths/waters
訓	湯	ゆ	hot water/bath; public bath
	湯気	ゆゲ	steam; vapor
	湯元	ゆもと	source of a hot spring

満 ⑫ 　 丶 丶 氵 氵 汁 泮 泄 洪 满 満 満

音	満	マン	full; abundant; Manchuria
熟	満員	マンイン	no vacancy; full
	満開	マンカイ	in full bloom
	満期	マンキ	expiration
	満月	マンゲツ	full moon
	満座	マンザ	the whole company; everyone present
	満州	マンシュウ	Manchuria
	満場	マンジョウ	the whole company/hall
	満身	マンシン	the whole body
	満水	マンスイ	filled to the brim with water —*vi.* be filled to the brim with water
	満足	マンゾク	satisfaction; contentment —*vi.* be satisfied/contented with
	満潮	マンチョウ	high tide
	満天	マンテン	the whole sky
	満点	マンテン	full marks; perfect score
	満腹	マンプク	full stomach/belly
	満々	マンマン	full of; brimming with
	満面	マンメン	the whole face
訓	満たす	みたす	*vt.* fill; satisfy; fulfill
	満ちる	みちる	*vi.* be full; (tide) come in; expire; be fulfilled
	満ち潮	みちしお	high tide

心 忄 戈 戸 手 扌 支 攵 文 斗 斤 方 日 曰 月 肉 月 木 欠 止 歹 殳 母 毋 比 毛 氏 气 水 氷 氵 火 灬 父 片 牛 犬 犭 王 礻 歩

652

漢 ⑬ ゛ ゙ ゙ ゙ ゙ ゙ ゙ ゙ ゙ ゙ ゙ 漢 漢

音	漢	カン	Han dynasty; fellow
熟	漢学	カンガク	study of Chinese classics
	漢語	カンゴ	Chinese word
	漢詩	カンシ	Chinese poetry
	漢字	カンジ	*kanji* (Chinese character)
	漢数字	カンスウジ	Chinese numerals
	漢文	カンブン	Chinese classics
	漢方薬	カンポウヤク	medicinal herb
	漢民族	カンミンゾク	the Han race; the Chinese
	漢和辞典	カンワジテン	Chinese-character dictionary with Japanese definitions; *kanji* dictionary

653

源 ⑬ ゛ ゙ ゙ ゙ ゙ ゙ ゙ ゙ ゙ 源 源 源

音	源	ゲン	source
熟	源泉	ゲンセン	source; origin
	源流	ゲンリュウ	source; origin
訓	源	みなもと	source; origin

654

準 ⑬ ゛ ゙ ゙ ゙ ゙ ゙ ゙ ゙ ゙ 準 準 準

音	準	ジュン	rule; standard; measure
熟	準じる	ジュンじる	*vi.* follow; conform
	準急	ジュンキュウ	local express
	準決勝	ジュンケッショウ	semi-final
	準備	ジュンビ	preparations —*v.* prepare; make preparations; get ready
	準用	ジュンヨウ	corresponding application —*vt.* apply correspondingly

心忄戈戸手扌支攴文斗斤方日曰月肉月木欠止歹殳母毌比毛氏气水氷氵火灬父片牛犬犭王礻老

4

333

左margin: 心 忄 戈 戸 手 扌 支 攵 文 斗 斤 方 日 曰 月 肉 月 木 欠 止 歹 殳 母 毋 比 毛 氏 気 水 氺 氵 火 灬 父 片 牛 犬 犭 王 礻 爿

655 演 ⑭

氵 氵 氵 汽 汽 沪 沪 涫 涫 涫 演 演 演

音	演	エン	state; act; apply
熟	演じる	エンじる	perform; play act; act
	演技	エンギ	acting; performance —*vi.* act; perform
	演芸	エンゲイ	performance; dramatic art
	演劇	エンゲキ	play; drama
	演算	エンザン	*math.* operation —*v.* operate; calculate; cipher; figure out
	演習	エンシュウ	seminar; practice; exercise —*vi.* practice; carry out exercises
	演出	エンシュツ	production —*v.* produce; stage; present
	演説	エンゼツ	public speech; oration; address —*v.* make a speech; address
	演奏	エンソウ	musical performance —*v.* give a musical performance

656 漁 ⑭

氵 氵 氵 氵 汽 沪 油 油 油 淄 漁 漁

音	漁	ギョ リョウ	fishing; angling
熟	漁業	ギョギョウ	fishery; the fishing industry
	漁具	ギョグ	fishing tackle
	漁港	ギョコウ	fishing harbor
	漁場	ギョジョウ	fishing ground
	漁村	ギョソン	fishing village/community
	漁夫	ギョフ	fisherman; fisher
	漁民	ギョミン	fishermen; fishing people
	漁師	リョウシ	fishermen

657 潔 ⑮

氵 氵 汁 汢 洁 渓 渓 潔 潔 潔 潔

音	潔	ケツ	pure
熟	潔白	ケッパク	innocence; purity
訓	潔い	いさぎよい	manly; frank; honorable; brave

658

潮 ⑮　氵 氵 氵 氵 浐 浐 浐 浐 渭 淖 淖 淖 潮 潮 潮

音	潮	チョウ	tide; salt water
熟	潮流	チョウリュウ	tide; current; trend; tendency
訓	潮	しお	tide; current; sea water; brine; opportunity; chance
	潮風	しおかぜ	sea breeze
	潮時	しおどき	tidal hour; opportunity; chance

659

激 ⑯　氵 氵 氵 氵 泸 泊 渔 渻 潟 潟 溿 激 激

音	激	ゲキ	violent; acute; sharp; sudden; excite; encourage
熟	激する	ゲキする	*v.* get excited; be agitated
	激化	ゲキカ	intensification —*vi.* become intense; intensify
	激減	ゲキゲン	sharp/marked decrease —*vi.* fall sharply; drop sharply
	激戦	ゲキセン	fierce battle
	激増	ゲキゾウ	sharp increase; sudden rise —*vi.* increase sharply; show a sudden increase
	激痛	ゲキツウ	acute/sharp pain
	激動	ゲキドウ	violent shaking/shock; excitement; turbulence —*vi.* shake violently; be excited/turbulent
	激変	ゲキヘン	violent/sudden change —*vi.* undergo a violent/sudden/rapid change
	激務	ゲキム	hard work; demanding job; pressing duties
	激流	ゲキリュウ	rapids; torrent; swift current
	激論	ゲキロン	hot argument; heated discussion
訓	激しい	はげしい	violent; extreme; severe; intense

4 火　ひ／ひへん　fire　灬 (p.338)

660

火 ④　丶 丷 少 火

| 音 | 火 | カ | fire; flame; light |

心
忄
戈
戸
手
扌
支
攴
文
斗
斤
方
日
曰
月
肉
月
木
欠
止
歹
殳
母
毋
比
毛
氏
気
水
氷
氵
火
灬
父
片
牛
犬
犭
王
礻
疒

熟	火気	カキ	fire; heat of fire
	火器	カキ	firearms
	火口	カコウ	(volcano) crater; muzzle (of a gun)
	火災	カサイ	fire; conflagration; large disastrous fire
	火山	カザン	volcano
	火事	カジ	fire; conflagration; disastrous fire
	火星	カセイ	the planet Mars
	火勢	カセイ	force of the flames
	火薬	カヤク	gunpowder; explosives
	火曜日	カヨウび	Tuesday
	火力	カリョク	heat; calorific force; thermal power
訓	火	ひ	fire; flame; light
	火加減	ひカゲン	how well/poorly a fire is burning
	火柱	ひばしら	pillar of fire
	火花	ひばな	sparks; hot glowing particles heated by friction
	火元	ひもと	origin of a fire
	火	ほ	fire

661

 灰 ⑥ 一 厂 厂 灰 灰 灰

音	灰	カイ	ash
訓	灰	はい	ash
	灰色	はいいろ	gray *fig*. hopelessness; uncertain attitude
	灰神楽	はいかぐら	cloud of ashes
	灰皿	はいざら	ashtray

662

 灯 ⑥ 丶 丷 少 火 火 灯

音	灯	トウ	light
熟	灯火	トウカ	light/lamplight
	灯下	トウカ	by lamplight
	灯心	トウシン	lampwick
	灯台	トウダイ	lighthouse/light/beacon
	灯油	トウユ	lamp oil; kerosene
訓	灯	ひ	light

663 災 ⑦

` ´ ´´ ´´´ ´´´ ´´´ ´´´ 災

音	災	サイ	calamity; disaster; misforturne
熟	災害	サイガイ	disaster; calamity
	災難	サイナン	misfortune; disaster; accident
訓	災い	わざわい	disaster; misfortune; calamity

664 炭 ⑨

` ´´ 山 屵 屵 屵 岸 炭 炭

音	炭	タン	charcoal; coal
熟	炭鉱	タンコウ	coal mine
	炭酸	タンサン	*chem*. carbonic acid
	炭酸水	タンサンスイ	*chem*. carbonated water
	炭水化物	タンスイカブツ	carbohydrate
	炭素	タンソ	carbon
	炭田	タンデン	coal field
訓	炭	すみ	charcoal

665 焼 ⑫

` ´ ´ 火 灯 灯 灶 灶 炉 焼 焼 焼

音	焼	ショウ	burn
熟	焼死	ショウシ	death by fire —*vi*. be burned to death
	焼失	ショウシツ	destruction by fire —*vi*. be burned down; be destroyed by fire
訓	焼く	やく	*v*. burn; heat; bake; grill; boil; roast
	焼ける	やける	*vi*. be burned/grilled/sun-tanned
	焼き物	やきもの	ceramic ware; pottery; porcelain; china

666 燃 ⑯

` ´ 火 火 灯 灯 灼 焛 燃 燃 燃 燃

音	燃	ネン	burn
熟	燃焼	ネンショウ	combustion; burning; ignition —*vi*. combust; burn; ignite

心 忄 戈 戸 手 扌 支 攵 文 斗 斤 方 日 曰 月 肉 月 木 欠 止 歹 殳 母 毋 比 毛 氏 气 水 氺 氵 火 灬 父 片 牛 犬 犭 王 礻 耂

燃料	ネンリョウ	fuel	

訓 燃える　もえる　***vi.*** burn; blaze; be in flames
燃す　もす　***vt.*** burn; light; kindle; ignite
燃やす　もやす　***vt.*** burn; kindle; ignite

4　灬　よつてん／れっか　fire in a row; four dots

667 点 ⑨

丶　卜　ト　占　占　占　点　点　点

音 点　テン　dot; spot; mark; grades; points; score; fault; defect; item; piece

熟 点火　テンカ　ignition; lighting —***vi.*** ignite; light; kindle; set off; fire

点眼　テンガン　dropping eyedrops in the eyes —***v.*** apply eyewash; drop eyedrops in the eyes

点検　テンケン　inspection; examination; checking; muster —***v.*** inspect; examine; scrutinize; check

点呼　テンコ　roll call; calling of the roll —***v.*** call the roll

点在　テンザイ　scattered —***vi.*** be dotted with; be scattered

点字　テンジ　braille type; braille; raised letters

点数　テンスウ　marks; points; score; number of articles

点線　テンセン　dotted/perforated line

点々　テンテン　here and there; sporadically; in drops

点灯　テントウ　lighting —***vi.*** light; light up; turn on a light

訓 点ける　つける　***vt.*** light; put a match to; turn/switch on

668 然 ⑫

ノ　ク　タ　タ　タ　タ　タ　然　然　然　然　然

音 然　ゼン　yes
ネン　nature

669 無 ⑫

ノ　ヒ　ニ　ケ　ニ　ニ　ニ　ニ　無　無　無　無

音 無　ム　nothing; without; (prefix) -less, -free, un-
ブ

熟 無愛想	ブアイソウ	unsociable; curt
無気味	ブキミ	ominous; eerie; uncanny
無器用	ブキヨウ	unskillful; clumsy
無骨	ブコツ	boorish; uncouth
無細工	ブサイク	clumsy; plain; ugly
無作法	ブサホウ	bad manners; rudeness
無事	ブジ	safe and sound
無精	ブショウ	idle; lazy
無勢	ブゼイ	numerical inferiority
無難	ブナン	safe; not dangerous; acceptable
無用心	ブヨウジン	carelessness
無礼	ブレイ	rudeness; discourtesy
無意義	ムイギ	meaningless; not significant
無意識	ムイシキ	unconscious; involuntary
無意味	ムイミ	meaningless; pointless
無医村	ムイソン	doctorless village
無一物	ムイチモツ	penniless; possessionless
無一文	ムイチモン	penniless
無益	ムエキ	useless; futile
無価	ムカ	priceless
無我	ムガ	selflessness; self-forgetfulness
無我夢中	ムガムチュウ	total absorption; being totally involved in; forgetting oneself
無害	ムガイ	harmless
無学	ムガク	uneducated; ignorant
無価値	ムカチ	worthless
無関心	ムカンシン	indifference; unconcern; apathy
無期	ムキ	indefinite (period of time)
無機	ムキ	inorganic
無傷	ムきず	undamaged; unblemished; unhurt
無記名	ムキメイ	unregistered
無休	ムキュウ	no holidays; always open
無給	ムキュウ	unpaid; non-salaried
無気力	ムキリョク	spiritless; flabby; gutless
無口	むくち	reticent; taciturn; laconic
無下	ムゲ	(refuse) flatly/roundly
無形	ムケイ	intangible
無形文化財	ムケイブンカザイ	intangible cultural assets (the skills of art, music and drama)
無欠	ムケツ	flawless; faultless
無限	ムゲン	infinite
無効	ムコウ	invalid; null; void; ineffective

心忄戈戸手扌支攴文斗斤方日曰月肉月欠止歹殳母毋比毛氏气水氺氵火灬父片牛犬犭王礻耂

無根	ムコン	groundless; unfounded
無言	ムゴン	silent; mute
無罪	ムザイ	innocent; not guilty
無差別	ムサベツ	indiscriminate
無産	ムサン	without property
無産者	ムサンシャ	proletariat
無残	ムザン	cruel; ruthless; pitiful
無私	ムシ	unselfish; disinterested
無視	ムシ	disregard —*v.* ignore; disregard
無地	ムジ	solid color; patternless
無実	ムジツ	false; unfounded; innocent
無上	ムジョウ	supreme; greatest; highest
無情	ムジョウ	unfeeling; callous; cruel
無常	ムジョウ	transitory; mutable; uncertain
無条件	ムジョウケン	unconditional
無色	ムショク	colorless; achromatic
無職	ムショク	no occupation; unemployed
無所属	ムショゾク	independent; unaffiliated
無心	ムシン	not thinking of anything
無神経	ムシンケイ	dull; insensitive; unfeeling
無人地帯	ムジンチタイ	no man's land
無人島	ムジントウ	uninhabited island
無数	ムスウ	innumerable; countless
無声	ムセイ	silent; mute; voiceless; noiseless
無税	ムゼイ	duty-free; tax-free
無制限	ムセイゲン	unlimited; unrestricted
無生物	ムセイブツ	inanimate object
無責任	ムセキニン	irresponsibility
無線	ムセン	wireless; radio
無銭	ムセン	without money; penniless
無造作	ムゾウサ	with ease; simple; artless
無断	ムダン	unannounced; unauthorized
無知	ムチ	ignorance
無茶	ムチャ	absurd; rash; excessive
無茶苦茶	ムチャクチャ	mixed up; confused; nonsensical; reckless
無賃	ムチン	free of charge
無敵	ムテキ	invincible; unrivaled
無二	ムニ	peerless; unequaled
無念	ムネン	regret; resentment; vexation
無能	ムノウ	incompetent; ineffective
無比	ムヒ	matchless; incomparable; unrivaled
無病	ムビョウ	well; healthy

	無風	ムフウ	windless; dead calm
	無分別	ムフンベツ	indiscrete; imprudent; thoughtless; rash
	無法	ムホウ	outrageous; unlawful; unjust
	無名	ムメイ	nameless; unknown; anonymous
	無用	ムヨウ	unnecessary; useless; prohibited
	無欲	ムヨク	unselfish; free from avarice
	無理	ムリ	unreasonable; impossible; beyond one's power; too difficult; by force; against one's will
	無理解	ムリカイ	lack of understanding
	無理算段	ムリサンダン	scraping together —*v*. scrape together
	無理難題	ムリナンダイ	unreasonable demand
	無理矢理	ムリやり	forcibly; under compulsion
	無料	ムリョウ	free of charge; free
	無量	ムリョウ	beyond measure; immense
	無力	ムリョク	powerless; ineffectual; feeble; incompetent
	無類	ムルイ	finest; choicest
	無論	ムロン	of course; naturally
訓	無い	ない	not; no
	無くす	なくす	***vt***. lose; get rid of
	無くなる	なくなる	***vi***. be gone/lost; run out of; die; pass away

670

照 ⑬

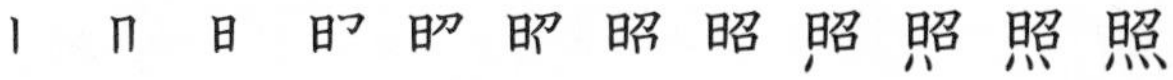

音	照	ショウ	shine; check
熟	照応	ショウオウ	correspondence; agreement; accordance —***vi***. correspond; agree; accord
	照会	ショウカイ	inquiry; reference —*v*. refer; inquire; make inquiries
	照会状	ショウカイジョウ	letter of inquiry
	照合	ショウゴウ	check; collation —*v*. check; collate
	照準	ショウジュン	aim; aiming
	照度	ショウド	illumination
	照明	ショウメイ	illumination; lighting —*v*. illuminate; light up
訓	照らす	てらす	***vt***. shine; light up; flash; consult; refer
	照らし合わせる	てらしあわせる	***vt***. check; confirm
	照る	てる	***vi***. shine; illuminate
	照れる	てれる	***vi***. feel self-conscious/shy; be embarrassed
	照れ屋	てれや	bashful person; person who blushes easily
	照り	てり	sunshine; glaze; glare

照り焼き　てりやき　　teriyaki (broiling meat/fish that has been soaked in soy sauce)

心忄戈戸手扌支攵文斗斤方日曰月肉月木欠止歹殳母毋比毛氏气水氺氵火灬父片牛犬犭王礻耂

671

熟 ⑮　　亠　亠　亠　亠　亯　亨　享　郭　孰　孰　孰　熟

音	熟	ジュク	ripen; mature; thorough
熟	熟する	ジュクする	*vi.* ripen; mature
	熟語	ジュクゴ	phrase; idiom; compound
	熟視	ジュクシ	intense stare
	熟成	ジュクセイ	ripe; mature —*vi.* ripen; mature; age
	熟達	ジュクタツ	mastering —*vi.* master; become proficient in
	熟知	ジュクチ	well-known; well-informed; familiar —*v.* know well; be familiar with; be well informed
	熟読	ジュクドク	careful reading —*v.* read carefully
	熟年	ジュクネン	middle-aged
	熟練	ジュクレン	skill; mastery —*vi.* be skilled/expert in
	熟考	ジュッコウ	consideration; deliberation —*v.* consider; deliberate
訓	熟れる	うれる	*vi.* ripen

672

熱 ⑮　　一　十　土　圭　圭　幸　幸　執　執　執　熱　熱

音	熱	ネツ	hot; heat; zeal; ardor; enthusiasm
熟	熱する	ネッする	*vt.* heat up *vi.* become hot/excited
	熱愛	ネツアイ	passionate love; devotion —*v.* love passionately/fervently; be madly in love
	熱意	ネツイ	zeal; ardor; enthusiasm
	熱演	ネツエン	ardent/impassioned performance —*v.* give an impassioned performance
	熱気	ネッキ	heat; ardor; hot air; heated atmosphere; feverishness
	熱血	ネッケツ	zeal; hot blood; enthusiasm; ardor
	熱源	ネツゲン	heat source
	熱効率	ネツコウリツ	*phy.* thermal efficiency
	熱射病	ネッシャビョウ	heatstroke
	熱情	ネツジョウ	fervor; ardor; passion; warmth; ardent love
	熱処理	ネツショリ	heat treatment
	熱心	ネッシン	enthusiasm; zeal; fervor; ardor; earnestness
	熱誠	ネッセイ	feverish; earnest; devoted; sincere; enthusiastic

熱戦	ネッセン	hot contest; hard fight
熱帯	ネッタイ	torrid zone; tropics
熱中	ネッチュウ	absorption; enthusiasm; zeal —*vi.* become enthusiastic; have a mania for
熱伝導	ネツデンドウ	*phy.* thermal conduction
熱湯	ネットウ	boiling water
熱病	ネツビョウ	fever
熱風	ネップウ	hot wind; blast of hot air; hot blast
熱弁	ネツベン	fervent speech
熱望	ネツボウ	ardent wish; eager desire —*v.* desire earnestly; be anxious for
熱量	ネツリョウ	*phy.* heat capacity; calorific value
訓 熱い	あつい	hot; heated; be madly in love
熱さ	あつさ	heat; warmth

---

4 父 ちち father

673

父 �
④
ノ ハ グ 父

音 父	フ	father
熟 父兄	フケイ	father and elder brother; guardians or parents of children
父母	フボ	father and mother; parents
訓 父	ちち	one's father
父親	ちちおや	father

---

4 片 かたへん right side

674

片 �ノ ゲ 广 片
④

音 片	ヘン	one half of a whole; one side; fragment; piece; pence (unit of British currency)
熟 片々	ヘンペン	in pieces; in small fragments
訓 片	かた	one (of two); one side; single
片足	かたあし	one leg/foot

343

4

心 忄 戈 戸 手 扌 支 攵 文 斗 斤 方 日 曰 月 肉 月 木 欠 止 歹 殳 母 毋 比 毛 氏 气 水 氺 氵 火 灬 ● 父 片 牛 犬 犭 王 礻 耂

心
忄
戈
戸
手
扌
支
攵
文
斗
斤
方
日
曰
月
肉
月
木
欠
止
歹
殳
母
毋
比
毛
氏
气
水
氵
火
灬
父
片
牛
犬
犭
王
礻
艹

片意地	かたイジ	stubborn; bigoted
片一方	かたイッポウ	one side/party; other side/party
片田舎	かたいなか	remote village in the country
片思い	かたおもい	unrequited love
片親	かたおや	one parent
片仮名	かたかな	*katakana* (the non-cursive syllabary)
片側	かたがわ	one side
片側通行	かたがわツウコウ	One Way (traffic)
片言	かたこと	baby talk; broken (English); few words
片便り	かただより	one-way correspondence
片付く	かたづく	*vi*. be tidied up; be put away; be settled; be disposed of; be married off
片付ける	かたづける	*vt*. tidy up; put away; settle; dispose of; marry off
片手間	かたてま	in one's spare time; on the side
片時	かたとき	a moment; instant
片腹痛い	かたはらいたい	ridiculous; absurd; laughable
片方	かたホウ	one side/party; other side/party
片身	かたみ	one side of the body
片道	かたみち	one-way (trip/ticket)
片目	かため	one eye; one-eyed
片面	かたメン	one side/aspect
片寄る	かたよる	*vi*. lean to one side; be unfair
片割れ	かたわれ	fragment; member of a group/gang (of criminals)

675

版⑧　丿　丿′　丿″　片　片′　片″　版　版

音	版	ハン	plate
熟	版画	ハンガ	print
	版権	ハンケン	copyright

4 牛 うし／うしへん cow

676

牛 ④ 　ノ　ヒ　二　牛

音	牛	ギュウ	cow; ox; beef; dairy
熟	牛飲馬食	ギュウイン バショク	heavy eating and drinking; immoderation in eating and drinking —*vi.* eat and drink heavily
	牛舎	ギュウシャ	cattle stall; cow barn
	牛耳る	ギュウジる	*vt.* take the lead; control
	牛肉	ギュウニク	beef
	牛乳	ギュウニュウ	cow's milk
訓	牛	うし	cow; ox; bull

677

物 ⑧ 　ノ　ヒ　牛　牛　牜　牞　物　物

音	物	ブツ	thing; object
		モツ	thing; object
熟	物議	ブツギ	public criticism/discussion
	物件	ブッケン	thing; article; object
	物故	ブッコ	death —*vi.* die; pass away
	物故者	ブッコシャ	the deceased
	物産	ブッサン	product; produce; commodity
	物資	ブッシ	goods; resources
	物質	ブッシツ	matter; substance
	物質的	ブッシツテキ	material; physical
	物色	ブッショク	ransacking; rummaging; looking for —*v.* ransack; rummage; look/search for; select
	物体	ブッタイ	body; object; substance
	物的	ブッテキ	material; physical
	物品	ブッピン	goods; article; commodity
	物欲	ブツヨク	worldly desires/ambition
	物理	ブツリ	law of nature; physics
	物理学	ブツリガク	physics
訓	物	もの	thing; object
	物入り	ものいり	expenses
	物語	ものがたり	story; narrative

345

心忄戈戸手扌支攵文斗方日曰月肉月木欠止歹殳母毋比毛氏气水氺氵火灬父片牛犬犭王礻耂

物心	ものごころ	discretion; judgment
物事	ものごと	things; matters
物好き	ものずき	curious; whimsical; eccentric
物足りない	ものたりない	unsatisfying; something missing
物干し	ものほし	(frame for) drying clothes
物見	ものみ	sightseeing; watchtower; scout; patrol
物見遊山	ものみユサン	pleasure trip; sightseeing tour
物々しい	ものものしい	showy; imposing; elaborate; overdone; excessive
物分かり	ものわかり	understanding
物忘れ	ものわすれ	forgetfulness

678

牧 ⑧　　丿 丶 牛 牛 牛 牧 牧 牧

音	牧	ボク	pasture
熟	牧牛	ボクギュウ	grazing/pasturing cattle
	牧師	ボクシ	pastor; minister
	牧舎	ボクシャ	cattleshed
	牧場	ボクジョウ	ranch; (cattle/sheep) farm
	牧神	ボクシン	Pan
	牧草	ボクソウ	grass; pasturage; meadow
	牧童	ボクドウ	cowboy; shepherd boy
訓	牧	まき	ranch; (cattle/sheep) farm
	牧場	まきば	ranch; (cattle/sheep) farm

679

特 ⑩　　丿 丶 牛 牛 牛 牜 特 特 特 特

音	特	トク	special; specific; particular
熟	特異	トクイ	unique; singular
	特技	トクギ	specialty; special talent/ability
	特産	トクサン	special product; specialty
	特使	トクシ	special envoy/express messenger
	特質	トクシツ	characteristic; property; special quality
	特集	トクシュウ	special edition (of a newspaper, magazine, etc.) —*v.* bring out a special edition
	特賞	トクショウ	special prize
	特色	トクショク	character; feature; distinguishing mark; idiosyncrasy

特性	トクセイ	special quality; characteristic; distinguishing mark
特製	トクセイ	special make/manufacture
特設	トクセツ	special establishment/installment/accomodation
特選	トクセン	special selection/approval; recognition
特大	トクダイ	outsize
特種	トクだね	scoop; exclusive news
特長	トクチョウ	merit; forte; strong point
特定	トクテイ	specific —*v.* specify
特典	トクテン	privilege; special favor; benefit
特電	トクデン	special telegram
特等	トクトウ	special/top grade
特派	トクハ	special dispatch —*v.* send a special dispatch; send; detail
特売	トクバイ	bargain/special sale; sale at a special price —*v.* sell at a special/reduced prices
特筆	トクヒツ	special mention —*v.* make a special mention/feature of
特別	トクベツ	special; extraordinary
特報	トクホウ	news flash —*v.* give a news flash
特約	トクヤク	special contract/agreement —*v.* make/come to a special agreement
特有	トクユウ	peculiar; characteristic; special
特例	トクレイ	special case/treatment; exception
特価	トッカ	special/bargain price
特急	トッキュウ	limited/super express
特許	トッキョ	patent; charter; license; special permission
特権	トッケン	privilege; special right; charter; option
特効薬	トッコウヤク	specific remedy

4 犬 いぬ dog; animal 犭 (p.348)

680

 一 ナ 大 犬 ④

音	犬	ケン	dog
熟	犬歯	ケンシ	canine teeth
訓	犬	いぬ	dog
	犬死に	いぬじに	unrewarded death —*vi.* die for nothing

心 忄 戈 戸 手 扌 支 攵 文 斗 斤 方 日 曰 月 肉 月 木 欠 止 歹 殳 母 毋 比 毛 氏 气 水 氺 氵 火 灬 父 片 牛 犬 犭 王 礻 爿

681

状 ⑦ 丶 丬 丬 丬 壮 状 状

音	状	ジョウ	condition; letter
熟	状勢	ジョウセイ	situation; state of affairs; conditions
	状態	ジョウタイ	state; condition

---

3 犭 けものへん animal

682

犯 ⑤ 丿 犭 犭 犭 犯

音	犯	ハン	offense
熟	犯行	ハンコウ	crime; offense; criminal act
	犯罪	ハンザイ	crime; offense
	犯人	ハンニン	criminal; offender
訓	犯す	おかす	*vt.* commit an offense; violate; attack; assault; rape

683

独 ⑨ 丿 犭 犭 犭 犭 犯 独 独 独

音	独	ドク	alone; by oneself; Germany
熟	独演	ドクエン	recital; single; solo performance —*v.* give a solo performance/recital
	独学	ドクガク	self-education; self-instruction —*v.* teach/educate oneself
	独語	ドクゴ	the German language
	独裁	ドクサイ	dictatorship; despotism; autocracy —*vi.* dictate; hold a country under despotic rule
	独裁者	ドクサイシャ	dictator
	独裁主義	ドクサイシュギ	dictatorship
	独裁的	ドクサイテキ	dictatorial; despotic; autocratic
	独自	ドクジ	original; peculiar; individual; oneself
	独習	ドクシュウ	self-teaching; self-study —*v.* teach oneself; study without a teacher
	独唱	ドクショウ	vocal solo; recital —*v.* sing a solo
	独身	ドクシン	single life; single; celibacy; bachelorhood

独善	ドクゼン	self-righteousness	
独走	ドクソウ	running alone; runaway; walkover —*vi.* run away; walkover	
独奏	ドクソウ	solo; recital —*v.* play a solo/alone	
独創	ドクソウ	originality	
独断	ドクダン	arbitrary decision; dogmatism	
独特	ドクトク	unique; peculiar; special; original	
独立	ドクリツ	independence; self-help; self-reliance; freedom; self-support —*vi.* become independent/free/ isolated	
独立心	ドクリッシン	independent spirit	
独立独歩	ドクリツドッポ	independence; self-reliance; self-help	
独力	ドクリョク	one's own efforts; single-handed	
独り	ひとり	alone; by oneself	
独り言	ひとりごと	monolog; soliloquy	

4 王　see ⇨p.350

4 礻　see ⇨p.378

4 耂　see ⇨p.416

5 玄 げん dark

684

率⑪ 　`, 亠 玄 玄 玄 洨 洨 滋 滋 率`

音	率	ソツ	lead; all; light; easy
		リツ	proportion; percentage; rate
熟	率先	ソッセン	taking the lead —*vi.* take the lead; be the first
	率然	ソツゼン	suddenly; unexpectedly
	率直	ソッチョク	frank; straightforward
訓	率いる	ひきいる	*vt.* lead; be in command of

5 玉 たま jewel 　　王 (p.350)

685

玉⑤ 　`一 丅 干 王 玉`

音	玉	ギョク	jewel; pearl; jewel like
熟	玉石混交	ギョクセキ コンコウ	good and bad
訓	玉	たま	jewel; gem

4 王 おう／たまへん／おうへん king

686

王④ 　`一 丅 干 王`

音	王	オウ	king; prince; lord
熟	王位	オウイ	the throne; the crown
	王宮	オウキュウ	king's palace; royal palace
	王国	オウコク	kingdom
	王座	オウザ	the throne
	王様	オウさま	king
	王子	オウジ	prince

王室	オウシツ	royal family
王者	オウシャ （オウジャ）	king; monarch; ruler
王女	オウジョ	princess
王政	オウセイ	imperial rule
王政復古	オウセイフッコ	*hist*. restoration of imperial rule (1867)
王族	オウゾク	royal family
王朝	オウチョウ	dynasty
王手	オウて	checkmate; *ote* (shogi)

687

班 ⑩　一 丁 王 王 玑 玑 玑 班 班

| 音 | 班 | ハン | group |
| 熟 | 班長 | ハンチョウ | squad/section/group leader |

688

球 ⑪　一 丁 王 王 王 玎 玎 玎 球 球 球

音	球	キュウ	ball; sphere; spherical; baseball
熟	球技	キュウギ	ball game
	球根	キュウコン	bulb
	球状	キュウジョウ	spherical shape; globe
	球場	キュウジョウ	baseball ground; ballpark
	球速	キュウソク	*bas*. (pitcher's) pace; speed of a pitcher's ball
訓	球	たま	ball

689

現 ⑪　一 丁 王 王 玑 玑 玑 玑 現 現 現

音	現	ゲン	appear; now; current; present
熟	現役	ゲンエキ	active service/duty
	現金	ゲンキン	cash; ready money *adj*. mercenary; calculating; selfish
	現行	ゲンコウ	current; present; existing
	現行犯	ゲンコウハン	flagrant offense; red-handed
	現在	ゲンザイ	now; the present; existing; current —*v*. exist; be current
	現実	ゲンジツ	reality; actuality; hard fact

玄玉王生用田疋疒癶白皮皿目矢石示礻禾穴立罒母水礻

351

玄
玉
王
● 生
用
田
疋
扩
癶
白
皮
皿
目
矢
石
示
礻
禾
穴
立
罒
母
氺
衤

現実化	ゲンジツカ	realization —*v.* realize; be realized; put into effect
現実主義	ゲンジツシュギ	realism
現住所	ゲンジュウショ	present address
現出	ゲンシュツ	appearance; emergence; revelation —*v.* appear; emerge; come out; reveal
現象	ゲンショウ	phenomenon; happening; phase; aspect
現状	ゲンジョウ	present state; actual situation; status quo
現職	ゲンショク	one's present post/office
現世	ゲンセ	this world/life; worldly; earthy; temporal; secular
現像	ゲンゾウ	film development —*v.* develop (a film)
現存	ゲンゾン	existence —*vi.* exist; be extant
現代	ゲンダイ	today; modern; the present age; contemporary
現地	ゲンチ	on the spot; locality; the field; the actual place
現地時間	ゲンチジカン	local time
現場	ゲンば	the spot; the field; the actual place
現品	ゲンピン	goods; the actual article

訓
| 現す | あらわす | *vt.* express; show; reveal |
| 現れる | あらわれる | *vi.* come out; appear; emerge |

690

 理 ⑪ 一 丁 千 王 玾 玾 玾 玾 玾 理 理 理

音 | 理 | リ | reason; justice; truth; principle |

熟
理科	リカ	science
理解	リカイ	understanding; comprehension —*v.* understand; comprehend
理化学	リカガク	physics and chemistry
理事	リジ	director; trustee
理性	リセイ	reason; reasoning power
理想	リソウ	ideal
理想郷	リソウキョウ	utopia; ideal land; Shangri-La
理想的	リソウテキ	ideal
理知	リチ	intellect; intelligence
理念	リネン	idea; doctrine; ideology
理非	リヒ	rights and wrongs; relative merits
理法	リホウ	law
理由	リユウ	reason; cause
理容	リヨウ	hairdressing
理路整然	リロセイゼン	logical; well-argued; cogent
理論	リロン	theory

5 生 うまれる life; birth

691

生 ⑤ ノ ヒ 牛 牛 生

音	生	ショウ	live; life
		セイ	life; living; birth; produce; grow

熟	生じる	ショウじる	v. develop; accrue; come about; engender
	生国	ショウゴク (ショウコク)	country/province of one's birth
	生育	セイイク	growth; development —v. grow; raise; be born and bred; vegetate
	生家	セイカ	one's parents' house; house one was born in
	生花	セイカ	real flower; flower arrangement
	生活	セイカツ	life; existence; livelihood —vi. live; exist; make a living
	生活水準	セイカツスイジュン	standard of living
	生活費	セイカツヒ	living expenses
	生気	セイキ	vitality; life; animation; vigor; spirit
	生計	セイケイ	living; livelihood
	生産	セイサン	production —v. produce; make; turn/put out
	生産高	セイサンだか	output; yield
	生産地	セイサンチ	producing center
	生死	セイシ	life or death; safety; fate
	生成	セイセイ	creation; formulation; generation —vi. be created/formed
	生前	セイゼン	while alive; during one's lifetime; before one's death
	生息	セイソク	inhabited —vi. inhabit; live
	生存	セイゾン	existence; being; life —vi. exist; live; survive; outlive
	生存競争	セイゾンキョウソウ	struggle for existence
	生存者	セイゾンシャ	survivor
	生態	セイタイ	mode of life; ecology
	生態学	セイタイガク	ecology
	生誕	セイタン	birth; nativity —vi. be born
	生地	セイチ	birthplace/home
	生年	セイネン	year of birth; age
	生年月日	セイネンガッぴ	date of birth
	生物	セイブツ	living thing; organism; creature; life
	生物学	セイブツガク	biology

玄玉王生用田疋疒癶白皮皿目矢石示ネ禾穴立罒母水衤

生別	セイベツ	eternal/lifelong separation —*v.* never meet again
生命	セイメイ	life; the soul
生来	セイライ	by nature; naturally; by birth
生理	セイリ	physiology; menstruation

訓

生きる	いきる	*vi.* live; exist; survive
生かす	いかす	*vi.* revive; resuscitate; bring to life; give life to
生ける	いける	*vt.* arrange flowers
生まれる	うまれる	*vi.* be born
生む	うむ	*vt.* bear; give birth to; produce
生う	おう	*v.* grow; come out
生える	はえる	*vi.* grow; come out
生やす	はやす	*vt.* grow; cultivate
生	き	pure; raw
生一本	きイッポン	pure; neat; straight; straightforward; honest
生糸	きいと	raw silk
生地	きジ	cloth
生真面目	きまじめ	honest; earnest; sincere
生	なま	raw; uncooked; rare; draft
生意気	なまイキ	conceit; self-conceit; selfishness
生演奏	なまエンソウ	live performance
生傷	なまきず	fresh wound
生々しい	なまなましい	fresh; green; vivid; graphic
生返事	なまヘンジ	vague answer; noncommittal reply
生放送	なまホウソウ	live broadcast

692

産 ⑪　 　丶　 亠　 产　 产　 立　 产　 产　 产　 产　 产　 産

音 産　サン　give birth to; produce; output

熟

産院	サンイン	maternity hospital
産科	サンカ	*med.* obstetrics; the obstetrical department
産気	サンケ	feeling that a baby is about to be born
産児制限	サンジセイゲン	birth control —*vi.* practice birth control
産地	サンチ	producing area/center
産婦人科	サンフジンカ	*med.* gynecology
産物	サンブツ	products; produce
産卵	サンラン	laying eggs; spawning —*vi.* lay eggs; spawn

訓

産む	うむ	*vt.* have a baby; bear; give birth to; produce
産まれる	うまれる	*vi.* be born; be established; be started
産	うぶ	naive; innocent; unsophisticated

5 用 もちいる using

693

用 ⑤ 　｜ 冂 月 月 用

音	用	ヨウ	business; errand; use
熟	用意	ヨウイ	preparations; arrangements
	用器	ヨウキ	instrument; tool
	用具	ヨウグ	equipment; kit
	用件	ヨウケン	business; things to be done
	用語	ヨウゴ	term; terminology
	用材	ヨウザイ	lumber; materials
	用紙	ヨウシ	(application) form; stationery
	用字	ヨウジ	use of characters
	用事	ヨウジ	business; errand; things to be done
	用心	ヨウジン	caution; care —*vi*. take care of; pay attention to
	用心棒	ヨウジンボウ	bodyguard
	用水	ヨウスイ	city/irrigation water
	用談	ヨウダン	business talk —*vi*. have an important business talk
	用地	ヨウチ	lot; site; land for some use
	用品	ヨウヒン	supplies
	用便	ヨウベン	going to the toilet —*v*. go to the toilet
	用法	ヨウホウ	how to use; directions
	用務	ヨウム	business
	用務員	ヨウムイン	janitor; custodian
	用命	ヨウメイ	command; order
	用例	ヨウレイ	example; illustration
訓	用いる	もちいる	*vt*. use

玄玉王生用田疋疒癶白皮皿目矢石示衤禾穴立罒母水衤

5 田 た／たへん rice field

694

⑤

音	田	デン	field
熟	田園	デンエン	fields and gardens; the country; rural districts
	田園生活	デンエンセイカツ	country life; life in the country
	田園都市	デンエントシ	rural city
	田楽	デンガク	*dengaku* (ritual music and dancing performed in Shinto shrines)
	田地	デンジ	rice paddies; state of mind; female genitals
	田畑	デンぱた	cultivated fields
	田野	デンヤ	cultivated fields
訓	田	た	rice field
	田植え	たうえ	rice planting
	田畑	たはた	rice field; farmland; fields

695

⑤ 申 ｜ 冂 日 日 申

音	申	シン	state; say; report; declare
熟	申告	シンコク	report; return; declaration —*v.* report; declare
	申告書	シンコクショ	report; declaration
訓	申す	もうす	*hum. vt.* say; speak; mention
	申し上げる	もうしあげる	*hum. vt.* tell; inform
	申し訳ない	もうしわけない	sorry; excuse me; thank you

696

⑤ 由 ｜ 冂 巾 由 由

音	由	ユ	reason; cause; significance; means; way
		ユウ	
		（ユイ）	
熟	由々しい	ユユしい	grave; serious
	由来	ユライ	origin; derivation; originally; by nature —*vi.* date back to; originate

訓 由　　　よし　　　reason; cause; significance; means; way

697

男 ⑦
丨 冂 冂 用 田 罗 男

音	男	ダン	man; male; baron
		ナン	man
熟	男子	ダンシ	male; man; boy; son
	男児	ダンジ	boy
	男女	ダンジョ	man and woman; couple
	男性	ダンセイ	male sex; man; masculinity; manliness
	男性的	ダンセイテキ	manly; masculine
訓	男	おとこ	man; boy

698

町 ⑦
丨 冂 冂 用 田 町 町

音	町	チョウ	town; street; block
熟	町家	チョウカ	town house
	町会	チョウカイ	town block association; town assembly
	町村	チョウソン	towns and villages; municipalities
	町長	チョウチョウ	town headman/manager
	町内	チョウナイ	town; streets; neighborhood
	町人	チョウニン	townsman; merchant
	町民	チョウミン	town resident
訓	町	まち	town; city; street
	町中	まちなか	the streets; the middle of the town
	町並み	まちなみ	row of stores and houses on a street
	町外れ	まちはずれ	outskirts of a town
	町役場	まちやくば	town hall/office

699

界 ⑨
丨 冂 冂 用 田 甲 艮 界 界

| 音 | 界 | カイ | border; circles; scope |
| 訓 | 界 | さかい | border; limit |

玄玉王生用田疋疒癶白皮皿目矢石示礻禾穴立罒母水礻

357

玄玉王生用田疋疒癶白皮皿目矢石示礻禾穴立罒母水礻

700

畑 ⑨

丶 ㇔ 丷 少 火 灯 烟 畑 畑

| 訓 | 畑 | はた | plowed field; farm; plantation |
| | 畑 | はたけ | plowed field; farm; plantation *fig.* specialty; one's field |

701

留 ⑩

丶 ㇗ 厶 幻 幻 幻 留 留 留

音	留	リュウ (ル)	stop; hold; fast; detain; keep
熟	留意	リュウイ	attention; mindful —*vi.* pay attention to; give head to; be mindful of
	留任	リュウニン	remaining in office —*vi.* remain in office
	留学	リュウガク	studying abroad —*vi.* study abroad
	留置	リュウチ	detention; custody —*v.* detain; lockup; hold in custody
	留保	リュウホ	reservation; withholding —*v.* reserve; withhold
	留守	ルス	absence; being away from home; neglecting
	留守番	ルスバン	looking after the house (while the owner is away); someone who looks after a house (while the owner in away)
	留守番電話	ルスバンデンワ	answering machine
訓	留まる	とまる	*vi.* stop; be fixed in one position
	留める	とめる	*vt.* stop; detain; fix in one position
	留め立て	とめだて	dissuasion

702

異 ⑪

丶 口 田 用 田 里 甲 甼 里 異 異

音	異	イ	different; unusual; curious; peculiar; uncommon
熟	異義	イギ	different/another meaning
	異議	イギ	objection; complaint
	異郷	イキョウ	strange/foreign land
	異境	イキョウ	foreign country/land
	異口同音	イクドウオン	with one voice/accord; unanimously
	異国	イコク	foreign land/country
	異質	イシツ	heterogeneity

異同	イドウ	difference
異動	イドウ	change; reshuffle
異物	イブツ	foreign matter
異変	イヘン	accident; mishap
異名	イミョウ	nickname; another name; alias
異様	イヨウ	strange; outlandish; fantastic; grotesque
異例	イレイ	exception; singular case
異論	イロン	different opinion; objection; controversial opinion
訓 異なる	ことなる	*vi.* differ; be different/dissimilar/unlike

703

略 ⑪ ｜ 冂 冂 用 田 田' 吥 昤 昤 略 略

音 略	リャク	omission; abridgement; abbreviation
熟 略する	リャクする	*vt.* omit; abbreviate; abridge; shorten
略画	リャクガ	rough sketch
略言	リャクゲン	abbreviated statement —*vi.* state briefly
略語	リャクゴ	abbreviation
略号	リャクゴウ	cable address
略字	リャクジ	simplified Chinese character
略式	リャクシキ	informal; summary
略述	リャクジュツ	brief account; outline —*v.* give a brief account; outline
略図	リャクズ	rough sketch; outline map
略装	リャクソウ	everyday clothes; informal wear
略伝	リャクデン	brief account; short history
略筆	リャクヒツ	abbreviated —*vt.* leave out formalities (in a letter)
略歴	リャクレキ	brief personal history; résumé
略記	リャッキ	brief account; outline —*v.* give a brief account; outline

704

番 ⑫ ノ ㇒ ㇒ 亚 平 乎 来 来 番 番 番

音 番	バン	watch; vigil; guard; turn; number
熟 番外	バンガイ	extra; outsize
番組	バンぐみ	program billing (of performers)
番犬	バンケン	watchdog; housedog
番号	バンゴウ	number

番台	バンダイ	watch stand; raised platform for a ticket seller, etc.
番地	バンチ	lot/house number; address
番茶	バンチャ	*bancha* (coarse green tea)
番付	バンづけ	program; list; ranking list
番頭	バントウ	clerk; secretary
番人	バンニン	guard; watchman
番兵	バンペイ	sentry; guard

5 疋 ひき animal counter

705 疑 ⑭

丶 ヒ ㇟ ㇟ 矣 矣 矣 矣 鈘 鈘 鈘 疑

音	疑	ギ	doubt
熟	疑似	ギジ	looking very alike
	疑点	ギテン	doubtful point; doubt
	疑念	ギネン	doubt; suspicion
	疑問	ギモン	question; problem; doubt
訓	疑い	うたがい	doubt; suspicion
	疑う	うたがう	*vt.* doubt; suspect; distrust
	疑わしい	うたがわしい	doubtful; questionable

5 疒 やまいだれ sickness

706 病 ⑩

丶 一 广 广 扩 疒 疒 疒 病 病

音	病	ビョウ（ヘイ）	disease; illness; sickness
熟	病院	ビョウイン	hospital; clinic; infirmary; doctor's office/surgery
	病気	ビョウキ	disease; illness; sickness *fig.* failing; weakness —*vi.* be ill/sick
	病苦	ビョウク	pain/suffering caused by illness
	病欠	ビョウケツ	sick leave —*vi.* be absent because of sickness
	病後	ビョウゴ	convalescence; after-care

病根	ビョウコン	cause of a disease; root of an evil
病死	ビョウシ	death from disease —*vi*. die from a disease
病室	ビョウシツ	sickroom; sick bay; infirmary
病弱	ビョウジャク	weak; sickly; weak constitution
病状	ビョウジョウ	condition of a disease; (patient's) condition
病身	ビョウシン	ill/poor health; sickly; susceptible to illness
病中	ビョウチュウ	during illness/sickness
病的	ビョウテキ	morbid; abnormal
病毒	ビョウドク	*med*. disease-causing virus; pathogen
病人	ビョウニン	sick person; invalid; patient; the sick
病理学	ビョウリガク	pathology

訓
病	やまい	sickness; illness; disease; bad habit; weakness
病む	やむ	be ill; get sick; suffer from
病み付き	やみつき	addicted to; hooked on; unable to give up

707
痛 ⑫　　｀ 宀 广 广 广 疒 疒 疒 病 病 痛 痛

音 痛　ツウ　ache

熟
痛快	ツウカイ	keen pleasure; thrill
痛感	ツウカン	strong/intense feeling; intuition —*v*. feel strongly; take to heart; fully realize
痛切	ツウセツ	keen; poignant; acute
痛風	ツウフウ	*med*. gout

訓
痛い	いたい	painful; sore; ache
痛む	いたむ	*vi*. feel/suffer pain; be wounded/injured
痛める	いためる	*vt*. hurt; injure; ache
痛手	いたで	serious wound; heavy blow

5　　はつがしら　departing head

708
発 ⑨　　フ 了 プ 癶 癶 癶 癶 癶 発 発

音
| 発 | ハツ | discharge; break out; disclose; start |
| | ホツ | occur |

熟
| 発する | ハッする | *vi*. discharge; fire; issue; publish; cry out; start off; leave |

発案	ハツアン	proposition; suggestion; motion —*v.* propose; suggest; move
発育	ハツイク	growth; development —*vi.* grow; develop
発音	ハツオン	pronunciation; articulation —*v.* pronounce; articulate
発芽	ハツガ	germination; sprouting; budding —*vi.* germinate; sprout; bud
発会	ハッカイ	first club meeting —*vi.* have the first club meeting
発覚	ハッカク	revelation; detection; discovery; disclosure; exposure —*vi.* be revealed/detected/discovered/exposed
発刊	ハッカン	publication; issue —*v.* publish; issue; bring out; start; launch
発揮	ハッキ	manifestation; exhibition; demonstration; display —*v.* make manifest; exhibit; demonstrate; display; show
発禁	ハッキン	prohibition of sale or publication
発見	ハッケン	discovery; revelation; detection —*v.* discover; detect; spot
発言	ハツゲン	utterance; speaking; speech; opinion —*vi.* speak; utter; open one's mouth; give an opinion
発光	ハッコウ	radiation; luminescence —*vi.* radiate; emit light; luminate
発行	ハッコウ	issue; publication; flotation —*v.* issue; publish; float
発効	ハッコウ	effectuation; coming in to effect —*v.* become effective; come/put into effect
発散	ハッサン	exhalation; radiation; diffusion; evaporation; divergence —*v.* exhale; emit; radiate; evaporate
発車	ハッシャ	departure (of a train, car, etc.) —*vi.* start; leave; depart
発射	ハッシャ	firing; shooting; lift-off —*v.* discharge firearms; fire; shoot
発信	ハッシン	dispatch of a letter, telegram, etc. —*vi.* send/dispatch a letter; telegraph; cable
発進	ハッシン	start; departure; take-off; launch —*vi.* start; depart; take-off; launch
発生	ハッセイ	occurrence; outbreak; appearance; birth; creation —*v.* occur; happen; come into existence
発声	ハッセイ	utterance —*vi.* utter; speak out; exclaim
発送	ハッソウ	sending; forwarding; shipping; dispatch —*v.* send out; forward; ship; dispatch
発想	ハッソウ	expression; conception; idea —*v.* conceive/come up with an idea
発達	ハッタツ	development; growth; progress —*vi.* develop; grow; make progress
発着	ハッチャク	departure and arrival —*vi.* depart and arrive

発注	ハッチュウ	ordering —*v.* order; give an order
発展	ハッテン	expansion; extension; progress; prosperity; dissipation —*vi.* expand; extend; develop; grow
発電	ハツデン	electricity generation; sending a telegram —*vi.* generate electricity; send a telegram; wire
発電所	ハツデンショ	power station/plant
発動	ハツドウ	motion; activity; exercise —*v.* move; put in motion; exercise
発熱	ハツネツ	fever; generation of heat **phy.** calorification —*vi.* break out into a fever **phy.** generate heat
発表	ハッピョウ	announcement; publication; statement —*v.* announce; publish; make public
発病	ハツビョウ	outbreak of a disease —*vi.* contract a disease; fall sick
発布	ハップ	promulgation; proclamation; issue —*v.* promulgate; proclaim; issue
発奮	ハップン	inspiration; stimulation —*vi.* be inspired/stimulated
発明	ハツメイ	invention; contrivance; cleverness; brightness —*v.* invent; devise; contrive
発令	ハツレイ	official announcement; proclamation —*v.* announce; proclaim
発起	ホッキ	proposal; suggestion —*v.* project; propose; suggest
発句	ホック	haiku poetry; first line of a *renga*
発作	ホッサ	spasm; fit
発足	ホッソク	starting; inauguration —*vi.* start; make a start; be inaugurated

709

ノ フ ヌ ㍗ 癶 癶 癶 癶 癶 癶 啓 発 登 登

⑫

音 登 ト climb; attendance
トウ

熟 登記 トウキ registration; registry —*v.* register; get on the register

登校 トウコウ school attendance; attending school —*vi.* go to/attend school

登場 トウジョウ entry; advent —*vi.* make an entrance; enter upon the stage; appear; show up

登頂 トウチョウ reaching the summit —*vi.* reach/climb to the summit

登板 トウバン **bas.** going up to the mound

登用 トウヨウ appointment; assignment; elevation; promotion; advancement —*v.* appoint; assign; designate; promote

玄玉王生用田疋疒癶
●白皮皿目矢石示礻禾穴立罒母水衤

	登録	トウロク	registration; record; entry —*v.* register; enter on a register; enroll
	登山	トザン	mountaineering; mountain climbing —*vi.* go up/climb/scale a mountain
訓	登る	のぼる	*vi.* climb; scale; go up; ascend; rise

5 白　しろい　white

710

　⑤　ノ　イ　白　白　白

音	白	ハク	white; clean; clear
		ビャク	white
熟	白衣	ハクイ	white robe
	白眼視	ハクガンシ	cold/indifferent look; frown —*v.* look coldly; frown upon; look with indifference
	白銀	ハクギン	silver
	白紙	ハクシ	blank paper; clean sheet of paper
	白日	ハクジツ	daytime; broad daylight; bright day
	白書	ハクショ	white paper; economic white paper
	白状	ハクジョウ	confession; avowal —*v.* confess; avow; own up to; admit to
	白色人種	ハクショクジンシュ	white race
	白人	ハクジン	white person
	白昼	ハクチュウ	daytime; broad daylight
	白昼夢	ハクチュウム	day dream
	白鳥	ハクチョウ	swan
	白銅	ハクドウ	nickel
	白熱	ハクネツ	climax; white heat; incandescence —*vi.* grow excited; climax; become white hot; be incandescent
	白票	ハクヒョウ	white/blank vote
	白米	ハクマイ	polished/cleaned rice
	白金	ハッキン	platinum
	白血病	ハッケツビョウ	***med.*** leukemia
	白夜	ビャクヤ	nights with the midnight sun
訓	白	しろ	white
	白い	しろい	white; fair; blank; spotless; immaculate; clean
	白身	しろみ	white meat/fish; white of an egg; albumen
	白	（しら）	white
	白木	しらき	plain/unpainted wood

白ける　しらける　*vi*. become chilled/spoiled
白々しい　しらじらしい　tense; awkward
白む　しらむ　*vi*. grow light

711

| 百 ⑥ | 一 ｢ ｢ 厂 百 百 百 |

音	百	ヒャク	hundred; numerous; many
熟	百害	ヒャクガイ	many evils; much harm
	百点	ヒャクテン	perfect score; full marks
	百人一首	ヒャクニンイッシュ	*hyakuninisshu* (Hundred Poems by One Hundred Poets)
	百年	ヒャクネン	one hundred years; century
	百聞	ヒャクブン	hearing many things
	百分	ヒャクブン	one hundred parts —*v.* divide into one hundred parts
	百分率	ヒャクブンリツ	percentage
	百万	ヒャクマン	million
	百万長者	ヒャクマンチョウジャ	millionnaire
	百面相	ヒャクメンソウ	all kinds of comic faces; many facial expressions
	百科事典	ヒャッカジテン	encyclopedia
	百貨店	ヒャッカテン	department store
	百発百中	ヒャッパツヒャクチュウ	never fail to hit the mark; all correct; right on target

712

| 的 ⑧ | ｀ ｀ 厂 白 白 白 的 的 |

音	的	テキ	target; exact
熟	的確	テキカク	exact; precise; accurate
	的中	テキチュウ	hit —*vi*. hit the bull's eye
訓	的	まと	target

玄玉王生用田疋扩癶白皮皿目矢石示ネ禾穴立罒母水ネ

713

⑨

´ ｀ 白 白 白 白 卑 皁 皇

音	皇	オウ	emperor; imperial
		コウ	emperor; lord; imperial
熟	皇子	オウジ	prince
	皇女	オウジョ	princess
	皇位	コウイ	the throne
	皇居	コウキョ	imperial palace
	皇后	コウゴウ	empress; queen; empress/queen consort
	皇室	コウシツ	imperial household; royal family
	皇族	コウゾク	imperial/royal family
	皇太后	コウタイゴウ	queen
	皇太子	コウタイシ	crown prince

5 皮 ひのかわ／けがわ leather; skin

714

⑤

） 厂 广 广 皮

音	皮	ヒ	skin; hide; leather; bark
熟	皮下	ヒカ	under the skin; subcutaneous
	皮下注射	ヒカチュウシャ	*med.* hypodermic injection
	皮革	ヒカク	hide; skin; leather
	皮相	ヒソウ	superficial; outward
	皮肉	ヒにく	irony; sarcasm
訓	皮	かわ	skin
	皮切り	かわきり	beginning; start
	皮算用	かわザンヨウ	count one's chickens before they are hatched

5 皿 さら dish; plate

715

皿 ⑤ 丶 冂 冖 冊 皿

訓 皿 さら dish; plate

716

益 ⑩ 丶 丷 䒑 𠂤 𠔁 𠔿 𠆢 𠔼 益 益

音	益	エキ	profit; gain; use; benefit
		（ヤク）	use; benefit
熟	益する	エキする	*vt.* be beneficial/useful
	益虫	エキチュウ	useful/beneficial insect
	益鳥	エキチョウ	useful/beneficial bird
	益金	エッキン	profit; gain
訓	益す	ます	increase; multiply; augment
	益々	ますます	increasingly; more and more

717

盛 ⑪ 丿 厂 厂 成 成 成 成 盛 盛 盛 盛

音	盛	セイ	prosperous
		（ジョウ）	
熟	盛夏	セイカ	midsummer; height of summer
	盛会	セイカイ	successful meeting
訓	盛る	さかる	*vi.* thrive; prosper; flourish; be popular

718

盟 ⑬ 丨 冂 月 日 冃 明 明 明 明 明 盟 盟

音	盟	メイ	pledge; oath; alliance
熟	盟約	メイヤク	pledge; pact; alliance
	盟友	メイユウ	comrade; sworn friend; staunch ally

5 目 め／めへん　eye

719

目 ⑤　｜ 冂 冂 月 目

音	目	モク （ボク）	eye; classification; order
熟	目算	モクサン	expectation; estimate; plan —v. expect; estimate; plan
	目次	モクジ	table of contents
	目前	モクゼン	before one's eyes
	目測	モクソク	measuring by eye —v. measure by eye
	目的	モクテキ	purpose; object; aim
	目標	モクヒョウ	aim; target; goal; objective
	目礼	モクレイ	eye greeting —v. greet by eye
	目録	モクロク	contents; catalog; list; inventory
	目下	モッカ	at present; now
訓	目	め （ま）	eye; look; judgment; pip; grain
	目当て	めあて	guide; aim
	目上	めうえ	one's superior/senior
	目移り	めうつり	waivering —vi. waiver/be at a loss what to choose
	目方	めかた	weight
	目先	めさき	before one's eyes; the near future; foresight
	目指す	めざす	vt. aim at/for
	目覚し時計	めざましどケイ	alarm clock
	目覚める	めざめる	vi. wake up; awaken
	目下	めした	one's inferior/subordinate/junior
	目印	めじるし	mark; sign
	目立つ	めだつ	vi. be conspicuous; stand out
	目玉	めだま	eyeball
	目付き	めつき	look; expression
	目鼻	めはな	eyes and nose
	目分量	めブンリョウ	by eye measure; by sight
	目星	めぼし	aim; object
	目盛り	めもり	graduation; scale
	目安	めやす	standard; yardstick

直 ⑧

一 十 十 亡 亢 亩 肖 肖 直

玄 玉 王 生 用 田 疋 疒 癶 白 皮 皿 目 ● 矢 石 示 礻 禾 穴 立 ⺫ 母 水 礻

音	直	ジキ	direct; at once; soon
		チョク	straight; directly; upright; frank
熟	直々	ジキジキ	personal; direct
	直筆	ジキヒツ	one's own handwriting; autograph
	直営	チョクエイ	direct management/control/operation —v. manage/control directly
	直言	チョクゲン	plain speaking; straight talking —v. speak plainly; speak without reserve; speak one's mind
	直後	チョクゴ	just/soon after
	直視	チョクシ	looking in the face —v. look a person directly in the face
	直射	チョクシャ	direct rays/fire —v. fire point-blank/directly
	直進	チョクシン	straight on —vi. go straight on; make straight for
	直接	チョクセツ	directly
	直線	チョクセン	straight line
	直前	チョクゼン	just before
	直送	チョクソウ	direct delivery —v. send directly
	直属	チョクゾク	under the direct control of —v. be under the direct control of
	直腸	チョクチョウ	med. rectum
	直通	チョクツウ	direct service/communication —vi. be in direct communication
	直配	チョクハイ	direct distribution —v. distribute directly
	直売	チョクバイ	direct sales —v. sell directly
	直面	チョクメン	confrontation —vi. confront; face; be up against
	直訳	チョクヤク	literal translation —v. translate/render literally
	直輸入	チョクユニュウ	direct import —v. import directly
	直立	チョクリツ	erectness —vi. stand erect; rise perpendicularly
	直立不動	チョクリツフドウ	standing at attention
	直流	チョクリュウ	direct current (DC)
	直下	チョッカ	directly/right under —vi. fall perpendicularly/down
	直角	チョッカク	math. right angle
	直感	チョッカン	intuition; hunch —v. know by intuition; have a hunch
	直観	チョッカン	intuition —v. know by intuition
	直系	チョッケイ	direct line of family descent
	直径	チョッケイ	math. diameter

玄
玉
王
生
用
田
疋
疒
癶
白
皮
皿
目
・
矢
石
示
ネ
禾
穴
立
罒
母
水
ネ

| 直結 | チョッケツ | direct connection —v. connect/link directly |
| 直行 | チョッコウ | going straight; uprightness —vi. go straight/direct |

訓

直す	なおす	vt. mend; repair; do over again
直る	なおる	vi. be mended; get better; recover; be corrected
直ちに	ただちに	at once; directly; immediately

721

看 ⑨ 一 二 三 手 手 手 看 看 看

音 看 カン　care; watch

熟

看過	カンカ	connivance (at wrong doing) —v. overlook an error
看護	カンゴ	caring; nursing —v. nurse; care for the sick
看護婦	カンゴフ	nurse
看守	カンシュ	guard; warder; jailer
看取	カンシュ	discernment; perception —v. discern; perceive; notice; detect
看破	カンパ	penetration —v. penetrate; see through
看板	カンバン	signboard; sign
看病	カンビョウ	nursing the sick —v. nurse; tend; care for a sick person

722

県 ⑨ 丨 冂 円 円 目 県 県 県 県

音 県 ケン　prefecture

熟

県営	ケンエイ	prefectural administration
県下	ケンカ	within a prefecture
県議会	ケンギカイ	prefectural assembly
県政	ケンセイ	prefectural government
県税	ケンゼイ	prefectural taxes
県知事	ケンチジ	prefectural governor
県庁	ケンチョウ	prefectural office
県道	ケンドウ	prefectural road
県立	ケンリツ	prefectural (school, hospital, etc.)

723

省 ⑨　⺌⺌小少少省省省省

音	省	ショウ	omit
		セイ	review; consider
熟	省略	ショウリャク	omission; abbreviation —*v.* omit; abbreviate
訓	省みる	かえりみる	*vt.* consider; think of; reflect on; worry about
	省く	はぶく	*vt.* omit; leave out; cut down; save

724

相 ⑨　一十才才机相相相相

音	相	ソウ	each other; reciprocal; aspect; phase; physiognomy
		ショウ	minister
熟	相応	ソウオウ	suitable; fitting —*vi.* be suitable/fitting
	相関	ソウカン	correlation —*vi.* correlate
	相関関係	ソウカンカンケイ	correlation; relation; relationship
	相関的	ソウカンテキ	interrelated
	相殺	ソウサイ	offset; counteraction; compensation —*v.* offset; countervail
	相似	ソウジ	similarity; resemblance; analogy —*vi.* be similar/analogous; resemble
	相続	ソウゾク	inheritance; succession —*v.* inherit; succeed
	相続人	ソウゾクニン	heir; heiress; successor
	相対	ソウタイ	relativity
	相対的	ソウタイテキ	relative
	相談	ソウダン	consultation; discussion —*v.* consult; confer; discuss
	相当	ソウトウ	fit; suitable; appropriate; equivalent —*vi.* be equivalent/correspond to
	相等	ソウトウ	equality; equivalence
訓	相	あい	together; fellow; each other
	相変わらず	あいかわらず	as usual
	相性	あいショウ	affinity; compatibility
	相対する	あいタイする	*vi.* facing each other directly
	相次ぐ	あいつぐ	*vi.* follow in succession
	相手	あいて	the other party; partner; opponent

玄玉王生用田疋疒癶白皮皿目●矢石示衤禾穴立罒母水衤

⑩ 一 十 广 市 市 古 直 直 真 真

真 シン truth; genuine; real

熟	真意	シンイ	one's real mind; real intention; true meaning
	真因	シンイン	true cause/motive
	真打ち	シンうち	star performer; headliner
	真価	シンカ	real value; true worth
	真紅	シンク	crimson
	真空	シンクウ	vacuum; evacuated
	真空包装	シンクウホウソウ	vacuum packing
	真実	シンジツ	truth; true; real; truly; really
	真情	シンジョウ	true feelings
	真性	シンセイ	genuine
	真正	シンセイ	genuine; true
	真善美	シンゼンビ	truth, good, and beauty
	真相	シンソウ	the truth; fact
	真底	シンテイ	bottom of one's heart; very bottom
	真否	シンピ	truth or falsehood; the truth
	真理	シンリ	truth

訓	真	ま	truth; sincerity
	真新しい	まあたらしい	brand-new
	真顔	まがお	serious look/face
	真心	まごころ	sincerity
	真四角	まシカク	perfect square
	真面目	まじめ	serious; earnest; honest; reliable
	真っ赤	まっか	deep red
	真っ青	まっさお	azure; deep blue; white as a sheet; pale
	真っ盛り	まっさかり	at their best
	真っ白	まっしろ	pure white; snow-white
	真っ直ぐ	まっすぐ	straight; in a straight line; in a beeline
	真夏	まなつ	midsummer
	真似	まね	imitation; mimicry; aping; copying; action; behavior —*v.* imitate; mimic; copy
	真似る	まねる	*vt.* imitate; mimic; copy; follow
	真昼	まひる	midday; high noon
	真冬	まふゆ	midwinter
	真水	まみず	fresh water
	真夜中	まよなか	middle of the night; at midnight

玄玉王生用田疋疒癶白皮皿目矢石示礻禾穴立皿母水礻

726

眼 ⑪ 丨 𝗌 𝗌 𝗌 目 目 目ㄱ 目ㅋ 目ㅋ 眼 眼 眼

音	眼	ガン	eye; point
		（ゲン）	
熟	眼下	ガンカ	under one's eyes
	眼科	ガンカ	*med*. ophthalmology
	眼球	ガンキュウ	eyeball
	眼光	ガンコウ	glitter of one's eyes; discernment; insight
	眼中	ガンチュウ	in one's eyes; consideration
	眼目	ガンモク	main point; gist; essence
	眼力	ガンリキ	insight; penetration; perception
訓	眼	まなこ	eye; eyeball

---

5 矢 や／やへん arrow

727

矢 ⑤ 丿 𝗅 𝗅 𝗌 矢

音	矢	シ	arrow
訓	矢	や	arrow
	矢先	やさき	arrowhead; moment; point; in time
	矢印	やじるし	arrow-shaped mark
	矢玉	やだま	arrows and bullets
	矢庭に	やにわに	on the spot; suddenly
	矢来	やライ	temporary bamboo and log fence

728

知 ⑧ 丿 𝗅 𝗅 𝗌 矢 知 知 知

音	知	チ	knowledge; wisdom; intellect; acquaintance
熟	知覚	チカク	perception; sensation; feeling —*v*. perceive; sense; feel
	知己	チキ	acquaintance; intimate friend
	知事	チジ	governor (of a prefecture)
	知識	チシキ	knowledge; information; know-how; learning; understanding

玄玉王生用田疋疒癶白皮皿目・矢石示礻禾穴立罒母氺衤

玄
玉
王
生
用
田
疋
扩
癶
白
皮
皿
目
● 矢
● 石
示
礻
禾
穴
立
罒
母
水
衤

知識階級	チシキカイキュウ	intelligentsia
知人	チジン	acquaintance; friend
知性	チセイ	intellect; intelligence
知的	チテキ	intellectual; mental
知能	チノウ	intellect; intelligence; mental faculties
知名	チメイ	noted; distinguished; famous; well-known

訓
知る	しる	***vt.*** know; be aware of; learn; understand; recognize; realize; feel
知らせ	しらせ	information; notice; report; news
知らせる	しらせる	***vt.*** inform; advise; notify; report
知らん顔	しらんかお	feigned ignorance; indifference; nonchalance
知り合い	しりあい	friend; acquaintance

729

短 ⑫ ' ト ヒ チ 矢 矢 知 知 知 知 短 短

| 音 | 短 | タン | short; brief; close |

熟
短歌	タンカ	*tanka* (31-syllable Japanese poem)
短気	タンキ	quick/short temper
短期	タンキ	short term
短縮	タンシュク	shortening; contraction; curtailment —*v.* shorten; contract; curtail
短所	タンショ	defect; fault; demerit; failing; shortcoming
短針	タンシン	the short hand (of a clock)
短調	タンチョウ	minor key (in music)
短波	タンパ	shortwave
短編	タンペン	short piece/story; sketch
短命	タンメイ	short life

訓
| 短い | みじかい | short; brief; abbreviated |

5 いし／いしへん　stone

730

石 ⑤ 一 ア 不 石 石

音	石	セキ	stone; jewel
	（コク）	*koku* (unit of volume, approx. 0.18 *ml*)
	（シャク）	

熟	石像	セキゾウ	stone image; statue
	石炭	セキタン	coal
	石仏	セキブツ	stone image of Buddha
	石油	セキユ	oil; petroleum; kerosene
	石灰	セッカイ	lime
	石器	セッキ	prehistoric/Stone Age tools
	石器時代	セッキジダイ	Stone Age
訓	石	いし	stone
	石頭	いしあたま	bigot
	石橋	いしばし	stone bridge

731

一 厂 イ 石 石 石 石 矼 研 研

⑨

音	研	ケン	polish; research
熟	研究	ケンキュウ	research; study; investigation; inquiry —*v*. study; make a study of; do research in; investigate
	研究員	ケンキュウイン	research worker
	研究科	ケンキュウカ	post-graduate course
	研究開発	ケンキュウカイハツ	R & D; (Research and Development)
	研修	ケンシュウ	study and training —*v*. study; be trained
訓	研ぐ	とぐ	*vt*. grind; sharpen; whet

732

砂

一 厂 イ 石 石 砂 砂 砂 砂

⑨

音	砂	サ	sand
		シャ	sand
熟	砂金	サキン	gold dust
	砂州	サす	sand reef
	砂鉄	サテツ	iron sand
	砂糖	サトウ	sugar
	砂利	ジャリ	gravel
訓	砂	すな	sand; dune
	砂時計	すなどケイ	hourglass
	砂場	すなば	sand pit

玄玉王生用田疋疒癶白皮皿目矢石示礻禾穴立罒母氺礻

•

375

玄
玉
王
生
用
田
疋
疒
癶
白
皮
皿
目
矢
● 石
示
礻
禾
穴
立
罒
母
水
衤

733

破 ⑩　一 厂 丆 石 石 刖 矿 矿 破 破

音	破	ハ	destroy; break; demolish
熟	破格	ハカク	exception
	破顔	ハガン	smiling face —*vi.* smile broadly
	破局	ハキョク	catastrophe; collapse
	破傷風	ハショウフウ	***med.*** tetanus; lockjaw
	破損	ハソン	damage; injury; breakdown; dilapidation —*v.* be damaged; breakdown; be dilapidated/destroyed
	破談	ハダン	cancellation; rupture; breaking off; rejection
	破片	ハヘン	fragment; splinter; broken piece
	破門	ハモン	expulsion; excommunication —*v.* expel; excommunicate
	破約	ハヤク	breach of promise/contract —*v.* break a promise; breach a contract
	ご破算	ごハサン	new calculation
訓	破る	やぶる	*v.* tear; rip; break; destroy; violate; infringe
	破れる	やぶれる	*vi.* be torn/ripped/broken/destroyed
	破れ	やぶれ	rupture; breach; failure; ruin; breakdown; collapse

734

磁 ⑭　一 厂 石 石 矿 矿 矿 磁 磁 磁 磁 磁

音	磁	ジ	magnet; pottery; ceramics
熟	磁気	ジキ	magnetism
	磁器	ジキ	porcelain; china; chinaware
	磁極	ジキョク	magnetic pole
	磁石	ジシャク	magnet; magnetite; compass
	磁針	ジシン	magnetic/compass needle
	磁性	ジセイ	magnetism
	磁場	ジば	magnetic field
	磁力	ジリョク	magnetic force

735

確 ⑮　一 厂 石 石 矿 矿 矿 砕 砕 砕 確 確

音	確	カク	certainty; steady; sure

熟	確実	カクジツ	certainty; reliability
	確証	カクショウ	corroboration; confirmation; positive proof
	確信	カクシン	conviction; firm belief; confidence —*v.* convince oneself; believe firmly; be confident
	確定	カクテイ	final settlement; decision —*v.* decide; settle; fix; confirm
	確認	カクニン	confirmation; validation —*v.* confirm; ascertain; validate
	確保	カクホ	guarantee; security —*v.* guarantee; secure
	確約	カクヤク	definite promise —*v.* give one's word; commit oneself to
	確立	カクリツ	establishment —*v.* establish; build up
	確率	カクリツ	probability
	確固	カッコ	firm; steady
訓	確か	たしか	sound; right; perhaps; firm; certain; probable
	確かめる	たしかめる	*vt.* ascertain

---

5 示 しめす show ネ (p.378)

736

示 ⑤ 一 二 テ 亍 示

音	示	シ	show; display; express; teaching
		ジ	
熟	示談	ジダン	private settlement; settlement out of court —*v.* settle out of court
訓	示す	しめす	*vt.* show; display; reveal; indicate; prove
	示し	しめし	display; revelation; example; indication; proof
	示し合わせる	しめしあわせる	*vt.* prearrange; conspire

737

祭 ⑪ ノ ク タ タ クア クス クタ クタ クタ 祭 祭

音	祭	サイ	festival; feast; deify; worship
熟	祭日	サイジツ	national holiday; festival day
	祭典	サイテン	festival
	祭礼	サイレイ	festival
訓	祭り	まつり	feast; festival

玄
玉
王
生
用
田
疋
疒
癶
白
皮
皿
目
矢
石
示
礻
禾
穴
立
罒
母
水
礻

祭る　　　まつる　　　*vt*. deify; worship

738

票 ⑪ 　一 一 戸 币 西 西 西 覀 覀 票 票

音 票　　ヒョウ　　slip of paper; ballot; vote
熟 票決　　ヒョウケツ　　voting; vote —*v*. vote

739

禁 ⑬ 　一 十 才 木 木 村 村 林 林 埜 埜 禁 禁

音 禁　　キン　　forbid; prohibit
熟 禁じる　　キンじる　　*vt*. forbid; prohibit
禁固　　キンコ　　imprisonment; incarceration; confinement
禁止　　キンシ　　prohibition; embargo; ban —*v*. forbid; prohibit; embargo; ban
禁酒　　キンシュ　　temperance —*vi*. be temperant; prohibit/forbid alcohol
禁制　　キンセイ　　prohibition; taboo; embargo; ban
禁足　　キンソク　　confinement —*vt*. confine
禁断　　キンダン　　prohibition; withdrawal
禁治産　　キンチサン　　incompetence; diminished responsibility
禁鳥　　キンチョウ　　protected bird
禁物　　キンモツ　　taboo; prohibited object
禁欲　　キンヨク　　obstinence; asceticism —*vi*. practice abstinence
禁漁　　キンリョウ　　no fishing
禁令　　キンレイ　　prohibitory decree; prohibition; ban

4 ネ　しめすへん　show to the left

740

礼 ⑤ 　丶 ラ 礻 礻 礼

音 礼　　レイ　　courtesy; politeness; salutation; bow
　　　　ライ
熟 礼拝　　ライハイ　　Buddhist worship/services —*v*. worhship Buddha
礼金　　レイキン　　honorarium; fee

玄玉王生用田疋疒癶白皮皿目矢石●示礻禾穴立罒母水礻

礼式	レイシキ	etiquette
礼状	レイジョウ	letter of thanks
礼節	レイセツ	decorum; propriety; politeness
礼装	レイソウ	formal/ceremonial dress; full dress
礼典	レイテン	ceremony; ritual; rites
礼拝	レイハイ	Christian worship/services —*v.* worship God
礼服	レイフク	formal dress

741

社 ⑦ 　 ` ラ ネ ネ ネ 礻 社 社

音	社	シャ	shrine; company; society
熟	社会	シャカイ	society; community; class; world
	社会運動	シャカイウンドウ	social movement
	社会科	シャカイカ	social studies
	社会学	シャカイガク	sociology
	社会主義	シャカイシュギ	socialism
	社会人	シャカイジン	public person; working adult
	社会的	シャカイテキ	social
	社会面	シャカイメン	general news page of a newspaper
	社会問題	シャカイモンダイ	social problem
	社訓	シャクン	company motto
	社交	シャコウ	social intercourse/contact; society
	社交家	シャコウカ	sociable person
	社交界	シャコウカイ	the fashionable world; high society
	社交性	シャコウセイ	sociability; outgoing; extrovert
	社主	シャシュ	company owner
	社説	シャセツ	editorial; leading article
	社宅	シャタク	company house/housing
	社団	シャダン	association; corporation
	社長	シャチョウ	company president
	社務所	シャムショ	shrine office
訓	社	やしろ	Shinto shrine

742

祝 ⑨ 　 ` ラ ネ ネ ネ 礽 礽 祝 祝

音	祝	シュク	celebrate
		（シュウ）	

玄玉王生用田疋扩癶白皮皿目矢石示ネ禾穴立罒母氺衤

熟 祝する　シュクする　*vt.* congratulate; celebrate
　　祝賀　　シュクガ　　celebration; congratulations
　　祝祭日　シュクサイジツ　public/national holiday
　　祝辞　　シュクジ　　congratulatory address/speeches
　　祝日　　シュクジツ　　public/national holday
　　祝典　　シュクテン　　festival; celebration; jubilee
　　祝電　　シュクデン　　congratulatory telegram
　　祝福　　シュクフク　　blessing —*v.* bless
訓 祝う　　いわう　　*vt.* congratulate; celebrate; observe
　　　　　　　　　　　an anniversary, etc.

743

⑨　　丶　ラ　礻　礻　礻　初　初　神　神

音 神　　シン　　god
　　　　ジン　　god
熟 神学　　シンガク　　theology
　　神格化　シンカクカ　deification —*v.* deify
　　神官　　シンカン　　Shinto priest
　　神宮　　ジングウ　　major Shinto shrine
　　神経　　シンケイ　　nerve; nervous; nerves
　　神経科　シンケイカ　neurology; department of neurology
　　神経質　シンケイシツ　nervous temperament; nervousness
　　神権　　シンケン　　divine right
　　神社　　ジンジャ　　Shinto shrine
　　神聖　　シンセイ　　holiness; sacredness; sanctity
　　神代　　ジンダイ　　mythological age; age of the gods
　　神通力　ジンツウリキ　magical power
　　神道　　シントウ　　Shintoism; Shinto
　　神秘　　シンピ　　mystery
　　神秘主義　シンピシュギ　mysticism
　　神秘的　シンピテキ　mystic; mysterious
　　神父　　シンプ　　Roman Catholic priest; Father
　　神仏　　シンブツ　　gods and Buddhas; Shintoism and Buddhism
　　神話　　シンワ　　myth; mythology
訓 神　　かみ　　god; deity
　　神風　　かみかぜ　　kamikaze
　　神業　　かみわざ　　act of God; divine work; miracle
　　神　　（かん）　　(prefix) Shinto
　　神主　　かんぬし　　Shinto priest

神　　　（こう）　　　divine; sublime
神々しい　こうごうしい　divine; sublime
神様　　かみさま　　god; deity

744

祖 ⑨　　` ラ ネ ネ ネ 礻 初 剂 剂 祖

音	祖	ソ	ancestor
熟	祖国	ソコク	homeland; fatherland
	祖先	ソセン	ancestor; forefathers
	祖父	ソフ	grandfather
	祖父母	ソフボ	grandparents
	祖母	ソボ	grandmother

745

福 ⑬　　` ラ ネ ネ 礻 礻 礻 祀 礻 福 福 福 福

音	福	フク	fortune; happiness; welfare; wealth
熟	福音	フクイン	the gospel; good news
	福運	フクウン	happiness and good fortune
	福利	フクリ	welfare; well-being
	福利厚生	フクリコウセイ	welfare program

5　禾　のぎへん　*no* (katakana) + tree

746

私 ⑦　　ー ニ 千 千 禾 禾 私 私

音	私	シ	I; private
熟	私案	シアン	one's private plan
	私意	シイ	personal opinion; selfish motive
	私益	シエキ	personal interest/gain
	私学	シガク	private school/college/university
	私見	シケン	personal view/opinion
	私語	シゴ	whisper; whispering
	私財	シザイ	private property
	私事	シジ	personal affairs; private matter

玄玉王生用田疋广癶白皮皿目矢石示礻・禾穴立罒母水衤

玄
玉
王
生
用
田
疋
疒
癶
白
皮
皿
目
矢
石
示
礻
● 禾
穴
立
罒
母
氷
衤

私室	シシツ	private room
私書	シショ	private document; personal letter
私書箱	シショばこ	post office box
私情	シジョウ	personal feelings
私小説	シショウセツ	"I" novel; novel based on the author's own life
私心	シシン	selfishness; one's own idea
私信	シシン	private letter/message
私生活	シセイカツ	one's private life
私生児	シセイジ	illegitimate child; love child
私設	シセツ	private establishment
私蔵	シゾウ	private ownership —*v.* own privately
私的	シテキ	private
私鉄	シテツ	privately-owned railway
私道	シドウ	private road; driveway; drive
私費	シヒ	one's own expense
私服	シフク	plain clothes; civillian clothes
私腹	シフク	one's own pockets; one's own profit or estate
私物	シブツ	private property; personal effects
私文書	シブンショ	personal writings; private documents
私有	シユウ	private ownership; —*v.* own privately
私用	ショウ	private use/business
私欲	ショク	self-interest; selfish desire
私利	シリ	self-interest; one's own interest
私立	シリツ	private; non-governmental
訓 私	わたし	I; me
私	わたくし	I; me; private
私事	わたくしごと	private matters

747

科 ⑨　　一　ニ　千　禾　禾　禾　禾　科　科

音 科	カ	course of study; offense
熟 科学	カガク	science; natural science
科目	カモク	academic subject; curriculum; items
科料	カリョウ	minor fine

748

秋 ⑨　一　二　千　千　乔　禾　禾'　秒　秋

音	秋	シュウ	fall; autumn
熟	秋季	シュウキ	fall; autumn
	秋期	シュウキ	fall season; autumn
	秋分	シュウブン	autumnal equinox
訓	秋	あき	fall; autumn
	秋風	あきかぜ	autumn breeze
	秋晴れ	あきばれ	fine autumn day
	秋雨	あきさめ	autumn rain

749

秒 ⑨　一　二　千　千　乔　利　利　秒　秒

音	秒	ビョウ	second (of time/arc)
熟	秒針	ビョウシン	second hand (of a watch/clock)
	秒速	ビョウソク	velocity per second
	秒読み	ビョウよみ	countdown —*vi*. count down

750

秘 ⑩　一　二　千　千　乔　禾'　利　秘　秘　秘

音	秘	ヒ	secret
熟	秘する	ヒする	*vt*. keep secret; conceal
	秘境	ヒキョウ	unexplored territory; land of mystery
	秘策	ヒサク	secret plot/plan/measures
	秘史	ヒシ	hidden history; historical secrets; unknown historical facts
	秘事	ヒジ	secret; mystery
	秘術	ヒジュツ	secret art; secrets/mysteries of
	秘書	ヒショ	(private) secretary
	秘書課	ヒショカ	secretariat; secretarial section
	秘書官	ヒショカン	minister's secretary
	秘蔵	ヒゾウ	treasuring —*v*. treasure; prize; cherish; keep (a thing) under lock and key
	秘伝	ヒデン	secret/esoteric mysteries; the secret/mystery of
	秘宝	ヒホウ	hidden treasure

玄玉王生用田疋疒癶白皮皿目矢石示礻禾穴立罒母水礻

383

玄玉王生用田疋疒癶白皮皿目矢石示礻禾穴立罒母水衤

	秘法	ヒホウ	secret method/formula
	秘本	ヒホン	treasured book; secret/hidden/forbidden book
	秘密	ヒミツ	secret; confidential; private
	秘薬	ヒヤク	secret medicine/remedy
	秘録	ヒロク	confidential notes; private papers
	秘話	ヒワ	secret story
訓	秘か	ひそか	secret
	秘める	ひめる	*vt.* conceal; keep secret

751

移 ⑪ 一 二 千 千 禾 禾 利 利 秒 秒 移 移

音	移	イ	move; shift; change
熟	移管	イカン	moving; transfer —*vt.* move; transfer
	移行	イコウ	uniform motion of a body in a straight line —*vi.* move; transfer; shift; switch
	移住	イジュウ	migration; emigration; transmigration —*vi.* migrate; emigrate; transmigrate; settle
	移出	イシュツ	export; shipment; clearance —*v.* export; ship out
	移植	イショク	transplantation; implantation; naturalization —*v.* transplant; implant; naturalize
	移転	イテン	moving; removal; transfer —*v.* move house; transfer
	移動	イドウ	movement; motion; locomotion; transfer —*v.* move; get around; be mobile
	移入	イニュウ	import; shipping in; introduction —*v.* import; ship in; introduce
	移民	イミン	emigration; immigration; settlement —*vi.* emigrate; immigrate; settle
訓	移す	うつす	*vt.* move; transfer; change; divert; turn; direct
	移り気	うつりギ	wandering mind; inability to concentrate
	移る	うつる	*vi.* move; remove; change; swift; be infected; spread

752

税 ⑫ 一 二 千 千 禾 禾 利 利 秒 秒 税

音	税	ゼイ	tax

753

程 ⑫ 　 ノ　ニ　千　千　禾　禾　秆　和　和　秆　秆　程

音	程	テイ	degree
熟	程度	テイド	degree; extent; measure; proportion
訓	程	ほど	extent; limit; time; distance
	程々	ほどほど	moderate; within bounds

754

穀 ⑭ 　 一　十　土　声　吉　壱　幸　彙　索　䊮　䊁　穀

音	穀	コク	grain
熟	穀倉	コクソウ	granary
	穀物	コクモツ	grain; cereal; corn

755

種 ⑭ 　 二　千　禾　秆　秆　秆　秆　秆　稆　種　種　種

音	種	シュ	seed; kind; type; variety
熟	種子	シュシ	seed; stone; pip
	種々	シュジュ	various; variety; all kinds
	種族	シュゾク	race; tribe
	種別	シュベツ	classification; class; kind —v. classify
	種目	シュモク	item; event
	種類	シュルイ	kind; sort; species
訓	種	たね	seed; stone; kernel; breed; stock; topic
	種明かし	たねあかし	revealing the secret (of magic, etc.)
	種油	たねあぶら	seed/rape oil
	種馬	たねうま	stud horse; stallion
	種切れ	たねぎれ	short of topics
	種本	たねホン	source of a written work, etc.

756

積 ⑯ 　 二　千　禾　禾　秆　秆　秸　秸　積　積　積　積

音	積	セキ	accumulate; product; size; area; volume

385

玄玉王生用田疋疒癶白皮皿目矢石示礻禾穴立罒母氺衤

● 穴
● 立

熟	積雪	セキセツ	fallen snow
	積分	セキブン	*math.* integral calculus
	積極的	セッキョクテキ	positive; active
訓	積む	つむ	*vt.* heap; load
	積もる	つもる	*vi.* accumulate; pile up; estimate
	積み上げる	つみあげる	*vt.* pile/heap up
	積み立てる	つみたてる	*vt.* save; lay aside; put by

---

5 穴　あな／あなかんむり　hole

757
穴 ⑤　 ` ` ⼧ ⼧ 穴

音	穴	ケツ	hole
熟	穴居	ケッキョ	cave dwelling —*vi.* live in a cave
訓	穴	あな	hole
	穴場	あなば	excellent but little known place

758
究 ⑦　 ` ` ⼧ ⼧ 究 究 究

音	究	キュウ	go to the end of; investigate thoroughly; end; terminate; reach an extreme
熟	究極	キュウキョク	extreme; ultimate
	究明	キュウメイ	study; investigation; inquiry —*v.* study; investigate; inquire into
訓	究める	きわめる	*vt.* go to the end of; master; go to extremes

759
空 ⑧　 ` ` ⼧ ⼧ 究 究 空 空

音	空	クウ	empty; useless; the sky; the heavens; aircraft
熟	空間	クウカン	space; the infinite
	空気	クウキ	air; atmosphere
	空軍	クウグン	air force
	空港	クウコウ	airport
	空車	クウシャ	empty car; For Hire; taxi for hire

空席	クウセキ	empty/vacant seat	
空前	クウゼン	unprecedented; unheard of	
空前絶後	クウゼンゼツゴ	the first and probably the last	
空想	クウソウ	daydream; fantasy —v. daydream; fantasize	
空中	クウチュウ	air; sky; space; midair	
空白	クウハク	blank; space; vacuum; void	
空費	クウヒ	waste —v. waste	
空腹	クウフク	empty stomach	
空輸	クウユ	air/aerial transport —v. transport by air	
空路	クウロ	air route/way	
空論	クウロン	empty theory	

訓	空く	あく	*vi*. open; be opened
	空ける	あける	*vt*. open（something）
	空	から	empty
	空回り	からまわり	skidding; racing; ineffective business activity; fruitless effort —*vi*. skid; race; prove/turn out ineffective
	空	そら	sky

760

窓 ⑪　　丶 ハ 宀 宀 空 空 空 空 窓 窓 窓

音	窓	ソウ	window
熟	窓外	ソウガイ	outside the window
訓	窓	まど	window
	窓際	まどぎわ	windowside; by the window
	窓口	まどぐち	（ticket）window

5 立 たつ standing

761

立 ⑤　　丶 ㇒ 十 亡 立

音	立	リツ	stand; rise
		（リュウ）	
熟	立案	リツアン	plan; devise; draft —v. make/form a plan; devise; design
	立夏	リッカ	first day of summer

387

玄玉王生用田疋疒癶白皮皿目矢石示礻禾穴●立罒母氺礻

立憲	リッケン	adopting a constitution	
立憲政治	リッケンセイジ	constitutional government	
立候補	リッコウホ	candidacy; running for office —*vi.* stand/run for office	
立国	リッコク	founding of a state	
立志伝	リッシデン	success story	
立秋	リッシュウ	first day of autumn	
立春	リッシュン	first day of spring	
立証	リッショウ	proof —*v.* prove; establish	
立身出世	リッシンシュッセ	success in life —*v.* succeed in life	
立像	リツゾウ	statue of someone standing	
立体	リッタイ	solid; three-dimensional	
立体感	リッタイカン	sense of depth	
立体交差	リッタイコウサ	grade separation	
立体的	リッタイテキ	three-dimensional	
立地	リッチ	location; siting	
立地条件	リッチジョウケン	geographical conditions	
立冬	リットウ	first day of winter	
立派	リッパ	splendid; fine; magnificient	
立腹	リップク	anger; offense —*vi.* get angry; lose one's temper	
立方	リッポウ	cubic; cube	
立方体	リッポウタイ	cube	
立法	リッポウ	legislation; law making	
立礼	リツレイ	standing and bowing	
立論	リツロン	argument —*vi.* put forth an argument	
立つ	たつ	*vi.* erect; rise; stand	訓
立ち会う	たちあう	*vi.* attend; witness	
立ち上がる	たちあがる	*vi.* stand up	
立ち入る	たちいる	*vi.* enter; interfere; go into (an issue)	
立ち往生	たちオウジョウ	*vi.* standing death —*vi.* come to a standstill; be in a dilemma	
立ち退く	たちのく	*vi.* leave	
立場	たちば	standpoint; viewpoint; position	
立ち回る	たちまわる	*vi.* act	
立ち向かう	たちむかう	*vi.* confront; fight; stand against	
立てる	たてる	*vt.* erect; set up; raise	
立行司	たてギョウジ	head sumo referee	
立札	たてふだ	signboard	

762 章 ⑪

` 一 十 立 立 产 音 音 音 音 章 章

音	章	ショウ	chapter; passage; writing
熟	章句	ショウク	passage of writing
	章節	ショウセツ	chapters and sections (of a thesis, etc.)

763 童 ⑫

` 一 十 立 立 产 音 音 音 音 竟 童 童

音	童	ドウ	child
熟	童顔	ドウガン	child's face; childlike face
	童心	ドウシン	child's mind; childlike heart
	童話	ドウワ	nursery tale; children's story
訓	童	わらべ	child

764 競 ⑳

一 十 立 音 产 竟 竞 竞 竞 竞 競 競 競

音	競	キョウ	rival; compete; dispute; quarrel
		ケイ	
熟	競泳	キョウエイ	swimming race/competition —*v.* compete in a swimming race
	競演	キョウエン	contest —*v.* contest; enter a competition
	競技	キョウギ	match; contest; competition —*v.* contest; compete
	競争	キョウソウ	competition; contest; rivalry —*vi.* compete; contest; be rivals
	競走	キョウソウ	race; running race —*vi.* run in a race
	競馬	ケイバ	horse race
	競輪	ケイリン	bicycle race
訓	競う	きそう	*vi.* compete; rival
	競る	せる	*vt.* compete with

玄玉王生用田疋疒癶白皮皿目矢石示礻禾穴立罒ⅠⅡ母氺礻

5 罒 あみがしら net

765

罪 ⑬ ⎟ 丶 冂 冂 冖 罒 罒 罪 罪 罪 罪 罪 罪

音	罪	ザイ	crime; sin
熟	罪悪	ザイアク	vice; crime
	罪人	ザイニン	criminal; offender; convict
	罪名	ザイメイ	offence; charge
訓	罪	つみ	sin; crime; act of wrong doing

766

署 ⑬ 丶 冂 冖 冖 罒 罒 甲 罒 罪 署 署 署

音	署	ショ	divide; office
熟	署長	ショチョウ	chief of police
	署名	ショメイ	signature —*vi*. sign

767

置 ⑬ 丶 冂 冖 冖 罒 罒 甲 罪 罪 罪 罪 置

音	置	チ	put; place; positon
訓	置き去りにする	おきざりにする	*vt*. leave (a person) in the lurch
	置場	おきば	yard; garage; shed; storage space
	置物	おきもの	ornament
	置き忘れる	おきわすれる	*vt*. mislay; misplace
	置く	おく	*vt*. put; place; position; leave; allow; let; keep; hold

5 母 see ⇨p.311

5 氺 see ⇨p.318

5 衤　see ➪p.431

6 竹 たけ／たけかんむり bamboo

768 竹 ⑥

ノ ⊢ ⊬ ⊬ ⊬ 竹

音	竹	チク	bamboo
熟	竹馬の友	チクバのとも	childhood friend
	竹林	チクリン	bamboo forest
訓	竹	たけ	bamboo
	竹の子	たけのこ	bamboo shoot

769 笑 ⑩

ノ ⊢ ⊬ ⊬ ⊬ ⊬ ⊬ 竺 竿 笑

音	笑	ショウ	laugh
訓	笑う	わらう	*v.* laugh; smile; chuckle; giggle
	笑い	わらい	laugh; smile
	笑話	わらいばなし	humorous/amusing story
	笑む	えむ	*vi.* come out; open; bloom; smile

770 第 ⑪

ノ ⊢ ⊬ ⊬ ⊬ ⊬ 竺 竿 笃 第 第

音	第	ダイ	(ordinal prefix)
熟	第一	ダイイチ	first; number one; foremost; primary
	第一印象	ダイイチ インショウ	first impressions
	第一人者	ダイイチニンシャ	first man; most talented person (in a group etc.)
	第一線	ダイイッセン	first line; front line; front
	第三者	ダイサンシャ	third party
	第六感	ダイロクカン	sixth sense

771 笛 ⑪

ノ ⊢ ⊬ ⊬ 竹 竹 竹 竹 笛 笛 笛

音	笛	テキ	pipe

訓 笛　ふえ　flute; whistle

772

筋 ⑫　丿 ナ ナ ケ 竹 竹 竹 竹 竹 笳 筋 筋

音	筋	キン	muscle; sinew
熟	筋骨	キンコツ	muscular; hard-muscled; well-built
	筋肉	キンニク	muscle
	筋力	キンリョク	ability; capacity; strength
訓	筋	すじ	muscle; sinew; blood vessel; line; stripe; streak; logic; coherence; plot (of a story); source (of information)
	筋書き	すじがき	synopsis; outline; plan
	筋金	すじがね	metal reinforcement
	筋道	すじみち	reason; logic; coherence
	筋目	すじめ	fold; crease; pedigree

773

策 ⑫　丿 ナ ナ ケ 竹 竹 笠 竹 竹 筆 筆 策

音	策	サク	plan; plot; whip stick
熟	策する	サクする	vt. plan; plot; scheme
	策略	サクリャク	plot; stratagem; trick

774

答 ⑫　丿 ナ ナ ケ 竹 竹 ゲ 咚 笅 笭 答 答

音	答	トウ	answer
熟	答案	トウアン	written answers; examination paper
	答辞	トウジ	formal reply
	答申	トウシン	report; reply (to one's superior) —v. report; submit a report (to a superior)
	答弁	トウベン	reply; answer; account; explanation —v. reply; answer; say something in self-defense
	答礼	トウレイ	return salute
訓	答え	こたえ	answer; reply; response
	答える	こたえる	vt. answer; reply; respond

竹米糸羊羽老耂耒耳肉自至舌舟色虫血行衣衤西艮

竹
米
糸
羊
羽
老耂
耒
耳
肉
自
至
舌
舟
色
虫
血
行
衣
衤
西
艮

775 等 ⑫

丿 亻 ← ←’ ⺮ ⺮ 竹 竺 笁 笁 等 等

音	等	トウ	equal
熟	等圧	トウアツ	uniform pressure
	等圧線	トウアツセン	isobar
	等価	トウカ	equivalence; parity
	等外	トウガイ	failure; also-ran
	等級	トウキュウ	grade; class; order; rank
	等号	トウゴウ	equal sign ($=$)
	等式	トウシキ	*math*. equality
	等時性	トウジセイ	*phy*. isochronism
	等質	トウシツ	homogeneity
	等身	トウシン	life size
	等分	トウブン	division into equal parts —*v*. divide into equal parts
訓	等しい	ひとしい	equal; similar; like

776 筆 ⑫

丿 亻 ← ←’ ⺮ ⺮ 竹 竺 笁 笁 筆 筆

音	筆	ヒツ	writing brush
熟	筆記	ヒッキ	note-taking; notes —*v*. take notes
	筆記体	ヒッキタイ	longhand (writing)
	筆耕	ヒッコウ	copying; copyist —*v*. copy
	筆算	ヒッサン	calculations on paper —*v*. do sums on a piece of paper
	筆写	ヒッシャ	copying; transcription —*v*. copy; transcribe
	筆者	ヒッシャ	author; writer
	筆順	ヒツジュン	stroke order (of Chinese characters)
	筆舌し難い	ヒツゼツ しがたい	beyond description
	筆談	ヒツダン	written communication —*vi*. communicate in writing
	筆頭	ヒットウ	tip of a writing brush; first on the list
	筆頭者	ヒットウシャ	head of a family (as recorded in a family register)
	筆答	ヒットウ	written answer —*vi*. answer in writing
	筆法	ヒッポウ	manner of using a writing brush *fig*. method; way of thinking
	筆名	ヒツメイ	pen name; pseudonym

筆力	ヒツリョク	power of the brush stroke/pen; powerful writing

訓	筆	ふで	writing brush
	筆入れ	ふでいれ	pencil case
	筆箱	ふでばこ	pencil box
	筆無精 (筆不精)	ふでブショウ	poor correspondent
	筆まめ	ふでまめ	ready pen; (someone who) likes writing letters, etc.

777

節 ⑬ 　ノ　ト　ケ　竹　竹　竺　笮　笳　笳　筲　節　節

音	節	セツ	season; occasion; section; paragraph; verse; joint; knot
		（セチ）	
熟	節句	セック	annual festivals
	節減	セツゲン	curtailment —v. curtail
	節制	セッセイ	moderation; temperance —v. moderate one's lifestyle
	節操	セッソウ	constancy; fidelity; integrity; chastity
	節度	セツド	moderation; rule; standard
	節分	セツブン	last day of winter
	節約	セツヤク	economy; saving; thrift —v. economize; save
訓	節	ふし	knot; joint; tune; point; item

778

管 ⑭ 　ノ　ト　ケ　竹　竹　竹　竺　笁　笞　管　管

音	管	カン	pipe; administer
熟	管楽器	カンガッキ	wind instrument
	管内	カンナイ	within the jurisdiction
	管理	カンリ	control; administration; supervision —v. control; administrate; supervise
訓	管	くだ	tube; pipe

779

算 ⑭ 　ノ　ト　ケ　竹　竹　竹　筲　管　管　笡　算　算

音	算	サン	count; calculation; reckoning; counting sticks
熟	算出	サンシュツ	calculation; computation —v. calculate; compute
	算数	サンスウ	arithmetic; calculation
	算段	サンダン	contrivance; thinking —v. contrive/think of a good way

竹 • 米 糸 羊 羽 老 耂 耒 耳 肉 自 至 舌 舟 色 虫 血 行 衣 衤 西 艮

算定	サンテイ	computation; calculation; estimate; estimation —*v*. calculate; estimate; appraise
算入	サンニュウ	item in an calculation —*v*. include in a calculation
算用数字	サンヨウスウジ	Arabic figures/numerals

780

箱 ⑮ ノ ト ヒ ㄏ ㄏ ㄏ ㄏ ㄏ 竻 箝 箱 箱

| 訓 | 箱 | はこ | box; case; casket |
| | 箱庭 | はこにわ | miniature garden |

781

築 ⑯ ノ ト ヒ ㄏ ㄏ ㄏ ㄏ ㄏ 筑 筑 竺 築

音	築	チク	construct; build
熟	築城	チクジョウ	construction of a castle; fortification —*vi*. fortify; build a castle
	築造	チクゾウ	construction
訓	築く	きずく	*vt*. build; make; construct; erect

782

簡 ⑱ ㇏ ヒ ㄏ ㄏ ㄏ ㄏ ㄏ ㄏ 節 節 簡 簡

音	簡	カン	letter; brevity
熟	簡易	カンイ	simplicity; ease; easiness
	簡潔	カンケツ	brevity; conciseness
	簡素	カンソ	simplicity
	簡単	カンタン	simplicity; simple; ease; easy
	簡便	カンベン	handiness; expediency; convenience; simplicity
	簡明	カンメイ	conciseness; brevity
	簡略	カンリャク	simplicity; conciseness

6 米 こめ／こめへん rice

783

米 、 ゛ ゛ 半 半 米 ⑥

音	米	ベイ	rice; eighty-eight years of age; America; meter (unit of measurement)
		マイ	rice
熟	米国	ベイコク	the United States
	米穀	ベイコク	rice; grain
	米作	ベイサク	rice cultivation/crop
	米収	ベイシュウ	rice crop/harvest
	米食	ベイショク	diet with rice as the staple
	米人	ベイジン	American person
	米兵	ベイヘイ	US soldier/sailor
訓	米	こめ	(uncooked) rice
	米所	こめどころ	rice-producing area
	米問屋	こめどんや	rice wholesaler
	米屋	こめや	rice dealer

784

粉 、 ゛ ゛ 半 半 米 米 米 米 粉 ⑩

音	粉	フン	flour; powder
熟	粉骨	フンコツ	assidiousness —*vi*. be assidious
	粉炭	フンタン	powdered coal
	粉本	フンポン	copy (for a painting/writing); rough sketch
	粉末	フンマツ	powder
訓	粉	こ	powder
	粉	こな	flour; powder
	粉薬	こなぐすり	powdered medicine
	粉々	こなごな	pieces; dust
	粉状	こなジョウ	powder form; powdered

785

精 ⑭ ` ´ ʾ ⺌ 米 籵 籵 籵 精 精 精 精 精

音	精	セイ （ショウ）	spirit; energy; vitality; semen; precise
熟	精進	ショウジン	devotion; diligence; purification —*vi.* abstain from meat or fish
	精進料理	ショウジン リョウリ	vegetarian cooking/cuisine
	精液	セイエキ	semen
	精確	セイカク	accurate; precise; exact
	精根	セイコン	energy; vitality
	精算	セイサン	exact calculation; settling of accounts —*v.* settle accounts
	精子	セイシ	sperm
	精神	セイシン	mind; spirit
	精神科	セイシンカ	psychiatry
	精神病	セイシンビョウ	mental disorder
	精製	セイセイ	refining; careful manufacture —*v.* refine
	精選	セイセン	careful/choice selection —*v.* choose/select carefully
	精通	セイツウ	well-informed; familiarity —*vi.* be familiar/well versed in
	精度	セイド	precision; accuracy
	精読	セイドク	careful reading —*v.* read carefully
	精分	セイブン	nourishment; vitality
	精米	セイマイ	polished rice —*v.* polish rice
	精密	セイミツ	precision
	精油	セイユ	refined/perfume oil —*vi.* refine oil
	精力	セイリョク	energy; vigor; vitality

786

糖 ⑯ ` ´ ʾ ⺌ 米 籵 籵 籵 籵 糖 糖 糖

音	糖	トウ	sugar; sweetened carbohydrate
熟	糖分	トウブン	sugar (content)
	糖類	トウルイ	saccharide

6 糸 いと／いとへん thread

787

糸 ⑥   く 幺 幺 争 弁 糸

音	糸	シ	thread
訓	糸	いと	thread; string; line
	糸口	いとぐち	end of a thread *fig.* first step; beginning; lead; clue
	糸切り歯	いときりば	canine tooth

788

系 ⑦   一 ㇅ 至 玄 卒 乑 系

音	系	ケイ	system; descent
熟	系図	ケイズ	genealogy; lineage
	系統	ケイトウ	system; lineage; genealogy; school; party
	系統的	ケイトウテキ	systematically; methodically
	系列	ケイレツ	order; series
訓	系ぐ	つなぐ	*vt.* connect; join

789

素 ⑩   一 十 丰 主 丰 夫 麦 麦 素 素

音	素	ス	naked; uncovered; simple
		ソ	element; beginning
熟	素足	スあし	barefoot
	素顔	スがお	unpainted face; face without makeup
	素性	スジョウ	birth; lineage; identity
	素手	スで	bare hands
	素敵	ステキ	splendid; marvelous; great; beautiful; nice
	素直	スなお	frank; gentle; meek; docile; honest
	素晴らしい	スばらしい	splendid; magnificent
	素因	ソイン	contributing factor; cause
	素行	ソコウ	behavior; conduct
	素材	ソザイ	material; subject matter
	素地	ソジ	groundwork; the makings of
	素質	ソシツ	quality; nature; makeup
	素数	ソスウ	*math.* prime number

| 素読 | ソドク | reading aloud without making any effort to understand what is written —*v.* read aloud without making any effort to understand what is written |
| 素養 | ソヨウ | culture; one's knowledge; attainments |

790

紀 ⑨ ＜ ＜ ＜ ＜ 糸 糸 糸 紀 紀 紀

音	紀	キ	account; writing; era; year
熟	紀元	キゲン	era; epoch
	紀行	キコウ	travelogue

791

級 ⑨ ＜ ＜ ＜ ＜ 糸 糸 糸 級 級 級

音	級	キュウ	class; grade; position; symbol; group
熟	級数	キュウスウ	*math.* series; progression
	級長	キュウチョウ	president of a class; homeroom president
	級友	キュウユウ	classmate

792

紅 ⑨ ＜ ＜ ＜ ＜ 糸 糸 糸 紅 紅

音	紅	コウ	crimson; rouge; red
		（ク）	
熟	紅一点	コウイッテン	only woman in a group
	紅顔	コウガン	rosy face; ruddy cheeks
	紅茶	コウチャ	tea
	紅潮	コウチョウ	blush; flush —*vi.* blush; flush; turn red/rosy
	紅白	コウハク	red and white
	紅葉	コウヨウ	autumnal leaves —*vi.* turn red/yellow
訓	紅	くれない	deep red; crimson
	紅	べに	rouge; deep red; crimson

約 ⑨

⟨ 纟 纟 纟 纟 糸 糸 糸 約 約

音	約	ヤク	promise; appproximately; curtail
熟	約する	ヤクする	*vt*. promise; reduce; abbreviate
	約言	ヤクゲン	contraction; summary
	約定	ヤクジョウ	promise; agreement; contract —*vi*. promise; make a contract; agree
	約数	ヤクスウ	*math*. divisor; factor
	約束	ヤクソク	promise; appointment —*v*. make a promise/appointment
	約分	ヤクブン	*math*. reduction of a factor to its lowest terms —*v. math*. reduce a fraction to its lowest terms

紙 ⑩

⟨ 纟 纟 纟 纟 糸 糸 紅 紙 紙 紙

音	紙	シ	paper; newspaper
熟	紙型	シケイ	paper mold/mat (used to make a printing plate)
	紙質	シシツ	paper quality
	紙上	シジョウ	in the press; in the papers; on paper
	紙片	シヘン	piece/strip/slip of paper
	紙面	シメン	the papers; the press
訓	紙	かみ	paper
	紙切れ	かみきれ	piece of paper
	紙一重	かみひとえ	very fine line

純 ⑩

⟨ 纟 纟 纟 纟 糸 糸 紅 紅 紅 純

音	純	ジュン	pure; naive; genuine; authentic
熟	純愛	ジュンアイ	pure/true love
	純化	ジュンカ	purification —*v*. purify
	純金	ジュンキン	pure gold
	純銀	ジュンギン	pure silver
	純潔	ジュンケツ	purity; chastity
	純血	ジュンケツ	pure-blooded; thoroughbred
	純情	ジュンジョウ	pure heart; naivete; innocence

竹
米
糸
羊
羽
老
耒
耳
肉
自
至
舟
色
虫
血
行
衣
衤
西
艮

純真	ジュンシン	pure heart; purity; naiveté
純正	ジュンセイ	pure; genuine
純然	ジュンゼン	pure; sheer; utter; absolute
純度	ジュンド	purity
純白	ジュンパク	snow-white
純文学	ジュンブンガク	serious literature
純綿	ジュンメン	pure cotton
純毛	ジュンモウ	pure wool
純良	ジュンリョウ	pure and good; grade A

796

納 ⑩　 く　幺　幺　幺　糸　糸　糸　紅　納　納

音 納　ノウ　offer; accept
　　　（トウ）
　　　（ナッ）
　　　（ナン）　put away

熟 納豆　ナットウ　*natto* (fermented soybeans)
納得　ナットク　understanding; consent; assent; compliance —*v.* understand; assent; give consent; agree
納屋　なや　barn
納戸　ナンど　closet; wardrobe; storeroom
納会　ノウカイ　last meeting of the year
納期　ノウキ　time of delivery; payment date
納骨　ノウコツ　laying a person's ashes to rest —*vi.* lay a person's ashes to rest
納税　ノウゼイ　payment of taxes —*vi.* pay one's taxes
納税者　ノウゼイシャ　taxpayer
納入　ノウニュウ　delivery; payment —*v.* deliver; pay; supply
納品　ノウヒン　delivery of goods —*v.* deliver; supply
納品書　ノウヒンショ　statement of delivery
納付　ノウフ　delivery; payment —*v.* deliver; supply; pay

訓 納まる　おさまる　*vi.* stay; be contented; be paid; settle down
納める　おさめる　*vt.* obtain; gain; acquire; deliver; supply

797

経 ⑪　く　幺　幺　幺　糸　糸　紅　奴　経　経　経

音 経　ケイ　elapse; pass; go through; normal; usual
　　　キョウ　sutra; mantra

402

熟	経文	キョウモン	sutra; text of a sutra
	経営	ケイエイ	management —*v.* manage; run; operate
	経過	ケイカ	progress; development; passage —*vi.* pass; elapse
	経験	ケイケン	experience —*v.* experience; go through; undergo
	経済	ケイザイ	economy; husbandry; the economy; finances
	経済的	ケイザイテキ	economical; frugal; thrifty
	経線	ケイセン	meridian
	経典	ケイテン	Scriptures; classics; literary works by the sages
	経度	ケイド	longitude
	経由	ケイユ	via; by way of; through —*vi.* go via/by way of/through
	経歴	ケイレキ	personal history; background; career
	経路	ケイロ	course; route; process
訓	経る	へる	*vi.* pass; elapse; go/pass through; experience

798

細 ⑪ ⟨ 纟 纟 纟 纟 糸 糸 紅 細 細 細

音	細	サイ	narrow; thin; fine; minute; detail
熟	細工	サイク	workmanship; handiwork; trick —*v.* use tricks; play tricks
	細事	サイジ	trifle
	細心	サイシン	very careful; scrupulous; meticulous
	細則	サイソク	bylaws
	細大	サイダイ	minutest detail; detailed; full
	細部	サイブ	details; particulars
	細分	サイブン	subdivision; segmentation —*v.* subdivide; segment
	細別	サイベツ	subdivision —*v.* subdivide
	細密	サイミツ	fine; close; minute
	細目	サイモク	details; particulars; specifications
訓	細かい	こまかい	small; fine; close; minute; delicate; subtle
	細か	こまか	small; fine; delicate; subtle
	細々	こまごま	in detail; minutely
	細る	ほそる	*vi.* become thin; slim down
	細い	ほそい	fine; thin; narrow; slender
	細面	ほそおもて	slender face
	細長い	ほそながい	slender; long and narrow
	細道	ほそみち	narrow lane

竹
米
糸 •
羊
羽
老
耂
耒
耳
肉
自
至
舌
舟
色
虫
血
行
衣
衤
西
艮

竹
米
糸
● 羊
羽
老
耂
耒
耳
肉
自
至
舌
舟
色
虫
血
行
衣
衤
西
艮

終 ⑪

く ㄠ ㄠ ㄠ 幺 糸 糸 糸 糽 終 終 終

音	終	シュウ	finish; last; complete
熟	終演	シュウエン	end of a performance
	終業	シュウギョウ	close of work/school —*vi*. close; break-up
	終曲	シュウキョク	finale; last song of a musical
	終極	シュウキョク	ultimate
	終局	シュウキョク	end; close
	終結	シュウケツ	conclusion; end —*vi*. end; be concluded
	終始	シュウシ	throughout; unchanged from beginning to end —*vi*. remain unchanged throughout
	終止	シュウシ	end; stop; termination —*vi*. stop; terminate; end; come to end
	終日	シュウジツ	all day long; from morning to night; throughout the day
	終生	シュウセイ	all one's life; life-long
	終戦	シュウセン	end of a war
	終着駅	シュウチャクエキ	terminal train station; terminus
	終点	シュウテン	terminal train station; end of the line; last stop
	終電	シュウデン	last train
	終幕	シュウマク	final scene; end of the performance
	終末	シュウマツ	end; conclusion
	終夜	シュウヤ	all night
	終夜営業	シュウヤエイギョウ	stay open all night
	終了	シュウリョウ	close; end —*v*. come to an end; be completed; finish
訓	終える	おえる	*vt*. finish; complete; go through with
	終わる	おわる	*vi*. end; be over; finish; be finished; come to an end

組 ⑪

く ㄠ ㄠ ㄠ 幺 糸 糸 糺 紀 紀 組 組

音	組	ソ	set; association; group; class; company
熟	組閣	ソカク	Cabinet formation —*vi*. form a Cabinet
	組織	ソシキ	organization; setup —*v*. organize; set up
	組織的	ソシキテキ	systematic
	組成	ソセイ	composition; makeup —*v*. compose; constitute; make up

訓	組	くみ	class; set; group; company
	組む	くむ	*v.* put together; assemble; cross one's legs; form; group

801

絵 ⑫　㇍ ㇗ 纟 纟 纟 糸 糸 糸 糸 給 絵 絵

音	絵	エ	picture
		カイ	picture
熟	絵図	エズ	graphic drawing; scale sketch
	絵の具	エのグ	water colors
	絵葉書	エはがき	picture postcard
	絵筆	エふで	paintbrush; drawing pen
	絵本	エホン	picture/illustrated book
	絵巻物	エまきもの	picture scroll
	絵文字	エモジ	pictorial symbol
	絵画	カイガ	pictures and paintings collectively

802

給 ⑫　㇍ ㇗ 纟 纟 纟 糸 糸 糸 糸 給 給 給

音	給	キュウ	give; allowance; salary; be enough/sufficient; serve; provide
熟	給仕	キュウジ	waiter; waitress; steward —*vi.* wait on; serve
	給食	キュウショク	provision of meals (at schools, etc.) —*vi.* provide/serve meals
	給水	キュウスイ	water supply/service —*vi.* supply water
	給付	キュウフ	presentation; delivery; benefit —*v.* make a presentation; deliver; pay
	給付金	キュウフキン	benefit
	給油	キュウユ	oil supply —*vi.* lubricate; refuel
	給料	キュウリョウ	wages; salary

803

結 ⑫　㇍ ㇗ 纟 纟 纟 糸 糸 糸 紸 結 結 結

音	結	ケツ	tie; join; union; conclusion
		（ケッ）	
熟	結果	ケッカ	result; effect; outcome; consequence
	結局	ケッキョク	after all; finally; ultimately; eventually

竹米糸羊羽老耂耒耳肉自至舌舟色虫血行衣衤西艮

結構	ケッコウ	fine; enough; sufficient
結合	ケツゴウ	union; combination —*v.* unite; combine
結実	ケツジツ	fruition —*vi.* bear fruit; realize
結成	ケッセイ	formation; organization —*v.* form; organize
結石	ケッセキ	*med.* stones (in the liver; gall bladder etc.)
結束	ケッソク	unity; union —*v.* unite; stand together
結末	ケツマツ	the end; conclusion; outcome
結論	ケツロン	conclusion —*vi.* come to/reach a conclusion

訓

結ぶ	むすぶ	*v.* tie; join; connect; link; conclude; bear (fruit)
結び	むすび	bow; end; conclusion
結び目	むすびめ	knot
結う	ゆう	*vt.* tie an *obi*; dress; put one's hair up in a traditional Japanese hairstyle
結納	ゆいノウ	betrothal gifts
結わえる	ゆわえる	*vt.* bind; fasten; tie

804

絶 ⑫ 　く　幺　幺　糸　糸　糸　糸'　糸勺　絽　絽　絶　絶

音

絶	ゼツ	die out; end; fail
	ゼッ	

熟

絶する	ゼッする	*v.* die out; end; fail
絶海	ゼッカイ	distant seas
絶景	ゼッケイ	splendid view
絶交	ゼッコウ	severance of relations; rupture —*vi.* sever one's relationship with
絶好	ゼッコウ	splendid; first rate
絶賛	ゼッサン	great admiration/praise —*v.* admire/praise greatly
絶食	ゼッショク	fasting; —*vi.* fast
絶世	ゼッセイ	peerless; unequaled
絶対	ゼッタイ	absolute; definite
絶体絶命	ゼッタイゼツメイ	desperate situation
絶大	ゼツダイ	immense; great
絶頂	ゼッチョウ	summit; peak; climax
絶版	ゼッパン	out-of-print —*v.* cease publication
絶筆	ゼッピツ	last piece of writing (before giving up, dying, etc.)
絶品	ゼッピン	superb article; masterpiece
絶望	ゼツボウ	despair —*vi.* despair; be full of despair
絶命	ゼツメイ	death —*vi.* die

訓	絶える	たえる	*vi*. cease; die out
	絶つ	たつ	*vt*. cut off
	絶やす	たやす	*vt*. exterminate

805

統 ⑫ く ∠ ٤ 乡 糸 糸 糸 紅 紆 紵 紵 統

音	統	トウ	control
熟	統一	トウイツ	unity; unification; uniformity; consolidation —*v*. unify; standardize; coordinate
	統計	トウケイ	statistics; figures; numerical statement —*v*. show statistically/numerically
	統合	トウゴウ	integration; unification; combination; consolidation —*v*. integrate; unify; combine; consolidate
	統制	トウセイ	control; regulation —*v*. control; regulate; govern
	統率	トウソツ	command; generalship; leadership —*v*. command; take the lead; lead; direct
	統率力	トウソツリョク	leadership
	統治	トウチ	rule; reign; government; administration —*v*. rule; govern; administer
訓	統べる	すべる	*vt*. generalize

806

絹 ⑬ く ∠ ٤ 乡 糸 糸 糸 糸 紀 絹 絹 絹

音	絹	ケン	silk
訓	絹	きぬ	silk
	絹糸	きぬいと	silk thread

807

続 ⑬ く ∠ ٤ 乡 糸 糸 糸 結 結 続 続 続

音	続	ゾク	continue
熟	続出	ゾクシュツ	successive appearances —*v*. occur in succession; appear one after another
	続々	ゾクゾク	successively; one after another
	続発	ゾクハツ	successive occurences —*v*. occur in succession/one after another
	続編	ゾクヘン	sequel
	続行	ゾッコウ	continuation —*v*. continue

竹 米 糸 羊 羽 老 耂 耒 耳 肉 自 至 舌 舟 色 虫 血 行 衣 衤 西 艮

407

6

竹米糸羊羽老耂耒耳肉自至舌舟色虫血行衣衤西艮

訓	続く	つづく	*vi.* continue
	続ける	つづける	*vt.* continue

808

総 ⑭

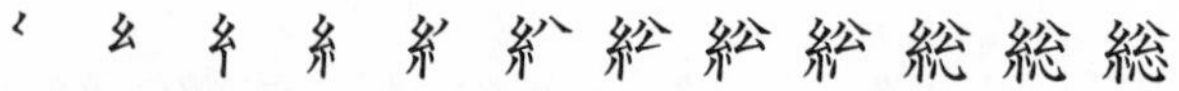

音	総	ソウ	general; overall
熟	総意	ソウイ	consensus
	総員	ソウイン	all hands; in full force
	総会	ソウカイ	general meeting; plenary session
	総画	ソウカク	the total stroke-count (of a Chinese character)
	総計	ソウケイ	total
	総合	ソウゴウ	synthesis; comprehensive —*v.* synthesize; integrate; put together
	総裁	ソウサイ	president; governor
	総菜	ソウザイ	everyday food; side dish
	総辞職	ソウジショク	mass resignation
	総数	ソウスウ	total number
	総勢	ソウゼイ	the whole army/group
	総選挙	ソウセンキョ	general election
	総体	ソウタイ	on the whole
	総代	ソウダイ	representative; delegate
	総長	ソウチョウ	president; chancellor
	総出	ソウで	in full force; all together
	総動員	ソウドウイン	general mobilization
	総本山	ソウホンザン	head temple
	総本店	ソウホンテン	head office
	総務	ソウム	manager; general affairs
	総理	ソウリ	prime minister
	総量	ソウリョウ	gross weight
	総領	ソウリョウ	heir; eldest child
	総領事	ソウリョウジ	consul general
	総力	ソウリョク	the whole strength; all one's might
	総和	ソウワ	(sum) total

809

綿 ⑭

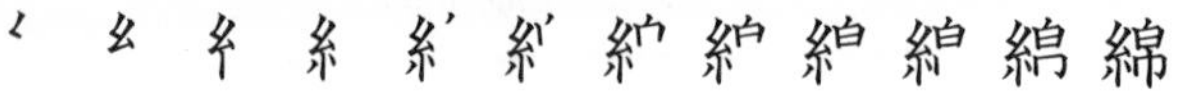

音	綿	メン	cotton
熟	綿織物	メンおりもの	cotton fabrics

綿花	メンカ	raw cotton
綿糸	メンシ	cotton yarn/thread
綿製品	メンセイヒン	cotton goods
綿布	メンプ	cotton (cloth)
綿密	メンミツ	minute; meticulous; detailed
綿々	メンメン	continuous; endless; unabating
綿羊	メンヨウ	sheep
訓 綿	わた	cotton

810 緑 ⑭

 く 么 乡 糸 糸 糽 糸 糸 糸 糸 緑 緑

音 緑	リョク	green
	(ロク)	green
熟 緑化	リョクカ	tree planting —*v.* plant trees
緑酒	リョクシュ	fine saké
緑樹	リョクジュ	greenery; lush, green tree
緑地	リョクチ	green track of land
緑地帯	リョクチタイ	green belt
緑茶	リョクチャ	green tea
緑青	ロクショウ	verdigris; green/copper rust
訓 緑	みどり	green

811 練 ⑭

く 么 乡 糸 糸 糸 糸 糸 絆 紳 練 練

音 練	レン	train
熟 練習	レンシュウ	practice; exercise —*v.* practice; exercise
練達	レンタツ	skill; dexterity
練乳	レンニュウ	condensed milk
訓 練る	ねる	*v.* knead; train; polish
練れる	ねれる	*vi.* be mellowed; be matured (of a personality, character)
練り物	ねりもの	paste; procession; parade float

812 線 ⑮

く　幺　幺　糸　糸　糽　紗　綧　綧　綧　綧　線

音	線	セン	line
熟	線	セン	line
	線画	センガ	line drawing
	線路	センロ	railway track

813 編 ⑮

く　幺　幺　糸　糽　綧　紗　紗　紗　絹　絹　編

音	編	ヘン	knit; compile; edit
熟	編曲	ヘンキョク	(musical) arrangement —v. arrange (a piece of music)
	編者	ヘンシャ (ヘンジャ)	editor; compiler
	編修	ヘンシュウ	compilation/editing (of books) —v. compile; edit
	編集	ヘンシュウ	compilation; editing —v. compile; edit
	編集者	ヘンシュウシャ	editor
	編集長	ヘンシュウチョウ	editor-in-chief
	編成	ヘンセイ	organization; putting into a systematic/logical form —v. organize
	編隊	ヘンタイ	formation flying
	編入	ヘンニュウ	entry; incorporation; transfer —v. enter; incorporate; transfer (to a new school, university department)
訓	編む	あむ	vt. knit; braid; compile; edit
	編み上げ	あみあげ	laceup (shoes, boots, etc.)
	編み出す	あみだす	vt. work out; think up; devise
	編み戸	あみど	(bamboo/wood) braided door
	編み針	あみばり	knitting needle; crochet hook
	編み棒	あみボウ	knitting needle/pin
	編み物	あみもの	knitting

814 縦 ⑯

く　幺　幺　糸　糸　糸　糽　綧　絆　絆　縦　縦

音	縦	ジュウ	length

熟	縦線	ジュウセン	vertical line
	縦断	ジュウダン	cutting vertically; running through
	縦列	ジュウレツ	column; file
訓	縦	たて	length; height; vertical; perpendicular
	縦書き	たてがき	vertical writing
	縦横	たてよこ	length and breadth; lengthwise and crosswise

815

縮 ⑰ 　く　幺　幸　糸　糸ˊ　紵　紵　綷　綷　縮　縮

音	縮	シュク	shrink; shorten; contract; reduce
熟	縮減	シュクゲン	reduction; cut back —v. reduce; cut back
	縮写	シュクシャ	reduced/miniature copy —v. make a reduced copy
	縮尺	シュクシャク	reduced scale —v. reduce the scale of; make smaller
	縮小	シュクショウ	reduction; curtailment —v. reduce; curtail; cut back
	縮図	シュクズ	reduced drawing; miniature copy
訓	縮む	ちぢむ	vi. shrink; contract; crinkle
	縮まる	ちぢまる	vi. shrink; contract
	縮み	ちぢみ	shrinkage
	縮める	ちぢめる	vt. shorten; cut down; reduce; condense
	縮らす	ちぢらす	vt. crinkle; curl; make frizzy
	縮れる	ちぢれる	vi. crinkle; be frizzled/curly

816

績 ⑰ 　く　幺　幸　糸　紵　紵　紵　結　結　績　績

| 音 | 績 | セキ | spin; achievements |

817

織 ⑱ 　く　幺　幸　糸　紵　紵　紵　絊　縎　織　織　織

音	織	シキ	organize
		ショク	weave; textiles
熟	織機	ショッキ	weaving machine; loom
訓	織る	おる	vt. weave; work at the loom
	織り地	おりジ	texture of woven fabric

竹米糸羊羽老耂耒耳肉自至舌舟色虫血行衣衤西艮

| 織物 | おりもの | textiles; fabrics; woven cloth |
| 織物業 | おりものギョウ | textile trade/business |

---

6 羊　ひつじ　sheep

818

羊 ⑥　丶　ソ　ソ　ソ　ソ　兰　兰　羊

音	羊	ヨウ	sheep
熟	羊皮	ヨウヒ	sheepskin
	羊皮紙	ヨウヒシ	parchment
	羊毛	ヨウモウ	wool
訓	羊	ひつじ	sheep
	羊飼い	ひつじかい	shepherd

819

美 ⑨　丶　ソ　ソ　ゾ　芒　羊　羊　美

音	美	ビ	beauty
熟	美化	ビカ	beautification; glorification; idealization —*v.* beautify (a city); glorify; idealize
	美学	ビガク	aesthetics
	美観	ビカン	fine view; beautiful scenery
	美形	ビケイ	beautiful; handsome
	美酒	ビシュ	delicious saké
	美術	ビジュツ	fine arts; art
	美術館	ビジュツカン	art gallery
	美女	ビジョ	beautiful/lovely woman; pretty girl
	美少年	ビショウネン	handsome youth; pretty boy
	美食	ビショク	delicious food —*vi.* live on/eat fancy food
	美食家	ビショクカ	gourmet; epicure
	美人	ビジン	beautiful woman
	美声	ビセイ	beautiful voice
	美談	ビダン	fine anecdote/story
	美的	ビテキ	aesthetic
	美点	ビテン	merit; virtue; good point
	美徳	ビトク	virtue; noble attribute
	美男	ビナン	handsome man

美男子	ビナンシ	handsome man
美風	ビフウ	fine/good custom
美文	ビブン	flowery/elegant prose
美文調	ビブンチョウ	ornate style
美味	ビミ	delicious; good; tasting
美名	ビメイ	good/reputable name
美容	ビヨウ	beautiful face; beautification of face or form
美容院	ビヨウイン	beauty parlor; hairdresser
美容外科	ビヨウゲカ	*med*. cosmetic surgery
美容師	ビヨウシ	beautician; hairdresser
美容整形	ビヨウセイケイ	cosmetic surgery
訓 美しい	うつくしい	beautiful

820

着 ⑫ 　　`ヽ ヾ ⺯ ⺷ ⺸ 羊 芦 芒 着 着 着 着

音 着	チャク (ジャク)	put on; wear; clothe; arrive; reach
熟 着衣	チャクイ	one's clothes
着眼	チャクガン	attention; notice; perception —*vi*. pay attention; notice; perceive
着眼点	チャクガンテン	point of view
着実	チャクジツ	steadiness; honesty
着手	チャクシュ	start; commencement; outset —*vi*. start; commence; begin
着順	チャクジュン	order of arrival
着色	チャクショク	coloration; coloring —*vi*. color; paint
着水	チャクスイ	alighting on the water; splashdown —*vi*. alight on the water; splashdown
着席	チャクセキ	taking a seat; sitting down —*vi*. take a seat; sit down
着想	チャクソウ	idea; conception
着地	チャクチ	landing —*vi*. land
着々	チャクチャク	steadily; step by step
着任	チャクニン	arrival at one's post —*vi*. arrive at one's post
着服	チャクフク	getting dressed; embezzlement; misappropriation —*v*. get dressed; misappropriate; embezzle
着目	チャクモク	attention; notice —*vi*. pay attention to; take notice of
着用	チャクヨウ	wearing (clothes) —*v*. wear (clothes)
着陸	チャクリク	landing; touchdown —*vi*. land; touchdown
着工	チャッコウ	commencement of construction work —*vi*. start construction work

竹
米
糸
• 羊
羽
老耂
耒
耳
肉
自
至
舌
舟
色
虫
血
行
衣衤
西艮

訓	着る	きる	*vt*. put on; wear
	着せる	きせる	*vt*. dress someone; clothe; put on; plate; coat; cover
	着付け	きつけ	dressing; fitting
	着物	きもの	kimono
	着く	つく	*vi*. arrive at; reach; come to hand
	着ける	つける	*vt*. put on; wear

821

義 ⑬

丶 ⺍ 丷 ⺷ 兰 美 羊 羊 羊 義 義 義

音	義	ギ	justice; meaning
熟	義眼	ギガン	artificial/glass eye
	義挙	ギキョ	righteous act; heroic deed
	義兄弟	ギキョウダイ	brothers-in-law; blood brothers
	義兄	ギケイ	(older) brother-in-law
	義姉	ギシ	(older) sister-in-law
	義歯	ギシ	false tooth/teeth
	義手	ギシュ	artificial arm
	義足	ギソク	artificial leg
	義弟	ギテイ	(younger) brother-in-law
	義父	ギフ	stepfather; father-in-law
	義母	ギボ	stepmother; mother-in-law
	義妹	ギマイ	(younger) sister-in-law
	義務	ギム	duty; obligation
	義務教育	ギムキョウイク	compulsory education
	義理	ギリ	obligation; justice; duty

822

群 ⑬

⊐ ⊐ ⊒ 尹 尹 君 君 君' 君彡 君彡 君彡 群

音	群	グン	gather; collect; many
熟	群居	グンキョ	living together in large numbers
	群衆	グンシュウ	large group of people
	群集	グンシュウ	crowd; multitude; throng
	群集心理	グンシュウシンリ	group psychology
	群小	グンショウ	insignificant; minor; petty
	群生	グンセイ	gregarious —*vi*. be gregarious
	群島	グントウ	group of islands
	群落	グンラク	group of villages; plant community

訓	群	（むら）	group; crowd; cluster; clump
	群がる	むらがる	*vi.* crowd (together); herd; flock; pack
	群れ	むれ	group; troop; crowd; herd; flock; pack
	群れる	むれる	*vi.* crowd (together); throng; flock together

---

6 羽 はね feather

823

羽 ⑥　　フ　フ　ヲ　羽　羽　羽

音	羽	ウ	feather; wing
熟	羽化	ウカ	emergence — *vi.* emerge; grow wings
	羽毛	ウモウ	feather; plume; feathering; plummage
訓	羽	はね	feather; wing
	羽	は	feather; wing; (counter for birds and rabbits)
	羽織	はおり	*haori* (Japanese overgarment)
	羽衣	はごろも	robe of feathers; winged jacket worn by angels

824

習 ⑪　　フ　ヲ　ヲ　羽　羽　羽　羽　羽　習　習　習

音	習	シュウ	study; custom
熟	習慣	シュウカン	custom; habit; practice
	習作	シュウサク	study (in art, music, etc.)
	習字	シュウジ	penmanship; calligraphy
	習熟	シュウジュク	mastering (a skill, etc.) — *vi.* master; become proficient
	習性	シュウセイ	habit; behavior; nature
	習得	シュウトク	learning; acquiring skills — *v.* learn; acquire a skill; master
訓	習う	ならう	*vt.* learn; train; take lessons
	習わし	ならわし	practice; custom; way; tradition

825

翌 ⑪　　フ　ヲ　ヲ　羽　羽　羽　羽　羽　翌　翌　翌

音	翌	ヨク	next/following

熟	翌月	ヨクゲツ	following month
	翌日	ヨクジツ	next/following day
	翌朝	ヨクチョウ	next morning
	翌年	ヨクネン	next/following year

---

6 老 おいがしら／おいかんむり old man 耂 (p.416)

826

老 ⑥ 一 十 土 耂 耂 老

音	老	ロウ	old age
熟	老眼	ロウガン	presbyopia
	老後	ロウゴ	in one's old age
	老骨	ロウコツ	one's old bones; old person's body
	老死	ロウシ	death by old age —*vi*. die of old age
	老中	ロウジュウ	*hist*. member of the shogun's council of elders
	老熟	ロウジュク	experienced; mature —*vi*. be experienced/mature
	老女	ロウジョ	old woman
	老人	ロウジン	old man; the elderly
	老体	ロウタイ	old body; elderly person
	老大家	ロウタイカ	veteran; authority
	老若	ロウニャク	young and old; young or old
	老年	ロウネン	old age; elderly person
	老練	ロウレン	experienced; veteran
訓	老いる	おいる	*vi*. grow old
	老い	おい	old age
	老いらく	おいらく	old age
	老ける	ふける	*vi*. grow old

---

4 耂 おいがしら／おいかんむり old man

827

考 ⑥ 一 十 土 耂 耂 考

| 音 | 考 | コウ | consider; reflect; think; contemplate; test; examine |

熟	考案	コウアン	conception; idea; plan; device; project —*v.* conceive; plan; design; devise; originate
	考課	コウカ	examination of personal records
	考究	コウキュウ	investigation —*vt.* investigate
	考古学	コウコガク	archaeology
	考査	コウサ	examination; test; consideration —*v.* test; examine; quiz; consider
	考察	コウサツ	contemplation; consideration; examination; study; inquiry —*v.* contemplate; consider; examine; study
	考試	コウシ	examination
	考証	コウショウ	historical research/investigation —*v.* carry out historical research
訓	考える	かんがえる	*vt.* think; consider; take a view; be of an opinion; regard
	考え	かんがえ	thinking; thought; ideas; conception; opinion
	考え方	かんがえかた	line of thought; point of view; solution
	考え事	かんがえごと	concern; worry

828

者 ⑧ 一 十 土 耂 耂 者 者 者

音	者	シャ	person
訓	者	もの	***hum.*** person

6 耒 すきへん plow

829

耕 ⑩ 一 二 三 丰 丰 耒 耒 耒 耕 耕

音	耕	コウ	till; plow; cultivate
熟	耕具	コウグ	farm implements
	耕作	コウサク	cultivation; farming; tillage —*v.* cultivate; farm; till
	耕地	コウチ	arable/cultivated/plowed land
訓	耕す	たがやす	*vt.* till; plow; cultivate

竹
米
糸
羊
耂
耒
● 耳
肉
自
至
舌
舟
色
虫
血
行
衣
衤
西
艮

6 耳　みみ／みみへん　ear

830

耳 ⑥　一 T F F E 耳

音	耳	ジ	ear
熟	耳目	ジモク	seeing and hearing; eyes and ears
訓	耳	みみ	ear; hearing; (bread) crust
	耳打ち	みみうち	whispering —*vi.* whisper
	耳学問	みみガクモン	hearsay
	耳寄りな話	みみよりなはなし	welcome news
	耳輪	みみわ	earring

831

聖 ⑬　一 T F E 耳 耴 耵 耵 聖 聖 聖

音	聖	セイ	saint; holy; sacred; sage
熟	聖域	セイイキ	sacred precincts
	聖火	セイカ	sacred flame; Olympic Flame
	聖者	セイジャ	saint; holy man
	聖書	セイショ	Bible
	聖人	セイジン	sage; saint; holy man
	聖地	セイチ	sacred land; Holy Land
	聖典	セイテン	holy book; scriptures
	聖母	セイボ	Holy Mother
	聖夜	セイヤ	Christmas Eve

832

聞 ⑭　丨 冂 冂 冃 冃 冃 門 門 門 門 門 聞 聞

音	聞	ブン	hear; listen to; heed; ask
		モン	
訓	聞く	きく	*vt.* hear; listen to; heed; ask
	聞こえる	きこえる	*vi.* hear; be heard/audible; be able to hear
	聞き入る	ききいる	*vi.* listen attentively
	聞き入れる	ききいれる	*vt.* accede to; comply with
	聞き納め	ききおさめ	last time to hear (somebody say something)

聞き落とす	ききおとす	*vt*. not hear; miss
聞き覚え	ききおぼえ	learning by ear; heard before
聞き返す	ききかえす	*vt*. ask back/again
聞き書き	ききがき	taking notes (from a talk/lecture)
聞き苦しい	ききぐるしい	offensive to the ear
聞き上手	ききジョウズ	good listener
聞き出す	ききだす	*vt*. ask about; begin to listen/ask
聞き付ける	ききつける	*vt*. hear; learn of; be used to hearing
聞き伝え	ききづたえ	hearsay
聞き手	ききて	listener
聞き取る	ききとる	*vt*. hear and understand; catch; follow
聞き流す	ききながす	*vt*. pay no attention to
聞き耳	ききみみ	attentive ears; listening carefully
聞き役	ききヤク	one who hears people's complaints
聞き分ける	ききわける	*vt*. distinguish between (sounds, stories, etc.); listen to reason; listen to and accept

833

職 ⑱　一 丆 耳 耳 耵 聀 聗 聸 聧 職 職 職

音	職	ショク	job; work; occupation
熟	職域	ショクイキ	one's job/occupation/area of responsibility
	職員	ショクイン	staff; personnel; member of staff
	職業	ショクギョウ	occupation; trade; profession
	職責	ショクセキ	one's work responsibility; duties
	職人	ショクニン	craftsman; workman; artisan
	職能	ショクノウ	professional ability; occupational function
	職場	ショクば	workshop; workplace; the office
	職務	ショクム	work duties
	職名	ショクメイ	official title
	職権	ショッケン	official authority
	職工	ショッコウ	worker; factory hand

6　肉　see ⇨ p.281

竹
米
糸
羊
羽
老
耂
耒
耳 ●
肉 ●
自
至
舌
舟
色
虫
血
行
衣
衤
西
艮

竹
米
糸
羽
老耂
耒
耳
肉
● 自
至
舌
舟
色
虫
血
行
衣
衤
西
艮

834

| 自 | ⑥ | ´ ˊ ⺁ ⺋ 自 自 自 |

| 音 | 自 | ジ | oneself |
| | | シ | natural; nature |

熟	自愛	ジアイ	self-love; self-indulgence —*vi*. take care of oneself
	自衛	ジエイ	self-defense; self-protection —*vi*. defend oneself
	自衛隊	ジエイタイ	the Self-Defense Force (SDF)
	自我	ジガ	the self/ego
	自害	ジガイ	suicide —*vi*. commit suicide
	自覚	ジカク	consciousness; self-awareness —*v*. be aware/conscious
	自画自賛	ジガジサン	self-praise —*vi*. sing one's own praises; praise oneself
	自画像	ジガゾウ	self-portrait
	自家製	ジカセイ	homemade
	自家用	ジカヨウ	for private use
	自活	ジカツ	self-support —*vi*. support oneself
	自給	ジキュウ	self-support; self-sustenance —*v*. provide for oneself
	自給自足	ジキュウジソク	self-sufficiency —*vi*. be self-sufficient
	自供	ジキョウ	confession —*v*. confession
	自決	ジケツ	self-determination; suicide —*vi*. determine/decide for oneself; commit suicide; kill oneself
	自己	ジコ	self; oneself
	自己暗示	ジコアンジ	autosuggestion
	自己中心	ジコチュウシン	egocentricity
	自己流	ジコリュウ	one's own way of doing something
	自業自得	ジゴウジトク	natural consequence of one's evil deed; asking for it; deserving what one gets
	自国	ジコク	one's own country/homeland
	自国語	ジコクゴ	native language; mother tongue
	自在	ジザイ	at will; freely
	自作	ジサク	one's own work; made by oneself —*v*. make something by oneself
	自作農	ジサクノウ	landed farmer
	自殺	ジサツ	suicide —*vi*. commit suicide; kill oneself
	自賛	ジサン	self-praise; narcissism —*vi*. praise oneself
	自首	ジシュ	surrendering —*vi*. give oneself up; surrender

自習	ジシュウ	self-study; learning by oneself —*vi.* teach oneself; study by oneself
自主的	ジシュテキ	independent; autonomous
自身	ジシン	oneself; personally; in person
自信	ジシン	self-confidence; confidence
自制	ジセイ	self-control —*v.* control one's emotions
自省	ジセイ	reflection; self-examination —*vi.* examine oneself
自責	ジセキ	self-reproach —*vi.* reproach oneself; have a guilty conscious
自説	ジセツ	one's own view/opinion
自然	シゼン	nature; natural; spontaneous; automatic
自然界	シゼンカイ	nature; the natural world
自然科学	シゼンカガク	natural science
自然現象	シゼンゲンショウ	natural phenomenon
自然主義	シゼンシュギ	naturalism
自然林	シゼンリン	natural/virgin forest
自尊心	ジソンシン	pride; self-respect
自他	ジタ	oneself and others; other people and oneself
自体	ジタイ	itself; the thing itself; one's own body
自宅	ジタク	one's house/home
自治	ジチ	self-government; autonomy
自治会	ジチカイ	student/town council
自治体	ジチタイ	self-governing body
自重	ジチョウ	self-respect; self-love —*vi.* be prudent
自転	ジテン	rotation —*vi.* rotate; revolve
自転車	ジテンシャ	bicycle
自伝	ジデン	autobiography
自動	ジドウ	automatic; mechanical
自動車	ジドウシャ	car; automobile; motorcar
自動的	ジドウテキ	automatically; mechanically
自認	ジニン	acknowledgment —*v.* acknowledge
自白	ジハク	confession —*v.* confess; make a confession
自発的	ジハツテキ	voluntarily; of one's own volition
自費	ジヒ	one's own expense
自筆	ジヒツ	one's own handwriting
自負	ジフ	self-confidence —*vi.* be self-confident
自分	ジブン	oneself; myself; me; I
自分自身	ジブンジシン	oneself; I; myself
自弁	ジベン	at one's own expenses —*v.* pay one's own way
自明	ジメイ	self-evidence; truism
自問自答	ジモンジトウ	questioning oneself; monolog —*vi.* talk to oneself

竹米糸羊羽老耂耒耳肉自至舌舟色虫血行衣衤西艮

自由	ジユウ	freedom; liberty
自力	ジリキ	self-effort; one's own efforts
自立	ジリツ	independence —*vi.* become independent; stand on one's feet
自律	ジリツ	autonomy —*vi.* be autonomous
訓 自ら	みずから	oneself

---

6 至　いたる　arriving

835

一 丆 云 至 至 至

⑥

音 至	シ	arrive; reach; extend
熟 至急	シキュウ	emergency; urgent; prompt
至近	シキン	point-blank; close range
至芸	シゲイ	unrivaled performance
至言	シゲン	wise saying
至高	シコウ	supremacy; highest; tallest
至極	シゴク	very; extremely
至上	シジョウ	supreme; urgent
至誠	シセイ	true sincerity; great devotion
至当	シトウ	highly appropriate; proper; right
至難	シナン	most difficult; almost impossible
至福	シフク	supreme bliss
至便	シベン	most convenient
至宝	シホウ	great treasure; valuable asset
訓 至る	いたる	*vi.* reach; arrive; come; extend; result in
至る所	いたるところ	everywhere; all over; throughout

---

6 舌　した　tongue

836

一 二 千 千 舌 舌

⑥

| 音 舌 | ゼツ | tongue |
| 熟 舌戦 | ゼッセン | verbal contest; war of words; quarrel |

舌頭	ゼットウ	tip of the tongue
訓 舌	した	tongue; language
舌打ち	したうち	clicking one's tongue —*vi.* click one's tongue
舌先	したさき	tip of the tongue
舌足らず	したたらず	unclear/mumbled speech

---

6 舟 ふね／ふねへん ship; boat

837

航 ⑩   ′ 亻 ナ 舟 舟 舟 舟' 舟 舟 航 航

音 航	コウ	cross; sail; navigate; fly; ship; airplane
熟 航海	コウカイ	voyage; navigation; sailing; crossing; passage —*vi.* sail; make a voyage/crossing; navigate; take a passage
航空	コウクウ	aviation; flying; flight; air traffic
航空機	コウクウキ	aircraft; airplane
航空書簡	コウクウショカン	aerogram
航空便	コウクウビン	airmail
航行	コウコウ	navigation; sailing; cruise —*vi.* navigate; sail; cruise
航程	コウテイ	distance covered; passage; flight; lap
航路	コウロ	course; sea route; line; service; run

838

船 ⑪   ′ 亻 ナ 舟 舟 舟 舟' 舟ハ 舟ハ 船 船

音 船	セン	vessel; ship
熟 船医	センイ	ship doctor
船員	センイン	crewman; seaman
船客	センキャク	ship's passenger
船号	センゴウ	ship's name
船室	センシツ	cabin
船主	センシュ	shipowner
船首	センシュ	bow; prow
船体	センタイ	hull; ship
船団	センダン	fleet; convoy
船長	センチョウ	captain
船底	センテイ	bottom of a ship

423

6

	船頭	センドウ	boatman
	船腹	センプク	tonnage; counter for ships; hold; bottoms
訓	船	ふね	ship; boat
	船	ふな	ship; boat
	船歌	ふなうた	chantey; song
	船賃	ふなチン	ship fare
	船出	ふなで	sailing —*vi*. set sail; put out to sea
	船乗り	ふなのり	sailor
	船人	ふなびと	seaman

6 色　いろ　color

839

色 ⑥　ノ ク ク ク 色 色

音	色	シキ	color; looks; sexual love
		ショク	color; aspect
熟	色感	シキカン	sense of color
	色紙	シキシ	square piece of fancy paper
	色弱	シキジャク	partial color blindness
	色情	シキジョウ	sexual desire
	色素	シキソ	pigment
	色調	シキチョウ	tone of color; hue
	色欲	シキヨク	lust; sexual desire
訓	色	いろ	color; complexion; expression; love affair
	色合い	いろあい	shade; hue
	色々	いろいろ	various; many kinds
	色男	いろおとこ	handsome man; ladykiller
	色女	いろおんな	mistress; beautiful woman
	色紙	いろがみ	colored paper
	色気	いろケ	sex appeal; sexual passion; inclination; ambitions
	色づく	いろづく	*vi*. color; turn (red, yellow, etc.); become sexy/attractive
	色っぽい	いろっぽい	sexy; attractive
	色眼鏡	いろめがね	colored/rose-tinted spectacles
	色物	いろもの	colored clothes/fabrics; variety entertainment; variety show

竹米糸羊羽老耂耒耳肉自至舌舟色虫血行衣衤西艮

竹米糸羊羽老耂耒耳肉自至舌舟色虫●血●行衣衤西艮

6 虫 むし insect

840

虫 ⑥

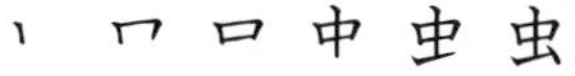

音	虫	チュウ	insect
熟	虫害	チュウガイ	damage done by insects; blight
	虫垂	チュウスイ	***med***. vermiform appendix
訓	虫	むし	insect; bug; worm; feeling
	虫食い	むしくい	vermiculation; damage by worms
	虫歯	むしば	decayed tooth
	虫眼鏡	むしめがね	magnifying glass

841

蚕 ⑩

音	蚕	サン	silkworm
熟	蚕糸	サンシ	silkwork
	蚕食	サンショク	encroachment; aggression —***v***. encroach on; make inroads; eat into
訓	蚕	かいこ	silkworm

6 血 ち blood

842

血 ⑥

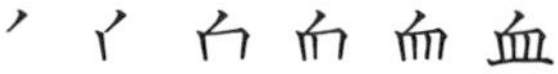

音	血	ケツ	blood
熟	血圧	ケツアツ	***med***. blood pressure
	血液	ケツエキ	***med***. blood
	血液型	ケツエキがた	***med***. blood type/group
	血液銀行	ケツエキギンコウ	***med***. blood bank
	血液検査	ケツエキケンサ	blood test
	血管	ケッカン	***med***. blood vessel
	血気	ケッキ	vigor; hotbloodedness; youthfulness

血球	ケッキュウ	*med*. blood corpuscle
血行	ケッコウ	*med*. circulation of the blood
血小板	ケッショウバン	*med*. (blood) platelet
血色	ケッショク	complexion
血清	ケッセイ	*med*. serum
血税	ケツゼイ	heavy taxes
血戦	ケッセン	bloody battle
血相	ケッソウ	expression
血族	ケツゾク	blood relative
血糖値	ケットウチ	*med*. blood sugar level
血統付き	ケットウつき	pedigreed
血肉	ケツニク	blood and flesh; living things
血便	ケツベン	*med*. bloody excrement
血脈	ケツミャク	*med*. blood vessel

訓
血	ち	blood
血潮	ちしお	blood
血筋	ちすじ	lineage; blood relationship
血走る	ちばしる	be bloodshot
血眼	ちまなこ	bloodshot eyes

843

衆 ⑫　ノ　ハ　ㄇ　血　血　血　血　衆　衆　衆　衆　衆

音 衆
| | シュウ | many; multitude; the people; the masses |
| | （シュ） | many |

熟
衆議	シュウギ	general consultation
衆議院	シュウギイン	the House of Representatives
衆人	シュウジン	the people/public
衆目	シュウモク	public attention
衆生	シュジョウ	*Bud*. living things

---

6 行 ぎょうがまえ　going

844

行 ⑥　ノ　ク　彳　彳　行　行

音 行
| | ギョウ | stroke; line |
| | コウ | go; going; do; exercise; conduct; line |

426

	（アン）	walking tour; pilgrimage	
熟	行間	ギョウカン	between the lines
	行司	ギョウジ	*gyōji* (referee in sumo wrestling)
	行事	ギョウジ	event; function
	行書	ギョウショ	semicursive style of writing *kanji*
	行商	ギョウショウ	peddling; hawking —*v.* peddle; hawk
	行状	ギョウジョウ	behavior; conduct; demeanor
	行水	ギョウズイ	ablution —*vi.* wash oneself
	行列	ギョウレツ	line; queue —*vi.* line up; queue up
	行軍	コウグン	march; marching
	行使	コウシ	exercise; use (of one's authority, etc.) —*v.* use; make use of; employ; exercise
	行進	コウシン	march; parade —*vi.* march; parade; proceed
	行進曲	コウシンキョク	parade; musical march
	行程	コウテイ	journey; distance; itinery
	行動	コウドウ	action; act; conduct; behavior —*vi.* act; behave; conduct; move
	行楽	コウラク	pleasure trip; excursion; picnic; outing
訓	行く	いく	*vi.* go; walk; depart
	行う	おこなう	*vt.* do; perform; conduct; carry out
	行く	ゆく	*vi.* go; pass
	行方	ゆくえ	destination; whereabouts
	行く先	ゆくさき	whereabouts
	行く末	ゆくすえ	future; forthcoming happening
	行手	ゆくて	destination

竹
米
糸
羊
羽
老
耂
耒
耳
肉
自
至
舌
舟
色
虫
血
行 ●
衣
衤
西
艮

845

術 ⑪ 　 ′ ㇒ ㇒ 彳 彳 休 休 術 術 術 術

音	術	ジュツ	means; art; skill
熟	術語	ジュツゴ	technical term; terminology
	術策	ジュッサク	stratagem; trick; artifice
	術中	ジュッチュウ	trick; trap

846

街 ⑫ 　 ′ ㇒ 彳 彳 彳 彳 往 徃 街 街 街

音	街	ガイ	street
		（カイ）	street; highway
熟	街道	カイドウ	highway; high road

竹米糸羊老耂耒耳肉自至舌舟色虫血行衣襾艮

街頭	ガイトウ	street
街灯	ガイトウ	street lamp
街路樹	ガイロジュ	roadside tree; trees lining a street

訓 街　まち　street; downtown

847
衛 ⑯　イ　イ′　イ″　彳″　彳″　街　街　街　徫　衛　衛　衛

音 衛　エイ　defend; guard

熟
衛視	エイシ	Diet guard
衛生	エイセイ	hygiene; sanitation
衛星	エイセイ	satellite
衛星放送	エイセイホウソウ	satellite broadcasting
衛兵	エイヘイ	sentry; guard

6　衣　ころも　clothes　　　　衤　(p.431)

848
衣 ⑥　ヽ　亠　ナ　亡　衣　衣

音 衣　イ　clothes; clothing; garments; robes

熟
衣装	イショウ	costume; apparel; dress
衣食	イショク	food and clothes
衣食住	イショクジュウ	food, clothing, and shelter; living
衣服	イフク	clothing; clothes
衣料	イリョウ	clothing; clothes
衣類	イルイ	clothes; garments

訓
衣	きぬ	clothes
衣	ころも	robes; garments

849
表 ⑧　一　十　丰　圭　主　丰　表　表　表

音 表　ヒョウ　table; chart; surface; express

熟
表する	ヒョウする	express/show (respect, regret, congratulations, etc.)
表意文字	ヒョウイモジ	ideograph; ideogram

428

表音文字	ヒョウオンモジ	phonetic symbol; phonogram
表記	ヒョウキ	written on the face/outside —*v.* write; transcribe; show
表敬訪問	ヒョウケイ ホウモン	courtesy call
表決	ヒョウケツ	vote; voting —*v.* make a decision by vote; vote
表現	ヒョウゲン	expression; representation —*v.* express; represent
表現主義	ヒョウゲンシュギ	expressionism (art, literature, etc.)
表札	ヒョウサツ	nameplate (on a door, gate, etc.)
表紙	ヒョウシ	cover/binding (of a book)
表示	ヒョウジ	indication; sign; expression —*v.* indicate; express; show on a chart; tabulate
表出	ヒョウシュツ	expression —*v.* express (one's feelings)
表象	ヒョウショウ	symbol; emblem; image; idea —*v.* symbolize
表情	ヒョウジョウ	expression
表題	ヒョウダイ	title (of a book, play, etc.); heading; caption
表土	ヒョウド	topsoil
表皮	ヒョウヒ	*med.* cuticle; epidermis
表明	ヒョウメイ	demonstration; manifestation; expression —*v.* demonstrate; show; manifest; express
表面	ヒョウメン	surface; face *fig.* superficial; appearances; pretext
表面化	ヒョウメンカ	coming to the surface —*vi.* come to the surface; attract public attention
表面積	ヒョウメンセキ	surface area
表裏	ヒョウリ	front and back; both sides *fig.* two faced; double-dealer
表裏一体	ヒョウリイッタイ	one and indivisible
訓 表す	あらわす	*vt.* express; show; reveal; manifest
表れる	あらわれる	*vi.* come out; appear; come in sight; show itself; be expressed
表	おもて	surface; right side; public; outside a house *bas.* top of an inning
表立つ	おもてだつ	*vi.* become public; be made public
表向き	おもてむき	openly; publicly; ostensibly; officially

竹 米 糸 羊 羽 老 耂 耒 耳 肉 自 至 舌 舟 色 虫 血 行 衣 衤 西 艮

850

⑫ 一 十 土 耂 圭 耂 耂 耂 表 裁 裁 裁

音 裁	サイ	cut; judge
熟 裁決	サイケツ	decision; verdict —*v.* decide; reach a verdict; judge
裁断	サイダン	cutting; judgment; decision —*v.* cut; decide; judge; pass judgment

竹
米
糸
羊
羽
老
耂
耒
耳
肉
自
至
舟
色
虫
血
行
● 衣
ネ
西
艮

裁定	サイテイ	decision; arbitration —*vt.* decide; judge
裁判	サイバン	trial; suit —*v.* try; judge; put to the courts to decide
裁判官	サイバンカン	judge
裁判権	サイバンケン	jurisdiction
裁判所	サイバンショ	court; law court
裁量	サイリョウ	discretion —*v.* use one's discretion

訓	裁く	さばく	*vt.* judge; sit in judgment; decide; pass verdict; punish
	裁き	さばき	judgment
	裁つ	たつ	*vt.* cut; cut out

851

装 ⑫　
ㅣ 丷 ㇠ 기 채 찬 壯 壯 裝 裝 裝 裝 装

音	装	ソウ	wear; feigh; pretend
		ショウ	
熟	装束	ショウゾク	dress; attire
	装具	ソウグ	equipment
	装身具	ソウシング	personal accessories
	装置	ソウチ	apparatus; device; equipment
	装着	ソウチャク	equipped; installed; fitted with —*v.* equip; instal; fit with
	装丁	ソウテイ	binding
	装備	ソウビ	equipment
訓	装う	よそおう	*vt.* wear; feigh; pretend

852

裏 ⑬　
亠 广 亠 卉 亩 审 审 重 重 裏 裏 裏

音	裏	リ	back; reverse side; opposite; rear
熟	裏面	リメン	back; reverse side; background
訓	裏	うら	back; reverse side
	裏表	うらおもて	both sides; reverse; inside out; two-faced
	裏方	うらかた	lady consort; stagehand
	裏側	うらがわ	back; reverse side; far side (of the moon)
	裏切る	うらぎる	*vt.* betray
	裏口	うらぐち	back door; rear entrance
	裏声	うらごえ	falsetto
	裏地	うらジ	lining

裏付ける	うらづける	*vt.* support; endorse
裏手	うらて	at the back; rear
裏話	うらばなし	inside story
裏腹	うらはら	reverse; opposite
裏町	うらまち	backstreet

853

製 ⑭ 　 ' 　 ⺊ 　 ⺊ 　 ⺊ 　 午 　 朱 　 制 　 制 　 制 　 製 　 製 　 製

音	製	セイ	manufacture; make
熟	製する	セイする	*vt.* manufacture; make
	製材	セイザイ	lumber; sawing
	製作	セイサク	work; manufacturing; production —*v.* work; product; make
	製図	セイズ	draftsmanship; drawing; cartography —*v.* draw; draft
	製造	セイゾウ	manufacturing —*v.* manufacture
	製鉄	セイテツ	iron manufacture
	製糖	セイトウ	sugar manufacture —*vi.* produce sugar
	製版	セイハン	(printing) plate making/engraving
	製品	セイヒン	product; manufactured goods
	製粉	セイフン	flour milling
	製法	セイホウ	manufacturing process; recipe
	製本	セイホン	bookbinding —*v.* bind books
	製薬	セイヤク	pharmacy; manufacturing drugs
	製油	セイユ	refining/processing oil

---

5 ころもへん　clothes at the left

854

補 ⑫ 　 ﹅ 　 ﹅ 　 ﾌ 　 ｲ 　 ネ 　 ネ 　 ネ 　 衤 　 衤 　 補 　 補 　 補

音	補	ホ	assist; supplement
熟	補する	ホする	*vt.* appoint; assign
	補角	ホカク	**math.** supplementary angle
	補完	ホカン	complement; supplement —*v.* complement; supplement
	補記	ホキ	appendage/addition (to an article) —*v.* add/append

	補給	ホキュウ	supply; replenishment —*v.* supply; replenish
	補強	ホキョウ	reinforcement —*v.* reinforce
	補欠	ホケツ	filling a vacancy; substitute; spare
	補血	ホケツ	***med.*** blood replenishment —*vi.* replenish one's blood
	補語	ホゴ	***gram.*** complement
	補修	ホシュウ	repair —*v.* repair; fix; mend
	補習	ホシュウ	supplementary lessons; extracurricular education
	補助	ホジョ	aid; assistance; supplement; subsidy —*v.* help; assist; supplement; subsidize
	補色	ホショク	complementary color
	補正	ホセイ	correction; revision —*v.* correct; revise
	補則	ホソク	supplementary rules
	補足	ホソク	supplement; supply; replenishment —*v.* supplement; supply; replenish
	補導	ホドウ	guidance; advice —*v.* guide; lead; advise
	補任	ホニン	appointment (to a post, vacancy) —*v.* appoint
訓	補う	おぎなう	*vt.* supply; make up/compensate for

855

複 ⑭ 　丶 　フ 　ラ 　ネ 　ネ 　ネ 　衤 　衤 　衤 　衤 　複

音	複	フク	double; multiple; composite
熟	複眼	フクガン	compound eye (of an insect)
	複合	フクゴウ	composite; compound; complex —*v.* compound; pound together
	複合語	フクゴウゴ	***gram.*** compound (word)
	複雑	フクザツ	complicated; complex
	複式	フクシキ	double-entry (bookkeeping)
	複写	フクシャ	copying; duplication; facsimile —*vi.* copy; duplicate
	複数	フクスウ	***gram.*** plural
	複製	フクセイ	reproduction; duplication —*v.* reproduce; duplicate
	複線	フクセン	double track
	複葉	フクヨウ	compound leaf

竹
米
糸
羊
羽
老
耂
耒
耳
肉
自
至
舌
舟
色
虫
血
行
衣
衤
西
艮

●

6 西 にし west

856

西 ⑥　一　 T　万　丙　西　西

音	西	セイ サイ	west
熟	西方	サイホウ	the West; Buddhist paradise
	西経	セイケイ	west longitude
	西方	セイホウ	(the) west; western
	西洋	セイヨウ	Western countries; the West; western; occidental
	西洋化	セイヨウカ	westernization; Europeanization —*v.* become westernized
訓	西	にし	west; western

857

要 ⑨　一　T　万　丙　西　西　亜　要　要

音	要	ヨウ	main point; principal; necessary; essential; important
熟	要する	ヨウする	require; need
	要因	ヨウイン	chief factor; principal cause
	要員	ヨウイン	essential personnel
	要求	ヨウキュウ	demand; requirement —*v.* demand; require
	要件	ヨウケン	requisite; essentials
	要港	ヨウコウ	important/strategic port
	要式	ヨウシキ	formal
	要所	ヨウショ	important/strategic place
	要職	ヨウショク	responsible position; important job
	要人	ヨウジン	leading figure; important person
	要素	ヨウソ	element; factor
	要地	ヨウチ	important strategic place
	要注意	ヨウチュウイ	requiring care/caution
	要点	ヨウテン	main point(s)
	要部	ヨウブ	principal/essential part
	要望	ヨウボウ	demand —*v.* demand
	要務	ヨウム	important business
	要目	ヨウモク	principal items

要約	ヨウヤク	summary —*v.* summarize
要領	ヨウリョウ	gist; purport; synopsis
訓 要る	いる	*vi.* need; cost

---

6 艮　ねづくり／こんづくり　good

858

良 ⑦　　' ウ ヲ ヲ 白 良 良

音	良	リョウ	good
熟	良好	リョウコウ	good; favorable; satisfactory
	良妻	リョウサイ	good wife
	良識	リョウシキ	good sense
	良質	リョウシツ	superior quality
	良種	リョウシュ	good breed; thoroughbred
	良書	リョウショ	good book
	良心	リョウシン	conscience
	良心的	リョウシンテキ	conscientious
	良知	リョウチ	intuition
	良否	リョウヒ	good or bad
	良品	リョウヒン	superior quality goods
	良民	リョウミン	good citizens
	良薬	リョウヤク	effective medicine
訓	良い	よい	good
	良し悪し	よしあし	good or evil; right or wrong; merits and demerits

7 見 みる seeing

859

見 ⑦ 丨 冂 冂 冃 目 貝 見

音	見	ケン	see; view; meet; show
熟	見解	ケンカイ	opinion; view; outlook
	見学	ケンガク	observation; tour (for educational purposes) —*v.* inspect; observe
	見学者	ケンガクシャ	visitor
	見識	ケンシキ	pride; self-respect; judgment; discernment; insight
	見地	ケンチ	standpoint; viewpoint; point of view
	見当	ケントウ	aim; direction; estimate; guess; about; approximately
	見物	ケンブツ	sightseeing —*v.* go sightseeing; see the sights
	見聞	ケンブン	information; experience; observation —*v.* go sightseeing
訓	見る	みる	*vt.* see; watch; look
	見える	みえる	*vi.* be seen; can see; seem to; visit; come; arrive
	見せる	みせる	*vt.* show; display; allow to be watched
	見合い	みあい	small party to introduce two prospective marriage candidates —*vi.* meet each other with a view to marriage
	見送る	みおくる	*vt.* see off one's guest
	見苦しい	みぐるしい	dishonorable; disgraceful; ugly; shabby
	見事	みごと	excellent; fine; splendid; superb; admirable
	見殺し	みごろし	leaving someone to his fate
	見境	みさかい	distinction
	見世物	みせもの	show; sideshow
	見所	みどころ	promise; good points; the point; highlight
	見習う	みならう	*vt.* follow a person's example; learn
	見本	みホン	sample; specimen; example; model
	見舞い	みまい	inquiry; expression of one's sympathy; visit to a sick person

860

規 ⑪ 一 二 ≠ 夫 夹 却 却 担 相 規 規

音	規	キ	regulation; rule

435

熟	規格	キカク	standard; norm
	規準	キジュン	criterion
	規正	キセイ	readjustment; correction; rectification
	規制	キセイ	regulation; control —*v.* regulate; control
	規則	キソク	rule; regulation
	規則的	キソクテキ	regular; systematic
	規定	キテイ	rule; regulations; stipulations; prescriptions —*v.* prescribe; ordain; stipulate
	規模	キボ	scale; scope
	規約	キヤク	rules; bylaws
	規律	キリツ	discipline; regulation; order; rules

861 視 ⑪

丶 ラ ネ ネ ネ 初 初 祁 袒 袒 視

音	視	シ	watch; regard
熟	視界	シカイ	field of vision; visibility; sight
	視覚	シカク	sense of sight
	視覚的	シカクテキ	visual; visually
	視察	シサツ	inspection; observation —*v.* inspection; make an inspection
	視察員	シサツイン	observer
	視線	シセン	one's gaze; one's line of vision
	視点	シテン	point of view; viewpoint
	視野	シヤ	field of vision; range of view; one's view
	視力	シリョク	sight; eyesight; vision
	視力検査	シリョクケンサ	eye test

862 覚 ⑫

丶 ツ ツ ツ ⺍ 学 学 党 覚 覚 覚 覚

音	覚	カク	sense; feel; comprehend
訓	覚える	おぼえる	*vi.* feel; remember; learn
	覚ます	さます	*vt.* awake; wake up
	覚める	さめる	*vi.* wake up; become sober; be enlightened

863

親 ⑯ 　 ㅗ　ㅜ　㔾　立　辛　辛　辛　亲　新　親　親　親

音	親	シン	parent; intimate
熟	親愛	シンアイ	affection; love
	親衛隊	シンエイタイ	bodyguards
	親近感	シンキンカン	sense of closeness
	親権	シンケン	parental authority
	親交	シンコウ	intimacy; friendship
	親切	シンセツ	kind; kindhearted; good; nice
	親善	シンゼン	friendship; goodwill
	親族	シンゾク	relative; relation
	親展	シンテン	confidential; personal
	親等	シントウ	degree of kinship
	親身	シンミ	kind; warm; tender; blood relation
	親密	シンミツ	intimacy; close friendship
	親友	シンユウ	bosom/close/good friend
	親類	シンルイ	relative; relation
	親和	シンワ	friendship; affinity
訓	親	おや	parent
	親方	おやかた	boss; foreman; master; home; parents
	親孝行	おやコウコウ	filial devotion/piety
	親心	おやごころ	parental love
	親父	おやじ	father; old man; the boss
	親潮	おやしお	Kurile Current
	親分	おやブン	gang leader; boss
	親元	おやもと	one's parents/home
	親指	おやゆび	thumb; big toe
	親しい	したしい	intimate; close; friendy; familiar
	親しむ	したしむ	*vi*. become familiar with; get to know; make friends with

864

覧 ⑰ 　 丨　厂　厂　戸　臣　臣　臣　臤　臤　臤　覧　覧

音	覧	ラン	inspect; see; look at

437

865

観 ⑱ ⺊ ⺊ ⺊ ⺊ ⺊ ⺊ 芹 雈 観 観 観 観

音	観	カン	observe; view; see; look
熟	観客	カンキャク	spectators
	観劇	カンゲキ	theatergoing —*v.* go to the theater; see a play
	観光	カンコウ	sightseeing; tourism —*v.* go sightseeing
	観光客	カンコウキャク	tourist
	観察	カンサツ	observation —*v.* observe; view; make observations
	観衆	カンシュウ	spectators; audience
	観賞	カンショウ	enjoyment; admiration —*v.* enjoy; admire
	観戦	カンセン	watch a battle/competition/contest
	観測	カンソク	observation; survey —*v.* observe; make an observation; survey
	観点	カンテン	standpoint; viewpoint; point of view
	観念	カンネン	idea; conception; notion
	観念的	カンネンテキ	ideal; ideological
	観音	カンノン	Kwannon, Avalokitesvara (Buddhist goddess of mercy)
	観望	カンボウ	sightseeing
	観覧	カンラン	viewing; inspection —*v.* view; inspect

7 角 つの horn

866

角 ⑦ ノ ク ケ 疒 角 角 角

音	角	カク	horn; angle; corner
熟	角界	カクカイ（カッカイ）	sumo wrestling world
	角材	カクザイ	square lumber
	角柱	カクチュウ	square pillar; prism
	角度	カクド	**math**. geometric angle
	角張る	カクばる	*vi.* be angular/square/sharp; become formal/ceremonious
訓	角	かど	corner; angle
	角	つの	animal's horn

解 ⑬ ⁿ ⁷ ⁿ 角 角 角 角ʳ 解ʳ 解ʳ 解ʳ 解

音	解	カイ	solve; untie; melt; understand; explain
		ゲ	realize; untie; melt
熟	解する	カイする	*vt*. interpret; understand
	解決	カイケツ	solution; settlement; conclusion —*v*. solve; settle; conclude
	解散	カイサン	breakup; dispersion —*v*. break up; disperse
	解除	カイジョ	release; cancellation; removal —*v*. release; cancel; remove
	解消	カイショウ	dissolution; cancellation; liquidation —*v*. dissolve; cancel; liquidate
	解説	カイセツ	commentary; explanation —*v*. make a commentary; explain
	解答	カイトウ	solution; answer —*vi*. solve; answer
	解読	カイドク	deciphering; decoding —*v*. decipher; decode
	解放	カイホウ	release; emancipation; liberation —*v*. release; emancipate; liberate
	解明	カイメイ	elucidation; solution —*v*. elucidate; solve
	解せない	ゲせない	incomprehensible
訓	解く	とく	*vt*. untie; relieve; answer; construe
	解かす	とかす	*vt*. melt
	解ける	とける	*vi*. loose; be dispelled; be relieved; melt
	解く	ほどく	*vt*. untie; undo; unfasten; loosen

---

7 言 げん／ごんべん word

868

言 ⑦ 丶 亠 三 言 言 言 言

音	言	ゲン	say; speak; word; language
		ゴン	word
熟	言外	ゲンガイ	implied; hinted
	言語	ゲンゴ	language; speech
	言語学	ゲンゴガク	linguistics
	言行	ゲンコウ	words and deeds; speech and behavior
	言質	ゲンシツ	pledge; promise
	言上	ゲンジョウ	statement —*vt*. state; convey

439

言動	ゲンドウ	speech and action; p's and q's
言明	ゲンメイ	declaration; assertion; positive statement —*v.* declare; assert; make a positive statement
言論	ゲンロン	expression of one's opinion through speech or writing
言論界	ゲンロンカイ	press; media
言論機関	ゲンロンキカン	organ of public opinion
言語道断	ゴンゴドウダン	outrageous; unspeakable; abominable; shocking
訓 言い返す	いいかえす	*vt.* talk back; retort
言い方	いいかた	expression; how to speak; one's words
言い張る	いいはる	*vt.* insist on
言い回し	いいまわし	(mode of) expression
言い訳	いいわけ	explanation; excuse; apology
言う	いう	*vt.* speak; say; mention; talk
言	こと	word
言伝て	ことづて	message
言葉	ことば	word; language; speech; phrase; statement

869

警 ⑲ 一 サ ナ 芍 苟 苟 荀 敬 敬 警 警 警

音 警	ケイ	warn; guard; vigilance; caution
熟 警句	ケイク	aphorism; epigram
警護	ケイゴ	guard —*v.* guard
警告	ケイコク	warning; caution —*v.* warn; caution; advise
警察	ケイサツ	police
警察官	ケイサツカン	policeman
警察署	ケイサツショ	police station
警察庁	ケイサツチョウ	National Police Agency
警笛	ケイテキ	horn; alarm whistle; foghorn
警備	ケイビ	guard; defense —*v.* guard; defend; keep guard
警備員	ケイビイン	security guard
警報	ケイホウ	alarm; warning

870

計 ⑨ 、 一 二 三 言 言 言 言 計

| 音 計 | ケイ | count; measure; plan; estimate; gauge |
| 熟 計画 | ケイカク | plan; project; scheme —*v.* plan; project; scheme |

440

計画的	ケイカクテキ	planned; scheduled; premeditated
計器	ケイキ	meter; gauge
計算	ケイサン	calculation; computation —*v.* calculate; compute; figure out; reckon
計算機	ケイサンキ	computer; calculator
計上	ケイジョウ	summing/adding up; aggregate —*v.* sum/add up; appropriate
計略	ケイリャク	stratagem; scheme; trick; plot
計量	ケイリョウ	weighing; measuring; gauging —*v.* weigh; measure; gauge
訓 計る	はかる	*vt.* time; measure; judge; estimate; guess
計り	はかり	measure; weight; scales
計らう	はからう	*vt.* take care; settle; handle

871

記 ⑩ 　 ` 　 ニ 　 三 　 言 　 言 　 言 　 言 　 訂 　 訂 　 記

音 記	キ	write down; record; note; remember
熟 記号	キゴウ	mark; sign; symbol
記事	キジ	news story/article
記者	キシャ	reporter; writer
記述	キジュツ	description; account —*v.* describe; give an account of
記帳	キチョウ	record; entry —*vt.* record; enter; register
記入	キニュウ	recording; entering —*v.* enter; make an entry; record; fill in
記念	キネン	commemoration; remembrance —*v.* commemorate; honor the memory of
記念日	キネンび	anniversary
記名	キメイ	signature —*v.* sign one's name
記録	キロク	record; document; archives —*v.* record; register; write down
記録的	キロクテキ	record-breaking
訓 記す	しるす	*vt.* write down; record; note

872

訓 ⑩ 　 ` 　 ニ 　 三 　 言 　 言 　 言 　 言 　 訓 　 訓 　 訓

音 訓	クン	teaching; lead; guide
熟 訓示	クンジ	instruction —*vi.* instruct
訓辞	クンジ	admonitory speech —*v.* give an admonitory speech

441

訓令	クンレイ	instructions; order; directive —*vi*. instruct; order; direct
訓練	クンレン	training; drill; practice —*v*. train; drill; practice
訓話	クンワ	moral discourse —*vi*. discuss morals

873

討 ⑩ ` ｽ ｽ ₹ ₹ ₹ 言 言 訂 討 討

音	討	トウ	attack
熟	討議	トウギ	discussion; debate; deliberation —*v*. discuss; deliberate; debate; hold a discussion
	討論	トウロン	debate; discussion; talk —*v*. debate; discuss; talk
	討論会	トウロンカイ	forum; discussion
訓	討つ	うつ	*vt*. strike; hit; attack; subjugate; conquer

874

許 ⑪ ` ｽ ｽ ₹ ₹ ₹ 言 言 計 計 許

音	許	キョ	forgive; permit; allow
熟	許可	キョカ	permission; license —*v*. permit; license; sanction
	許容	キョヨウ	permission; allowance; permit —*v*. permit; allow
訓	許す	ゆるす	*vt*. forgive; allow; permit; approve

875

設 ⑪ ` ｽ ｽ ₹ ₹ 言 言 計 訳 設 設

音	設	セツ	set up; establish; provide; prepare
熟	設営	セツエイ	construction; preparations —*v*. put up (a tent, etc.)
	設計	セッケイ	design; planning —*v*. design; plan
	設置	セッチ	establishment; founding; institution —*v*. establish; found
	設定	セッテイ	fixation; establishment; creation —*v*. fix; establish; create
	設備	セツビ	facilities; equipment; accommodations —*v*. facilitate; equip; accommodate
	設問	セツモン	question —*vi*. ask questions; question
	設立	セツリツ	founding; establishment —*v*. found; establish
訓	設ける	もうける	*vt*. prepare; provide; establish; set up

876 訪 ⑪
` ⺊ ⻌ 訁 訁 言 言 言' 訮 訪 訪

音	訪	ホウ	visit
熟	訪客	ホウキャク	visitor; guest
	訪日	ホウニチ	visiting Japan
	訪問	ホウモン	visiting; visit —v. visit
訓	訪れる	おとずれる	*vi.* visit
	訪ねる	たずねる	*vt.* visit

877 訳 ⑪
` ⺊ ⻌ 訁 訁 言 言 訂 訳 訳 訳

音	訳	ヤク	translation
熟	訳する	ヤクする	*vt.* translate
	訳語	ヤクゴ	*gram.* translated term; equivalent
	訳者	ヤクシャ	translator
	訳文	ヤクブン	translation; translated literature
訓	訳	わけ	meaning; reason; cause; meaning; circumstances; the case
	訳無い	わけない	easy; simple

878 詞 ⑫
` ⺊ ⻌ 訁 訁 言 言 訂 訂 訶 詞 詞

音	詞	シ	word; writing

879 証 ⑫
` ⺊ ⻌ 訁 訁 言 言 訂 訂 訮 証 証

音	証	ショウ	proof
熟	証する	ショウする	*vt.* prove; guarantee; supply evidence
	証言	ショウゲン	testimony —v. testify; give evidence
	証書	ショウショ	bond; deed; certificate
	証人	ショウニン	witness; guarantor

見角言谷豕豸貝赤走足⻊身車辛辰酉里臣

証明	ショウメイ	proof; evidence; testimony; demonstration —*v.* prove; testify; certify; demonstrate
証明書	ショウメイショ	certificate
証文	ショウモン	bond; deed

880 評 ⑫
` ゝ ｽ ㍘ 言 言 言 訢 訅 評 評

音	評	ヒョウ	criticism; comment
熟	評する	ヒョウする	*vt.* criticize; comment on; speak of (a person) as
	評価	ヒョウカ	valuation; estimate; assessment; evaluation; appraisal —*v.* value; estimate; assess; evaluate; appraise
	評議	ヒョウギ	conference; discussion; council; meeting —*v.* hold a conference/council/meeting; discuss
	評決	ヒョウケツ	verdict (of guilty/not guilty) —*v.* pronounce a verdict; sentence
	評者	ヒョウシャ	critic; reviewer
	評注	ヒョウチュウ	annotation; (critical) notes —*v.* annotate
	評定	ヒョウテイ	evaluation; rating —*v.* evaluate; rate
	評点	ヒョウテン	(examination) marks/grades
	評判	ヒョウバン	(public) estimation; reputation; popularity; rumor; gossip; fame
	評論	ヒョウロン	criticism; review; comment —*v.* review; comment
	評論家	ヒョウロンカ	critic; reviewer; commentator; publicist

881 試 ⑬
` ゝ ㍘ 言 言 言 訪 訣 訣 試 試

音	試	シ	try
熟	試合	シあい	match; game; tournament —*vi.* play/have a match/game; have a tournament
	試案	シアン	tentative plan; proposal
	試運転	シウンテン	test/trial run —*v.* make a test/trial run; run a trial
	試金石	シキンセキ	touchstone; test; test case
	試験	シケン	examination; test; experiment —*v.* experiment; put a thing to the test; test
	試験管	シケンカン	test tube
	試験的	シケンテキ	experimental; tentative
	試作	シサク	trial manufacture/production —*v.* make on an experimental basis

試作品	シサクヒン	trial product
試写	シシャ	preview —*v.* give/hold a preview of
試乗	シジョウ	test ride/drive —*v.* test drive a car
試食	シショク	tasting; sampling —*v.* taste; sample; try
試着	シチャク	trying clothes on —*v.* try on
試着室	シチャクシツ	fitting room
試用	シヨウ	trial —*v.* try; make a trial
試練	シレン	ordeal; trial
訓 試みる	こころみる	*vt.* try; attempt
試み	こころみ	trial; test; experiment; temptation (biblical sense)
試す	ためす	*vt.* test; try

882

詩 ⑬ 　 ` 　 亠 　 ミ 　 言 　 言 　 言 　 言 　 計 　 計 　 計 　 詩 　 詩

音	詩	シ	poetry; verse; Chinese poem
熟	詩歌	シイカ	poetry; verse
	詩作	シサク	writing poetry —*vi.* write poetry
	詩集	シシュウ	collection of poems; poetry anthology
	詩情	シジョウ	poetic sentiment
	詩人	シジン	poet
	詩的	シテキ	poetic

883

誠 ⑬ 　 ` 　 亠 　 ミ 　 言 　 言 　 言 　 訂 　 訂 　 訪 　 誠 　 誠 　 誠

音	誠	セイ	sincerity; fidelity; truth
熟	誠意	セイイ	sincerity; good faith
	誠実	セイジツ	sincere; faithful; loyal
訓	誠	まこと	sincerity; fidelity; truth

884

話 ⑬ 　 ` 　 亠 　 ミ 　 言 　 言 　 言 　 訂 　 訐 　 計 　 話 　 話

音	話	ワ	story; conversation; talk
熟	話術	ワジュツ	storytelling
	話題	ワダイ	topic; subject (of a story/discussion)

見角言谷豆豕貝赤走足𧾷身車辛辰酉里臣 •

| 話法 | ワホウ | speech; parlance |

訓
話	はなし	talk; conversation; story
話す	はなす	*vt.* talk; speak
話し中	はなしチュウ	while speaking; (phone is) busy/engaged
話し手	はなして	speaker

885

語 ⑭ 　二 ﾖ ﾖ 言 言 訂 訓 訝 語 語 語 語

音
| 語 | ゴ | speak; word; language |

熟
語意	ゴイ	meaning of a word
語学	ゴガク	linguistics; language study
語感	ゴカン	nuance; shade of meaning
語気	ゴキ	tone of voice
語義	ゴギ	mearing of a word
語句	ゴク	words and phrases
語源	ゴゲン	etymology
語順	ゴジュン	*gram.* word order
語調	ゴチョウ	tone of voice
語法	ゴホウ	diction; usage; expression; wording
語録	ゴロク	analects; collection of sayings

訓
| 語る | かたる | *vt.* talk; recite; narrate |
| 語らう | かたらう | *vt.* talk over |

886

誤 ⑭ 　二 ﾖ ﾖ 言 言 訂 訳 誤 誤 誤 誤

音
| 誤 | ゴ | mistake; error |

熟
誤解	ゴカイ	misunderstanding —*v.* misunderstand
誤差	ゴサ	error; difference; margin of error; tolerance
誤算	ゴサン	miscalculation —*vi.* miscalculate
誤字	ゴジ	wrong letter; erratum; misprint
誤報	ゴホウ	false report; misinformation
誤訳	ゴヤク	mistranslation —*v.* mistranslate; make an error in translation
誤用	ゴヨウ	misuse —*v.* misuse; use improperly

訓
| 誤る | あやまる | *v.* err; make a mistake |
| 誤り | あやまり | mistake; error |

887
誌 ⑭
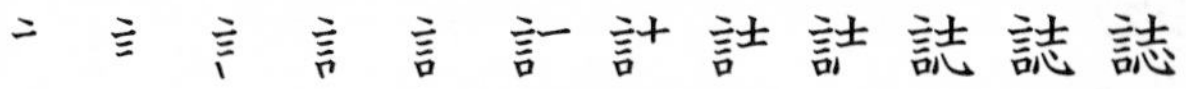

音	誌	シ	record; magazine
熟	誌上	シジョウ	in a magazine
	誌面	シメン	in a magazine

888
説 ⑭
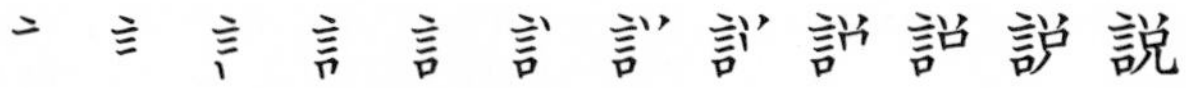

音	説	セツ	explain; view; theory; opinion
		（ゼイ）	explain; persuade
熟	説教	セッキョウ	preaching; sermon —*vi*. preach; sermonize
	説得	セットク	persuasion —*v*. persuade
	説明	セツメイ	explanation —*v*. explain
	説明文	セツメイブン	written explanation
	説話	セツワ	legend; tale; narrative
訓	説く	とく	*v*. explain; persuade

889
読 ⑭
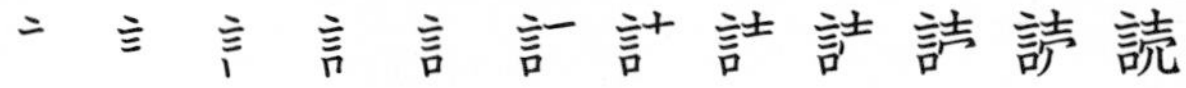

音	読	ドク	read
		トク	read
		（トウ）	
熟	読点	トウテン	comma
	読経	ドキョウ	sutra-chanting —*vi*. chant sutras
	読者	ドクシャ	reader (of books)
	読書	ドクショ	reading —*vi*. read books
	読破	ドクハ	reading through a book —*v*. read/go through a book
	読本	トクホン	reader; reading book
訓	読む	よむ	*vt*. read; peruse; chant; recite
	読み	よみ	reading; judgment; calculation
	読み書き	よみかき	reading and writing
	読み方	よみかた	reading; pronunciation
	読み切る	よみきる	*vt*. read through; finish reading
	読み物	よみもの	reading; reading matter; literature

890

認 ⑭ 　ニ　ミ　言　言　言　訂　訒　訒　認　認　認　認

音	認	ニン	recognize; approve; consent
熟	認可	ニンカ	sanction; approval; authorization; license; permission —v. approve; authorize; permit
	認識	ニンシキ	recognition; cognition; perception; knowledge; understanding —v. recognize; cognize; perceive; know; understand
	認証	ニンショウ	authentication; certification; validation; confirmation —v. certify; atest; authenticate; confirm
	認知	ニンチ	recognition; acknowledgment —v. recognize; acknowledge
	認定	ニンテイ	recognition; acknowledgment; identity —v. admit; recognize; find; deem
	認容	ニンヨウ	admission; acknowledgment —v. admit; acknowledge; accept
訓	認める	みとめる	vt. see; witness; recognize; approve; accept; judge; conclude

891

課 ⑮ 　ニ　ミ　言　言　訂　訊　訊　訊　課　課　課　課

音	課	カ	allot; section; impose
熟	課外	カガイ	extracurricular
	課業	カギョウ	class lesson
	課題	カダイ	subject; theme; problem; task; assignment
	課長	カチョウ	section chief
	課程	カテイ	curriculum
	課目	カモク	subject
訓	課す	かす	vt. impose; assign
¥	課税	カゼイ	imposition of taxes —vi. impose taxes
	課徴金	カチョウキン	surcharge

892

諸 ⑮ 　ニ　ミ　言　言　言　計　詳　詳　諸　諸　諸　諸

音	諸	ショ	various
熟	諸行無常	ショギョウ ムジョウ	all things pass; everything is transient

諸君	ショクン	Gentlemen!; Ladies and gentlemen!; Boys and girls!; Boys!
諸芸	ショゲイ	accomplishments
諸国	ショコク	various countries
諸説	ショセツ	various views
諸島	ショトウ	archipelago; group of islands

893 誕 ⑮

⎯ ⎯ ⎯ ⎯ ⎯ ⎯ ⎯ ⎯ ⎯ ⎯ 誕 誕 誕

音 誕　　タン　　be born

熟 誕生　　タンジョウ　　birth; nativity ―**vi**. be born; come into the world

　　誕生日　　タンジョウび　　birthday

894 談 ⑮

⎯ ⎯ ⎯ ⎯ ⎯ ⎯ ⎯ 談 談 談 談 談

音 談　　ダン　　talk; conversation; story; tale

熟 談じる　　ダンじる　　**vt**. talk

　　談合　　ダンゴウ　　consultation; conference ―**vi**. consult; confer

　　談笑　　ダンショウ　　chat; intimate conversation ―**vi**. chat

　　談判　　ダンパン　　negotiation; bargaining ―**vi**. negotiate; bargain

　　談話　　ダンワ　　talk; conversation ―**vi**. talk; chat; converse

895 調 ⑮

⎯ ⎯ ⎯ ⎯ ⎯ 訓 訓 詞 調 調 調 調

音 調　　チョウ　　inspect; survey; examine; tune; tone; pitch

熟 調印　　チョウイン　　signing; signature; sealing ―**vi**. sign; seal

　　調教　　チョウキョウ　　horse training/breaking; train a wild animal ―**v**. break in a horse; train a wild animal

　　調合　　チョウゴウ　　compounding; mixing; preparation; concoction ―**v**. compound; mix; prepare; concoct

　　調査　　チョウサ　　examination; investigation; inquiry; survey; research ―**v**. investigate; inquire; survey

　　調子　　チョウシ　　tune; tone; key; way; manner; style; condition; order

　　調子者　　チョウシもの　　person who is easily carried away

449

見
角
言
●
谷
豆
豕
貝
赤
走
足
⻊
身
車
辛
辰
酉
里
臣

調書	チョウショ	protocol; written evidence; record
調整	チョウセイ	regulation; adjustment; correction; modulation; tuning —v. regulate; adjust; rectify; govern; control
調節	チョウセツ	regulation; adjustment; control; governing —v. regulate; adjust; control; govern
調達	チョウタツ	supply; procurement; provision —v. supply; provide; furnish; purvey; procure
調停	チョウテイ	mediation; arbitration; intercession —v. mediate; arbitrate; intercede; intervene
調度品	チョウドヒン	personal/household effects; furniture
調味	チョウミ	seasoning; flavoring —v. season; flavor; spice
調味料	チョウミリョウ	seasoning; flavoring
調理	チョウリ	cooking; cookery —v. cook; arrange; organize
調律	チョウリツ	tuning (a musical instrument) —v. tune (a musical instrument)
調律師	チョウリツシ	piano tuner
調和	チョウワ	harmony; accord; agreement —v. harmonize; match; agree; fit in well

訓

調べる	しらべる	vt. investigate; examine; survey; inspect; check
調べ	しらべ	melody
調う	ととのう	vi. be prepared/arranged/settled/concluded
調える	ととのえる	vt. prepare; make ready; arrange; settle; conclude

896

論 ⑮ 　 亠 言 言 言 訃 訃 論 論 論 論 論

音 論　ロン　argument; discussion; thesis

熟

論じる	ロンじる	vt. discuss; argue; dispute; debate
論外	ロンガイ	out of the question; irrelevant
論客	ロンカク (ロンキャク)	disputant; polemicist
論議	ロンギ	discussion; argument —v. discuss; argue
論告	ロンコク	prosecutor's summation —v. address (the court) for the last time
論述	ロンジュツ	statement; enunciation —v. set forth; enunciate; state
論証	ロンショウ	proof/demonstration (by argument) —v. proof/demonstrate (by argument)
論説	ロンセツ	editorial; dissertation
論戦	ロンセン	verbal battle; war of words —vi. have a verbal battle; exchange views
論争	ロンソウ	argument; dispute; controversy —v. argue; dispute

450

論点	ロンテン	point at issue
論破	ロンパ	refutation —*v.* refute
論評	ロンピョウ	criticism; comment; review —*v.* criticize; comment; review
論文	ロンブン	thesis; essay
論弁	ロンベン	argument —*vi.* argue
論法	ロンボウ	argument; reasoning; logic
論理	ロンリ	logic

897

講 ⑰

`⊃ ⸓ 言 訁 訁 訃 訃 諽 講 講 講 講 講`

音	講	コウ	lecture; speech; interpretation; training
熟	講じる	コウじる	*vt.* lecture; give a speech; read out aloud; devise; workout
	講演	コウエン	lecture; address; discourse; talk —*vi.* give a lecture; address; lecture
	講義	コウギ	lecture; exposition; explanation —*v.* lecture on; give a lecture
	講師	コウシ	lecturer; speaker; reader; instructor
	講習	コウシュウ	short course; class
	講談	コウダン	storytelling; narration
	講堂	コウドウ	auditorium; lecture hall/theater
	講読	コウドク	exigesis/study of sutras
	講評	コウヒョウ	criticism; commentary; review —*v.* criticize; comment on; review
	講和	コウワ	peace; reconciliation —*vi.* make peace; bury the hatchet
	講話	コウワ	lecture; discourse; address —*vi.* lecture; deliver a lecture; address

898

謝 ⑰

`⊃ ⸓ 言 訁 訃 訇 訇 謝 諽 謝 謝`

音	謝	シャ	thanks; apologize; decline; refuse
熟	謝する	しゃする	*vt.* thank a person for their help; apologize; decline; refuse
	謝意	シャイ	gratitude; thanks; apology
	謝恩	シャオン	expression of gratitude; appreciation
	謝金	シャキン	honorarium
	謝罪	シャザイ	apology —*vi.* apologize; beg a person's forgiveness
	謝罪状	シャザイジョウ	written apology

451

見
角
言
谷
豆
豕
貝
赤
走
足
⻊
身
車
辛
辰
酉
里
臣

謝辞	シャジ	address of gratitude; a few words of thanks; apology
謝状	シャジョウ	letter of thanks/apology
謝絶	シャゼツ	refusal —v. refuse; decline
謝肉祭	シャニクサイ	carnival
謝礼	シャレイ	thanks; reward; renumeration
訓 謝る	あやまる	v. apologize

899

識 ⑲　　　一　三　言　言　言′　計　評　評　語　諳　識　識　識

音 識	シキ	discern; sight; consciousness
熟 識見	シキケン	discernment; judgment; insight; view; opinion
識者	シキシャ	intellectual; person of intelligence; intelligentsia
識別	シキベツ	discrimination —v. discriminate; distinguish; tell apart

900

議 ⑳　　　一　言　言　言′　計′　詳　詳　詳　議　議　議

音 議	ギ	talk over; consultation
熟 議する	ギする	vt. talk over; consult
議案	ギアン	bill; measure; proposal for discussion
議員	ギイン	elected representative; Diet member
議院	ギイン	houses of parliament; lower and upper houses
議会	ギカイ	assembly; national assembly; Diet
議決	ギケツ	decision; resolution —v. decide; resolve; pass a vote
議事	ギジ	proceedings; agenda
議事堂	ギジドウ	Diet building
議席	ギセキ	parlimentary seat
議題	ギダイ	subject for discussion; agenda; program
議長	ギチョウ	chairperson; president; speaker
議論	ギロン	argument; discussion; debate; dispute —v. argue; discuss; debate; dispute
訓 議る	はかる	vt. consult; confer; deliberate

901

護 ⑳ 　 ニ　ニ　言　言　言'　言'　言'　言'　誰　誰　護　護

音	護	ゴ	protect; guard
熟	護衛	ゴエイ	bodyguard; escort —v. guard; escort
	護身	ゴシン	self-protection/-defense
	護送	ゴソウ	escort —v. escort; send under guard
訓	護る	まもる	**vt**. protect; guard

---

7 谷 たに valley

902

谷 ⑦ 　 ′　ハ　グ　父　父　谷　谷

音	谷	コク	valley; river valley; ravine
訓	谷	たに	valley
	谷底	たにぞこ	the bottom of ravine; valley floor
	谷間	たにま	ravine; gorge; chasm; valley

---

7 豆 まめ bean

903

豆 ⑦ 　 一　厂　一　豆　戸　豆　豆

音	豆	トウ （ズ）	bean
熟	豆乳	トウニュウ	soya milk
訓	豆	まめ	bean; pea; soybean
	豆知識	まめチシキ	bits of knowledge/information
	豆電球	まめデンキュウ	miniature/small bulb

453

見
角
言
谷
● 豆
● 豕
● 貝
赤
走
足
⻊
身
車
辛
辰
酉
里
臣

904

豊 ⑬ 　 丶 冂 曲 曲 曲 曲 曲 豊 豊 豊 豊 豊

音	豊	ホウ	abundant; rich
熟	豊作	ホウサク	good/abundant harvest
	豊熟	ホウジュク	ripening of crops —*vi.* (crops) ripen abundantly
	豊年	ホウネン	fruitful/good year
	豊富	ホウフ	abundance; affluence
	豊満	ホウマン	plump; corpulent; full-figured
	豊漁	ホウリョウ	big/abundant catch (of fish)
訓	豊か	ゆたか	abundant; rich

7 豕　ぶた／いのこ　pig

905

象 ⑫ 　 ノ ⺈ ⼙ 冎 冎 台 争 争 象 象 象 象

音	象	ショウ	shape
	象	ゾウ	elephant
熟	象形	ショウケイ	hieroglyph
	象形文字	ショウケイモジ	hieroglyphic

7 貝　かい／かいへん　shell

906

貝 ⑦ 　 丨 冂 冂 月 目 貝 貝

音	貝	（バイ）	shellfish; shell
訓	貝	かい	shellfish; shell
	貝細工	かいザイク	shellwork

907

負 ⑨ ノ ク ケ 豸 豸 角 角 負 負

音	負	フ	bear; suffer; sustain; lose; be defeated
熟	負荷	フカ	bearing a burden; taking over a company
	負傷	フショウ	wound; injury —*vi.* be wounded; get injured
	負数	フスウ	***math.*** minus/negative number
	負担	フタン	charge; responsibilty; burden; onus —*v.* bear; stand; shoulder; carry
訓	負ける	まける	*vi.* be defeated/beaten/overcome/daunted *vt.* make something cheap
	負かす	まかす	*vt.* beat; defeat; vanquish; get the better of
	負う	おう	*vt.* bear; carry; be charged/accused of; suffer; sustain

908

貨 ⑪ ノ イ イ 化 化 化 作 貨 貨 貨 貨

音	貨	カ	goods; coin
熟	貨客船	カキャクセン	cargo-passenger ship
	貨車	カシャ	freight car; goods wagon

909

責 ⑪ 一 十 キ 主 丰 青 青 青 青 青 責

音	責	セキ	condemn; censure; torture
熟	責任	セキニン	responsibility; liability
	責任感	セキニンカン	sense of responsibility
	責務	セキム	duty; obligation
訓	責める	せめる	*vt.* duty

910

貧 ⑪ ノ 八 分 分 分 分 咎 咎 咎 貧 貧

音	貧	ヒン	poverty
		ビン	poor
熟	貧苦	ヒンク	poverty; hardship of poverty

	貧血	ヒンケツ	*med*. anemia —*vi*. be anemic; suffer from anemia
	貧困	ヒンコン	poverty *fig*. lack (of proper government, ideas, etc.)
	貧者	ヒンジャ	poor person; the poor
	貧弱	ヒンジャク	poverty; poor; weak; shabby; feeble; scanty; meager
	貧相	ヒンソウ	poor appearance; poor-looking
	貧富	ヒンプ	wealth and poverty; rich and poor
	貧乏	ビンボウ	poverty; poor —*vi*. be poor/badly off
	貧民	ヒンミン	the poor/needy
訓	貧しい	まずしい	poor

911

賀 ⑫　　フ　カ　カ　加　加　加　智　智　智　賀　賀

音	賀	ガ	congratulations
熟	賀春	ガシュン	spring greetings
	賀正	ガショウ	A Happy New Year!; New Year's greetings
	賀状	ガジョウ	greeting card; New Year's card

912

貴 ⑫　　丶　ワ　ロ　中　虫　卑　昔　青　青　書　貴　貴

音	貴	キ	noble; precious; high
熟	貴金属	キキンゾク	precious metals
	貴族	キゾク	nobility; aristocracy
	貴重	キチョウ	valuable; precious
	貴重品	キチョウヒン	valuables
	貴婦人	キフジン	lady
訓	貴い	たっとい	noble; precious; exalted; valuable
	貴ぶ	たっとぶ	*vt*. respect; honor; value; esteem
	貴い	とうとい	noble; precious
	貴ぶ	とうとぶ	*vt*. respect; honor; value; esteem

913

貸 ⑫ ノ イ イ 代 代 代 伐 伐 俗 貸 貸

音	貸	タイ	lend
熟	貸借	タイシャク	debit and credit; lending and borrowing; loan —v. lend and borrow; debt and credit
訓	貸切	かしきり	reserved; chartered
	貸す	かす	**vt**. lend; give credit

914

買 ⑫ 丶 冖 冂 皿 皿 罒 罒 胃 胃 買 買

音	買	バイ	buy
訓	買う	かう	**vt**. buy; purchase
	買い物	かいもの	purchases; shopping; bargain

915

費 ⑫ 一 弓 弓 弗 弗 弗 弗 弗 費 費 費 費

音	費	ヒ	expenses; cost
熟	費用	ヒヨウ	expenses; cost
訓	費やす	ついやす	**vt**. spend; waste; use up
	費える	ついえる	**vi**. be wasted/used up

916

貿 ⑫ 丶 丘 丘 邱 邱 邱 留 留 留 貿 貿

音	貿	ボウ	trade; exchange
熟	貿易風	ボウエキフウ	trade wind

917

資 ⑬ 丶 冫 冫 沪 沪 次 次 资 资 资 資 資

音	資	シ	fund; nature; resources
熟	資格	シカク	qualification
	資源	シゲン	resources

見
角
言
谷
豆
豕
貝 ●
赤
走
足
身
車
辛
辰
酉
里
臣

資材	シザイ	materials
資質	シシツ	nature; one's nature
資料	シリョウ	data; materials
資力	シリョク	means; funds; money

918

賃 ⑬　ノ　イ　仁　仁　二　任　任　任　侟　侟　侟　賃　賃

音	賃	チン	price; fare; fee; hire; wages; rent
熟	賃銀	チンギン	compensation; remuneration
	賃借	チンシャク	hire; hiring; lease —v. hire; lease; rent
	賃貸	チンタイ	lease; hiring out —v. lease; hire out

919

替 ⑮　一　二　弄　夫　夫ニ　夫ヂ　夫夫　梺　梺　替　替　賛

音	賛	サン	praise; dedication; inscription; tribute; help; support; agree
熟	賛意	サンイ	one's approval/assent
	賛歌	サンカ	song of praise; paean
	賛辞	サンジ	praise; tribute
	賛助	サンジョ	support; patronage —v. support; patronize
	賛成	サンセイ	approval; agreement —vi. approve; agree; support; favor
	賛同	サンドウ	approval; support; endorsement —vi. approve; support; endorse
	賛美	サンビ	praise; glorification —v. praise; glorify
	賛美歌	サンビカ	hymn
	賛否	サンピ	approval and disapproval; yes or no

920

質 ⑮　ノ　ア　ヂ　斤　斤ノ　斤ヶ　斦　斦　斦　斦　筲　筲　質

音	質	シチ	pawn
		シツ	nature; disposition; temperament; matter; quality
		(チ)	
熟	質屋	シチや	pawnshop; pawnbroker
	質疑応答	シツギオウトウ	questions and answers —vi. have a question-and-answer session

質素	シッソ	simple; plain; modest
質的	シツテキ	qualitative
質点	シツテン	*phy.* particle
質問	シツモン	question —*v.* question; ask questions
質量	シツリョウ	mass; quality and quantity

921

賞 ⑮　` ` `` ``` ``` ``` ``` ``` ``` ``` 賞 賞

音	賞	ショウ	prize; reward
熟	賞金	ショウキン	prize money; prize; reward
	賞賛	ショウサン	praise; admiration —*v.* praise; admire; applaud
	賞状	ショウジョウ	certificate of merit; honorary certificate
	賞品	ショウヒン	prize; award
	賞味	ショウミ	relishment/enjoyment of food —*v.* relish; enjoy food

922

財 ⑩　丨 冂 冂 月 目 貝 貝 貝 財 財

音	財	ザイ （サイ）	property; finance; business
熟	財貨	ザイカ	wealth
	財界人	ザイカイジン	big businessman; financier
	財布	サイフ	purse; pocketbook; wallet
	財宝	ザイホウ	treasures; riches
	財力	ザイリョク	financial power

923

貯 ⑫　丨 冂 冂 月 目 貝 貝 貝 貝 貯 貯 貯

音	貯	チョ	store; stock; save; savings
熟	貯金	チョキン	savings; deposit —*vi.* save money; put money by
	貯水	チョスイ	storage of water; impoundment; reservoir water
	貯水池	チョスイチ	reservoir
	貯蔵	チョゾウ	storage; storing; preservation —*v.* store; put aside; conserve; preserve
訓	貯える	たくわえる	*vt.* save; store; conserve

7 赤　あかい　red

924
赤 ⑦　一　十　土　ナ　ナ　赤　赤

音	赤	セキ（シャク）	red
熟	赤銅	シャクドウ	gold-copper alloy
	赤外線	セキガイセン	infrared rays
	赤軍	セキグン	Red Army
	赤十字	セキジュウジ	Red Cross
	赤心	セキシン	sincerity; true heart
	赤道	セキドウ	equator
	赤飯	セキハン	rice with red beans
	赤貧	セキヒン	dire poverty
	赤面	セキメン	blush —***vi***. blush; go red in the cheeks
	赤化	セッカ	making Communist —***v***. make Communist
	赤血球	セッケッキュウ	red corpuscles
訓	赤	あか	red
	赤字	あかじ	deficit; in the red
	赤ちゃん	あかちゃん	baby
	赤い	あかい	red
	赤らむ	あからむ	***vi***. become red; blush
	赤らめる	あからめる	***vt***. make red

7 走　はしる／そうにょう　running

925
走 ⑦　一　十　土　キ　キ　赤　走

音	走	ソウ	run; run away
熟	走者	ソウシャ	runner
	走破	ソウハ	running the whole distance —***vi***. run the whole distance

走法	ソウホウ	form of running; running style
走馬灯	ソウまトウ	revolving lantern
走路	ソウロ	running track/course
訓 走る	はしる	*vi*. run; run away
走り書き	はしりがき	scribbling —*v*. scribble; write hurriedly

926

起 ⑩

一 十 土 キ キ 走 走 起 起 起

音 起	キ	get up; be stirred up; happen
熟 起案	キアン	draft; charter; plan
起因	キイン	origin; cause; attribute —*vi*. originate in; be caused by; be attributable to
起源	キゲン	origin; beginning; source
起工	キコウ	start of construction work —*vi*. begin construction
起草	キソウ	drafting —*v*. draft; draw up
起点	キテン	starting point
起用	キヨウ	appointment; employment —*v*. appoint; employ
起立	キリツ	rising; standing up —*vi*. rise; stand up
訓 起きる	おきる	*vi*. get up; rise
起こす	おこす	*vt*. raise up; awake; bring about; wake up
起こる	おころ	*vi*. happen; come to pass

7 足 𧾷 あし／あしへん leg

927

足 ⑦

ヽ 口 口 ア ア 足 足

音 足	ソク	foot; leg; suffice; add
熟 足下	ソッカ	at one's foot; you
足労	ソクロウ	trouble of coming
訓 足	あし	leg; foot
足音	あしおと	sound of footsteps
足首	あしくび	ankle
足場	あしば	foothold; scaffold
足元	あしもと	at one's feet
足す	たす	*vt*. add; supply

461

足りる	たりる	*vi*. be enough; suffice
足る	たる	*vi*. be enough; suffice

928

路 ⑬

ロ ロ 尸 尸 尸 足 足 足 跫 跫 路 路

音	路	ロ	road; path; way
熟	路地	ロジ	alley; lane; path
	路上	ロジョウ	on the road
	路線	ロセン	route; line; alignment
	路頭	ロトウ	road side; wayside
	路面	ロメン	road surface
訓	路	じ	road; path; way

7 身 み body

929

身 ⑦

ノ イ 冂 冃 自 身 身

音	身	シン	body
熟	身上	シンジョウ	personal reasons; merit; asset
	身上書	シンジョウショ	personal information form
	身上持ち	シンショウもち	fortune; wealthy person; housekeeper; handling the household budget
	身心	シンシン	body and mind
	身体	シンタイ	body; physical; bodily
	身体検査	シンタイケンサ	physical examination; medical check-up; search; frisking —*vi*. have a check-up; be searched/frisked
	身体障害者	シンタイショウガイシャ	physically handicapped/disabled person
	身代	シンダイ	total estate; being wealthy
	身長	シンチョウ	height; stature
	身辺	シンペン	personal
訓	身	み	body; position; place; status
	身内	みうち	relative; family; fellow; all over the body
	身重	みおも	pregnant; expecting; with child
	身構え	みがまえ	posture; attitude
	身軽	みがる	light; agile; nimble

462

身代わり	みがわり	subsitution; substitute
身近	みぢか	near/close to oneself
身投げ	みなげ	suicide by drowning or jumping —*vi*. drown oneself; throw oneself from a high place
身の上	みのうえ	history; personal circumstances
身分	みブン	social position; rank; means; circumstances; birth
身元	みもと	one's identity; background
身元引受人	みもとひきうけニン	surety; guarantor; guarantee

---

7 車　くるま／くるまへん　car

930
車⑦　一 ㄷ 厅 両 亘 亘 車

音	車	シャ	car; vehicle
熟	車検	シャケン	car inspection; safety check on a motor vehicle
	車庫	シャコ	garage; car port; bus depot
	車種	シャシュ	type/model of car
	車線	シャセン	traffic lane
	車窓	シャソウ	car/train window
	車体	シャタイ	the body of a car; bicycle frame
	車中	シャチュウ	in a train/car
	車道	シャドウ	roadway; road
	車内	シャナイ	in a car/train
	車両	シャリョウ	cars; vehicles; rolling stock; coach; car; carriage
	車輪	シャリン	wheel
訓	車	くるま	wheel; vehicle; car
	車座	くるまザ	sitting in a circle

931
軍⑨　丶 冖 冖 罒 罕 罕 宭 軍 軍

音	軍	グン	military; army; soldiers
熟	軍医	グンイ	military physician; army doctor; medic
	軍港	グンコウ	naval station

見角言谷豆豕貝赤走足跫身車辛辰酉里臣

軍国主義	グンコクシュギ	militarism
軍事	グンジ	naval and military; military
軍資金	グンシキン	war/campaign funds
軍縮	グンシュク	arms reduction —*vi.* reduce arms/military expenditure
軍人	グンジン	soldier; serviceman; service woman
軍隊	グンタイ	troops; forces; army
軍配	グンバイ	stratagem; tactics
軍備	グンビ	armaments; military preparation

932

転 ⑪ 一 厂 亓 戸 亘 亘 車 車 軒 転 転

音	転	テン	roll; tumble; move
熟	転じる	テンじる	*v.* turn round; revolve; rotate; shift; alter; convert; remove
	転位	テンイ	transposition; dislocation; displacement
	転移	テンイ	change; transition; transfer —*v.* change; transfer
	転化	テンカ	change; transformation; inversion; conversion —*vi.* change; be transformed/inverted
	転回	テンカイ	revolution; rotation; evolution —*v.* revolve; rotate; evolve
	転記	テンキ	copying information into another (family) register —*v.* copy information into another (family) register
	転機	テンキ	turning point; point of change
	転居	テンキョ	moving; change of address —*vi.* move; change one's address
	転業	テンギョウ	change of trade; change of occupation —*vi.* change one's employment/trade
	転勤	テンキン	transferal (to another city, etc.) —*vi.* be transferred (to another city, etc.)
	転向	テンコウ	conversion; turn; turning —*vi.* turn; be converted; abandon an idea
	転校	テンコウ	change of schools —*vi.* change one's school
	転写	テンシャ	transference; copying; transcription —*v.* transfer; copy; transcribe
	転出	テンシュツ	transfer out; moving out —*vi.* be transferred out; move out
	転職	テンショク	change of occupation —*vi.* change one's occupation
	転身	テンシン	turnover; complete change —*vi.* change over; change completely
	転成	テンセイ	transformation; transmutation —*vi.* be transformed; change into

転送	テンソウ	transmission; forwarding —v. transmit; forward; send on
転地	テンチ	moving away for a change of air; trying a change of climate —vi. go somewhere for a change of air; try a change of air
転調	テンチョウ	modulation (music); transition —vi. modulate
転々	テンテン	from one place to another; from hand to hand —vi. go from one place to another; pass from hand-to-hand
転入	テンニュウ	transference in; moving in —vi. be transfered in; move into
転任	テンニン	transferal (to another city, etc.) —vi. be transferred (to another city, etc.)
転変	テンペン	mutation; change
転用	テンヨウ	diversion —v. divert; convert
転落	テンラク	fall; degradation —vi. fall; have a fall; degrade

訓
転がす	ころがす	vt. roll; trundle
転がる	ころがる	vi. roll; tumble; fall; lie down
転げる	ころげる	vi. roll; tumble; fall
転ばす	ころばす	vt. roll over; knock down
転ぶ	ころぶ	vi. roll; tumble; fall over

933

軽 ⑫ 一 厂 厂 戸 亘 亘 車 軒 軒 軽 軽 軽

音
軽	ケイ	light; light-hearted; slight; easy; casual

熟
軽音楽	ケイオンガク	light/easy-listening music
軽快	ケイカイ	light; cheerful; casual
軽金属	ケイキンゾク	light metals
軽減	ケイゲン	reduction; commutation; alleviation —v. reduce; commute; lighten; alleviate; relieve; ease
軽視	ケイシ	making light of; slighting; belittling —v. make light of; slight; belittle
軽傷	ケイショウ	slight injury/wound
軽少	ケイショウ	slight; trifling
軽食	ケイショク	light meal; snack
軽装	ケイソウ	light/casual dress —vi. be lightly/casually dressed
軽卒	ケイソツ	rashness; haste; carelessness; imprudence
軽度	ケイド	slight

訓
軽い	かるい	light; agile; slight; mild; easy
軽やか	かろやか	lightly
軽んじる	かろんじる	vt. look down upon; make light of

934

輪 ⑮ 一 厂 厅 百 亘 車 軒 軒 軒 軩 輪 輪

音	輪	リン	wheel; circle; rotate; (counter for flowers/wheels)
熟	輪作	リンサク	crop rotation
	輪唱	リンショウ	canon (in music); round —*v*. sing a canon
	輪状	リンジョウ	circular; ring-shaped
	輪転	リンテン	rotation; revolution
	輪転機	リンテンキ	rotary press
	輪読	リンドク	reading a book in turns —*v*. take turns reading a book
	輪番	リンバン	rotation; taking turns
訓	輪	わ	ring; wheel; circle; hoop; loop
	輪切り	わぎり	round slices

935

輸 ⑯ 一 厂 厅 百 亘 車 軒 軒 軩 輪 輸

音	輸	ユ	transport; send
熟	輸血	ユケツ	blood transfusion —*vi*. give a blood transfusion
	輸出	ユシュツ	exports —*v*. export
	輸送	ユソウ	transport —*v*. transport; convey; carry; forward
	輸入	ユニュウ	imports —*v*. import

7 辛 からい bitter

936

辞 ⑬ 一 二 千 千 舌 舌 舌' 舌゛ 舌゛ 辞 辞 辞

音	辞	ジ	word; address; resign; give up
熟	辞する	ジする	*vi*. resign; give up (one's post)
	辞意	ジイ	intention to resign
	辞去	ジキョ	departing —*vi*. take one's leave
	辞書	ジショ	dictionary; lexicon; thesaurus
	辞職	ジショク	resignation; giving up one's job —*vi*. resign one's post; hand in one's notice; give up work

辞世	ジセイ	one's dying poem; one's death
辞退	ジタイ	declination; refusal —v. refuse; decline; turn down
辞典	ジテン	dictionary
辞任	ジニン	resignation; notice —v. resign; hand in one's resignation
辞表	ジヒョウ	one's resignation
辞令	ジレイ	written appointment to a position
訓 辞める	やめる	*vi.* resign; retire; give up

7 辰 しんのたつ small dragon

937

農⑬

丶 冖 冂 曲 曲 曲 声 芦 芦 農 農 農 農

音 農	ノウ	cultivate; farming; agriculture
熟 農園	ノウエン	farm; plantation
農家	ノウカ	farmhouse; farming family
農機具	ノウキグ	agricultural implement
農業	ノウギョウ	farming; agriculture
農業国	ノウギョウコク	farming country
農具	ノウグ	farm implements
農耕	ノウコウ	farming; agriculture
農作	ノウサク	cultivation of land; tillage of soil; farming
農作物	ノウサクモツ (ノウサクブツ)	crops; farm produce
農産物	ノウサンブツ	farm produce; agricultural products
農場	ノウジョウ	farm
農村	ノウソン	farm village; rural community
農地	ノウチ	farm/agricultural land
農地改革	ノウチカイカク	farmland/agrarian reform
農夫	ノウフ	farmer
農民	ノウミン	farmers
農薬	ノウヤク	agricultural chemicals
農林	ノウリン	agriculture and forestry

見
角
言
谷
豆
豕
貝
赤
走
足
跙
身
車
辛
辰
酉
里
臣

7 酉 さけづくり／とりへん liquor; sake

938 酒 ⑩
`、 ゛ ミ ミ 沪 汀 沪 洒 酒 酒

音	酒	シュ	saké; wine; liquor
熟	酒気	シュキ	smell of alcohol
	酒色	シュショク	wine and women
	酒精	シュセイ	alcohol
	酒席	シュセキ	banquet; drinking party
	酒造	シュゾウ	saké brewing; wine making; distilling
	酒乱	シュラン	drunken fit; ugly drunk
訓	酒	さけ	rice wine; saké; liquor
	酒飲み	さけのみ	drinker
	酒	さか	rice wine; saké; liguor
	酒蔵	さかぐら	room for storing saké
	酒代	さかダイ	beer money; money for drinks
	酒場	さかば	bar; pub
	酒盛り	さかもり	drinking party
	酒屋	さかや	wine shop; liquor store

939 配 ⑩
一 厂 厂 丙 丙 酉 酉 酉ˊ 酉ˊ 配

音	配	ハイ	distribute
熟	配する	ハイする	*vt.* allot; arrange; match; exile; place under
	配下	ハイカ	followers; subordinates
	配管	ハイカン	installment of gas/water pipes
	配給	ハイキュウ	distribution; supply; rationing —*v.* distribute; supply; deal out; ration
	配合	ハイゴウ	combination; harmony; match; mixture; blending —*v.* combine; distribute; arrange; match; tone
	配車	ハイシャ	car allocation —*v.* alllocate cars
	配色	ハイショク	color scheme
	配水	ハイスイ	water supply —*vi.* supply/distribute water
	配線	ハイセン	electric wiring —*vi.* wire (a house) for electricity
	配属	ハイゾク	assignment; job allocation —*v.* assign (a person to a position)

配達	ハイタツ	delivery —*v.* deliver
配置	ハイチ	arrangement; disposition; posting; placement —*v.* arrange; distribute; post; station; detail
配電	ハイデン	supply of electric power; power distribution —*vi.* supply electricity; distribute power
配備	ハイビ	(troop) positioning —*vt.* position (troops)
配布	ハイフ	distribution —*v.* distribute
配付	ハイフ	distribution; division; handing out —*v.* distribute; give/hand out
配分	ハイブン	distribution; division; allotment; allocation —*v.* distribute; divide; share; allot; allocate
配本	ハイホン	book delivery to subscribers
配役	ハイヤク	the cast; casting
配列	ハイレツ	arrangement; disposal; grouping —*v.* arrange; dispose; put in order; array
訓 配る	くばる	*vt.* distribute; deliver; hand out

940

酸 ⑭　一 丆 兀 西 酉 酉 酉 酉 酉 酚 酵 酸

音 酸	サン	sour; acid
熟 酸化	サンカ	*chem.* oxidation —*vi.* be oxidized
酸性	サンセイ	*chem.* acidity
酸性雨	サンセイウ	acid rain
酸素	サンソ	*chem.* oxygen
酸味	サンミ	sourness; sour taste; acidity
訓 酸い	すい	sour; acidic; vinegary
酸っぱい	すっぱい	sour; acidic; vinegary

---

7 **里** さと／さとへん　village

941

里 ⑦　丨 冂 冋 曱 里 里 里

音 里	リ	village; *ri* (unit of length, approx. 3.9 km)
熟 里程	リテイ	distance; milage
里程標	リテイヒョウ	milepost; milestone
訓 里	さと	village; the country; hometown

里親	さとおや	foster parents
里帰り	さとがえり	bride's first call at her old (parent's) house
里子	さとご	foster child
里心	さとごころ	homesickness; nostalgia

942

重 ⑨ 一 二 一 亡 亡 言 言 言 重 重 重

音	重	ジュウ	heavy; steady; pile up; important
		チョウ	heavy
熟	重圧	ジュウアツ	strong pressure
	重厚	ジュウコウ	solid; dignified
	重罪	ジュウザイ	felony; grave offense/crime
	重視	ジュウシ	attaching greater importance —*v.* attach greater importance; take seriously
	重々	ジュウジュウ	very; well; fully
	重傷	ジュウショウ	serious wound/injury
	重心	ジュウシン	center of gravity/mass
	重責	ジュウセキ	heavy responsibility; important mission
	重体	ジュウタイ	serious condition; critically ill
	重大	ジュウダイ	serious; grave; critical; important
	重点	ジュウテン	important point; great importance; emphasis; priority
	重病	ジュウビョウ	serious illness
	重油	ジュウユ	heavy oil
	重要	ジュウヨウ	importance; essential; key; vital
	重量	ジュウリョウ	weight
	重力	ジュウリョク	gravity
	重労働	ジュウロウドウ	hard/heavy labor
	重複	チョウフク	duplication; repetition; redundancy —*vi.* duplicate; repeat; make redundant
	重宝	チョウホウ	convenient; handy; useful —*v.* be convenient/handy to use
訓	重	え	fold
	重い	おもい	heavy; important; serious
	重々しい	おもおもしい	solemn; grave; dignified
	重さ	おもさ	weight; emphasis; importance
	重たい	おもたい	heavy
	重んじる	おもんじる	*vt.* regard highly; hold in high esteem
	重荷	おもに	heavy load; burden
	重なる	かさなる	*vi.* be on top of; be piled up; come in succession

重ねる　かさねる　*vt*. pile/stack up
重ね重ね　かさねがさね　repeatedly; over and over again

943

野 ⑪　丶　口　日　日　甲　甲　里　野　野　野　野

音	野	ヤ	field; the opposition; rustic; wild
熟	野営	ヤエイ	camp; bivouac —*vi*. camp out; make camp
	野外	ヤガイ	the open air; outdoor
	野球	ヤキュウ	baseball
	野犬	ヤケン	stray dog
	野菜	ヤサイ	vegetables
	野次	ヤジ	hooting; jeering
	野次馬	ヤジうま	curious crowd
	野心	ヤシン	ambition
	野人	ヤジン	rustic; bumpkin; uncouth person
	野性	ヤセイ	wild nature; uncouthness; wild (animal, beast, etc.)
	野戦病院	ヤセンビョウイン	field hospital
	野鳥	ヤチョウ	wild fowl/birds
	野党	ヤトウ	the Opposition; opposition party
	野暮	ヤボ	senseless; booric
	野望	ヤボウ	ambition
訓	野	の	field
	野宿	のジュク	camping out —*vi*. spend the night outdoors; sleep in the open
	野天	のテン	open air
	野中	のなか	in a field
	野原	のはら	field; plain
	野火	のび	burning off grass and weeds
	野武士	のブシ	*hist*. marauding samurai and groups of farmers who stole armor, etc., from defeated samurai
	野山	のやま	hills and fields
	野良	のら	wild; stray; outdoors

944

量 ⑫　丶　口　日　日　旦　早　景　昌　昌　量　量　量

| 音 | 量 | リョウ | quantity |
| 熟 | 量感 | リョウカン | volume; bulk; massiveness |

量産	リョウサン	mass production —*v.* produce in large quantities
量的	リョウテキ	quantitative
量目	リョウめ	weight
訓 量る	はかる	*vt.* weigh; measure

---

7 臣 しん minister

945

臣 ⑦ 丨 厂 厂 尸 臣 臣 臣

音 臣	シン	subject
	ジン	
熟 臣下	シンカ	subject; retainer
臣民	シンミン	subject

946

臨 ⑱ 丨 厂 厂 尸 尸 臣 𦣻 𦣻 𦣻 𦣻 𦣻 臨 臨

音 臨	リン	be present at; look out over; go to; copy; rule
熟 臨海	リンカイ	seaside; coastal; marine
臨機応変	リンキオウヘン	adaptation to circumstances
臨月	リンゲツ	the last month of pregnancy
臨時	リンジ	extra; temporary; provisional
臨終	リンジュウ	one's last moment
臨席	リンセキ	attendance; presence —*vi.* attend; be present
臨地	リンチ	on-site
訓 臨む	のぞむ	*vt.* face; attend; be present

8 金 かね／かねへん　metal; money

947
金 ⑧　ノ 𠂉 𠆢 A 今 仐 刽 金 金

音	金	キン	gold; currency; metal; coin
		（コン）	gold
熟	金貨	キンカ	gold coin/currency
	金科玉条	キンカ ギョクジョウ	golden rule
	金言	キンゲン	wise saying; watchword
	金庫	キンコ	safe
	金鉱	キンコウ	gold mine
	金策	キンサク	raising money; getting a loan —*vi*. raise money; get a loan
	金星	キンセイ	the planet Venus
	金銭	キンセン	money
	金属	キンゾク	metal; metallic
	金品	キンピン	money and other valuables
	金曜日	キンヨウび	Friday
	金利	キンリ	interest
	金色	コンジキ	gold color
訓	金	かね	metal; money
	金目	かねめ	(monetary) value
	金持ち	かねもち	rich; having a lot of money
	金	かな	(prefix) metal; money
	金具	かなグ	metal fittings; metallic parts

948
針 ⑩　ノ 𠂉 𠂉 𠂉 𠂉 仐 刽 金 金 針

音	針	シン	needle
熟	針小棒大	シンショウ ボウダイ	exaggeration; making a mountain out of a mole hill
	針葉樹	シンヨウジュ	coniferous tree
	針路	シンロ	course
訓	針	はり	needle; hook; pin
	針金	はりがね	wire
	針仕事	はりシごと	needlework

949

鉱 ⑬ ノ ノ ノ ゲ 牟 金 金 金 釒 釒 鉱 鉱

音	鉱	コウ	ore; mineral; mine
熟	鉱業	コウギョウ	the mining industry; mining
	鉱区	コウク	mining region
	鉱山	コウザン	mine
	鉱石	コウセキ	ore; mineral; crystal
	鉱泉	コウセン	mineral spring/water; spring
	鉱毒	コウドク	mineral/copper poisoning
	鉱夫	コウフ	miner
	鉱物	コウブツ	mineral
	鉱脈	コウミャク	vein of ore/mineral; ore/mineral deposit

950

鉄 ⑬ ノ ノ ノ ゲ 牟 金 金 金 釒 釒 鈇 鉄

音	鉄	テツ	iron; steel
熟	鉄火	テッカ	red-hot iron; gunfire; swords and guns; cuisine that uses raw tuna and *wasabi*
	鉄管	テッカン	iron pipe/tube
	鉄器	テッキ	ironware; hardware; ironmongery
	鉄橋	テッキョウ	iron bridge
	鉄筋 コンクリート	テッキン コンクリート	reinforced concrete
	鉄工	テッコウ	ironworker; blacksmith
	鉄鉱	テッコウ	iron ore
	鉄鋼	テッコウ	steel
	鉄格子	テツゴウシ	iron-barred window
	鉄骨	テッコツ	steel frame
	鉄材	テツザイ	iron material
	鉄製	テッセイ	made of steel/iron
	鉄線	テッセン	steel wire
	鉄則	テッソク	iron rule
	鉄道	テツドウ	railroad; railway
	鉄板	テッパン	hot plate
	鉄板焼	テッパンやき	*teppanyaki* (meat and vegetables grilled on a hot plate)
	鉄分	テツブン	iron content
	鉄面皮	テツメンピ	impudence; brazeness; shamelessness

951

銀 ⑭ 　 ハ ｸ ﾉﾆ 乍 金 金 針 釘 銀 銀 銀 銀

音	銀	ギン	silver; money; banking
熟	銀貨	ギンカ	silver coinage
	銀河	ギンガ	Milky Way
	銀行	ギンコウ	bank
	銀製	ギンセイ	made from silver; silverware
	銀世界	ギンセカイ	silver world; snow-covered scenery
	銀幕	ギンマク	silver screen

952

銭 ⑭ 　 ハ ｸ ﾉﾆ 乍 金 金 金 銭 銭 銭 銭

音	銭	セン	coin
熟	銭湯	セントウ	bathhouse
訓	銭	ぜに	coin; change

953

銅 ⑭ 　 ハ ｸ ﾉﾆ 乍 金 金 釘 銅 銅 銅 銅

音	銅	ドウ	copper
熟	銅貨	ドウカ	copper coin
	銅器	ドウキ	copper utensil; copperware
	銅山	ドウザン	copper mine
	銅像	ドウゾウ	bronze statue
	銅版	ドウバン	copperplate

954

鋼 ⑯ 　 ハ ｸ ﾉﾆ 乍 金 釘 鋼 鋼 鋼 鋼 鋼

音	鋼	コウ	steel
熟	鋼管	コウカン	steel tubing
	鋼材	コウザイ	steel materials; structural/rolled steel
	鋼鉄	コウテツ	steel
訓	鋼	はがね	steel

955

録 ⑯ ⌒ ⌒ ⌒ 午 余 金 釒 鉅 針 鈩 録 録

音	録	ロク	record; catalog
熟	録音	ロクオン	sound recording —*v.* make a sound recording
	録画	ロクガ	videotape recording —*v.* record on videotape

956

鏡 ⑲ ⌒ ⌒ 午 余 金 釒 釒 鈩 鎞 鎞 鏡

音	鏡	キョウ	mirror; lens; spectacles; mirrorlike
熟	鏡台	キョウダイ	dressing table; dresser
訓	鏡	かがみ	mirror; looking glass

8 長 ながい long

957

長 ⑧ 1 ⌐ ⌐ 「 ⴺ 長 長 長

音	長	チョウ	long; far; stretch; head; chief; headman; merit; strong point
熟	長じる	チョウじる	*vi.* grow up; be older; excel; be clever
	長音	チョウオン	long vowel/sound
	長官	チョウカン	director; president; administrator; head; chief
	長期	チョウキ	long period/term
	長子	チョウシ	oldest son
	長者	チョウジャ	millionaire
	長所	チョウショ	merit; strong point; forte
	長女	チョウジョ	oldest daughter
	長身	チョウシン	tall figure; great stature
	長針	チョウシン	the long/minute hand (of a clock)
	長大	チョウダイ	long and stout; huge
	長短	チョウタン	relative length; merits and demerits
	長調	チョウチョウ	major key (in music)
	長男	チョウナン	oldest son; heir
	長編	チョウヘン	long novel/movie/poem

長方形	チョウホウケイ	*math*. rectangle; oblong
長命	チョウメイ	longevity; long life
長老	チョウロウ	senior; elder

訓

長い	ながい	long; lengthy; lanky
長さ	ながさ	length
長雨	ながあめ	long period of rain
長居	ながい	long stay/visit —*vi*. stay too long; make a long visit
長生き	ながいき	long life; longevity —*vi*. live long; enjoy longevity
長続き	ながつづき	long lasting —*vi*. last long
長年	ながネン	long time; many years
長引く	ながびく	*vi*. be prolonged/protracted/delayed
長持ち	ながもち	durability; endurance —*vi*. endure; be durable; last long

---

8 門 もんがまえ gate

958

門 丨 冂 冂 冃 冃 門 門 門
⑧

音 門 モン gate

熟

門衛	モンエイ	guard; gatekeeper
門下	モンカ	one's disciple/pupil
門外漢	モンガイカン	outsider; layman
門限	モンゲン	curfew
門戸	モンコ	doorway
門札	モンサツ	name plate
門歯	モンシ	incisor; front teeth
門人	モンジン	pupil; disciple
門前	モンゼン	before the gate
門柱	モンチュウ	gatepost
門弟	モンテイ	disciple; pupil
門灯	モントウ	gate light
門番	モンバン	gatekeeper
門標	モンピョウ	name plate

訓

門	かど	gate; house
門口	かどぐち	front door; entrance
門出	かどで	departure —*v*. depart; set out

959

閉 ⑪ 丨 厂 户 户 户' 門 門 門 門 閈 閉

音	閉	ヘイ	close; shut; confine; end
熟	閉会	ヘイカイ	closing/adjournment (of a meeting) —*v.* close/adjourn a meeting
	閉館	ヘイカン	closing (hall/building) —*v.* close (hall/building)
	閉口	ヘイコウ	troublesome; confoundment —*vi.* be troubled/confounded by
	閉店	ヘイテン	closing a shop (for the day) —*vi.* close the shop
	閉幕	ヘイマク	falling of the curtain; end of a play —*vi.* curtain falls; play ends
	閉門	ヘイモン	locking up the gate; house arrest (Edo period) —*vi.* lock up the gate; be confined to one's home
訓	閉まる	しまる	*vi.* be shut/closed/locked
	閉める	しめる	*vt.* shut; close; lock
	閉ざす	とざす	*vt.* close; shut; lock
	閉じる	とじる	*vt.* close; shut; lock
	閉じこもる	とじこもる	*vi.* stay indoors; be confined to one's house

960

開 ⑫ 丨 厂 户 户 户' 門 門 門 門 閈 開 開

音	開	カイ	open; begin; civilize; unfold; expand; open up land; develop; reclaim
熟	開運	カイウン	improvement of one's fortune
	開演	カイエン	opening of a performance; raising of the curtain —*vi.* start a performance; raise the curtain
	開化	カイカ	Westernization; becoming civilized —*vi.* become Westernized/civilized
	開花	カイカ	fluorescence; bloom; flourishing —*vi.* flower; bloom; flourish
	開会	カイカイ	opening of a meeting —*v.* open/begin a meeting
	開口	カイコウ	opening; aperture
	開校	カイコウ	opening of a new school —*v.* open a new school
	開港	カイコウ	opening of a port to (foreign trade) —*v.* open a port (to foreign trade)
	開国	カイコク	opening of a country to the world; foundation of a country —*v.* open up a country to the world; found a nation

開始	カイシ	beginning; start; commencement —v. begin; start; commence
開場	カイジョウ	opening (of the doors to a hall, etc.) —vi. open; open the doors (to a hall, etc.)
開設	カイセツ	opening; establishment; setting up —v. open; establish; set up
開戦	カイセン	outbreak of war; commencement of hostilities —vi. make/wage war
開通	カイツウ	opening up to traffic —v. open up to traffic
開発	カイハツ	development; exploitation —v. develop; open up; exploit
開票	カイヒョウ	ballot counting —v. count votes; open ballot boxes
開閉	カイヘイ	opening and shutting —v. open and shut
開放	カイホウ	opening —v. open; throw open
開門	カイモン	opening of a gate —vi. open a gate

訓

開く	あく	vi. open
開ける	あける	vt. open; begin; bore (a hole, etc.)
開く	ひらく	v. open; solve; start
開ける	ひらける	vi. develop; be open; be civilized

961

間 ⑫

丨 冂 冂 冃 冃' 門 門 門 門 間 間 間

音 間

| | カン | interval; between; gap; opportunity |
| | ケン | between; middle |

熟

間食	カンショク	eating between meals; snack —vi. eat between meals
間接	カンセツ	indirectness
間接的	カンセツテキ	indirect
間断	カンダン	pause; interval

訓

間	あいだ	interval; middle; gap
間	ま	space; leisure; room; pause; interval; (counter for rooms)
間口	まぐち	front; facade; width of a building, etc.
間近	まぢか	nearby; close at hand
間取り	まどり	plan of a house; room arrangement
間引き	まびき	thinning out of plants

962

閣 ⑭ 　 丨 冂 冃 冃 門 門 門 門 閁 閛 閣 閣 閣

音	閣	カク	Cabinet; tower
熟	閣議	カクギ	Cabinet meeting/council
	閣下	カッカ	Your Excellency

963

関 ⑭ 　 丨 冂 冃 冃 門 門 門 門 閁 閆 関 関

音	関	カン	barrier; bolt
熟	関する	カンする	*vi*. be related/connected to
	関係	カンケイ	relation; connection; relationship —*vi*. be related/connected; be involved in a relationship
	関西	カンサイ	Kansai district
	関心	カンシン	concern; interest
	関数	カンスウ	*math*. function
	関節	カンセツ	joint of the body
	関知	カンチ	concern —*vi*. be concerned with
	関東	カントウ	Kanto district
	関白	カンパク	*hist*. *Kampaku* (chancellor or chief adviser to the emperor)
	関門	カンモン	gateway; gate
	関連	カンレン	involvement; correlation; connection; reference —*vi*. be connected/associated/correlated
訓	関	せき	checkpoint; barrier
	関所	せきショ	checkpoint; barrier
	関取	せきとり	high-ranking sumo wrestler

8 ふるとり　old bird

964

集 ⑫ 　 ノ イ イ 广 什 仹 隹 隹 隹 隼 集 集

| 音 | 集 | シュウ | assemble; collect; gather |
| 熟 | 集荷 | シュウカ | cargo collection —*v*. collect cargo |

集会	シュウカイ	meeting; assembly; gathering
集計	シュウケイ	total; sum; aggregate —v. total; sum; collect together
集結	シュウケツ	collecting things in one place; gathering in one place —v. mass; gather; assemble
集合	シュウゴウ	meeting; gathering; assembly **math**. set —v. meet; gather; assemble
集札	シュウサツ	ticket collection —v. collect tickets
集散	シュウサン	collecting and distribution —v. meet and part; collect and distribute
集積	シュウセキ	accumulation; pile —v. accumulate; pile up
集大成	シュウタイセイ	collection; compilation —v. compile (various texts) into one book
集団	シュウダン	group; body
集中	シュウチュウ	concentration —v. center on; concentrate
集配	シュウハイ	collection and delivery —v. collect and deliver
集約	シュウヤク	putting/collecting together —v. put together
集落	シュウラク	village **bio**. colony
集録	シュウロク	compilation of written records —v. compile

訓

集まり	あつまり	meeting; gathering; party; congregation; crowd; attendance
集まる	あつまる	v. gather come; get together; mass; be collected/concentrated
集める	あつめる	vt. gather; get together; collect; accumulate; attract; draw together
集い	つどい	gathering; meeting; get-together
集う	つどう	vi. gather; come; get together; amass

965

雑 ⑭ 　ノ 九 九 杂 杂 杂 架 刹 剎 刹 剎 雑

音

| 雑 | ザツ | miscellaneous; sloppy; slipshod; messy |
| | ゾウ | miscellany; various |

熟

雑役	ザツエキ	odd jobs; chores
雑音	ザツオン	noise; static; interference (on radio, etc.)
雑貨	ザッカ	sundry/miscellaneous goods; general merchandise; sundries
雑貨屋	ザッカや	general store
雑学	ザツガク	general knowledge
雑感	ザッカン	miscellaneous thoughts; casual impressions
雑記帳	ザッキチョウ	notebook
雑穀	ザッコク	miscellaneous cereals (excluding rice and wheat)
雑誌	ザッシ	magazine; journal; periodical

雑事	ザツジ	household chores; routine work
雑種	ザッシュ	cross; hybrid; mongrel
雑食性	ザッショクセイ	omnivorous
雑然	ザツゼン	untidy; messy; in disorder
雑草	ザッソウ	weeds
雑多	ザッタ	miscellaneous
雑談	ザツダン	chitchat; chat; light conversation; small talk —*vi*. chitchat; chat
雑念	ザツネン	idle thoughts
雑務	ザツム	odd duties; routine; trivial tasks
雑用	ザツヨウ	odd business; various chores
雑木林	ゾウきばやし	growth of trees; copse; coppice

966

難 ⑱ 一 艹 艹 艹 芑 苎 莫 莫 蓳 鄞 艱 難

音	難	ナン	difficult
熟	難易	ナンイ	hardness; difficulty
	難解	ナンカイ	difficult to understand; unintelligible
	難関	ナンカン	barrier; obstacle; hurdle; difficult situation
	難行苦行	ナンギョウクギョウ	penance; asceticism; religious austerities
	難局	ナンキョク	difficult situation; crisis; deadlock
	難曲	ナンキョク	challenging piece of music
	難航	ナンコウ	stormy voyage; rough passage —*vi*. have a difficult sailing/rough passage
	難産	ナンザン	hard labor; complicated birth —*vi*. have a difficult/complicated delivery
	難事	ナンジ	difficult matter; hard task; tough job
	難所	ナンショ	dangerous spot; place hard to pass
	難色	ナンショク	disapproval; reluctance; unwillingness
	難船	ナンセン	shipwreck; wreck; ship in distress —*vi*. be shipwrecked; be wrecked
	難題	ナンダイ	unreasonable terms; unfair proposal
	難点	ナンテン	crux; difficult point; weakness; fault; flaw
	難無く	ナンなく	without difficulty; with ease
	難破	ナンパ	shipwreck
	難病	ナンビョウ	serious/incurable disease
	難物	ナンブツ	bothersome object/person
	難民	ナンミン	sufferers; refugees
	難問	ナンモン	puzzling question; question that is hard to answer
	難路	ナンロ	hard pass; rough road

| 訓 | 難い | かたい | hard; difficult |
| | 難しい | むずかしい | hard; difficult; troublesome; problematic |

8 雨　あめ／あめかんむり　rain

967

雨 ⑧

一　ナ　ヮ　币　币　雨　雨　雨

音	雨	ウ	rain
熟	雨季	ウキ	rainy season
	雨後	ウゴ	after the rain
	雨天	ウテン	rainy weather; wet day
	雨量	ウリョウ	rainfall; rain; precipitation
	雨量計	ウリョウケイ	rain gauge
訓	雨	あめ	rain
	雨上がり	あめあがり	after the rain
	雨	あま	(prefix) rain; rainy
	雨合羽	あまガッぱ	raincoat
	雨具	あまグ	rainwear
	雨雲	あまぐも	rain cloud
	雨戸	あまど	sliding door; shutter
	雨宿り	あまやどり	sheltering from the rain —*vi*. take shelter from the rain; get out of the rain

968

雪 ⑪

一　ナ　ヮ　币　币　币　币　雪　雪　雪　雪

音	雪	セツ	snow
熟	雪害	セツガイ	snow damage
	雪原	セツゲン	snowfield; expanse of snow
	雪中	セッチュウ	in/through the snow
訓	雪	ゆき	snow
	雪男	ゆきおとこ	abominable snowman; yeti
	雪女	ゆきおんな	snow fairy
	雪合戦	ゆきガッセン	snowball fight
	雪解け	ゆきどけ	thawing; solution of a problem —*v*. thaw; solve a problem

金長門佳
●雨青非
食

969

一 ニ 一 〒 币 币 币 靊 雪 雲 雲 雲 ⑫

音	雲	ウン	cloud
熟	雲海	ウンカイ	sea of clouds
	雲母	ウンモ	mica
	雲量	ウンリョウ	cloudiness; amount of cloud
訓	雲	くも	cloud
	雲行き	くもゆき	sky; weather; circumstances; state of affairs

970

一 ニ 一 〒 币 币 币 雨 雪 霄 雷 電 ⑬

音	電	デン	lightning; electricity
熟	電圧	デンアツ	voltage; tension; electric pressure
	電化	デンカ	electrification —*v.* electrify; install electricity
	電荷	デンカ	electric charge
	電界	デンカイ	electric field
	電解	デンカイ	electrolysis —*v.* electrolyze
	電気	デンキ	electricity; electric light
	電球	デンキュウ	electric light bulb
	電極	デンキョク	electrode
	電源	デンゲン	source of electricity; power/electric source
	電工	デンコウ	electrician
	電光	デンコウ	electric light; lightning
	電子	デンシ	electron
	電子工学	デンシコウガク	electronics
	電磁気	デンジキ	electromagnetism
	電磁石	デンジシャク	electromagnet
	電磁場	デンジば	electromagnetic field
	電車	デンシャ	train
	電信	デンシン	telegraph; telegram; wire; cable
	電信柱	デンシンばしら	telegraph pole
	電線	デンセン	electric wire/cable; telegraph wire
	電送	デンソウ	electrical transmission —*v.* telegraph; wire; cable
	電池	デンチ	battery; electric cell
	電柱	デンチュウ	utility/telephone/telegraph pole
	電灯	デントウ	electric light

電動	デンドウ	electromotion
電動機	デンドウキ	electric motor
電熱	デンネツ	electric heat
電波	デンパ	electric/radio wave
電文	デンブン	telegram
電報	デンポウ	telegram; wire
電流	デンリュウ	electric current
電流計	デンリュウケイ	galvanometer
電力	デンリョク	electric power; electricity
電話	デンワ	telephone
電話局	デンワキョク	telephone office
電話線	デンワセン	telephone wire
電話帳	デンワチョウ	telephone directory
電話番号	デンワバンゴウ	telephone number

---

8 青 おあ／あおへん blue; green

971

青 ⑧ 一 十 キ 主 丰 青 青 青 青

音	青	セイ （ショウ）	blue; green; young; immature
熟	青果	セイカ	fruit and vegetables; fresh produce
	青春	セイシュン	youth
	青少年	セイショウネン	young people
	青銅	セイドウ	bronze
	青年	セイネン	youth; young man
訓	青	あお	blue; azure; green
	青い	あおい	blue; azure; green; pale (face)
	青々	あおあお	deep blue; lush green; verdant
	青海原	あおうなばら	wide blue sea
	青写真	あおジャシン	blueprint
	青白い	あおじろい	pale; pallid
	青空	あおぞら	blue sky
	青空市場	あおぞらいちば	open-air market
	青二才	あおニサイ	young and inexperienced fellow
	青葉	あおば	green leaves
	青物	あおもの	greens; vegetables
	青み	あおみ	blueness; greeness

| 青む | あおむ | turn blue/green |
| 青ざめる | あおざめる | turn pale |

972

静 ⑭ 一 十 主 丰 青 青 靑 靗 靜 静 静 静

音	静	セイ （ジョウ）	calm; quiet; peaceful; still
熟	静脈	ジョウミャク	vein
	静観	セイカン	watching calmly —*v*. watch calmly; wait and see
	静止	セイシ	standstill; still; at rest; stationary —*vi*. come to rest/a standstill; be at rest/stationary
	静的	セイテキ	static
	静電気	セイデンキ	static electricity
	静物	セイブツ	still life
	静養	セイヨウ	rest; recuperation —*vi*. rest; recuperate
訓	静	しず	quiet; peaceful; still
	静か	しずか	calm; quiet; peaceful; still
	静まる	しずまる	*vi*. become quiet; subside; die down
	静める	しずめる	*vt*. calm; soothe; quell

8 非 あらず negative

973

非 ⑧ ノ ナ ヲ ヺ 非 非 非 非

音	非	ヒ	(prefix) non-; un-; wrong; not
熟	非運	ヒウン	misfortune; bad luck
	非金属	ヒキンゾク	nonmetallic
	非行	ヒコウ	misdeed; misconduct; delinquency
	非業	ヒゴウ	*Bud*. untimely/unnatural death
	非公開	ヒコウカイ	private/closed (meeting); closed-door (session)
	非公式	ヒコウシキ	unofficial; informal
	非公認	ヒコウニン	unauthorized
	非合法	ヒゴウホウ	illegal
	非合理	ヒゴウリ	irrational; unreasonable
	非国民	ヒコクミン	traitor; unpatriotic person

非才	ヒサイ	lack of ability; incompetence
非情	ヒジョウ	unfeeling; coldhearted; inanimate
非常	ヒジョウ	emergency; extraordinary; very; exceeding; extremely
非常勤	ヒジョウキン	part-time work
非常口	ヒジョウぐち	emergency exit
非常時	ヒジョウジ	emergency; crisis
非常識	ヒジョウシキ	lack of common sense; absurd
非常手段	ヒジョウシュダン	emergency means
非戦論	ヒセンロン	pacifism
非道	ヒドウ	inhuman; unjust; cruel; tyrannical
非難	ヒナン	blame; reproach —*v.* criticize unfavorably; censure; blame; reproach
非売品	ヒバイヒン	article not for sale; Not for Sale
非番	ヒバン	off duty
非武装	ヒブソウ	demilitarization; unarmed
非力	ヒリキ	incapable; powerless; useless; incompetent
非礼	ヒレイ	impoliteness
訓 非ず	あらず	not; not so

8　食　see ⇨p.495

9 面 めん face

974

面⑨　一　ｱ　尸　币　而　而　而　面　面

音	面	メン	face; mask; surface; aspect; facet; page
熟	面する	メンする	*vi.* face; front; look on
	面会	メンカイ	interview; meeting —*vi.* interview; meet and talk with
	面識	メンシキ	acquaintance
	面積	メンセキ	area
	面接	メンセツ	interview —*vi.* interview; meet and talk with
	面前	メンゼン	in the presence of; before (someone)
	面相	メンソウ	looks; face
	面談	メンダン	interview —*vi.* meet and talk with
	面目	メンボク(メンモク)	honor; face; dignity
	面々	メンメン	each one; all
	面容	メンヨウ	countenance; looks
訓	面	おも	surface; face
	面白い	おもしろい	interesting; amusing
	面長	おもなが	long-faced
	面	おもて	face; surface
	面	つら	surface; face (impolite)
	面当て	つらあて	insinuating/spiteful remark; innuendo

9 革 かくのかわ／つくりのかわ shoe leather

975

革⑨　一　十　廿　廿　芇　苫　苫　萆　革

音	革	カク	hide; leather; renew
熟	革命	カクメイ	revolution
訓	革	かわ	leather; skin

488

9 音 おと noise

976

音⑨ 　 丶 亠 ナ 立 产 咅 咅 音 音

音	音	オン	sound; pronunciation; music
		（イン）	sound; tidings
熟	音域	オンイキ	singing range; register
	音階	オンカイ	the whole series of recognized musical notes; musical scale; gamut
	音楽	オンガク	music
	音感	オンカン	sense of sound/pitch
	音曲	オンキョク	music; songs
	音訓	オンクン	Chinese and Japanese readings of kanji
	音質	オンシツ	tonal quality; tonality
	音信	オンシン	correspondence; communication
		（インシン）	
	音声	オンセイ	voice; audio sound
	音声学	オンセイガク	phonetics
	音節	オンセツ	syllable
	音速	オンソク	velocity of sound; sonic speed
	音程	オンテイ	musical interval; step
	音頭	オンド	leading a song
	音読	オンドク	reading aloud —*v.* read aloud
	音波	オンパ	sound waves
	音便	オンビン	euphonic change; euphony
	音律	オンリツ	tune; rhythm; pitch
	音量	オンリョウ	sound volume; volume
訓	音	おと	sound
	音	ね	sound
	音色	ねいろ	tonal quality; tonality

9 頁 おおがい big shell; page

977

頂 ⑪

一 丁 丁 厂 厂 厂 币 币 币 頂 頂 頂

音	頂	チョウ	top of the head; top; peak; summit
熟	頂角	チョウカク	**math**. vertical angle
	頂上	チョウジョウ	top; summit; crest; crown; peak
	頂点	チョウテン	apex; vertex; zenith; climax
訓	頂	いただき	top; summit; peak
	頂く	いただく	**vt**. wear a crown; be crowned **hon**. receive; get; be given; eat; drink

---

978

順 ⑫

丿 刂 刂 川 川 川 川 順 順 順 順 順

音	順	ジュン	submit; order; series
熟	順位	ジュンイ	ranking; order
	順延	ジュンエン	postponement —**v**. postpone; put off
	順化	ジュンカ	adapting (to climate, etc.)
	順次	ジュンジ	in order; one by one; one after another
	順々	ジュンジュン	by turns; one by one; one after another
	順序	ジュンジョ	order; procedure
	順調	ジュンチョウ	smooth; satisfactory; favorable
	順当	ジュントウ	proper; right
	順応	ジュンノウ	adaptation; adjustment —**vi**. adapt; adjust; conform
	順番	ジュンバン	order; turn; place
	順風	ジュンプウ	favorable wind
	順法	ジュンポウ	law-abiding
	順列	ジュンレツ	permutation
	順路	ジュンロ	route

979

預 ⑬

フ マ ヌ 予 予 予 別 預 預 預 預

音	預	ヨ	deposit; entrust

490

熟	預金	ヨキン	deposit; bank account —*v.* deposit money in a bank
訓	預かる	あずかる	*vt.* receive for safekeeping
	預ける	あずける	*vt.* deposit; entrust; hand over for safe-keeping; leave in someone's care

980 領 ⑭

ノ 人 ㇒ 今 令 令 令 卸 領 領 領 領

音	領	リョウ	govern; rule; territory
熟	領域	リョウイキ	domain; territory
	領海	リョウカイ	territorial waters
	領解	リョウカイ	understanding; consent —*v.* understand; consent
	領空	リョウクウ	territorial airspace
	領事	リョウジ	consul
	領事館	リョウジカン	consulate
	領主	リョウシュ	*hist.* feudal lord (Edo period)
	領収書	リョウシュウショ	(written) receipt
	領収証	リョウシュウショウ	receipt; proof of payment
	領地	リョウチ	territory
	領土	リョウド	territory
	領分	リョウブン	territory; domain; sphere of influence
	領有	リョウユウ	possession (of land/territory) —*v.* possess (land/territory)

981 頭 ⑯

一 ㇒ 干 日 豆 豆 豆 豆 頭 頭 頭 頭

音	頭	ズ	head
		トウ	head; beginning
		（ト）	
熟	頭上	ズジョウ	overhead; above the head
	頭痛	ズツウ	*med.* headache
	頭脳	ズノウ	brain
	頭角	トウカク	top of the head; crown; talent
	頭取	トウどり	president; manager
	頭領	トウリョウ	boss
訓	頭	あたま	head; brains; mind; hair; chief; leader
	頭打ち	あたまうち	(highest) limit; peak; ceiling
	頭数	あたまかず	headcount; number of persons

頭ごなし	あたまごなし	merciless
頭割り	あたまわり	equal share
頭	かしら	head; hair; leader
頭文字	かしらモジ	initial; first letter

982

額 ⑱ 　 ` 宀 宀 安 安 客 客 客 客 額 額 額

音	額	ガク	forehead; amount; frame
熟	額面	ガクメン	face value
訓	額	ひたい	forehead

983

顔 ⑱ 　 ` 亠 产 产 立 产 彦 彦 彦 顔 顔 顔

音	顔	ガン	face; looks
熟	顔色	ガンショク	complexion
	顔面	ガンメン	face
訓	顔	かお	face; looks; honor
	顔色	かおいろ	expression; countenance; color of a person's face
	顔役	かおヤク	boss

984

題 ⑱ 　 丨 日 旦 早 早 昰 是 是 是 題 題 題

音	題	ダイ	title
熟	題する	ダイする	*vi.* entitle
	題材	ダイザイ	subject matter; theme
	題字	ダイジ	title (of a book, etc.)
	題名	ダイメイ	title (of a book, etc.)
	題目	ダイモク	prayer of the Nichiren sect; theme

985

類 ⑱ 　 ` ′ ′ 半 米 米 米 类 类 類 類 類

| 音 | 類 | ルイ | kind; type; genus |

熟	類する	ルイする	*vi.* classify
	類火	ルイカ	spreading fire
	類型	ルイケイ	type; pattern
	類語	ルイゴ	*gram.* synonym
	類似	ルイジ	resemblance; similarity —*vi.* resemble; be similar
	類書	ルイショ	books of the same kind
	類焼	ルイショウ	spreading fire —*vi.* spread fire
	類推	ルイスイ	analogy —*v.* analogize
	類同	ルイドウ	similar
	類比	ルイヒ	analogy; comparison —*v.* analogize; compare
	類別	ルイベツ	classification —*v.* classify
	類例	ルイレイ	similar example

986
願 ⑲　一　厂　厂　庐　庐　原　原　原　原　願　願　願

音	願	ガン	desire; prayer
熟	願書	ガンショ	written application/request
	願望	ガンボウ	desire; wish
訓	願い	ねがい	*vt.* wish; favor; request
	願う	ねがう	pray; wish; request politely

9　飛　とぶ flying

987
飛 ⑨　乀　乁　乁　飞　飞　飛　飛　飛　飛

音	飛	ヒ	fly; jump
熟	飛語	ヒゴ	groundless rumor
	飛行	ヒコウ	flight; flying; aviation —*vi.* fly
	飛行士	ヒコウシ	airman; aviator; flier
	飛散	ヒサン	scattering; dispersement —*vi.* scatter; disperse; fly
	飛来	ヒライ	by air/airplane —*vi.* come flying
訓	飛ぶ	とぶ	*vi.* fly; jump; hurry; progress rapidly
	飛ばす	とばす	*vt.* fly; spatter; drive fast; skip (pages, etc.); omit

飛び上がる	とびあがる	*vi*. fly/jump up; take off
飛び歩く	とびあるく	*vi*. run/rush about
飛石	とびいし	steppingstone
飛板	とびいた	springboard; diving board
飛び移る	とびうつる	*vi*. fly/jump from one place to other
飛び降りる	とびおりる	*vi*. jump/leap out
飛び出す	とびだす	*vi*. spring/bolt out; run away; protrude
飛び出る	とびでる	*vi*. protrude; project; fly/jump out; appear suddenly; run/pop out; be exorbitant

---

9 食 しょく food 食 (p.495)

988

食 ⑨ ノ 人 ヘ 今 今 今 食 食 食

音	食	ショク（ジキ）	eat; food; meal; appetite
熟	食塩	ショクエン	table salt
	食言	ショクゲン	*vi*. go back on one's words; tell lies
	食後	ショクゴ	after a meal
	食指	ショクシ	index finger
	食事	ショクジ	meal; diet —*vi*. eat; dine
	食傷	ショクショウ	sick and tired; fed up; food poisoning —*vi*. be sick and tired of; get fed up; get food poisoning
	食前	ショクゼン	before a meal
	食中毒	ショクチュウドク	food poisoning
	食通	ショクツウ	gourmet
	食堂	ショクドウ	dining room; eating house; canteen; cafeteria
	食道	ショクドウ	*med*. gullet; esophagus
	食費	ショクヒ	food costs/expenses
	食品	ショクヒン	food
	食物	ショクモツ	food
	食用	ショクヨウ	edible
	食欲	ショクヨク	appetite
	食料	ショクリョウ	food; provisions
	食料品	ショクリョウヒン	foodstuff
	食器	ショッキ	tableware; dishes, plates and bowls
訓	食う	くう	*vt*. eat (used mainly by men and in some regional dialects)

食らう	くらう	**vt**. eat; drink
食べる	たべる	**vt**. eat
食べ物	たべもの	food; diet

989
養 ⑮　　　ソ ソ ソ 芦 美 美 美 莠 莠 養 養 養

音	養	ヨウ	foster; bring up; rear; adopt; support; cultivate; develop
熟	養育	ヨウイク	fostering; rearing —**v**. foster; bring up; near; support
	養育者	ヨウイクシャ	guardian
	養魚	ヨウギョ	fish breeding/farming
	養護	ヨウゴ	protection; care —**v**. protect
	養蚕	ヨウサン	sericulture; silkworm raising/culture
	養子	ヨウシ	adopted child
	養女	ヨウジョ	adopted daughter
	養生	ヨウジョウ	health care —**v**. take care of one's health
	養成	ヨウセイ	training; education; cultivation —**v**. train; educate; cultivate
	養父	ヨウフ	adoptive/foster father
	養分	ヨウブン	nourishment
	養母	ヨウボ	adoptive/foster mother
	養老	ヨウロウ	provision for old age; caring for the aged
	養老金	ヨウロウキン	old-age penision
訓	養う	やしなう	**vt**. foster; bring up; rear; adopt; support; cultivate; develop

8　食　しょくへん　food

990
飲 ⑫　　　ノ 人 ケ 今 今 今 食 食 食 飲 飲 飲

音	飲	イン	drink
熟	飲酒	インシュ	drinking alcohol
	飲食	インショク	eating and drinking; food and drink —**v**. eat and drink; take refreshments
	飲用	インヨウ	use for drinking purposes; potable
	飲料	インリョウ	drink; beverage

飲料水	インリョウスイ	drinking/potable water
訓 飲む	のむ	*vt*. drink; swallow; accept
飲み物	のみもの	drink

991

飯 ⑫　　ノ　ヘ　ケ　今　今　今　食　食　飣　飣　飯　飯

音 飯	ハン	rice; food; meal
熟 飯台	ハンダイ	dinner/dining table
飯場	ハンば	workmen's quarters; construction camp
訓 飯	めし	boiled rice; food; meal

992

飼 ⑬　　ヘ　ケ　今　今　今　食　食　飣　飣　飣　飼　飼

音 飼	シ	raise; breed
熟 飼育	シイク	breeding; raising (domestic animals) —*v*. breed; raise
飼料	シリョウ	feed; fodder
訓 飼う	かう	*vt*. breed; raise; keep (animals)
飼主	かいぬし	pet owner; animal keeper

993

館 ⑯　　ノ　ケ　今　今　食　食'　飣　飣　飣　飭　館　館

音 館	カン	mansion; inn; hall
熟 館長	カンチョウ	superintendent; director; librarian; curator
館内	カンナイ	inside the building; on the premises

9　首　くび　neck

994

首 ⑨　　丶　丷　䒑　䒑　产　斉　斉　首　首

| 音 首 | シュ | head; first; chief |
| 熟 首位 | シュイ | first place |

首相	シュショウ	premier; prime minister
首席	シュセキ	first/top (of the class); chief
首都	シュト	capital city; metropolis
首脳	シュノウ	head; leader
首班	シュハン	head; premier; prime minister
首府	シュフ	capital city
首領	シュリョウ	leader

訓

首	くび	neck; head
首切り	くびきり	dismissal
首筋	くびすじ	scruff of the neck

面
革
音
頁
飛
食
食
首 ●

10 馬　うま／うまへん　horse

995

馬　⑩　｜　厂　广　г　斤　臣　馬　馬　馬　馬　馬

音	馬	バ	horse
熟	馬具	バグ	harness; horse gear; trappings
	馬耳東風	バジトウフウ	utter indifference; praying to deaf ears
	馬車	バシャ	coach; carriage; omnibus
	馬術	バジュツ	horsemanship; equestrian skill
	馬上	バジョウ	horseback; mounted
	馬場	ばば	riding ground; racecourse; race track
	馬力	バリキ	horsepower; energy
訓	馬	うま	horse
	馬面	うまづら	horseface; long face
	馬乗り	うまのり	horse riding; rider; horseman
	馬屋	うまや	stable
	馬	ま	horse
	馬子	まご	wagon driver

996

駅　⑭　｜　厂　广　г　斤　臣　馬　馬　馬　駅　駅　駅　駅

音	駅	エキ	post-road stage; train station
熟	駅員	エキイン	station employee
	駅長	エキチョウ	station master
	駅伝	エキデン	long-distance relay race
	駅頭	エキトウ	at or near the train station
	駅弁	エキベン	packed lunch sold at railway stations

997

験　⑱　｜　厂　г　斤　馬　馬　馬　駖　駖　験　験　験

音	験	ケン	effect; test; examine
		ゲン	effect
熟	験算	ケンザン	verification of accounts

10 骨　ほね／ほねへん　bone

998

骨　⑩　｜　冂　冂　冃　冎　冎　骨　骨　骨　骨

音	骨	コツ	bone; ashes; spirit; looks
熟	骨格	コッカク	framework; skeleton; frame; build; physique
	骨子	コッシ	gist; essential part; main part
	骨折	コッセツ	bone fracture —*v.* fracture a bone
	骨頂	コッチョウ	the height of; the uttermost
	骨肉	コツニク	blood relatives; flesh and blood
訓	骨	ほね	bone; frame; spirit; backbone
	骨折る	ほねおる	*vi.* make efforts; put oneself out
	骨身	ほねみ	flesh and bones; marrow
	骨休め	ほねやすめ	rest; relaxation —*vi.* rest; relax

10 高　たかい　tall; high

999

高　⑩　｀　亠　亠　古　古　宮　高　高　高　高

音	高	コウ	high
熟	高圧	コウアツ	high pressure/tension; coercion; oppression
	高圧的	コウアツテキ	high-handed; coercive; overbearing
	高位	コウイ	high rank; honors
	高遠	コウエン	lofty; noble; exalted
	高音	コウオン	high-pitched tone
	高温	コウオン	high temperature
	高価	コウカ	expensive; costly; high price
	高額	コウガク	large sum/amount (of money)
	高官	コウカン	high official
	高貴	コウキ	noble; precious; valuable
	高気圧	コウキアツ	high atmospheric pressure
	高級	コウキュウ	high-class; seniority
	高給	コウキュウ	high salary/pay
	高潔	コウケツ	noble/high-mindedness; loftiness; purity

499

馬
骨
●高

高原	コウゲン	plateau	
高山	コウザン	high mountain	
高所	コウショ	high ground; broad view	
高層	コウソウ	altostratus	
高速度	コウソクド	high speed	
高速道路	コウソクドウロ	expressway; highway; motorway	
高低	コウテイ	high and low; uneven; rugged	
高度	コウド	altitude; height; high degree	
高等	コウトウ	high-grade/class	
高等学校	コウトウガッコウ	senior high school	
高等裁判所	コウトウ サイバンショ	high court	
高熱	コウネツ	high fever/temperature; intense heat	
高名	コウメイ	fame; repute; renown	
高率	コウリツ	high rate/interest rate	
訓 高	たか	amount; quantity; volume	
高い	たかい	tall; high; eminent; lofty	
高潮	たかしお	flood/high tide; tidal wave	
高台	たかダイ	heights; high ground; high, flat area	
高々	たかだか	at most; at the best; no more than	
高鳴る	たかなる	*vi.* throb; beat	
高根の花	たかねのはな	unattainable object; prize beyond one's reach	
高飛車	たかビシャ	high-handed; overbearing	
高ぶる	たかぶる	*vi.* be highly wrought-up; be excited; be conceited	
高まる	たかまる	*vi.* rise; be raised; increase	
高める	たかめる	*vt.* raise; lift; promote; elevate	

11 魚 うお fish

魚 ⑪ 　 ᐟ ᐟ ク ク 个 甶 甶 魚 魚 魚 魚

音	魚	ギョ	fish
熟	魚類	ギョルイ	fishes
訓	魚	うお (さかな)	fish

11 鳥 とり bird

鳥 ⑪ 　 ᐟ ア 户 戸 鸟 鳥 鳥 鳥 鳥 鳥

音	鳥	チョウ	bird
熟	鳥類	チョウルイ	birds
訓	鳥	とり	bird
	鳥居	とりい	*torii* (gateway to a Shinto Shrine)

鳴 ⑭ 　 丶 ロ ロ ロᐟ ロ゙ ロ冖 ロ户 ロ皀 鳴 鳴 鳴

音	鳴	メイ	cry; sing; howl
熟	鳴動	メイドウ	rumbling —*vi.* rumble; move with a loud noise
訓	鳴く	なく	*vi.* cry; sing; howl; chirp
	鳴き声	なきごえ	cry; call; chirping
	鳴る	なる	*vi.* sound; ring
	鳴らす	ならす	*vt.* sound ring

11 黄 きいろい／き yellow

1003

黄 ⑪ 一 十 艹 艹 共 芦 芐 莆 菐 苗 黄 黄

音 黄 コウ yellow; gold
オウ

熟 黄金 オウゴン gold; money
黄金時代 オウゴンジダイ golden age; age of gods
黄色人種 オウショクジンシュ yellow race
黄水 オウスイ bile; gall
黄鉄鉱 オウテッコウ iron pyrite; fool's gold
黄熱病 オウネツビョウ *med*. yellow fever
黄河 コウガ Yellow River
黄土 コウド（オウド） loess; yellow soil

訓 黄 き yellow
黄色 きいろ yellow
黄身 きみ yolk
黄金色 こがねいろ gold (color)

11 黒 くろい／くろ black

1004

黒 ⑪ 丶 冂 冂 曰 甲 甲 里 里 黒 黒 黒

音 黒 コク black; darkness; bad; wrong

熟 黒人 コクジン black person
黒点 コクテン sunspots; black spots
黒板 コクバン blackboard

訓 黒 くろ black
黒い くろい black; dirty; dark
黒船 くろふね *hist*. 'black ships' (term used to refer to all Western ships that visited Japan from 1600 to 1868)
黒星 くろぼし black mark; bull's-eye
黒幕 くろマク wirepuller; behind-the-scenes man

12 歯　は　tooth

1005

歯 ⑫　　丨　ト　止　止　歩　歩　歩　歩　歯　歯　歯　歯

音	歯	シ	tooth; age
熟	歯科	シカ	dentistry
	歯科医	シカイ	dentist
	歯石	シセキ	tartar; plaque
訓	歯	は	tooth; teeth
	歯医者	はイシャ	dentist
	歯車	はぐるま	gear wheel
	歯向かう	はむかう	*vi*. rise/turn against

14 鼻 はな nose

1006

鼻 ⑭　　´ 亻 冂 自 自 皀 鼻 鼻 畠 畠 鼻 鼻

音	鼻	ビ	nose
熟	鼻音	ビオン	nasal sound
	鼻下	ビカ	under the nose; area between nose and mouth; upper lip
訓	鼻	はな	nose
	鼻息	はないき	breathing through the nose; mood; temper
	鼻歌	はなうた	humming
	鼻毛	はなげ	nostril hairs
	鼻声	はなごえ	nasal voice
	鼻先	はなさき	tip of the nose; under one's nose
	鼻白む	はなじろむ	*vi.* look disappointed/bored
	鼻筋	はなすじ	line of the nose
	鼻高々	はなたかだか	proudly; triumphantly
	鼻血	はなぢ	nosebleed *med.* epistasis
	鼻水	はなみず	nasal mucus; runny nose
	鼻持ちならない	はなもちならない	intolerable; detestable; disgusting; stinking

RADICAL INDEX

RADICAL INDEX

(by radical and kanji number)

---

1 STROKE

一

一 1
七 2
丁 3
下 4
三 5
上 6
万 7
不 8
世 9
両 10

二(二) 20
十(十) 141
才(扌) 459
友(又) 159
五(二) 21
天(大) 239
戸(戸) 454
可(口) 181
平(干) 332
正(止) 598
再(冂) 98
死(歹) 602
百(白) 711
西(西) 856
否(口) 174
束(木) 553
求(水) 618
豆(豆) 903
表(衣) 849
事(亅) 19
画(凵) 103
雨(雨) 967
面(面) 974

丨

中 11
半(十) 144
旧(日) 504
申(田) 695

丶

丸 12
主 13
以(人) 27
永(水) 615
州(川) 315
良(艮) 858

ノ

久 14
乗 15
九(乙) 16
千(十) 142
午(十) 143
手(手) 456
欠(欠) 593
毛(毛) 610
牛(牛) 676
失(大) 242
生(生) 691
矢(矢) 727
先(儿) 83
向(口) 186
年(干) 333
有(月) 529
気(气) 613
舌(舌) 836
系(糸) 788
受(又) 161
垂(土) 209

重(里) 942

乙

九 16

乚

乱 17
乳 18
丸(丶) 12
札(木) 563
礼(ネ) 740

亅

事 19
丁(一) 3
予(マ) 163
争(ク) 162

2 STROKES

二

二 20
五 21
来 22
天(大) 239
仁(イ) 36
干(干) 331
元(儿) 80
夫(大) 240
未(木) 551
示(示) 736

亠

亡 23
交 24
京 25

市(巾) 321
立(立) 761
衣(衣) 848
忘(心) 432
言(言) 868
卒(十) 146
夜(夕) 235
育(月) 536
変(夂) 230
高(高) 999
商(口) 193
率(玄) 684
産(生) 692
裏(衣) 852
六(八) 89
文(文) 495
方(方) 499

人

人 26
以 27
内(冂) 96

八

今 28
令 29
会 30
全 31
余 32
舎 33
倉 34
合(口) 170
命(口) 189
念(心) 434
金(金) 947
食(食) 988

イ

化 35
仁 36
仏 37
仕 38
他 39
代 40
付 41
仮 42
休 43
件 44
伝 45
任 46
位 47
何 48
作 49
似 50
住 51
体 52
低 53
価 54
供 55
使 56
例 57
係 58
信 59
便 60
保 61
個 62
候 63
借 64
修 65
値 66
俳 67
倍 68
俵 69
健 70
側 71
　 72

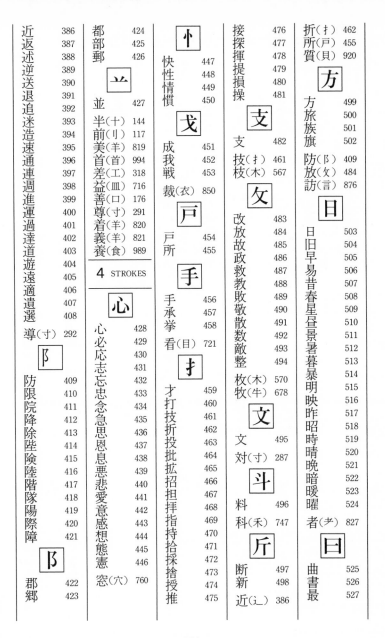

畑(田) 700
秋(禾) 748

灬
点 667
然 668
無 669
照 670
熟 671
熱 672
馬(馬) 995
魚(魚) 1000
鳥(鳥) 1001
黒(黒) 1004
蒸(艹) 382

爫
受(又) 161
愛(心) 441

父
父 673
交(亠) 24

片
片 674
版 675

牛
牛 676
物 677
牧 678
特 679
件(亻) 44

犬
犬 680
状 681

犭
犯 682
独 683

5 STROKES

玄
率 684

玉
玉 685
宝(宀) 272
国(囗) 204

王
王 686
班 687
球 688
現 689
理 690
主(丶) 13
全(入) 31
皇(白) 713
望(月) 532
聖(耳) 831

生
生 691
産 692
性(忄) 448
星(日) 509

用
用 693

田
田 694
申 695

由 696
男 697
町 698
界 699
畑 700
留 701
異 702
略 703
番 704
里(里) 941
画(凵) 103
果(木) 554
思(心) 436
胃(月) 537
富(宀) 283
奮(大) 244

疋
疑 705

疒
病 706
痛 707

癶
発 708
登 709

白
白 710
百 711
的 712
皇 713
泉(水) 617
習(羽) 824
楽(木) 561

皮
皮 714
波(氵) 628

破(石) 733

皿
皿 715
益 716
盛 717
盟 718
血(血) 842

目
目 719
直 720
看 721
県 722
省 723
相 724
真 725
眼 726
見(見) 859
貝(貝) 906
具(八) 92
着(羊) 820

矛
務(力) 133

矢
矢 727
知 728
短 729
医(匸) 140

石
石 730
研 731
砂 732
破 733
磁 734
確 735
岩(山) 311

示
示 736
祭 737
票 738
禁 739
宗(宀) 269

ネ
礼 740
社 741
祝 742
神 743
祖 744
福 745
視(見) 861

禾
私 746
科 747
秋 748
秒 749
秘 750
移 751
税 752
程 753
穀 754
種 755
積 756
番(田) 704
和(口) 190
委(女) 246
利(刂) 113
季(子) 259

穴
穴 757
究 758
空 759
窓 760
容(宀) 278

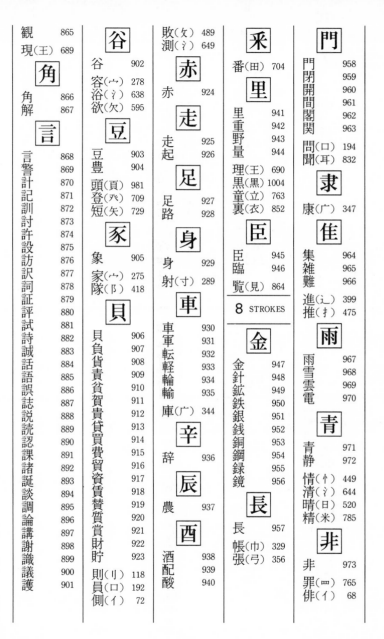

515

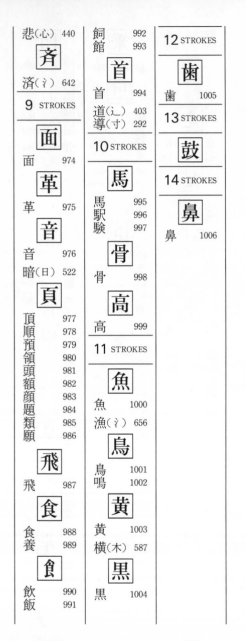

悲(心) 440

斉

済(氵) 642

9 STROKES

面

面 974

革

革 975

音

音 976
暗(日) 522

頁

頂 977
順 978
預 979
領 980
頭 981
額 982
顔 983
題 984
類 985
願 986

飛

飛 987

食

食 988
養 989

食

飲 990
飯 991

飼 992
館 993

首

首 994
道(辶) 403
導(寸) 292

10 STROKES

馬

馬 995
駅 996
験 997

骨

骨 998

高

高 999

11 STROKES

魚

魚 1000
漁(氵) 656

鳥

鳥 1001
鳴 1002

黄

黄 1003
横(木) 587

黒

黒 1004

12 STROKES

歯

歯 1005

13 STROKES

鼓

14 STROKES

鼻

鼻 1006

ON/KUN INDEX

ON-KUN INDEX

(by ON／KUN and kanji number)

519

535

536

STROKE INDEX

STROKE INDEX

(by stroke number and kanji number)

539

漢字	No.
備	74
割	120
創	121
勤	134
勝	135
博	148
喜	175
善	176
報	210
場	220
寒	282
富	283
尊	291
営	299
就	301
属	308
復	367
葉	380
落	381
運	400
過	401
達	402
道	403
階	404
隊	417
陽	418
悲	419
揮	440
提	478
敬	479
散	490
景	491
暑	511
晴	512
晩	520
最	521
期	527
朝	533
森	534
極	560
検	580
植	581
棒	582
温	583
	645

漢字	No.
清	644
率	684
球	688
現	689
理	690
産	692
異	702
略	703
盛	717
眼	726
祭	737
票	738
移	751
窓	760
章	762
第	770
笛	771
経	797
細	798
終	799
組	800
習	824
翌	825
船	838
術	845
規	860
視	861
許	874
設	875
訪	876
訳	877
貨	908
責	909
貧	910
転	932
野	943
閉	959
雪	968
頂	977
魚	1000
鳥	1001
黄	1003
黒	1004

12

漢字	No.
基	212
堂	213
域	219
婦	253
寄	279
宿	280
密	281
巣	298
常	328
帳	329
康	347
強	355
張	366
得	378
菜	379
著	398
週	399
進	415
険	416
郷	423
都	424
部	425
郵	426
悪	439
情	449
採	472
捨	473
授	474
推	475
接	476
救	477
教	487
敗	488
族	489
望	497
脳	501
械	532
欲	544
液	579
混	595
済	640
深	641
	642
	643

漢字	No.
梅	578
残	603
殺	605
消	637
浴	638
流	639
特	679
班	687
留	701
病	706
益	716
真	725
破	733
秘	750
笑	769
粉	784
素	789
紙	794
純	795
納	796
耕	829
航	837
蚕	841
記	871
訓	872
討	873
財	922
起	926
酒	938
配	939
針	948
馬	995
骨	998
高	999

11

漢字	No.
健	71
側	72
停	73
副	119
動	132
務	133
唱	180
商	193
問	194

漢字	No.
宮	277
容	278
射	289
将	290
党	296
展	307
島	313
差	318
帰	324
師	325
席	326
帯	327
庫	344
座	345
庭	346
弱	354
従	364
徒	365
荷	377
造	394
速	395
通	396
院	397
降	411
除	412
陸	413
郡	414
恩	422
息	437
挙	438
料	458
旅	496
時	500
書	519
朗	526
能	531
胸	539
脈	542
案	543
桜	559
格	573
株	574
校	575
根	576
	577

漢字	No.
県	722
省	723
相	724
研	731
砂	732
祝	742
神	743
祖	744
科	747
秋	748
秒	749
紀	790
級	791
紅	792
約	793
美	819
要	857
計	870
負	907
軍	931
重	942
面	974
革	975
音	976
飛	987
食	988
首	994

10

漢字	No.
倉	34
個	63
候	64
借	65
修	66
値	67
俳	68
倍	69
俵	70
勉	131
原	153
員	192
夏	231
孫	260
家	275
害	276

（新装版）教育漢英熟語辞典
KODANSHA'S ELEMENTARY KANJI DICTIONARY

2001年5月11日　第1刷発行

編　者　　講談社インターナショナル株式会社

発行者　　野間佐和子

発行所　　講談社インターナショナル株式会社
　　　　　〒112-8652 東京都文京区音羽 1-17-14
　　　　　電話　03-3944-6493（編集部）
　　　　　　　　03-3944-6492（営業部・業務部）
　　　　　ホームページ　http://www.kodansha-intl.co.jp

印刷所　　凸版印刷株式会社

製本所　　凸版印刷株式会社

© 講談社インターナショナル 2001
Printed in Japan
ISBN4-7700-2752-4

KODANSHA INTERNATIONAL DICTIONARIES

Easy-to-use dictionaries designed for non-native learners of Japanese.

KODANSHA'S FURIGANA JAPANESE DICTIONARY
JAPANESE-ENGLISH / ENGLISH-JAPANESE　ふりがな和英・英和辞典

Both of Kodansha's popular furigana dictionaries in one portable, affordable volume. A truly comprehensive and practical dictionary for English-speaking learners, and an invaluable guide to using the Japanese language.
• Basic vocabulary of 30,000 entries　• Hundreds of special words, names, and phrases
• Clear explanations of semantic and usage differences　• Special information on grammar and usage
Hardcover, 1318 pages, ISBN 4-7700-2480-0

KODANSHA'S FURIGANA JAPANESE-ENGLISH DICTIONARY
ふりがな和英辞典

The essential dictionary for all students of Japanese.
• Furigana readings added to all *kanji*　• Comprehensive 16,000-word basic vocabulary
Vinyl flexibinding, 592 pages, ISBN 4-7700-1983-1

KODANSHA'S FURIGANA ENGLISH-JAPANESE DICTIONARY
ふりがな英和辞典

The companion to the essential dictionary for all students of Japanese.
• Furigana readings added to all *kanji*　• Comprehensive 14,000-word basic vocabulary
Vinyl flexibinding, 728 pages, ISBN 4-7700-2055-4

KODANSHA'S CONCISE ROMANIZED JAPANESE-ENGLISH DICTIONARY
コンサイス版 ローマ字和英辞典

A first, basic dictionary for beginner students of Japanese.
• Comprehensive 10,000-word basic vocabulary　• Easy-to-find romanized entries listed in alphabetical order
• Definitions written for English-speaking users
• Sample sentences in romanized and standard Japanese script, followed by the English translation
Paperback, 480 pages, ISBN 4-7700-2849-0

KODANSHA'S ROMANIZED JAPANESE-ENGLISH DICTIONARY
ローマ字和英辞典

A portable reference written for beginning and intermediate students.
• 16,000-word vocabulary　• No knowledge of *kanji* necessary
Vinyl flexibinding, 688 pages, ISBN 4-7700-1603-4

KODANSHA'S BASIC ENGLISH-JAPANESE DICTIONARY
日常日本語バイリンガル辞典

An annotated dictionary useful for both students and teachers.
• Over 4,500 entries and 18,000 vocabulary items　• Examples and information on stylistic differences
• Appendixes for technical terms, syntax and grammar
Vinyl flexibinding, 1520 pages, ISBN 4-7700-2628-5

THE MODERN ENGLISH-NIHONGO DICTIONARY
日本語学習英日辞典

The first truly bilingual dictionary designed exclusively for non-native learners of Japanese.
• Over 6,000 headwords　• Both standard Japanese with *furigana* and romanized orthography
• Sample sentences provided for most entries　• Numerous explanatory notes and *kanji* guides
Vinyl flexibinding, 1200 pages, ISBN 4-7700-2148-8

KODANSHA'S ELEMENTARY KANJI DICTIONARY

新装版 教育漢英熟語辞典

A first, basic *kanji* dictionary for non-native learners of Japanese.
• Complete guide to 1,006 *Shin-kyōiku kanji*   • Over 10,000 common compounds
• Three indices for finding *kanji*   • Compact, portable format   • Functional, up-to-date, timely
Paperback, 576 pages, ISBN 4-7700-2752-4

KODANSHA'S COMPACT KANJI GUIDE

常用漢英熟語辞典

A functional character dictionary that is both compact and comprehensive.
• 1,945 essential *jōyō kanji*   • 20,000 common compounds   • Three indexes for finding *kanji*
Vinyl flexibinding, 928 pages, ISBN 4-7700-1553-4

THE KODANSHA KANJI LEARNER'S DICTIONARY

漢英学習字典

The perfect kanji tool for beginners to advanced learners.
• Revolutionary SKIP lookup method   • Five lookup methods and three indexes
• 2,230 entries & 41,000 meanings for 31,000 words
Vinyl flexibinding, 1060 pages (2-color), ISBN 4-7700-2335-9

KODANSHA'S EFFECTIVE JAPANESE USAGE DICTIONARY

新装版 日本語使い分け辞典

A concise, bilingual dictionary which clarifies the usage of frequently confused words and phrases.
• Explanations of 708 synonymous terms   • Numerous example sentences
Paperback, 768 pages, ISBN 4-7700-2850-4

A DICTIONARY OF JAPANESE PARTICLES

てにをは辞典

Treats over 100 particles in alphabetical order, providing sample sentences for each meaning.
• Meets students' needs from beginning to advanced levels
• Treats principal particle meanings as well as variants
Paperback, 368 pages, ISBN 4-7700-2352-9

THE HANDBOOK OF JAPANESE VERBS

日本語動詞ハンドブック   *Taeko Kamiya*

An indispensable reference and guide to Japanese verbs aimed at beginning and intermediate students. Precisely the book that verb-challenged students have been looking for.
• Verbs are grouped, conjugated, and combined with auxiliaries
• Different forms are used in sentences
• Each form is followed by reinforcing examples and exercises
Paperback, 256pages, ISBN 4-7700-2683-8

A DICTIONARY OF BASIC JAPANESE SENTENCE PATTERNS

日本語基本文型辞典

Author of the best-selling All About Particles explains fifty of the most common, basic patterns and their variations, along with numerous contextual examples. Both a reference and a textbook for students at all levels.
• Formulas delineating basic pattern structure   • Commentary on individual usages
Paperback, 320 pages, ISBN 4-7700-2608-0

JAPANESE LANGUAGE GUIDES

Easy-to-use guides to essential language skills

13 SECRETS FOR SPEAKING FLUENT JAPANESE

日本語をペラペラ話すための13の秘訣　*Giles Murray*

The most fun, rewarding and universal techniques of successful learners of Japanese that anyone can put immediately to use. A unique and exciting alternative full of lively commentaries, comical illustrations, and brain-teasing puzzles.

Paperback, 184 pages; ISBN 4-7700-2302-2

ALL ABOUT PARTICLES

新装版 助詞で変わるあなたの日本語　*Naoko Chino*

The most common and less common particles brought together and broken down into some 200 usages, with abundant sample sentences.

Paperback, 128 pages; ISBN 4-7700-2781-8

BEYOND POLITE JAPANESE
A Dictionary of Japanese Slang and Colloquialisms

新装版 役にたつ話ことば辞典　*Akihiko Yonekawa*

Expressions that all Japanese, but few foreigners, know and use every day. Sample sentences for every entry.

Paperback, 176 pages; ISBN 4-7700-2773-7

JAPANESE CORE WORDS AND PHRASES
Things You Can't Find in a Dictionary

新装版 辞書では解らない慣用表現　*Kakuko Shoji*

Some Japanese words and phrases, even though they lie at the core of the language, forever elude the student's grasp. This book brings these recalcitrants to bay.

Paperback, 144 pages; ISBN 4-7700-2774-5

JAPANESE VERBS AT A GLANCE

新装版 日本語の動詞　*Naoko Chino*

Clear and straightforward explanations of Japanese verbs—their functions, forms, roles, and politeness levels.

Paperback, 180 pages; ISBN 4-7700-2765-6

THE JAPANESE WRITTEN WORD
A Unique Reader

「読む」日本語　*Glenn Melchinger & Helen Kasha*

A collection of original texts and material in a broad spectrum of styles and themes, utilizing a unique (and patented) method to allow students to read original Japanese easily.

Paperback, 248 pages; ISBN 4-7700-2126-7

BITS AND PIECES
51 Activities for Teaching Japanese K-12

日本語教材・アクティビティ集　*Japan Council of International Schools*

Practical, educational, and interesting activities prepared by veteran teachers, each presented in bilingual format with material ready to copy for immediate use in the classroom.

Paperback, 208 pages; ISBN 4-7700-2029-5

www.thejapanpage.com

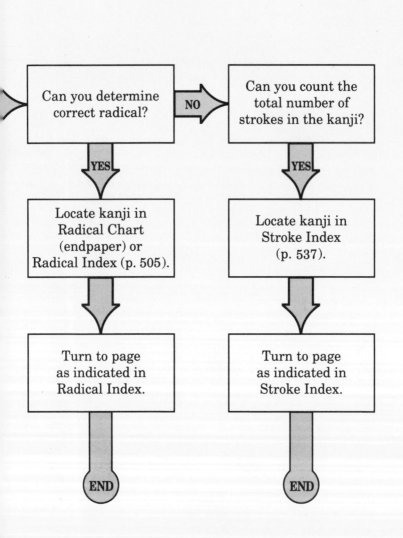